THE LIFE AND WORK OF

ROBERT GIBBINGS

BY MARTIN J. ANDREWS

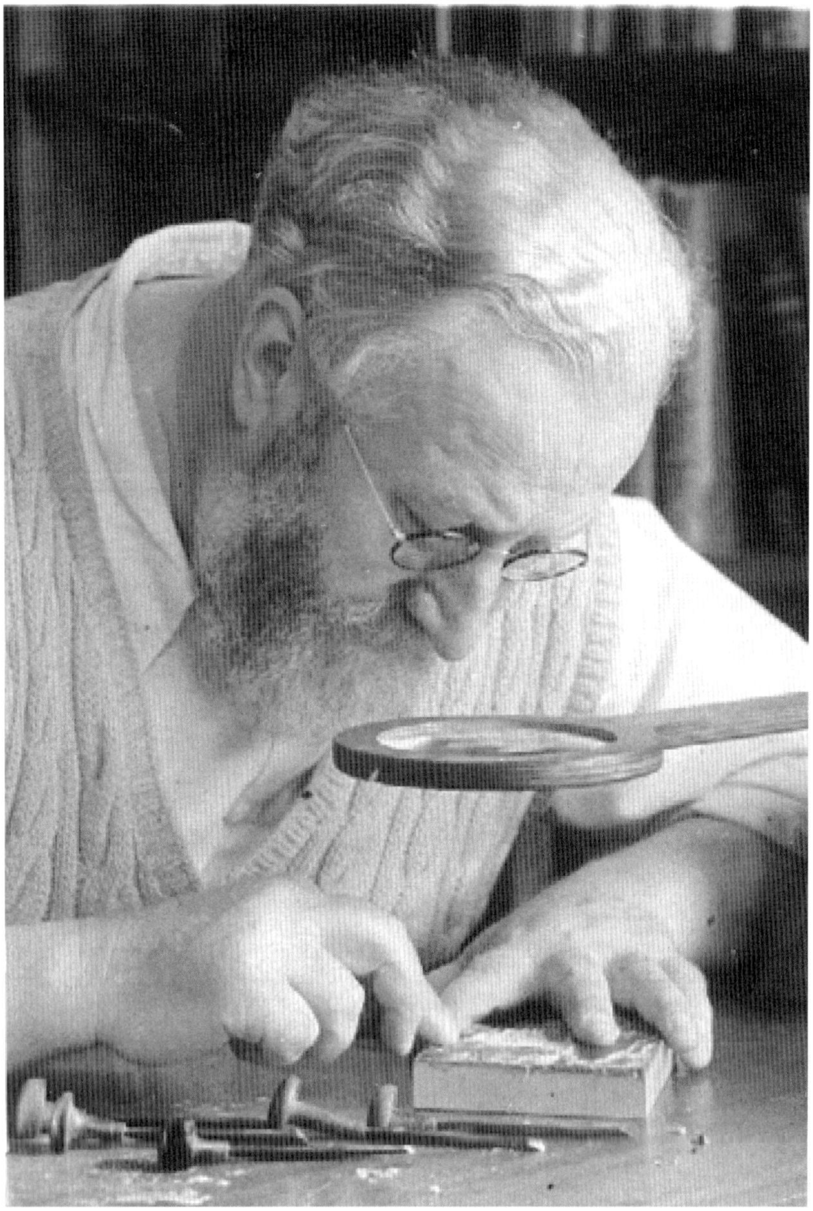

Robert Gibbings wood-engraving, 1949.

THE LIFE AND WORK OF

ROBERT GIBBINGS

BY MARTIN J. ANDREWS

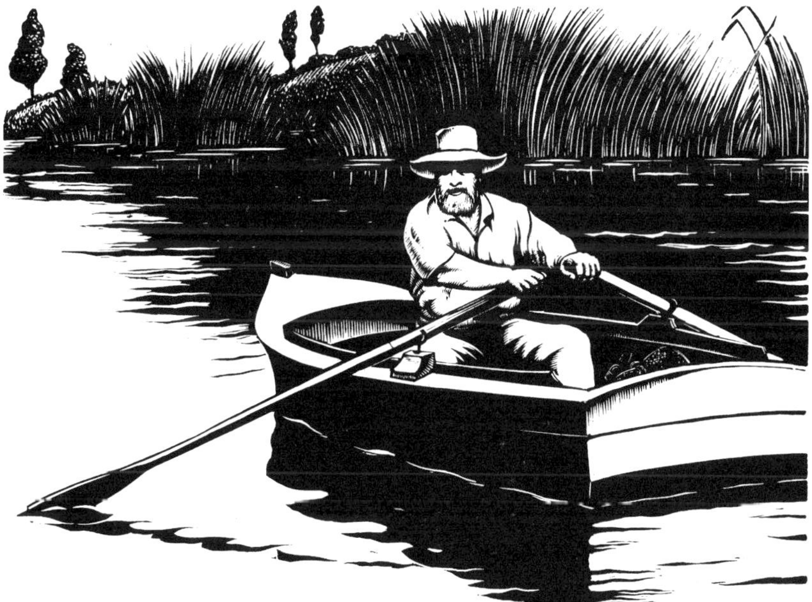

BICESTER • PRIMROSE HILL PRESS

Published in Great Britain by Primrose Hill Press, Bicester, 2003.

Designed and set by Derek Brown at Oblong
Wetherby

ISBN 1 901648 31 1

British Library Cataloguing-in-Publication Data.

A Catalogue record for this book is available
from the British Library.

Printed in Great Britain by
Henry Ling Ltd, The Dorset Press
Dorchester

Contents

This book is dedicated
to Patience Empson and
to my wife, Verity

Acknowledgements

My involvement with the work of Robert Gibbings began in 1975 but the serious research for this book has taken over ten years. In that time I have been generously helped by a vast number of institutions and individuals, some of whom, sadly, are no longer alive. I have attempted to include everyone in this acknowledgement but if I have unintentionally omitted anyone, I would like to apologise and say that if it had not been for everyone's generous help and support, this book would not have been completed.

I would like to thank the following institutions, archives, libraries and museums: British Pathé News; the Society of Wood-Engravers; BBC Archives; John Lewis Partnership Archive; Penguin Archive, Bristol University Library; the Library, University College Cork; Reading University Library; John Johnson Collection, Bodleian Library, University of Oxford; Gleeson Library, University of San Francisco; the William Andrews Clark Memorial Library, UCLA, for generously awarding me a short term Fellowship and to the staff for all their help and patience; Cathy Henderson and the staff at the Harry Ransom Humanities Research Center, University of Texas at Austin; the Houghton Library; Harvard College Library; Walpole Library, The King's School, Canterbury; Reading Local Studies Library; Jonathan Riddle at the London Transport Museum; Prints and Drawings Collection, British Museum; Imperial War Museum; Sylvia Backemeyer, Central School of Art; Crawford Art Gallery, Cork; Whitworth Gallery, Manchester; Prints and Drawings Collection at the Victoria & Albert Museum.

I would also like to thank Laurence Pollinger, Gibbings's literary agent, and the following publishers and companies: Orion Books and in particular, Simon Cobley, archivist, for their permission to use material from J. M. Dent & Sons Ltd; Penguin Books; John and Virginia Murray; John Randle at the Whittington Press; Oxford University Press; Random House; Gerald Duckworth & Co. Ltd; Parker Pen Company; API Foils.

It is one of the joys of writing such a book that you meet a wealth of fascinating and kind people, and many of them become friends. I am enormously grateful to the following for information or permission to use letters or illustrations: Robert Avis, Michael Black, Harry Blacker, John Blatchly, Ronald Blythe, Victor Bond, Joan L. Carter, Tony Cox, Dr M. Ian Crichton, Hilda Dale, Helen Davis, John Dreyfus, Howard Duckworth, Charles Ede, Olivia Fitzpatrick, Peter Foden, Steve Hare, Jean Harrison, Annetta Hoffnung, Anthony Humphreys, Lawrence Hutson, May M. Knight, John Kurtz, the late Professor William Lacey, the late John Lewis, Fiona MacCarthy, Elizabeth McIntyre, Craig McKechnie, Patricia Medley, Mrs Seamus Murphy, Hilary Paynter, R. Pleydell-Bouverie, Susan Pollen, the Ravilious family, the late Michael Renton, Ian Rogerson, Judith Russell, T. F. S. Scott, the late S. Maberly Smith, Mr Somerville, Eric Stanford, Mrs Strachan, Amoret Tanner, Margaret Till, S. P. Tuohy, David van Rest, Joan and the late William Wilder, Graham York and Edward Young.

A special thank you is due to Cal Hyland for his hospitality and support over the years; to Albert Gibbings and his family for looking after me so well; to the late Albert and Dorothy Cooper for their friendship and for giving me so much Gibbings material; to Joanna Selborne for her encouragement and expertise; to the late John Hadfield, whom it was a privilege to have known, and to Roderick Cave for his invaluable advice and for generously letting me read the manuscript of Cave & Manson's history of the Golden Cockerel Press (to be published shortly).

It would have been impossible to have written this book without the support of the Gibbings family and in particular I would like to mention Diana and the late Patrick Gibbings for wonderful days in Northumberland and for making so much material available to me. I would also like to thank Laurence Gibbings, Vahine Gibbings and Shaun Gibbings.

Over the years I have had enormous support and encouragement from colleagues in the Department of Typography & Graphic Communication at The University of Reading. The University itself has been generous in awarding me a number of grants to help my research but it is to past and present Heads of Department that I owe gratitude for their unfailing support and advice. Professor Michael Twyman has been an inspiration as a writer and historian and it was he who encouraged Professor Sue Walker (now Head of Department) and myself to work on Robert Gibbings as students in 1975 — a period with many happy memories. Dr Margaret Smith has offered great encouragement and valued comments; David Knott (Keeper of Rare Books, Reading University Library) has been wonderfully patient and generous in making the collections available to me and helping with my research. I would like to thank Dr Christopher Burke for his proof reading and editorial advice. But the greatest thanks must go to Michael Bott, the University's Archivist, who in his official capacity and as a long term friend has shown unfailing patience in his editorial role. Mike has read endless drafts and without his expertise and editorial skills the book would never have been fit for publication.

In carrying out such a project, family love and support is invaluable. George Andrews, my father, has been a great help in checking and ferreting out factual details; my wife, Verity, has not only been so patient and understanding but has also corrected drafts and spent many hours helping with the typing. To my daughter and son, Beth and Joe, I apologise for what they had to put up with while I was working on this book — often stressed and bad tempered, I may sometimes have seemed a distant father at a time when they deserved my attention.

I have been very fortunate in my publishers, who have invested so much in this book. I would like to thank Professor William Butler for making this book possible, Dr Brian Hill who was so immediately enthusiastic about the project. Rose Siviter has been a meticulous editor and I would especially like to thank her for all the time and effort she has contributed. Thanks too to Derek Brown for all his care and attention in the design and to Jill Ford for compiling the index.

Finally I would like to thank Patience Empson for having faith and trust in me and for giving me the privilege to write about Robert Gibbings with her co-operation and blessing. It has taken many more years than we expected but I hope she feels it has been worth it.

Note

In all references and footnotes, Reading University Library is referred to as RUL; the William Andrews Clark Memorial Library, UCLA, Los Angeles, as Clark; the Harry Ransom Humanities Research Center, University of Texas at Austin, as HRHRC; the Gleeson Library, University of San Francisco, as Gleeson.

Bibliographical details and size of editions are based on Kirkus, A., Mary, *Robert Gibbings: a Bibliography*, ed. Patience Empson and John Harris , London: J. M. Dent & Sons Ltd, 1962.

Introduction

BROWSING ALONG THE SHELVES in second-hand bookshops, one is almost bound to come across a copy of a book written and illustrated by Robert Gibbings and published by J. M. Dent. This is an indication of just how popular these books were in the 1940s and 50s. The books could be shelved in many different sections: natural history, travel, illustrated books or art — which only goes to show how diverse they are in subject matter and how they appealed to a wide range of readers. Many of the copies will be tired and worn late editions or book club reprints. Pristine first editions are more likely to be found in the rare and antiquarian sections, locked in glass cabinets alongside examples of fine typography, book production and illustration. It is possible that those cabinets will also contain other books for which Gibbings was responsible — the now highly-valued limited editions of the Golden Cockerel Press.

Much has been written and published about the period when Gibbings was the owner and director of the Golden Cockerel Press and articles have documented other aspects of his career. However, to date, nothing has been published encompassing his whole life, providing a context for his work and achievements. Gibbings is often described as having been a larger than life, colourful and adventurous character but he was also responsible, perhaps more than anyone, for bringing the art of wood-engraving to the attention of the general public.

One of the main concerns of this book is to provide a critical analysis of Gibbings's style and technique and to trace the development of his work as an artist and wood-engraver, particularly in the field of book illustration. From his earliest days as an illustrator, Gibbings pursued a passionate belief that illustration should be visually integrated and harmonious with the text and not simply a decorative afterthought. Thus, his ambition was to control all aspects of design and production as the best way to achieve his goal, and as director of the Golden Cockerel Press he was in an ideal position to fulfil it. It is widely acknowledged that he was responsible for some of the finest books of the private press movement in the twentieth century. Later he attempted to bring these ideals to the world of the popular paperback, both as an author and illustrator, and as art editor of the Penguin Illustrated Classics. Eventually, after a short period as a teacher of wood-engraving and book production at The University of Reading, he achieved remarkable success with books which he wrote, illustrated and designed, working in close collaboration with his publisher J. M. Dent & Sons. These books made him a best-selling author in both Britain and America and sold all over the world.

In addition to his wood-engraving, I have explored other aspects of his life as an artist, including his sculpture and painting. Gibbings's gregarious nature ensured he had a wide circle of friends and associates in the art world. During the period when he was a student at the Slade, from 1911 to 1913, the school was experiencing one of its 'periodical triumphal flows', and among his fellow students were Stanley Spencer, William Roberts, C. R. W. Nevinson and Paul Nash. Through the Society of Wood Engravers (of which he was a founder member) and the Golden Cockerel Press, Gibbings became friends with, and commissioned work from, many leading British artists, including David Jones, Eric Ravilious, Paul and John Nash and Blair Hughes-Stanton. Of greatest significance was his close personal relationship with Eric Gill and their working collaboration culminated in the production of *The Four Gospels*, which is considered to be a masterpiece of book design and production. His social circle also encompassed figures from the worlds of music, literature and the theatre.

But there were many other dimensions to his life. He was recognised as a natural historian, not in an academic way, but through his life-time passion for the outdoor life, his fascination with flora and fauna and his remarkable powers of observation and description. Given his love of nature, it is not surprising that Gibbings was a keen nudist and a founder member of the British naturist movement, with others such as Bernard Shaw and A. E. Coppard. Above all, Gibbings was a great communicator — a brilliant public speaker, he also broadcast on radio and appeared on television in its pioneering days. His easy manner and natural way with words made him able to capture and fascinate an audience. Through his books, talks, journalism and broadcasts he did much to popularise the subject of natural history. Gibbings paved the way for broadcasters and writers such as David Attenborough, who revealed, in a *Radio Times* article celebrating sixty years of Penguin Books, that *Blue Angels and Whales*, by Gibbings, was the first Penguin he owned.

Gibbings lived life to the full and was a traveller and adventurer. He journeyed around the world seeking material for his books and wood-engravings — often to exotic places. He spent two years living with the people of Polynesia, taking part in rituals and ceremonies (he was made a honorary chief), pearl diving and shark fishing and he spent almost a year sailing between the islands on a masted schooner. Closer to home, he floated down the River Thames in a boat he designed himself and went on to explore the rivers Wye, Lee and Seine, enjoying the landscape, history, food and wine, and, most of all, the people he met on the way. With the success of his popular river books, all profusely illustrated with his own wood-engravings, Gibbings became something of a household name in the 1940s and 1950s, and his books brought the art of wood-engraving to a mass audience. His work achieved similar success in America, where his books were published by E. P. Dutton & Co. of New York.

Robert Gibbings would have been surprised and possibly annoyed at the prospect of anyone writing his biography; partly through a natural desire for privacy, but more likely because he would have been frustrated at the idea of someone spending over ten years retracing and piecing together the activities of *his* lifetime, rather than living their own to the full. My reply would be that I have tried to respect his privacy and not sensationalise, but to give an honest and factual account, and simply to say that in writing this book I have travelled to so many places, met so many fascinating people and learnt so much about a rich period in Irish and British art and literature, that this is surely justification enough and one with which he would sympathise.

Whenever possible I have deliberately used Gibbings's own words to tell his story; quoting extensively from his books and letters, allowing his own voice and engaging style to be always present. The majority of his published books are based on accounts of his own adventures and experiences and are full of autobiographical references; a large part of the task in writing this book has been to bring together and organise them chronologically. In 1949 his friend, Tom Balston, outlined his career to date in an introduction to his book of Gibbings's engravings, based on conversations he had with him. Gibbings himself began writing more detailed autobiographical notes for a large volume of his collected wood-engravings but this remained unfinished at his death; both of these have been invaluable sources.[1] Aspects of bibliographical detail, in particular the dates and size of editions of Gibbings's books, are largely based on another essential source of information about his work — the bibliography written by Dr Mary Kirkus, and extended and edited by Patience Empson and John Harris.[2]

Unfortunately I never met Gibbings, but my wife, as a young child, moved to Long Wittenham, the village where Gibbings had a cottage, in the year that he died. She later introduced me to his books and as a student at Reading University, first in the Department of Fine Art and then the Department of Typography & Graphic Communication, I was made aware of his influence and became fascinated by his life and work. So much so that in 1975 a major exhibition of his work was mounted in the University Library by myself, together with a fellow student, Sue Walker, and the University's then Assistant Archivist, Michael Bott. In the course of carrying out research for this exhibition and gathering material, I became friendly with Patience Empson and with Albert Cooper, the pressman at the Golden Cockerel Press, and was introduced to many of Gibbings's family and friends. In 1989 I helped to organize a centenary exhibition of Gibbings's work at The Museum of Reading, again in conjunction with the University Library. Shortly after this I joined the staff at the Department of Typography & Graphic Communication and the idea of writing a biography developed.

For the past ten years, since the project was first suggested, I have been working closely with Patience Empson. During regular visits to Footbridge Cottage, where she still lives, we have sipped tea (and whisky), sitting by the window looking out onto the garden, surrounded by Robert's books and prints, as we have discussed the past. Patience has been a generous collaborator and over this period has passed over to the University of Reading an extensive archive of material which, in her role as secretary and personal assistant, she had filed in an orderly fashion in Gibbings's studio. This includes much of Gibbings's correspondence from 1945 onwards and manuscripts, typescripts, woodblocks, prints, drawings, paintings and photographs — many of which are published here for the first time. The letters generally consist of original letters from correspondents writing to Gibbings with carbon copies (typed by Patience) of his letters. This material, together with the collections in the William Andrews Clark Memorial Library, UCLA, in Los Angeles and the Harry Ransom Humanities Research Center, The University of Texas at Austin, Texas, have been major sources for this study.

Gibbings was a person so concerned with the visual world that it seems appropriate to tell the story of his life in pictures as well as in words and the book also brings together a wealth of illustrations, both of Gibbings's own work and photographs recording his life. Many of the images included are primarily here to illustrate the narrative, others are reproduced as works of art. In order to include as many of the former as possible it has been necessary to reduce many of them in size; the latter have been kept as close to the originals as possible.

His influence as a wood-engraver is acknowledged by contemporary engravers. Simon Brett, one of the leading engravers in this country today, recently commented on Gibbings's strengths and weaknesses: he describes him as a hugely prolific but uneven artist, recognising his early work as 'stunning' and 'radical' but criticising his later work as anecdotal and banal, while noting his 'vivid sense of the shape of the page'. But what is undisputed is his 'impresario's contribution'; Brett asks: 'Where would any of us be without him?'.[3] Gibbings produced over fifteen hundred wood-engravings in his lifetime and his role in popularising and promoting the medium is unrivalled.

Gibbings had many friends and his social circle was extraordinarily wide. People from all backgrounds and occupations were drawn to him; this has made it possible to mention only some of those who knew him. Indeed, his output of work means that there must be many examples of his engraving, publishing and broadcasting that I have not documented, and being such a compulsive letter writer, there must be collections of letters I have not seen. However, I have made the book as comprehensive as I can and attempted to give an accurate account of an amazingly rich and varied life, perhaps only possible in the era in which he lived, and to cover the great diversity of his talents and achievements.

Chapter One
An Irish Childhood 1889–1910

For Robert Gibbings Ireland was a spiritual home. Most of his adult life was spent in England or travelling the world, but he never lost his love of County Cork. Much later in his life, he wrote to a friend (an American publisher), outlining ideas for his next book: '... it really does seem best that I should go back to Ireland, where I belong, and do my next book there. ... In Ireland I know the idiom as well as I know the people, and they all know me, and will be only too anxious to help. ... It is superb country all round there, to my mind the finest in the world ...'.[1] Gibbings had a great sense of place and despite his love of travel and exotic lands, he was always proud and anxious to acknowledge his 'Irishness'. The book referred to was *Sweet Cork of Thee*, published in 1951, in which Gibbings created a rich and affectionate picture of the landscape and people with whom he grew up.

The Gibbings family roots in the south of Ireland date back to Elizabethan times. Advancement and an increase in family fortunes took place after the English Civil War when, owing to their support of Cromwell's cause and service in the Parliamentary army, they were rewarded with grants of land in County Cork. The land eventually passed out of the family's possession and many of the male members became clergyman in the Protestant Church of Ireland. So Gibbings was born into a religious family — not wealthy but comfortable and well respected. His father, the Reverend Edward Gibbings, was the son of John George Gibbings of Montenotte in the city of Cork. Born in 1859, Edward was educated at Queen's College, Cork, and Trinity College, Dublin, and following the family tradition was ordained in 1883 as a Deacon, and in 1884 as a Priest, in St Finn Barre's Cathedral in Cork, where he later became a canon.

Edward's first post was as Curate of St Luke's Church in Cork. Now that he had a living he was in a position to marry and on 15 June 1886 he took Caroline Rouvière as his bride and the couple moved into a house in Clarence Terrace. Caroline was the daughter of Robert Day, a distinguished and successful businessman who, among a number of enterprises, had become head of the family firm, a renowned saddlery and tackle business in Patrick Street, Cork. He had married the daughter of Robert Scott, the owner of another major business in the city, of which Day had then become managing director. Apart from business, Robert Day was a passionate collector and gained a considerable and widespread reputation

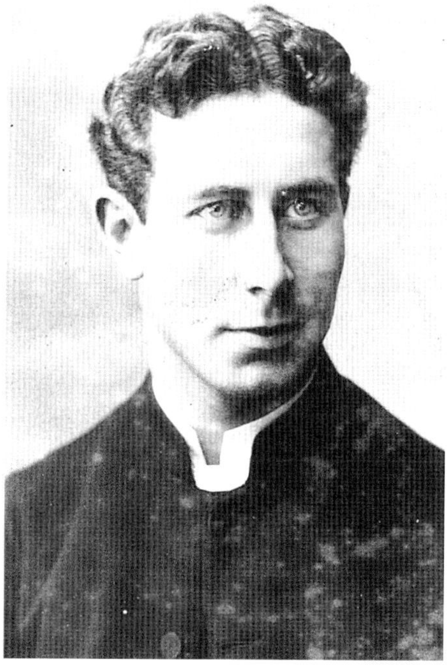

1 Robert's father, the Reverend Edward Gibbings.

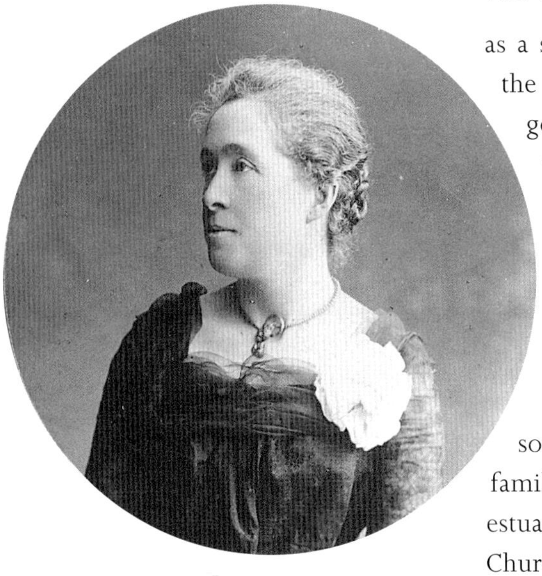

2 Robert's mother, Caroline Rouvière Gibbings (née Day).

as a scholar and antiquarian. The family home, Myrtle Hill House, overlooked the river Lee and was a treasury of beautiful objects, ranging from ancient gold ornaments of Ireland to ethnographic curiosities from around the world.

Edward and Caroline Gibbings soon started a family: first born was Edward Maurice, followed two years later by Robert John, who was born on 23 March 1889. After a gap of some years the couple had two daughters: Caroline May in 1893, and Rebecca Aimée in 1897 (always called May and Aimée by the family and friends).

In 1890, Edward was given his own parish in Carrigaline, a small village south of Cork, half-way between the city and the coast. Five years later the family moved to the beautiful coastal town of Kinsale, overlooking the winding estuary of the Bandon river, where Edward was appointed Rector of St Multose Church. An ancient building dating from the thirteenth century, the church had a much bigger congregation than his previous parishes and the living also provided a comfortable residence called the 'Glebe'.

It was a caring and secure home that Robert grew up in. There was a certain discipline and he was expected to attend church but outside these limitations Robert was free to wander, to explore and to ramble, and to develop a strong feeling for the landscape and wildlife. His father, Edward, although large in stature (as Robert was to become), was a kind and gentle man with a simple and innocent nature — much loved by the local people. Robert had a great affection for his father despite his rather pious and puritan approach to life. Through example Edward instilled in his son a love of living things: 'He loved his fellow creatures. Never in my life did I hear him say an unkind word about man, woman or child. He loved, also, every manifestation of nature.'[2] Edward Gibbings was a staunch believer in temperance, among other virtues, which perhaps accounts for Robert's rebellious nature and later love of good wines and whiskey. Of his father, Robert wrote:

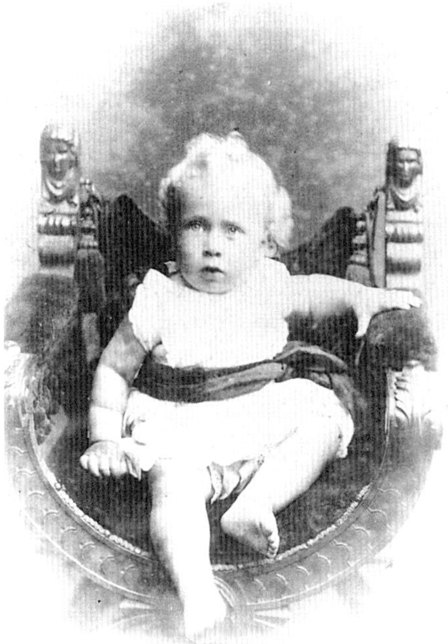

3 Robert Gibbings at one or two years of age.

> During 'the bad times,' just after the Irish Free State came into being, my people were living in the south of Ireland. My father, as I've said before, was a parson, and one of the things he believed was that 'a parson had no business to be mixing himself up in politics.'
>
> Whatever he might think, it was better for him to mind his own business. And so, beyond voting occasionally for William O'Brien, he never uttered a political opinion, but ministered to all with the kindliness which filled his soul.
>
> To give you an idea of the man I ought to tell you that he prayed in season and out of season. He could hardly put on his boots without muttering a prayer, and the queer thing was that, when he prayed, he groaned aloud as if in the travail of his soul. I've heard him groaning in the larder, I've heard him groaning in the stable, and at all queer times of the day he would retire to his bedroom and drop on his knees for a few moments.
>
> I remember one occasion, just after we had got a new housemaid. Soon after her arrival, in the middle of a morning, she came running to my mother.
>
> 'Come quickly, mam, the master is above in his bedroom, and he's dying of pain.'
>
> 'That's nothing, Mary,' said my mother, 'tis only praying he is.'
>
> 'Lor, mam, but isn't he the holy man!'[3]

In later life Robert was recognised by an old woman to whom he had given a lift:

'And aren't you a fine strong man, God bless you. Yerra, there's nothing like them Protestant clergy for bringing up families. Sure, aren't they decent, honest men, every one of them, and don't they set a fine example to their children. Oh then, I remember your father well — as quiet and sober a man as I ever met.'[4]

His father never discriminated between Protestant and Catholic, rich or poor: 'Ah, sure, there's never been any one like the canon. Didn't he do as much for us as his own?' a local Roman Catholic parishioner remarked years later, 'And wouldn't he be down on his knees on the cottage floors playing with the children?'[5] Although a Protestant, his father's conviction went far beyond any sectarianism — his religion was of the heart. Yet despite this, and the fact that the family had been in Ireland for many generations, the Gibbingses could never be considered anything other than Anglo-Irish. Still some years before the partition of Ireland, their social standing inevitably associated them with the Anglo-Irish Protestant ascendancy. But the Protestant community was a long established one in southern Ireland and people of both the Protestant and Catholic faiths had lived together in tolerance and acceptance for many years.

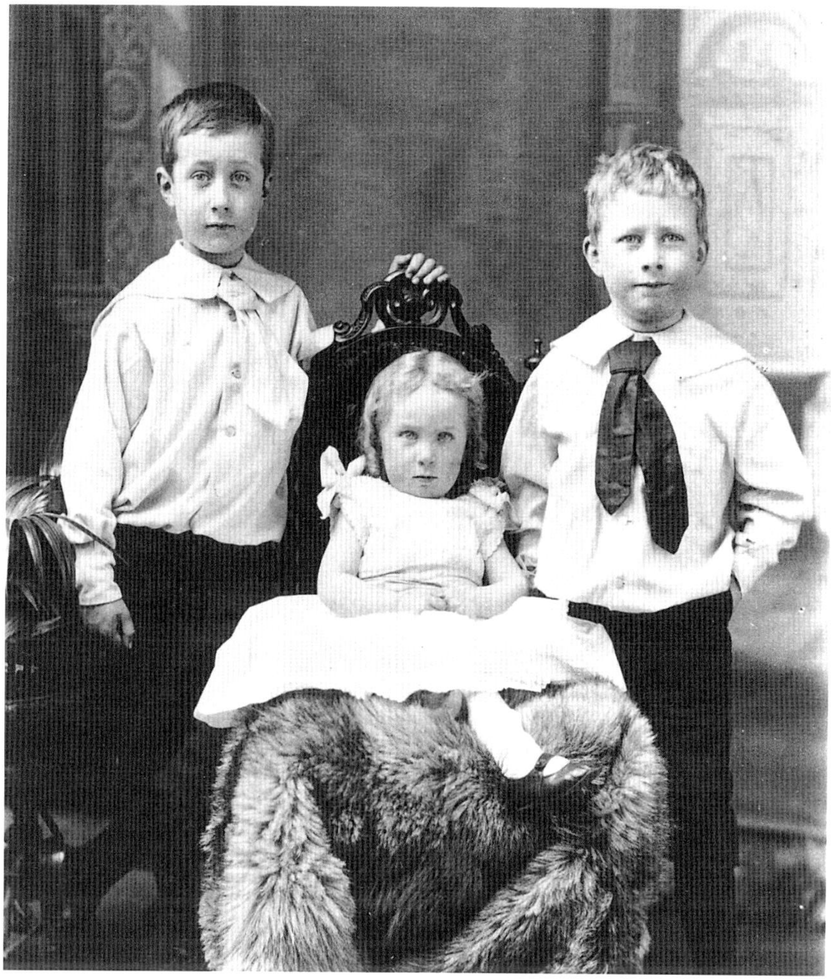

4 Robert Gibbings (*right*) with his brother Edward Maurice (*left*) and sister Caroline May (*centre*).

Robert attended a Dame School in Kinsale run by a Miss Eleanor, assisted by her sister, Miss Harrie Orr, who had given him his first lessons in drawing — copying geometric patterns. Apart from education he recalled that much of his energies were 'taken up in shivering at early morning bathing parties and sweating at midday bicycle picnics, for I was the youngest among my companions and I found it very hard to keep up with them'.[6]

Robert described Kinsale as a prosperous town at that time, an historic place with fine star-shaped fortresses on either side of the harbour. It was a thriving fishing port: boats from Scotland, Cornwall, and the Isle of Man following the herring and mackerel jostled in the harbour. During the week 'the quay would be alive with men and women salting and packing the fish, while at the week-end the inner harbour would be solid with smacks. At that time, too, a British regiment stationed in the town brought a considerable revenue to the business community'.[7] Outside the bustling town the surrounding countryside and coastline offered a richness of nature and history to explore. For the young Gibbings it must have been a paradise, and here began his passion for water and boats that stayed with him all his life. He was fascinated by the local boat builder's yard: 'As a boy I used to watch racing yachts growing out of a foam of shavings ... as a young man I used to hire yachts ... for a couple of shillings a day.'[8]

Both his parents were involved in the community. Reminiscing with an old childhood friend, Robert remembered '... the model yacht regatta which my mother organized each year for the young people, and the Saturday-night prayer meetings which my father organized when the fishing fleets were in harbour'.[9]

Robert loved his mother dearly but she died at the tragically young age of forty-seven, when he was just eighteen, of a bowel obstruction complicated by appendicitis. She was a woman full of energy and fun, always organizing some event. Picnic parties were a particular enthusiasm, as Robert recalled on a visit to Garrettstown close to Kinsale:

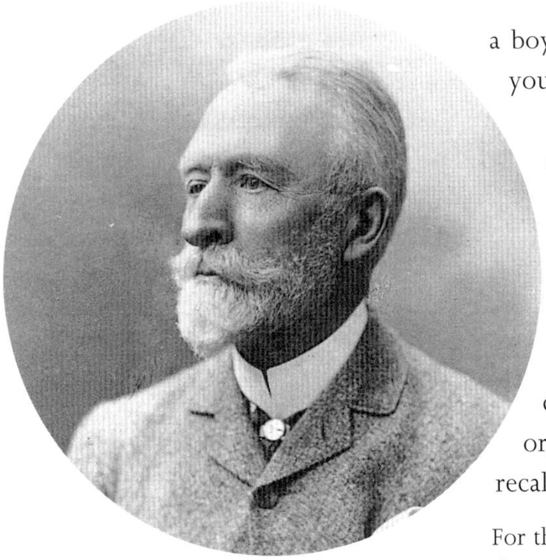

5 Robert Day (1836–1914). Robert Gibbings's grandfather was a successful businessman and prominent citizen of Cork. A Justice of the Peace, he was also an Alderman of the city and for one year its High Sheriff. A man of great intellect and scholarship, he was a Fellow of the Society of Antiquaries; he also founded and was president of the Cork Historical and Archaeological Society and was a member of the Royal Irish Academy. Reflecting his broad interests, he was Vice-President of the Ex Libris Society and Fellow of the Numismatic Society, at one time the President of the Cork Literary and Scientific Society, and a Trustee and Governor of various banks and commercial institutions. In the photograph he looks rather grave but he had a generous and outgoing personality. A confident and fluent public speaker, he was described as an excellent raconteur. He enjoyed imparting facts and minute detail – all qualities that were to be passed on to his grandson, Robert, on whom he undoubtedly had a great influence.

> For the seven years that my father was rector of Kinsale, Garrettstown was to us children the summit of our ambition for picnics. It was seven miles from the town, a long distance for small boys, but my mother would organize parties, hiring a two-horse waggonette for the occasion. 'Oh, boys, do you smell the sea?' she would say with delight, as we drove along the last mile of tree-shaded road that brought us to the strand. Then there would be paddling and bathing and the building of sand castles, and old Joaney who lived in a cottage on the cliff near by would boil kettles for our tea. My mother loved the wildness of that strand, not only in summer but in the winter, and when in Kinsale after a south-westerly gale she could hear the distant rumble of the storm-flung shingle, she would hire a side-car and, taking a few of us with her, drive out 'to see the waves.'[10]

A childhood acquaintance later described Robert's mother as a 'handsome rather sentimental woman' with a 'fine voice'[11] — her musical talents were inherited by her daughter Aimée. Robert was very close to his mother, and much of her spirit and sensuality, her love of the hugeness and force of nature, lived on in him. Robert's character was also greatly influenced by his maternal grandfather, Robert Day. The young boy must have been fascinated and overawed by the curiosities and books that filled Myrtle Hill House — objects that told of far away places and people that stimulated his young imagination. Robert described his Grandfather as:

> ... a remarkable man if ever there was one. I don't suppose there are many antiquarians alive who haven't heard of Robert Day of Cork — not important ones, anyway. Wherever you go you'll find traces of his collection: Roman beads in the museum at Cirencester: Fijian flesh-eating forks in New Zealand: medals wherever medals are to be found .... The trouble with some grandparents is that they die too soon. There he was, with his hall filled with Polynesian clubs, and his study packed with everything from old gold ornaments downwards, and now they are all dispersed, and all that I remember of him is a fine hearty handsome man with great knowledge.[12]

Visits to an uncle added to Robert's sense of wonder and curiosity about distant lands. Exploration of his uncle's house led to 'a scarce-used room, wherein were treasures innumerable. Fantastic shells from foreign shores. Cabinets of tropic butterflies, cases of exotic beetles, ships inside bottles'.[13]

Although this was a cultured environment for Robert, his immediate family were not academic or intellectual. Gibbings had a deep and instinctive feeling for history, for physical objects but also for myths and legends and the spirit and atmosphere of the past, which seems to have been with him from childhood. In the country he was surrounded by ancient remains which he would explore and it was on such an expedition to the ruin of Ringroan Castle, a few miles from Kinsale, that Robert made his first serious attempt at sketching at the age of ten.

With another boy, now a Very Revd., I crept away shyly, complete with notebook and pencil, and later in the day was not displeased by my parents' comments when I ventured to show them what I had done. This was my first practical adventure into the realms of art, though a year earlier when on holiday at Baltimore, a sea port some fifty miles from Kinsale, my eyes had been opened by a friend of my mother's who could do what seemed to me wonders with a box of water-colours. She must have been about thirty-five years of age and I was about nine, and I used to stand behind her for hours while she sketched, watching the miracles she worked on paper, watching, too, the lights in the rather prim coils of her flaxen hair.[14]

On occasions the freedom he enjoyed as a boy inevitably led to misdemeanours. Gibbings later delighted in recounting one such incident when he found some gun cartridges in the loft of the rectory:

I opened the lot, about two dozen, and having extracted the powder I put a heap of it under the kitchen table and laid a trail from that to the back door. We had a large fat cook called Mary, in my parents' estimation a little inclined to swearing and drink but otherwise an angel. Waiting till she was bending over the table, I put a match to the end of the trail. Then I nearly died of fright. There was a rush of flame and the next moment a screeching and a swearing from the kitchen such as I'd never heard in all my ten years of life. Smoke poured out of the kitchen door into the passage where I was hiding, and through the half-opened window into the stable yard. I thought it wiser to hide in a remnant of hay that had also been left behind in the loft. When next Mary saw me she came after me with a broom. 'May the divil crack your bones!' I heard her shouting. She cornered me in the loose-box and was about to murder me, as I thought, when suddenly she stopped, threw her arms round me, and hugged me. 'Your father was wild with you,' she said, 'but sure, I told him 'twas only an accident.'[15]

Robert was to be wrenched from this secure and idyllic world of childhood when at the age of eleven, too old for the cosseted and protected nest of the Dame School, he was sent away to boarding school, and experienced his 'first pangs of loneliness'. The school was in the town of Fermoy, about twenty miles north of Cork on the banks of the River Blackwater. This was a new experience, standing on his own feet, but Robert seems to have adapted, albeit reluctantly, to his new life. Two impressions of this time stayed with him: one to do with the mysteries of women and childbirth, the other with sport — both topics of fascination for young schoolboys.

I liked the headmaster and I admired his wife. She had a baby during my first term, a complete surprise to me, though some of the senior boys said that of course they knew. This business of babies was very mystifying to me just then. Twice it had occurred in my own family without apparently a word of warning. It just happened. I had gone to bed as usual the night before, and next morning there was my mother with a baby in her arms. After the second of these events, I determined that I would keep a very close watch, and I did so for several months without results. Then the idea went out of my head. And now at Fermoy almost the very same thing had occurred again!

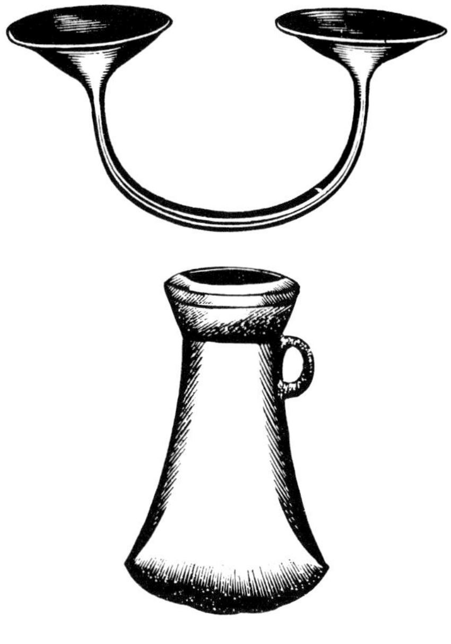

6 Wood-engraved illustrations (actual size) by Robert Gibbings of a gold fibula and bronze axe head from *Sweet Cork of Thee*, 1951. These objects were found by local farmers and became part of Robert Day's archaeological collections. Day kept meticulous hand-written catalogues of his material, illustrated with watercolours of objects mainly drawn by himself. However, one of the catalogues contained a pencil sketch of a silver crucifix, signed and dated, R. J. Gibbings 1907, so it would seem Robert occasionally helped his grandfather document his collections.

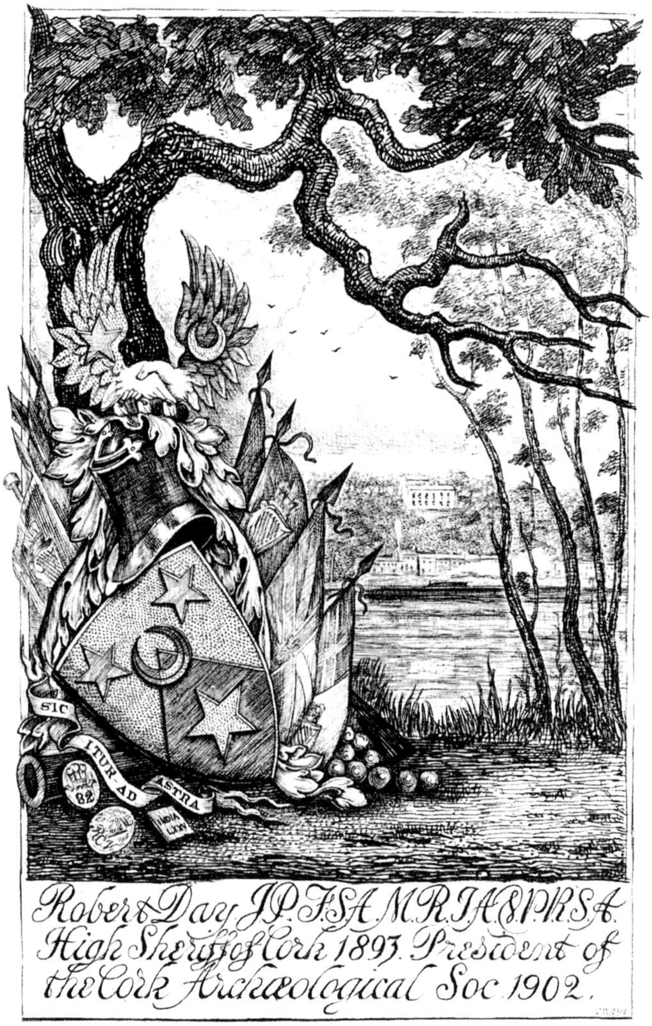

7 One of Robert Day's bookplates with a view of Myrtle Hill House where Robert visited his grandfather and was fascinated and intrigued by the collections of archaeological material and exotic ethnographical artefacts from far off places. After his death in 1914 most of his collections were sold at auction and dispersed, much of the material ending up in major museums.

At that school I first learned of compulsory games. Till I went there I thought games were pastimes to be enjoyed when one felt like playing; I hadn't realized that they were more important than classroom study. And it took me a long while to understand why, having run all over the field till I hadn't a breath left in my body, I should get a furious kick in my bottom from a husky full-back, twice my size, with the injunction, 'Play up!' I was never built for such violent and continued exertion, but shone at the end of a tug-of-war rope where my instructions were 'Lie on it!'[16]

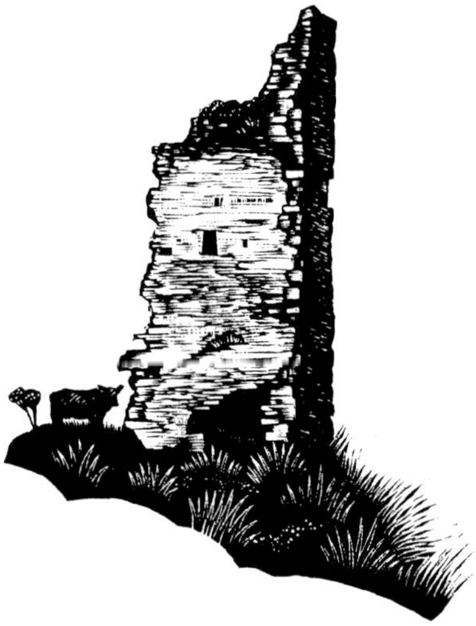

8 The ruins of Ringroan Castle. A wood-engraved illustration (actual size) by Robert Gibbings from *Sweet Cork of Thee*, 1951. The ruins were the subject of his first serious attempts at sketching as a young boy.

Already, in his early teens, Robert was tall and well-built, but although impressive and strong, he was never physically aggressive by nature, rather being a genial and warm personality, quick to make friends, inheriting his father's gentleness. Robert also failed to distinguish himself at cricket, only managing to be selected as the twelfth man in the fourth eleven. But not all activities caused him stress: in quieter moments he had made friends with a boy who enjoyed copying prints and illustrations from books using pen and ink and before long Robert was inspired enough to try this himself.

His exile at boarding school was to last for only two years, for in July 1902, when Robert was thirteen, his father was appointed Rector of Carrigrohane, and

Robert became a pupil at the day Grammar School in Cork. Carrigrohane was a larger parish, although still modest in size, centred on the Victorian Gothic church of St Peters — but, most importantly, the Parish provided a substantial Rectory. The village of Carrigrohane is on the western outskirts of Cork, a few miles from the city, beside the River Lee. Robert no longer had the sea but now he had the gentle waters of the river to explore — long days of messing about in boats, fishing, lying in the grass on the banks watching the birds and animals.

The Rectory was a real family home, surrounded by farmland and open country, and, with a small domestic staff, life was comfortable in a modest way. Memories of the house were always held in great affection by Robert, as too were memories of one old retainer:

> The rectory at Carrigrohane was a 'pretty' house, with plenty of eaves and creepers. A nice sweep of a drive, with meadows on either side, swung up from the road to its porch, and behind the house a flower garden framed in thick beech hedges was backed by an acre of vegetables. There was a coach-house, stabling for three horses, and lots of sheds for sticks and coal and dogs and rabbits. All that was the domain of an elderly retainer, Mr George Payne. He had seen long service at the rectory before my father was appointed to the parish, so that Boss Payne was indeed a part of the eleven acres that went with the house. For quite a long while we had growing in our garden only the particular vegetables that he and his family liked. He had a cottage rent free at our gate, and for working without thought of time for six and a half days of the week, my father paid him eleven shillings over a period of many years.[17]

The land around the Rectory was sufficient to support a small amount of livestock and Robert was involved with their care:

> I have spoken of Boss Payne because among his other duties was the care of Spot, a red-and-white cow whose name describes her appearance. Many a time of an evening, leaning over the haggard gate with Payne, I would share his anxieties about the family cattle. There was a time when one of our two cows had to have an inch cut off the tip of her horn because it was curling inwards to the skull. While he held the animal's head I did

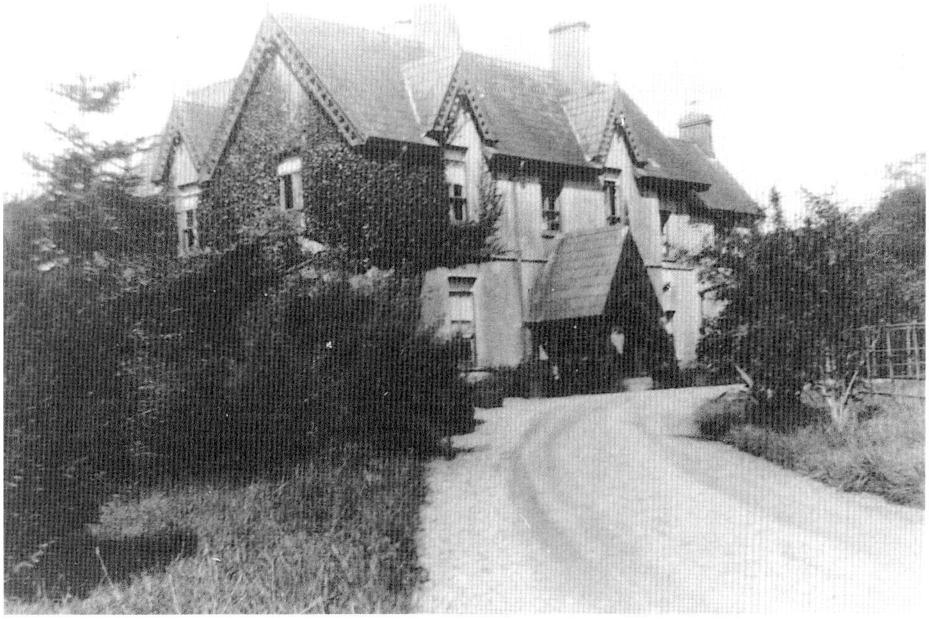

9 The Rectory at Carrigrohane, Robert's family home from 1902 when his father became Rector of St Peter's Church in the village.

the operation with a hacksaw, all the more interesting because in school that day the chemistry master had told us that horn, hair, and finger or toe nails were rich in ammonia and when heated gave off that gas. Next day in the lab I tested this with an inch of horn and nearly asphyxiated the school.[18]

The headmaster at the Grammar School was another clergyman, a rather eccentric man who 'wore rubber-soled shoes and had glass filled in the doors of all the rooms. In his class school began each day with gabbled prayers, the prayer merging without a pause into the subject of the first hour's teaching: "... through Jesus Christ our Lord Amen $x^2 + y^2$ + something-or-other equals what? Hands up when you've got it. Come on, get on your seats quickly!" I learned nothing there except the answers to a few questions that enabled me to pass matric'.[19] A school friend recalled Robert as a pupil:

Bob Gibbings was my contemporary and we were classmates at the Grammar School under Harvey. Owing to the fact that he lived in the country at Carrigrohane Rectory, his attendance was not very regular, and consequently he was not a star pupil. He was a genial, popular boy and enjoyed a certain prestige by the sort of intimate knowledge that city boys only acquire later, when they arrive at the trout-fishing, snipe-shooting stage. His genius for drawing was evident at an early age. A lightning sketch of a master on the blackboard was always recognisable and sometimes, no doubt, brilliant.[20]

Formal lessons, learning facts by rote, cramming for exams, this was not the kind of learning Robert responded to. He absorbed things through his own discovery, from experience, sensations, and a passionate fascination with nature and the people around him. The classroom held no interest for him and Gibbings himself admitted that he was really educated in the snipe bogs and trout streams of Munster. Every available moment was spent out in the countryside, fishing, rummaging about in manure heaps to find red-and-white ringed brandings as bait for the hook, stalking the undergrowth with his dog (a pointer bitch), letting off the occasional shot (although in later life Gibbings regretted his hunting: '... I now get far greater pleasure walking the country, armed only with a pair of field-glasses, than ever I did when carrying a double-barrelled gun'),[21] often causing concern when arriving home dirty and wet after a day rambling with one of the local boys. But equally he would spend time alone, '... searching for places where there was no sign of human existence, no roads or cottages or even smoke from cottage fires, no cultivated fields, no hedges ...'.[22]

Robert was eager to learn, he had a real thirst for knowledge, but only on his own terms:

Up in the hills of Ballyshoneen and out in the Muskerry bogs; those were the places where I learnt anything that has been of value to me ever since.

I had a friend called Rafferty, Tom Rafferty. When I knew him first he was a middle-aged man, and a teacher in the village school, but my father, who had been at Trinity College, Dublin, with him, used to tell of the man's brilliance as a student. Apparently Greek and Latin came as naturally to him as his mother's milk, but there was one other thing that came easier still, and it wasn't in a milk bottle. ... he dropped farther and farther from grace until he had been glad to earn a few shillings grinding the Latin into unwilling heads. But sometimes he would come shooting with me, though he never brought a gun and always insisted on carrying the bag. On these occasions it was his great delight as we went along to recite stories from the classics. Any excuse would set him off. A few moments' shelter in a cottage and I would hear about Baucis and Philemon.[23]

Life in the village inevitably revolved around work on the farms. Robert helped in the fields, forking the wheat onto the horse-drawn carts, enjoying the ritual of raising the rick and the skill of the labourers, and attending to the animals. Spot the cow was an important member of the household, Gibbings recalled:

It was early one Sunday morning that Boss Payne ... woke me with stones against my window. 'Come down, Mister Bob,' he said. 'Spot is bad.' She was certainly in pain when I reached the cowshed, and I could do no more than I was told. I won't go into details. The calf was born by means that still seem to me incredible, and then I just had time to find the helping farmer a drink before rushing off to teach in Sunday school.[24]

His position as the son of the Rector meant that he had obligations and had to conform to the practices of the church. Sunday service, prayer meetings, Sunday school, he was made to attend them all. Perhaps this forced piety led him to reject any formal religious beliefs and positively avoid any involvement with the established church. As a child he had been frightened by the descriptions of hell and damnation: 'I have always had a horror of the fate of Korah, Dathan, and Abiram. The idea of earth opening and swallowing, and then slowly squashing one to death, has terrified me ever since as a child I heard some monstrous sermon on the subject.'[25] Gibbings did have a deep spiritual belief, which rested more in a broader sense of the power of nature, not confined to the strictures of any dogma. His father had a fundamental belief in the power of evil, which seemed to Gibbings confusing given his almost naive and trusting character. Gibbings had heard him say from the pulpit '... that the devil was waiting outside the church door like a black cat ready to jump on our shoulders as we went out'.[26]

At the early age of fourteen or fifteen, Gibbings had already decided that his ambition was to be an artist. In such a religious and puritan family this suggestion was bound to meet with opposition. To become an artist was an outrageous thought to his father — after all it would mean looking at naked ladies and was bound to result in starvation! It was his mother who defended him: '"Leave the boy alone." That's what she used to say when uncles, aunts, and other loving relatives ballyragged me for wanting to be an artist. I still remember the scorn with which one of them, an aunt by marriage, said to me: "You don't suppose *you* could be an artist."'[27]

Overwhelmed by the opposition, Gibbings had no option but to give in to his father's wishes, and in 1907, the year that his mother died, he was sent to University College in Cork to study medicine. Why this was to be the preferred profession is uncertain. It seems a strange choice given Robert's lack-lustre academic career to date, but it was a respectable profession, offering the chance to make a worthy contribution to society, and one which also offered security. Perhaps his family had hopes that he would follow the distinguished medical career of his namesake and probable relative, Dr Robert Gibbings, in whose memory a wing of the North Charitable Infirmary in Cork had been named and built with money bequeathed by his daughter, Lady Combermere in 1893. Perhaps Robert's fascination for everything to do with natural history and biology seemed to suggest an aptitude for the subject.

Things did not work out. In his first year he passed the First Arts Examination, but during the next two years he failed the First Medical Board three times in succession. He had problems in getting on with his professors: 'It wasn't that there was any ill will between us, it was just that they couldn't agree with my answers to their questions. The professor of Zoology lamented that I seemed more interested in the outside than the inside of a rabbit.'[28] It was not all wasted time; in an article he published many years later with the ironic title 'My Career in Medicine' he wrote:

> ... I owe much in later life to those early researches in zoology, botany, chemistry and physics. Many a day I spent in the Irish bogs studying the flight of snipe, and many an evening in practical experiments in the feeding habits of trout. For chemistry I gave up hours to the boiling of liquids in which exquisite crystals would form when they cooled. The aesthetics of physics — or is it geometry? — appealed to me too and have remained a life-long interest: only the other day I was excited to learn that a spiral corresponding to the arrangement of seeds on a sunflower head could be formed from the Golden Rectangle of Pythagoras.[29]

Robert was only too willing to be distracted from his studies and spend time with the local youths. He had an ability to make friends with people from every background and level of society. A particularly close relationship was with Dan Corcoran, a local railway station master, with whom Robert spent many days and nights wandering by the river, through bogs, or over hills with their dogs. But he was also occasionally invited to tennis-parties and dances in the big country houses around Cork and experienced something of the eccentric society portrayed in the books of Somerville and Ross.

Gibbings had never taken to academic study nor did he cut himself off from the outside world and fresh air to become absorbed in books. While sailing around the islands of Polynesia on board a schooner in 1948, Gibbings listed the authors to whom he turned to fill the moments of tedium of the open sea but also confessed:

> Not that I am 'a great reader.' On the contrary, like Montaigne, I rarely read 'except at those hours when the tedium of doing nothing drives me to it.' Then I like sufficient of a book to stimulate my thoughts, not enough of it to jade my mind. Long hours of study do not suit my temperament. I am far from being one of those who, as Seneca says, 'carry intemperance into the study of literature.' I am more in sympathy with Emerson's idea that 'the rich mind lies in the sun and sleeps'.[30]

10 A view of the river Lee near Carrigrohane. A wood-engraved illustration (actual size) by Robert Gibbings from *Lovely is the Lee*, 1945.

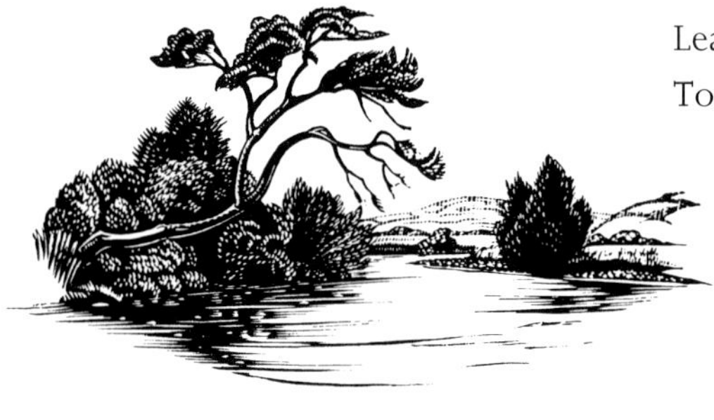

Learning through experience was another matter. He later explained to his friend Tom Balston that he had felt none of the usual qualms in the dissecting room, discovery of the workings of the body was a fascination in the sterile and isolated environment of the laboratory, but he found that he had a sensitivity and horror towards the plight of the real people on the wards that he could not cope with. But more than this, his heart was not in it, as he still cherished his ambition to be an artist. Although Robert registered for his third year of medical studies it became clear that he would never reach graduation. Eventually, despite the investment already made, his father was forced to recognise that medicine was the wrong career for his son. It was a hopeless cause even if he were allowed to sit the exams yet again, and Robert left the University towards the end of the academic year in 1910.

The financial investment had been considerable and now there was limited money available for Robert to pursue his true vocation. All that could be afforded was a year's tuition from a local landscape and genre painter, Harry Scully. Scully had been trained at the Crawford Municipal School of Art in Cork and then went to Heatherley's Art School in London. He travelled widely throughout England and the continent and returned to Ireland to establish a studio on the upper floor of an old house opposite the Crawford Art School in Nelson's Place.[31]

Scully painted many scenes around County Cork and particularly enjoyed atmospheric and moody compositions, specialising in evening light and moonlit landscapes, marshlands and expansive moorlands. Although essentially conventional in style, Scully had spent some time in Penzance and Newlyn and was, for a while, associated with the Newlyn School, and shared their sense of open air and fresh colour. He had achieved recognition and was elected an academician in the Royal Hibernian Academy in 1906. As a teacher he was also reasonably successful, holding classes in his studio for a number of local pupils. Robert had already attended some classes with Scully while at the University, and now he was able to concentrate and put all his creative energy into his drawing and painting. The teaching was not inspired but at least Robert was able to develop as a draughtsman and learn about technique, colour, and tone. And so a year passed at home with the support of his family but not their active encouragement. His father tolerated his studies for at least Scully's establishment was respectable — a number of local families sent their daughters there and under Scully's roof Robert was reasonably safe from the temptations of the bohemian life. By chance Gibbings met a fellow student some fifty years later and recalled Scully's teaching:

'How that man cared for tone!' said de Lacey.

I agreed with him. Drawing, colour, and every other desirable attribute would be added, Scully assured us, if at first we got our tones right; he nearly broke our hearts with the relative values in black and white of what we were trying to put down in colour.

'Good at colour but not a draughtsman,' suggested de Lacey.

I agreed again. Scully had little sympathy for attempts at precision. 'Don't give yourself away: feel it out,' he would say. He had been caught in the tag ends of Impressionism.

'You have travelled a different road,' said de Lacy.

'No good groping,' I said. 'Engraving has taught me that. A stroke should be a stroke, not a fumble.'

We laughed at the memory of how Scully would put us men to draw the cast of Hercules and the women that of the Venus de Milo. A nude model was not to be heard of in Cork. Scully, a Protestant puritan, said it was the fault of the priests; but on the only occasion that I was allowed to draw the Venus, he could not bring himself to mention the word 'breasts,' but explained the significant angles of the hemispheres by dumb gestures.[32]

Chapter Two

London: the Slade and the Central School of Arts and Crafts 1911–1913

THE TRAINING that Scully could provide was very limited and could not satisfy Gibbings's ambition. London was the place to study art and with financial support from his father he saved up enough money to cross the water for just one term of tuition at the Slade School of Art. At twenty two years of age it must have seemed a great adventure to be leaving the sheltered, rural existence in Ireland. Gibbings was familiar with the city of Cork but one can only imagine the excitement, mixed with trepidation, that he must have felt experiencing the scale, sophistication, and grandeur of the bustling city of London on his own.

On his arrival in London, Gibbings signed up for classes in figure drawing for six days a week, at a fee of eight guineas, and arranged lodgings at the University College Hall, Ealing. Normally it was a strict rule at the Slade that students had to reach a proficiency in drawing from casts in the 'Antique Room' before progressing to drawing from the live model. Somehow Gibbings managed to persuade Professor Brown, the Principal, to let him enter the Life Class straight away. Perhaps Brown was impressed by the drawing he had already done from casts in Scully's studio or felt sympathetic to Gibbings as he could only be there for such a short time. The teaching staff of the Slade included Frederick Brown as Professor, Henry Tonks and Philip Wilson Steer (who concentrated on painting) as his assistants, with Roger Fry as a visiting lecturer on Art History. But it was Professor Brown and Henry Tonks who dominated the school. Both men had reputations for being irascible and difficult. Brown was a 'somewhat gruff, hard-bitten man, of great feeling, with something of the Victorian military man about him'[1] — not the sort of person who usually bent the rules. Tonks appeared rather formidable too, very tall and daunting in character, capable of acid comments and scathing criticism of students' work. He had become a practising artist relatively late in life, having previously pursued a very successful medical training (unlike Gibbings). He had devoted himself to the study of anatomy and physiology and became more and more absorbed in drawing the human body, both alive and dead! Although he had eventually been appointed a senior resident medical officer, he abandoned his medical career in his early thirties to pursue his passion for painting and drawing and naturally brought his specialist knowledge and skill to his teaching. Based on the French tradition, which put great emphasis on working from the live model, it was in the teaching of drawing that Tonks and the Slade excelled. However, although 'the training ground for Britain's finest young painters, the Slade was a divided institution ... while receptive to the developments of modern art, it remained hostile to change .... Hard work and diligent study of the old masters was required for every pupil if they were to achieve the excellence in draughtsmanship which was the Slade's goal'.[2]

Tonks was an inspirational teacher, and despite his grim exterior underneath he was shy, patient and caring, taking great pains to explain his methods and his belief that to draw the figure you had to start with the structure and direction of the bones in order to appreciate the contour of the flesh and muscle — 'the word "outline" did not exist for him, and he would not allow it'.[3] In the studio students sat astride 'donkeys' (wooden stools with an easel attached), while the tutors wandered around observing their progress; teaching was done mainly through demonstration, with corrective drawings being made on the margins of the student's work. Students were encouraged to work at speed, with the point of a pencil rather than charcoal, and not to draw an exact outline to be filled in with laborious texture and shading, which they felt only masked poor draughtsmanship, but to make considered and bold marks, leaving the drawing 'open' until the student was confident of where the drawing was going. Tonks's passion, style and theories on drawing were to influence a whole generation of young artists, including Gibbings.

As in Scully's studio, men and women were segregated — female students having a separate and smaller studio than the men. The men's life room was a vast space in the basement that in height occupied two floors with skylights and tall windows extending almost from floor to ceiling in the north wall. At ground-floor level a balcony ran the width of the room leading to the Professor's office and from this vantage point Tonks or Brown could survey the class — the students becoming conscious of their scrutiny from on high. Empty, this cavernous space, part underground, had a rather gloomy atmosphere; full of students it was different: 'Here they worked, in a thick atmosphere of tobacco smoke, warmed by a coke stove on the model's throne and hot water pipes on the north wall.'[4]

On 2 October 1911, Gibbings left his hall of residence in Ealing to cross the city to the Slade. Passing from the rush and noise of Gower Street through the college gates he entered a tranquil courtyard and was confronted by imposing neo-classical buildings and neat lush lawns; he then turned left to enter the wing that was occupied by the Slade through a small semi-circular portico hung with ivy. In the entrance hall was a large attendance book — his signature appears regularly but often some way down the list — and at this point the male and female students separated as fraternisation between the sexes was discouraged even in the echoing corridors or on the lawns. Entering the hallowed ground of the men's life room to be confronted by rows of silent workers all deep in concentration staring intently through the fug of heat and tobacco at a naked woman must have filled the inexperienced Gibbings with apprehension. This was what his father had feared and Gibbings later confessed that '... I couldn't see anything wrong in that myself. I'll admit, though, that when I did reach the door of the life-room I had a slight quickening of the pulse. That all disappeared when I got inside, for there, on the throne, was the loveliest thing I'd ever seen, pink and white and fresh and natural ...'.[5]

Gibbings had entered the Slade at a remarkable period. It was almost unrivalled by any other school in England and had a growing reputation among the students for breaking new ground and supporting the *avant-garde*. Tonks, Brown and Wilson Steer were not radical in their ideas but Frederick Brown, together with others such as Roger Fry, had formed the New English Art Club in 1886, which championed the move towards 'open air realism of diffused light', following the recent developments in French art and Impressionism, and thus challenging 'the historical, allegorical and literary works produced and promoted by the Royal Academy'.[6] Augustus John, a student in the 1890s, had marked an earlier period of flourishing reputation, but the generation of students studying in the years 1910 to 1912 included an amazing array of names which were to become the leading British artists of the twentieth century. Paul Nash, in his autobiography *Outline*, described the Slade as experiencing one of its 'periodical triumphal flows'. The circle in which Gibbings found himself included Stanley Spencer, Mark Gertler, Edward Wadsworth, Adrian Allinson, William Roberts, David Bomberg, Paul Nash, Jacob Kramer, Ben Nicholson and Christopher Nevinson. Contact with female students was restricted but Dora Carrington and Dorothy Brett were students in 1911 and no doubt friendships and liaisons were formed in spite of the official attitude.

It must have been daunting to be thrown into this remarkable and diverse group of people — many of whom were unconventional and intense characters. Paul Nash compared the atmosphere in the life class as being similar to a public school, describing Nevinson as the 'school bully', who was the ringleader of his circle encouraging verbal ragging and taunting with nicknames of the 'New boys'.[7] Gibbings might well have been such a target. His large frame (by now he was just over six feet in height but had a large barrel of a chest which made him seem impressive) and Irish country ways would have made him stand out. Gibbings was quiet and somewhat shy in such circumstances but he seems to have found a solution to his vulnerability by befriending a fellow student who had already stood his ground. At this time Paul Nash was looking for a suitable model for one of his paintings. Still under the influence of the Pre-Raphaelites, the subject was to be 'Lavengro teaching Isopel Armenian in the Dingle'. But where to find his Lavengro?

A conspicuous figure at the Slade at this time was a personage known as the Man from Mexico, so-called from his habit of arriving each morning in Gower Street riding an elderly bicycle and wearing some sort of equestrian leggings and a wide brimmed hat. He was not, however, a person to stand for ridicule as the Slade wits soon found out. He had a power of caustic reprisal and was capable of aggression. His usual companion was an immense blond Irishman. After a while the Slade left them alone. But I had become interested in the Man from Mexico and was beginning to study him. His name, I discovered, was Lee, perhaps of the gypsy family? Certainly, he had in those days a gypsy look about him. At the same time his face had an intellectual structure and his finely modelled features a serious, half-sarcastic expression. He was largely built with a big head for his wide hat. Suddenly, I felt convinced that here was my model.[8]

The 'immense blond Irishman' was of course Gibbings with his new companion, Rupert Lee.

In conversation with his friend Tom Balston years later Gibbings remembered, Balston notes, '... how little they all thought of his abilities until Spencer happened to see one of his drawings of a cow'.[9] Spencer was another student who stood out through his eccentricity and stature — he was the opposite of Gibbings, being particularly small. He was nicknamed 'Cookham' but Gibbings remembered him by another name when he unexpectedly met him again more than forty years later:

... Giotto Junior, as we used to call him because of his obsession with the early Florentine artists and because of the intensity of his own religious paintings. ... Giotto was the master draughtsman among the students of our generation at the Slade. Form and its interpretation obsessed him: I remember when a huge South African joined us in the life room, Giotto who was short of stature stood looking up at his face. 'May I stroke your nose?' he asked at length, and having run his finger along the high crest of that feature returned to his easel and drew it.

Life drawing was the beginning and but a step removed from the end of all study at the Slade in those days. Colour didn't matter; it was something laid on afterwards, almost as a house decorator works. To see men scrubbing colours together on their palette until they found a flat dull tone of mud used to distress me, for I had worked under a man who couldn't draw a finite line to any form but could make his pigments sparkle almost as the French Impressionists had done. Clean, cold, unrelenting drawing with a hard pencil was the order: no 'sketching,' none of the charcoal don't-give-yourself-away school: and Giotto, though physically the smallest student in the class, was with pencil in his hand the biggest man among us.[10]

This reference to his days at the Slade is one of only a few of any significance in his writing — for some reason Gibbings rarely spoke about his experiences there. It is only in the accounts of others that fleeting mention is made of him. The impression given is that Gibbings was on the periphery of the 'in crowd'. Physically attractive as well as impressive, Gibbings had a warm and gregarious character but also took great pleasure in being solitary and was not anxious to be part of a particular group. Also he was working among a group of students of great vigour and vision, uncompromisingly pushing out the boundaries of art, and this was perhaps intimidating for a young man who had genuine talent and skill but whose vision was more simple, less intellectual or revolutionary; more based on his intuitive and sensual response to nature and form. His desire was to become competent enough to be able to make a living and pursue his rather romantic and naive ideal of life as an artist.

After only one term Gibbings returned home to Ireland for Christmas. Unfortunately at the beginning of the New Year, his father announced that he could not afford the fees to enable a return to London but the determined student proposed a compromise:

> 'If I raise fifteen quid will you do the rest?' I asked.
>
> 'I will,' he said, thinking himself safe. He forgot that, a year before, I'd bought a Hereford calf for a pound, and now it was worth eight. I had a pointer bitch, too .... She produced a litter of seven pups, and I sold them at a pound apiece. There was my fifteen pounds, and I went back to the Slade.[11]

As if to confirm his belief in himself and his chosen profession, just as he was leaving, he was given his first commission:

> ... by way of a kindly send-off, a Mrs Onslow living in the parish gave me my first commission. She asked me to design a bookplate for her husband, then a colonel, later to become Major-General Sir William Onslow, K.C.M.G. Three guineas I was to be paid for it, and when I sailed down Cork Harbour on my way, as I hoped, to 'fame,' I already seemed to have found the beginnings of fortune. Never mind the motto, *Festina lente* [the motto of the Onslow family], I was going ahead at full speed.[12]

Gibbings returned to the Slade in April 1912 for the Summer term and this time he signed up for classes for three days a week. Once again he entered the social world of student life in London which was, as ever, full of youthful energy and fun. The beginnings of a new liberation and egalitarianism meant that outside the college young men and women could mix more easily, and a bohemian lifestyle could be enjoyed without much money. Students wandered through the streets of Bloomsbury frequenting cheap restaurants and cafés and attending exhibitions and concerts. The Slade itself sponsored dances and picnics and fancy dress parties were all the rage. Many students found lodgings among the artists' quarters and, perhaps to be nearer the college and at the centre of things, Gibbings moved from the hall in Ealing to the fringes of Chelsea. He found rooms in a large Victorian town house with grand steps leading to the front door flanked by columns and situated near a small leafy square. Fifty-one Courtfield Gardens was just off the Cromwell Road and within easy walking distance of many of his new friends.

Soon after his arrival in London, Gibbings started on the Onslow commission. He wrote a detailed account of its faltering progress:

> In London I completed the design in pen and ink and sent it to have a line block made and a hundred copies printed, hoping that in the photography the somewhat poor qualities of my pen line might be mitigated. They weren't: the reduction in size enlarged the faults. My hopes were blasted. Here at the first chance given to me I had fulfilled the gloom of prophecies. 'You don't think *you* could be an artist? Why not go into the army and be a man?'

Having already spent twelve shillings on the block Gibbings reluctantly parcelled up the results. Almost immediately after he put the package in the post he regretted letting poor work out of his hands and rushed to the post office to retrieve it.

> Next morning at the Slade, where I was then working three days a week, I showed one of the proofs to another student.
>
> 'Your line is weak and broken,' he said. 'Heraldry is virile — it needs strength.'

'What can I do?' I asked.

'It ought to be engraved,' he said. 'Get some fellow at the Central School to go snags with you. There's a good etching class there.'

So that evening I found myself asking Luke Taylor, the head of that department, if among his students there was one who would take on the job.

'Why not put it on copper yourself?' he asked.

'Don't know how,' I said.

'You'll soon learn,' he said. 'Come and try.'

So he enrolled for two evening classes a week to learn the art of etching. But he still had two days free and could just about afford two half-days in a design class at the Central:

Noel Rooke was in charge of that department. 'Why not do wood engraving?' he said. 'It would help you.'

I had never heard of engraving on wood and was not drawn to the idea. There would be further outlay on gravers, and even at that time wood cost 1½d. or 2d. a square inch, and what was it all about anyway. I tried to excuse myself, but Rooke prevailed.

'It is what your work needs,' he said, 'and that design of the man on the hill top would be a suitable subject. We'll get your poem set up in the typography department downstairs and print the whole lot together.'

The drawing was of a naked man stretched his full length on a mountain top with vast billowing clouds passing over him, and the lines that I had written to go with it began,

Out on the mountain's breast I lie
While endless aeons onward roll,

and the idea was that, drawing strength from nature, I would one day

... rise as Adam that first day
God breathed the breath of life.

I was always a close-to-nature man. Rooke thought it should be a colour print.

So I engraved a 'key' block, and then I cut at least two more for colour, and then we printed them all together with the poem added, and still I wondered what all this business of engraving was about; and I thought so little of my first effort that I threw away all the proofs, and I doubt if there is one in existence to-day.

Meanwhile I had etched the bookplate and to my surprise it had 'come off.' With it delivered and paid for, I had just enough money to get myself home to Cork, though I had to borrow from Pat Lehane, the guard of the local line, my eightpenny rail fare to Carrigrohane where we lived.[13]

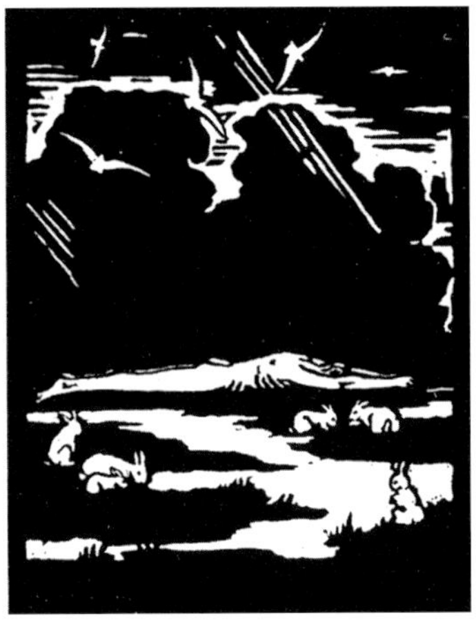

11 Untitled, c. 1912, wood-engraving, 120 x 90 mm. This image of a naked man stretched out on a mountain top was Gibbings's first attempt at wood-engraving. Gibbings claimed he thought so little of the result that he threw the proofs away. However, a print of the black 'key' block (the print was over-printed with at least two colours) has survived. The print was given to family friends and a poem written and printed by Gibbings and set in Caslon type (see below) has been pasted to the back of the frame. The print is signed and dated 1914 but this is probably the date that he gave the print away. *Reproduced with permission of C. E. Fleury.*

Out on the mountains breast I lie
While endless aeons onward roll,
Drinking that food the gods supply
Drawing my strength from nature's soul.

And when all time has passed away
With envy, hatred, lust and strife,
I'll rise, as Adam, that first day
God breathed the breath of life.

Balston described Rooke as the 'pioneer of modern wood-engraving in England' and this introduction was to have a lasting effect on Gibbings's career. If he had any doubts at that point about becoming an artist, Rooke's advice was to make the decision simple:

'Is it very foolish of me,' he [Gibbings] asked in a moment of desperation, 'to try to be an artist?'

'What else could you do?'

'Nothing.'

'Isn't that the answer?' Rooke said kindly, being convinced that Gibbings had an aptitude for art.[14]

Rooke had also trained at the Slade and in 1905 he joined the staff of the Central School of Art under William Lethaby. As the School's first principal (he was appointed in 1896), Lethaby was set on introducing his own clear philosophy and approach to the teaching of art and design. His ambition was to develop the Central 'to become for design and the crafts what the Slade School or the Royal Academy Schools were for the fine arts'.[15] Firmly based in the arts and crafts tradition, he was none the less clear in his own mind that design had to work in terms of production and, unlike some of his contemporaries, he was prepared to work with the new technology rather than to oppose it. Lethaby showed great skill in attracting talented staff to support him, and in 1899 Edward Johnston was appointed to set up a course in calligraphy. The course started with seven students, including two pupils who were to have a significant influence on Gibbings — Noel Rooke and Eric Gill. A foundation of Johnston's teaching was his simple concept that the form of a letter was determined by the form of the tool used to make it. His teaching had a profound and lasting impact on both Rooke and Gill. About this time, Rooke developed an interest in book illustration and, dissatisfied with illustrations produced using photo-mechanical processes as a means of artistic expression,[16] began to experiment with wood-engraving, encouraged by Lucien Pissarro. It was quite natural that he should apply Johnston's concept to this medium — that the marks made in the wood to create an image should be the marks naturally created by the tools used. This simple idea was in fact an important re-discovery and was to become one of the central beliefs of the movement which brought about the revival of wood-engraving in the twentieth century.

The art of wood-engraving had changed throughout the course of the nineteenth century. Since Thomas Bewick, who had engraved his own images which were full of originality, expressive energy and narrative skill, the medium had developed as a reproductive process. The engraver became someone merely employed to produce a printing block of an image created by someone else. In book illustration the engraver's task was to match the tone and line of an artist's work as faithfully as possible. The technical expertise involved was considerable but even at the highest level, with the work of such men as Joseph and John Swain or the Dalziel brothers, the engraver's reputation was still based on how well he interpreted the work of another person on wood, often in imitation of another medium. In terms of illustration it was the pictorial magazine or journal that had greatest impact on the general public in the nineteenth century. If one looks at a cartoon from *Punch* of the second half of the nineteenth century, the engraving resembles an ink drawing, even the spontaneous scribble of the artist's nib is reproduced. To achieve this effect, once the image has been drawn onto the wood-block, the engraver had to cut away all the white space either side of the drawn line, leaving the line raised as the relief printing surface. In areas of cross-hatching it was the minute areas of white space between the lines that had to be removed. This technique became known as 'black line' — one can admire the skill but the result was that as a creative medium in its own right, wood-engraving declined.

Dissatisfied with this development, a number of artists began to experiment with wood-engraving and re-discover its potential as an art form. Following on from William Morris, artists such as Edward Gordon Craig, Charles Ricketts, William Nicholson, Thomas Sturge Moore, Charles Shannon, and from abroad, Lucien Pissarro and Lepère, in their own ways were reviving interest in the artistic and expressive use of wood-engraving. But their work was still essentially based on the black line tradition; although Gwen Raverat had been doing pioneering work, it was Noel Rooke who explored the specific qualities of line and texture that belong to wood-engraving alone. Looking again at the technique of Bewick, Rooke put more emphasis on the use of the 'white line' in engraving. Using the white line technique, the engraver creates the image by cutting line and texture out of the solid black of the printing surface — a much more natural process and one which allows the artist to exploit the marks directly made by the variety of shapes cut by the tools. Above all, it was now the artists themselves who were working directly onto the block, burin in hand, no longer simply supplying drawings or paintings to be reproduced.

The course which Rooke then set up at the Central School was on book illustration. As the sole teacher, Rooke was able to direct the course towards his own interests, which included introducing wood-engraving as a subject. Had Lethaby been aware of this at an early stage, he might have objected, as his ideas about wood-engraving were still coloured by reproductive commercial engraving. There was a tradition of print-making already established at the Central, by Frank Morley Fletcher and Sidney Lee,[17] of wood-cutting in the Japanese style. Rooke, who also taught woodcutting techniques, was sensitive to the politics of the situation and started by unofficially teaching wood-engraving and limiting its use to the design of initial letters, and other embellishments of the book. Once Lethaby had resigned as Principal in 1911, Rooke was in a position to expand and develop his teaching with enthusiasm and energy, and, still in the face of some opposition, formally set up a course in Lettering and Wood-engraving. It was this course that Gibbings joined in 1912, at a significant moment, for through his teaching Rooke was to inspire a generation of engravers. Fellow pupils in the Rookery, as the class was affectionately known, were later to include Vivien Gribble, Rachel Marshall (later Mrs David Garnett) and Margaret Pilkington.

12 *Spot*, 1913, wood-engraving (actual size). Gibbings described this image of one of the cows belonging to the family as his first *real* wood-engraving.

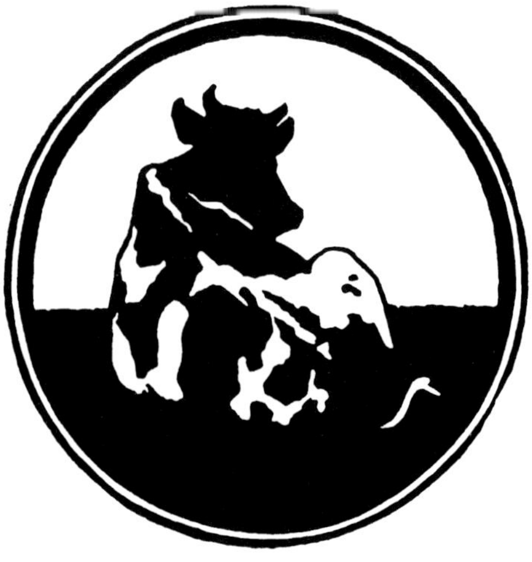

Rooke was keen to create interest in wood engraving among commercial publishers and, with this in mind, he introduced his students to modern printing techniques using powered presses and working with type. When Rooke sent Gibbings to the typography department to set his poem in type, Gibbings had come under the instruction of J. H. Mason who ran the class. Mason, an experienced and masterly typographer, had previously worked at the Doves Press and the style and design of that Press strongly influenced the printing and binding at the Central School. 'Simplicity' was the 'keynote of the printing, the placing of the type on the page taking priority.'[18] Mason had a passion for the typeface Caslon Old Face and it was used for nearly all the books printed by the School at that time. This brief but invaluable contact with Mason helped to shape Gibbings's approach to typography.

One day, back in Carrigrohane during the vacation, Gibbings looked out of a window of the Rectory and his eye was taken by the sight of the family cow, Spot, grazing on the grass:

> ... liking the pattern of her markings, I made a drawing of them in simple black and white, no attempt at lighting. That evening, looking at my drawing, I thought, 'That makes sense with wood engraving.' I hurriedly wrote to London for a block and when it came I engraved it. Then, using an old letter-press from my father's study, I took proofs. That was really, I think, my first wood engraving.
>
> Finding how well Spot lent herself to wood, I followed our second cow, a large half-Kerry, about the field as she grazed, hoping to get movement into another engraving. All went well except that as during her feeding she constantly changed direction, the shadows were now on one side, now on the other, and eventually it seemed best to turn her into a silhouette. Then, not long after this, as I was cycling along the back road from Cork, I saw in a field about a mile from home two enormous pigs sitting up on their hind quarters looking into each other's eyes over an empty food trough. I hadn't got paper and pencil with me so I pedalled my hardest to the rectory, picked up the necessary materials, and hurried back to the monumental scene. There the two of them were, still motionless, serene. But I had achieved only a bare outline of their anatomies when a farmer appeared at the other end of the field with a bucket. That was the signal for action. What had been classic was now comic, as with squeals, grunts, and flapping of ears they hurtled towards the swill. Again I had to be content with a silhouette.[19]

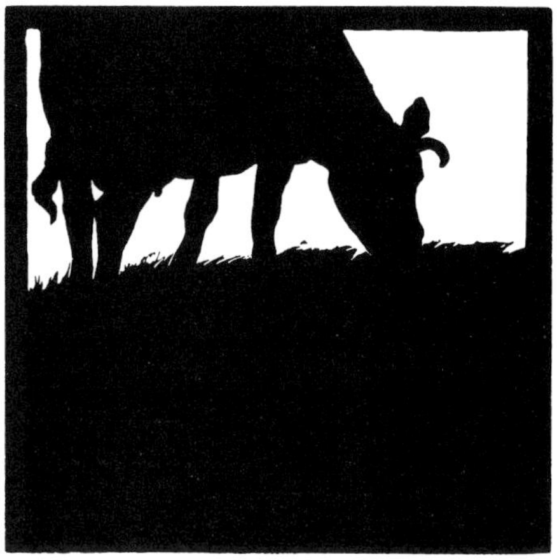

13 *The Crest of the Hill*, 1913, wood-engraving, 100 x 103 mm.

That Gibbings described these as his first *real* engravings is not surprising. His earlier attempt was naive and clumsy in execution. These three engravings, although so simple in concept, have a directness and strength of design combined with accurate observation and, in the engraving of the pigs, a wit that makes them complete and successful as images. Despite his amusing explanation for the use of silhouette, as a beginner the approach enabled him to avoid too many technical difficulties. The effect is simple and could have been achieved equally well using woodcutting techniques, for as yet Gibbings had not mastered the delicate qualities associated with wood-engraving — these would come later. The confidence and instinctive sense of design, the understanding of the balance of black and white that can already be seen in these early attempts, show that Gibbings had found his natural medium.[20] Looking back at this time he wrote:

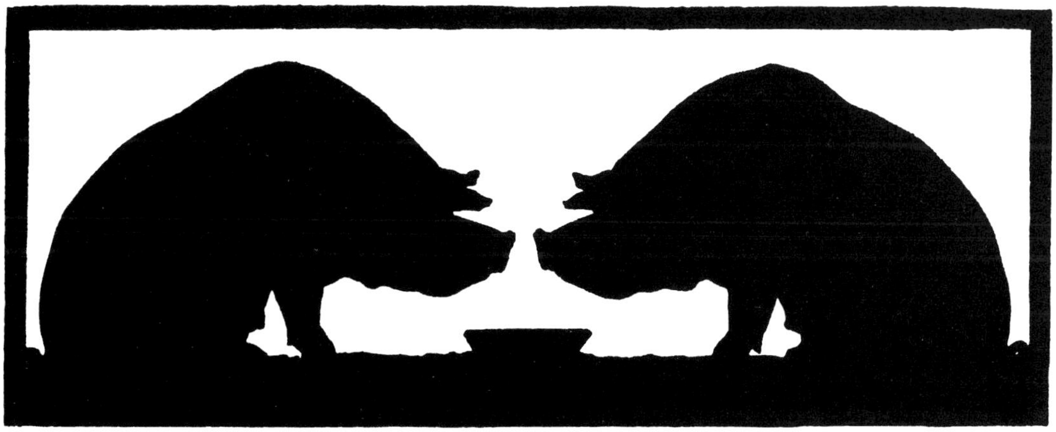

14 *The Two Pigs*, 1913, wood-engraving, 55 x 142 mm. This engraving was later entitled *An Irish Question* and appeared in volume one of the literary journal, *The Apple of Beauty and Discord*, in 1920.

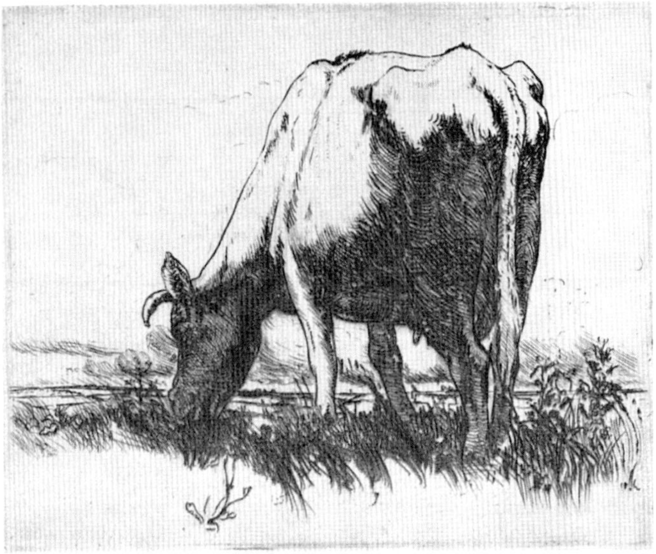

15 A cow, 1913, etching, plate size 100 x 125 mm.

When I came over from Ireland ... I found Rooke at the Central School of Arts not only teaching the craft but emphasizing to youngsters like myself that it provided a discipline of thought that was necessary to every artist. Discipline in art: was that what I'd come to London for? Impressionism was what I thought I was after. I couldn't think what all this hard labour on wood was about. There was no tradition at the time; it seemed a lot of finicky gouging to get a few lines that might have been obtained more easily with a pen or brush. But slowly a love of the wood came over me. I began to enjoy the crisp purr of the graver as it furrowed the polished surface. I began to appreciate the cleanness of the white line that it incised: even the simplest silhouettes had an austere quality, a dignity, that could not be achieved by other means. Clear, precise statement, that was what it amounted to. Near enough wouldn't do: it had to be just right.[21]

Paul Nash, in his autobiography *Outline*, has left us a rare glimpse of Gibbings as a student. Nash had left the Slade in the December of 1911 feeling that he could no longer be a financial burden on his father and soon after held a moderately successful exhibition at the Carfax Gallery. A stylish friend had wickedly fooled Nash into over-dressing for the private view — a silk top hat and a silver topped cane. This friend was Rupert Lee, whose other friendship, with Gibbings, had also continued on the latter's return to London. Although Gibbings does not seem to have become close to Nash, they did meet through their mutual friendship with Lee. Nash recorded a tea party at Lee's lodgings: 'Tea was ready by the time we reached South Parade. Rosalind was there and Rupert's Slade friend, the huge blond Irishman, Bob Gibbings. After tea Rupert played Bach to us ...'.[22]

A favourite haunt of art students was the plush surroundings of the Café Royal. Whenever they could afford it, they were able to brush shoulders with the artistic élite of London. Augustus John regularly held court there. Gibbings also quickly developed a taste for such surroundings and he was to become a regular customer throughout his life when in town and flush with money.

16 A pig, 1914, etching, plate size 76 x 100 mm.

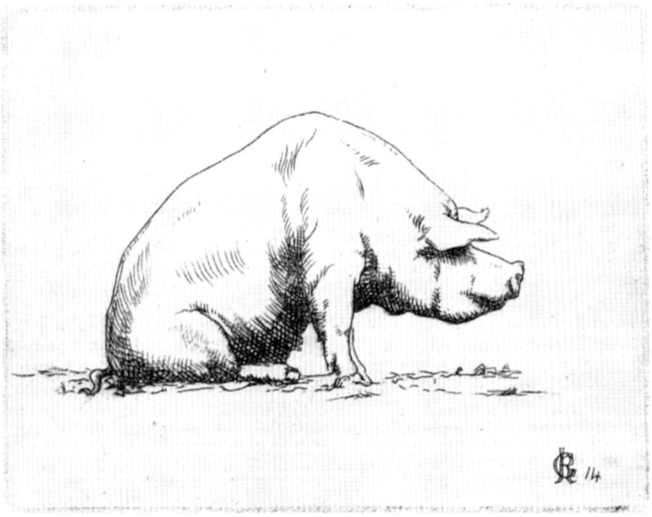

According to Nash, the London scene was still dominated by 'three rather more than life-size personalities ... Augustus John, the painter; Jacob Epstein, the sculptor; and [Edward] Gordon Craig, son of Ellen Terry, the theatrical designer'.[23] To young students they still represented something romantic, dangerous, and brilliant. Nash respected Craig above the other two. In the spring of 1913, Craig was recruiting personnel for his proposed School of the Art of the Theatre. Rupert Lee had been offered a post as musical director by Craig, and Nash recorded a meeting with Craig and Lee at the Café Royal some months later:

As I entered the Café I spied him [Craig] at the far end of the Brandy Square, but safely coupled to the dining part of the Café, with his back to the engine, as it were, with a marble table before him, from which, although he seemed to have finished his meal, the cloth was still not yet drawn. This was because Craig was still drawing all over it with a very heavy black pencil. However, the space was now so full of Theatres in the air, not unlike illustrations for De Quincey's dream and other dizzy imaginings, that an impatient waiter who had been watching him for some time, rudely snatched the table cloth almost from under the Master's pencil. Craig took no notice but merely continued his drawing upon the white marble table which from thence became transformed and animated by what looked to be a quite transposed architectural complex which even held the waiters spellbound. Meanwhile he talked. He was flanked on either side by two of our friends, Rupert Lee and Robert Gibbings, who were eagerly listening and watching. Craig asked us what we were doing or what we were going to do. 'What about you?' he said to G. 'I'm an artist,' said G. who had not yet left the Slade. 'Nonsense,' said Craig at once. 'You're too tall for an artist.' G. protested in a vigorous brogue, we all in fact demurred.[24]

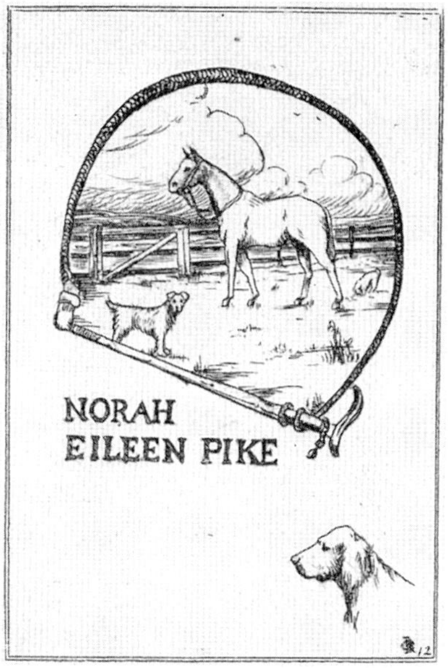

17 Bookplate: Norah Eileen Pike, 1912, etching, image size 76 x 52 mm.
Norah Pike and her brother Hubert were childhood friends of Gibbings.

Gibbings was a student at the Slade at a time which was not only significant in terms of the college itself but also in terms of British art generally. It was an era of controversy and change; Roger Fry had mounted his first Post Impressionist exhibition at the Grafton Gallery in 1910, which although a great success had stirred strong feelings amongst the establishment and the public. He was planning another exhibition for the autumn of 1911 and had a proposal to appease his more conventional colleagues: 'To make it strong I would have to devote one or two rooms to the conservatives, Steer, Tonks and Co., and then allow *les jeunes* a free opportunity in the others.'[25] However Tonks and Co. declined the offer and the exhibition never took place. 'This lack of co-operation forced Fry, when organising the 1912 Post-Impressionist exhibition, to adopt a more separatist position, thereby antagonising the old guard still further.'[26] The passion and extremism of the views that raged throughout the press and the art world must have had a heady effect on the young students at the Slade. They must have felt excitement at witnessing the beginnings of a new modernist age. The impact of seeing paintings by Cézanne, Matisse, Picasso, works from Russia, and being introduced to new ideas such as cubism, must have been enormous and shown the way forward for many of the students. Nevinson, Bomberg, Roberts and Wadsworth were to throw themselves into the modern movements. Post-Impressionism had taken hold at the Slade and a group of radical students had already collected around Mark Gertler and Nevinson calling themselves the 'Neo-Primitives'. Tonks and some of his colleagues attempted a rearguard action against cubism and recommended that students stayed away from the Grafton Galleries.[27] Gibbings could not have been unaffected by these events. The atmosphere was intense — he must have been party to discussions and arguments among his colleagues and yet he seems to have stood back from allying himself to any particular group — only later did elements of the new thinking influence his work.

18 Bookplate: the arms, crest and motto of Leslie, Earls of Rothe, 1913, image size 87 x 76 mm.

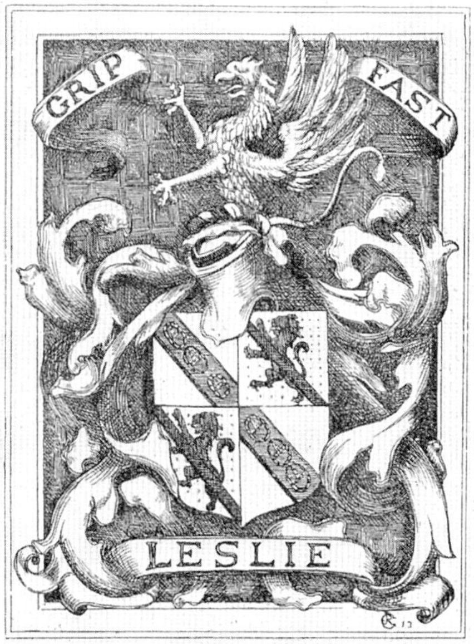

His enthusiasm for wood-engraving was growing but he still attended classes in etching where he was becoming increasingly proficient. Cows and pigs figured prominently as subject matter and his developing skill as a draughtsman shows clearly in the confidence of his line. His first commission for a bookplate had led to others. In 1912 he had designed a bookplate for Norah Pike, the sister of Hubert Pike, both childhood friends from Carrigrohane. The design is weak and

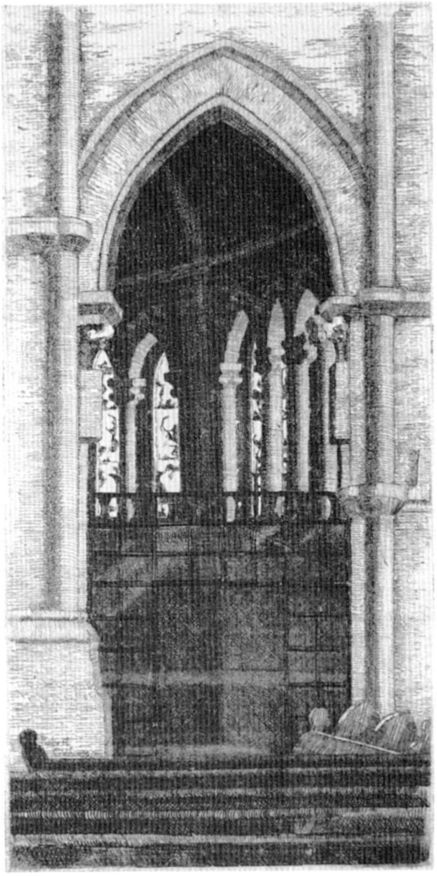

19 *Cork Cathedral*, 1914, etching, image size 171 x 88 mm.
An interior view of St Finn Barre's Cathedral in Cork where Gibbings's father was a Canon.

contrived and the horse and dog portrayed are stiff and lifeless, so different from the animals he was etching a year later. But this commission was to please a friend and not to be judged as a work of art. A year later he designed a more impressive bookplate for J. F. Leslie, an armorial design based on the arms, crest and motto of Leslie, Earls of Rothe. Bookplates were a useful commercial application for the print-maker, but the suggestion to design bookplates might well have come from his grandfather, Robert Day, who was a founder member of the Ex Libris Society and who wrote many articles on the subject.[28] In 1913, Gibbings succeeded in having a bookplate accepted for the annual exhibition of the Royal Hibernian Academy.

After three more terms Gibbings's money ran out and he returned to Ireland with a certificate in drawing from the Slade and a diploma from the Central School, but with his future uncertain. Back home, according to the people around him, he began to drift: '... in general local opinion I did nothing. "Ah sure, poor master Bob, isn't it a pity he can't settle to anything!" said Boss Payne's wife at the lodge. "There's a job in the Savings Bank here at £50 a year I could get for you," said my rich Godfather. "Better for you than loafing about at home doing nothing," he added. In fact I was working very hard with pencil and brush'.[29]

He was surrounded by people who had little knowledge or appreciation of art. Whatever they made of his activities, he had not been idle; he had produced a number of etchings of the interior of St Finn Barre's Cathedral and had been commissioned to design an heraldic bookplate for the library of his old college — University College Cork. From his own account, he had also been drawing and painting, but no trace of this work has been found.

Gibbings was now twenty-five; what was he to do next? Uncertainty about his future and his apparent listlessness were to be abruptly ended. World events were about to take over.

20 Bookplate: The Library, University College Cork, 1914, etching, diam. 83 mm. The bookplate was reproduced in an article on heraldic bookplates in *The Studio*, vol. 75, 1918, p. 86.

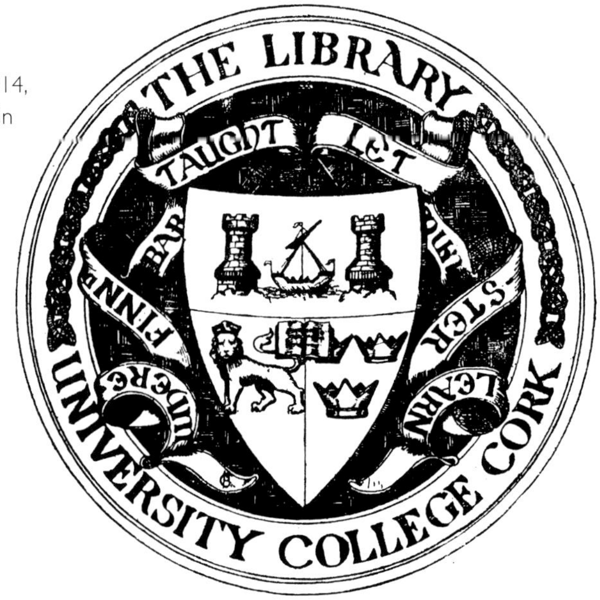

Chapter Three
War and Marriage 1914–1919

ON 1 AUGUST 1914, Gibbings was cycling home along a stretch of road beside the river Lee, when an overtaking car slowed down:

> 'Hallo, Bob, what are you going to do if war breaks out?' asked the cheery R.A.M.C. major who was driving.
> 'What war?' I asked.
> 'Against Germany,' he said. 'Any day now, looks mighty like it.'
> 'I suppose I'll come along and enlist,' I said.
> 'Nonsense, man,' he answered; 'get a commission. Go down to the Munster depot at Kinsale and they'll give you one. Of course they will.'
> That evening I felt restless. 'I'll go down and sound them,' I thought. So next morning I got on my bike and rode the twenty miles to the depot in Charles Fort — bastions and all — overlooking Kinsale harbour.
> 'Will you give me a commission if there's a war?' I asked the adjutant.
> 'We'll give you one whether there's a war or not,' he said. 'We have several vacancies.'
> 'Only if there's a war,' I replied.
> Two days later, 4th August, I was in the orderly room again. 'What about that commission?' I asked.
> 'Your name is down,' he said.
> On 15th August I was gazetted second lieutenant in the 4th Battalion Royal Munster Fusiliers .... Some time in September I reported in shining new uniform, not knowing with which hand I ought to give or take a salute. Six months later I was confirmed in my commission with high marks, the troops temporarily at my disposal being determined to make the right manoeuvres however wrong my commands.[1]

Gibbings had rejected previous advice to pursue a military career when it was given by those cynical of his artistic ambitions, but a call to duty and the possibilities of adventure, as his own choice, was another matter. Perhaps unclear in his own mind how to develop his career, he saw this as an opportunity to prove himself in the eyes of his nagging relatives. Ebenezer Pike, J. P., a wealthy Cork businessman and the father of his friend Hubert, had provided him with a good character reference and immediately on enlisting Gibbings had been sent on a training course, along with forty or so other young officers. Accusations that he was a 'loafer' were soon dispelled and his Father was to be 'surprised and pleased to get a private report that he was the most efficient of his class'.[2] Nine months after enlisting he was promoted to a full Lieutenant.

In April 1915, the first troop landings had taken place at 'V' beach on the peninsula of Gallipoli, as part of the early stages of the Allied campaign to gain

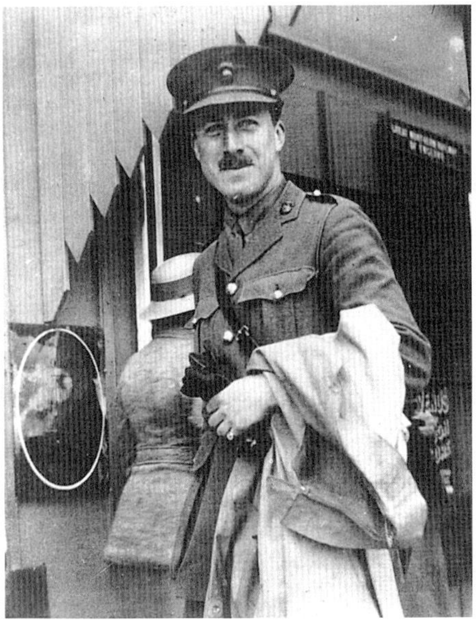

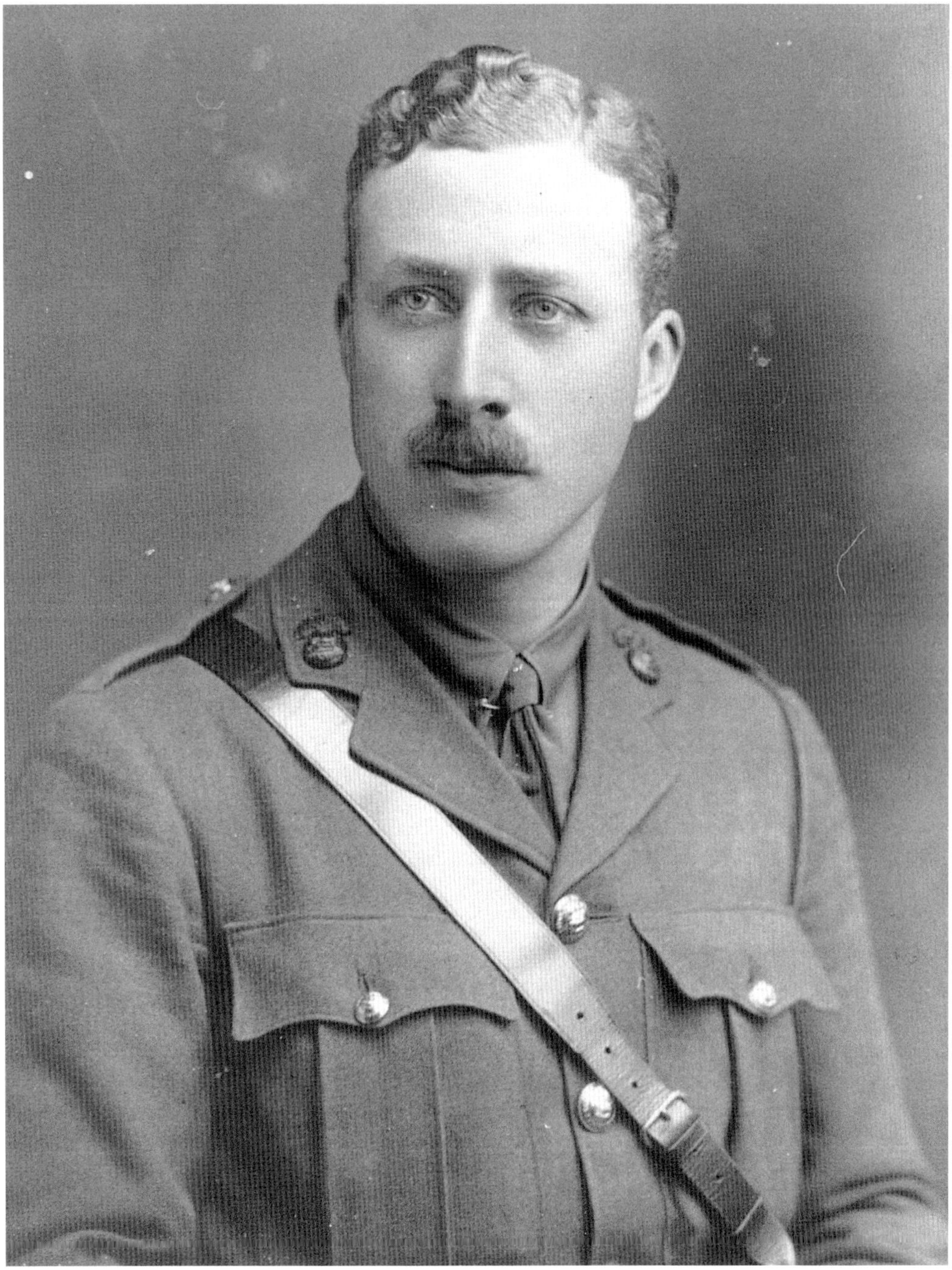

21 & 21a Gibbings in uniform c. 1915. He had joined up with the 4th Battalion Royal Munster Fusiliers on 15 August 1914.

control of the Dardanelles. This narrow spit of land had been heavily fortified by the Turks in order to cut off the sea passage and vital supply route to Russia, Britain's ally. The terrain was difficult and the coastline precipitous — concealed trenches and gun emplacements on the hills surrounding the few possible landing places gave the Turks a commanding position. To help rapid disembarkation a tramp steamer, the *River Clyde*, was to perform the function of a bridge or landing stage, and was run aground on 'V' beach. A gangway was to connect the sally ports cut in her bows with a floating bridge made from lighters and thence to the beach. At the last minute there were unexpected difficulties manoeuvring the lighters into position. The first wave of troops included the Dublin Fusiliers and the Munster Fusiliers. It fell to the Munsters to try to manoeuvre the lighters into position under the unrelenting rain of fire from the Turks. The horrendous tally of dead and injured was graphically described by John Masefield: 'They were killed as they worked, but others took their places; the bridge was made, and some of the Munsters dashed along it from the ship and fell in heaps as they ran.'[3]

More men were needed and at the end of April Gibbings and a group from his battalion sailed for the Dardanelles as part of a draft of reinforcements. For so many young men at the time, this was their first chance to travel, and despite the horror that was to come, the experience held excitement: 'I had my first sight of Malta with its medieval battlements and then of the Aegean Islands, unsubstantial as mist, rising from a mirror-like sea. "Almost worth it even if we don't come back," I thought.'[4]

By 5 May he was in the trenches. Writing home he reported, despite some minor wounds to a few men, 'so far nothing but a few spent bullets & a little shrapnel'. His main concern was that his father should send out a box of fifty packets of Woodbine cigarettes for his men, all 'awfully good fellows', and to thank his sister May for sending cocoa rations.[5] However, it was not long before the action became more intensive and in a letter of 10 June, he told his father that he was expecting to move up into the front line any day. Dug into their trenches they were now suffering from heavy shelling, 'clouds of earth' raining down on them; he also reported that a friend had been gravely wounded. Gibbings himself had had a narrow escape when sitting on the edge of the trench; on shifting position a bullet hit the very spot he had occupied.

Now second in command of his company, under a Captain Smithwick, his rank did not stop him from valuing the 'cheery' character and companionship of the soldiers around him. At night he lay awake listening to their chatter: 'Be japers when this war is over if I see as much as two dogs fighting in the street, I'll dig myself a dug out on the spot'. Another fellow looking at a great hunk of shell said 'Well now aren't they dangerous things after all'.[6] The noting and recounting of tales and anecdotes with an ear for dialect and a warm respect for the people around him was to become a natural habit throughout Gibbings's life. Later such stories provided a rich source for his own writing and added to his own convivial conversation. Boring rations, bad tasting water (Gibbings requested a supply of lime juice or lemon squash tablets), mild dysentery and the extreme heat of the day, accompanied by dust and flies, were frustrations only made bearable by cooler nights. He was anxious for news from home; how was his brother Maurice who was serving in the Navy? Could newspapers, however old, be sent? To keep in touch with the art world he asked May to send copies of *The Studio*.

By 14 June, Gibbings wrote 'everything is going strong'. His troops had moved forward behind the firing line and he was familiarising himself with the new trenches: 'They are not bad except to put it crudely for the smell of "dead Turk" which is noticeable practically everywhere .... There are a lot of dead lying about still unburied.' His Captain had been slightly wounded and Gibbings was now temporarily in command of his company and feeling somewhat daunted by the responsibility. He recorded seeing some terrible sights but tried not to dwell on them, preferring to concentrate on the many fine qualities he saw in his men and their numerous acts of bravery and compassion. He was impressed by two men who risked their lives under heavy fire to rescue a horse harnessed to a wagon that had been hit by a shell, and by the affection shown for a small mongrel terrier that had been smuggled all the way from Bere Island in Bantry Bay by one of the troopers.

The morning of 28 June was the date for a major attack in the area of Gully Beach and Gibbings was with the first few of his company moving forward. Taking cover from the shelling and the hail of shrapnel he suddenly felt 'what seemed like a blow from a sledge hammer tearing my whole throat away & at the same time a heavy bang on the left arm'.[7] Gibbings had been hit, a shrapnel bullet had passed clean through his neck just below the jaw narrowly missing his wind pipe and vital nerves and arteries and had buried itself in his forearm. His wound was hurriedly bandaged and with help from a Red Cross orderly he crawled to a dressing station where he was left lying on a stretcher for eighteen hours before he was transported by various boats to a hospital in Lemnos. Very weak to begin with he was unable to swallow more than a few sips of water and it was decided to delay operating on his arm until he gained a little strength. The bullet was removed on 12 July and Gibbings kept it with him as a lucky charm for the rest of his life.

The attack had ended in partial success and in fact was one of the more effective actions of an otherwise desperate and ill-judged campaign; it was of great tactical importance but casualties had been much heavier than expected. Writing to his father from his sick bed in Lemnos, Gibbings expressed his gratitude for being 'away from the continual noise. I had exactly 4 weeks of it & I never want to see any more. ... I am glad I was hit early in the day as I hear the bloodshed was awful on both sides but we took our 5 lines of trenches as ordered. I believe the 4 other officers in my company were hit & they say one was killed & I believe there is scarcely a man left'.[8] He had been extremely fortunate, but the injury was very serious and it was to put an end to his active soldiering; he admitted: 'I may be coming home, I sincerely hope so, I don't feel capable of any more fighting.'

From Lemnos he was transferred to a hospital in Alexandria to convalesce and he was soon fit enough to be aware of his surroundings, taking in the 'oriental colour' and making sketches. After about six weeks he was granted sick leave and sailed to Southampton on the *Letitia* and then on to Cork. Gibbings recovered physically from his wounds relatively quickly and only suffered from a soreness in his throat and temporary huskiness in his voice. But mentally his scars went much deeper — he was in shock. Later he was to be formally diagnosed as suffering from neurasthenia and the experience in Gallipoli had left him with severe nervous tension. Medical records show that his symptoms included a buzzing in his ears; he was tremulous and rapidly became fatigued at the slightest exertion; he had lost concentration and had defects of memory; his sleep was disturbed and full of horrific dreams which led to irritability and depression. It was to be some years before his mental state was fully recovered.[9]

In later life Gibbings rarely referred to his experiences of action in any detail, never wanting to dwell on its horror. He would recount the story of his injury in an almost matter-of-fact way but avoided any deeper or darker description unless he was able to distance himself and tell the story through the words of another. Gibbings certainly never referred to his mental stress. But he did benefit by his experiences in some way, for the following years of his military service were to give him opportunities to expand his visual ideas and mature as an artist; whenever possible he made drawings and notes of what he saw.

Back in his family home in Carrigrohane, Gibbings was granted convalescent leave but had regular check-ups at a military hospital in Cork. The doctors noted that his wounds had healed but that he was still suffering from shock. Early in the new year of 1916, Gibbings was thumbing through a copy of the *Illustrated London News* when he was impressed by a photograph which captured an incident during the retreat from Serbia. The picture showed the aged Marshal Putnik being carried in a primitive sedan chair at the head of a line of straggling soldiers over the Bridge of the Viziers.[10] Inspired by the image, he used the photograph as the basis for the design of a large wood-engraving in two colours. He printed it on a letter-copying press in his father's study using flat colours, but when making subsequent copies he used graduated colour on each of the blocks, more in the Japanese style. Gibbings was pleased with the result and commented that it was 'illustrative admittedly, but my first success'.[11]

The Retreat from Serbia – see colour plate 2b.

In the Autumn of 1916, he had recovered sufficiently to return to light duties. He was posted to Bere Island which was garrisoned by British troops guarding the passage into Bantry Bay. This was a remote place and with little to do, life was tedious and dull — only relieved by such highlights as the local regatta when the regimental band provided music. Hoping to escape winter on the island and following the recommendation of his medical officer, Gibbings volunteered for

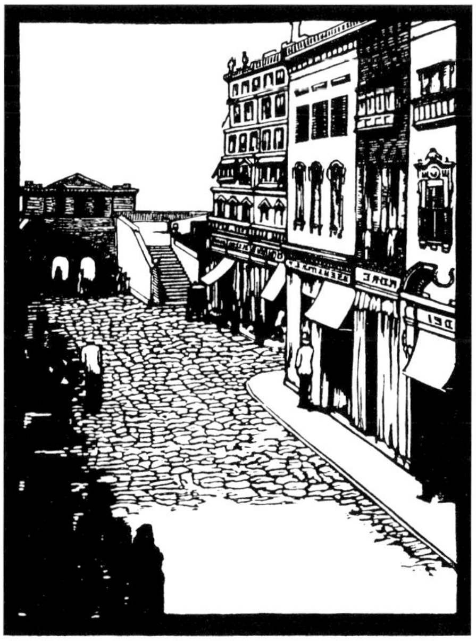

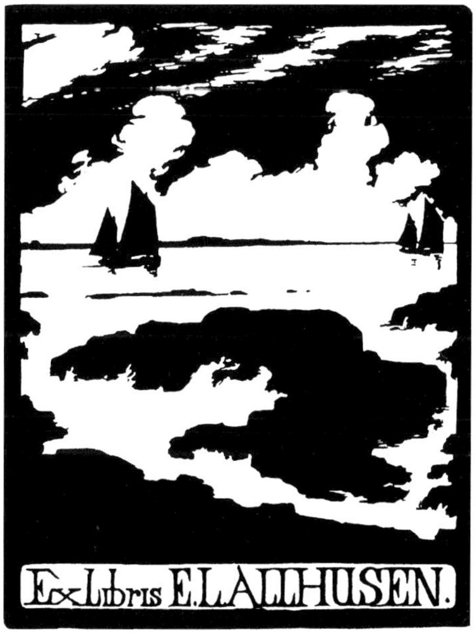

22 *left* *A Street in Malta*, *c.* 1915, wood-engraving, 127 x 96 mm. A copy of this print exists in which the shutters in the right hand corner have been coloured green suggesting that Gibbings was experimenting with this as a coloured wood-engraving. Although the print is dated 1915, it was probably based on a drawing Gibbings made when his ship stopped at Malta on the way to the Dardanelles and engraved at about the same time as *The Retreat from Serbia*.

23 *right* Bookplate, 1916, wood-engraving, 96 x 75 mm.

garrison duty in Egypt but, owing to administrative delay, he was stationed for a short time at the Royal Barracks in Dublin. Winter weather had now set in. A view from the window of the mess-room in the barracks took in the roof-tops of Dublin covered in snow and inspired Gibbings to make a drawing which he later engraved. In the drawing and subsequent print he began to experiment and develop a new abstract quality in his design.

In February 1917 he eventually set out on the voyage to his new post but, because of an error, the destination was not Egypt but Salonica and on arrival he found the weather conditions similar to Dublin — snow and blizzards. Almost straight away the conditions affected his health and aggravated his wound and he found himself back in hospital with more time to draw. This brief spell of only about six weeks in Salonica was ended when, to aid his recovery, he was shipped to a convalescent camp in Malta to undertake further light duties. In Malta 'life took a happy turn'; he had by now been promoted to the rank of Captain and he found himself '... the senior executive officer in a camp of about 100 junior officers and 4,000 men ...'.

The commandant was a Harley Street gynaecologist with a slight experience of peace-time yeomanry; provided he could hire a couple of *carrozzo* nags and ride, with me alongside as his A.D.C., at the head of his force, he was perfectly happy. My time, apart from these circus marches, was entirely my own.[12]

With time on his hands Gibbings was able to make drawings of his surroundings. The architecture and strong Mediterranean light made a powerful visual impression on him and suggested images that were to enforce and stimulate new ideas. After four months recuperating, with only minor duties, his condition was assessed by a medical board which decided that although he was physically fit, he was still suffering from neurasthenia and so he was passed fit for home service only. It was decided to send him to England to take up an administrative post in the Ministry of Munitions in London. The voyage home was on the ship *Llandovery Castle*, and, as always, Gibbings took advantage of his spare time to make drawings and designs to be developed later:

Then home in the hospital ship *Llandovery Castle* .... I made a drawing of her after-deck with the casualties in hospital blue, and later I did an engraving of the subject in three colours; but though it was exhibited in a Bond Street window, I fear the interest was entirely topical and I hope few copies survive.[13]

The *Llandovery Castle* – see colour plate 2a.

Back in London, with a safe desk job pushing paper around as a 'Controller of gun ammunition filing', Gibbings was ironically to find himself again involved in enemy action; the hotel in which he had temporary accommodation was bombed one evening during an air-raid. Five people were killed and the windows of his room were smashed, but fortunately Gibbings was at a concert in the Queen's Hall at the time.[14]

His post was as boring as the title suggests — he was a lowly administrative assistant in a sub-section of the department dealing with the paperwork for medium gun and heavy Howitzer ammunition. He retained his Captain's salary but a more unsuitable and tedious activity for a young and frustrated artist can hardly be imagined. Gibbings was desperate to get back to the world of art. To make his new job tolerable, he immediately signed up for evening classes with Noel Rooke. Rooke had been made Head of the School of Book Production at the Central and had been able to openly develop his teaching of wood-engraving in relation to book illustration. Working on military affairs during the day, Gibbings needed to get back into the artistic community and so rented rooms near his old address in Courtfield Gardens. By the end of October he had moved to the Bolton Studios in Chelsea. These were a complex of purpose-built artists' studios (over twenty in number), situated between Redcliffe Road and Gilston Road and running in a line between the ends of the gardens of the houses in both streets. A long corridor linked the studios, which had entrances from both roads. Now, with a permanent space of his own, Gibbings was able to equip himself with a printing press. With Rooke's advice, he purchased a Crown Albion Press for proofing his engraved blocks and for printing editions of his prints. During his active service and periods of convalescence he had built up a sizeable portfolio of drawings that were to provide subjects for wood-engravings over the next few years. He now set about selecting designs that would be suitable for engraving and started work on a series of prints. The engraving, *Dublin under Snow*, was based on his drawings made at the Royal Barracks:

> This was the first of my engravings in which pattern took ascendancy over subject; the first, too, in which I used what has since been called the vanishing line. Where one white surface, such as of snow, is seen against another, the line of demarcation is often so faint that it is all to the good if it can be omitted and the variety in plane or perspective expressed by other means. An accidental shadow, or a window or doorway, may give all that is needed of definition. I think I brought it off in this print and that is why I still have a liking for it.[15]

From the drawings made in hospital, he engraved *The City Walls, Salonica*, for which he adopted a similar approach but in which the figurative treatment of the

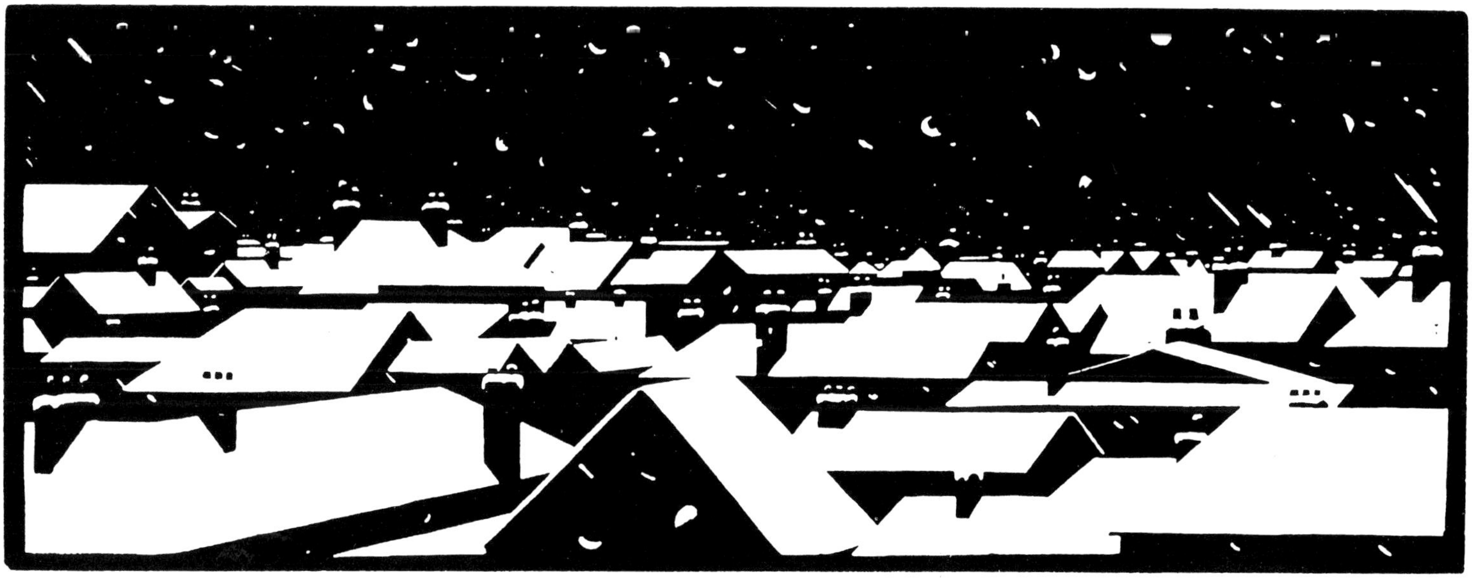

24 *Dublin under Snow*, 1918, wood-engraving, 91 x 243 mm.
Based on a drawing of the view from the officers' mess at the Royal Barracks in Dublin, which Gibbings made in 1917. In this print Gibbings developed his use of the 'vanishing line'.

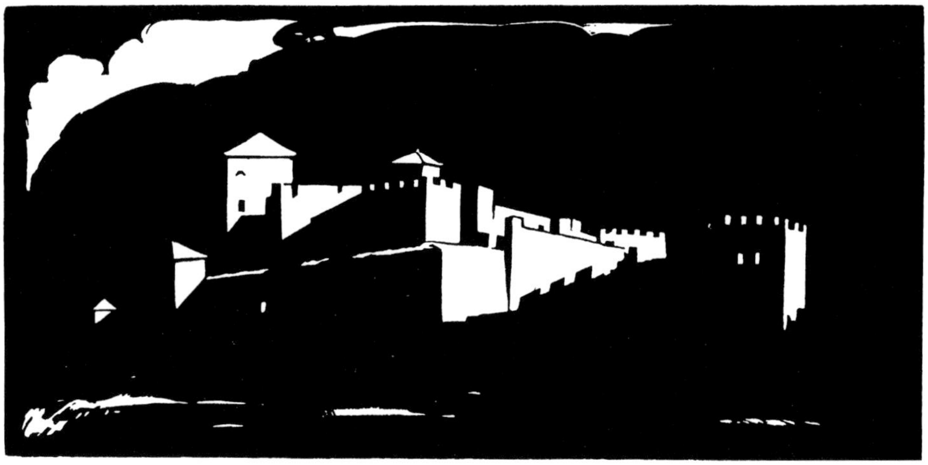

25 *The City Walls, Salonica*, 1918, wood-engraving, 75 × 153 mm.

sky and foreground undermined the abstract quality; Gibbings himself, looking back, had doubts about the print, 'which I now feel to be weak and pseudo-dramatic, though many copies were sold at its first appearance'.[16]

Unfortunately Gibbings could not escape the effects of his war experiences and still suffered nervous symptoms, including a lack of concentration, which seemed to threaten his ambitions as an artist. He made light of his condition when writing to his father and relatives but the reality was that he was still ill. Close to a breakdown, Gibbings went before a medical board at the beginning of April 1918. In a recorded statement to the board he declared that he had a 'distinct ... repugnance to destroying life ... during his service in the firing line he did not once fire a shot and even charged without firing'. He admitted that he had been 'relieved in his mind when he was wounded as then he felt he could not be expected to even try to take life'. Earlier in the war such a statement from a soldier in the ranks might have resulted in serious disciplinary action but Gibbings had shown bravery and was an officer. The board interpreted his statement as evidence of his continued neuropathic tendencies and recommended that he be immediately invalided out of the army.[17] Gibbings was awarded a generous gratuity, a large portion of which, according to Balston, he lost by investing in a French loan.[18]

At last Gibbings could concentrate on making his way as a full-time artist — but he needed money. In October he had called at the Ministry of Information offering his services as an official war artist, asking the Principal of the Central School, Frederick Burridge, who had taken over from Lethaby, to provide a reference.

> Capt. Robert Gibbings, late 4th Royal Munster Fusiliers who has seen a deal of service in Gallipoli & Salonica being now invalided is anxious still to be of what service he may. He was a student here & at the Slade for some time, is a good draughtsman & woodcutter & I recommend him to the favourable consideration of the Ministry of Information as an official artist at one of the fronts.[19]

Unfortunately Lord Beaverbrook was ill on the day of his visit and, although he left a portfolio of work, the next month he received a letter finally declining his offer — the war had already ended. However Gibbings was persistent in his search for work. A letter of 17 January 1919, makes it clear he had a new motivation to earn a decent income; in it Gibbings mentioned that he now had a fiancée — a Miss Pennefather.[20] Gibbings had arranged for his fiancée to deliver three prints to the Imperial War Museum on approval with the hope that they might buy them. The prints on offer were *The Retreat from Serbia* and another coloured engraving done from the drawings made on board the *Llandovery Castle* (which had been torpedoed and sunk in June 1917), at a price of three guineas each, and a small etching of a view of 'W' beach in Gallipoli at fifteen shillings. The purchasing committee needed to know whether the images were drawn from personal observations, and, once Gibbings had assured them that, apart from *The Retreat from Serbia*, they were, they bought them for the collections, having extracted a considerable discount from the struggling artist!

The hardness of the bargain was relieved a little by the committee's interest in commissioning an oil painting or a watercolour on a 'Gallipoli theme'. With great speed, Gibbings replied with a proposal in the form of a written description of a composition for an oil painting — based on a larger version of the scene of

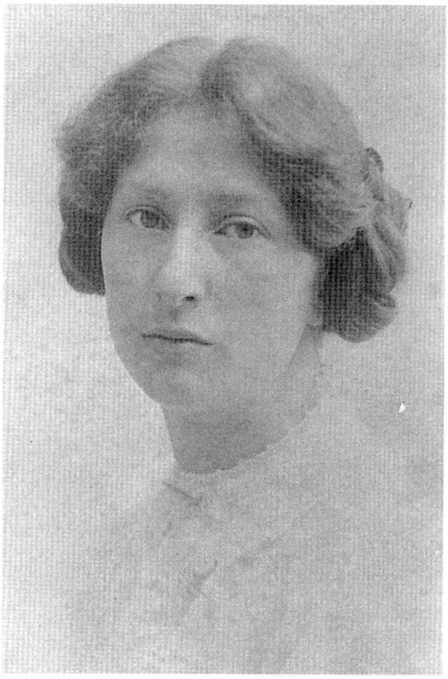

26 Photograph of Mary Pennefather (always known as Moira) in her early twenties.

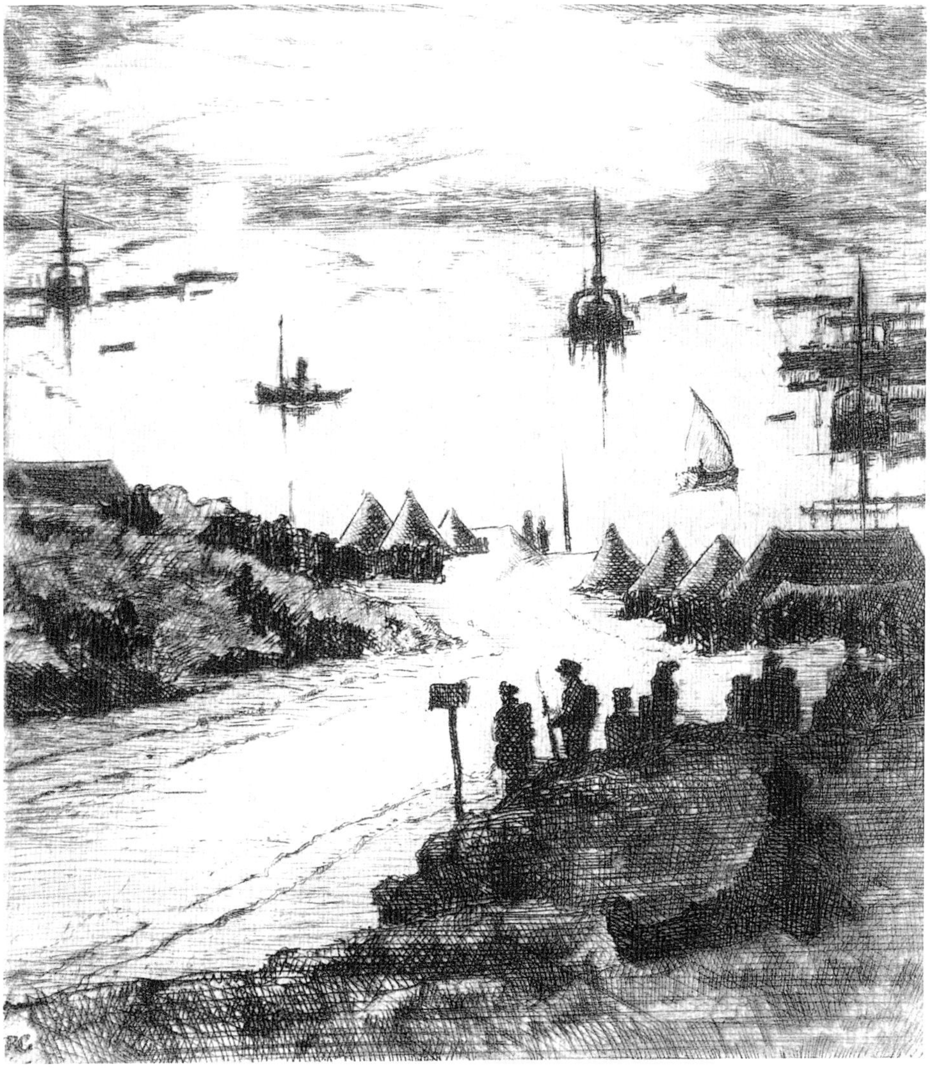

27 *'W' Beach, Gallipoli*, 1918, etching, plate size 99 x 89 mm. Gibbings made a sketch of this scene in 1915 while on active service which he later made into an etching.

'W' beach depicted in his etching. The painting was to be approximately thirty by twenty-four inches and the price unframed, fifty pounds. The commission was confirmed and on the 6 August 1919 the painting, *Sunset over Lemnos*, was delivered. Unfortunately, as the committee was very firm in pointing out, the picture differed from that proposed by Gibbings and at first the committee refused it. Realising he had made a mistake in promising too much, Gibbings offered a reduction in price to thirty-five guineas including a frame. Interesting from an historical point of view, the painting is conventional in treatment, very similar in the handling of the dramatic sunset to the kind of painting he had been familiar with in Scully's studio. It is a polished and professional piece of work although lacking any real passion, but after all it had been painted to raise money and the only similarity with his graphic work of the time is the dramatic use of silhouette and deep shadow. Unlike many of his contemporaries, he never depicted the brutal reality of war in his paintings or wood-engravings. Some months later, while sorting through old work, Gibbings found three drawings of Gallipoli which he offered to the Museum, they included a view of 'Achi Baba, the crux of the situation at Cape Helles, from our own reserve trenches in June 1915',[21] which he had also made into an etching, but they were refused by the Museum. Days later his confidence was given a boost when the *Daily Sketch* printed a note entitled 'The Soldier Artist' with a small photograph of Gibbings announcing that the Victoria & Albert Museum had honoured him by purchasing a copy of *The Retreat from Serbia* together with another coloured wood-engraving, *Evening at Gaza*.[22]

Sunset over Lemnos – see colour plate 2c.

Evening at Gaza – see colour plate 4b.

On 30 April 1919, Gibbings married Mary Pennefather in the Parish church of Wyke Regis, a village on the outskirts of Weymouth, where Mary lived with her parents. Robert was thirty years old and Mary, who always used the name Moira, was twenty-four. Her family background was one of formal respectability and military service. Her father, Lieutenant-Colonel Edward Graham Pennefather, was the son of a clergyman, who in turn was the second son of a Lord Chief Justice of Ireland. Edward Pennefather was brought up in County Wexford in Ireland and it is possible that there was some acquaintance with the Gibbings family through the Church. Edward had a distinguished military career and spent much of his service in Africa, where he had an important role in the history of Rhodesia, working with Cecil Rhodes. Edward later returned to England and was stationed with his regiment in Brighton but in 1896 resigned his commission on being appointed as Inspector General of Police in Singapore. Moira and a younger brother went with him to Singapore and stayed until his retirement in 1910.

How the couple met is uncertain — perhaps Gibbings had known of her brothers during the war or it is possible that the families were acquainted — but the marriage caused 'equal distress to the two families concerned. "They'll starve," said one. "Why couldn't he have stayed in the army with promotion before him?" said the other'.[23] The idea that Robert could support the both of them through his art seemed most unlikely; it was not seen as a suitable or respectable occupation by any of the parents. Given such opposition, it says much for the strength of character and independent spirit of Moira, and the determina-

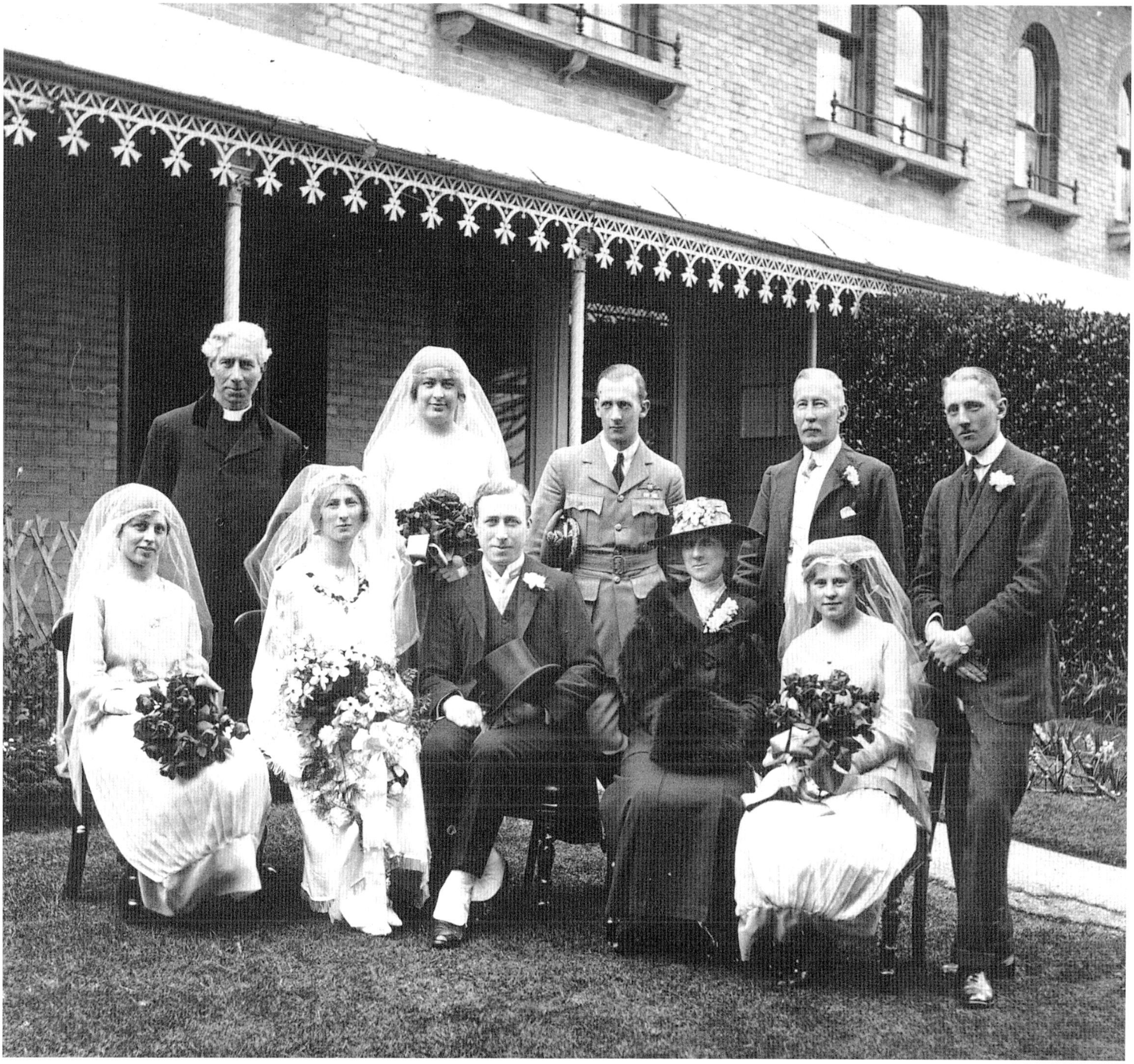

28 Moira and Robert on their wedding day, 30 April 1919.
The family group includes on the left Robert's father, Edward Gibbings with his daughter May to his left, and the Pennefathers on the right. Lieutenant-Colonel Pennefather is flanked by two young men who are probably his sons. Moira had three brothers and the eldest, William, was a Commander in the Royal Navy and might well have known Robert's brother, Maurice, also serving in the navy. The married couple might therefore have been introduced through their brothers. Robert's father-in-law had had a distinguished military career. Educated at Harrow and Oxford, Edward Pennefather went on to enlist with the Inniskilling Dragoons, serving in South Africa during the Zulu war of 1879. He later became Commander of the military contingent that accompanied the Pioneer Column to the territory that became Rhodesia and he worked closely with Cecil Rhodes.

tion of Gibbings not to be dissuaded from his belief in himself as an artist, that they persevered. Moira was to be a great support: an attractive woman, tall, long-legged and rather stylish, she enjoyed wearing fashionable clothes and make-up and shared Gibbings's love of the good things in life.

The wedding photograph suggests that it was a small family occasion, Gibbings himself uncharacteristically dressed very formally in tails, spats and a silk top hat, perhaps with the intention of impressing his in-laws, who seem somewhat severe.

For the struggling artist, marriage brought new responsibilities.

Chapter Four

Getting Established and the Society of Wood Engravers 1920–1923

THE COUPLE'S FIRST HOME consisted of rooms in a large Victorian town house, overlooking a church and surrounding gardens, at 35 Redcliffe Square, a few streets away from the Bolton Studios. Gibbings now had a wife to support and the lack of confidence shown in the couple by their parents must have made him all the more determined to prove them wrong.

His work was beginning to attract attention. The library bookplate for University College Cork was reproduced in *The Studio* in December 1918 and the following year a design for an anniversary address, with extravagant patterns and hand-lettering in a Celtic style, was also illustrated in the magazine.[1] Other journals began to notice his work; *Change: The Beginning of a Chapter*, a new literary journal, used five of his wood-engravings, including *The Little Copse* and *The Power Station*, in its first two issues. Gibbings also took the initiative in promoting his services as a designer of bookplates and risked placing an expensive advertisement in *The Studio* in the hope that it might generate work.[2]

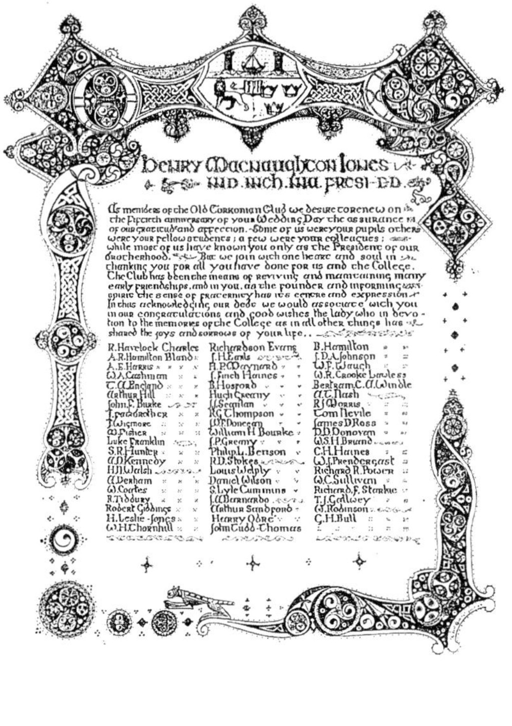
Henry Macnaughton Jones
M.D. M.Ch. M.A. Presi-dent

As members of the Old Corkonian Club we desire to renew on the Fiftieth anniversary of your Wedding Day the assurance of our gratitude and affection. Some of us were your pupils others were your fellow students; a few were your colleagues; while most of us have known you only as the President of our brotherhood. But we join with one heart and soul in thanking you for all you have done for us and the College. The Club has been the means of reviving and maintaining many early friendships, and in you, as the founder and informing spirit the sense of fraternity has its centre and expression. In thus acknowledging our debt we would associate with you in our congratulations and good wishes the lady who in devotion to the memories of the College as in all other things has shared the joys and sorrows of your life.

R. Havelock Charles	Richardson Evans	B. Hamilton
A.R. Hamilton Bland	J.H. Earls	J.D. Johnson
A.E. Harris	H.P. Maynard	W.F. Waugh
W.A. Cashman	J. Finch Haines	W.R. Crooke Lawless
T.A. England	B. Hosford	Bertram C.A. Windle
Arthur Hill	Hugh Creamy	A.T. Nash
John F. Burke	J.J. Scanlan	R.J. Morris
J. Fairbrother	R.G. Thompson	Tom Nevile
J. Wigmore	J.W.F. Donegan	James D. Ross
M. Fisher	William H. Bourke	D.D. Donovan
Luke Franklin	J.P. Creamy	W.S.H. Briand
S.R. Hunter	Philip L. Benson	C.H. Haines
A.N. Kennedy	R.D. Stokes	W.J. Prendergast
H.N. Walsh	Louis Welply	Richard R. Power
A. Derham	Daniel Wilson	W.C. Sullivan
W. Coates	G. Lyle Cummins	Richard F. Starkie
R. Tidbury	J.A. Bernardo	T.J. Galwey
Robert Gibbings	Arthur Sandford	G. Robinson
H. Leslie-Jones	Henry Dore	G.H. Bull
W.H. Thornhill	John Todd-Thomas	

29 An anniversary address, designed and executed by Gibbings, presented by the Old Corkonian Club of the University College, Cork, to their President to celebrate his Golden Wedding. The address was reproduced in *The Studio*, with the comment that the Celtic ornament and hand-lettering were harmonious and 'admirably utilized'.

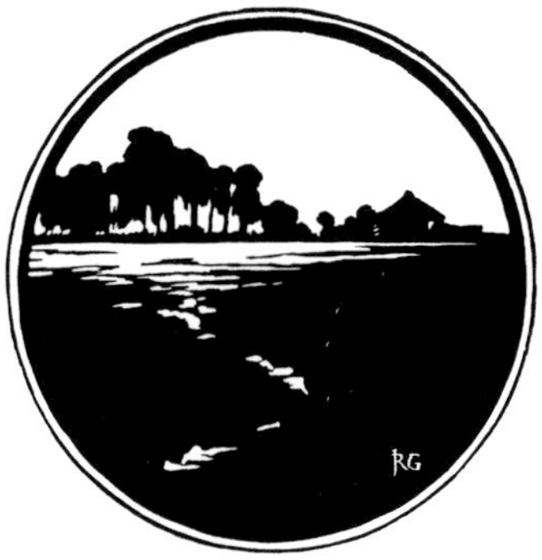

30 *Little Copse*, 1918, wood-engraving, diam. 80 mm.

The popularity of wood-engraving and coloured woodcuts as decorative prints to adorn the homes of the general public was growing. The art critic Malcolm Salaman added impetus to this trend when he wrote the first article about a wood-engraver of the modern movement to appear in *The Studio* in February 1919 — the article featured the up-and-coming artist, Robert Gibbings.[3] Salaman began with the observation that 'With the pleasanter and happier conditions of living which must result from the social and industrial reconstruction, promised with the hard-won Peace, art will surely have a wider and more pervasively intimate part to play in the homes of the people.' He predicted that improved economic and living conditions and a 'growing appreciation of tasteful environment,' would 'induce a desire for more artistic craft-work and pictorial art of genuine quality at moderate cost'. Salaman recognised that 'good painting' would probably be beyond the means of the average small householder and that wood-engravings and colour prints were an ideal way to satisfy the needs of 'happy workers', who, 'pretending to no connoisseurship' were 'moved by new impulses to love the products of sincere and charming art as part of their expression of joy in life'. However he also predicted that black and white prints had limited appeal and that the more obviously decorative qualities of the 'Artistic colour-print' would prove to be the way forward.

While acclaiming the work of other printmakers, Salaman cites Gibbings as being an example of a new generation of artists who might fulfil this vision. Salaman is full of praise: 'His work is artistically interesting, his simple and straightforward craftsmanship being admirably at the service of his design, which

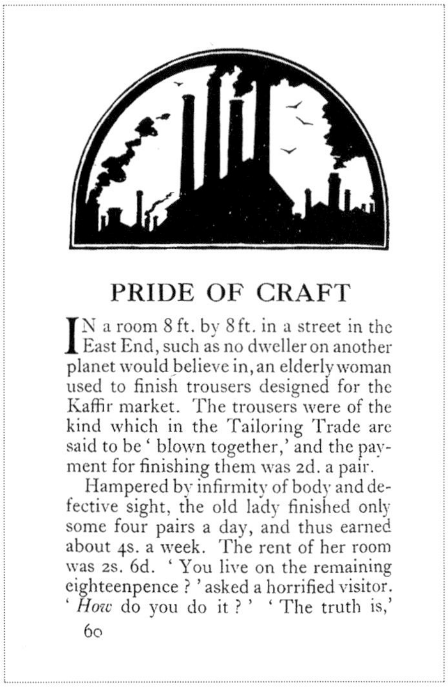

PRIDE OF CRAFT

IN a room 8 ft. by 8 ft. in a street in the East End, such as no dweller on another planet would believe in, an elderly woman used to finish trousers designed for the Kaffir market. The trousers were of the kind which in the Tailoring Trade are said to be 'blown together,' and the payment for finishing them was 2d. a pair.

Hampered by infirmity of body and defective sight, the old lady finished only some four pairs a day, and thus earned about 4s. a week. The rent of her room was 2s. 6d. 'You live on the remaining eighteenpence?' asked a horrified visitor. '*How* do you do it?' 'The truth is,'

60

31 *The Power Station*, 1918, wood-engraving, 71 x 43 mm. (page size 165 x 102 mm.) Page from the literary journal *Change*, 1919. Wood-engravings by artists such as Eric Gill, Philip Hagreen and Vivien Gribble also appeared in the journal.

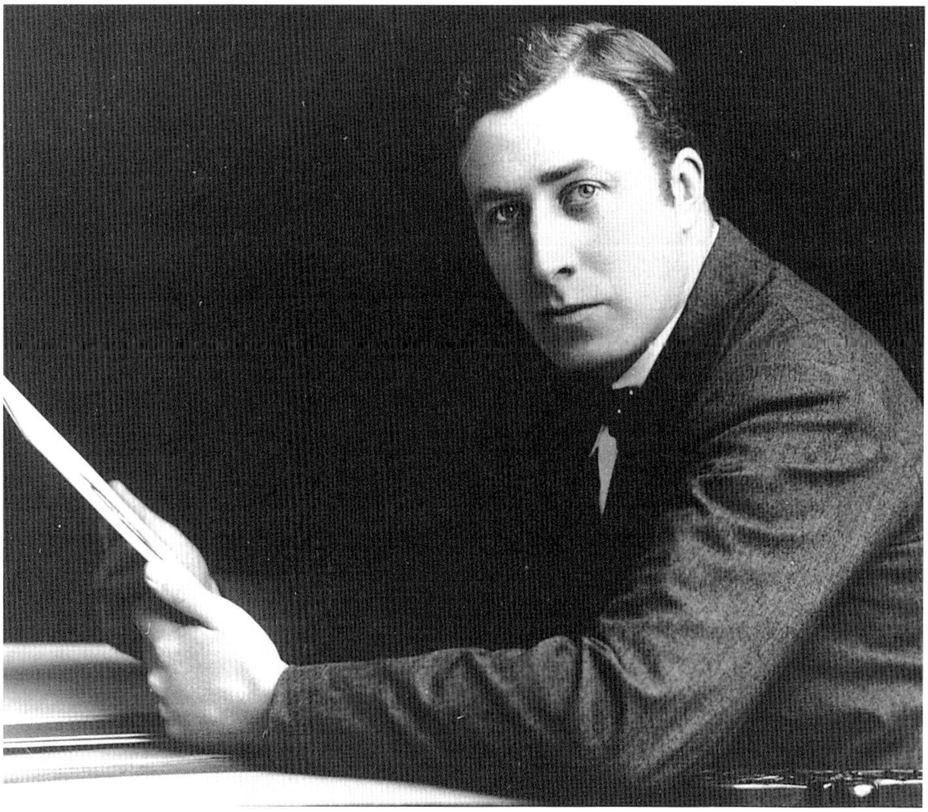

32 Robert Gibbings, c.1920, holding a mounted wood-engraving.

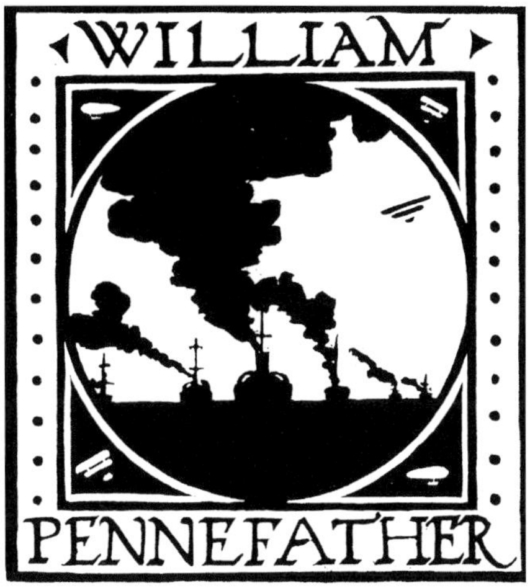

33 Bookplate for William Pennefather, 1919, wood-engraving, 60 x 56 mm. William, Moira's brother, was a Commander in the Royal Navy during the First World War.

he invariably conceives with a sense of decoration.' Salaman's style of writing is rather gushing but he is sensitive to Gibbings's strengths: 'A remarkable instinct for spacing with unfailingly effective balance of black-and-white masses, and a command of form in silhouette, characterizes all the woodcuts Captain Gibbings has so far wrought.' Salaman uses the term 'woodcuts' loosely, as in fact he was referring to Gibbings's wood-engravings, but it was common to use the same term for the two processes at that time.[4] The article is illustrated with a number of Gibbings's black and white prints including a bookplate he had designed and engraved for his brother-in-law, William Pennefather; but keeping to his argument, it is Gibbings's coloured engravings that Salaman puts forward as being of most interest. Gibbings needed to sell work and, perhaps in response to the perceived market, he had produced a number of coloured prints during this period. Reproduced in colour in the article were *The Retreat from Serbia* and *Evening at Gaza*, an evocative image based on his sketches made while staying in Alexandria. Salaman described *Evening at Gaza* as being 'of charming appeal, with elegance of design and an emotional beauty of luminous tone'. *Llandovery Castle*, and another coloured print, *A Corner in Malta*, were reproduced in black and white.

A Corner in Malta – see colour plate 4a

The article includes a detailed description of Gibbings's technique for coloured prints:

> He limits himself usually to two blocks, the key-block for the design and another for the colour, and, manipulating his tone-gradations with his rollers, he takes the impressions with an Albion printing press. Discarding the water-colour and rice-paste of the Japanese, he mixes his colour-powders with varnish; and boxwood is generally his material, though he sometimes uses chestnut.

Balston points out that 'though his designs were not lacking in strength, the printer's varnish ink with which they were printed, being only semi-transparent, devitalized the colouring, especially where one colour was superimposed upon another'.[5] This was a period of experimentation and serious debate amongst printmakers who were trying to decide the future of the art; Gibbings had adopted what has been termed the European style, which lent itself to more

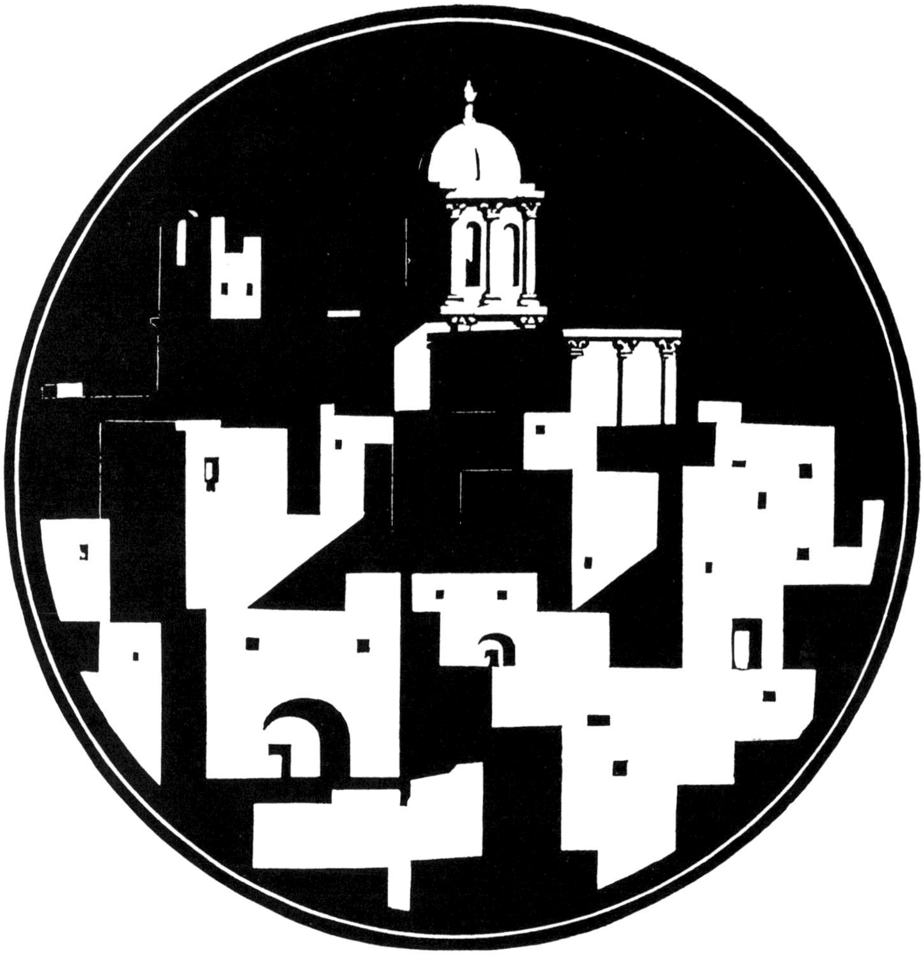

34 *Melleha*, 1919, wood-engraving, diam. 193 mm.

commercial applications; others championed the Japanese technique which was directed towards producing prints to be framed and hung on walls.[6]

Salaman's article ends with the comment that 'Captain Gibbings wisely recognizing the universal call for brightness and charm, is engaged upon some delightful schemes for colour-prints, with the pictorial graces of childhood and girlhood decoratively appealing'. This encouragement to produce popular coloured images might explain two rather strange large and circular coloured prints, using a style and subject matter that were quite uncharacteristic of his usual work, that date from this period. The prints were obviously aimed at children and possibly intended to decorate the nursery wall.

Play, a coloured wood-engraving of a rabbit designed to appeal to children – see colour plate 4c.

If Gibbings had been persuaded that his future lay in coloured prints, then his conviction did not last long. It seems that he was dissatisfied with his next colour-print, *Albert Bridge, Chelsea*. This familiar local landmark is given an almost Whistler-like aesthetic treatment by Gibbings and the print was reproduced in colour as a full-page plate in a special number of *The Studio*.[7] Following this disappointment, he began once again to concentrate on developing his ideas for black and white engravings. He returned to the sketches he had made in Malta where he had noted the effects of the Mediterranean sunshine:

Albert Bridge, Chelsea – see colour plate 1.

> Here it was that I began to see the strong patterns of light and shade on rectangular houses almost in terms of music — major chords, minor chords, small windows or archways as the accidentals. The proportions of one rectangle were important in themselves: they were equally important in their relation to adjacent shapes.[8]

Two ambitious engravings from this period, *Melleha* and *Hamrun*, are large, confident, and strong in design. The images have been simplified to patterns of black and white but Gibbings commented later: 'In the former I now feel that I should have been more abstract in my treatment of the culminating pillars; in the latter I should have done likewise with the trees.'[9] Gibbings's use of the vanishing line technique reached full maturity with his first significant engraving of a figure, *Clear Waters* of 1920. Here the delicate outline of the body is never defined by a line other than the boundary of one area of highlight with that of shadow; the eye naturally completes the shape by implication and all unnecessary detail is eliminated — it is a lyrical image.

Gibbings was not the only artist to be experimenting with such effects. Edward Wadsworth, who had been a fellow student at the Slade, had developed a similar approach and in 1918 he produced a famous series of images based on the 'dazzle' effect of camouflage paint on warships.[10] These images, and earlier ones, clearly exploit the vanishing line but push the idea to the boundaries of representation and abstraction with a dynamism and energy which is not found in the gentler interpretation explored by Gibbings, who put more emphasis on the decorative effects of pattern. Gibbings later became familiar with the work of Wadsworth but their ideas evolved independently of each other. Gibbings's images were based on visual ideas developed from his observations abroad

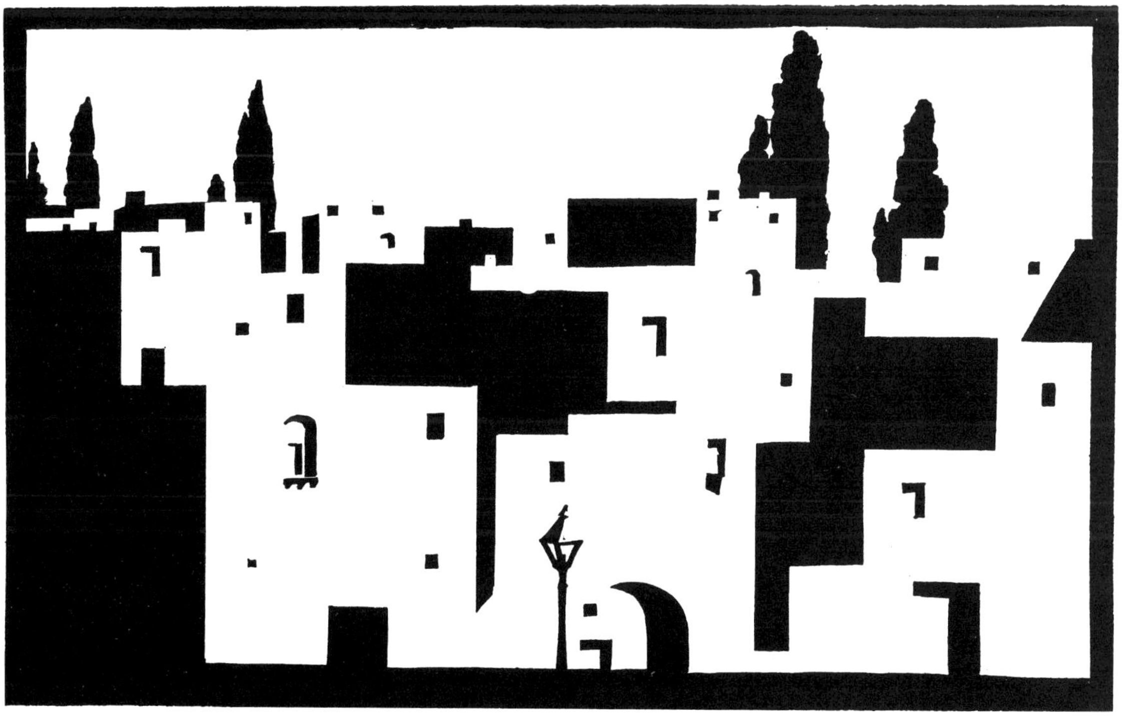

35 *Hamrun*, c.1919, wood-engraving, 177 x 292 mm.

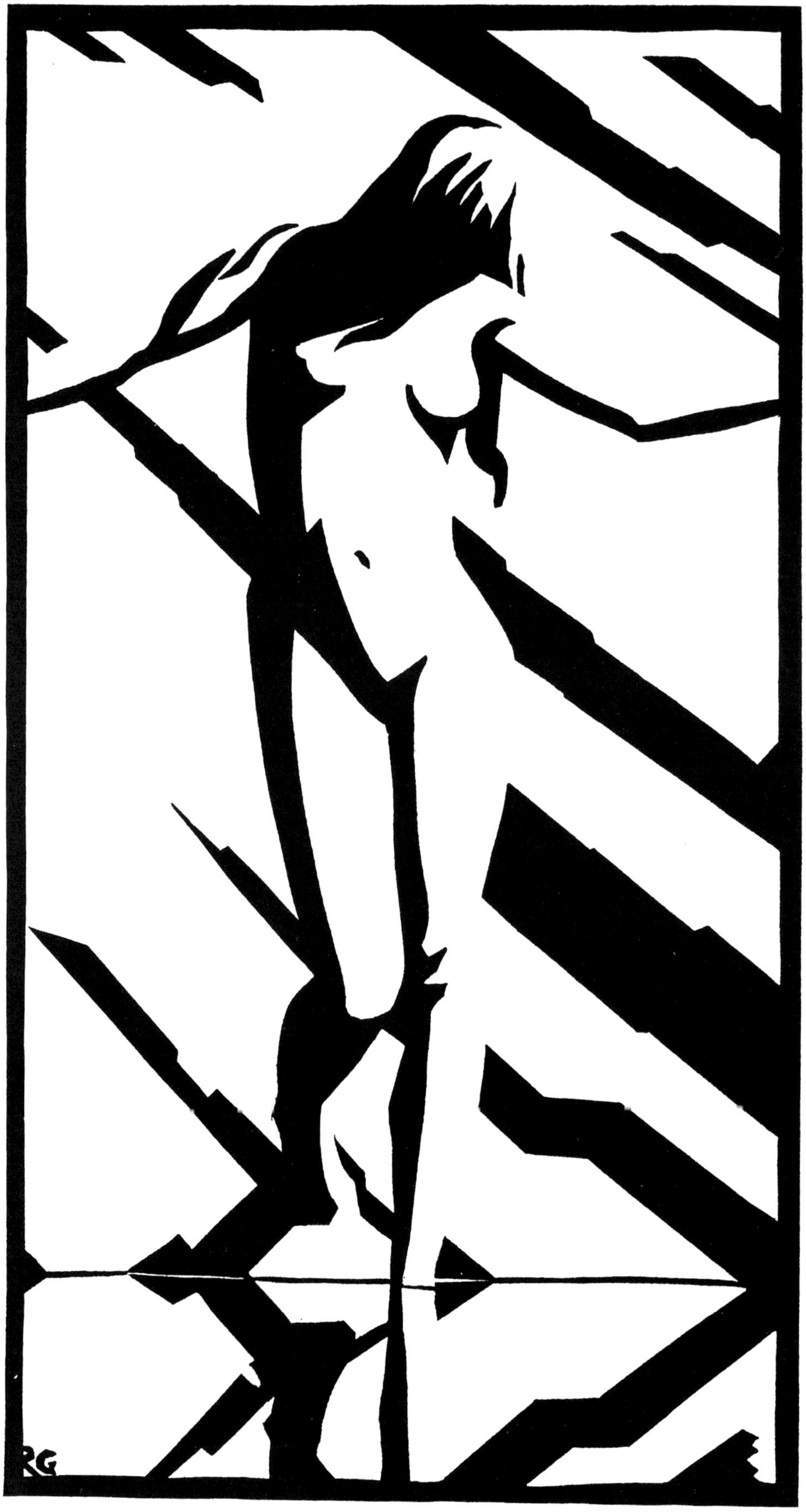

36 *Clear Waters*, 1920,
wood-engraving,
247 x 134 mm.

during the war years when he was cut off from other influences. He had not seen Wadsworth's early prints and, although he was aware of the Futurist and Cubist movements, he still made no conscious effort to ally himself with the Vorticist group or other modernist movements in art.

ESTABLISHED IN CHELSEA, Robert and Moira now enjoyed an expanding group of friends and contacts in artistic circles. Gibbings's ebullient character and natural enthusiasm made him a popular figure and Moira was also attracted to this intriguing world and anxious to play her part. The publicity in *The Studio* and the success of his recent prints added to Gibbings's growing reputation as one of the leading new print-makers. Engravings by Gibbings appeared in a variety of new literary journals which were springing up, such as *Voices* and *The Apple of Beauty and Discord*.[11] Recognition had even spread abroad and in June 1919 Gibbings had dispatched a selection of his prints for sale in America; the Dunster House Bookshop in Cambridge, Massachusetts, was one of the first to stock his work. Limited editions of his engravings had been selling so well that he contemplated making further editions just for sale in America.[12]

But Gibbings was only one of an increasing circle of artists who were stimulated by the possibilities of this revived medium and were consequently receiving greater public recognition. Rooke's teaching had produced a nucleus of enthusiastic young engravers, but more established artists such as Sidney Lee, Edward Gordon Craig, Gwen Raverat, Eric Gill and Paul and John Nash, had been developing the medium quite independently of the teaching at the Central School. Despite the growing number of practitioners, wood-engraving was only just becoming recognised and taken seriously by critics and gallery owners and so their work was still relatively unknown to the general public. They needed exposure and more opportunities to exhibit — how could they promote their work and increase public awareness? Artists working in other media, such as etching and lithography, had been very successful in establishing popular appeal, benefiting from the increased strength and influence gained by joining forces and forming societies such as the Royal Society of Painter-Etchers and Engravers (later re-named The Royal Society of Painter-printmakers) and the Senefelder Club.[13] In 1920 Frank Morley Fletcher and J. D. Batten, and other artists who had adopted the Japanese tradition, had formed the Colour Woodcut Society and a wave of other arts and crafts established societies for mutual support. In the light of all this activity it is hardly surprising that the idea should have emerged of forming a society of wood-engravers. Gibbings, naturally looking for ways to promote his own work, was one of the first to see the advantages of joining together. He decided to take the lead and owing to his energy and enthusiasm 'began to emerge as a spokesman'.[14] Balston attributes the idea of forming a society to Gibbings, and he then put the suggestion to Rooke, Sidney Lee, and Philip Hagreen.[15]

At this early stage, initial reactions to the idea were sought from a wide range of artists and print-makers and Balston records a meeting held by Mrs Austin

Brown, the wife of a colour-woodcutter in the Japanese style, during which the establishment of a society was proposed, to be headed by Pissarro, Lee and Rooke. But it soon emerged that it would be impracticable to base the society on too broad a range of styles and techniques. A planning meeting took place in Philip Hagreen's studio on 27 March 1920 and a society was set up with the title 'The Bewick Club'. The minutes of this inaugural meeting, written by hand in an old exercise book, list the provisional members: Mr Lucien Pissarro, Mr Robert Gibbings, Mr Philip Hagreen, Mr E. M. O'Rourke Dickey, Mr Noel Rooke and Mr Sidney Lee, and goes on to list 'woodcutters' who were to be invited to join: Mr Shannon, Mr Ricketts, Mr Sturge Moore, Mr Wadsworth, Mr Brangwyn, Mr Ginner, Mr Gordon Craig, Mr Gill, Mrs Raverat, Mr John Nash. Those who accepted were Gill, Nash, Raverat, Sturge Moore and Gordon Craig — Wadsworth, Shannon, Ricketts and Ginner refused. Ludovic Rodo provisionally joined but resigned after the first meeting.[16] The membership represented a range of ages and styles — this was not to be a body led by revolutionary ideas but one more intent on becoming established and promoting itself. At the same meeting Moira Gibbings was invited to become the Honorary Secretary. She was anxious to be fully involved with her husband's activities and, although not a practising

37 *A Cornish Harbour*, 1920, wood-engraving, 160 x 236 mm. This print and *Cornwall's Cliffs* (opposite) were exhibited at the first annual exhibition of the Society of Wood Engravers in November 1920. Moira and Robert made a number of visits to Cornwall during the early years of their marriage.

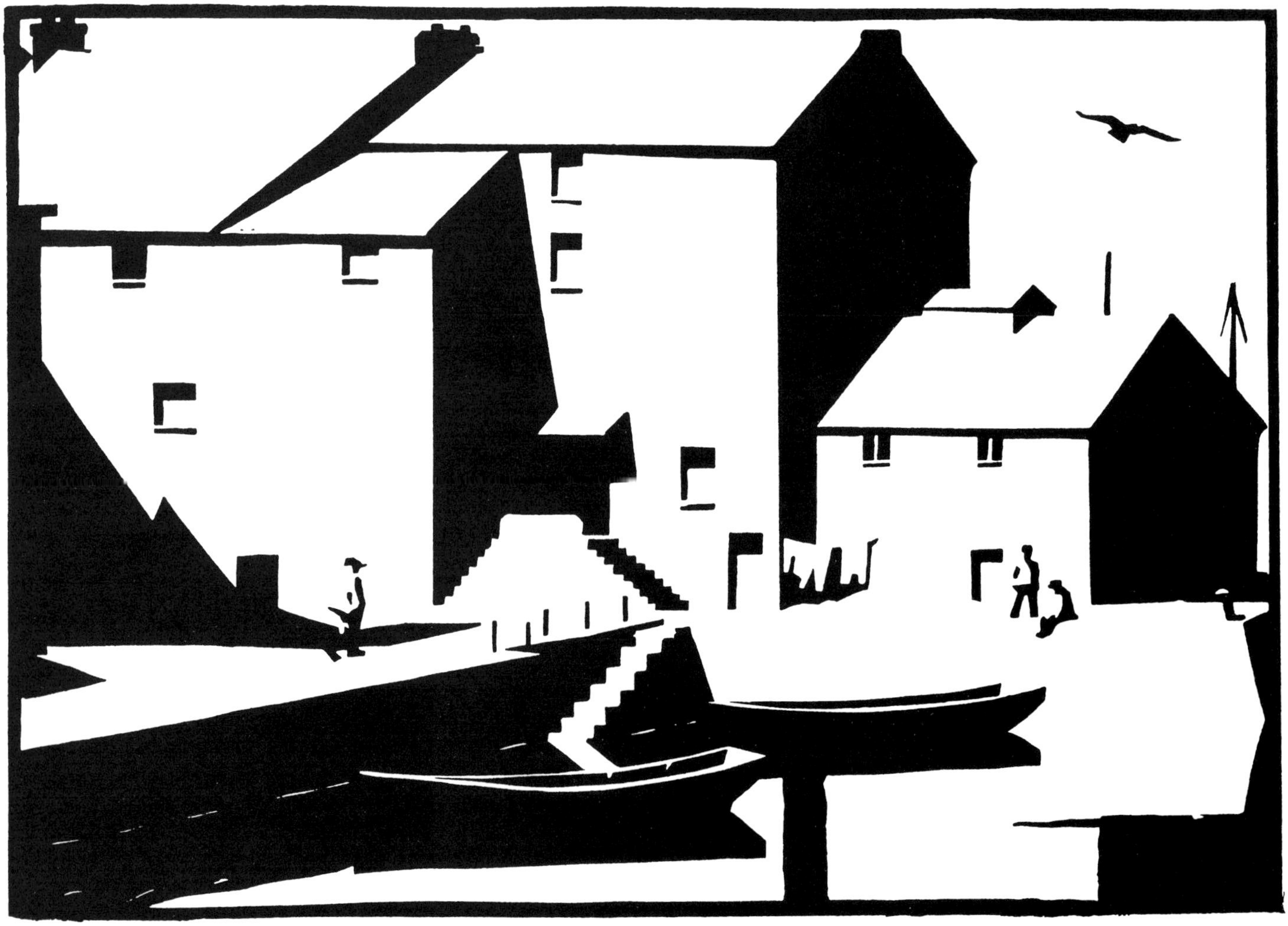

artist, she had valuable skills as an organiser. The minutes also mention a proposed circular which was to contain a clear statement of the Society's aims: 'The purpose of the Society is to hold exhibitions devoted solely to woodcutting & engraving by the European method'.

At a later meeting on 13 May the name The Bewick Club, with its symbolic but rather historical meaning, was dropped in favour of the more general title — The Society of Wood Engravers. A decision was also made to hold their first exhibition at the Chenil Gallery in the King's Road and an announcement later appeared in *The Studio*.[17] The first annual exhibition opened in November 1920 with ninety-one wood-engravings and woodcuts on show.[18] Seven non-members were invited to exhibit: Desmond Chute, Eric Daglish, Dorothy Elliot, Rupert Lee (Gibbings had taught him to engrave), Margaret Pilkington, Ludovic Rodo, and Ethelbert White; together they contributed eighteen prints. Gibbings had the largest number on show: his twelve prints included *A Cornish Harbour*, *Melleha*, *Hamrun*, *Clear Waters*, *Fowey Harbour* and *Cornwall's Cliffs*; *A Corner in Malta* was one of a small number of coloured prints exhibited.

A printed catalogue with a foreword by Campbell Dodgson, Keeper of Prints and Drawings at the British Museum, accompanied the exhibition. Dodgson was a major establishment figure and a champion of printmakers; a great collector of

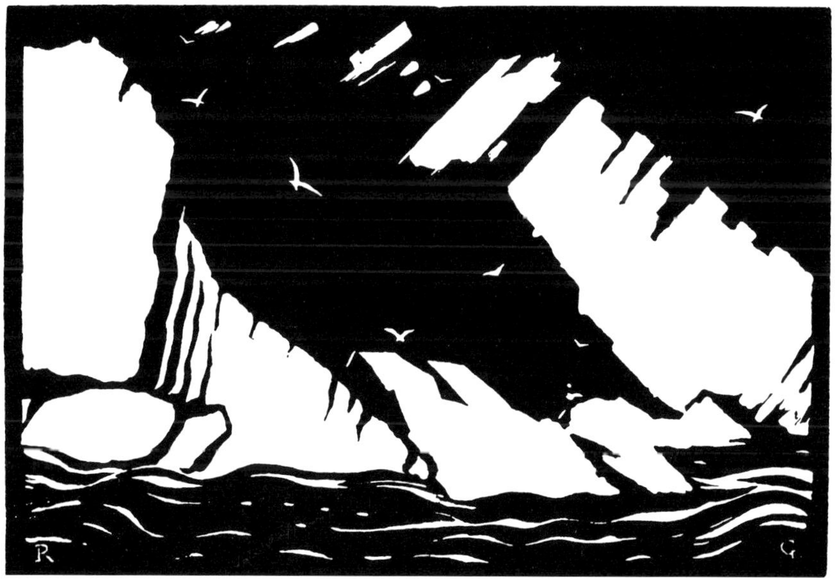

38 *Cornwall's Cliffs*, c.1919, wood-engraving, 76 x 111 mm.

prints, he wrote many articles supporting the art. In his foreword, Dodgson heralded the birth of the Society with optimism as the next in line of a succession of such initiatives. He ended his introduction with the plea that contemporary engravers should learn from the 'glorious record' of European engraving but not try to imitate it; 'Let them be themselves, frankly of their own time, and develop a modern style. … The woodcuts must be good, and now, tomorrow if not today, they will be bought and prized'. Dodgson's assumption, in keeping with Salaman, was that the market was for prints to be hung on walls rather than for book illustrations.

The exhibition was widely reported in the Press as an event of significance and both the revival of the medium and the modern approach were greeted with enthusiasm. Reviews were encouraging but the critics were not without their reservations. Frank Rutter, in particular, raised the question of popular appeal:

> ... while many of the works are impressive and scholarly it is to be feared that few will be really popular in their pictorial appeal. There is a tendency to preciousness which should be guarded against, for if the new society is to be of real service it must appeal not only to collectors but also to the general public.[19]

Rutter bemoaned the lack of colour, predicting that the public would want decoration to brighten their walls 'in so gloomy a land as England' and the mass market would not be with collectors buying prints 'to put away in boxes'. Gibbings had of course entered one of the few coloured images and this and a number of his other prints were picked out for praise. Rutter described *Clear Waters* as a 'model of a woodcut in its simplicity and expressiveness'; another review commented that 'Mr. R. Gibbings' brilliant "Dublin under Snow" is already deservedly well-known'. His use of the vanishing line technique gave his prints undoubted impact; a review in the *Yorkshire Post* observed that Gibbings had 'evolved a very ingenious style using heavy shadows against the white in almost geometrical form. The effect at a short distance is most fascinating, and akin to that of the stencil'.[20] Other critics were less convinced: 'The many cuts by Mr. Robert Gibbings show a pleasant feeling for distribution of black and white masses, but his exclusive use of straight lines and curves gives them a monotonous stiffness.'[21]

Amongst all the argument and debate that surrounded the setting up of the Society, Moira announced she was expecting a baby. Patrick Edward Pennefather Gibbings was born on the 16 December 1920, adding to Gibbings's responsibilities and increasing the need to find regular work. There can be no doubt that the exhibition generated interest, not least amongst commercial firms who recognised the potential of the medium for advertising purposes and for use on packaging. Compared to the income made through selling prints, companies were willing to pay well for such work and for Gibbings, just starting out on married life and parenthood, every commission was of importance.

He had been approached by an agent, Joseph Thorp, to whom he had been recommended by the 'Headmaster' of the Central School. Thorp was acting on behalf of Eno's Fruit Salt:

> 'We have this idea for a badge,' he said when he came to see me, 'a badge of health. Here is a little boy holding in either outstretched hand a bunch of grapes. We want it engraved with the sun rising behind him.'
>
> 'If the sun is behind him, he will have to be in silhouette,' I said.
>
> 'I think,' said Thorp, 'that we may postulate a light on his chest.' And so was born the badge which until recently adorned the Eno's cork.[22]

Through Thorp, Gibbings was also introduced to the Imperial Tobacco Company, the proprietors of Matinée cigarettes:

> 'You have been in the Balkans,' he said.
>
> 'A month in hospital,' I told him.

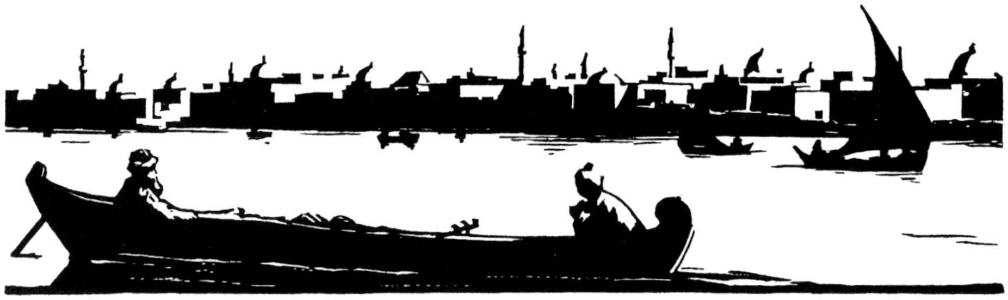

39 One of six wood-engravings designed for the Imperial Tobacco Company and used to advertise Matinée cigarettes, 1920, image size 45 x 163 mm. G. M. Ellwood commented in an article in the *Penrose Annual*, that Gibbings was one of the first artists of the new movement in wood-engraving to be commissioned for an English advertising campaign. He described the prints as being 'very simply conceived scenes … giving the necessary Eastern atmosphere'. See 'Wood-and Lino-cuts in Advertising', *Penrose Annual*, vol. 35, 1933, pp. 92–95.

'Never mind, you've got the colour. They want six engravings,' and he mentioned a price that would suit me well to-day.[23]

Commercial work, so necessary to support his young family, continued to increase. Another commission was for George M. Whiley Ltd, a company which manufactured gold and silver leaf. Gibbings designed trade marks for their 'Old London' and 'Beaters' brands. Another company to recognise the potential of Gibbings's engraving was Findlaters:

> Then, I can't remember how, Findlater's approached me, asking for some engravings of London's bridges, to advertise their port. Four biggish ones I did for them, with which they seemed greatly pleased.
>
> And now the year was drawing to its close and Christmas was soon to be upon us. Matinée cigarettes, Findlater's port, I mused — would there be a token from either of them? Sure enough, on Christmas Eve I found a large package in my hall: half a dozen of port, I thought. I was wrong — it was a full dozen of Eno's, and with it a card wishing me a healthy New Year.[24]

His commercial work was by necessity more conservative in style. His engravings of London bridges were strong in design and robust enough to be photographically reduced and printed from process line blocks and used in a range of brochures and advertisements.

Boosted by the amount of work that was coming in, and with further commissions promised, life seemed a little more secure. Flush with money from his commercial activities, Gibbings felt in a position to invest in a personal project to promote his own studio work. In the following year, 1921, he decided to publish privately a selection of his most recent small prints in book form, including a number of engravings which had already been published or exhibited. *Twelve Wood Engravings by Robert Gibbings* was printed 'at the Baynard Press by Sanders Philips & Co. Ltd,' in a signed and limited edition of one hundred and twenty-five copies.[25] Apart from the title and contents page the book had no text and was simply bound in grey boards and printed on damped hand-made paper. In engravings from the book such as *The Rick Yard* and *Scraps*, Gibbings found a startling simplicity, giving a powerful sense of design to domestic and everyday subjects.

As with all privately published books, the problem was one of marketing and distribution. No doubt Gibbings took every opportunity to sell copies to his acquaintances but he needed to recoup his money. In a letter offering the *Twelve Wood Engravings* to the Dunster House Bookshop in America he reported that he had sold forty copies in about six weeks after publication.[26] In October 1922 he

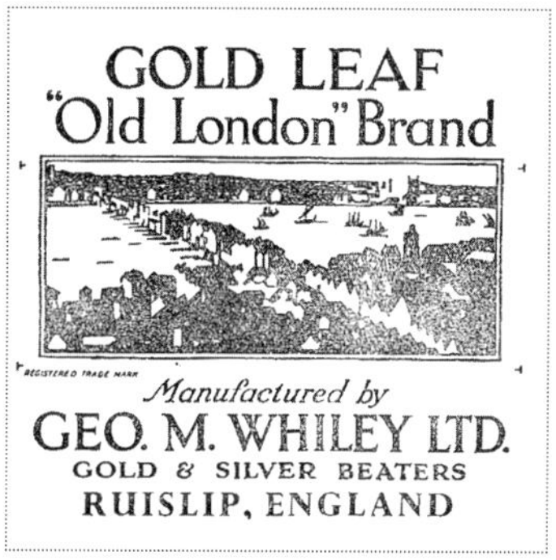

40 Wood-engraving of the old London Bridge used as a trade mark on the cover of books of gold leaf produced by G. M. Whiley, c.1920, cover size 90 x 91 mm. Reproduced with permission of API Foils.

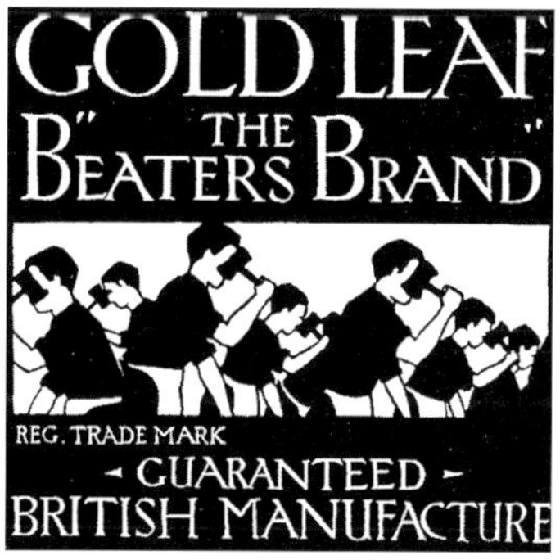

41 Wood-engraving used as a trade mark for G. M. Whiley's Beaters Brand of gold leaf, c.1920, 70 x 70 mm. Reproduced with permission of API Foils.

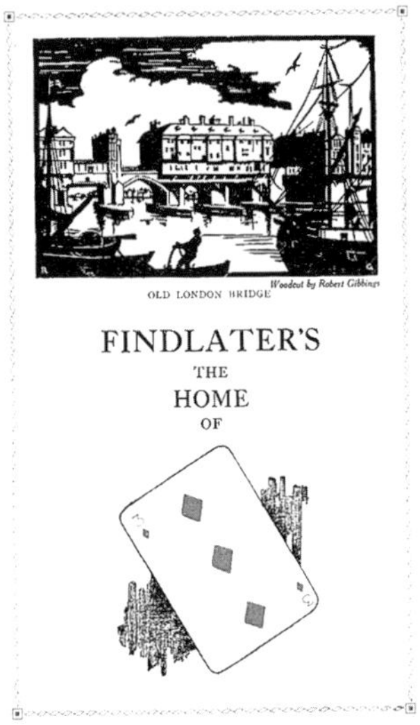

42 *above* Cover of a small publicity leaflet, *c.* 1920 produced for Findlater's illustrated with a reproduction (reduced) of a wood-engraving of the old London Bridge. The original print measures 137 x 200 mm. Reproduced with permission of the John Lewis Partnership Archive.

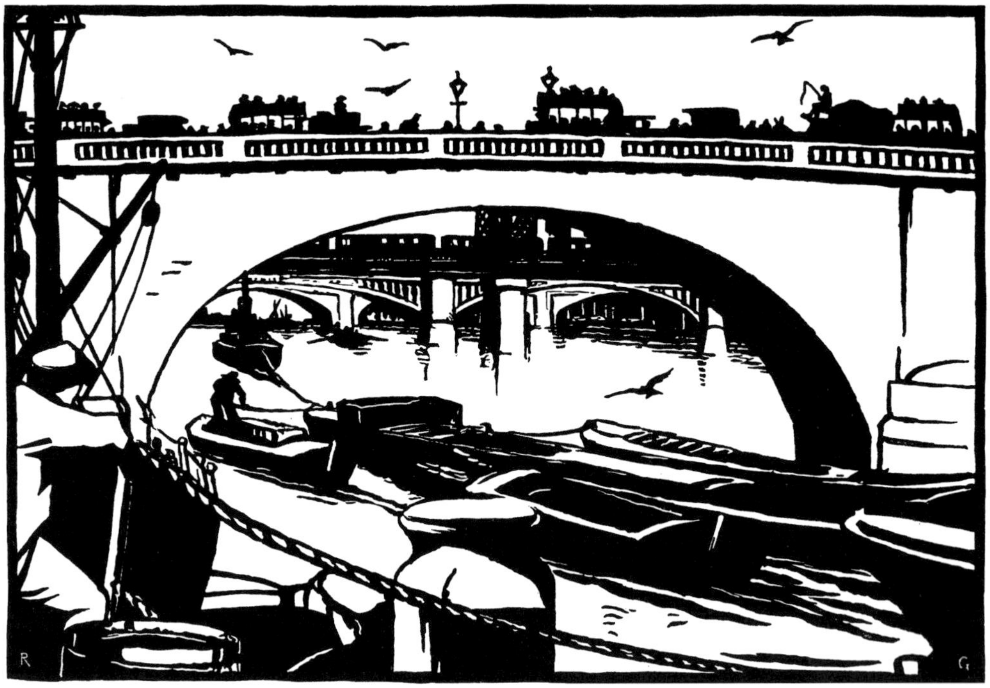

43 *right London Bridge To-day*, *c.* 1920, wood-engraving, 133 x 196 mm. One of four wood-engravings of London bridges designed to advertise Findlater's port.

placed an advertisement in *The Studio* offering the remaining copies for sale 'to be had from the artist' — price one guinea. Until publishing his collection of engravings, his work mainly focused on producing studio prints to be framed. Now that Gibbings could see his work in the format of a book, even though one without words, he could appreciate the feel of the book as an artefact and as a context for engraving.

His engravings continued to appear in a variety of journals; *Nude in a Pool* appeared in volume two of *The Apple of Beauty and Discord* in 1921, and *Clear Waters*, and a very striking engraving of William Walcot, the architect and water-colourist, appeared in *The Studio*.[27] In contrast to his commissioned work, Gibbings was experimenting with ideas of composition and the balance of shapes. *The House Painters*, with one figure cut off at the waist, is a 'snap-shot' image from an unusual viewing point of a mundane subject, which Gibbings turns into a powerful visual statement.

Part of the summer of 1921 was spent in Cornwall, staying in a friend's house as a break from the pressures of life in the city. Here Gibbings was able to concentrate on his engravings for the next annual exhibition of the Society of Wood Engravers. The Society had expanded its activities and during May and June 1921 an exhibition had been held at the Rymans Galleries in Oxford. In October the critic Herbert Furst gave the Society further publicity in an article he published on 'The Modern Woodcut'.[28] Tracing the development of the medium over the last century, Furst analysed the work of the artists of the 'old school', and then discussed the work of the young generation or the 'Artist-Venturers ... out to discover new fields'. Furst, rather conservative in his views, felt that 'a multitude of theories' had sprung up in this century which had enticed the artist 'away from the pursuit of practical artistry into the pastures of aesthetic speculation'. He

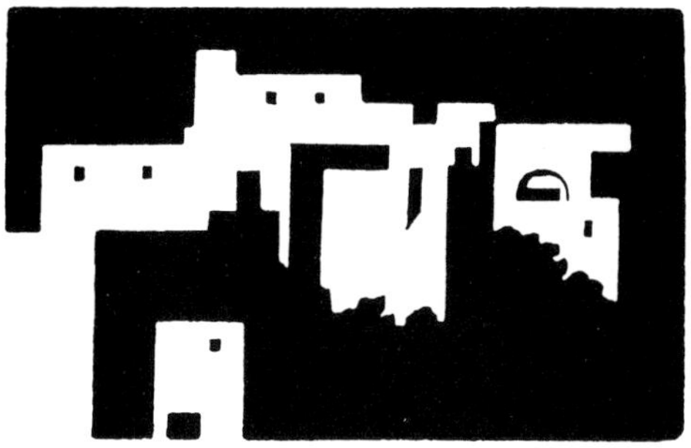

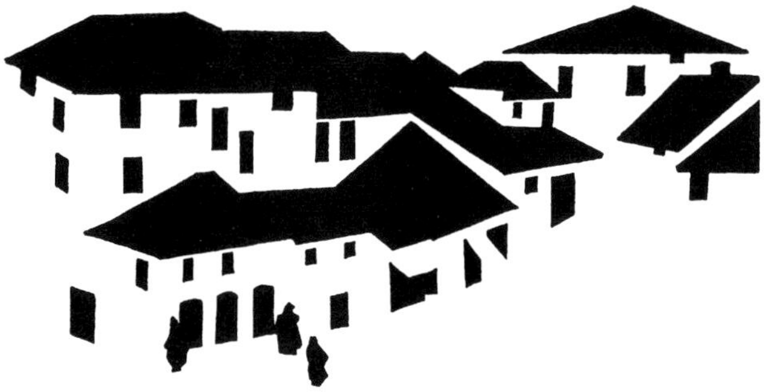

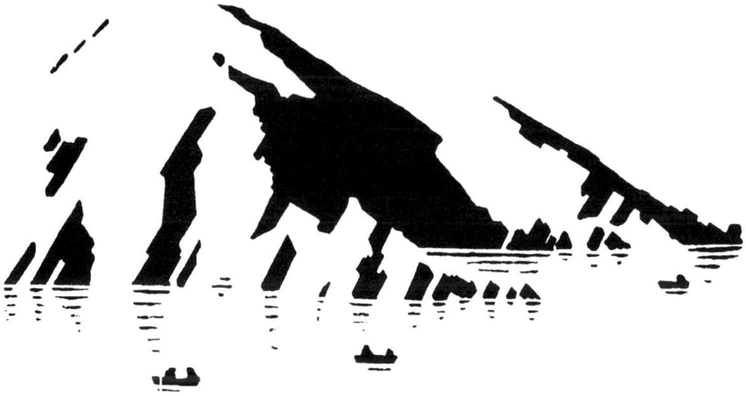

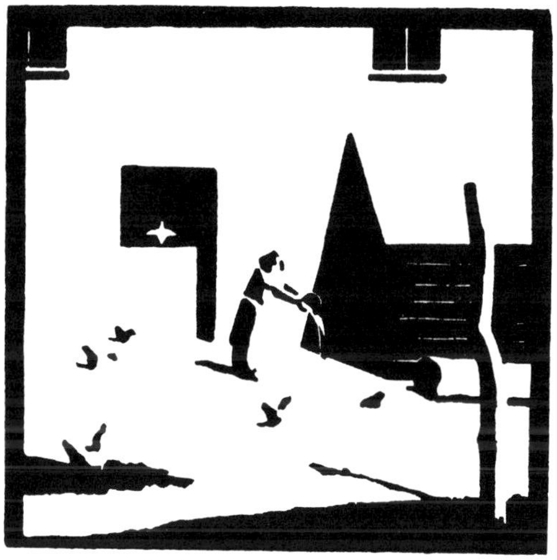

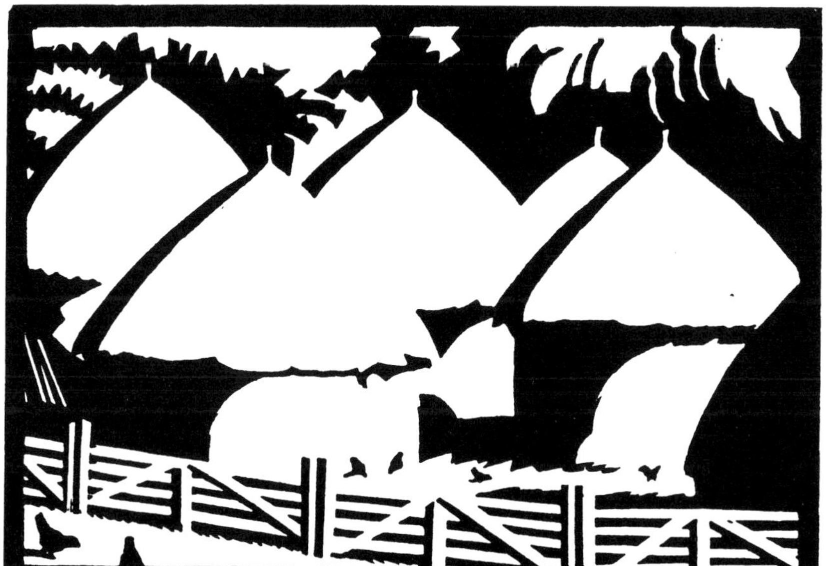

44 *top left Tigne, Malta, c.* 1919, wood-engraving, 39 × 63 mm.

45 *top right A Street in Macedonia,* 1920, wood-engraving, 48 × 96 mm.

46 *middle left Evening Sunshine,* c. 1920, wood-engraving, 52 × 100 mm.

47 *middle right Scraps, c.* 1920, wood-engraving, 64 × 66 mm.

48 *bottom The Rick Yard, c.* 1921, wood-engraving, 77 × 110 mm.

44–49 (*next page*) were all prints included in the book *Twelve Wood Engravings by Robert Gibbings* which he published privately in 1921.

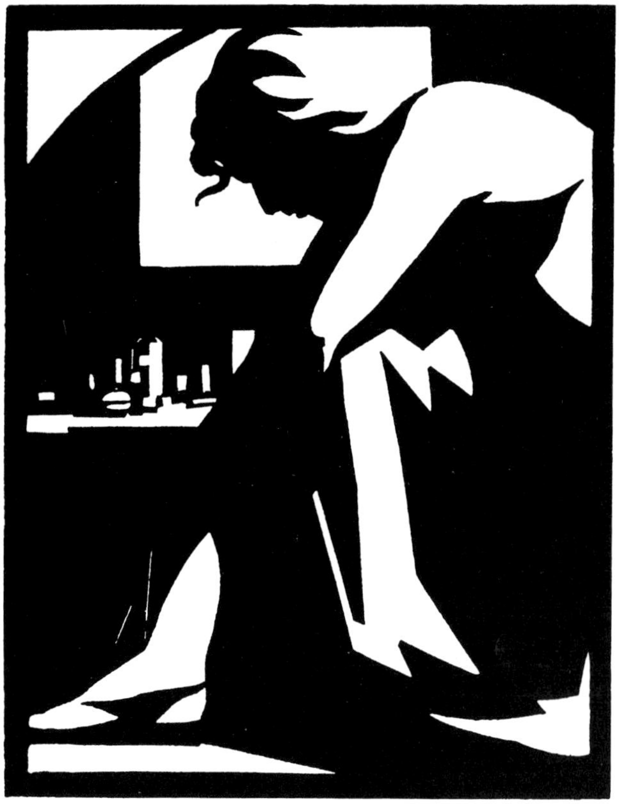

49 *The Girl in the Garret*, 1921, wood-engraving, 105 x 82 mm.

appreciated that the brutality of war had made it impossible for the young artists to return to the 'aesthetic sensibility — sentimentality they would call it' of previous generations. Furst was troubled by what he saw as the machine-like new vision with a preference for 'decided and unequivocal forms, unbroken and unsoftened by the atmosphere of nature or the mist of dreams'; even those seeking inspiration from the past looked to the 'harsh Byzantine gloom or the angular Egyptian rhythm rather than the suave Renaissance grace …'. Amongst others of the young generation, Furst picked out Eric Gill and Gibbings as followers of the 'Byzantine mannerisms' but worthy of praise for their skill. He responded to Gibbings's work, recognising that his vision was rooted in nature, commenting that his 'geometric and vigorous simplifications of landscapes and figure subjects are conceived with imagination … the degree of naturalism combined with a satisfying aesthetic pattern is sometimes quite remarkable'.

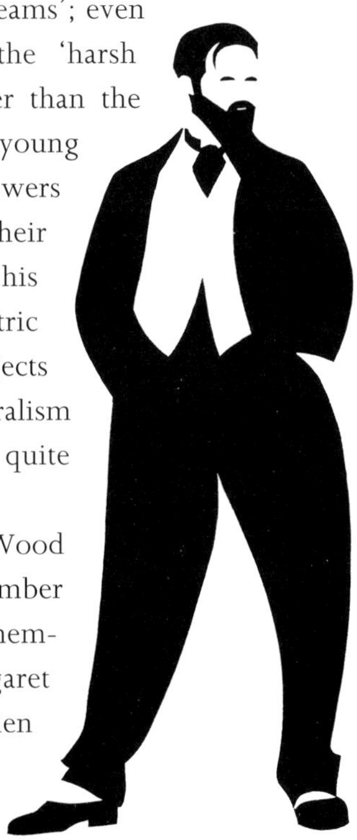

50 *William Walcot*, 1921, wood-engraving, 296 x 142 mm.

At the second annual exhibition of the Society of Wood Engravers, which opened at the Chenil Gallery in November 1921, the number of contributors had increased; new members included Ethelbert White, Charles Ginner and Margaret Pilkington, and invited exhibitors included Paul Nash, Vivien Gribble, Hester Sainsbury and Claude Flight.[29] The selection of exhibits was decided in a democratic way at

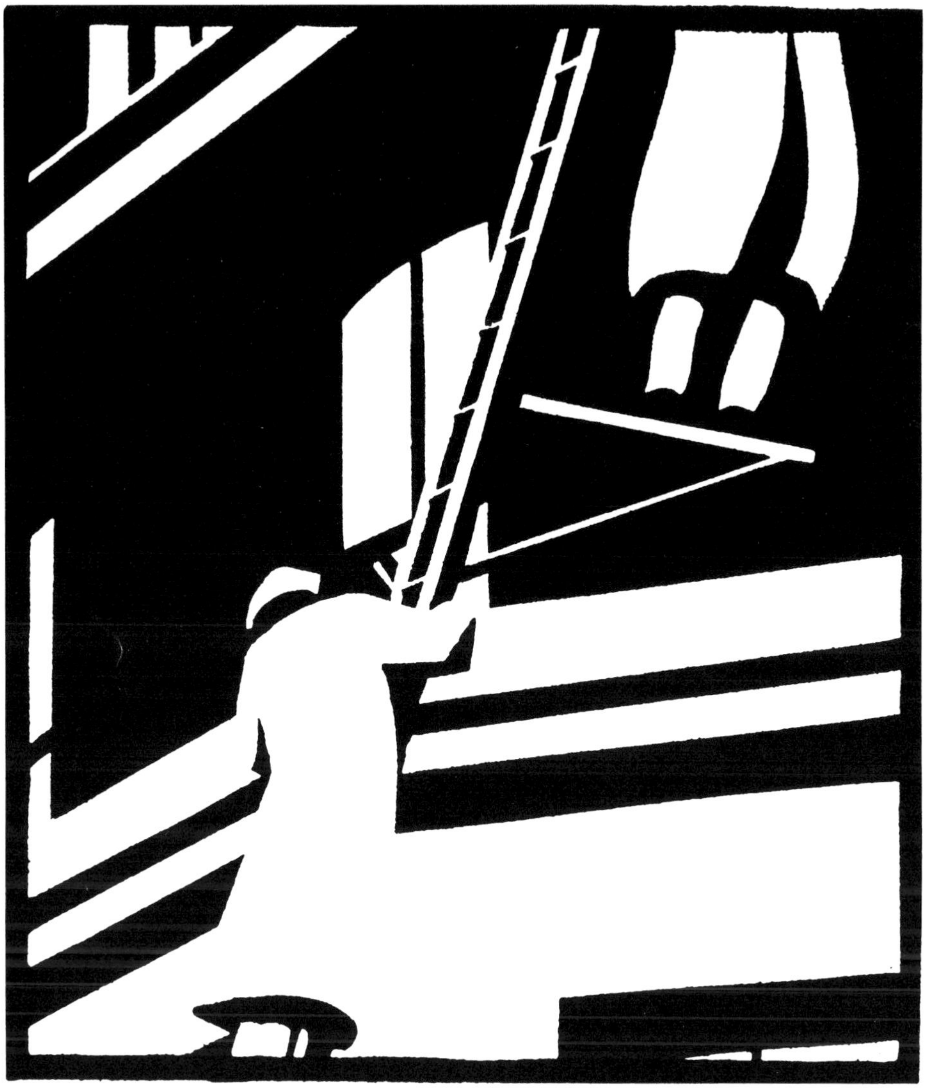

51 *House Painters*, 1921, wood-engraving, 142 x 124 mm.

a general meeting — a hanging committee was then elected which consisted of two members plus the Honorary Secretary, the 'Honorary' role now falling to Robert while Moira still carried on with the basic hard graft of administration and secretarial support.

The year 1922 brought with it a continuing stream of commercial work for Gibbings. The publishers Chatto & Windus commissioned book jackets for *The Oppidan* by Shane Leslie and *The Camomile* by Catherine Carswell; for the firm Henry Hope & Sons, Gibbings produced a large engraving of County Hall in London for use in advertisements, and the Orient Shipping Line commissioned a set of twelve decorative wood-engraved borders for use on their publicity, cruise itineraries and menus. Also, the literary and art journals *Today*, *The Beacon*, and *The Golden Hind* were publishing engravings by Gibbings.

London Underground commissioned Gibbings to design a poster advertising the gardens at Wisley. Following this, Moira and Robert worked together on another piece of publicity for the London Underground — a twenty-page booklet

Wisley poster – see colour plate 3.

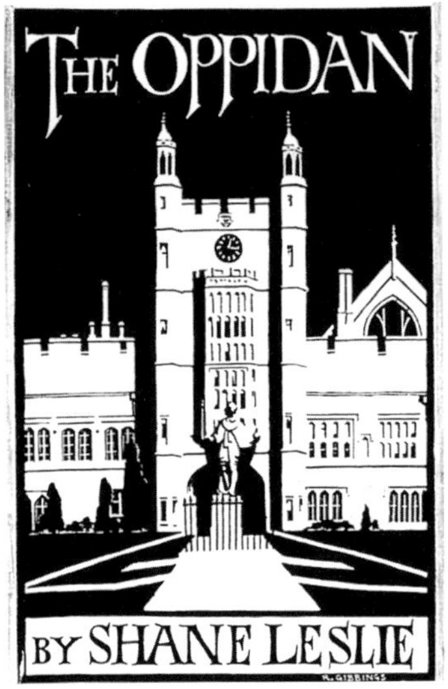

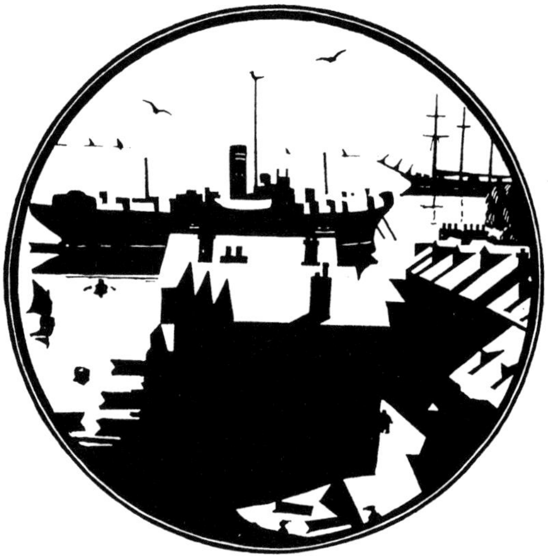

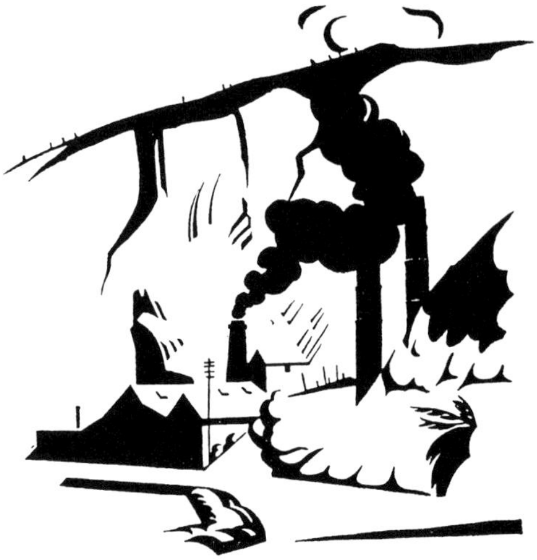

52 *above* Wood-engraved illustration used on the dust-jacket of *The Oppidan*, published by Chatto & Windus in 1922. Image size 183 x 117 mm.

53 *above right* *Fowey Harbour*, c. 1919, wood-engraving, diam. 102 mm. Published in the art and literature magazine *The Golden Hind*, vol. 1, no. 1, October 1922, p. 24.

54 *right* Untitled wood-engraving, 100 x 97 mm., which was published in *The Golden Hind*, vol. 1, no. 4, July 1923, p. 9.

The Zoo – see colour plate 4d.

promoting London Zoo and predictably titled *The Zoo*. To what extent it was a true collaboration is uncertain. Perhaps Gibbings was anxious to make Moira feel involved; the style of writing suggests it was Robert's work and maybe Moira's role was that of researcher and organiser. The text, clearly aimed at children, takes the form of a lively and light-hearted account of a day trip to the zoo by two children with their well-travelled 'Uncle Max'. The creatures encountered are given almost human personalities and names. There is no title page, but a reference to the author is to be discovered in the text: 'I bet the Gibbons are wide awake'; a footnote then comments, 'Please note — no relation to author or artist'. Full of dialogue and questions from the inquisitive children, the apparent informality of the text is balanced by accurate description and information about the animals; these educational elements, although effort has been made to blend them in naturally, seem over earnest in the typical style of the period. But for the first time, Gibbings was expressing his enthusiasm and love of foreign parts and his fascination for flora and fauna in writing and integrating his words and images.

IN APRIL 1922 Gibbings began to correspond with Thomas Balston, who was to prove a great friend and supporter in the years to come. The correspondence started with an approach by Balston asking if Gibbings was interested in commissions for book illustrations. After distinguished military service in the First World War, Balston had joined the publishing firm of Gerald Duckworth, becoming a partner in 1923 and a director a year later. John Dreyfus has described Balston as a 'lively-minded, wiry, energetic and affluent bachelor'.[30] He was an avid collector of English paintings and ceramics and had a 'keen artistic sense'; in later life he took up painting himself, taking lessons from Mark Gertler, whose work he admired and collected. Balston attended the exhibitions of the Society of Wood Engravers and became very enthusiastic about what he saw. It started him off on a life-long passion for wood-engraving and he became a keen collector and writer on the subject. Balston saw the potential of reviving wood-engraving as a medium for book illustration and, taking something of a lead, had already commissioned illustrations from Vivien Gribble and Ethelbert White.

Gibbings, always in need of work, responded eagerly to Balston's approach: 'I should very much like to do some decorations for really first class books, especially when it would be possible to keep in touch with the printer and treat the book as a whole, not so many pages of letterpress with so many illustrations.'[31] This simple desire was deeply felt by Gibbings and would be a motivation and goal for the rest of his life. The following week, Gibbings wrote to Balston sending him his last copy of *Clear Waters*, which Balston had bought for his collection; he continued with the suggestion of publishing a book on Spain. Gibbings would provide the illustrations: 'The whole thing is just an idea and I should very much like to have your opinion on it. Spain has always attracted me but so far I have not got there.'[32] However, not long before, Gibbings had journeyed to the Pyrenees in a side-car belonging to his friend the composer E. J. Moeran. Moeran was a passionate and expert motorcyclist and Gibbings accompanied him on this adventure just after he had composed his first symphonic impression, *In the Mountain Country*.[33] Despite the commitment to family and home, Gibbings had a constant desire for travel and adventure but on this occasion he was disappointed as the project on Spain was never taken up.

From 10 May to 7 June the Society of Wood Engravers held an exhibition in the Whitworth Gallery in Manchester, organised by Margaret Pilkington, who had connections with the gallery.[34] A review in the *Manchester City News* remarked that the medium would 'not please everybody — there are those people to whom mere black and white are more or less anathema', and one or two artists were picked out as being too avant-garde for general tastes; 'particularly in the studies by Paul Nash, there are tendencies which we do not like, so freed do they seem from the commonly accepted rules of pictures'. So some work was challenging, although the reviewer found nothing in Gibbings's prints to shock or disturb.

By then Balston was working on another publishing project, a collection of wood-engravings by leading contemporary artists. Gibbings was keen to contribute but worried that he had used his most recent small images in his own book.

However, he informed Balston that he hoped to get away to the country for the summer months and intended to do a lot of 'fresh work'. He had grown to enjoy the pace and society of London, despite being a countryman at heart, but the demands of such a life added to the pressure he already felt owing to his heavy commitment to the Society of Wood Engravers. Consequently he needed a period of escape in order to concentrate on his own work. But as a newly married couple the need for financial stringency meant that Robert and Moira relied on friends to help with alternative accommodation.

Balston's project, fired by his own enthusiasm for the subject, progressed quickly; Campbell Dodgson had agreed to write the introduction to the book and Balston was seeking contributions from his selected artists. Gibbings agreed to approach Rooke, who unfortunately was abroad, but he was hesitant about approaching Eric Gill with whom he had worked on Society matters:

> In three years I've pestered him with every form of letter to make him do what he does not want to do, till I'm almost afraid to meet him face to face. I certainly will be after this as I've written to him to-day, sandwiching the question of the moment [Gill's contribution to the book] between a cheque due to him for sales and some noble words about the cause.
>
> He is a very difficult man to manage and I could not say very much but my poor effort may have some slight effect if he is inclined to waver. I pretended that I had not had your last letter & asked him if he had heard from you saying he was bound to do so etc. etc. & that his work was essential to the book. That although we got no immediate advantage that it ought to interest a new public in the medium & so on. I hope very much for all our sakes he comes in.[35]

Gibbings stayed in a house borrowed from a friend in Alfriston, Sussex in July, August and September, returning for short visits to Redcliffe Square. He had suffered from 'rotten weather' in the country and was behind in engravings for Balston's book. In October, he arranged to let the flat in London and spent another four months in Sussex, this time at 'Bungalow Cottage' in the village of Iden. Gibbings explained to Balston that he wanted to get on with some painting but was aware that this would lose him some commercial work. He had also been collecting together some fifty examples of his work for a proposed exhibition in Brighton, in November of 1922.

In December, Gibbings wrote to Balston to thank him for a present of a copy of Theocritus's *Sixe Idillia*, published by Duckworth and illustrated with woodcuts by Vivien Gribble — a gift which had left him 'speechless':

> Yes indeed! I am delighted to have it, & would have had one long ago on my own account only that the world has been very much with us just lately & unfortunately much more in the spending than the getting line. I find that half the year I have infinitely more work than I can do & the other half I have none at all & I've just come through the latter half.[36]

Gibbings enclosed two designs for book-jackets (which were eventually not used) but was clearly experiencing financial difficulties.

Towards the end of 1922 *Contemporary English Woodcuts* was published by Duckworth. Gibbings had eventually fallen back on two of his already successful prints, *Hamrun* and *Clear Waters*, as his contribution. A review in *The Studio* pointed

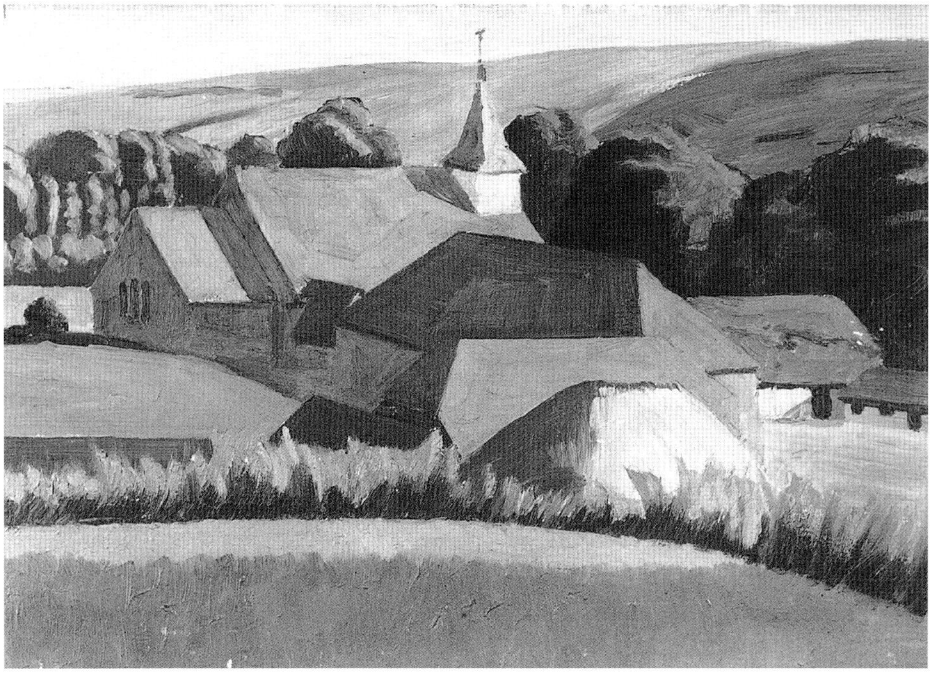

55 *Village Church in Sussex*, c. 1923, oil on board, 222 x 324 mm. Painted while Gibbings was staying in Sussex for some months in 1922 and the spring of 1923. Very few of Gibbings's early paintings have survived and this work was given to a friend, Professor Denis Gwynn, who later presented it to the Hugh Lane Municipal Gallery of Modern Art in Dublin. Another painting with the same title was exhibited at the Crawford School of Art, Cork, in 1960, on loan from a Mrs V. Rickard.

out that of the eighteen artists included, about half were members of the Society of Wood Engravers: 'With one exception they all belong to the younger school, and the selection is intended to convey an idea of the variety of talent and accomplishment possessed by this generation of artists who have found in the woodblock a congenial medium for original expression.'[37] The review goes on to describe the different stylistic 'tendencies' to be found: 'Cubistic design has a fascination for Mr. Gibbings, Mr. Kauffer and Mr. Wadsworth; but most of them seem to prefer less powerful contrasts of black-and-white.' Gibbings's images do have a strong 'cubist' reference, but his style was still essentially figurative — the effect was a development of the artist's careful observation of reality, responding to and exploring the powerful graphic quality that could be produced; he never pursued the abstract qualities he had observed in nature as an end in itself, nor did he intellectualise about it. Yet many of the images made at this period are 'modernist' and, in comparison to his later work, are challenging. They provoked reaction and remain some of the most dramatic and progressive images of the period.

Not all the reviews of the book were favourable; an anonymous reviewer had written, 'In Mr. Gibbings we get the unsophisticated "stunt"; he contributes a townscape ["Hamrun"] and a nude ["Clear Waters"]: every shadow is stuck on like a postage stamp, as though cut out in black paper; all outline, all half-tone is scrupulously omitted. If you restored them you would have two perfectly commonplace studies. Why Mr Campbell Dodgson should include such rubbish is the only mystery about it ...'. Gibbings was greatly annoyed at these comments and wrote to Balston: 'Have you any idea who was the idiot who wrote those two columns in *The Times Lit Supplement* Dec 7th [1922]. The only reply suitable is a box of liver pills which I would very much like to send with my compliments, if I could find out his name. Do let me know if you can.' The 'anonymous idiot' has later been identified as Thomas Sturge Moore, an engraver of the 'old school'.[38]

In the spring of 1923, Gibbings was still staying at Iden, Sussex, having sublet his flat in London. He was getting more work from Balston, including a commission for a jacket for a book entitled *Aquarium* by Harold Acton and the publishers Chatto & Windus commissioned another jacket design for the book *Nature and Men* by Arthur McDowall. Over the following years Gibbings was to design at least four more book-jackets for Jonathan Cape, Chatto & Windus and Constable.

Yet for the last year or so the country's economy had been experiencing a slump. Recession was biting and financial worries were a great concern for the young family. Some of the commissions that Gibbings was relying on were cancelled so he turned to the teaching of wood-engraving to supplement his income. He had already taught Rupert Lee and given tuition to the American art student, Marion Mitchell. A welcome respite had come in the autumn of 1922 with a substantial commission from Jonathan Cape. Gwen Raverat had been approached by Cape for a set of engravings to illustrate an edition of *Erewhon* by Samuel Butler; she had turned them down and the work was offered to Gibbings instead. *Erewhon*, published in November 1923, was Gibbings's first commission as a book illustrator and writing to Balston he explained, '... it is the kind of stuff I want to do, much more satisfactory than aperients [referring to his work for Eno's Fruit Salt]'.[39]

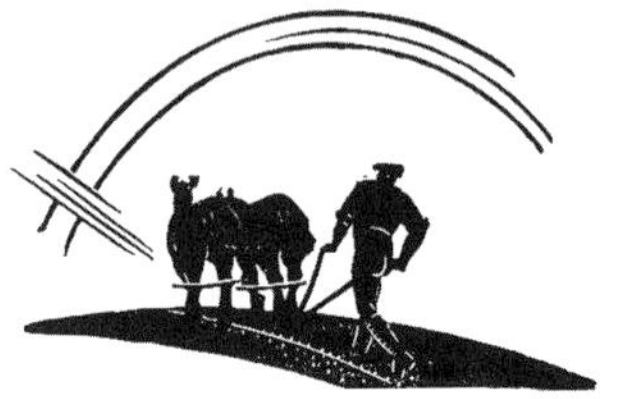

Chapter XXV : The Machines—
continued

HERE followed a very long and untranslatable digression about the different races and families of the then existing machines. The writer attempted to support his theory by pointing out the similarities existing between many machines of a widely different character, which served to show descent from a common ancestor. He divided machines into their genera, subgenera, species, varieties, subvarieties, and so forth. He proved the existence of connecting links between machines that seemed to have very little in common, and showed that many more such links had existed, but had now perished. He pointed out tendencies to reversion, and the presence of rudimentary organs which existed in many machines feebly developed and perfectly useless, yet serving to mark descent from an ancestor to whom the function was actually useful.
263

56 Headpiece at the opening of chapter 15 of *Erewhon*, 1923, wood-engraving, page size 203 x 138 mm., image size 54 x 88 mm. A number of the engravings from the book were given titles and exhibited at the annual exhibition of the Society of Wood Engravers in 1924. To comply with the Society's new regulations the prints were identified as 'illustrations' in the catalogue.

Gibbings produced thirty-eight blocks for *Erewhon*, made up of head- and tail-pieces using black silhouette with a few indications of detail rather hesitantly cut as 'white line' in the black solids. Limited editions of a selection of these engravings were printed and put into small portfolios for sale as a special edition of prints.[40] Despite his desire to show his abilities as an engraver, in retrospect, Gibbings himself was rather disappointed and critical of his work:

> My first book! Must do my utmost,' I thought. But eagerness when not controlled may be more of a curb than a spur. Looking back now, it seems that the desire to do well put a brake on my ability to do so. Though the firm were appreciative and generous when I delivered the blocks, I still have twinges of remorse when I think of the paltry efforts with which I served them.[41]

Constrained by his need to support his family, Gibbings was still hankering after travel. In a letter to Balston from Iden, while working hard on *Erewhon*, he wrote:

> I again have hopes of the Pyrenees, a sea journey on a tramp [steamer] to Spain, and then a wander through the country on a motor bike, with a couple of weeks walking in the Pyrenees. At the last moment I shall probably have to buy a new bootlace or something and won't be able to afford it, but I'm busy building castles.[42]

He was right about having no money, in fact things were becoming increasingly difficult and again his plans for travel had to be abandoned.

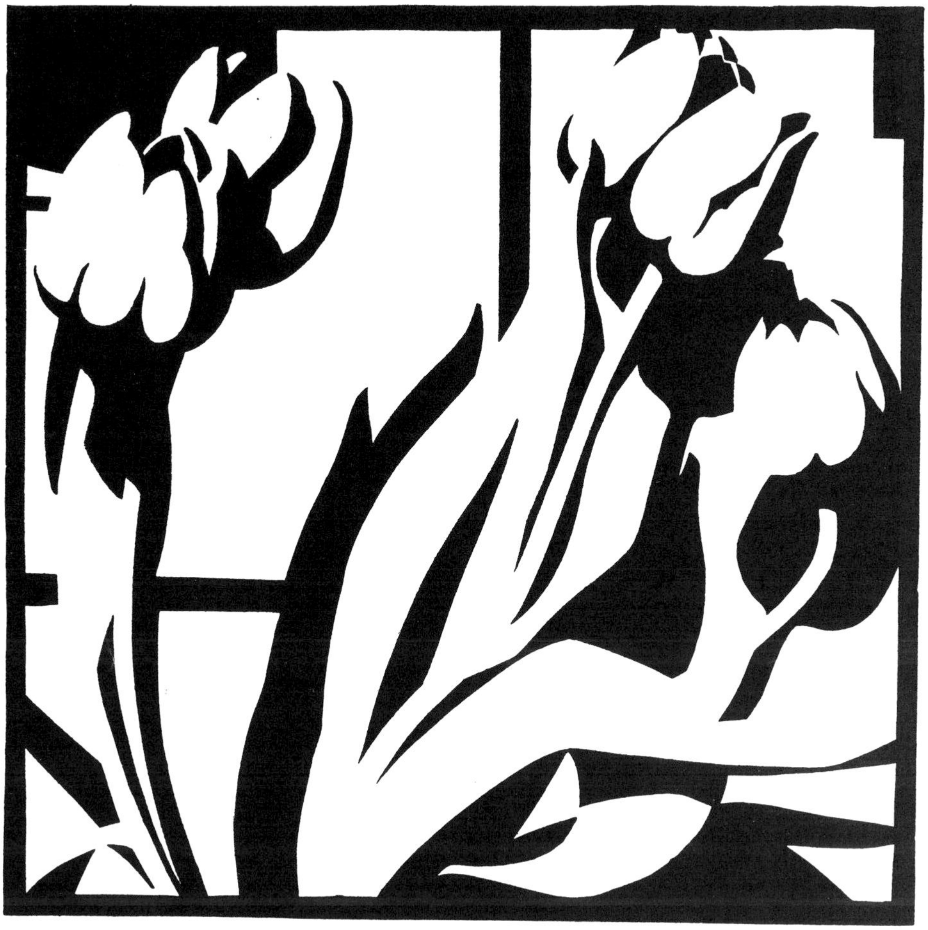

57 *Tulips*, 1922, wood-engraving, 175 x 180 mm. *Tulips* and *The Downs* were exhibited at the annual exhibition of the Society of Wood Engravers in 1922.

Robert and Moira continued to be heavily involved with the Society of Wood Engravers. As with most societies, a small group of 'regulars' formed the motivating force and Gibbings rarely missed a committee meeting. He only exhibited five prints at the annual exhibition of 1922, including his portrait of William Walcot and two large new engravings entitled *Tulips* and *The Downs*.[43] Increasingly, the Society was organising exhibitions in other towns and cities in Britain but in April 1923 exhibitions took on a more international flavour when the Society sent an exhibition to the Carnegie Institute in Pittsburgh, USA.

Heated debate amongst members of the Society over issues of policy and the definition of the role of wood-engraving was common. The best way to promote their work was the subject of continual discussion. Craig, in his familiar cantankerous way, considered posters 'rather a waste', suggesting greater effort in publishing articles or interviews in journals prior to the opening of a show. He also proposed that exhibitions should be held in 'all university towns', hoping for support and backing from the V&A. At a later meeting, it was decided to ask Paul Nash 'to write a pamphlet inviting London publishers to the next annual exhibition explaining the advantages of the woodcut as a medium of expression'. Initially the focus of the Society had been on encouraging studio prints to be framed and hung on walls — the idea of exhibiting and promoting wood-engravings, designed as illustrations for books, was a new and controversial one.

It was decided at a committee meeting, in October 1923, to form a sub-committee, to be called the 'Book work committee', chaired by Eric Gill, who believed passionately in wood-engraving as book illustration, with the purpose of organising a specialised exhibition to 'rouse public interest in the woodcut for book decoration'.[44]

In 1923 the venue for the annual exhibition moved to the St George's Gallery, Hanover Square. John Nash had suggested the move, reasoning that a more central location would attract more visitors. Gibbings showed seven new images including *Painting the Myosotis* and *Cutting Herrings*, in which a modernist approach is taken, with the composition and treatment of the figures reminiscent in some ways of the work of William Roberts or Nevinson, and marking a move away from the vanishing line. New contributors to the 1923 exhibition included Clare Leighton and Marion Mitchell and a special feature that year was a collection of ten woodcuts by Paul Gauguin, reprinted from the original blocks. These images from Gauguin's life in Polynesia were to have echoes in Gibbings's own life in the future.

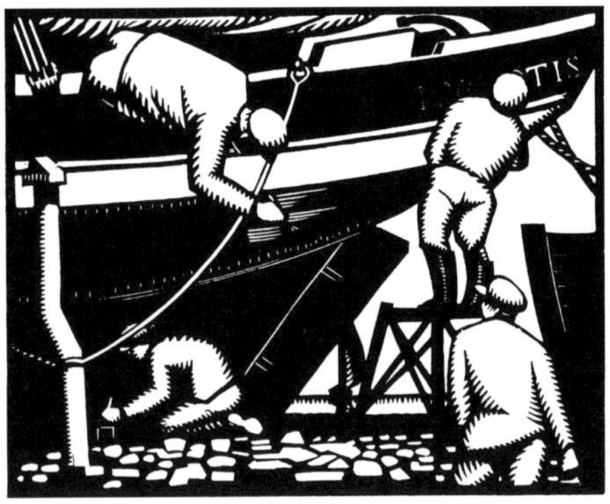

58 *above* *Painting the Myosotis*, c. 1923, wood-engraving, 101 x 126 mm.

59 *right* *Cutting Herrings*, c. 1923, wood-engraving, 132 x 93 mm. A few years later Gibbings engraved a larger version of this composition using finer lines to introduce greater tone and detail. Empson gave this engraving an alternative title of *On the Slip*.

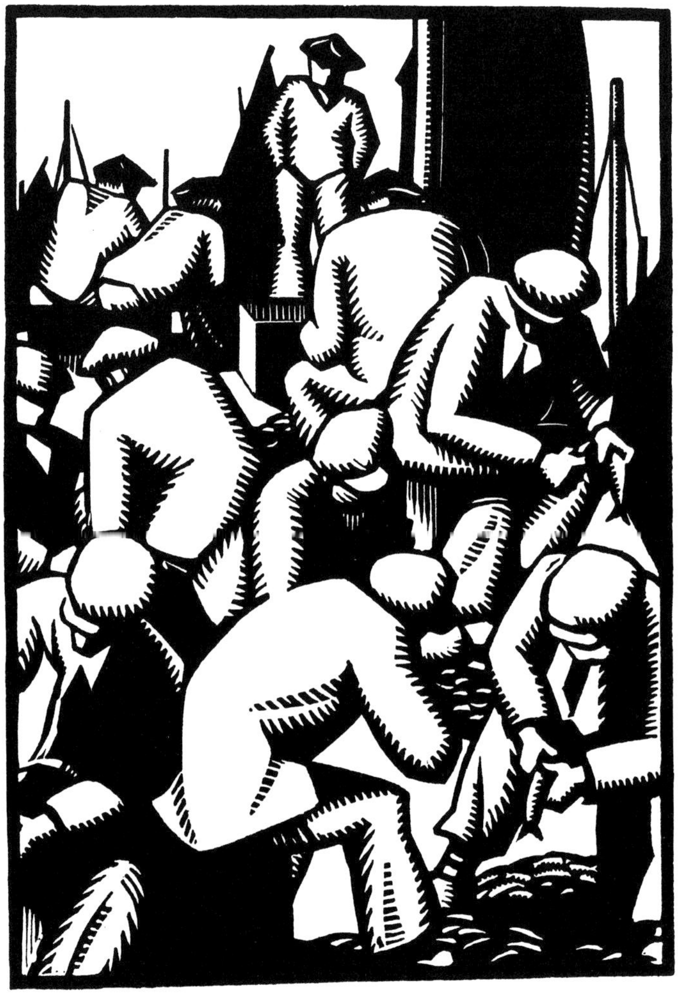

Although they were very busy with the activities of the Society, Robert and Moira could not disguise the fact that financially they were struggling — it was impossible to live solely on money generated by the sale of prints. No new commissions were in the offing and, to add to the pressure, another baby was on the way. The only temporary solution was to move in with Robert's in-laws. For a few weeks after they vacated their flat in London they stayed with relatives in Cheltenham[45] and in October 1923 Robert and Moira joined the Pennefathers in Bloxham near Banbury at their home called 'The Paddocks'. No doubt this felt like an admission of failure but the outlook was suddenly to improve with the arrival of a letter. Gibbings recalled: 'Suddenly there came a request from an unknown firm, the Golden Cockerel Press: would I do ten engravings for a limited and *de luxe* edition of Brantôme's *La Vie des Dames Galantes*? In my innocence I had never heard of this classic. A hundred guineas — why, of course I would. And the domestic atmosphere lightened.'[46]

The reason for his lack of knowledge was that this was an erotic tale, a 'top shelf' book as Gibbings later described it. Although mild by today's standards, the sensual nature of the illustrations needed presented Gibbings with a dilemma; how to do full justice to the subject matter under the close scrutiny of his 'puritanical' father-in-law? The solution was to find a room for himself back in Chelsea where he could work in some privacy.

The Golden Cockerel Press was owned and directed by Harold Midgley Taylor and his wife, Gay. Originally, full of youthful idealism, the intention had been to establish the Press as a co-operative involving young writers, who were unable to get commercial publishers to take their work, in the printing and publishing of their own books. By 1923 this policy was obviously failing and, in a desperate effort to make money, Hal Taylor had decided to try a new and more lucrative market — that of publishing expensive, fine editions of erotic texts. One of the suggested titles was *The Lives of Gallant Ladies* and a prospectus issued early in 1923 had announced the forthcoming edition 'with woodcuts by Ethelbert White'. White had already provided illustrations for an edition of *The Wedding Songs of Edmund Spenser*, published in the August of that year, but he eventually pulled out of this project leaving the Taylors anxious to find another artist. White was a friend of Gibbings through the Society of Wood Engravers and perhaps it was he who suggested him as his replacement.

Back in Chelsea Gibbings was able to concentrate on the new commission in earnest, only to be shocked and disappointed when a second letter came from the Press. Gay Taylor wrote: 'I am awfully sorry to tell you ... that my husband has had a bad relapse of T. B. and is now in a sanatorium. We do not expect him to recover, and are closing down the Press next Thursday.'[47] This was a major setback and one that had come at a very bad time. Low in spirits, Gibbings was able to spill out his frustration to his old friend, Hubert Pike, with whom he was dining that evening:

'How's things?' he asked.

'Rotten,' I said. 'Just lost the only decent job I've had for months,' and I explained what had happened. 'It's a pity too,' I added, 'because the Press was beginning to do good printing.'

Hubert, who came from a wealthy family, and Robert had grown up together and naturally he was concerned and sympathetic about Robert's predicament. He was now a successful businessman and in 1921 had become a director of Bentley Motors and was in a position to help his friend. Impressed by Robert's enthusiasm for the project, Hubert suggested a startling solution to the problem:

'Why don't you buy the Press?' said Hubert. 'It's just what you want.'
'Haven't got the money,' I answered.
'I'll lend it to you,' he said. 'Go down on Monday and, if you like it, buy it.'
I went down on the Monday, as he had suggested, and found the men packing the type into boxes, ready for closing down. On Tuesday I sent a wire to Mrs Taylor, saying 'Keep on the men,' and when I went down on the following Monday the two compositors and the machine minder were all in their several ways busy with the Brantôme. In the following financial year I had a letter from H. M. Inspector of Taxes at Reading. 'Would you please explain the item in your balance sheet, "Profits X.Y.Z. by Gallant Ladies."' 'I am sorry to inform you,' I replied, 'that they refer only to the title of a book.'[48]

Although Pike's offer was totally unexpected, in retrospect the plan to buy the Press does seem a natural and inevitable consequence of a number of factors in Gibbings's life at the time. He had already been involved in the debate about the promotion of engraving as a medium for book illustration; typography and the integration of text and image had been until now a latent interest since working with Rooke and Mason at the Central. Above all, he had expressed the desire to be able to control quality and all aspects of production himself. Taking over the directorship of the Golden Cockerel Press was the perfect opportunity to satisfy his desire and also rid himself of the pressure and insecurity of looking for work from others — now he could generate his own.

Chapter Five
Early Days at Waltham 1924–1925

'I THINK,' GIBBINGS WROTE TO BALSTON, 'it is going to be very jolly. There is a very pleasant cottage with about ¾ acre of garden, and with any luck I should have quite a lot of spare time for my own work.'[1] Although happy to be in the country, experience would very quickly moderate his optimistic expectations of 'spare time' but, in terms of his family life, moving to the gentle and beautiful surroundings of rural Berkshire and into a home of their own must indeed have filled Robert and Moira with hope for the future. After years of moving from one temporary address to another, at last the family now had some sense of permanence and could plan for the longer term. For Moira in particular it must have been a relief as she had a new baby to look after.

Just a few days after his third birthday, their son Patrick was presented with a sister. On 20 December, 1923, Brigid Elaine Jacqueline Gibbings had been born in the maternity ward at Banbury Hospital. With such a young baby it had been sensible to delay the move to Waltham for a short while — despite Gibbings's anxiety to end his dependence on his in-laws. Also, sensitive to the difficult circumstances in which Gay Taylor found herself, the family did not take over the cottage until late February 1924, giving Gay some time to clear the house and settle her affairs. Gibbings took rooms in the village a few days before the move to organise and oversee the arrival of the furniture and he was shortly joined by the family. He was in buoyant mood; in his own words it was 'a case of Yo Ho Ho and some printer's ink!'[2] In response to an offer of another commission from the publishers Chatto & Windus, he wrote: 'You will probably be surprised to hear that I am now head cook & bottle washer down here. ... We only moved down last week but look forward to many years among fruit trees, flowers & printing presses.'[3]

The cottage, grandly named 'Four Elms', was to prove a splendid family home and a blissful environment for children. Waltham Saint Lawrence remains a picturesque village today, with many old vernacular buildings typical of the Thames Valley. But in 1924 it was very rural and relatively untouched; a small mixed community with some wealthy and professional families — the close proximity to the GWR railway into Paddington at Twyford made commuting to the city possible — as well as farmers and agricultural workers. The old centre of the village clusters around the church and a fourteenth-century timber-framed

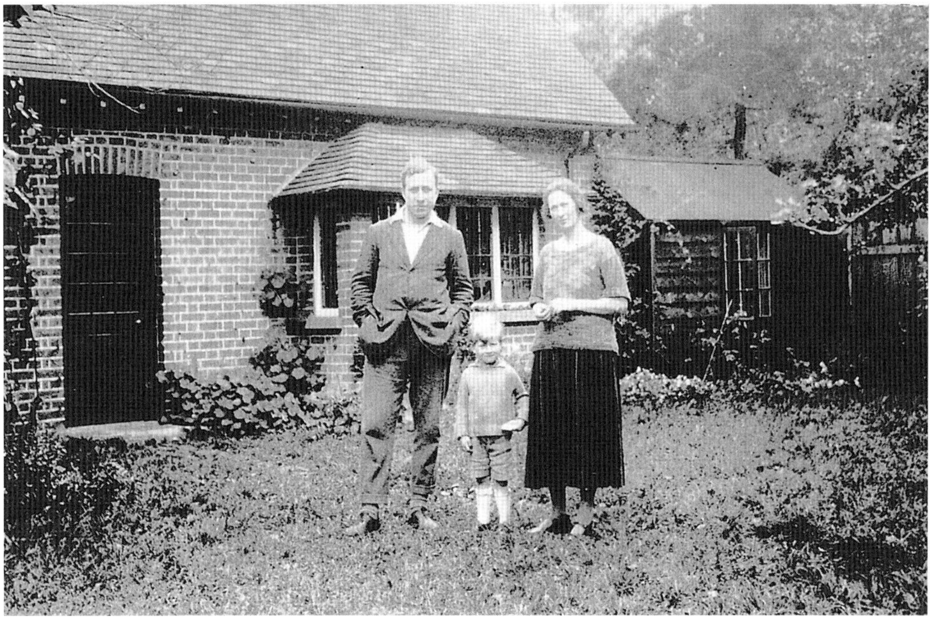

60 Robert, Patrick and Moira Gibbings at Four Elms, c. 1924. Clark Library.

public house, the Bell, which was to become a familiar haunt for Gibbings; Four Elms was on the fringes of the village on a corner of a winding road leading to Wargrave, and about three miles away from the banks of the Thames.

The cottage was small, only consisting of a ground floor (and therefore technically a bungalow), not old but sturdily built in red brick with a tile roof. In addition to the garden, the property included an orchard, a meadow and wooded ground which amounted to about eleven acres. The Press was housed in a converted army hut where Albert Cooper, the pressman, and Frank Young and Harry Gibbs, the compositors, were hard at work — Gibbings not only took over all the machinery and equipment, he also kept on the small professional staff. At the time of the sale, figures showed that technically the Golden Cockerel Press, named after the Russian ballet 'Coq d'Or' which Harold Midgley Taylor admired, had shown a recent profit. But this was only on paper and in fact running the Press had proved an exhausting and ill-fated enterprise, despite all the idealism and energy with which it had been started.

Taylor had originally taken over the land as a smallholding, setting up a fruit farming business as an investment and renting out the cottage to tenants. This enterprise was to prove a failure and, in any case, Taylor's real passion and ambition was directed towards the world of literature. After a short and passionate courtship, Taylor had married Gay in the spring of 1920, and, together with two of Gay's flatmates, the printing and publishing co-operative had been set up. None of them had any experience or practical knowledge of printing so the Taylors spent the summer months with Hilary Pepler, hard at work at the St Dominic's Press in Ditchling, learning the basic skills.

Their first few months in Waltham were hard; the cottage was still occupied by tenants so primitive temporary accommodation was found in outbuildings; the winter was particularly cold. Equipment and machinery were purchased; for type they bought cases of Caslon Old Face together with a few other founts and everything was installed in the army hut erected for the purpose near to the cottage. Conditions were so bad that morale was affected; for anyone without Hal Taylor's literary zeal the work must have often seemed full of drudgery and tedium and by the summer of 1921 the partnership had collapsed and Hal and Gay were left to carry on alone.[4] But there had been some success — their first book, a collection of short stories by A .E. Coppard, *Adam & Eve & Pinch Me*, was published in April 1921 and quickly sold out; a second edition followed in June. Taylor had also persuaded a friend to have his literary magazine, *Voices*, typeset and printed at the Press. However, although this had been a much needed commission, the pressures of time and the amount of labour involved in production proved too much for such inexperienced staff and subsequent issues were printed elsewhere. Despite their enthusiasm, their lack of training and limited understanding of typography resulted in books that were naive and rather dull in their design: line lengths too long for the size of type, poor justification, the lack of leading, the over-use of swash letters, the choice of inappropriate paper and poor press work clearly demonstrated that they were well-meaning amateurs.

Taylor had been impressed by a story of Coppard's that he had read in *Voices* and later Coppard recounted how Taylor cycled twenty-five miles on a hot summer's day to beg him to let him 'begin his publishing campaign' with a collection of his stories. Coppard described Taylor as 'an extremely intelligent and likeable man' and was impressed by him as a 'fellow of exquisite taste and discrimination' in having the foresight to recognise his talents and offer him the chance to have his first book published. Coppard regularly visited the Press during the preparation of his book and joined in the work himself:

> I set just one row of the type, besides doing some of the printing, folding, pasting, binding, and labelling. In the end my eyes were so bedazed by the title page that they were blind to the inadequacies of the rest; the type was poor, the paper bad, the leaves fell out, the cover collapsed, but I was not to blame for anything except the contents, and it happened that we were all kindly commended by the reviewers.[5]

Despite these rather exaggerated faults the book was a success and recognised as being of literary importance; the production genuinely embodied the ideals set out in the Press's manifesto that it was to be a '… co-operative in the strictest sense. Its members are their own craftsmen, and will produce their books themselves in their own communal workshops ….' These were fine intentions but the reality was bound to fall short. Only Coppard offered any substantial support to the Taylors as he also helped with the financial accounting;[6] most authors were to prove only too willing to leave the grind to Hal and Gay.

To add to their problems Hal's health deteriorated. He had suffered since childhood from attacks of tuberculosis and these now re-occurred, forcing him to leave the Press to recuperate. The pressure had also affected his relationship with Gay, arguments were frequent and, partly due to his own views on 'open marriage', Gay embarked on an affair with Coppard, which despite Hal's liberal attitude caused all concerned anxiety and unhappiness. Books produced in 1922 had

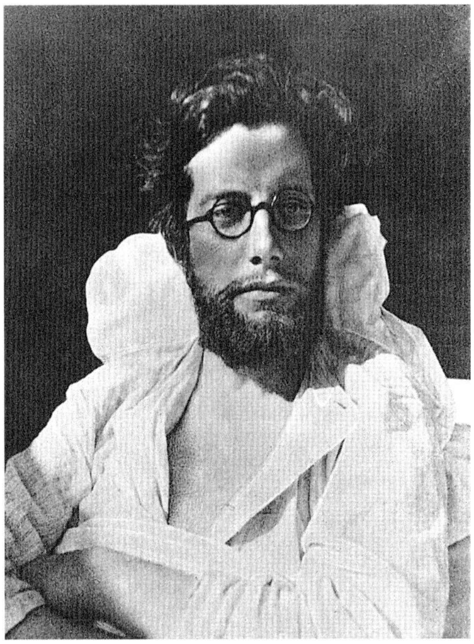

61 Harold Midgely Taylor in bed suffering from an attack of tuberculosis. Albert Cooper Collection, RUL.

slow sales and authors increasingly complained of errors in their printed texts. The situation demanded a radical re-think. The decision was taken to abandon the co-operative idea, employ qualified tradesmen and concentrate on the production of fine and limited editions of the classics, printed on damped hand-made papers (previously books had been printed on ordinary stock or dry antique paper). The quality of production improved but filling wage packets created new demands to provide enough work to keep the compositors and pressman occupied.

Most of their books were not illustrated but for the edition of *The Wedding Songs of Edmund Spenser* Ethelbert White had produced some coloured wood-engravings. At the time it was generally felt that White's engravings failed to harmonise well with the type and purists dissapproved of the use of colour and so White's commission to illustrate Brantôme's *The Lives of Gallant Ladies*, although already announced, was dropped. Towards the close of 1923, Taylor was again hit by a bad attack of tuberculosis. Albert Cooper recalled that Hal's office was often bitterly cold as he always sat by an open window. As things got worse, Taylor had to take to a bed set up in a summerhouse:

> It was on wheels on a circular base and he could turn that south so as to get the lee side against the wind. There was a mantelpiece and pictures hanging up, and his bed, and everything was just like a little room in itself only with one side open. After a day's work I used to go across. He liked to see the progress of what was going on in the Press.[7]

By Christmas 1923, Taylor's condition had deteriorated so much that he was admitted to a local sanatorium.[8]

With Hal too ill to contribute to the day-to-day running of the Press, it fell to Gay and Coppard to struggle on. The publishing programme became haphazard, proposed projects were dropped and others substituted. They had lost their way in both their personal lives and in the running of the Press and it was inevitable that they should have considered selling up. Advertisements for the sale of the Press appeared in *The Times* and *The London Mercury*.

Charles T. Jacobi was one person who inquired about the sale and Gay Taylor's reply to his letter, dated 6 November 1923, gives a brief description of equipment and facilities at the Press:

> The workshops, stock-room and office are of about 875 sq. feet floor-space, and are equipped with a small Wharfedale, a crown broadside Phoenix platen machine, about 3000 lbs of Caslon Old Face type, guillotine and hand and standing presses, power, and very complete accessories for the production of fine letterpress printing. The printing staff is at present three; the full complement would be seven.
>
> I enclose profit and loss accounts for the three years of working. The total capital we invested was £2800, but plant and building values have, of course, fallen considerably since 1920. We are now willing to sell at £1800 for plant, buildings, stocks and goodwill.
>
> The workshops stand near a small house, and we would either sell or let this to the purchaser of the Press, with one to twelve acres of garden and meadows, including the ground rent of the workshops.[9]

The profit and loss account for the Press accompanied the letter. For the first eighteen months, until 31 March 1922, there was a loss of £252 4s 10d, the next year ended with a loss of £68 14s 7d, but for the seven months up to 31 October

1923, the figures show a profit of £520 6s 11d. This seems to have been the result of a little 'creative' accounting as the figures not only included the running costs of the Press but various rather vague estimates of the capital value of materials and existing stock, which, when added in, made it appear there was an encouraging operating profit. It is clear from pencilled notes on Jacobi's copy that he questioned some of the detail of these figures — particularly the valuation of existing stock and the effects of depreciation, but at face value, the change in policy to the production of fine editions of the classics had turned the finances of the Press around.

So this was the state of affairs when Gibbings's casual dinner date with Hubert Pike led to his spontaneous decision to buy the Golden Cockerel Press. Seventeen books had been published by the Press itself but other books and journals had been printed by them. The Press had published some worthwhile texts which had met with some success and despite the poor production and errors of the early work, it had gained a certain respect and created interest in literary circles. Now, with professional tradesmen on the staff, production quality was improving and, on paper at least, the Press was showing a profit.

The asking price was £1800 but values had declined steeply and Gay was desperate to sell. Cave and Manson state that a price of £850, a fair and realistic evaluation in the circumstances, was agreed for the premises (the huts), the plant and goodwill and £200 for the materials and work already done on the *The Lives of Gallant Ladies*.[10] Without Pike's financial help the purchase would have been impossible; Pike was to receive interest on his investment but otherwise had little involvement in the Press, of which Gibbings was sole manager on an annual salary of £500 — any additional profits were to be shared equally between the two partners.[11]

The cottage offered rather inadequate accommodation, consisting of a small hall, a large living room, a small kitchen, outside timber-built toilet and two small bedrooms. Adjoining the house was a timber-built summerhouse which initially they used as an additional bedroom for one of the children. Later, in 1926, Gibbings had a wing built on to provide room for his expanding family, and various timber outbuildings were erected which were used for studio space. The

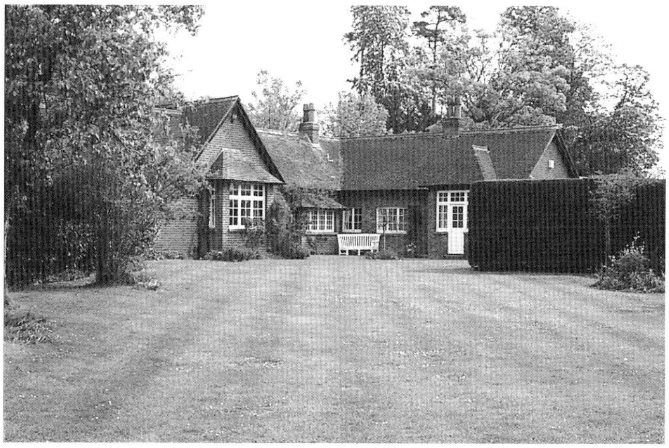

62 View of Four Elms showing the extension Gibbings had built on to increase the accommodation. Photograph taken in 1989.

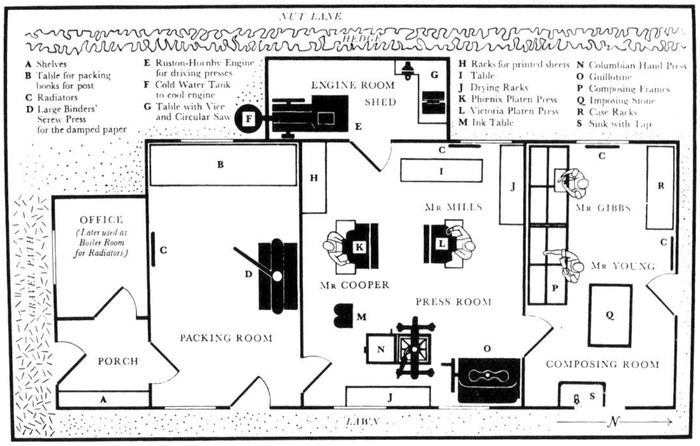

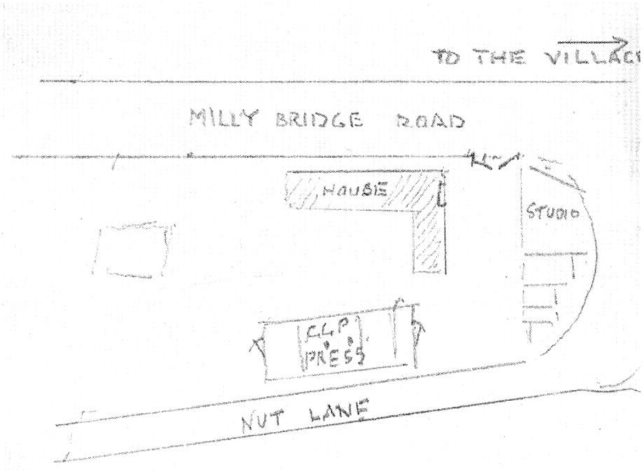

63 *left* Plan of the Golden Cockerel Press based on a sketch by Albert Cooper and published to accompany his 'Notes on the printing methods of the Golden Cockerel Press' in *Robert Gibbings, a Bibliography*, 1962, p. 153.

64 *right* Sketch map drawn by Albert Cooper from memory, showing the layout of buildings at Four Elms and the Golden Cockerel Press. Author's collection.

army hut which housed the Press had been partitioned to provide a composing room, press-room, office and packing room. Many years later Albert Cooper wrote a brief description :

It was lined inside and well heated, and situated at the rear of his house. ...As there was no electric light laid on in Waltham in those days, the lighting for the evenings in the winter was hanging paraffin oil lamps, and the heating system was by two anthracite closed stoves, one in the press-room and one in the composing-room, with a Valor oil stove in the packing-room when it was used. Later Mr Gibbings had central heating installed with radiators in each room, and also Aladdin incandescent-mantle oil lamps for better efficiency. ... The machine was a Double Crown size Wharfedale cylinder with flat-bed, which was power driven by an oil-engine (Ruston-Hornby) in a shed attached to the hut. There was a bookbinding stitching machine, as they bound books too. Later Mr Taylor bought a Victoria heavy platen press from a London printing machine company [Cooper is confused in his account here, it was a Phoenix platen press which was acquired by Taylor as listed in Gay Taylor's description of the Press to Jacobi; the Victoria was purchased by Gibbings to replace the Wharfedale a few years later].[12]

65 Albert Cooper, pressman, at work on one of the platen presses. RUL.

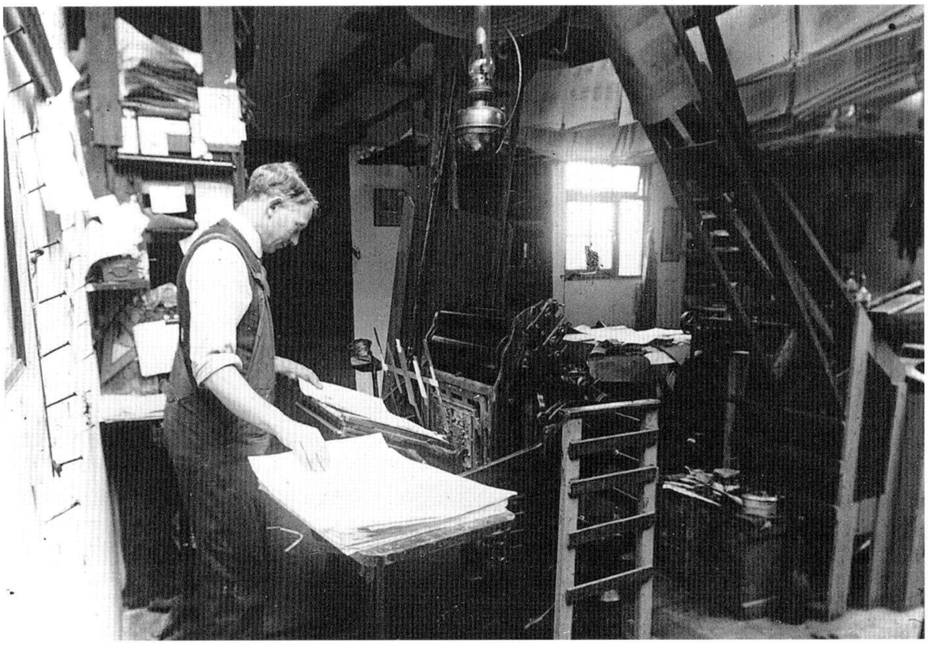

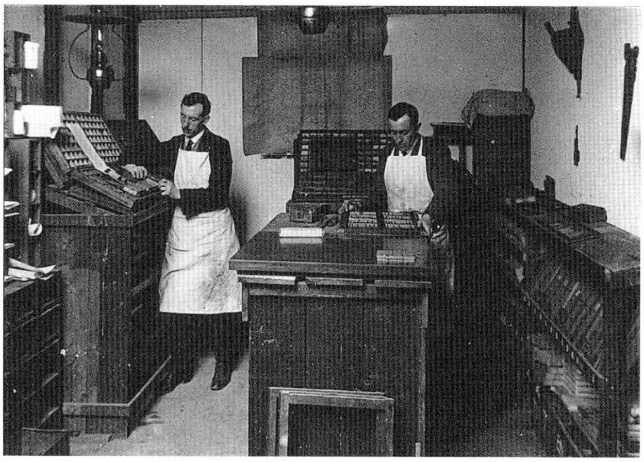

66 Frank Young and Harry Gibbs, compositors at the Golden Cockerel Press. RUL.

There was also a Columbian hand-press on which the compositors pulled proofs for author's corrections and which Gibbings and Cooper used for proofing wood-engravings.

MOIRA AND ROBERT intended to run the Press together as a team, Moira taking on much of the administration and business matters (she was a good organiser), and Robert dealing with the more creative side and production. Yet neither had any great experience of commercial printing. The Taylors had at least spent a few months with Pepler but Gibbings only had his time at the Central School with Rooke and his brief contacts with J. H. Mason on which to draw. But he was fortunate in having inherited a very professional staff; all three were experienced tradesmen and keen and interested in the future of the Press. It was largely their advice and support that enabled Gibbings to take over as director with such apparent ease.

> So then I suddenly found myself printer and publisher, with a duty to the public, and many other responsibilities of which I had never dreamt, and for some time the going was hard. As I was almost completely ignorant of typography, disaster was only averted by the efficiency of the staff. There were no studios at that time; the house was minute, and all my early illustrating was done with the children playing under my feet.[13]

Their first task was to finish the *Gallant Ladies*. Gibbings completed the engravings, no doubt enjoying the sensuality of the subject matter. Quite what decisions had already been taken by Taylor in the design of the book are uncertain but work was in progress when Gibbings took over. He produced ten large and fairly heavy engravings and used 14pt Caslon Old Face to try to balance their weight. The whole format of the book was large, with a square feel to the page and a very generous bottom margin. Coloured initial letters were used but the design was hardly adventurous — the engravings appearing opposite the text pages with no integration. But this book had been Taylor's choice and Gibbings had no fixed views about his own selection of texts; things happened in a rather haphazard way. *The Lives of Gallant Ladies* was published in July in two volumes and was only available to private subscribers. In May 1924, Gibbings had sent out his first piece

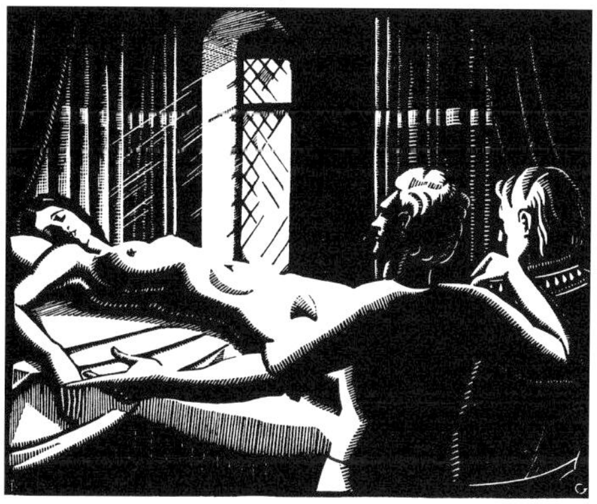

67 Illustration from *The Lives of Gallant Ladies*, wood-engraving, 106 x 133 mm, depicting a scene from the *Tale of the Proud but Imprudent Husband*.

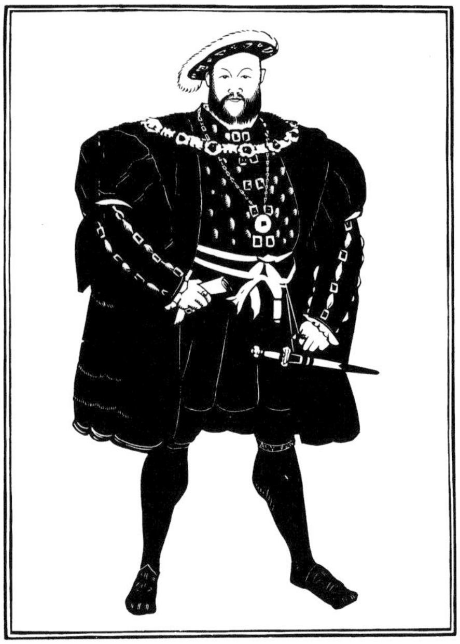

68 Frontispiece to *Miscellaneous Writings of Henry the Eighth*, 1924, wood-engraving, border size 161 x 118 mm.

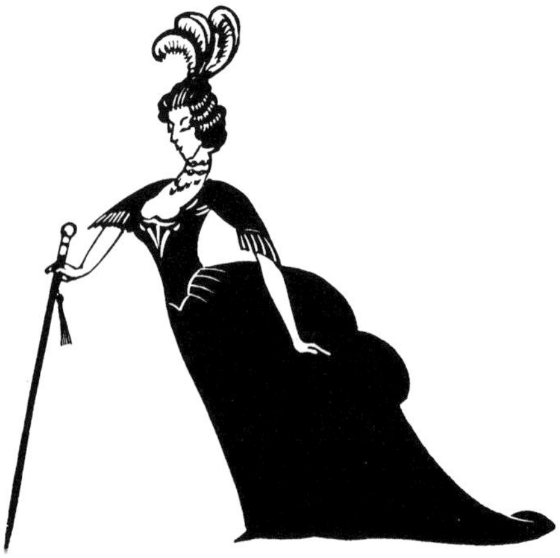

69 Illustration from *Songs and Poems of Henry Carey*, 1924, wood-engraving, 90 x 95 mm.

of printing — a prospectus announcing that he had taken over 'complete direction' of the Press:

It is hoped in every way to maintain the high standard already established by this Press and to continue to produce fine editions of fine books in increasingly fine technique. Following the traditions of the best periods of typography the type will as formerly be completely set up by hand, the paper used whether hand-made or otherwise will be the best of its kind, and by limiting the number of each edition it will be possible to supervise personally every volume printed.

The cover of the prospectus bore an engraving of a cockerel, designed and cut by Desmond Chute for Hal Taylor. It included a list of Taylor's publications that were still available and an invitation to subscribers for books in preparation. *Moral Maxims* by Duc de la Rochefoucault, which was published in August, was the first book for which Gibbings was entirely responsible, and *Miscellaneous Writings of Henry the Eighth*, a project presumably suggested to them by Francis MacNamara, who was the editor, was completed on 30 October but not published until December.[14] *Henry the Eighth* was the last book to appear in their first year; five had been produced in total and all but *Moral Maxims* were illustrated with engravings by Gibbings, who had taken over the packing room as a temporary workroom and studio. During the summer, work was also in progress on an edition of the *Songs and Poems of Henry Carey*, a light-hearted book, delightfully decorated with twenty-four engravings by Gibbings and with pages of songs and music drawn by Gladys Evans and engraved by W. M. R. Quick. Balston criticised the use of Arnold paper for being 'too hard and white for the 18 pt. type and very black engravings', but it was used for a number of the early books until the inherited stock ran out.[15] Moira made the selection, wrote a preface, and edited the text; the colophon states that the book was 'made' by her which suggests it was her particular choice. The printing was by Cooper, assisted by W. R. Mills, another local trade printer, who was occasionally brought in to help when pressure of work demanded. With a limited range of typefaces and type sizes available, a small press was bound to run into production problems; Gibbings now had type locked up for a number of books. The negative reply to an inquiry from Frank Young as to whether the *Carey* proofs had been returned from the reader left Gibbings with a problem of how to use the men's time profitably:

One of our great troubles in those days was shortage of any size of type over 11 pt., so that any hold-up by editor or artist created idle days. One morning before breakfast we discovered such a situation: no type free but the small 11 pt. My wife being approached for help put her hand to the nearest bookshelf, drew out the first book, Thoreau's 'Walden', and opening at random came on the essay 'Where I lived and what I lived for'. Crown paper folded many times gave a small enough page; the type was set and printed, leaving space for the engravings to be added later. So came into being this minute volume, & another unemployment problem was solved.[16]

Despite coming into being as the result of such a random choice, *Where I Lived and What I Lived For* is a charming book, all the more appealing for its diminutive scale. The engravings were carefully designed and printed in blue in order not to overwhelm the delicate type.

It was a very encouraging start, Golden Cockerel books were selling well, but there was a price to pay — a new sense of reality had tempered their optimism, as Gibbings explained in a letter to Balston on 6 October 1924:

Very many thanks for your letter and handsome order. I have put you down for them at 25% off & you may expect the first of them 'Carey' in a few weeks & the others at short intervals afterwards. Yes! it's great fun down here & quite surprising how easy it is to make the books go, but I'm tied by the leg as I watch everything & every sheet is passed before going through the press. It's hard work when I'm illustrating 3 books but to-day I finished the last block for two of them so am going to have things a bit easier. I'll certainly look you up if I have a moment when in town but generally it's a flying visit. Lucky beggar to get to Sicily. I see no chance of a holiday for myself much as I'd like one. Why don't you come & see us? Don't you ever take a walk of a Saturday or Sunday — its just 3 miles from Twyford station to here. We haven't a domestic at the moment or I'd fix a date but when if ever we find a wench you must come & lunch & spend a rural afternoon. Glad to hear Mabel Annesley has been working for you. I sent a message to her a few weeks ago saying she must do something for us.[17]

Hal Taylor had arranged for the distribution of his books through Birrell & Garnett in London and Brentano's in New York and presumably Gibbings had a similar arrangement. Cockerel books were also available at the Oxford Street bookshop of John and Edward Bumpus in London and he continued to deal direct with the Dunster House Bookshop in Massachusetts. A request for supplies of older titles from the Dunster House Bookshop was unsuccessful — stocks had sold out: '... in fact the only copies we have of anything are a few copies of the *Gallant Ladies*. I am sending you herewith copies of our new list. On the back of one of them I have marked those of which the last copies were sold while the list was in the press. ... The Rochefoucault was fully subscribed a month before publication & the same is the case with Henry Carey which won't be ready for another fortnight'.[18] Gibbings suggested that if they wanted to reserve copies a standing order would be the best arrangement.

Desperate to make a go of things, despite their apparent success, the Gibbingses had to take on as much work as possible. Following Taylor's example, Gibbings also printed work for other publishers and *Bright Island* by Arnold Bennett was printed that summer for Vine Books. He had also made time to design a jacket for Chatto & Windus for *Mark Only*, by T. F. Powys. Pressure of work meant that Gibbings had found little opportunity to make engravings as studio prints. *Gossips* and *Lonely Rocks*, both engraved the year before, were published in a new arts and crafts journal, *Artwork*, in which sculpture and an article by Eric Gill also appeared.

Gill and Gibbings had occasional contact through the Society of Wood Engravers, but not socially. Gill's committee, set up to look into whether book illustrations should be eligible for inclusion in the annual exhibition, must have reached a decision because Gibbings exhibited engravings from the books he was working on at the Press that year. The exhibition was again held at the St George's Gallery. A critic in the *Observer* questioned the value of the revival of the engraving medium in the light of new technology and the process block, challenging artists to explore the special qualities of the wood itself:

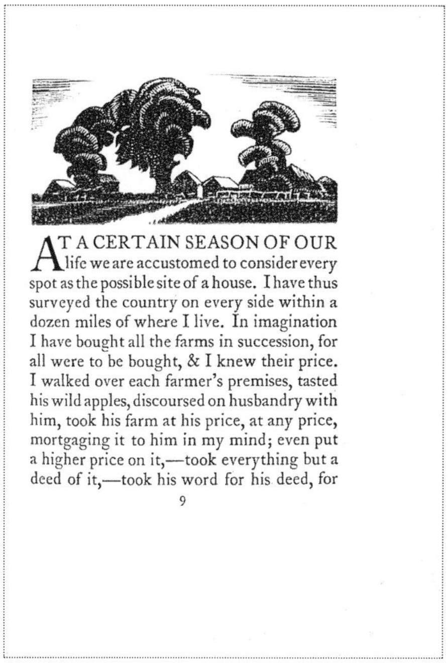

AT A CERTAIN SEASON OF OUR life we are accustomed to consider every spot as the possible site of a house. I have thus surveyed the country on every side within a dozen miles of where I live. In imagination I have bought all the farms in succession, for all were to be bought, & I knew their price. I walked over each farmer's premises, tasted his wild apples, discoursed on husbandry with him, took his farm at his price, at any price, mortgaging it to him in my mind; even put a higher price on it,—took everything but a deed of it,—took his word for his deed, for

9

70 Chapter opening from Henry Thoreau's *Where I Lived and What I Lived For*, page size 130 x 95 mm. Reproduced by permission of the Golden Cockerel Press Ltd.

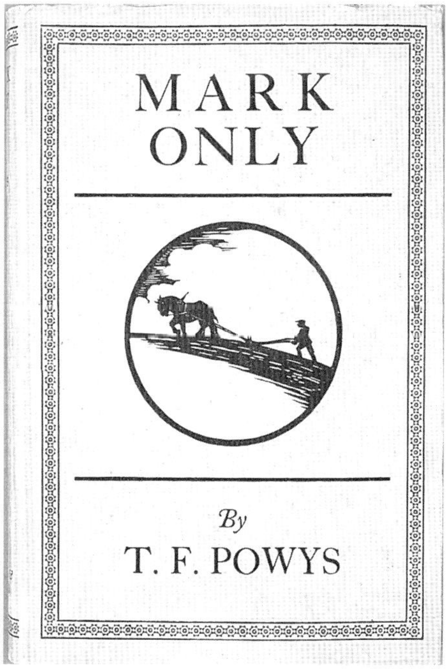

71 Bookjacket illustrated with a wood-engraving by Gibbings for *Mark Only* by T. W. Powys, published by Chatto & Windus, 1924.

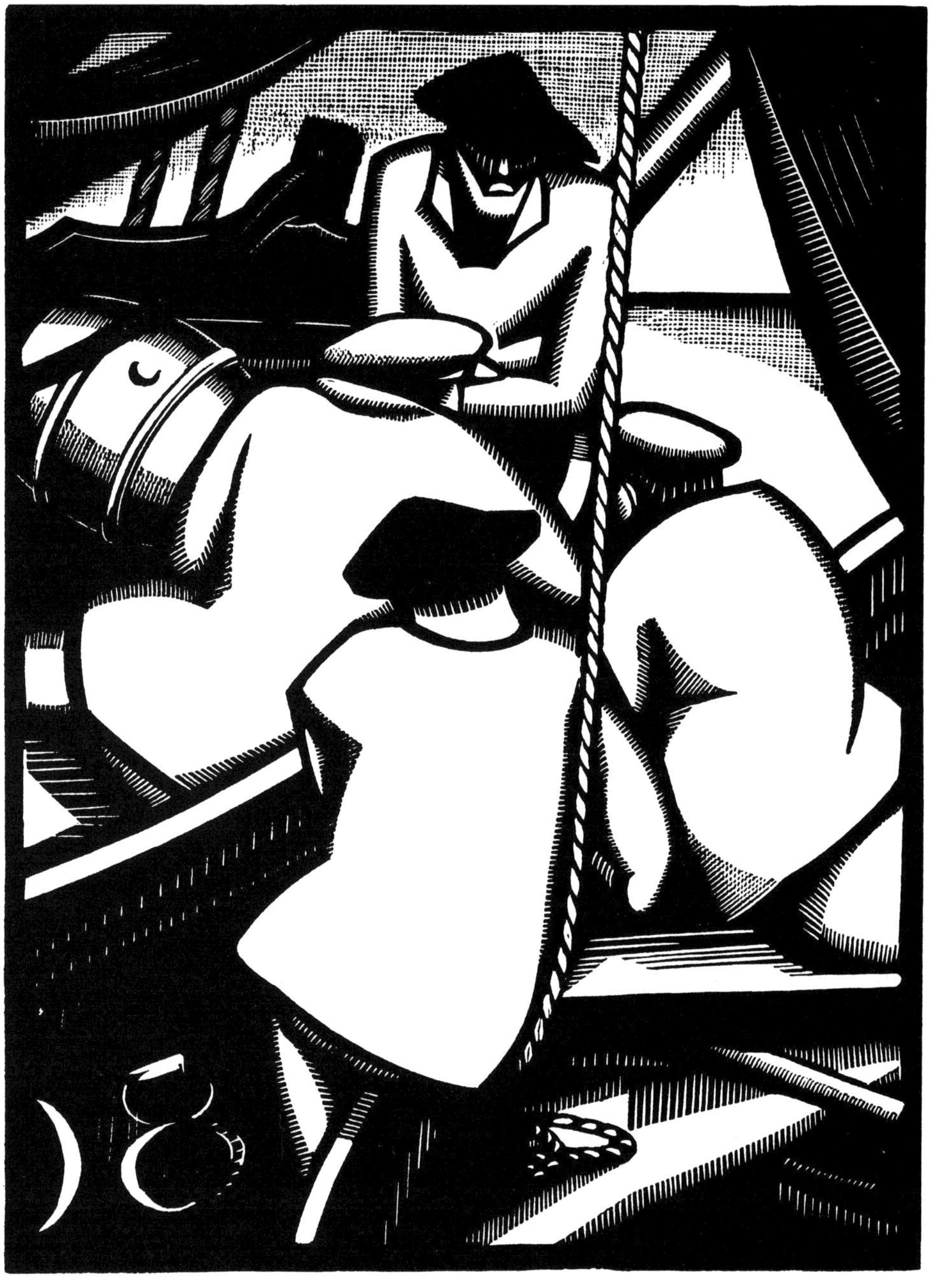

72 *Gossips*, *c.* 1925, wood-engraving, 171 x 127 mm.

When it is remembered that, with photographic reproduction of drawings, the look of any phase of wood engraving in the past can be got without touching the block at all, the futility of this will be evident. Like all revivals, that of wood engraving is affected by the change of conditions in the interval; that which was once a virtue of necessity having become a matter of aesthetic choice; and the reasonable thing to do is to pursue the choice regardless of any limitations but those inherent in the method.[19]

With these comments in mind the reviewer noted a change in Gibbings's work, 'From this point of view one is glad to see Mr. Robert Gibbings getting away from a treatment which suggested saddling wood engraving with the special difficulties of the stencil rather than tackling its own' — clearly a reference to the critic's preference for Gibbings's greater use of tone and figurative approach in his book illustrations compared to his earlier, more abstract, prints.

The impression might be formed that all innovations in wood-engraving evolved in the Society of Wood Engravers, but this would be a false view as in many ways the Society was rather conventional in outlook. Many individual artists, both in Britain and Europe, were working with the medium and other groups of artists were joining together to form recognised 'schools' or societies. One such group had recently been formed when wood-engraving had been introduced to the circle of students and artists associated with Leon Underwood by one of his pupils, Marion Mitchell. Although differing in their approach to wood-engraving, their rivalry with the Society of Wood Engravers was friendly enough for Marion Mitchell and her colleague Gertrude Hermes to exhibit with the Society that year.

Gibbings worked very hard in his first year at the Press, providing all the illustrations used. Presumably to get projects off the ground with the minimum of cost and planning, it was easier for him to do the work himself. As the momentum built up, however, he needed illustrators of vision and originality and it was natural that in the Society of Wood Engravers he should find a perfect source of young and enthusiastic engravers to commission. He wrote to several of his fellow artists, outlining his plans and aspirations for the Press and inviting their co-operation. Later Gibbings recalled:

> Strangely enough, in view of later events, the only one to reject my invitation was Eric Gill. He wrote a very nice letter but gave several reasons for refusal, the chief of which appeared to be that I was not a Catholic. But a few months later there came to me a letter from my friend John Wilson of Messrs Bumpus, in which he suggested that I should print a selection of poems by Enid Clay, a sister of Eric Gill, adding that her brother would do some engravings for the volume. This idea fitted in very happily with my programme ....[20]

Gibbings's relations with Gill until then had been awkward and rather formal. Gill, seven years older, was already well established, and Gibbings was perhaps a little unsure of how to handle this apparently temperamental character whom he had already found rather difficult. Enid Clay had asked her brother to illustrate her book of poems, which originally was to be published in association with Bumpus early in 1924, but Gill's initial response had been rather negative:

> If I do the engravings, the printing of the book must be done here [Ditchling]. I only do engraving for St. Dominic's Press & not otherwise. This is not a contract between me and Mr Pepler, but is simply because I find that unless the printing & Typography & engraving are all done to match and under one control the result is a failure. You see, engravings are as much a part of *book making* as of *illustration*. They don't merely illustrate the text, they also decorate the book. Therefore the engraver & printer *must* be one 'firm'.[21]

Gill insisted that the printing should be done at Ditchling but he had recently broken off from Pepler after a bitter quarrel; later there was mention of Blackwell's publishing Enid's book, and finally, through John Wilson's[22] recommendation, it was decided that it should be printed and published at the Golden Cockerel Press. Gill's convictions about book illustration exactly matched those of Gibbings, which boded well for the success of their collaboration. In November 1924, Gill wrote to Enid saying he was sending all the blocks for the book to

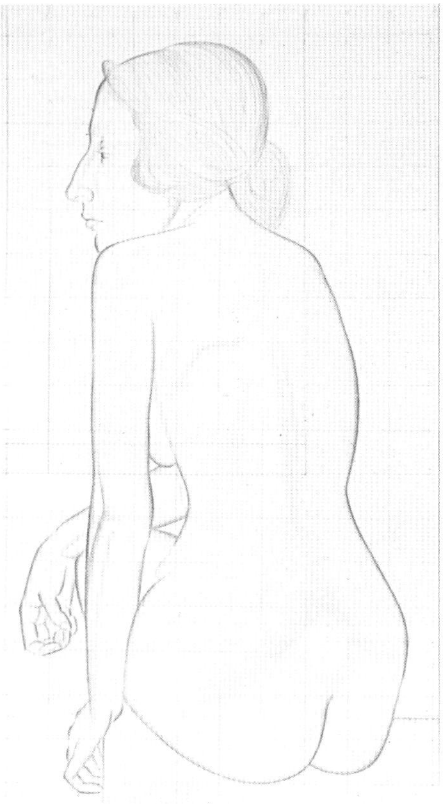

73 Pencil drawing of Moira Gibbings by Eric Gill, signed and dated December 1924, 480 x 265 mm. Gill also made an etching of Moira's head and shoulders which was based on a section of this drawing. Art Collection, HRHRC.

Gibbings and offering to send his copy of the manuscript as well. On 29 November he gave a lecture to the Society of Wood Engravers in London and after the meeting Gibbings drove him home to Waltham to stay for the weekend. The next day was spent viewing the press and carrying on intense discussions about printing and planning Enid's book; the evening was filled with life drawing. Moira and Robert acted as models — neither had any inhibitions about being naked. Gill, also nude, noted in his diary that he had found the whole experience 'v. exhilarating and good'.[23] The next day Gill worked on a more finished life drawing of Moira on which he based a portrait print, a delicate etching, finding a certain beauty in her strong profile. This was the first of many such weekends. Their intimacy and friendship seems very sudden — something clicked between the two men and there was obviously a mutual attraction with Moira, who was too strong a character to have been involved in sexual frolics with Gill against her will. On reflection, Gill and Gibbings did have circumstances in common which would account for a certain empathy between them. Both had recently moved and embarked on new projects; the craftsman community at Ditchling which Gill had set up with Hilary Pepler had broken up as a result of their feud, and Gill had moved to the remote Capel-y-ffin in the Black Mountains of Wales. They were both struggling to support their families on small and precarious incomes. Both men had fathers who were Protestant clergymen, although their own attitudes to the church were very different, Gill having converted to Catholicism. Fiona MacCarthy suggests they were also suffering from a certain instability:

> ... their immediate mutual rapport was not just a simple matter of their shared professional interests. They answered an emotional need in one another. Gill and Gibbings were prize boosters of one another's ego. They let each other off, and they cheered each other up. They shared a particular kind of love of life, a talent for 'high jinks': the not unlikely outcome of their common background of religion and rebellion.[24]

They discovered in each other the excitement and stimulation of shared aspirations for their work. Gill was attracted by Gibbings's love of physical sensuality, his open, natural freedom, with no hint of piousness or reverence, despite his church upbringing. In Gibbings's company he could relax and indulge himself in the pleasures of life, for Gibbings also enjoyed a touch of decadence — good food, good wine — which was shared by Moira with her taste for fashion and style. Fun and laughter, and the physical exhilaration of abandoning clothes and rejoicing in freedom and exercise — this is what Waltham meant. Fun and play was also part of life at Capel-y-ffin, but it was so much more comfortable in the gentle landscape and climate of the home counties — a relief from the grey, stoic and sparse discomfort of the stone half-ruin in Wales.

The art world in England at this period was very close knit, especially amongst the wood-engraving fraternity. The Gibbingses' social life was busy and their circle of friends spread wide. Robert and Moira were gregarious and amiable, and many others as well as Gill enjoyed the relaxed and genial hospitality at Waltham. Guests were welcome, although accommodation was restricted, and artists were encouraged to visit Waltham while work on the books they were illustrating was in progress. In September 1924, Gibbings wrote a witty letter to the actress Colette O'Neill inviting her to visit. Gibbings explained the lack of 'bed or maid' meant that she would have to stay at the village pub, the Bell, but otherwise '... we at the golden cockerel expect you to tea & supper daily'. Gibbings, always susceptible to the presence of interesting young women, ends by expressing his hope that '... I may at last have a chance of drawing you'.[25]

Visits by Gill to Waltham became regular and frequent over the next year. In January, Gill was working on drawings for an alphabet of wood-engraved initial letters for use by the Golden Cockerel Press to enrich the page and add variety to the Caslon Old Face, and Enid Clay's book was still in production. Often linked to Society of Wood Engravers' meetings in London, weekends at Waltham were necessary to discuss projects in hand and plans for the future. Both men worked with concentration and energy during what were very productive days, but the evenings often ended in dancing and games in the nude. Gill was in the rather dubious habit of making detailed notes of all his sexual experiences in his diaries, and on the 24 January 1925 the diary entry notes with obvious and almost schoolboy glee that Moira came to his bedroom and stayed for a 'goodnight hug' and fondle, noting that Robert had told him that 'he would not trust any other man on earth to enjoy such intimacy ...'. Not surprisingly, the next morning Gill also notes that he had to miss his usual attendance at Mass — excusing himself as there was no local Catholic Church that was convenient, but on another occasion he admitted that the activities of the previous night had resulted in oversleeping! So Waltham also relieved him of his usual religious observance.

In February, Jonathan Swift's *Directions to Servants* was published with twelve wood-engravings by Gibbings's colleague and friend from the Society of Wood-engravers, John Nash. The unusual layout of this book, using a double column on a page was an experiment and not very successful, but was arrived at as a way of using the smaller typesizes which were not in use on other projects, while retaining a large format. This was the first book published under Gibbings's direction to use illustrations by another artist, but the Press's *Spring List* announced books illustrated by Eric Gill, Mabel Annesley and John Farleigh, and later that year other titles were published with engravings by Noel Rooke and David Jones.

Directions to Servants was followed by *Sonnets, with Folk Songs from the Spanish* by Havelock Ellis and Enid Clay's *Sonnets and Verses*, both published in April. Gibbings was pleased with *Sonnets and Verses*, feeling that Gill's blocks harmonised well with the type '... but beautiful as are the engravings, the technique of such very fine white line is not one to be recommended for letterpress printing'.[26] Gill had used a technique of creating the image from very fine white lines cut into the heavy solid black of the block in a number of the images. Prone to filling in with ink, these blocks had to be printed with great care and skill. Desmond Chute gave his opinion of the book in a letter to Gill from Rapallo in Italy: 'The blocks are beautifully printed and they fit in with the type, as they never did under Hilary [Pepler].'[27]

The book received further acclaim when the Double Crown Club selected *Sonnets and Verses* for the award of the club's prestigious 'crown' for 1925. Gibbings had been elected to the club in 1924, no doubt thinking that he would make contacts to help him in his new enterprise, but unfortunately the award was tarnished by an ill-tempered dispute which arose over the eligibility of private press books to be crowned; Gibbings resigned as a result of the bad feeling.[28]

In an article written for *The Woodcut*, on the Golden Cockerel Press in 1927, Gibbings was forthright in laying out his approach to wood-engraving as a medium for book illustration and his aims for the Press:

> Most of the work of the Press is experimental. Efforts are made that each book shall not merely repeat a former success, but shall develop one on its own merits. The artists who design for the Press are chosen on account of their work considered as Art, and not for their appeal to a conservative public. They are encouraged to work in close touch with the compositors, and many of them spend days at a time at the Press while their books are being printed. It is paradoxical that wood engravings, which are pre-eminently suitable as book decoration, should to-day be amongst the most difficult of illustrations to combine with type; and this is the fault of the artists and, in many cases, the critics. The contemporary engraver-illustrator is content to take a piece of wood and carve thereon a design having no reference whatever, beyond the subject matter, to the type it is intended to adorn. Sufficient is it if it should be obvious to the world that it was cut on wood, and here the critics praise him loudly. In fact, the one quality demanded in recent years of wood engraving is that it should have the appearance of rough wood worked on by a blunt gouge. This is called 'the quality of the wood'! As well ask for the smell of nitrous fumes from etching, so that the quality of the acid may be retained. A great deal of this is reaction against the hack engraving of the late nineteenth century, but we surely have had time to grow up. Bad workmanship is not a quality of wood, and slovenliness is not Art. Wood can be cut as cleanly and very much more easily than copper. Spontaneity in Art is seldom spontaneous.[29]

Gibbings went on in the article to champion wood-engraving as book illustration; he argued that prints as decoration on walls have a limited life whereas books survive for centuries.

> Type itself is not of to-day or yesterday. It has taken centuries to reach its present form, and its chief fault is its almost too perfect finish. And if engravings are to harmonize with type, they must in some way approximate to its finish. Wood engravings for books are not ends in themselves, they are ornaments for the *Book*, and on this account a more rigorous discipline on the part of the artist is necessary. Very few contemporary engravers have considered what may be known as the unit of texture. Type when properly printed requires a very nicely adjusted quantity of ink per square inch: a fraction too much, and it fills up; a fraction too little, and it prints grey. It must be obvious that a block set amongst type must, for success, approximate to the texture of the type, otherwise one or the other must suffer in printing. But even if the area of the actual printing surface of a block conforms to that of the type, there is need that the unit of texture should in some degree approach the unit of texture of the type. A few coarse lines left standing on a block may *print* well with small type, but they won't *look* well. Something of the relationship of the thick and thin of type must be observed in the block. ... An entirely successful example of harmony between blocks and type will be found in Mr. Gill's engravings for many pages of the *Song of Songs*, recently published at the Press.[30]

Gill and Gibbings had started planning *The Song of Songs* as early as March that year, but Gill was working intensively on the engravings for most of the summer and it was published in October.

Despite his strong views about book illustration and the fact that books were now the basis of his income, Gibbings continued to produce some studio prints unrelated to any book. His engravings were still occasionally appearing in journals such as *The Beacon* and in March 1925 *Dreams*, alternatively titled *Caryatid*, was reproduced together with *Clouds and Geese*; both prints were shown in an exhibition of Gibbings's work held at the Redfern Gallery from 6 March to 3 April that year. On the same page as *Clouds and Geese*, a short poem by Gibbings entitled 'They Built a Tower' was published.[31] This rare and perhaps rather naive excursion into verse puts his aspirations about art and the achievements of mankind into perspective when compared to his deep empathy with nature which was always the bedrock of his life.

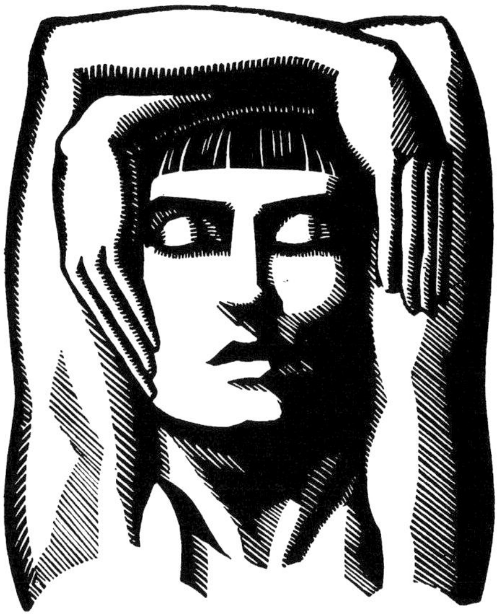

74 *Dreams* or *Caryatid*, c. 1925, wood-engraving, 85 x 73 mm.

They built a tower, these proud, these clever men;
High, with a massive plinth, and then
Along its length carved emblems of the dead,
'For play of light,' they said.
And around the crest as finish for the same
O'erlappings, juttings, called by some learned name.
With lines like these, thought they, with Art so fair
Nature could never in the least compare.
But they forgot — that growing quite close by
A little poplar-tree stood up against the sky.

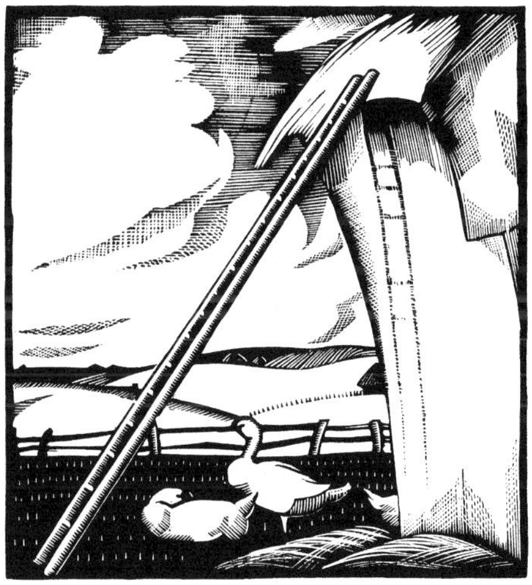

75 *Clouds and Geese*, c. 1925, wood-engraving, 93 x 88 mm. Gibbings also made a smaller version of the same composition which appeared as an illustration to *Pelagea* by A. E . Coppard published by the Golden Cockerel Press in 1926.

Five more books were published before October 1925: *Pictor Ignotus, Fra Lippo Lippi, Andrea Del Sarto* by Robert Browning, with initial letters by Gill, *Selected Essays* by Jonathan Swift, with engravings by John Farleigh, *Songs from Robert Burns*, selected and with a preface by A. E. Coppard, with illustrations by Mabel Annesley, *An Apology for the Life of Colley Cibber* by himself, again with initials by Gill, and *Samson and Delilah* from the Book of Judges, with six wood-engravings by Gibbings. In an article in *The Manchester Guardian*, *Songs from Robert Burns* was described as '... one of the most beautiful books yet issued from the Golden Cockerel Press, which in enterprise and accomplishment is steadily taking the first place among English private presses'.[32] In November appeared *The Nativity*, taken from Luke's Gospel, with engravings by Noel Rooke and the exhausting programme ended with an edition of Swift's *Gulliver's Travels*, illustrated by David Jones.

In his article in *The Woodcut* already quoted, Gibbings went on to review a number of the books produced in 1925. Pursuing the ideal of the balance between type and the block, he cited Noel Rooke's rather heavy black images used in *The Nativity* as an example of another approach:

> But it must not be understood that uniformity as to texture and colour of block and type are the only possible solutions of the difficulty. On the contrary, contrast, the exact opposite, can be entirely successful; but where this is employed, it is essential that a certain space of white should separate the heavy black of the wood from the grey of the

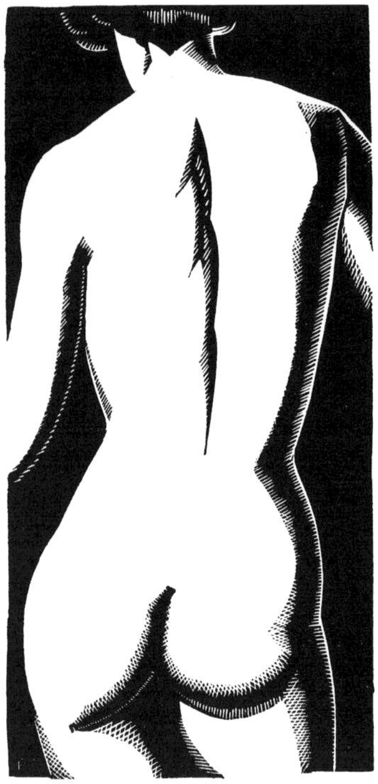

type. Excellent examples of the use of heavy black used in this way may be found in *The Birth of Christ*, designed throughout for the Press by Mr. Noel Rooke.[33]

While praising others, Gibbings was an objective and honest critic of his own work: 'Thoroughly bad examples from the same point of view are the writer's own engravings for *Samson and Delilah*, which are far too black and heavy to be so near the type.'[34] He had chosen this text because it occurred to him that '... here was a chance to express human strength and human weakness. But I think I put a little too much of the former into the blocks, for though I like most of the designs the contrasts of blacks and whites were too heavy to go with the type. I had not yet begun to think of "unit of texture"'.[35] The engravings do indeed overwhelm the type, which, unusually, was set unjustified, but in themselves the images are powerful and graphic designs, working within the squared-up frame of the engraving; dynamic but simple in the balance of solid blacks and whites and areas of texture. The images demand attention rather than being polite decorations to the page. Gibbings had no reservations about David Jones's illustrations for Swift's book: 'For a really perfect illustration, aesthetically, typographically, and any other way the reader may choose, see page 112 of Vol. I of *Gulliver's Travels*, and many others throughout the book.'[36]

David Jones had been accepted as a new member of the Society of Wood Engravers in November, together with Charles Ginner, John Farleigh, Enid Marx

76 *left* *A Girl's Back*, *c.* 1925, wood-engraving, 125 × 62 mm.
77 *below left* *Nude Torso*, *c.* 1924–5, wood-engraving, 169 × 75 mm. Proof found in the Albert Cooper collection, RUL.
78 *below right* *Les Femmes Damnées*, *c.* 1925, wood-engraving, 106 × 131 mm. Author's collection.

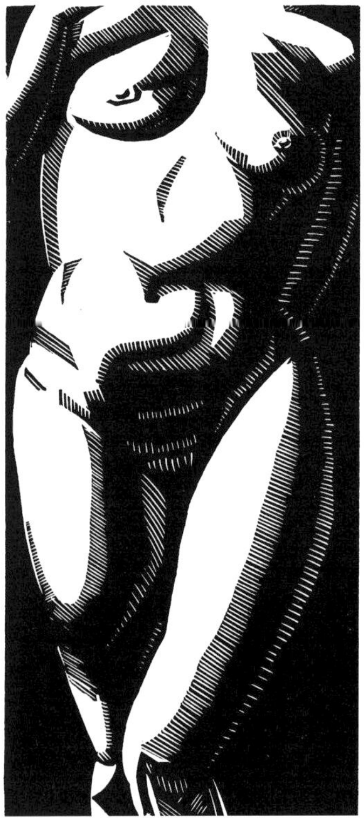

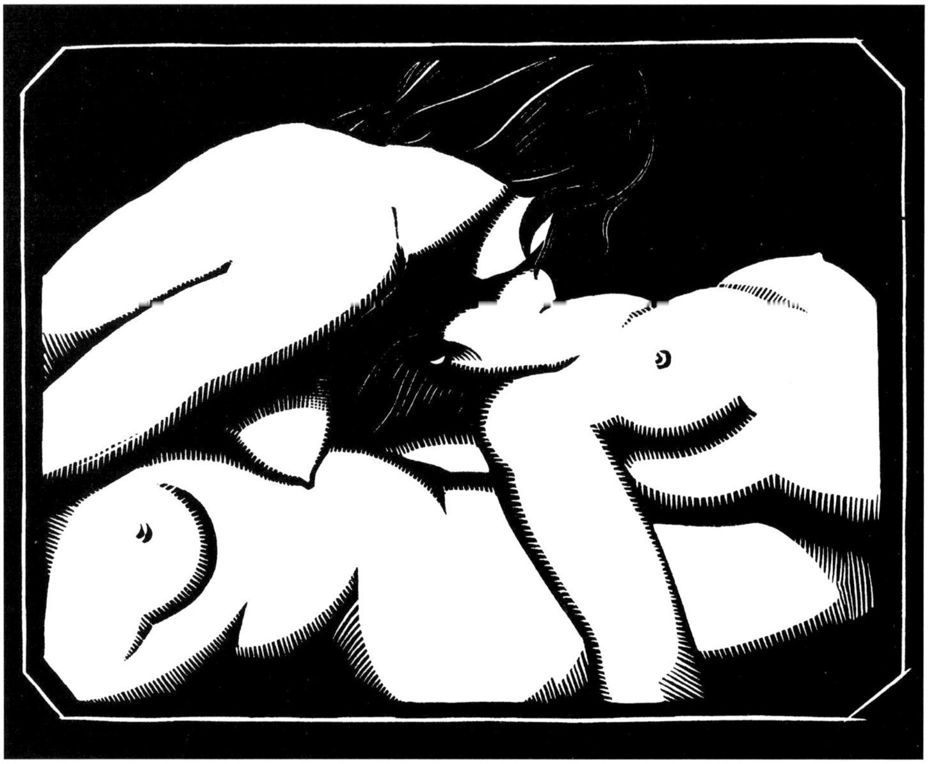

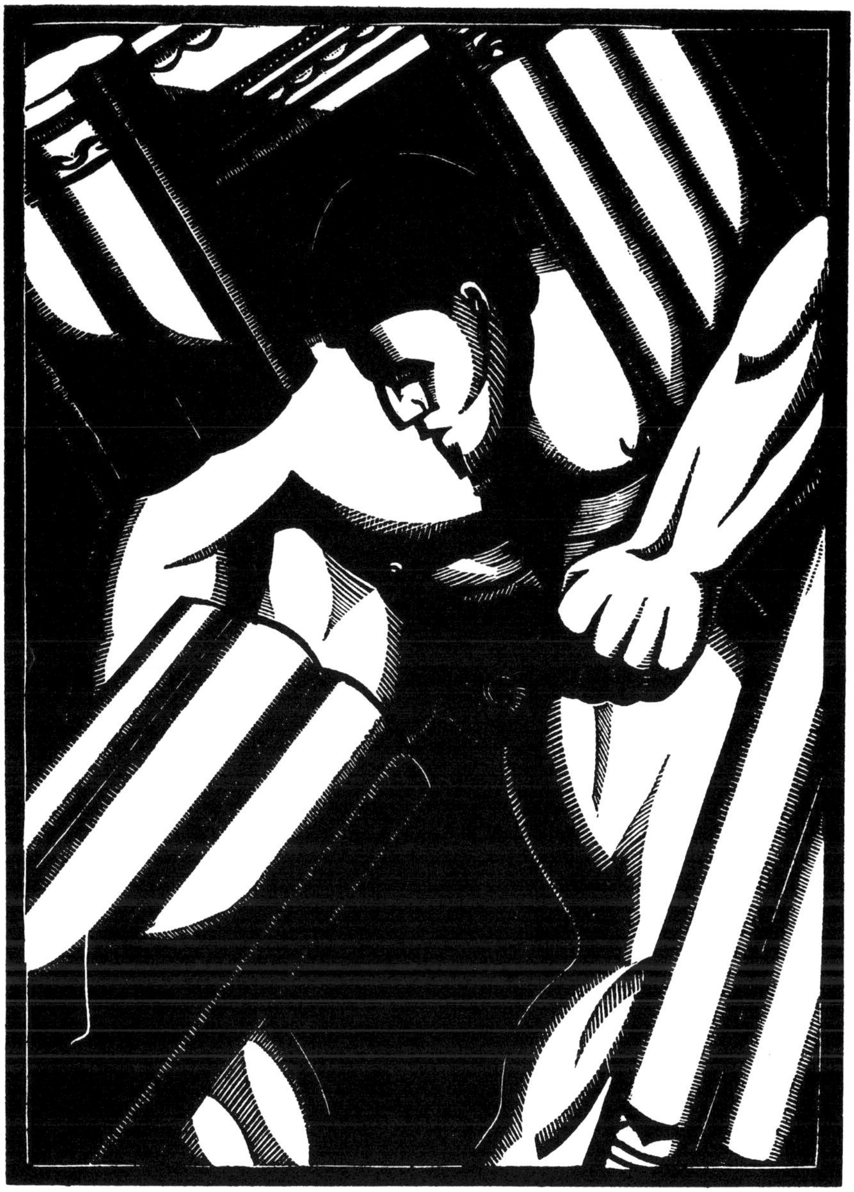

79 Illustration from *Samson and Delilah*, 1925, wood-engraving, 156 x 113 mm.

and Eric Ravilious, who was proposed by Paul Nash. Jones was living and working with Gill at Capel-y-ffin and in August Moira and Robert went to spend a week in the rather primitive and remote surroundings of the artist community. It was not all bleak — lively discussions about work in hand and a picnic in the woods were high spots. Gibbings later had mixed memories of this visit to Wales. The soulful and mournful presence of Jones, silently adoring Gill's daughter, Petra, over the refectory table; Mary Gill, so patient and kind but homely and plain in contrast to the stylish elegance of Moira — all this made rather dull company for the Gibbingses. Robert recalled:

The Black Mountains rise up sharp to the west of Llangorse, and at the head of the Honddu valley is Capel-y-ffin (The Chapel at the Boundary). ... Close to the chapel is Llanthony Abbey .... In recent times Eric Gill lived at the abbey for a few years, and it is certainly as cold a spot as any anchorite could wish for. I can still remember the dinners

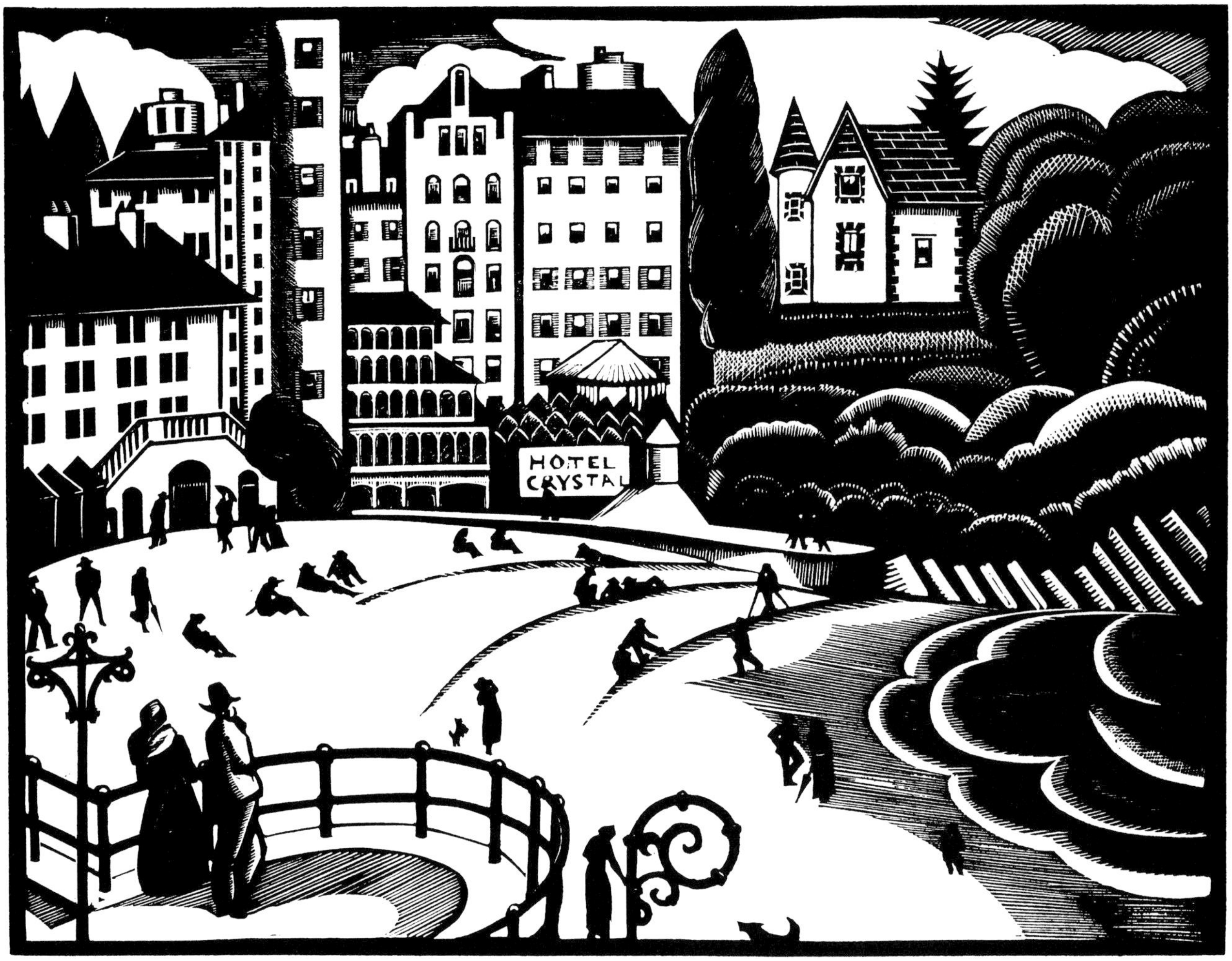

80 *The Seafront at Dinard*, France, c. 1925, wood-engraving, 165 × 220 mm. Author's collection.

by candlelight at the long refectory table, every one wearing overcoats or shawls, while members of Gill's family took it in turn to read the Epistle and Gospel for the Day and a chapter from the *Martyrology*. But if the stone floors were cold, hearts were warm; Eric was as loveable a man as you could meet.[37]

Their close friendship at this time meant that matters of business were conducted in a very casual and haphazard way — nothing much in writing but more a matter of a gentleman's agreement, as demonstrated in a letter from Gill to Gibbings, dated 3 October 1925, concerning his illustrations for *The Song of Songs*:

My dear Robert — you told me you were relying upon my memory in the matter of the arrangements between you and me. I am afraid my memory is a little bit hazy on the subject, but as far as I can recollect the understanding is that I am to have £60 cash for the engravings and a half share of the extra profits on the sales of the *coloured* edition. In addition I have the right to issue and if possible sell 12 prints of each illustration. I think this is all — I do not know whether the initial letters are supposed to be an extra. Moreover if you find the splitting of profits on the coloured edition is a complicated way of doing things, please suggest anything else which seems to you better. I am writing this so as to have the thing clear in both our minds.[38]

Following *The Song of Songs* an agreement was made that Gill should engrave exclusively for the Golden Cockerel Press — an arrangement which was to prove so crucial to the success of the venture. But their personal relationship was still full of boyish naughtiness; on the back of the envelope for the letter above Gill had written:

> D. J. is sending his Cock by the same post
> Do you know Bach's organ works?
> but his works are better than his Bach
> so D. J.'s 'crow' is better than his cock.

Late in October, David Jones and Gill again enjoyed the delights of Waltham and their stay followed the familiar formula of days spent on serious work in planning books (new projects were *The Passion* and *Procreant Hymn*), followed by nude dancing. The privacy offered by the gardens at Waltham encouraged the Gibbingses in their passion for nudism — what could be more natural than shedding clothes when the weather permitted? Gossip about their bohemian antics soon spread amongst the villagers and the neighbouring children were told to knock loudly on the door when coming to play, just in case they should surprise anybody naked! One bashful nudist was the publisher John (Jock) Murray, who relished recounting his experiences at the Golden Cockerel Press. During a vacation, while a schoolboy at Eton, he stayed at Waltham to learn a little about printing and modestly declared 'My main claim to fame, is that I am the only publisher who has typeset in the nude. Unfortunately I hit the period when Gibbings was in his nudist phase, and as I was only 15 I found this embarrassing.'[39]

But the impression that life was all fun at Waltham is a false one as the undoubted success of the press meant increasing demands on both Robert and Moira.

Chapter Six
The End of the Apprenticeship 1925–1927

ALTHOUGH IT WAS ROBERT who represented the public face of the Press, Moira was beside him and took a full part in the work. Behind the scenes she dealt with most of the administration, writing to suppliers, bookbinders and booksellers or drafting letters for Robert to sign, as well as selecting and transcribing texts. All this was in addition to coping with housework, guests and young children and so it is hardly surprising that she decided to resign as secretary to the Society of Wood Engravers. Robert also gave up the role of Honorary Secretary and both posts were filled by Margaret Pilkington.

Margaret Pilkington was one of a group of enthusiastic and talented wood-engravers who were financially independent and thus could devote their time to wood-engraving, free from the pressures of making a living. Through her connections with the Whitworth Art Gallery in Manchester another exhibition for the Society was organised there in March 1924; a review in the *Manchester Guardian* picked out Gibbings's figure subjects for praise, recognising a certain 'play of humour'. A quiet and unassuming person, Margaret was full of generosity and anxious to help her fellow artists; she proved to be a constant support to the Society of Wood Engravers over the coming years, contributing both time and money. Robert remained a dominant personality in the Society; Margaret later recalled that 'Robert still presided over the meetings, a large handsome and genial figure with his golden beard, rosy complexion and blue eyes, clad usually in light tweeds with a bright blue knitted sweater, his conversation larded with Irish humour. In sharp contrast Eric Gill, short and pale, would come in a short black cassock or tunic.'[1] Gibbings had grown the beard partly to cover the scars from his throat wound and it became a characteristic feature for the rest of his life. Most commentators are similar in their descriptions of Robert and seem to have been impressed by the same qualities — women in particular nearly always found him attractive and captivating.

Although united by a common cause, the minutes of the Society of Wood Engravers reveal that disagreements were frequent: 'The most lively were not those of philosophy and aesthetics, but more mundanely, about gallery conditions, exhibiting terms, commissions and fees.'[2] At a meeting in May 1924, John

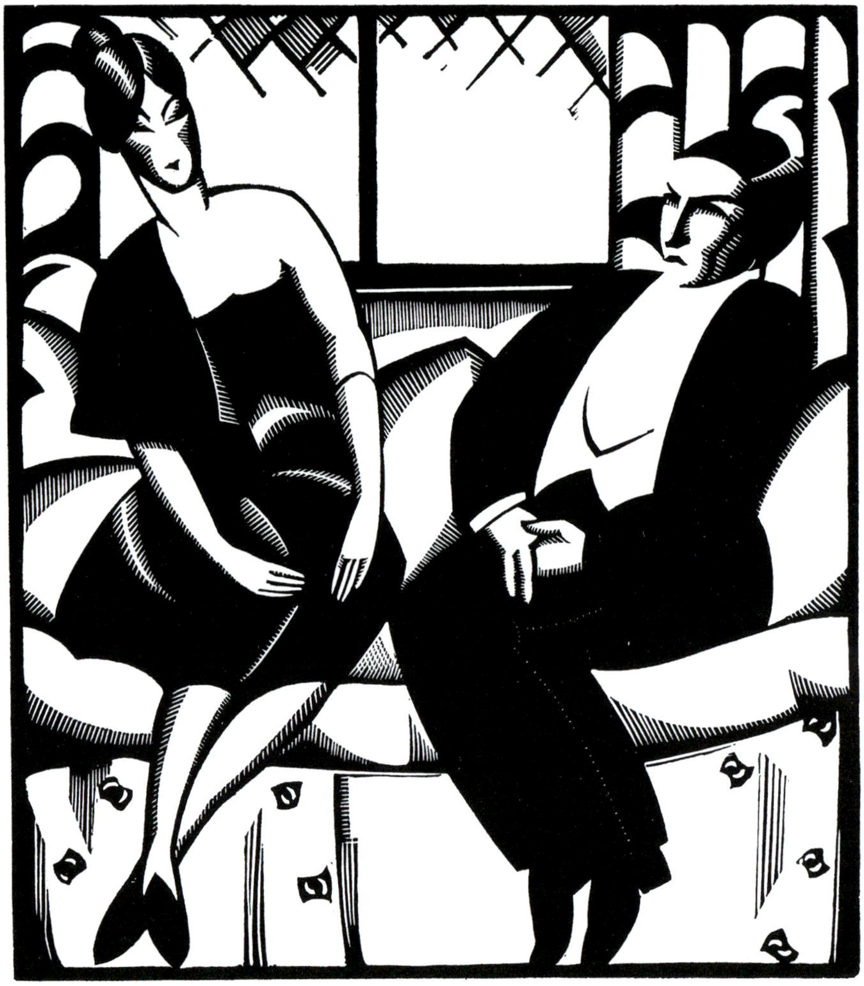

81 *Sitting Out*, 1925, wood-engraving, 130 x 114 mm.

Nash had proposed yet another move of the annual exhibition to a new venue, the Redfern Gallery, then in Old Bond Street, which was considered to have advantages both 'in position and the actual room, and also in the clientele'. Gill did not like the St George's Gallery and its director, Arthur Howell. Gill and Gibbings disagreed with Howell over his wish to exclude book illustrations from exhibitions, but a compromise was arrived at and it was felt unfair to change venues that year at such short notice — besides, Howell had already arranged three provincial exhibitions for the coming year. Howell wanted a monopoly on their activities and arguments also arose over conditions and commission rates. On 19 March 1925, the minutes record that the decision was made to hold the annual exhibition at the Redfern Gallery. Predictably not all members were happy about the move. Gordon Craig was tetchy and blunt in his objections, favouring the more overtly commercial approach, as he saw it, of the St George's Gallery. There was no doubt that sales at the gallery had been good; it was more a matter of a clash of personalities and philosophies.

Partly as a result of this argument and partly because there was a feeling amongst some of the members that the Society was already beginning to be rather staid and conventional, a number of members resigned. They wanted to be more radical and anti the establishment which, in its short life, they felt the Society of Wood Engravers had come to represent. Clifford Webb, Gertrude Hermes and Blair Hughes-Stanton contributed prints to the 1924 exhibition for the first time, but the following year these young artists deserted the Society for a new rival group, the English Wood Engraving Society, taking with them Craig, Claughton Pellew and Ethelbert White.

The success of the revival of wood-engraving was gaining momentum and was attracting the attention of an ever wider circle of artists and art students. This new blood was bound to bring about experimentation in both style and technique. Marion Mitchell had studied engraving in Paris for a year with Dmitri Galanis and he had introduced her to the multiple tool[3] which had a great effect on the colour and tone of her images. On her return from Paris she had joined the Brook Street Art School in London, run by the sculptor Leon Underwood. Through her,

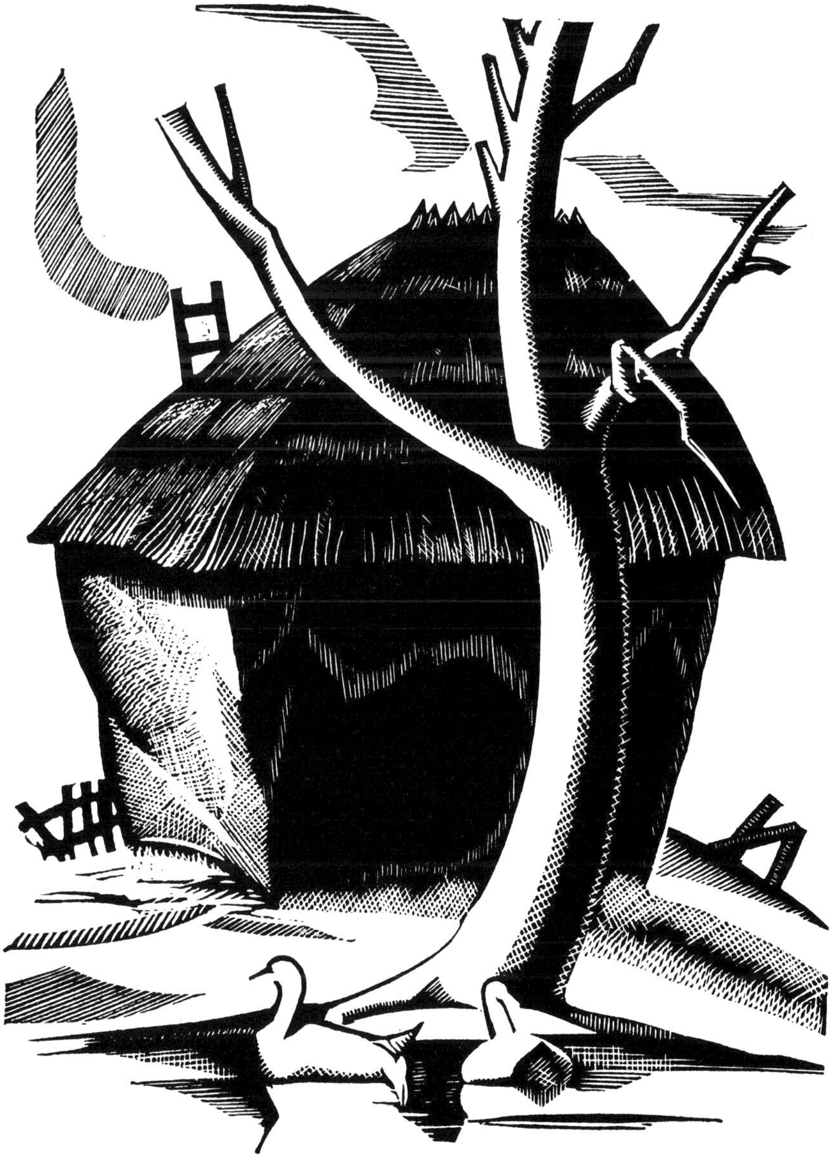

82 *Blogg's Pond*, c. 1925, wood-engraving, 152 x 112 mm.

Underwood and some of his pupils, such as Gertrude Hermes and Blair Hughes-Stanton, took up the medium and, influenced by the more fluid and abstract ideas of Underwood, developed a recognisably new style:

> Their technical virtuosity and silvery grey tones, often achieved with the use of the multiple tool, and their fondness for semi-abstract symbolic subject matter, particularly in the thirties, was in great contrast to the blacker, more representational style typical of the wood engravers of the early twenties, and was cause for yet more controversy amongst purists.[4]

The older members of the Society of Wood Engravers found it difficult to accept these new approaches and so in November 1925, Marion Mitchell became the driving force in founding the English Wood Engraving Society. They held their first exhibition at the St George's Gallery to coincide with that of the Society of Wood Engravers at the Redfern. Critics noted the rivalry between the two societies: *The Observer* saw both shows as 'equally fascinating'. Although there must have been some animosity, members of both societies saw no reason not to remain friendly and Gibbings, for one, felt quite happy to exhibit with both groups.

Some members had left the Society of Wood Engravers but others joined; John Farleigh, David Jones and Hester Sainsbury became associates, together with Eric Ravilious who had studied engraving under Paul Nash at the Royal College of Art, and who was introduced to the Society by him. Gibbings exhibited six prints at the annual exhibition that year but had already exhibited work at the Redfern Gallery in March in a two-man show which he shared with Eric Daglish. Provincial exhibitions had been held at Southport and selection was under way for work to be shown in forthcoming exhibitions at Pontypool, Toronto, Glasgow and New York. It was recognised that sales at these exhibitions would be small but they were 'an excellent form of propaganda and advertisement' — most sales came through dealers. In November 1925 the Society held an exhibition at John Magee's Gallery in Belfast, in which Gibbings contributed five engravings including *Sitting Out* and *Blogg's Pond*.

THE MONTH OF NOVEMBER also brought sadness and problems. On the eighth, Robert's father died, aged 65. Gibbings also had to deal with changes in his partnership with Hubert Pike; he and Robert had decided to dissolve their partnership and seek new financial backers. It is possible that Hubert had run into money problems — Bentley Motors experienced financial difficulties in the mid-twenties.[5] But it is more likely that Gibbings needed to raise some capital in order to buy the cottage and build the extension. Hal Taylor had died in March and in June Gibbings had purchased the land and property through the executors.[6] With an investment of £1700, a Miss M. H. Wiggin took over from Pike in financing the press.[7] She was a wealthy property owner from Cork, who, like Pike, was to have no active role in the workings of the Press but who luckily was able to step in with the necessary finances. New partnership documents were drawn up in January 1926, and this time Moira, who quite rightly wanted recognition for her major contribution to the Press, also became a formal partner. Miss Wiggin had made a promising investment as the balance sheet at the Press showed a healthy profit.

Despite problems behind the scenes the reputation of the Press was growing. The books were receiving favourable reviews with references to their quality and 'exquisite' decoration and typography. Stanley Morison[8] selected the title page from *Moral Maxims* as an illustration in his prestigious and sumptuous volume, entitled *Modern Fine Printing*. Early in the new year, the Press published a prospectus for 'forthcoming publications'. On the cover Gibbings used an engraving by Albert Cooper, entitled *Morning*. This kind gesture was typical of the support and respect Gibbings gave his workmen. Gibbings encouraged Cooper to wood-engrave and through him Cooper had had prints accepted for the Society of Wood Engraver's annual exhibition.[9] Gibbings was generous to give Cooper's print such prominence — it was a dramatic composition but showed weaknesses that hinted of the amateur. Gill was less generous: in a letter to Desmond Chute he referred to Cooper's engraving in cutting tones but with a certain affection: 'That engraving by A. C. — well, poor old Cooper. It was a mistake to put it out!'[10] However on other occasions Gill was happy to praise Cooper's printing. But Gill's rather patronising criticism was not just aimed at Cooper; in the same letter Gill wrote of Gibbings: 'Some of Robt Gibbing's engravings are good but he hasn't weaned himself yet of a bad past. He himself is the dearest creature ever known ....' In an extensive list of itemised comments, Gill went on to give his opinion on various projects in the rest of the letter. Concerning *The Song of Songs*, Gill was pleased with Chute's approval: 'I'm glad you think the black & white of the engravings is typographically right'. Another comment was about the first book to be published by the Press that year, *Red Wise* by Powys Mathers: 'Powys-Mathers is a fat man who lives in Lincoln's Inn Fields. I scarcely know him. "Red Wise" is very good & and very naughty — I think it probable that P-M is the same!'.

Gibbings described Edward Powys Mathers as 'floating' into his world and in the new prospectus it was announced that the Press would publish three of his books, *Red Wise*, *Procreant Hymn*, and *Maxims & Considerations of Chamfort*. Powys Mathers had recently completed a translation of *The Arabian Nights* and, pursuing his enjoyment of exotic oriental prose, had written a short tale 'in eastern vein', recounting fictional episodes in the life of Abu Nowas, entitled *Red Wise*. Love of wine, art, passion, and desire are themes that fill a tale with which Gibbings could readily identify and so he happily enjoyed 'cutting a few sensuous blocks'. His illustrations for this book have a light touch, full of delicate line and pattern that cleverly exploit the marks made by the engraving tool. Most critics praised the book and even Gill approved and designed a special binding for his own copy.

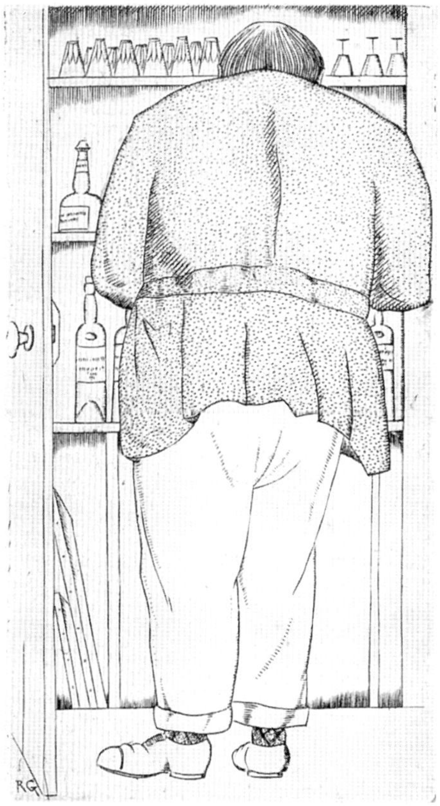

83 E. Powys Mathers, *c.* mid–late 1920s, etching, plate size 145 x 80 mm.

Following the success of *The Song of Songs* and *Samson and Delilah*, two further volumes of stories from the Bible were in preparation, *The Passion* and *The Book of Jonah*, which were to be uniform in style. Gill had been working hard on a set of initials and six engravings for *The Passion*. In January he wrote to Gibbings, outlining progress:

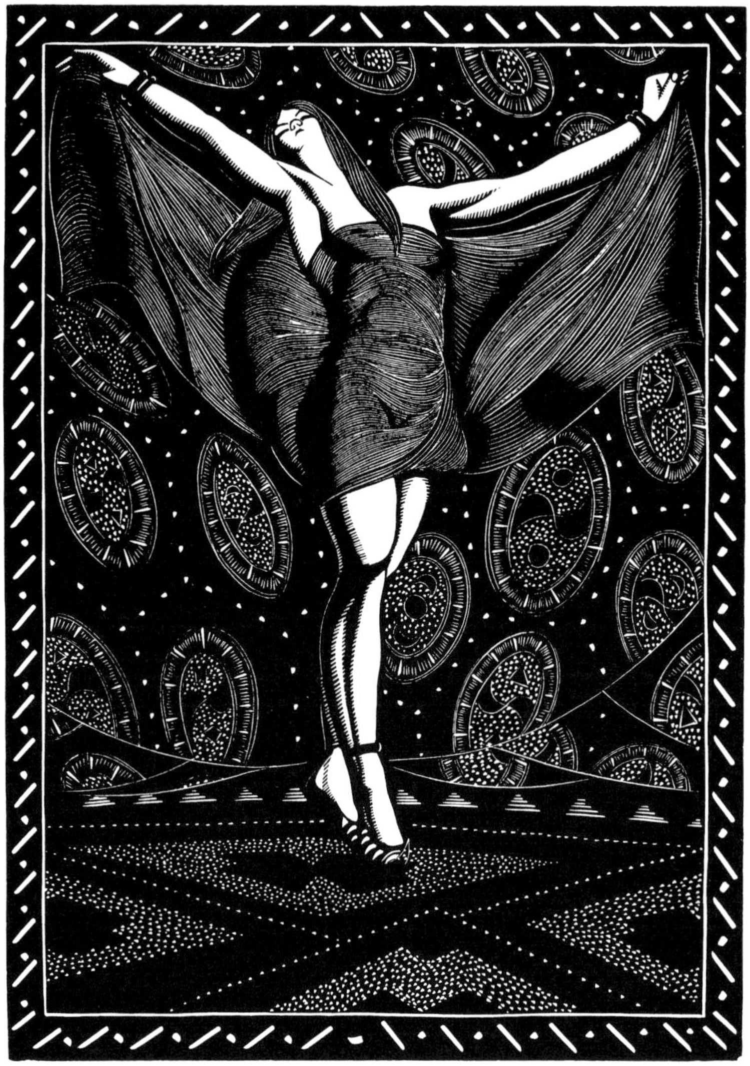

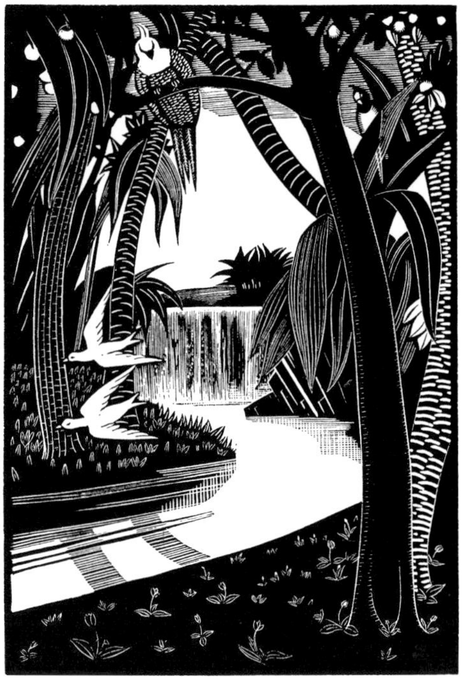

84 *left* Illustration from *Red Wise* by E. Powys Mathers, 1926, wood-engraving, 138 x 98 mm. A highly decorative design in which Gibbings has exploited the marks naturally made by the engraving tool to create rich and fine patterns.
85 *above* Illustration from *Red Wise* by E. Powys Mathers, 1926, wood-engraving, 145 x 100 mm. Although figurative in treatment Gibbings has carefully arranged the foliage to produce a highly controlled design – a feature of his wood-engraving which was to become very characteristic in his later work.

Herewith initials: A E E M & P. I hope you will like them & find them the right size. I have tried to make the 'bodies' so that you won't need any packing above or below — but I fear they're not frightfully square.

I tried to design floral backgrounds. But came to the conclusion they'd be better plain. I hope you'll agree. I also send the block for the title page "Mary Magdalene" I hope you'll like this & find it suitable & printable. I've made all the designs for the other 5 blocks & am going straight ahead. We're a bit behind in time — but I had to wait while I heard from you approving the paste up! I'm anxiously awaiting letter from you re various things ....[11]

The 'paste up' mentioned tells something of the working method between the two men. Both were striving for a perfect integration of text and image, but how was this to be achieved? Gibbings admitted that initially planning and design had been minimal:

In the printing of *Sonnets and Verses* there was little that could be called planning between artist and printer. The author sent me her manuscript, Eric sent me his blocks, and I put them together as best I could; and in the books that followed soon after, such as *The Song of Songs* and *The Passion*, decorated for me by Gill, there was not as far as I can remember a

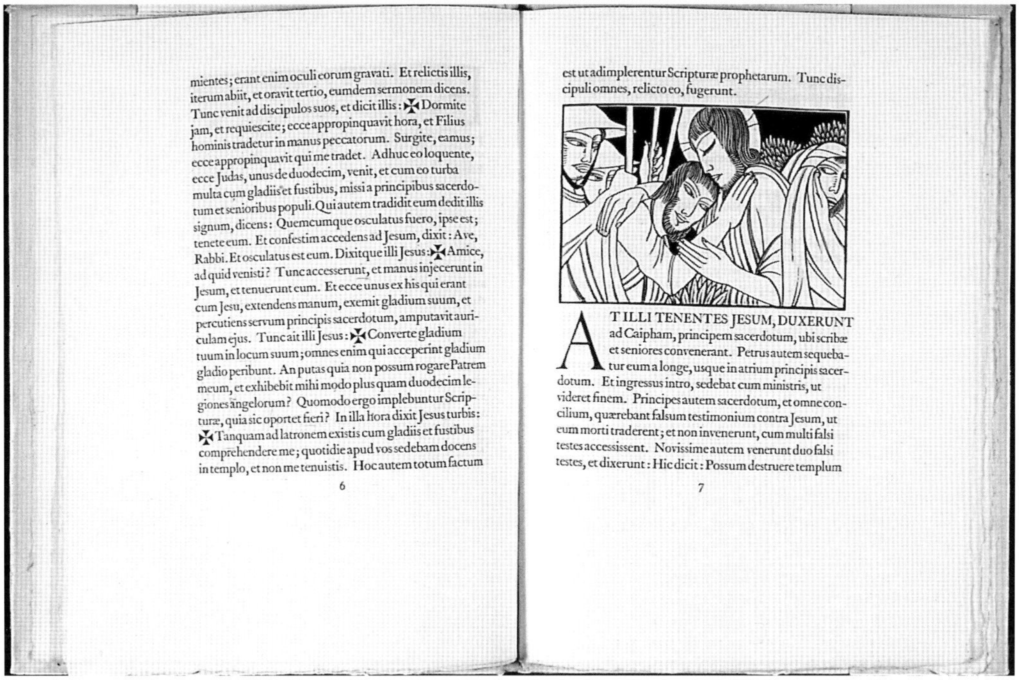

mientes; erant enim oculi eorum gravati. Et relictis illis, iterum abiit, et oravit tertio, eumdem sermonem dicens. Tunc venit ad discipulos suos, et dicit illis: ✠ Dormite jam, et requiescite; ecce appropinquavit hora, et Filius hominis tradetur in manus peccatorum. Surgite, eamus; ecce appropinquavit qui me tradet. Adhuc eo loquente, ecce Judas, unus de duodecim, venit, et cum eo turba multa cum gladiis et fustibus, missi a principibus sacerdotum et senioribus populi. Qui autem tradidit eum dedit illis signum, dicens: Quemcumque osculatus fuero, ipse est; tenete eum. Et confestim accedens ad Jesum, dixit: Ave, Rabbi. Et osculatus est eum. Dixitque illi Jesus: ✠ Amice, ad quid venisti? Tunc accesserunt, et manus injecerunt in Jesum, et tenuerunt eum. Et ecce unus ex his qui erant cum Jesu, extendens manum, exemit gladium suum, et percutiens servum principis sacerdotum, amputavit auriculam ejus. Tunc ait illi Jesus: ✠ Converte gladium tuum in locum suum; omnes enim qui acceperint gladium gladio peribunt. An putas quia non possum rogare Patrem meum, et exhibebit mihi modo plus quam duodecim legiones angelorum? Quomodo ergo implebuntur Scripturæ, quia sic oportet fieri? In illa hora dixit Jesus turbis: ✠ Tanquam ad latronem existis cum gladiis et fustibus comprehendere me; quotidie apud vos sedebam docens in templo, et non me tenuistis. Hoc autem totum factum

6

est ut adimplerentur Scripturæ prophetarum. Tunc discipuli omnes, relicto eo, fugerunt.

AT ILLI TENENTES JESUM, DUXERUNT ad Caipham, principem sacerdotum, ubi scribæ et seniores convenerant. Petrus autem sequebatur eum a longe, usque in atrium principis sacerdotum. Et ingressus intro, sedebat cum ministris, ut videret finem. Principes autem sacerdotum, et omne concilium, quærebant falsum testimonium contra Jesum, ut eum morti traderent; et non invenerunt, cum multi falsi testes accessissent. Novissime autem venerunt duo falsi testes, et dixerunt: Hic dicit: Possum destruere templum

7

86 A double page opening from *The Passion*, 1926, with wood-engravings by Eric Gill, page size 267 × 190 mm. Reproduced by permission of the Golden Cockerel Press Ltd.

great deal if any of the close co-operation that came later. My memory is that in *The Song of Songs* and possibly also in *The Passion* I may have sent Eric proofs of the type in galley slips and asked him to paste them up as he thought fit with the illustrations that he had already engraved. But in none of these volumes was there any real marriage of wood and metal. The blocks and the type had little more than a brotherly-sisterly relationship; that is to say, the designing and cutting of the wood did not await the setting of the type.[12]

Working with Gill heightened Gibbings's sensitivity towards typography and encouraged him to experiment with layout and text setting:

... 'The Passion', which was interesting from the fact that being printed in Latin there was a predominance of round generous letters such as m n u, with very few bearing ascenders and descenders. Added to this we avoided justification of lines in order to have close even spacing, thus retaining the interplay of forms between words as between letters. There is a very great deal to be said for this method of composition .... The justified right-hand edge is entirely a convention, and the pleasant colour of the even close-spaced page more than makes up for any other deficiency.[13]

Gibbings wrote this in 1931, and although his style of typographic design is far from that of the central European 'new typography' movement, his views on unjustified text setting are radical and show a sensitivity towards spacing on the page. This position must have been arrived at through discussion between the two men. Gill expressed similar views in his book *An Essay on Typography*, also published in 1931, which was another very early example of a book published with unjustified setting. Gibbings had no thought of deliberately being avant-garde; many of the values and character of the private press movement and the 'book beautiful' appeal to a rather conventional clientele, exploiting qualities of traditional craftsmanship. Gibbings, greatly influenced by Gill, arrived at this view as a natural consequence of his passionate pursuit of the balanced page and he was prepared to take the risk and design the books as he wished.

The Passion was published in March followed by *An Apology for the Life of Mrs Shamela Andrews*. But work was already in progress on a number of other projects. Gill had been rather put out by the announcement of the *Procreant Hymn* which appeared in the *Spring Prospectus*. To Gibbings he had written: 'I received yesterday your new "list" ... I was glad to see Cooper in evidence [rather hypocritical in the light of his earlier comments]. I hope what you say re Procreant Hymn won't frighten the right people away.'[14] To Desmond Chute, Gill had been far less diplomatic in his comments: 'Procreant Hymn. Yes: that "puff" in the GCP press "announcement" was very low. I'm awfully sorry about it — thoroughly disgusting — But the Hymn is very good. You shall have a copy — even if only to burn — for you may think it unacceptable. I think no modern writer or few old ones have got as close to that subject as PM has done without falling into either coarseness or obscurity — mere animalism or mere verbiage ....'[15] What Gill was objecting to was the rather florid description of the book's contents: 'This is a lyrical exultation in praise of the generative principle in man, in nature, and in deity. It celebrates the spirit, process, and intention of the creative act, in stanzas of inevitable beauty, and with a detailed daring which is as new as it is pure.'[16] Gibbings clearly felt the need to justify and thinly veil the contents of the book which was in essence an erotic description of the sexual act in verse, overlaid with an oriental style. It was decided to use copper engravings as the medium for the illustrations and Gill's early designs matched the erotic nature of the text. Gill produced a number of versions of the illustrations — varying in explicitness. One illustration depicted a man and a woman making love with an image of God looking on in approval; the first version shows the couple fully exposed; in the second a blanket covers the lower parts of their bodies; in the final version, which was published in the book, the couple are modestly covered — always knowing his market, Gill made it known that limited editions of the alternative versions were for sale!

Robert and Moira had been friends with Powys Mathers and his wife for some while. Both were accomplished translators and Mathers had a reputation as a distinguished authority on eastern texts and culture — which led to his passion for erotic texts and his own original writing with a similar flavour. As a couple they were good fun and happy to be involved in the Press, suggesting ideas for new books as well as providing translations. Letters from Mathers to the Gibbings family are full of innuendo and barely comprehensible double meanings, playful and affectionate — often bordering on the flirtatious. Letters to Moira were addressed to 'Dearest Viret' and to Robert as 'Don Roberto'.[17] Delighted with the Cockerel editions of his work, Mathers pushed his ideas to the limit of what was acceptable as decent and Gibbings, who thoroughly enjoyed such work, was nonetheless sensitive to the fact that *Procreant Hymn* was close to the borderline.

Gill also shared Gibbings's enjoyment of erotica which was further stimulated by a visit to France. At the end of April, Moira and Robert managed to get away together from the constant pressure of the Press and took a well-earned holiday in Paris. Moira needed the break — Robert, now that the routines of the Press were established, had already managed to get away for the occasional trip abroad and had been 'on his travels' for a week in February to do some drawing and painting.[18] On the first of May, Gill joined the couple at their hotel, breaking a journey to Salies-de-Béarn, a spa town at the foot of the Pyrenees. Gill later returned to spend some more time in Paris and days were spent visiting galleries and studios, and life drawing at the Académie Chaumière with Gibbings; evening excursions included the Folies Bergères to see Josephine Baker and night-clubs and casinos. Another couple, referred to as E & P in Gill's diary, also joined the party. This was presumably Elizabeth Bill, Gill's secretary and mistress who owned a house in Salies-de-Béarn, accompanied by her fiancé. Clearly enjoying the risqué aspects of Parisian night life, Gill recorded one evening when Elizabeth, himself, Robert and Moira all went to a 'strange place of which RG had been given the address and saw some girls nude posturing in lascivious manner'.[19] Allowing themselves time for frivolity on another night, Moira and Robert decided to attend a fancy dress dance at Juliana's and Robert, according to a little sketch Gill made in his diary, dressed in a grass skirt and allowed Gill to paint a face all over his bare chest and ample stomach — nipples became eyes and navel became a mouth; the two men seemed to encourage each other in such vulgarities. A day excursion to Luxembourg and an outing to see the famous clown, Grock, perform ended their stay. On their return to Waltham, Gill stayed a night and was picked up by René Hague the next day.[20] Holiday over, work began immediately on new projects.

Gibbings wanted a decorative border for his *Autumn List*,[21] Gill was already correcting proofs of his own book, *Id Quod*, due for publication later that year and now ambitious plans were being discussed for a major new venture — an edition of Chaucer's *Troilus and Criseyde*. Gibbings was very excited by the project. Writing to Gill in June he outlined his views on format and the treatment of illustrations.

> Since last writing about TROILUS, I have thought much and often, and am now of the following opinion.
>
> First, that the enclosed pages are much better in shape than the Crown 4to originally thought of. The verses fit better and it has the advantage that we can get it all into one volume instead of two. But on the other hand I feel that copper engravings are not really suitable for a book of this size, and that it would be far better from every point of view to let ourselves go with wood. I am inclined to think that we ought to have at least a couple of full pages, about half a dozen of the area of two verses, and then about two dozen small ones, of the size of one verse .... I don't know whether you will consider this much more work than the original scheme of large coppers, but I suggest that we pay you £100, and that for that you make the book as sumptuous as you can, either on the lines I have indicated, or in any other way that may occur to you. We are proposing to do a small edition at an expensive price, and I am very anxious to make it a really swish volume.[22]

While these plans were developing production continued: the *Procreant Hymn* appeared in June, followed by *Cupid's Whirligig* by Edward Sharpham and *Osmond the Great Turk* by Lodowick Carlell which were produced as uniform editions (another work by Carlell, *The Fool Would be a Favorit*, was published in August as part of the series). In July *The Book of Jonah* with wood-engravings by David Jones was published followed by *Maxims and Considerations of Chamfort,* translated by Powys

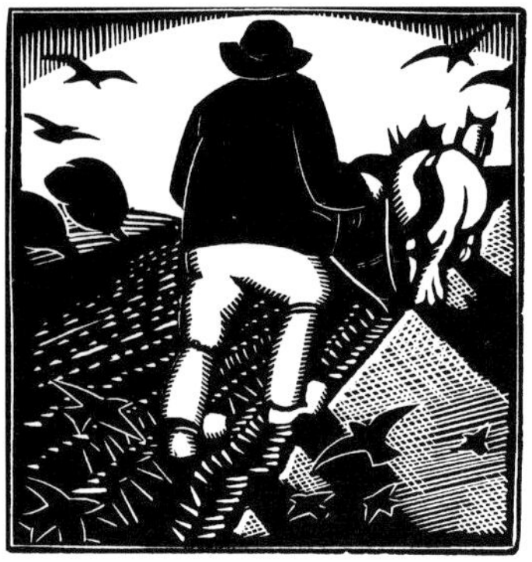

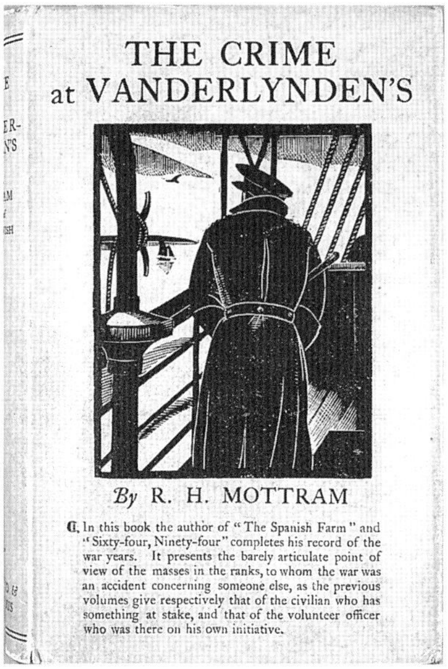

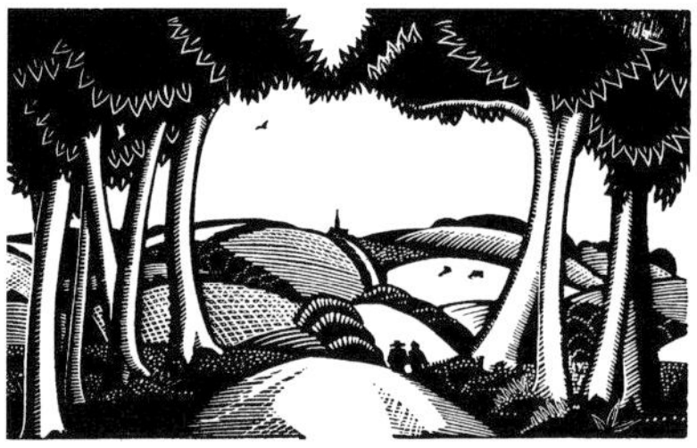

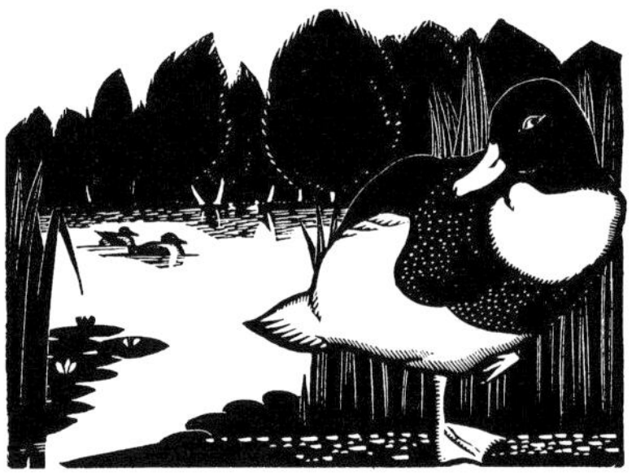

87 *left* Illustration from *Pelagea & Other Poems* by A. E. Coppard, 1926, wood-engraving, 54 x 51 mm.

88 *centre* Bookjacket illustrated with a wood-engraving by Gibbings for *The Crime at Vanderlynden's* by R. H. Mottram, published by Chatto & Windus, 1926.

89 *top right* Illustration from *Fallodon Papers* by Viscount Grey of Fallodon, 1926, wood-engraving, 55 x 90 mm.

90 *bottom right* Illustration from *Fallodon Papers* by Viscount Grey of Fallodon, 1926, wood-engraving, 66 x 90 mm. The themes of this book allowed Gibbings to explore images relating to his love of nature and in particular, birdlife.

Mathers. Gibbings was also working on his own wood-engravings to illustrate *Pelagea & Other Poems* by Coppard, which was published in October. Coppard continued to be a supporter and frequent visitor at the Press; he had become a close friend of Robert and Moira and he was paid a small retainer for his help with the accounts.

Gibbings still found time to undertake designs for book jackets for other publishers. The previous year he had worked on jackets for Jonathan Cape, Constable, and Chatto & Windus[23] but a more significant commission was for illustrations for a collection of lectures given by Viscount Grey of Fallodon to be published under the title *Fallodon Papers*, by Constable. The subjects covered included 'Pleasure in Nature', 'Waterfowl at Fallodon' and 'The Fly-fisherman', all topics which greatly appealed to Gibbings and gave him the opportunity to engrave images of wild-life, a theme to which he was soon to return, in the form of charming and simple vignettes and tailpieces.

Through September 1926, Gill worked on the blocks for *Troilus*, visiting Waltham late in the month to discuss progress and final arrangements for the printing of his own book, *Id Quod*.[24] Over the same weekend, Gill showed Robert and Moira a sketch of an idea he had had for a carved stone doorway in the new extension at Four Elms, consisting of two columns supporting a lintel stone which was to be carved in low relief. Gill now frequently used Waltham as a convenient stopping-off point on his trips to the Goupil Gallery in London to discuss the sales of his work, occasionally being driven there by Robert or Moira. Following Paris, theatre visits were also enjoyed — not highbrow drama, but glamorous shows or variety. The relationship between Gill and the Gibbingses, as well as being intensely creative and productive, was also about gaiety and fun — frequent references in Gill's diaries note evenings out: 'To supper with RG & M at Brice's — To "Pavilion" to see Florence Mills'.[25] From September until the end of the year, Gill continued to concentrate on the border engravings for *Troilus*. On

18 December, Gill noted that he was 'finishing & printing T & C borders in eve' and had sent off the stones for the doorway, cut and shaped for the builders.

Id Quod was printed in October 1926, followed by *Pompey the Little*, an amusing tale of the adventures of a lap-dog, written in the eighteenth century, with two wood-engravings by David Jones. The year ended with an edition of *The Fables of Aesop*, with illustrations by Celia Fiennes[26] and John Marston's *Metamorphosis of Pigmalion's Image* [*sic*], with engravings by René Ben Sussan.

So far the list of publications at the Golden Cockerel Press had mainly consisted of new editions of classic and biblical works, with only the occasional new translation or original piece. But Robert and Moira were always seeking new titles and to that end approached many leading authors. In turn, they received suggestions from others. Ford Madox Ford, Siegfried Sassoon, Aldous Huxley, Lytton Strachey and J. B. Priestley were all asked if they would like to publish something with the Press but for various reasons refused.[27] On 28 July 1926, Gibbings had written to Bernard Shaw, enclosing a copy of *The Passion* and a sample page of *Troilus*, and sounding him out on a proposal that the Press should publish a 'monumental' edition of his complete works. Gibbings made an appeal as a compatriot: 'If you should consider this matter at all perhaps the fact that I too am proletarian Irish, hailing from Cork, with a Tipperary wife, may incline the balance in our favour.' Shaw's secretary replied that 'as an old comrade of William Morris', Shaw was interested in the art of printing. Gibbings followed his letter up in November, pointing out that the press made books of the highest quality:

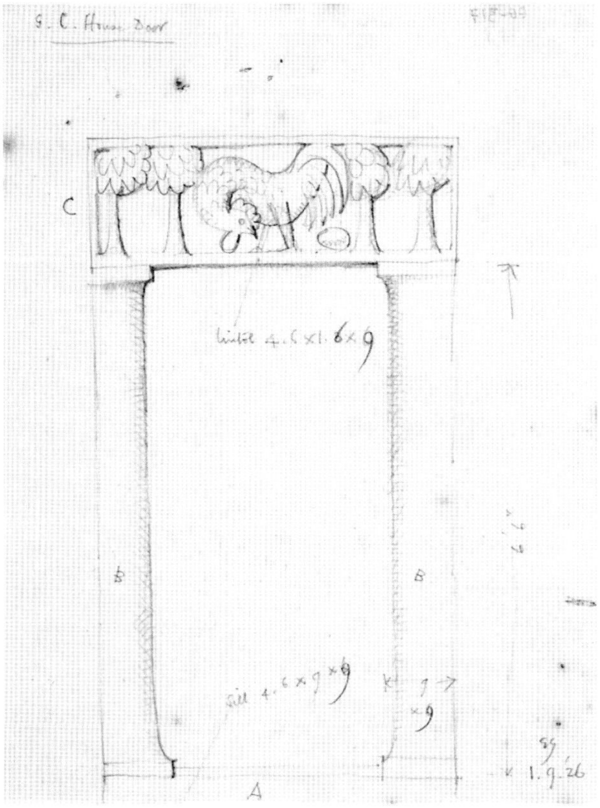

91 Pencil sketch of a design for the doorway at Four Elms by Eric Gill, dated 1 September 1926, 165 x 127 mm. Clark Library.

We do not believe in the unlimited limited edition, a business ramp by which people are enabled to sell double the quantity they could otherwise dispose of. Our editions are limited only to secure excellence of workmanship, and not to obtain the fictitious value of scarcity.

Again the reply was from Shaw's secretary but she expressed his view that type set by machine could be excellent: 'Now that they have Caslon on the machines hand setting is pure superstition. When Morris died he was on the point of discarding his hand press. Mr Shaw adds that the Golden Cockerel Press is not really up to date'. Gibbings's annoyance at this comment is obvious in his reply sent on 21 November; he was quick to point out 'that Caslon on the "Mono" is not even the same face as Caslon hand set, though professed to be, neither is it as good. Also, that although the Golden Cockerel sets by hand, it prints on platen machines such as, in all probability, Morris would have used, and that it has not the slightest wish to be "really up to date" — it prefers to do good work'.[28]

Plans for their edition of *Troilus* had become increasingly ambitious. Gill's illustrations grew in number and concept and a lavish arrangement of decorative borders had been decided upon — Gibbings's desire that this should be a 'swish' edition was being fulfilled. Gill was busily occupied on the project for the next few months and letters passed to-and-fro, Gill outlining progress on the blocks and explaining his selection of subjects: 'No. 159 shows Troilus spying Cressida with Dromede. Cressida does not appear to have wholly surrendered yet ... No. 157 Troilus thoroughly fed up with Cupid chases him off the earth ... No. 158 Cupid in flight, above in the tree are seen Pan & an ape. These display the natural indifference of their kind for the affairs of humanity.'[29]

Early in 1927, family affairs were again to interrupt work at the Press. On 30 March, Moira gave birth to twin boys, Lawrence and Finnbar. Gibbings later attributed their conception to the fact that he and Moira had been reading the *Procreant Hymn*. He warned of the book's potent effects: 'If you can find a copy read it. But be careful. I knew a couple who did so and they had twins within a year.'[30] A scribbled announcement from Gibbings to Gill, sent the next day, expressed his joy at this event: 'TWIN BOYS & "gallant little swearers" too arrived this early morning at half an hour's notice & with no more trouble to Moira than walking across the road to the doctor's, GLORIA IN EXCELSIS DEO, Fondly, affectionately, humbly & proudly Robert. ... The loveliest little things you ever saw & and all three doing grand. On my knees I say God be praised.'[31]

Gibbings's joy was clearly genuine but later that year he was feeling the strain of his growing responsibilities; writing to Tom Balston in October 1927, he commented: 'By the way, if you should hear of anyone wanting a typographical advisor say one day a week at a vast salary, let me know. With four brats growing up, it behoves me to earn a bit more, & I don't want to alter the lines on which this place is run.'[32] If Robert felt the pressure then, it must have been all the more exhausting for Moira — now with four children, a house, and business to run, Moira needed help. Some of that help came in the form of Mary O'Sullivan, a country girl from Ireland who had been a domestic servant in the house of one of Robert's aunts in Cork, who had come to work at Waltham. Robert's relief at her arrival is obvious in his praise of her in a letter to Gill:

... but now let me tell you of the most marvellous thing in the world, one Mary O'Sullivan from Skibbereen who has come over to us as domestic. Tis as queen she ought to have come, she has the face of a madonna & in her voice there's 50,000 years of kindness. I just can't keep the tears out of my eyes when I hear it. ... Tisn't her brogue so much, tis just the same softness that you can catch between your hands in the Irish air thats in her voice, tis mountains & mountains of atlantic waves of kindness that's in her speech that you can only cry in pity for the rest of the world.[33]

This visitor from his native Ireland provoked in him passionate feelings of nostalgia for the country and people who had accepted the intrusion of earlier generations of his family and allowed them to become Anglo-Irish. His letter continued:

You mustn't mind all this, its only because I'm a poor bloody Englishman who was allowed to live a few generations near heaven and am now back again not very far from Hell.

If you ever leave Wales lets all go to Ireland. There's no living there for such as us but even the thorn tree in the hedge gets its chance there so why shouldn't we & if there are clouds they don't form in the next county but come up from the other side of the world & if it does rain its the dew of heaven and not the sweat of Essex. I wish I could be down to-night in the 'Green Valley' & if I did whether I wake again there or in Heaven would be very little different.

By now another person had joined the team at Waltham and was employed by the Press. Lucy Cook came as a secretary to help Moira with administration, taking up residence in a hut, converted into living quarters, which had formerly been used as a house for the geese that roamed the orchard. Lucy was a bright young woman and a South African educationalist of advanced views. Her good humour was highly appreciated by visitors to the Press; an added advantage was that she could give lessons to Patrick and Brigid'.[34]

Despite these important family events, work at the Press had carried on. Gibbings was in discussion with Douglas Cleverdon over the possibility of publishing Gill's essay *Art and Love* and of sharing lists of subscribers and commercial travellers between their publishing activities. Production was underway on *A Rapture* by Thomas Carew, with copper engravings by J. E. Laboureur, and *Men and Matters* by William Shenstone which appeared in May 1927. Gill had provided an engraving for the front cover of the *Spring Prospectus* which, as well as announcing forthcoming titles, also advertised a series of postcards printed by the Press, featuring wood-engravings from various publications.[35] In the February, Gibbings wrote an article on the Golden Cockerel Press for a new annual called *The Woodcut*, edited by Herbert Furst. This was important publicity and a list of available books, illustrated with wood-engravings, followed the article. In the text Gibbings outlined the 'origins, aims, and achievements of the Press' and pages from key Cockerel books were reproduced. In the last paragraph, Gibbings stated his views about producing limited editions and his dislike of pretension; he ended with a tribute to his staff:

Concerning the limitation of editions. It is a pity that commercial speculation should pursue the art of printing. Publishers find that, by calling an edition limited, they sell double the number they might otherwise dispose of. The only real reason for limitation is quality of workmanship. ... The Golden Cockerel is very proud of its staff. Mr. F. Young and Mr. A. H. Gibbs have set up all the fine editions of the Press, and Mr. A. C. Cooper, himself an artist and a wood engraver, has printed them. Many mistakes have been made at the Press and many will be made, but as Mr. Gill has said, 'A live worm is better than a dead angel'. The Golden Cockerel rises early and hopes to catch the worm.[36]

LIFE AT THE PRESS was by no means inward-looking or isolated. The intense relationship with Gill did not monopolise Robert and Moira's lives and their friendships ranged well beyond the confines of the wood-engraving and printing fraternity — artists, writers, musicians and interesting and creative people of all kinds were part of their circle, and they, in turn, were welcome and popular guests at social gatherings. Interest in the theatre and amateur dramatics was another of their enthusiasms and in July 1927 Robert and Moira were persuaded to 'tread the boards', or in this case the dusty floor of a barn, in a production of the morality play *Everyman*. Their friend Katherine Pleydell-Bouverie, nicknamed Beano, was one of the producers of the play. Her real talent was as a potter and she studied ceramics with Bernard Leach in his studio at St Ives. In 1924 she set up her own pottery at her family home of Coleshill in Berkshire, working in partnership with Ada Mason (known as Peter), a fellow student, and her co-producer. On the family estate was a famous historic building, the Great Barn at Great Coxwell, a vast, ancient, cathedral-like space, rustic and full of atmosphere, which was to be the perfect setting for such a play. The cast were all drawn from Katherine's friends and the guest book at Coleshill House documents the gathering together of the players for what must have been something of a house party. Robert was cast as 'God', Moira as 'Beauty' and Robert revelled in the role for which his stature and bearing made him a natural choice. Katherine's cousin Doris recalled the occasion:

Robert and Moira were, I remember, in the honeymoon room as we called one of the bedrooms, in the large four-poster Chippendale bed, & she *couldn't* learn her lines, so the story went she kicked him awake in the middle of the night saying 'God, hear Beauty!' He looked with his red beard, like a Russian ikon & he and Michael Cardew (another potter) who was very beautiful, were up in the hayloft in Heaven, Michael playing his recorder to the intermittent clucking of a hen who was also up there![37]

Although only an amateur production, a review appeared in the *Manchester Guardian* which described the performance as 'curiously successful'. Despite Moira's problems with her lines, all the actors were judged as good, and the effectiveness of the production was attributed to the producers, who gave the play 'just as of old, the right tragic effect of outward expression purged down and refined to its barest essentials by a chastening intensity of feeling'. Performances took place on Saturday 23 and Sunday 24 of July in the afternoon, in front of a supportive audience that included many friends such as Bernard Leach and his wife. Serious though their performances were, no doubt it was also an occasion for backstage humour and bonhomie. Gibbings greatly enjoyed the experience

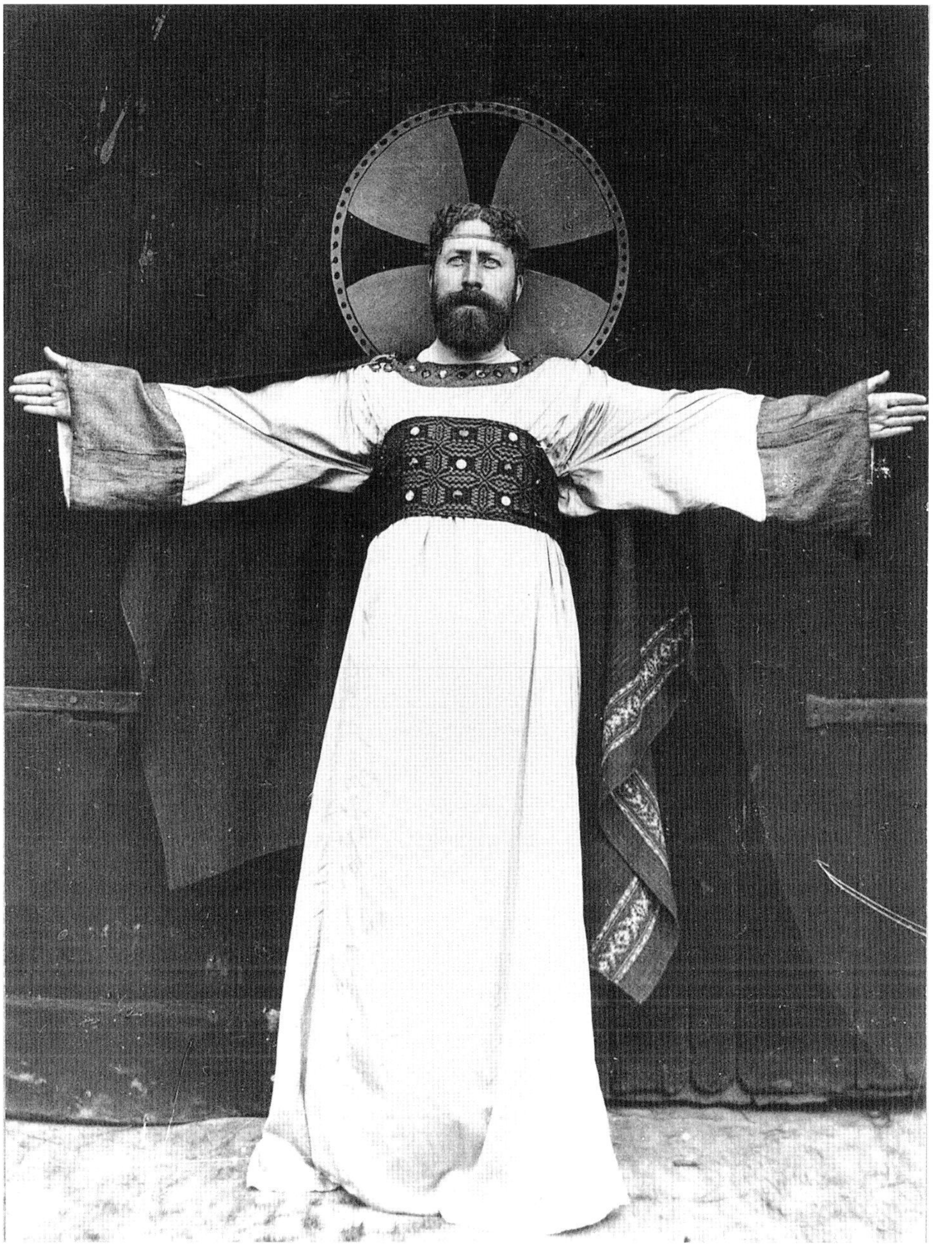

92 Robert Gibbings playing the role of God in a production of the morality play *Everyman*, performed at the Great Barn at Great Coxwell in July 1927.
Reproduced with permission of R. W. Pleydell-Bouverie.

and was fond of boasting in later years that on a return visit to the Great Barn he was recognised: 'I know you — you're God'. Amused, Gibbings agreed.

No more books were published until September when *A Ballad Upon a Wedding* by Sir John Suckling, with illustrations by Eric Ravilious, appeared. Gibbings had written to Ravilious inviting him to illustrate a book for the Press at the end of the previous year and asked for his suggestions for suitable titles. One can perhaps imply from this that, to some extent, Gibbings chose books that would show off the talents of the illustrators, texts that would appeal and stimulate them, rather than being so concerned with literary content. Rejecting Ravilious's suggestions but sharing his interest in early literature, Gibbings proposed this seventeenth century work. Ravilious had enjoyed a visit to the Press in January and already had ideas for the look of the book, so he wrote to Gibbings with suggestions. Ravilious had difficulty in finding a copy of the text but was getting carried along by his enthusiasm, thinking of possibilities for future publications, and, going far beyond discussing his own engraving, he considered the design of the whole book. Gibbings was encouraging but at the same time careful to make it clear that he was in control:

I think our best plan would be for me to set up the poem in question and send you a proof of it. The particular volume it is in is one of a set which I do not want to risk in the post, besides finding it rather useful here for reference in connection with other matters.

I think it would be excellent if you could do four engravings as well as one of the music.

I think to have a patterned paper extra would cost too much for this small volume, besides which it would not be uniform with the others, which form I am anxious to retain.[38]

Although both men enjoyed giving vent to creative ideas, Gibbings was responsible for keeping tightly to realistic budgets:

We must not have more than four verses to a page, and of course the more pages we can manage, thanks to your engravings, the better, but don't let me in for more than £12.12.0 which I would like to include the block with the music.[39]

Further letters concerned technical matters and by May time was getting short and the late delivery of some blocks was causing Ravilious anxiety; Gibbings wanted two blocks to be softened by vignetting and there were further problems with the shallow cutting of one block which made it difficult to print without appearing too black:

The blocks and your letter arrived this morning. I'm awfully glad they weren't lost .... I will certainly mend the two blocks and I'm glad you thought of it and sent them to me. The edges are rather aggressive, and I must make them more in harmony with the rest of the book .... I am rather sorry I didn't cut deeper in the thing on page 3 — the head of the girl; this is a bit too black for the others don't you think? I don't know if anything could be done to remedy this in the printing — if it could in some way be printed lighter? Everything else has printed jolly well.[40]

A number of other titles were in preparation but efforts were still being concentrated on *Troilus*. Gill was regularly sending blocks and Gibbings was supervising the page make-up with the help of the compositors, in particular Frank Young, who was making suggestions and resolving problems of fitting the blocks with the type. Work on initial letters and plates for Gill's book *Art and Love*, which they now had agreement to print, filled spare moments and some jobbing work included a marriage announcement for Gill's eldest daughter Betty and ordination cards printed for Desmond Chute.

In Britain an increasing number of bookshops were stocking Cockerel books but distribution was always a problem. Outside Britain, there were some direct sales to bookshops on the continent and countries throughout the Empire including India, Australia and New Zealand. But by far the biggest market was in America, where sales had become increasingly important to the Press but distribution was disorganised.[41] Gibbings's heart was in the design and production of

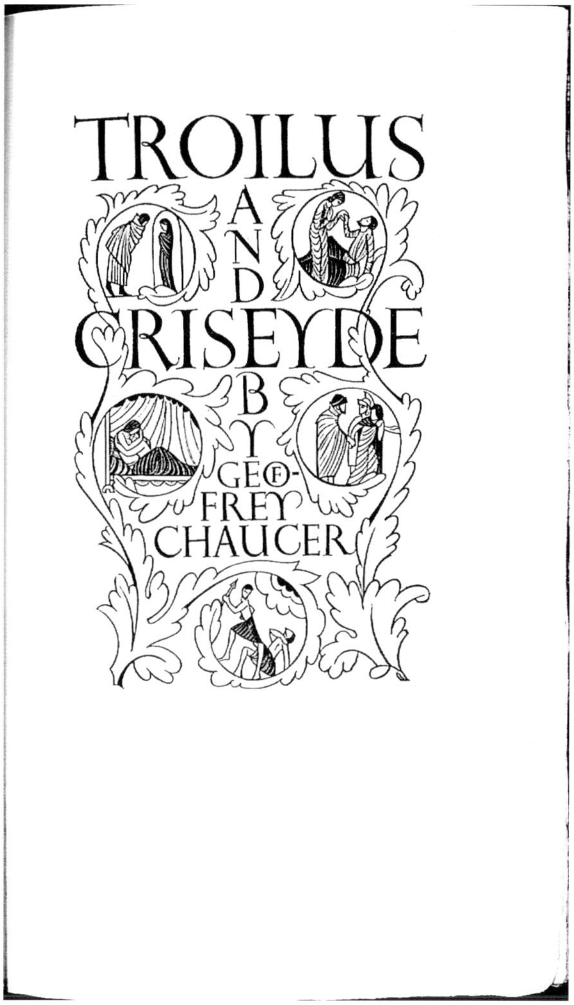

93 Title page from *Troilus and Criseyde* by Geoffrey Chaucer, with lettering and wood-engraved decorations by Eric Gill. Published by the Golden Cockerel Press in September 1927, page size 317 x 190 mm. Reproduced by permission of the Golden Cockerel Press Ltd.

fine books — the business side was a necessary duty — so in the summer of 1927 he found an easy solution to the problem and signed a contract with Random House for them to be sole distributor of Cockerel books in America.

Interest in and anticipation of the *Troilus* was high following the issue of a prospectus, and the edition was heavily subscribed. In a postscript to a letter to Gibbings, Gill mentioned he had heard from Count Kessler, owner of the distinguished Cranach Press, who wanted to reserve a copy, hoping it was not too late. Final details were being decided; Sangorski and Sutcliffe, the well-known bookbinding firm that the Press invariably used,[42] were experimenting with bindings and Gibbings was consulting Gill on the design of the lettering on the cover, suggesting he might try a special monogram of the GCP initials, later changed to a T and C in combination. He was also organizing Gill to sign the colophon page of the special edition printed on vellum. In the midst of all this activity the family managed to get away for a fortnight's holiday in late August. A few weeks later the much heralded *Troilus and Criseyde* appeared.

Recognised as the most ambitious piece of book production yet attempted by the Press, every one of its three hundred or so pages was decorated with wood-engravings by Gill: a title page, five full-page illustrations, five half-page

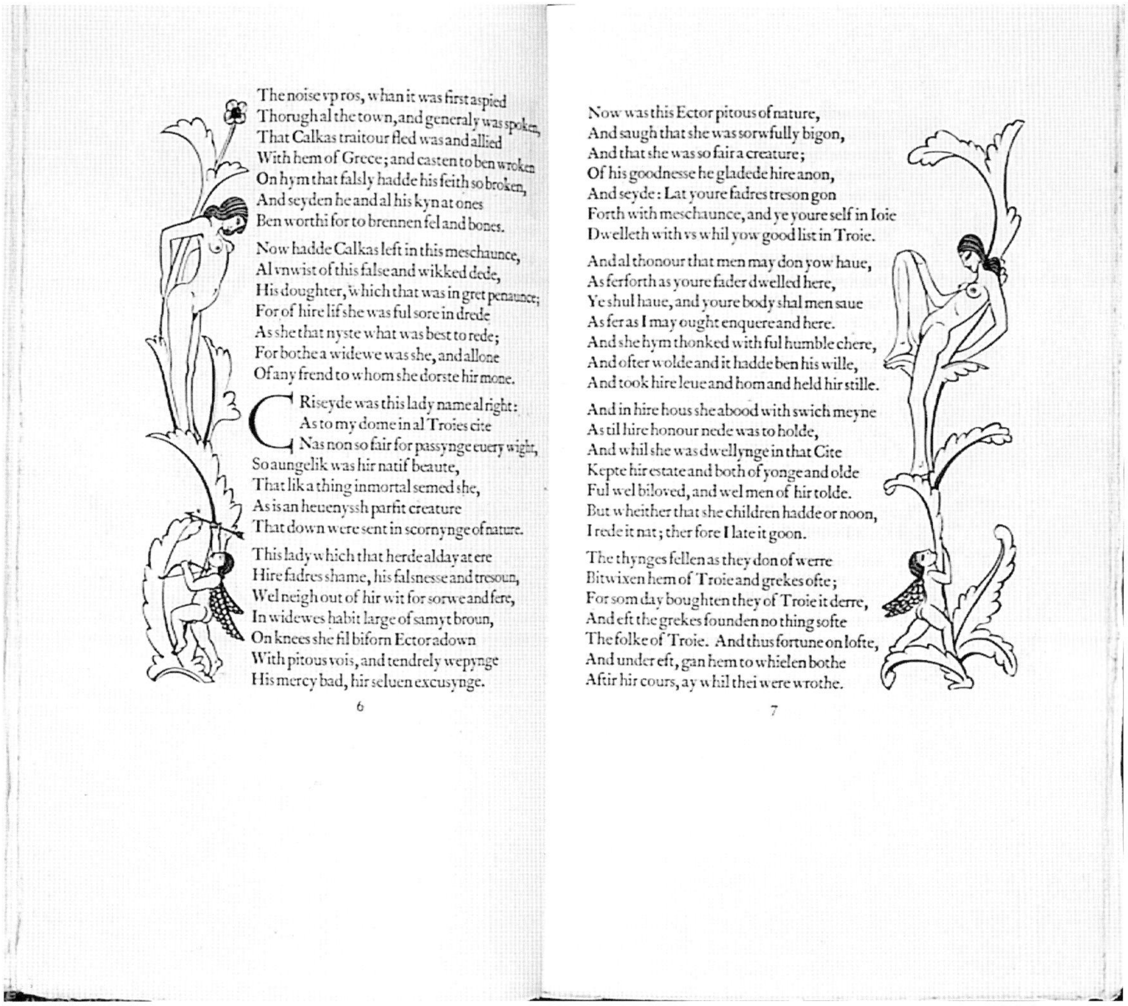

The noise vp ros, whan it was first aspied
Thorugh al the town, and generaly was spoken,
That Calkas traitour fled was and allied
With hem of Grece; and casten to ben wroken
On hym that falsly hadde his feith so broken,
And seyden he and al his kyn at ones
Ben worthi for to brennen fel and bones.

Now hadde Calkas left in this meschaunce,
Al vnwist of this false and wikked dede,
His doughter, which that was in gret penaunce;
For of hire lif she was ful sore in drede
As she that nyste what was best to rede;
For bothe a widewe was she, and allone
Of any frend to whom she dorste hir mone.

CRiseyde was this lady name al right:
As to my dome in al Troies cite
Nas non so fair for passynge euery wight,
So aungelik was hir natif beaute,
That lik a thing inmortal semed she,
As is an heuenyssh parfit creature
That down were sent in scornynge of nature.

This lady which that herde alday at ere
Hire fadres shame, his falsnesse and tresoun,
Wel neigh out of hir wit for sorwe and fere,
In widewes habit large of samyt broun,
On knees she fil biforn Ector adown
With pitous vois, and tendrely wepynge
His mercy bad, hir seluen excusynge.

6

Now was this Ector pitous of nature,
And saugh that she was sorwfully bigon,
And that she was so fair a creature;
Of his goodnesse he gladede hire anon,
And seyde: Lat youre fadres treson gon
Forth with meschaunce, and ye youre self in Ioie
Dwelleth with vs whil yow good list in Troie.

And al thonour that men may don yow haue,
As ferforth as youre fader dwelled here,
Ye shul haue, and youre body shal men saue
As fer as I may ought enquere and here.
And she hym thonked with ful humble chere,
And ofter wolde and it hadde ben his wille,
And took hire leue and hom and held hir stille.

And in hire hous she abood with swich meyne
As til hire honour nede was to holde,
And whil she was dwellynge in that Cite
Kepte hir estate and both of yonge and olde
Ful wel biloved, and wel men of hir tolde.
But wheither that she children hadde or noon,
I rede it nat; ther fore I late it goon.

The thynges fellen as they don of werre
Bitwixen hem of Troie and grekes ofte;
For som day boughten they of Troie it derre,
And eft the grekes founden no thing softe
The folke of Troie. And thus fortune on lofte,
And under eft, gan hem to whielen bothe
Aftir hir cours, ay whil thei were wrothe.

7

94 Double-page opening from Chaucer's *Troilus and Criseyde*, 1927, with wood-engraved borders and illustrations by Eric Gill. Reproduced by permission of the Golden Cockerel Press Ltd.

decorations and numerous initials. Gibbings felt that they had got the balance of the page just right: '... the engravings are in the form of very delicate borders almost identical with the weight of the type, so that the page is of an entirely even texture picked out here and there with accents of rubrication and coloured initials'.[43] *Troilus* was well received by the critics; John Rothenstein wrote a review full of praise but balanced with some reservations:

This imposing *Troilus and Criseyde* is the most ambitious piece of book-production The Golden Cockerel Press has yet attempted. ... The text, which has been admirably printed from eighteen-point Caslon Old Face type, combines great dignity with extreme legibility. ... Mr. Gill has been faced by a difficulty which inevitably confronts illustrators of works remote from their own time. Fitness, upon the one hand, demands that the style of the illustrations shall conform in some measure to the text, which it is its chief function to amplify. While upon the other, the artist's desire to interpret his text, to translate it, as it were, into contemporary terms, must always be a strong one if his interest is deeply involved.[44]

Rothenstein felt Gill's images illustrated this dilemma and 'just fail to achieve the complete harmony for which he has sought'. Another inconsistency that worried Rothenstein was Gill's 'misplaced naturalism', he felt that Gill's masterly

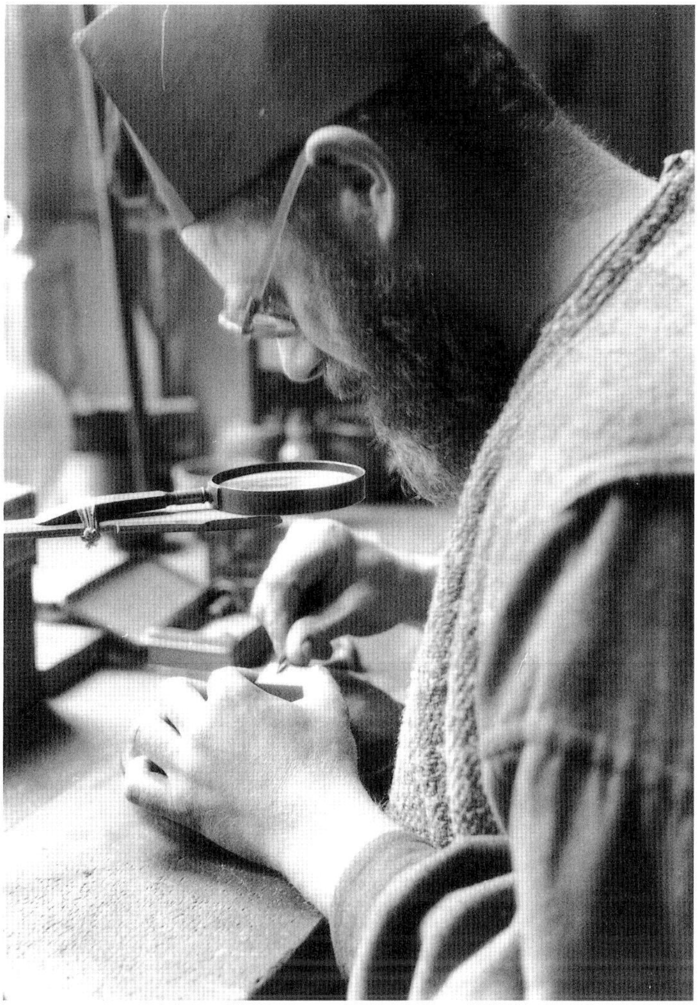

95 Eric Gill engraving, 1928, photograph by Howard Coster. By courtesy of the National Portrait Gallery.

control of design and pattern which gave the page a unity was occasionally broken by 'too great an insistence upon the human body. Real women of flesh and blood recline unsuitably upon the fragile leaves of formal, almost heraldic plants'. Gill himself had some criticisms of his own work, especially of the borders: 'In the *Troilus*, in fact, there was *too much* variety in the borders — too many different sorts. The book was "jumpy".'[45]

On the domestic front, life was complicated by the fact that Mary O'Sullivan left the household, returning to Cork to get married. She had proved to be a real treasure in the community at Waltham; everyone was deeply fond of her, as can be seen by the comments and good wishes entered into her autograph album. They all wrote touching laments at her departure — Coppard, the children, Lucy Cook, and the staff in the press room.

In October 1927, a major exhibition of the work of the Press was organised at the St George's Gallery and later moved to the Whitworth Art Gallery in the spring of 1928. Ninety-three framed, engraved illustrations were shown (twenty-three by Gibbings himself) and twenty-two of the books. The loyal Campbell Dodgson provided a preface to the catalogue which gave fulsome praise to the work, opening with the words 'The Golden Cockerel Press has surpassed its predecessors among the recent English presses directed by artists or printers animated by high motives for the reform of their craft, in the zeal that it has shown for the art of original engraving'. Dodgson continued his eulogy:

Then one has to consider Mr. Gibbings as occupied, not only with engravings (on copper, recently, as well as wood), but also with the serious problem, which he owns to having only partially solved in some early productions of the press, of adjusting, with a nice sense of proportion, the exact style of the block to be employed (not too black, not too white, the lines neither too thick nor too thin) to the type that has to go with it, and to the size of the page. And he has to impress the necessity of such adjustments, not only on himself but on other artists. What opportunity, what need, for tact!

The fact that the press is not a separate thing from the publisher's office, but in close connection with it — in Mr. Gibbings' own garden ... enables him to exercise the strictest supervision over ink and paper, and to bring artists and compositors into the close contact & co-operation that are needed for the successful production of books illustrated by wood blocks. And of artists he has enlisted already a goodly company, as this exhibition will shew.[46]

Gibbings added a note at the end of the catalogue that he and his partners

... regard the first seven years' work not only with humility in spite of Mr Dodgson's complimentary preface, but as a term of apprenticeship, of which the recently published *Troilus and Criseyde* is offered as a qualifying certificate and as an index of the main direction it is hoped to pursue during the forth-coming years.[47]

Chapter Seven
Building on Success 1927–1928

THE APPRENTICESHIP was indeed over. In three years under Gibbings's direction the Press had built up an international reputation for quality and artistic distinction and established a style and character of its own. Leading writers on typography were recognising its work as significant — Stanley Morison included Golden Cockerel Press publications in *A Review of Recent Typography in England, the United States, France and Germany*, 1927.[1] Five books had been published in their first year but production had quickly increased and eleven books appeared in 1925, and thirteen in 1926; only seven books were to appear in 1927, but this can be explained by the efforts put into *Troilus* — still, the average of ten books a year over the three years was the result of working at a hectic pace.

The remaining months of 1927 saw the completion of a number of significant projects.[2] In October, Hodder & Stoughton published *The Charm of Birds* by Viscount Grey of Fallodon, for which they had commissioned Gibbings to provide head- and tail-pieces. Similar in style to the engravings he had produced for *Fallodon Papers* the previous year, these small but delicate images seem to be early indications of how his later work would develop. In the best of the engravings one can see how confident Gibbings was in the depiction of wildlife. His draughtsmanship seemed assured, more so than when he drew the human figure; the accuracy and simplicity of his drawing came through careful observation and his affinity with the subject matter. Gibbings himself described these two books as 'a signpost on my road'; through them he began to see 'not only the decorative quality of birds but the suitability of wood engraving for their clearly defined textures'.[3] But he felt he was only 'groping', aware that the proportions of his

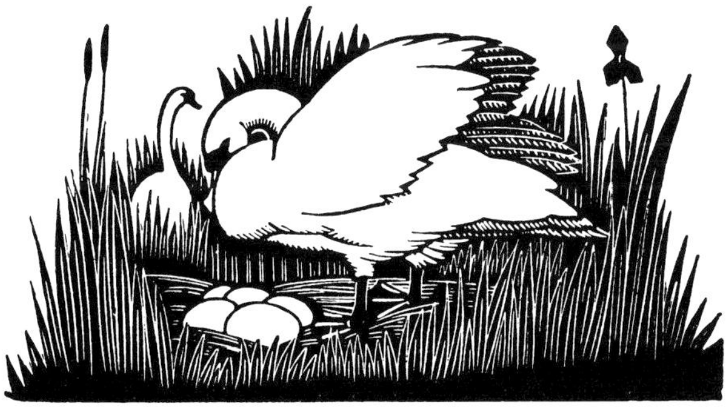

96 Illustration from *The Charm of Birds*, 1927, wood-engraving, 43 x 79 mm.

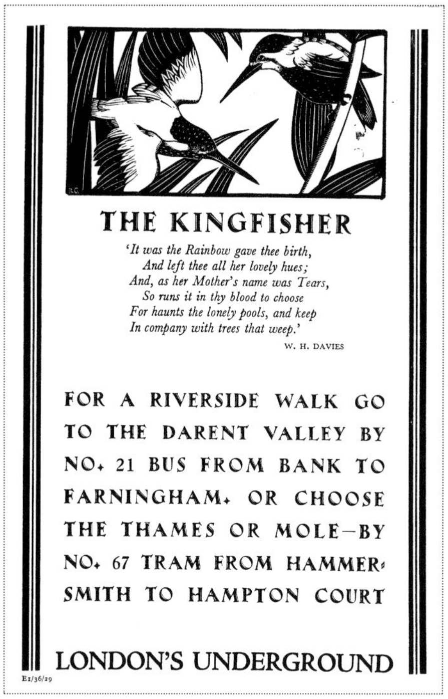

97 Advertisement for London's Underground illustrated with a wood-engraving by Gibbings, 1929, sheet size 210 x 140 mm., image size 52 x 101 mm. At least six advertisements were produced and appeared widely in magazines and newspapers. Another advertisement from the series, with an image of an owl and a verse from Shakespeare, was illustrated in *Modern Publicity 1930*, a commercial art annual published by The Studio Ltd, p. 26. Reproduced with permission of the London Transport Museum.

drawings '... lacked accuracy and my textures variety. Those strong black-and-whites of earlier days still had their hold on me'. The book was an immediate success; four impressions were made before the end of the year, a limited edition was oversubscribed before publication and it continued to sell for many years.[4]

Gibbings was also able to pursue this interest in birdlife in a more overtly commercial way. In 1929 the London Underground devised an advertising campaign, using quotations about birds by famous poets. He was commissioned to engrave a series of illustrations to accompany the verses, depicting birds that could be seen in the country accessible by public transport.

December 1927 saw the culmination of activity on three books ready for the Christmas market: *The Twelve Moneths* illustrated by Eric Ravilious, *The Chester Play of the Deluge*, illustrated by David Jones and *The True Historie of Lucian the Samosatenian* with engravings by Gibbings. *The Twelve Moneths*, a seventeenth century text written by Nicholas Breton, the minor Elizabethan poet, consisted of short pieces of satirical, religious, and romantic and pastoral subjects, organised as a calendar. It had been planned earlier in the year and by June Ravilious was working on the illustrations to fit Gibbings's layout:

I have made a few drawings for the 'Nicolas Breton' [*sic*] calendar to the sizes you have worked out. You should have the engravings — I mean the three or four you mention in, say two to three weeks? The arrangement looks well I think; there may be a small difficulty I foresee that perhaps the calendar side may look too *rich*. I shall try to make the top rectangle as simple in design as I can .... Thanks very much for the pulls for 'January'; they should be useful.... Certainly I will 'get really down to it'.[5]

Ravilious seems to have had faith in Gibbings's judgement and certainly shared the philosophy of the Press and appreciated the care and attention to detail that Gibbings showed — the two men worked well together. A solution proposed by Gibbings to a problem with the opening pages of the book was readily accepted by Ravilious:

We find when we come to set up January that it is rather longer than a single page. As it happens this is all to the good in one way, as it enables us to continue the usual tradition of beginning the book on the right hand side; but in order to keep the second page pretty full we can only put a dozen lines on page one, and after much cogitation as to how to fill the top of said page, we have decided to use a half title, as shown, surrounded by some form of border, which we should like you to do for us. This will of course be extra to the others. I am inclined to think in this case that it ought to have irregular edges, and all that seems to me to be wanted is some rather non-committal floreated effect, in which possibly the leaves should suggest the difference between winter and summer. You might, for instance, start at the bottom with two branches which gradually come into rather fuller leaf as they wind round to the top, but I leave it to you. I think it wants to be kept rather lighter in weight than the others. Could you do this for us fairly soon? We shall then be able to get a dummy made up of the first pages and send it to our travellers.[6]

Ravilious was co-operative and prompt with delivery and by the end of September had completed all the blocks, and the book was already being printed. In May the following year, Ravilious wrote a gentle reminder that he had not yet been paid for his work; he was often short of money. It was Moira who replied with forty pounds on account but asking for a delay in paying the balance — however successful the Press, cash flow was always a problem.[7]

The collaboration with David Jones and his illustrations for *The Chester Play of the Deluge* had a less successful outcome. The quality and extremely individual style and imagery used by Jones in these engravings was not matched by the standard of printing for the book. Jones was so intensely concerned with his art that perhaps he was less able to adapt and consider aspects of production; as Cave and Manson observe: 'Triumphs of design and imagery, Jones's blocks for *The Chester Play* were shallow in their engraving, so shallow that they would not print well on the paper Gibbings intended to use. The sad fact was that ... the superb blocks were badly printed; even Albert Cooper's skills as pressman were not enough.'[8]

The idea to publish an edition of *The True Historie of Lucian* might well have been that of Ravilious. He had submitted a selection of classical stories to Gibbings as possible publications but Gibbings, having consulted 'an expert on classical yarns', had rejected some as being 'dull', and others as being too well known.[9] Included in this last category was the *Lucian* but it would appear that later Gibbings changed his mind and decided to illustrate it himself. In a note in *Chanticleer*, a bibliography of the Golden Cockerel Press,[10] the resulting book is described thus: 'Whether or not of a progressive format, this is a very beautiful book.' The format might not indeed have been progressive, as it drew on the layout of many manuscripts and early printed books for its inspiration, but it was inventive in its revival of a solution to the problem of combining dual texts (English and Greek). The page layout and design must have presented a challenge to the compositors, especially as Gibbings's illustrations fit closely into the text area. The English text occupied the central text area partly surrounded by the Greek in a smaller size. This arrangement left uneven gaps so Gibbings designed his illustrations to fit the spaces left — an intricate exercise. Gibbings later observed: 'Such a game ... can only be played where the artist and compositors are in daily touch — here-in, at least, lies one advantage of being printer and artist at one and the same time.'[11] The Greek type was set at Oxford University Press and then the pages were assembled at Waltham.[12] Each spread was carefully organised and a true integration of text and image was achieved; the engravings matched the texture of the type while still being images of energy and drama.

The *Lucian* had involved fifty-five engravings and Gibbings was understandably beginning to tire of the medium. He complained 'I'd willingly consign all wood to the flames in favour of the oil, but needs mustn't when the twins drive.'[13] His thoughts had turned to oil painting, partly because Balston had admired one of his earlier pictures and, writing in December 1927, Gibbings offered to send a painting to him '... I am tempted to send you for inspection the only one I've done in the last 18 months. It has at least a "scarcity" value, but personally I like it a little, and other people whose opinion I value do the same .... I showed it at the "Chenil" last year ...'[14] His life seemed dominated by wood-engraving — a medium that demands control, precision and close concentration. For a man so full of energy and with a love of colour, it is hardly surprising that he sometimes

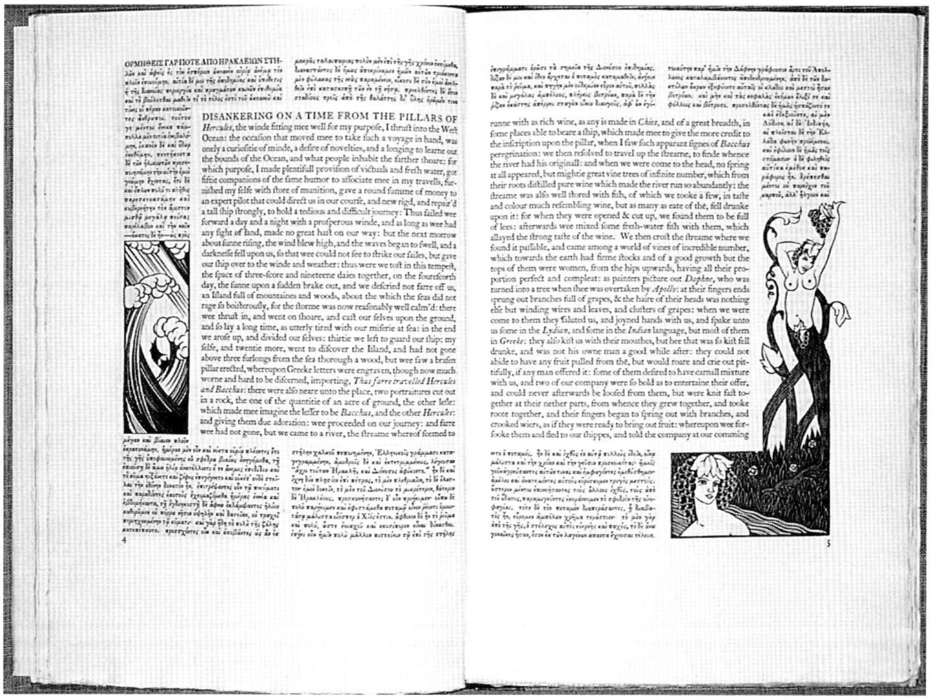

DISANKERING ON A TIME FROM THE PILLARS OF *Hercules*, the winde fitting mee well for my purpoſe, I thruſt into the Weſt Ocean: the occaſion that moved mee to take ſuch a voyage in hand, was onely a curioſitie of minde, a deſire of novelties, and a longing to learne out the bounds of the Ocean, and what people inhabit the farther ſhoare: for which purpoſe, I made plentifull proviſion of victuals and freſh water, got fiftie companions of the ſame humor to aſſociate mee in my travells, furniſhed my ſelfe with ſtore of munition, gave a round ſumme of money to an expert pilot that could direct us in our courſe, and new rigd, and repair'd a tall ſhip ſtrongly, to hold a tedious and difficult journey: Thus ſailed wee forward a day and a night with a proſperous winde, and as long as wee had any ſight of land, made no great haſt on our way: but the next morrow about ſunne riſing, the wind blew high, and the waves began to ſwell, and a darkneſſe fell upon us, ſo that wee could not ſee to ſtrike our ſailes, but gave our ſhip over to the winde and weather: thus were we toſt in this tempeſt, the ſpace of three-ſcore and nineteene daies together, on the foureſcorth day, the ſunne upon a ſudden brake out, and we deſcried not farre off us, an Iſland full of mountaines and woods, about the which the ſeas did not rage ſo boiſterouſly, for the ſtorme was now reaſonably well calm'd: there wee thruſt in, and went on ſhoare, and caſt our ſelves upon the ground, and ſo lay a long time, as utterly tired with our miſerie at ſea: in the end we aroſe up, and divided our ſelves: thirtie we left to guard our ſhip: my ſelfe, and twentie more, went to diſcover the Iſland, and had not gone above three furlongs from the ſea thorough a wood, but wee ſaw a braſen pillar erected, whereupon Greeke letters were engraven, though now much worne and hard to be diſcerned, importing, *Thus farre travelled Hercules and Bacchus*: there were alſo neare unto the place, two portraitures cut out in a rock, the one of the quantitie of an acre of ground, the other leſſe: which made mee imagine the leſſer to be *Bacchus*, and the other *Hercules*: and giving them due adoration: wee proceeded on our journey: and farre wee had not gone, but we came to a river, the ſtreame whereof ſeemed to

4

runne with as rich wine, as any is made in *Chios*, and of a great breadth, in ſome places able to beare a ſhip, which made mee to give the more credit to the inſcription upon the pillar, when I ſaw ſuch apparant ſignes of *Bacchus* peregrination: we then reſolved to travel up the ſtreame, to finde whence the river had his originall: and when we were come to the head, no ſpring at all appeared, but mightie great vine trees of infinite number, which from their roots diſtilled pure wine which made the river run so abundantly: the ſtreame was alſo well ſtored with fiſh, of which we tooke a few, in taſte and colour much reſembling wine, but as many as eate of thē, fell drunke upon it: for when they were opened & cut up, we found them to be full of lees: afterwards wee mixed ſome freſh-water fiſh with them, which allayed the ſtrong taſte of the wine. We then croſt the ſtreame where we found it paſſable, and came among a world of vines of incredible number, which towards the earth had firme ſtocks and of a good growth but the tops of them were women, from the hips upwards, having all their proportion perfect and compleat: as painters picture out *Daphne*, who was turned into a tree when ſhee was overtaken by *Apollo*: at their fingers ends ſprung out branches full of grapes, & the haire of their heads was nothing elſe but winding wires and leaves, and cluſters of grapes: when we were come to them they ſaluted us, and joyned hands with us, and ſpake unto us ſome in the *Lydian*, and ſome in the *Indian* language, but moſt of them in *Greeke*: they alſo kiſt us with their mouthes, but hee that was ſo kiſt fell drunke, and was not his owne man a good while after: they could not abide to have any fruit pulled from thē, but would roare and crie out pitifully, if any man offered it: ſome of them deſired to have carnall mixture with us, and two of our company were ſo bold as to entertaine their offer, and could never afterwards be looſed from them, but were knit faſt together at their nether parts, from whence they grew together, and tooke roote together, and their fingers began to ſpring out with branches, and crooked wiers, as if they were ready to bring out fruit: whereupon wee forſooke them and fled to our ſhippes, and told the company at our comming

5

98 Double-page spread from *The True Historie of Lucian*, 1927, page size 317 x 229 mm. Reproduced by permission of the Golden Cockerel Press Ltd.

felt the desire to break out and express himself in a more spontaneous and free way and on a different scale. Little of his painting has survived but in his later work Gibbings showed a vigorous style, using fresh colour with free and energetic brush strokes. Sculpture also had an appeal — the liberation of working on a large scale and the physical enjoyment to be had when cutting into stone had impressed him on a visit to Eric Gill at a London studio in Glebe Place, close to his familiar haunts in Chelsea. He himself had recently rented a studio at his old address in the Boltons, Redcliffe Road, as a retreat from Waltham. Gill was busy working on a monumental sculpture of a female figure, later to be entitled *Mankind*. During the early months of 1928, Gibbings was a frequent visitor to Gill's studio, and he became fascinated to see the huge female torso slowly emerge from the block of stone:

He [Gill] said that he didn't want to be bothered with head, arms, and legs, he just wanted to enjoy carving a body which would represent his ideal of feminine beauty. ... I remember that, in his eagerness to see some part of the stone finished, he went ahead with the chisel before he had finished all over with the claw, so that at one time there were three different states to be seen: the deep ridges, encircling the forms, from the punch, the 'combed' surface from the claw, and the smooth stone almost polished by his amazing skill with the chisel. It was at this stage that he shocked two somewhat puritan visitors by telling them, when they remarked on the hardness of the work, that in reality it was great fun. It was like undressing a girl, he said, each layer of stone a garment, first one got rid of the rough woollies, finally the delicate silk. Eric liked these little innocent naughtinesses.

Gibbings even claimed to have had a creative input to the work:

One day when I was with him he told me that he was worried about the thighs of the torso, which at knee height struck rather awkwardly into the supporting base. He felt that whereas such abruptness in a classical torso, mutilated by time, was entirely reasonable, the same thing carved deliberately would be lacking in design and less acceptable. While we debated the question, viewing the work from all angles, I noticed that his mason had for the time being allowed a quantity of stone to remain behind the knees, to give the figure greater strength, while it was being carved. 'Why not make it a kneeling torso?' I suggested. 'There's plenty of stone there, and it will give more of an architectural base to the figure.' Eric thought this was a good idea. It would be something new and 'rather fun.' Next day when I went to see him he had roughed it out as I had suggested, and the alteration seemed to solve his problem.[15]

Mankind was to form the centrepiece of a major exhibition of Gill's sculpture held at the Goupil Gallery; rather embarrassed, Gill admitted 'the blooming show is an absurd success — monstrous.'[16] Gibbings was full of congratulations: '... don't forget the poor bally old cock in your greatness. We want reflected glory at least.' But in the same letter Gibbings expressed his growing frustration at being tied down: 'I'm trying to get away .... Fact is I must paint, however badly, or burst & if I can manage 6 or 8 weeks away I'll come back in good fettle to get on with the job here which I really like enormously but its hard to keep alive in Waltham.'[17] Gibbings stayed with Gill in London for a week in the December of 1927, mainly life drawing during the day, sharing a model occasionally with David Jones and other artists. No doubt they enjoyed the delights of London's nightlife too, and also had time to discuss future projects. Social meetings between the friends in London became more frequent; after a supper and evening together with Gill in early January, Robert and Moira went on to the Chelsea Arts Club Ball. The following week, Moira went out with Gill on her own and they saw a performance of *Maya* at the recently re-opened Gate Theatre, followed by supper. This was not by chance as there was a connection between the Gate Theatre and the Golden Cockerel Press. How it began is uncertain: it might have been through theatrical contacts as a result of their participation in *Everyman* or more likely simply through the reputation of the Press as one linked strongly with contemporary artists and wood-engravers. One of the theatre's directors was Velona Pilcher, an American who had also been a pupil of Leon Underwood's and knew Blair Hughes-Stanton and probably Gertrude Hermes well. Through Velona, Hughes-Stanton had been commissioned to engrave illustrations for the cover of the theatre's programmes for the 1927–28 season. A note on one of these programmes, signed by 'V. P.', announced:

> The Gate Theatre Press invites playgoers to observe that these playbills they are reading are held in increasing esteem by people interested in hand printing ... and appreciative of modern wood-engravings. Sets for the Season 1927–28 are being collected by connoisseurs .... There are nine of these playbills altogether. Seven have wood-engravings, especially designed for each play, by Blair H–S; and two — the first two in the seven — are particularly acceptable, having been printed by the Golden Cockerel Press.[18]

The Gate was the first private theatre club in London and it specialised in experimental and foreign plays, unacceptable to mainstream commercial theatres or the Lord Chamberlain's censors.[19] It also put on intimate reviews which

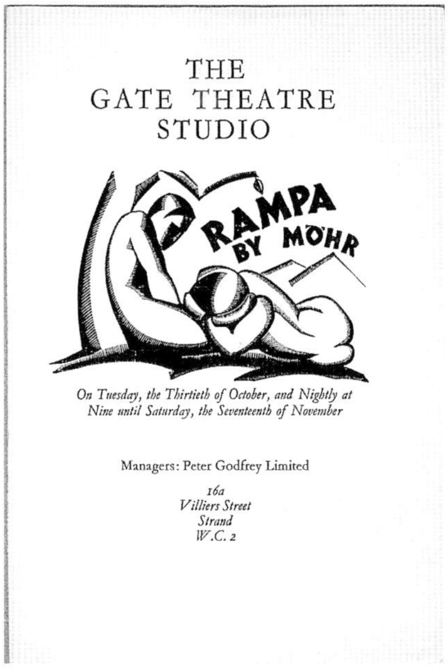

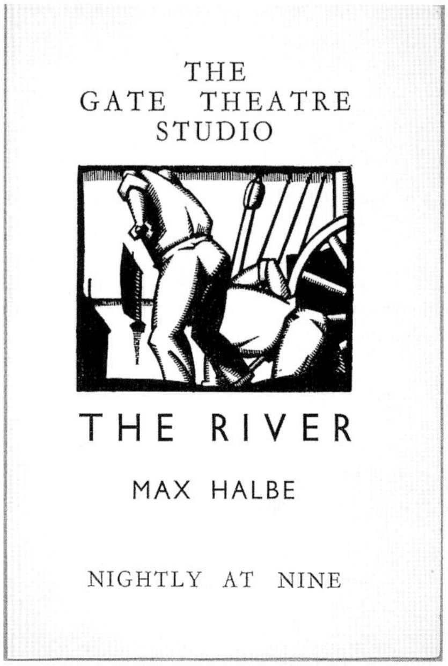

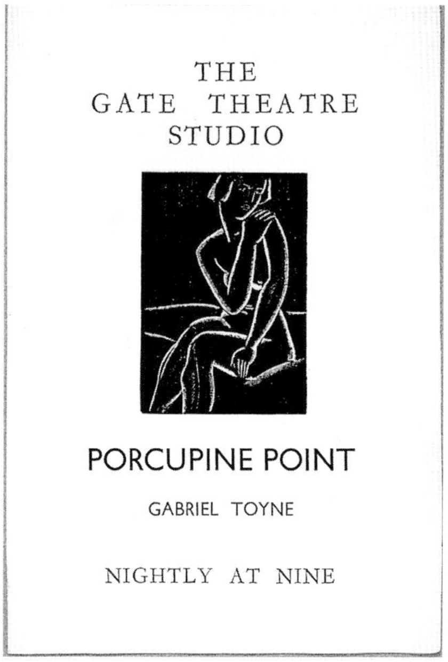

99, 100 & 101 Programme covers for the Gate Theatre Studio illustrated with wood-engravings by Gibbings, page size 283 x 190 mm: *Rampa*, October 1928; *The River*, November 1930; *Porcupine Point*, September 1931. A few of Gibbings's images might have been designed especially for the plays – the majority were re-used blocks, some dating back to 1920, selected to be appropriate for the play in hand. Programmes dating from 1929 frequently use the typeface Gill Sans. RUL.

became an institution amongst the more avant-garde London theatre audience. The Gate Theatre Studio had opened with the play *Maya* by Simon Gantillon which Moira and Gill had enjoyed. It was an outstanding success and ran for fifty-three performances in that first season. The Golden Cockerel Press became the regular printer of the theatre's programmes, which led Gibbings to come into contact with Charles Spencer, one of the partners in the theatre, who was mainly responsible for overseeing the production of programmes. Spencer enjoyed working with artists and he and Gibbings became firm friends. In the first few seasons notable artists such as McKnight Kauffer and Ashley Havinden produced modernist designs in keeping with the character of the theatre. In October 1928, the programme that accompanied the play *Rampa* by Max Möhr was illustrated on the cover by a large and powerful wood-engraving by Gibbings of a naked couple lying under a tree. The following year *Maya* was revived and this time Gibbings provided a more delicate image, again of a naked couple, simple but effective in design. Gibbings engraved blocks for at least a dozen of the programmes until 1932, when Charles Spencer gave up his partnership and the standard of design and production of the programmes declined.

But the talk was not all about sculpture or the theatre. In December, Gill had noted in his diary that shortly after Gibbings had spent the week with him in London, he had started designing specimen borders for an edition of *The Canterbury Tales*, and no doubt this had been another topic for discussion. Following the success of *Troilus*, this was to be even more ambitious and demanding and, as if this were not enough, plans were also being made for a yet bigger project — an edition of *The Four Gospels*. Gibbings retained a clear mental picture of Gill sitting on the divan in his Boltons studio, working on the budget for *The Canterbury Tales*:

Apart from the title-pages for the four volumes, we had planned a number of blocks all of approximately the same size, which could be transposed in varying repetitions. 'Well,'

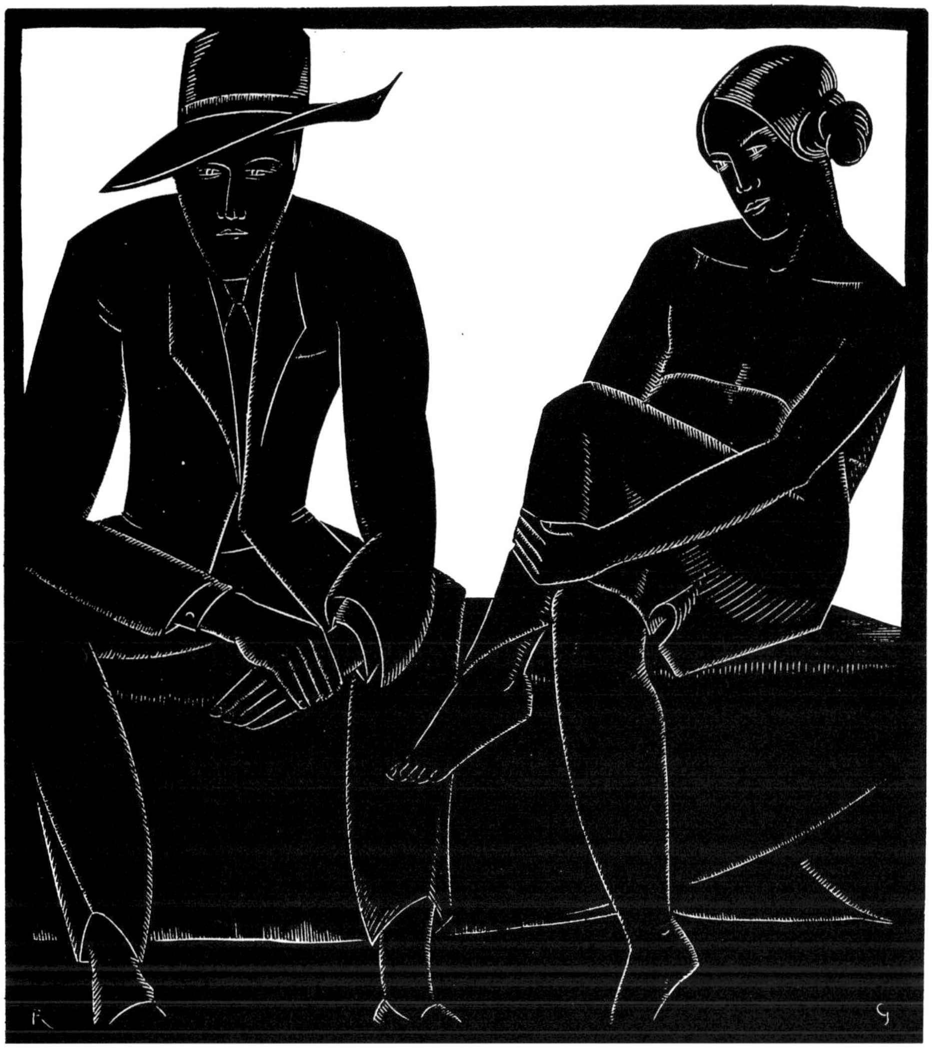

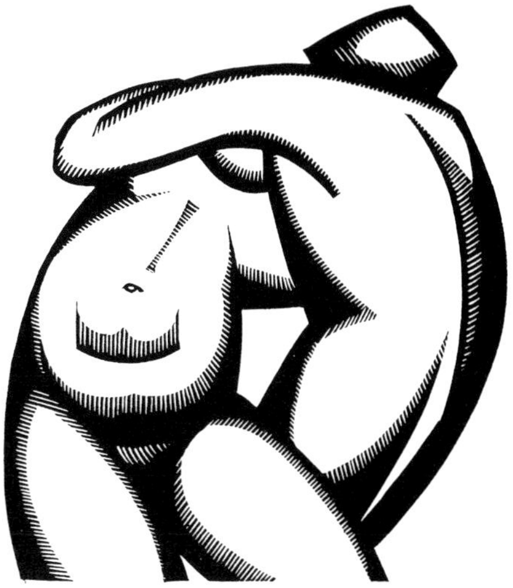

102 *left* Untitled wood-engraving, *c.* 1928, 153 x 140 mm. Proof found in the Albert Cooper Collection, RUL.

103 *above* Untitled wood-engraving, *c.* 1928, 104 x 94 mm. Proof found in the Albert Cooper Collection, RUL.

said Eric, 'there are so many blocks of such and such a size. That means a total of so many inches. With that kind of design, I can engrave a square inch in so long, and at so much an hour the total would come to so much.' I cannot remember what the figure was, but I do remember that it fell about fifteen or twenty pounds short of one of the hundreds. 'Let's make it even money,' I said. 'That's jolly generous of you,' said Eric. In fact, I thought I was getting a jolly good bargain, and had a pang of conscience that I hadn't offered more. Our agreements were scarcely more than a scrap of paper on which one or other of us had scribbled the details.

Those were idyllic days. It was my boast then, and I am still happy to think of it, that I never had a formal agreement with an artist or an author who worked for me, and I never had a disagreement.[20]

Casual and trusting as both men were about matters of business, something in writing was necessary and in January Gibbings sent a note laying out the terms in which Gill agreed to 'do engraving for all kinds of bookwork for us [GCP] exclusively, but when ever you particularly wish to take on some outside work we shall probably be able to come to terms if you consult us in the matter'.[21] Gill was paid a retaining fee but Gibbings was anxious to be liberal about the arrangement and added a postscript 'As they say on one's lease, "No reasonable

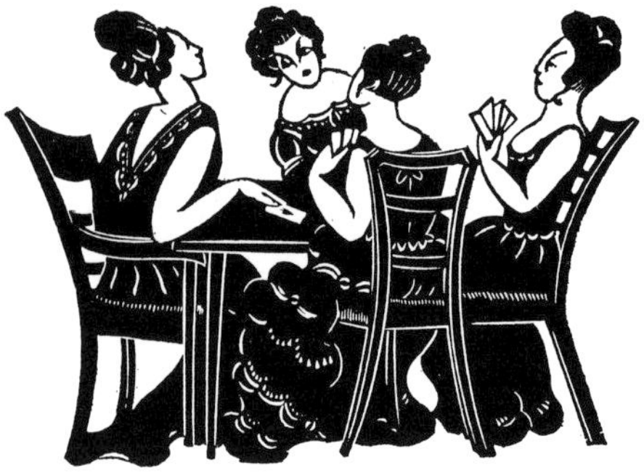

104 Illustration from *Miscellaneous Poems of Jonathan Swift*, 1928, wood-engraving, 60 x 82 mm.

permission will be refused".' Gill's work was in demand and it was not long before the agreement was tested.[22] With two major book projects under way, Gill's time was limited; for the months until *The Canterbury Tales* appeared in February 1929 and even until 1931, when *The Four Gospels* was published, much of both men's time was occupied on these projects. Letters to and fro were frequent and during periods of intense activity were sent almost daily. It demanded perseverance and enormous sustained effort and enthusiasm. The working relationship between them reached a new level of understanding and the result was a maturing of their ideas concerning the balance and harmony of type and image. On reflection, Gibbings thought that the title pages of *The Canterbury Tales* showed the first indications of the 'ideal partnership that was achieved in *The Four Gospels*'.[23]

In April, Gill and Gibbings allowed themselves a short break from 'bookwork', and spent a week in Paris, mainly life drawing at the Académie Chaumière. Gibbings was away again in May on another trip to Europe.[24] The *Spring Prospectus* announced the forthcoming publication of *The Canterbury Tales* with four specimen pages from the book loosely inserted. While Robert was away, it fell to Moira to deal with correspondence and keep everything going. From the many letters to and from Moira on Press business, it becomes clear just how closely involved she was on these projects, and how much she was responsible for editorial issues. As well as the Chaucer, proofs of *Art and Prudence*, an essay by Gill, were being corrected and work was in progress on an edition of *The Utopia of Sir Thomas More*, for which Gill was designing some floreated initials. Gill was in the thick of work on *The Canterbury Tales* and wrote to Gibbings on his return about his ideas for a border at the beginning of each tale and sent sketches of his proposal. He also asked Gibbings to have 'set up the first 42 lines of the Prologue; the last 36 of the same; and the first 7 or 8 of the Knight's Tale. That will do for a start'.[25] This enabled Gill to design borders to fit exactly the ragged ends of the lines. He also queried the extent of the book and exactly how many tales would fit into each volume. Gibbings happily agreed with his suggestions and expressed pleasure that Gill had liked *A Sentimental Journey* and the Swift. Both these books had been published in May: *Miscellaneous Poems of Jonathan Swift*[26] had engravings by Gibbings himself and *A Sentimental Journey*, by Laurence Sterne, was illustrated by J. E. Laboureur. An edition of *Count Stefan*, also illustrated by Gibbings, had already appeared in March with four engravings, including a portrait of its author, A. E. Coppard, in which Gibbings captured a good likeness.

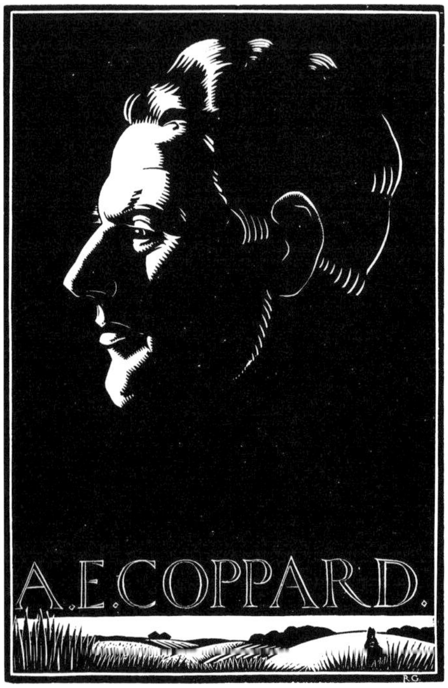

105 Portrait of A. E. Coppard, wood-engraving, frontispiece to *Count Stefan*, 1928, 132 x 89 mm. Gibbings was pleased with this portrait: '... the only likeness that I have ever got in engraving'. Quoted from a series of typed comments Gibbings provided for Balston, who was preparing his book on Gibbings's engravings published by Art and Technics in 1949. Clark Library.

Because books are referred to by their date of publication, it is easy to forget the time scale involved in preparation and while the design and engraving work was under way on the Chaucer, Gibbings was also hard at work on several other projects including some engravings for an edition of Keats's *Lamia*, which had been announced for publication towards the end of the year. In June he reported to Gill that '*Lamia* goes ahead well and life is really quite serene.'[27] Perhaps this feeling of optimism had been brought about by his recent jaunts abroad because he continued, 'I think the solution of various problems will be for me to get away a little more often. Eighteen months on end at Waltham would give stronger men than me the pip. A few weeks now and again should bring back the colour to my faded cheeks.' He might have hoped for a sympathetic response from Gill, who was also perhaps thankful for the occasional break from the enclosed world of Capel-y-ffin, but his claim to have been eighteen months on end in Waltham was an exaggeration, given his frequent visits to London and trips to Ireland and the continent. His reference to 'various problems' might also hint that he was unhappy about other aspects of his life at the Press. It was really Moira who had most to complain of, as her input to the Press was just as committed yet she was expected to run the house and be a mother as well. For her there were no retreats to London and little opportunity to indulge her own passions; perhaps it was their relationship that was also under pressure?

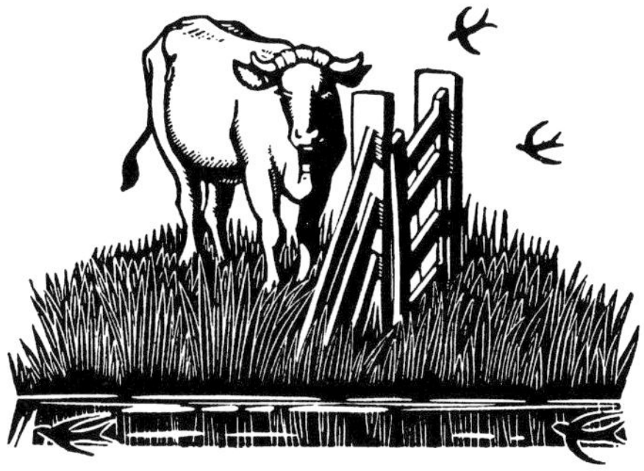

106 Illustration from *Count Stefan*, 1928, wood-engraving, 48 x 70 mm.

For Robert, a few days away was clearly not enough. His ever present desire to travel would only be satisfied by an adventure, a few weeks to himself, not days. The constant need to hit deadlines; the problems of dealing with artists and authors; the complexities of having to co-ordinate a number of projects at one time; the feeling that his immediate future was already scheduled in — just being responsible for it all made Gibbings feel tied down. Wood-engraving itself was a tiring activity, demanding endless hours of concentration, especially when being pushed by deadlines — both Gill and Gibbings prided themselves on their professional attitude in keeping to delivery dates. As well as *Lamia*, Gibbings had been working on some engravings for another project earlier in the year. Houghton Mifflin, the Boston publishers, had issued an American edition of *The Charm of Birds* and as a result had asked Gibbings to illustrate a book by Esther Forbes called *A Mirror for Witches*.

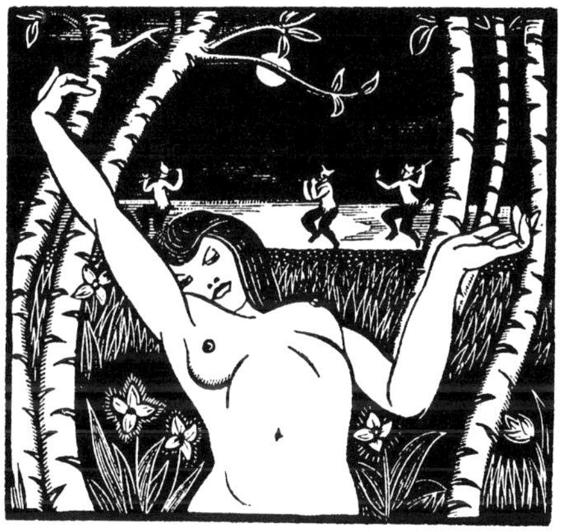

107 Illustration from *A Mirror for Witches*, 1928, wood-engraving, 72 x 79 mm. The engravings used in the English edition, published by Heinemann also in 1928, must have been printed from process copies as the images are reproduced slightly larger.

The novel was the story of a little French girl whose parents were burned as witches. Taken to Salem, in America, the tale recounts the 'life, machinations & death of the witch Doll Bilby' as she was called. Full of witchcraft and Satanism, this strange story was published in early April 1928 and was a great success.[28] In the publicity, Gibbings was heralded as the 'most celebrated of living English artists in the field'. His engravings are more erotic and playful than sinister but worked well with the page design and typeface. Esther Forbes's first novel had been taken by the Book-of-the-Month Club the previous year, which had guaranteed large sales and established her as a 'hot' author; *A Mirror for Witches* was thus eagerly awaited and had received good reviews; consequently the cheaper, standard edition went to three large printings before the formal publication date. The Golden Cockerel Press already had a high reputation with American collectors but for Gibbings personally the publicity resulting from the book's success must have helped to establish his name there.[29]

Gibbings recounted how when he had finished the blocks and was about to put them into the post he decided to write a covering letter:

'Dear Houghton Mifflin, Herewith the blocks which I hope you will like, also the invoice. Yours truly.' Then it seemed to me that that was a bit curt for the long distance that lay between us, so I tore it up and wrote another. This time, by way of conversation, I added: 'Next time you give me a job, for God's sake send me to the South Seas — I'm sick of

English fogs.' It was a cold and dirty February day when I wrote: my mention of the South Seas was merely that having read Rupert Brooke's account of his stay in Tahiti I harboured a longing to follow in his steps.[30]

This heartfelt plea was later to receive a surprising response from the publishers!

THROUGHOUT JUNE 1928 work was intense; letters from Gibbings to Gill are full of discussion of typographic detail and layout for the Chaucer but also about binding.[31] The following letter from Gibbings, sent in June, demonstrates the complexity of the task:

I send herewith, proofs of the Knight's Tale, and the beginning of the 'Miller's Prologue'. The latter consists of 3 full pages and the 18 lines that we have printed, so that the Miller's Tale can, by this arrangement, begin at the top of the page. If we do this, the Miller's Tale will end with 10 lines on a page and we can then carry on with another decoration and a few lines of the 'Reeves Prologue', which, being 66 lines, will be a full page and 6 lines, leaving you 14 lines for your decoration. I hope this is clear. ... In the meantime, I take it, you have enough to carry on. ... I also include a 'Table of lines', made out by the men for vol. 1, which may be of use to you.[32]

Working at such distances (Gill had returned to Wales) on such detailed issues was a considerable nuisance to both men and increased the possibility of time-wasting misunderstandings. Gibbings was finding the arrangement difficult and was anxious for a meeting to sort things out:

If you could come along and bring all sketches and everything else as far as you have proceeded, we could go into matters quietly and get it all into absolute order, thereby saving anxiety and risk. Why not do this and charge your railway fare to the GCP. The sooner you can manage it the more we'll be delighted. I have so many things in my head that I find myself a little out of my depth. If I came down to you, it would mean we should not have Young and Co. [the compositors], who are very important in the discussion and really much more intelligent than I can hope to be regarding the imposition. Once we had fixed on all the details, it would be much easier for each of us to proceed, even though separated. ... Why not bring your gravers with you and so be able to do any oddments that might be required, while you were here.[33]

Gill did manage to get to Waltham at the end of June but on this rare occasion it was Moira who was away; 'Moira won't be back till the 29th, but I will endeavour to make you comfortable if you come before that'. Gill took the opportunity to meet with Stanley Morison at Waltham to discuss Monotype matters as he had recently been taken on by the Monotype Corporation as a consultant.[34] The day after his arrival in Waltham, Gibbings drove Gill and his daughter Joan to Piggots, a farm near High Wycombe, in Buckinghamshire. The intention was that Gill should buy it — perhaps he had had enough of isolation in Wales. He had recently sold his sculpture *Mankind* and was therefore able to afford a deposit. Writing to Gill a few days after the visit, Gibbings was clearly very keen for Gill to move closer; 'I hope you'll take Piggots'.[35] Gill was back at Waltham in the middle of July and took a bus into Reading to consult his solicitors over the purchase of Piggots (Gill later changed the spelling to Pigotts because it was easier to write) and in his diary noted that the previous evening a supper party had been held on the lawn at Waltham with every one wearing swimming costumes — dancing followed! It is possible that René Hague joined in the party as he was courting Joan Gill and had been working at the Golden Cockerel Press during the year, learning about printing.[36]

On 25 August, Gill noted that Gibbings had just returned from a trip to Germany. He had been visiting a new nudist camp at Motzenmuhle with a group of British naturists. Many years later Gibbings 'confessed' this fact to his readers:

> I trust that I have by now established sufficiently with the reader the natural innocence and uprightness of my soul to confess that I once visited a nudist colony. Indeed, I lived there for a fortnight. It was by a lake, among pine woods, and there were only two rules of conduct:
>
> Thou shalt not carry a camera.
> Thou shalt not wear clothes.
>
> First thing in the morning we tumbled into the lake. Then, with towel wrapped about us, we drank hot coffee and ate rolls and butter. After that we laid aside the towels and played games: good hard games that stretched every muscle. Into the lake again before lunch. After lunch, a siesta in the sun, and then more games. In the evening, songs around a camp fire. In that camp there was no consciousness of age, or class, or sex. The essential spirit of the community was one of honesty. Coyness could not exist. All the ordinary complications of life faded away. It was the nearest thing to Eden that I expect to find this side of the Styx.[37]

Given the freedom of the lifestyle at Waltham, it was entirely consistent with his personal views that Gibbings should take up the cause of naturism and he was to become a committed and pioneering member of the movement. He returned with a collection of German naturist magazines, full of photographs of athletic men and women posing and performing energetic feats, but which with hindsight, one cannot help but associate with the way such health propaganda would be turned to the cause of fascism.[38]

Lamia was published in November and was a beautiful book, 'almost perfectly-proportioned',[39] and the engravings are some of the best Gibbings produced for the Press. The balance of text and image on the page shows a level of control and elegance that is masterly. The weight of the line used in the engravings matches the weight of the type perfectly and fulfils Gibbings's aspirations and struggle for that ideal. Gill had designed a series of elegant initial letters for the book but his influence is to be seen most significantly in the style of Gibbings's engraving.[40] Gibbings admired Gill's work; Gill had a consistency and strength of vision in his work that Gibbings perhaps lacked. Gibbings was more versatile, more able and willing to adapt his style to the demands of the job, which made him more effective as an illustrator for a wider range of subject matter. As an artist it was likely that Gibbings would be influenced by Gill rather than the other way around.

Gill was to stimulate Gibbings to follow in other artistic directions too. It is hardly surprising that the experience of seeing *Mankind* emerge from the block of stone should have inspired Gibbings to try his hand at sculpture; what is surprising is that Gibbings seems to have mastered the craft of stone cutting at his first attempt.

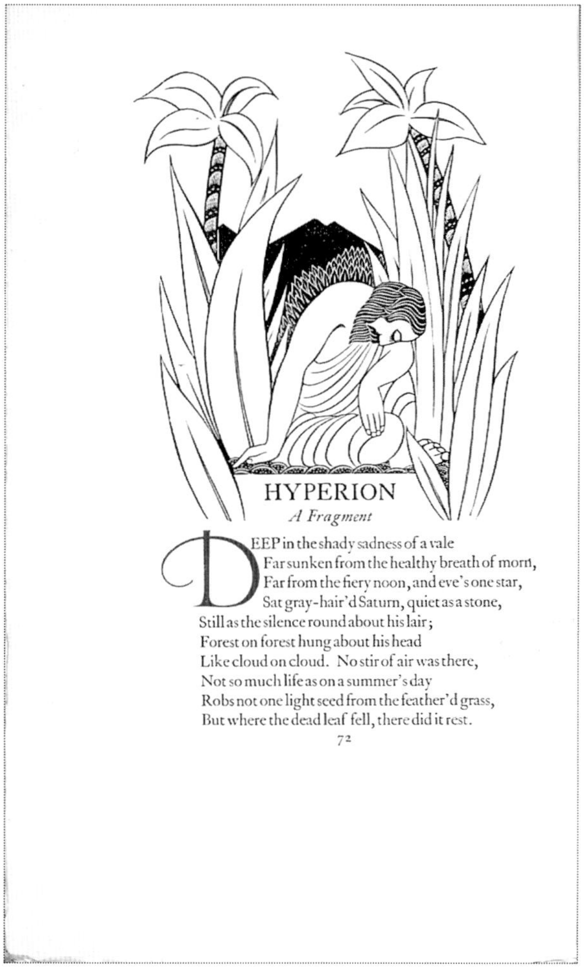

HYPERION

A Fragment

DEEP in the shady sadness of a vale
Far sunken from the healthy breath of morn,
Far from the fiery noon, and eve's one star,
Sat gray-hair'd Saturn, quiet as a stone,
Still as the silence round about his lair;
Forest on forest hung about his head
Like cloud on cloud. No stir of air was there,
Not so much life as on a summer's day
Robs not one light seed from the feather'd grass,
But where the dead leaf fell, there did it rest.

72

108 Page from *Lamia*, 1928, page size 317 x 190 mm. Reproduced by permission of the Golden Cockerel Press Ltd.

The first piece that ever I touched with chisel came from the Portland quarries, a slab some four feet square and about six inches thick. It was to be a low relief. Several people have since called it a very low relief. It began with a photograph that I saw in the souvenir programme of a Paris music-hall — two girls dancing, their arms interlocked to make a geometric pattern. From that, with the substitution of a male figure for one of the dancers, a composition of more virile implication evolved on paper.[41]

Gibbings had in fact already used a very similar figure composition as the frontispiece to *A Mirror for Witches*. The impressive quality of his first sculpture might well be attributed to the fact that the strong outline and stylisation of the figures in very low relief could be handled in a similar way to his engraving — just on a very different scale. The actual technique of cutting stone was not such an obstacle for him given his natural craftsmanship — he also had a good teacher. Gill was happy to give advice: '… when we met in London he took me to a toolsmith and chose for me chisels, claws, points, a pitching tool, and a couple of hammers, and on his next visit to my home showed me how they should be used. It looked simple enough as I watched him'.[42] Despite his enthusiasm, sculpture had to be fitted into spare moments:

Pauses in any work are wonderful opportunities for the digestion of new ideas concerning it, and at that time, busy as I was with the Golden Cockerel Press and the artists and

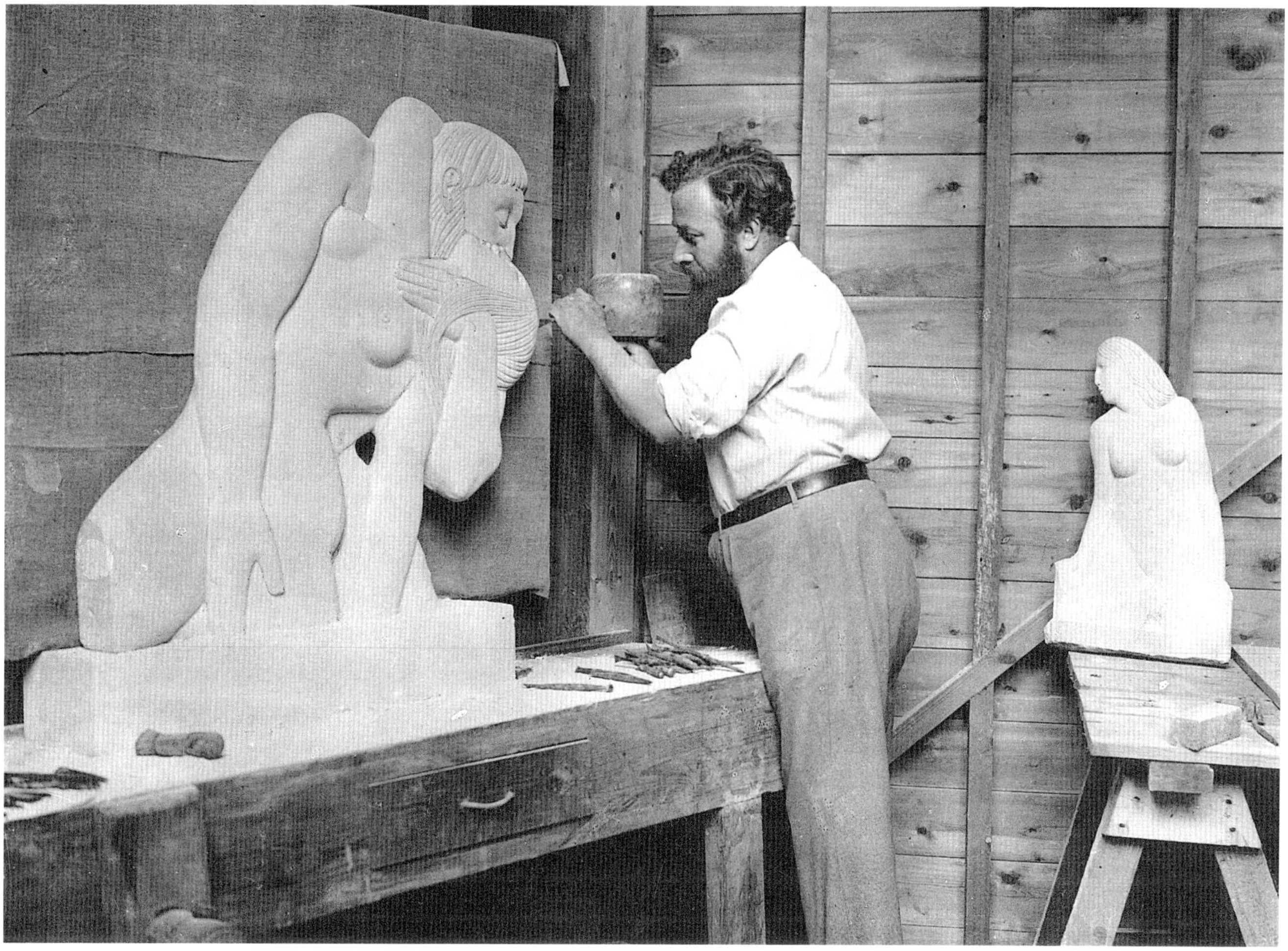

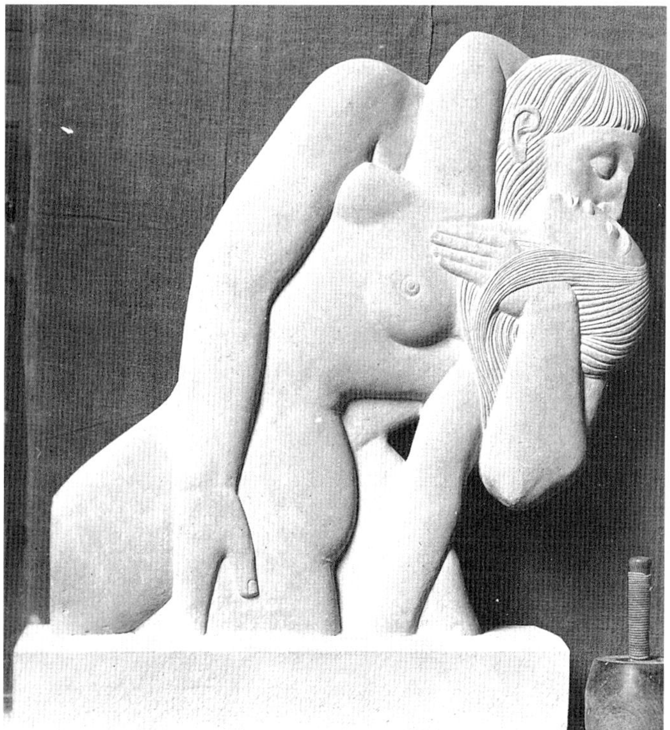

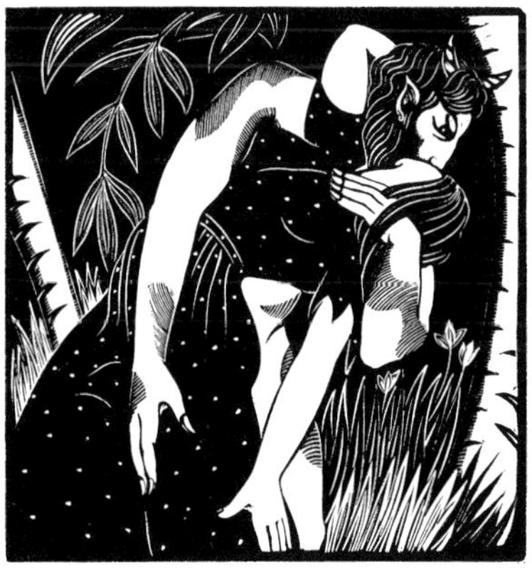

109 *top* Gibbings working on his sculpture (see 110 *left*) in the studio at Waltham St Lawrence. Sculpture *c.* 1928–29; the photograph was taken later for publicity purposes. RUL.
110 *left* Embracing couple, *c.* 1928–29, Portland stone, 1100 mm in height. This was his first sculpture and is now in the collections of the Museum of Reading. Photograph, Author's collection.
111 *right* Frontispiece from *A Mirror for Witches*, 1928, wood-engraving, 87 x 83 mm. Gibbings clearly based his sculpture on this composition.

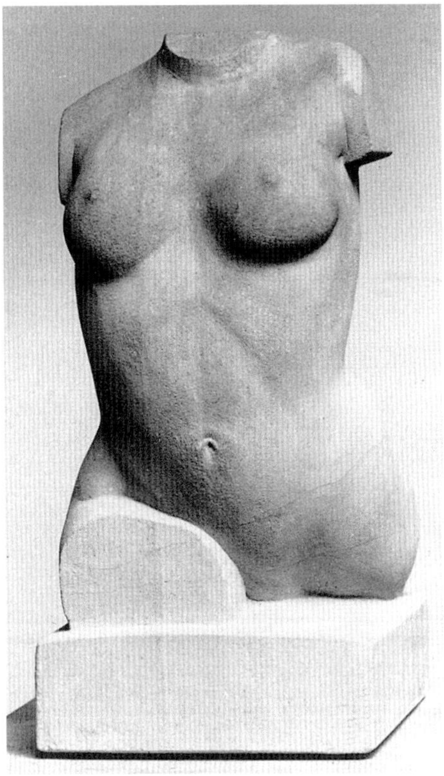

112 *Female Torso*, c. 1928–29, Bath stone, height unknown. This sculpture was based on drawings Gibbings made of an acrobatic dancer. It has now been lost. Photograph, RUL.

authors who worked for it, there were many enforced interludes during which, with sleeves unrolled and attending only to books, I got the feel of the stone better than if my biceps had been bulging. Eventually there came a day when I felt that to take away any more stone from my carving would not add to its significance, so with a prayer for the mellowing of time and weather I put it in my garden. To-day it stands on the lawn of the Hind's Head Hotel at Bray-on-Thames, whence visiting connoisseurs of art sometimes write me appreciative letters; others, less literate, put their mark direct upon the stone.[43]

Once his retreat in the Boltons studios had been established, Gibbings found subjects for further sculpture:

From an entrance hall decorated with plaster casts of figures in the classic style, modelled by a relative of the lady proprietor, there stretched a corridor with some thirty studios opening from it at regular intervals. There, in Number 14, I could work in peace, with any meals that I might need brought to me on a tray by Milly, daughter of the housekeeper and as lovely a girl as ever Renoir painted. The only interruptions to my thoughts were the succession of tappings at the studio door. 'Want a model?' was the inevitable greeting when I answered a summoning rap. There was unemployment at that time, and men and women of every age sought shillings for a few hour's work. ...It was from one such girl that I did my next carving. She told me that she was training to be an acrobatic dancer, but had a stiffness in the hips that prevented her getting as low in 'the splits' as she would have liked.

'Get as low as you can on the floor,' I said, 'and I'll do a drawing.'

From several that I made, fore and aft, I carved a torso in Bath stone. Then there came to me a lady of title who said that she did not wish to be paid; she just felt that her figure would be of interest to an artist. It was, and from it I did a small relief, with water lapping at the thighs.[44]

None of these distractions could be allowed to stop production at the Press. In June, Paul Nash's only illustrations for the Press were published in an edition of *Abd-er-Rhaman in Paradise*, by Jules Tellier; in August *Art and Prudence* was printed for Douglas Cleverdon and *A Tale of Rosamund Gray and Old Blind Margaret* by Charles Lamb was printed at the Press for Frank Hollings. Good publicity came in the form of an article by Charles Jacobi on the Golden Cockerel Press in a series on private presses for the *Penrose Annual*. The article outlined the character of the Press, its history, and some technical and bibliographical details. Generally admiring in tone, in quoting Gibbings on his aims and objectives for the Press, Jacobi had one criticism:

Mr. Gibbings, the controlling partner of the Press, confided to me that he hopes some day to acquire a special and distinctive typeface for the exclusive use of the Press. This gentleman has some very marked theories as to the production and marketing of books. These, perhaps, may be readily applied to the work of his Press, or to those working on the same lines. His work is more or less experimental, he tells me, and his endeavour is that each book shall not repeat a former success. His views on the subject of harmony between illustration or decoration and the type employed I generally agree with, but I am afraid that it is not always possible to put such ideas into actual practice, because I find in some instances that even the Golden Cockerel Press departs from that 'counsel of perfection' by the letterpress sometimes being overweighted by the designs, the extreme heaviness or solidity of the engravings being responsible for this when used on the same page. He abhors commercialism in the ordinary way and would create a spirit of working fellowship between author, artist and printer, which spirit may be more easily cultivated by those responsible for the control of private presses than those working under more commercial conditions.[45]

Although the article appeared in the annual for 1928, Jacobi had written it after a visit to the Press in the previous year, before the *Troilus* and *Lucian* had been published. Entries in Gill's diaries show that Jacobi had been correct in reporting Gibbings's wish for a 'special' and 'distinctive' typeface. Earlier that year Gill had been working on a typeface which had been commissioned by the Monotype Corporation and which later would become the classic face bearing his name — Gill Sans. In September, Gill recorded that he had started work on a new and exclusive typeface for the Golden Cockerel Press.

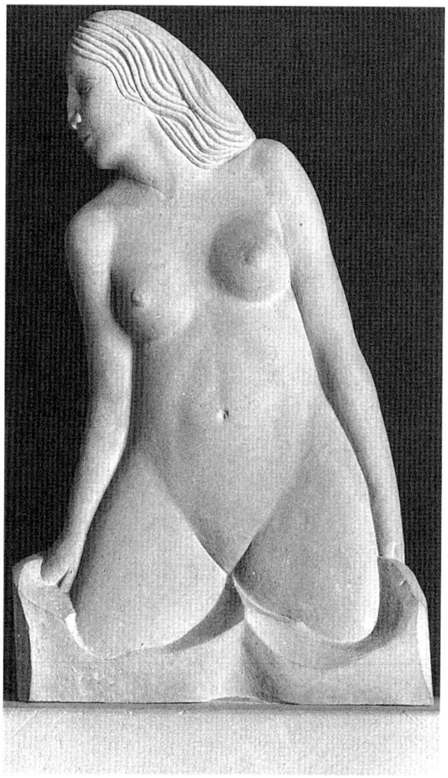

113 *Tahitian Woman*, c. 1929–30, Hopton Wood stone, 737 mm. in height. The sculpture, which Gibbings claimed was based on 'a lady of title' who was the model, was eventually bought by the Victoria & Albert Museum from its original owner and given this title. It is now on display in the gallery of Twentieth-century British Art and Design. Photograph, RUL.

Chapter Eight
New Horizons 1929–1931

IN THE MIDDLE of intense activity at the Press, and with so many projects underway, on 5 January 1929 Gibbings boarded a steam-liner bound for the South Seas. A belated notification appeared in the *Spring Prospectus*: 'Mr. Robert Gibbings is glad to announce that he is shortly making a trip to the South Pacific, and during his absence the typography of the Press will be under the most excellent supervision of Mr. Eric Gill.' The explanation behind his departure was not some kind of mid-life crisis, although he was only a few months away from his fortieth birthday, but that Gibbings had received a reply from the publishers, Houghton Mifflin, to his light-hearted, but no doubt inwardly genuine plea, to be allowed to escape the 'English fogs' for distant and exotic climes. Such good fortune rarely comes to ordinary people but Gibbings had a personality that seems to have attracted the interest and support of others; he recalled that the reply came 'in no time at all'. The publishers were full of enthusiasm:

> 'We are delighted with your idea of going to the Pacific. When will you be free to go? Find out what it will cost you, our partner will be in London in a month's time.'
>
> In a month's time I met the partner. 'We'll give you half your fee in advance,' he said, 'and the other half when you come back. Of course, we don't expect you ever *will* come back, but go out there anyway and make contact with James Norman Hall who lives there, and do a book together — anything you like.'
>
> In due course I sailed, in sleet and snow, from Tilbury, in the Orient Line *Otranto* for Sidney, and after a few days there I sailed again in the Union Line *Makura* bound for Tahiti.[1]

However, this was not some rash act of generosity. Houghton Mifflin had been delighted with the reception of *A Mirror for Witches* and had been quick to appreciate the potential of investing in Gibbings's work. They came up with the concept of a book which was to be a collaborative effort, combining the illustrative talents of Gibbings with the words of the author James Norman Hall. Gibbings signed a contract with the publishers in October 1928 and in the new year found himself on the way to Tahiti, where Hall lived, with a brief to plan a book.[2] Hall, later to become well known as the author of the highly successful novel about the mutiny on the *Bounty*,[3] had settled in Tahiti shortly after the First World War and had married a local Tahitian girl. On docking, Gibbings was greeted by Hall's wife who explained that her husband had a bad leg caused by coral poisoning and was unable to travel into the port of Papeete but was waiting to welcome him at their home a few miles outside the town. Gibbings had planned to stay for four months, after which he must return to the Press. He was given an old thatched beach house, built in native style, close to the seashore with views out over the coral reef and the lagoon, near to Hall's house which was on the inland side of the coastal road.

He was soon comfortably settled. Hall and Gibbings quickly became warm friends; writing in 1952 shortly after Hall's death, Gibbings remembered him with affection: 'Slight of build and gentle in manner, he was strong in kindness: 'Jeemee' to his Tahitian wife, 'Papa Halli' to the natives of the island, 'my best friend' to every man that I have met who had ever met him.'[4] As yet Hall had written nothing but he outlined to Robert his plans for a volume of essays on local life. Unfortunately, Hall was for the moment preoccupied with work on an American edition of the *Bounty* story and could spare no time for this new project. Given that his visit was limited, Hall advised Gibbings not to wait for him but to spend the time available absorbing impressions of the life and landscape of the place and in making as many drawings as possible. If Gibbings's sketches covered enough subject material, something was bound to be appropriate to illustrate his text once it had been written.

Four months later, in April, the time arrived for Gibbings to return to England. He had fulfilled his side of the contract and accumulated plenty of visual material and reference for the proposed book, but Hall still showed no sign of starting the text. If Robert felt frustrated by this uncertainty about the project he had at least achieved his ambition to visit the South Seas. The people, landscape, and way of life had made a lasting impression — he felt a deep affinity with the lifestyle of the native folk, and was saddened by the threat to it from newcomers. But he had also hatched an idea for another publication entirely:

> ... I had material for a little book of my own, a tale told to me on the quay at Papeete almost as my ship sailed, by a local character, Bill Bambridge, and relating how his grandfather had survived shipwreck among cannibals and 'lived happily ever after.' Sitting in a deck-chair in the French mail-boat that took me as far homewards as Martinique, I put the story into 189 words and 15 drawings.[5]

The finished book entitled, *The Seventh Man*, was published by the Press the following year.

Not long after his return to Waltham, Gibbings received a letter from Hall in which he wrote that he had pulled down the old house that Robert had stayed in and was building a new and bigger one in its place: '... it is yours whenever you come back. We call it "The House that waits for Robert"'.[6] In years to come he would return but now he had to face coming back to the life at Waltham; how had things gone in his absence?

Gibbings returned to 'abominable spring weather' and must have found it hard to adjust. The *Autumn Prospectus*, again belatedly, announced: 'Contrary to the fears of a few and the expectations of many, the *Golden Cockerel*, alias Robert Gibbings, has returned from Tahiti bringing a store of material which he hopes to make use of in future publications of the Press.' — The tone is light hearted but underlying the comment there was perhaps a more serious recognition of the impact the trip had made on Robert. The cover of the prospectus was adorned by a new depiction of the cockerel, engraved by Gibbings.[7] The cockerel is shown on the run, perhaps symbolic of his feelings, against the background of a tropical tree.

In his absence things had carried on much as normal. Gill had moved with his family into Pigotts and was therefore able to keep in closer contact with the Press. The declaration that the Press was under his 'supervision' while Gibbings was away must have annoyed Moira, as she was effectively in charge on a day-to-day basis, but happy to seek Gill's advice on design matters. It was left to Moira to see through the final production and launch of volume one of *The Canterbury Tales* which appeared in February 1929. The edition was already 'out of print' before publication. It was seen as something of an event by the book buying public and attracted the attention of the press. This first volume used very much the same formula and design as had been used for *Troilus* and was received with similar acclaim.

Work was well advanced on the subsequent volumes of the Chaucer but other projects were in progress too. Moira needed an additional illustration for an edition of Sir Thomas More's *Utopia*, for which Gill had engraved some floreated initials. The editor wanted to include symbols of the Utopian alphabet, so Moira appealed to Gill: 'As far as I can see the only way would be for you to engrave them on wood ... but is it worth it? ... Let me know what you think and what it would cost ... also how long ... I don't want to hold up publication for a mere whim. ... Young has been away for a week with the flu, so work has not been rushing along.'[8] Gill's advice was also needed on volume two of the Chaucer: '... the men might begin setting up the prose tale next week. Do you want them to justify the lines or not, and do you know yet what space you require at the beginning, middle or end for decorations? You did tell me these things once before but I fear that I have forgotten them — abject apologies'. Gill dictated his reply to his wife as he too was suffering from flu but he was anxious to help: '... I can easily do an engraving of the Utopian Alphabet. ... I think it will make a handsome little decoration as well as of literary interest'.[9] By return of post, Moira hastily thanked Gill, for she was '... just tearing off to town for the day but have left orders for the men to pull you a set of proofs of the final pp. of *Utopia*, showing the general arrangement of all the catchy bits and the space at your disposal for the alphabet at the end'.[10] Moira was coping but finding it hard going; in March she sent another SOS:

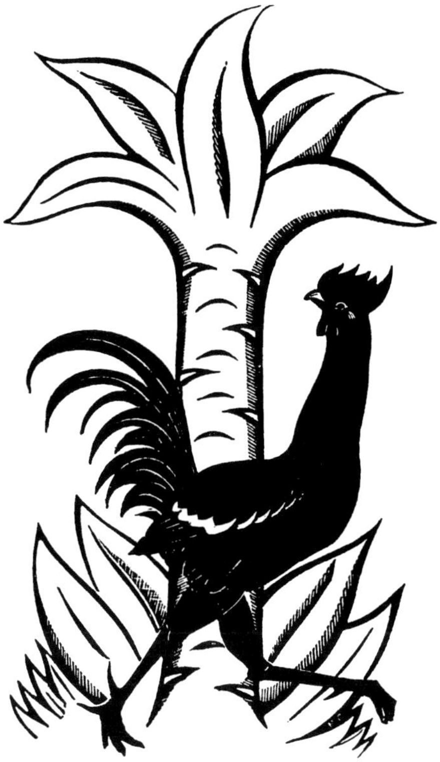

114 A running cockerel, 1929, wood-engraving, 109 x 60 mm. This device was used on the cover of the October list. Gibbings made several versions of this device.

> Will you regard me as the most pernicious pest if I throw myself on your mercy and ask you to help me out with a couple of jobs of a like nature — please not! Its like this. There are in *Tristram Shandy* one page of just a marbled design and three with a few lines of calligraphic scrawls which have to be reproduced somehow. Bob told me to write to Laboureur about it, which I did, but he says that he never touches wood these days, and in any case that he was never sufficiently proficient to play such tricks as these. Bob was going to do them himself on wood if he had been here, but as he isn't, would you be so kind?[11]

All the illustrations Laboureur had produced for the Press had been intaglio prints on copper. The same medium had been used by Gill in the *Procreant Hymn* but generally Gibbings intended that they should concentrate on wood-engraved

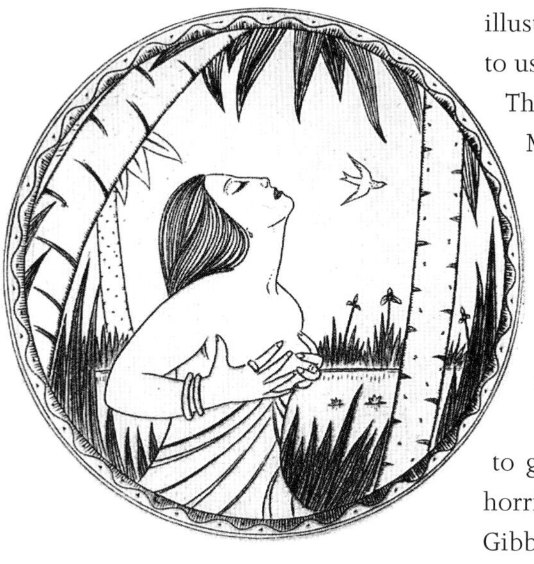

115 Illustration from *A Circle of the Seasons*, 1929, copper engraving, image diameter 81 mm.

illustration.[12] Gibbings declared that 'Strictly speaking it is against our principles to use copper plates ... we hope as time goes on to do fewer of these books ...'.[13] This might have been his intention but in February an edition of Powys Mathers's prose poem based on oriental sources, *A Circle of the Seasons*, was also published, with four copper-engravings by Gibbings, representing each season. Engraved before he set off for Tahiti, Gibbings was disappointed with the result when he returned to see the finished book. Perhaps his comments about intaglio printing were the result of his awareness that, however successful the images were on their own, they did not comfortably match the weight of the italic type.

By May, Gibbings was back in harness and Moira had taken the opportunity to get away for a break, leaving Robert to manage on his own: 'I miss Moira horribly but I do think she deserves a jolly good holiday and I hope she gets it.'[14] Gibbings was writing to Gill about an accounting error; going through the books they discovered they had overpaid Gill, who seemed little concerned and happily agreed to the amount being deducted from his next invoice. Gibbings's letter also refers to some initial letters which Gill was working on. Frank Young, the compositor, was unhappy about the way one of these letters was working: '... he wants you to see the "A" as he thinks perhaps you might like to remove that initial altogether. He thinks very diffidently, it looks wrong and feels that you might not want it to go through'. The 'A' was dropped; both men respected the views of the tradesmen at the Press and Gibbings happily acknowledged the importance of the compositor's contribution.

Sir Thomas More's *Utopia* appeared in April, followed by the first of the three volumes of Laurence Sterne's *Tristram Shandy*, with engravings by Laboureur. Later in the year *Abyss* by Leonid Andreyev with wood-engravings by Ivan Lebedeff, a leading Russian engraver who was living in France, was published. Two further volumes of the Chaucer and *Tristram Shandy* were scheduled to appear in November and in the same month *The Atrocities of the Pirates* by Aaron Smith was published, with ten wood-engravings by Eric Ravilious. This last book, first published in 1824, described the true adventures of the author, who had been captured by pirates off the coast of Cuba.

Gibbings had approached Ravilious about the commission in October 1928, and the book had been planned before he left for Tahiti. Gibbings had his own precious volume of the tale which he sent to Ravilious for his opinion; Ravilious was enthusiastic and the swashbuckling story appealed to him. Fees were negotiated for a series of small blocks to fit the measure: 'We will be doing the book crown octavo and the measure of the type will be about 3¼" so that the blocks ought to be 3¼" by about 1½" or 2" '.[15] Ravilious seems to have reacted with boyish excitement at the possibility of illustrating such melodramatic but true events: 'I want to do the fight with knives, and also the occasion when Aaron comes upon four of them playing cards under a tree in the middle of the night. The mangrove swamps would be good too'.[16] Gibbings encouraged him: 'I quite agree that the more "bloody" they are, the better!'[17] While Gibbings was away in the following year, Moira had to check on the progress of the illustrations because by March 1929 Ravilious was a little behind.[18] Towards the end of April, knowing that she was shortly going on holiday, Moira was pushing to tie up last minute details. It is possible that she was intending to leave before Robert's return, as she informed Ravilious that she was leaving Gill in charge in her absence. Ravilious had further requests for a bright red cover, which the Press readily agreed to, but when three months later 'he was anxiously begging for payment', the secretary, Lucy Cook, had to put him off. Both Moira and Robert were away at the same time in July and Lucy felt that she could not authorise payment herself, making the excuse that the Press only paid after publication — it is more likely that again it was a problem of cash flow. Lucy wrote to Ravilious in July with an explanation: 'We are sending you herewith a cheque for £50. We regret that we could not let you have the cheque some weeks ago when you asked for it but just then the state of our exchequer made it quite impossible'.

Another book appeared in November which, although printed at the Golden Cockerel Press, bore another imprint — Four Elms Press — with Lucy Cook named as the printer. Entitled *When Grandmama was Young*, it was a collection of Victorian verses for children. In fact, this book was intended as the first in a series of children's books to be published under this imprint and edited by Moira. It was to be her own enterprise supported by Lucy Cook, and was possibly intended to gave Moira some independence and a chance to develop her own ideas without being overshadowed by her husband. A prospectus for the Four Elms Press, announcing their first book, was published in April 1929. On the cover was a specially designed device, followed by a statement of aims and objectives. 'Value as reading matter' was the overriding criterion for selection; the intention was to publish books that 'children themselves like' rather than 'books which grown-ups like for children'. The book was illustrated with lino-cuts by William McCance[19] which were hand coloured by the pochoir method, a 'pleasing effect for modern book decoration in France'.[20] The book had a fresh and contemporary feel but perhaps the climate was not right for limited edition books aimed at children. For what ever reason, *When Grandmama was Young* was the only book to be produced under this imprint.

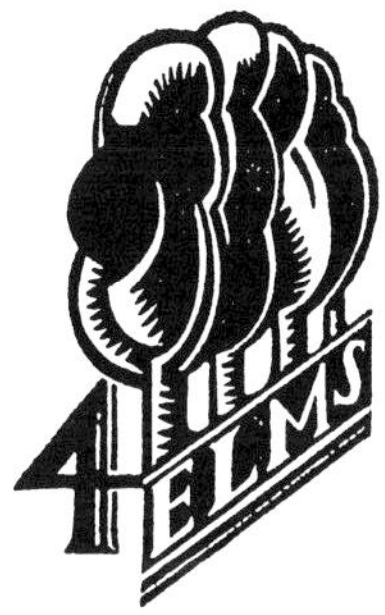

116 Device for the Four Elms Press used on a prospectus for *When Grandmama was Young*, 1929. Designed by William McCance. Gibbings Collection, Department of Typography & Graphic Communication, The University of Reading.

EARLIER IN 1929, in the February issue of *The Studio*, an article by Robert appeared in his absence. He wrote a short piece on the Golden Cockerel Press; in answer to his own question 'Why do we publish limited editions?' Gibbings gave a similar reply to the one he had given in the article in *The Woodcut* in 1927: 'Once interest flags, quality deteriorates … an edition of 500 is the most that any man can be expected to print with interest. Printing dry on machine-made paper is another story. A modern machine can do 4,000 per hour. At the Golden Cockerel Press we do about 4,000 per week.'[21] He went on to describe the delicate process of printing on damped hand-made papers; with dampening '… the minimum of ink and pressure are required, thereby achieving a really clean impression of each individual letter, and thus preserving its character'. For an artist and wood-engraver, Gibbings's concern for the quality of printing went far beyond the images — he was concerned about the type itself. His experience of typefaces had been strictly limited; from his hesitant efforts in handsetting with J. H. Mason, he was only familiar with Caslon Old Face and this was the main typeface in use at the Press when he took over. Mason and others had revived Caslon and made it popular again, especially with the private presses. 'Why do we use only Caslon Old Face type?' Gibbings asked; 'Because we do not know of a better design', he answered. His lack of familiarity with other typefaces had led to him to be rather conservative in the past but surprisingly passionate in his views:

> It has been suggested from time to time that a new type should be designed to go with modern woodcuts, but they who do so forget that even if type could be produced to go with every 'ism' of the studios (and at present the answer appears to be in the negative), very few printers, least of all the private Presses, could afford to stock quantities which might perhaps be used for one book, and then discarded. As has been said, Type is traditional: its forms are as static as the forms of our legs and arms. Indeed, it seems that both lettering and legs, alphabets and arms, achieved their highest perfection at the same period. (*Vide* Trajan column.) But why that is so is outside the present article. Let those who demand new types remember that Giotto was content to decorate the buildings he was offered, neither did Michelangelo nor Pisano object to the current shape of bricks.[22]

However his views had modified by the time he wrote the article in *The Studio*: 'If we could find a type face more beautiful or more suitable to print the classics, we would certainly use it and to this end we are now experimenting, in collaboration with Mr. Eric Gill, to find a design which will suit our needs even better than the above-named [Caslon].'

Initially Gibbings had just wanted an italic to go with the Caslon Old Face. Gill, writing to Morison in June 1928 in reply to his request for an italic to accompany Gill's 'Roman' (Perpetua), pointed out that his '... agreement with the G.C.P. specially bars me from designing new founts of type except for the G.C.P. and they are particularly anxious that I shd. do a new italic to go with the Caslon l.c. & yet be an improvement on the existing Caslon italic'.[23] This was awkward for Gill who had recently been appointed Monotype's type consultant but he was loyal: 'I think it's all fair and square. G.C.P. wants me to do for them various types. I agree. So they say well give us the bloody things then & don't go spreading yourself on other people till you've done ours.'[24]

Gill, an amazingly industrious person, was in a period of intense activity. Wood-engraving was only one facet of his professional life — he was becoming an internationally known sculptor; there was constant work as a letterer in stone for commemorative and memorial work; he was always writing, on top of which, through Stanley Morison and the Monotype Corporation, he was finding a new enthusiasm for type design.[25] Gill's technical knowledge of the intricacies of letter spacing and the finer details of punch-cutting was limited; he freely admitted the letterforms he had designed were based on those he used when lettercutting in stone or signwriting. He relied on the experts at Monotype to make presentable and functioning typefaces of them. But this had been invaluable experience for him to draw upon when designing the Golden Cockerel type. Plans for an edition of *The Four Gospels* were taking shape and Gibbings and Gill were both unsure whether Caslon was quite right for what they had in mind — such a prestigious book demanded something special. A large format had been chosen for the book which allowed for a large typesize; 18-point type was decided upon and working on this generous scale meant that Gill could sketch out his ideas for the letters using an ordinary square-nib pen. He started the design by writing out a part of the Lord's prayer, at the exact 18-point size, as a base which he then had photographically enlarged to eight times the original size. On these prints he was able to correct and build up the letter accurately by touching up in black ink and process white — the prints could then be reduced again to see what corrections were needed. Next, Gill made drawings of each letter at 1½" in height. The general look and shape of the letters that emerged were clearly influenced by his designs for Perpetua, but were heavier and more robust, specifically to take into account the need to harmonise with modern wood-engravings, or in Gill's words, 'a heavy, closely massing type'. But Gill was also influenced by two other typefaces which he greatly admired — the inevitable Caslon and a Jenson style Roman. He had examples of both typefaces blown up to his working size to allow direct comparisons with his own letters.

After some initial work in September 1928, perhaps preoccupied with his move to Pigotts, Gill's diary does not record any more progress on the Cockerel type until December, but in March and April 1929 Gill worked consistently on the project and completed most of the work. Early summer was taken up with engraving for volume two of *The Canterbury Tales* and in late August he started on those for volume three. In September, work on the type was entering a production phase; on the ninth, Robert and Moira visited Gill at Pigotts to discuss the

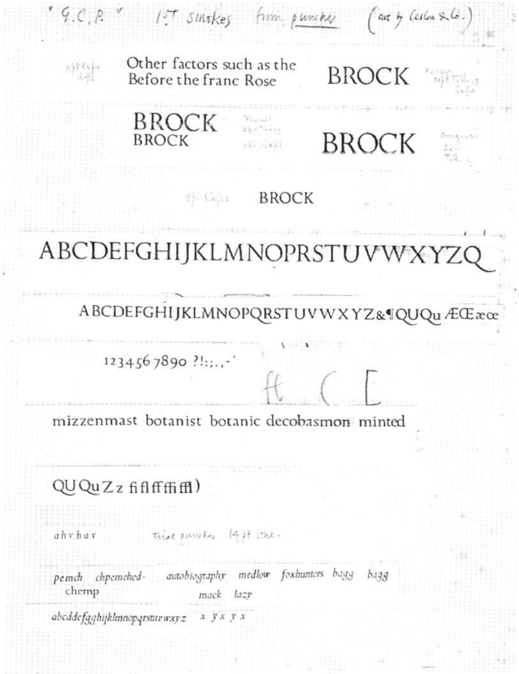

117 First smoke proofs from the punches for the Golden Cockerel type designed by Eric Gill and cut by H. W. Caslon & Co. in 1929. Clark Library.

final details and Gill worked on them the next morning. On 17 September, Gill visited Gibbings at his London studio and they both went to the typefoundry of H. W. Caslon & Co. to arrange the punch cutting; they visited again in October and a number of times in November and December. Brass patterns had been made from Gill's drawings and, using a pantographic device, punches for different sizes were cut. Matrices were subsequently made and two text founts successfully cast on 18 and 14-point bodies. Gibbings also ordered a titling fount of capitals on a 24-point body using the same brass patterns to cut the punches.[26] Unfortunately there was a problem:

> ... I had ordered 24 point titling from the same designs. But when this arrived, we found that it lacked something of the distinction of the 18 point. The thicks and thins had lost a little of their balance in the larger size. And yet the work was mathematically correct. It was an interesting demonstration to us both that mathematics and aesthetics do not always agree, and that one of the greatest changes you can make in a design is to alter its scale. For the 36 point titling which I commissioned soon afterwards, Eric worked again on his designs, reducing the weight of the horizontals in proportion to that of the verticals, and so retrieved the lost elegance of the design.[27]

The October prospectus had announced:

> With regard to the long promised sample page of the *Four Gospels*, this has only been held up by the fact that the Press was particularly anxious that this volume should be the first to be printed in the new Golden Cockerel type, designed by Mr. Eric Gill. The drawings are now with the punch cutter, and it is confidently expected that the appearance of this new fount will constitute a very important event in typographic history. Delivery of the type has been promised early in January ....

WITH GIBBINGS AWAY for so much of 1929 it was fortunate that the running of the workshops was professionally organised. His supportive staff were well able to carry on without him but his absence inevitably had the effect that fewer new publications were planned for the coming year. Most of their effort was dedicated to work on *The Four Gospels*, yet Gill was also occupied with initial designs for an edition of *The Phaedo of Plato*, and was still working on further volumes of *The Canterbury Tales* and *Tristram Shandy*. The *Spring Prospectus* for 1930 opened with words of buoyant optimism: 'Of editions de luxe there is no end and much fine printing is a weariness to the purse, nevertheless the Golden Cockerel hails the New Year with radiant comb and bristling spurs, fortified by the ever-increasing appreciation of connoisseurs.'[28] This rousing greeting was perhaps an attempt to revive Gibbings's own flagging spirits. Sample pages from *The Four Gospels* and *The Canterbury Tales* were included in the prospectus, together with a sample page for a proposed edition of *Paradise Lost* which was later dropped.[29] The pages from *The Four Gospels* and *Paradise Lost* were set in the much heralded Golden Cockerel type; Gibbings was anxious that 'its first encounter with the world' should be 'associated with the richest of English prose'.

At the end of the previous year Gibbings had cut a wood-engraved frontispiece for *The Man from Kisheelan* by A. E. Coppard which appeared in January 1930, but only produced engravings for one other book that year — his own story *The*

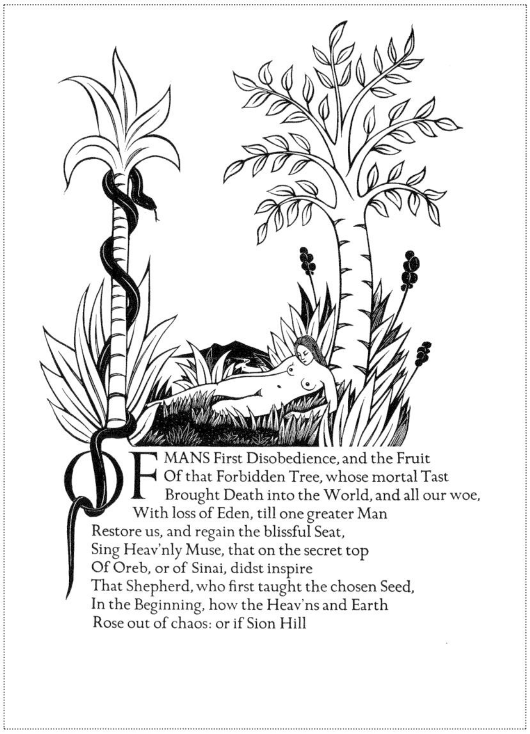
OF MANS First Disobedience, and the Fruit
Of that Forbidden Tree, whose mortal Tast
Brought Death into the World, and all our woe,
With loss of Eden, till one greater Man
Restore us, and regain the blissful Seat,
Sing Heav'nly Muse, that on the secret top
Of Oreb, or of Sinai, didst inspire
That Shepherd, who first taught the chosen Seed,
In the Beginning, how the Heav'ns and Earth
Rose out of chaos: or if Sion Hill

118 Specimen page for Milton's *Paradise Lost.* This project was never completed but the specimen was one of the first pages to be set in Golden Cockerel type. Reproduced by permission of the Golden Cockerel Press Ltd.

Seventh Man, which did not come out until August. Business was booming; Robert's own reputation and that of the Press seemed established. Yet he was not settled, something in his character rebelled against responsibilities that restricted him. He was restless and beginning to tire of being a printer and publisher. In a letter to Balston in June 1930, Gibbings mentions that he had been trying to organise an exhibition of his paintings; but yet again the demands of the Press had overwhelmed him:

> Alas! I've had to postpone my show, simply can't get enough time from here, so much that I feel tempted to sell this blooming bird. I've worked out that on a price which would enable me to clear out there is at least an easy 10% or 12% after paying a manager. So if you know any one with an itch to print, let me know. We are completely sold out for the next twelve months, so now would be an easy time to start. I'd really clear out tomorrow if I got a buyer though actually the show is 100% better than it has ever been before.[30]

Business had been so good that Robert and Moira had recently taken a financial risk and bought the Press themselves. Mary Wiggin had married and in January 1929 documents had been drawn up dissolving their partnership; Robert had raised new finance for the business by arranging a mortgage and had taken out a loan with Barclays Bank. The Bank manager was encouraging, helped by the fact that he was an enthusiastic collector of Golden Cockerel books himself. Now they were financially independent of sleeping partners but the Bank was to prove a less sympathetic backer. Regular repayments had to be met and for Gibbings, already feeling oppressed, this obligation must have increased his feeling of being trapped. As Cave and Manson point out, large projects such as *The Canterbury Tales* and *The Four Gospels* tied up working capital 'for uncomfortably long periods' and cash flow continued to be a problem. At times the Gibbings household would suffer periods of desperate lack of money and struggle to keep up payments. Cave and Manson have commented on how the couple were coping with the growing financial pressure:

> Neither Robert nor Moira was temperamentally able to handle this. The ever faithful Coppard still gave advice, and still spent a day or two each month keeping the Press's accounts, but they needed more than this part-time help. It was hard for Robert to take the frustration of having to devote a lot of his time to business or editorial matters which didn't interest him at all, when all he wanted was to be able to get on with creating his own engravings, or paintings, or sculpture.[31]

Two articles on book illustration appeared in *The Studio* in 1930 and both featured work by the artists commissioned by the Press and by Gibbings himself. Maximilien Vox wrote on contemporary wood-engraving and reproduced a print by Gibbings of tropical fish entitled *Oiri and Friends*.[32] The second article on modern illustrated books included an illustration of the sample page of *Paradise Lost*, greatly reduced. The caption praises the book as 'incomparably the most ambitious and "superb" of the books here mentioned' and with publication expected in the autumn, the book was anticipated to be 'a well-nigh perfect example of the high peaks of British book-work ....'[33] — with such publicity it must have been an embarrassment when it failed to appear! Even greater praise came in an article by Malcolm Salaman in *The New Woodcut*, which was the special Spring number of *The Studio* for 1930. Again heavily illustrated with wood-engravings by artists working for the Golden Cockerel Press, Gibbings's work was represented by *Pandanus Grove, Tahiti*, which, together with *Oiri and Friends*, was one of the illustrations Gibbings had engraved from drawings made on his trip to Tahiti. In his article, Salaman acknowledges Gibbings's influence in the world of wood-engraving and his skill and vision in commissioning so many leading artists and finding just the right texts to allow them to show their talents. Gibbings's technical skill and his ability to adapt his style and mood is commended:

> His touch on the wood is eminently individual in its combination of black and white masses with the informing line, he handles the medium as its master, and confides his expression to it with light-hearted faithfulness. What ironic humour he has infused into his little illustrations to Swift's poems, as, for instance, the austere quartet of lady card-players, with what noble beauty he has caught suggestions from Keats's 'Eve of St. Agnes' and 'Hyperion,' how freshly he has let his imagination play in decorating the charming page of English and Greek type that gives us *The True Historie of Lucian, the Samosatenian*, very choice books all these.[34]

The Phaedo of Plato, with exuberant floreated initials by Gill, printed in red, appeared in April 1930, followed by *Lucina Sine Concubitu*, a peculiar little book published as a companion volume to the book of etiquette for young ladies, which reprinted an address given to the Royal Society in 1750 on the subject of whether 'women may conceive and be brought to bed without any commerce with men'. It was illustrated with three copper-engravings by Hester Sainsbury who also designed a special paper for the binding consisting of a repeat

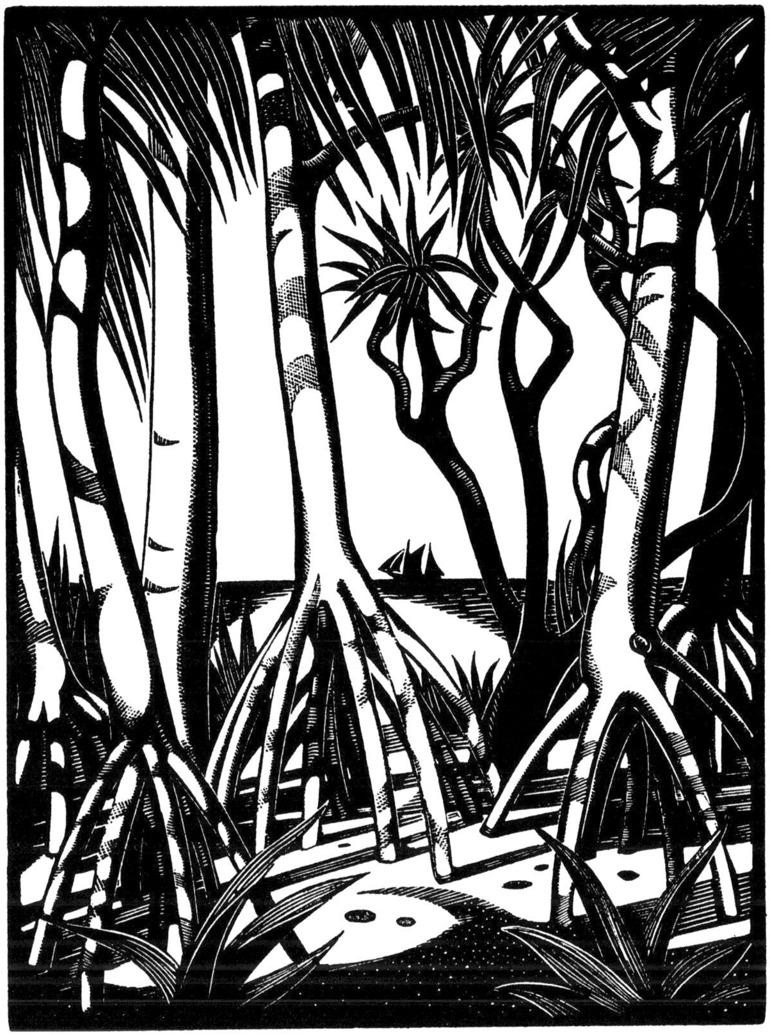

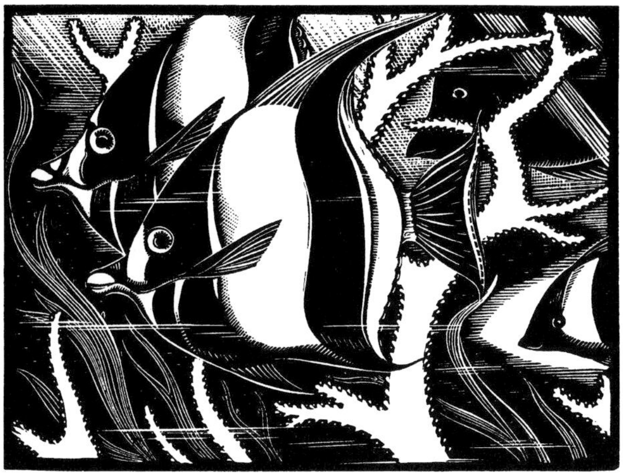

119 *left Pandanus Grove*, Tahiti, *c.* 1930, wood-engraving, 135 x 102 mm. Intended as an illustration for a book by James Norman Hall but eventually used in *Iorana*.

120 *above Oiri and Friends*, *c.* 1930, wood-engraving, 75 x 102 mm. This engraving was based on drawings Gibbings had made in Tahiti and was used as an illustration in his book *Iorana*.

wood-engraved pattern of a stylised naked figure printed in sepia on a deep buff paper. In June an edition of *Maya* was published with thirteen wood-engravings by Blair Hughes-Stanton. When Gibbings arranged for permission to publish the play through the Gate Theatre, its author, Simon Gantillon, who had been pleased with the Hughes-Stanton engravings for the programme of the 1928 Gate production, suggested that he would like the same artist to illustrate this new edition. Blair Hughes-Stanton was an artist of very personal vision and had an individual approach to wood-engraving. Gibbings was impressed by his work, describing some illustrations Hughes-Stanton had done for an edition of *The Pilgrim's Progress* as 'the outstanding event' of a recent exhibition held by the Society of Wood Engravers. His images were much more complex in conception than the literal illustrations which were more the norm with other illustrators used by the Press. He experimented with abstract elements of pattern and shape and delicate texture, introducing subtle grey tones into his often highly symbolic compositions. The plot of *Maya* provided an opportunity to explore his interest in the human form and the complexities of the relationships between men and women. The play revolved around the life of a prostitute, 'a moth or butterfly whose

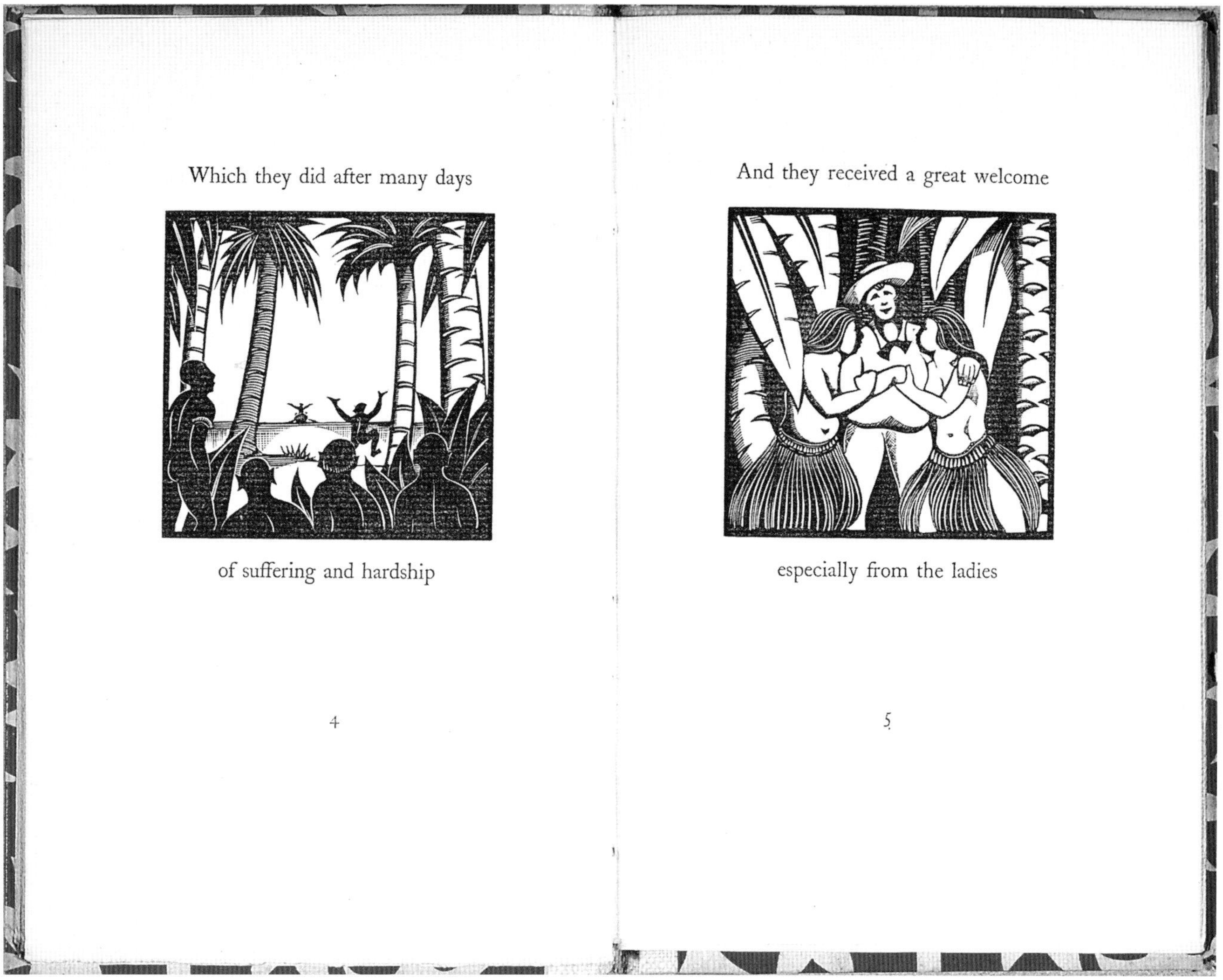

121 Double page spread from *The Seventh Man, a True Cannibal Tale of the South Seas*, 1930, page size 190 x 125 mm. A powerful design of a stylised skull and palm tree printed in black and red was used on the binding. Reproduced by permission of the Golden Cockerel Press Ltd.

wings are painted by every man in the colours of desire'. Original though the engravings were, they presented difficulties for the printer — as with David Jones's engraving in *The Deluge*, Cooper had problems holding the fine white lines. Hughes-Stanton was a difficult person at the best of times and his dissatisfaction with the reproduction of his blocks led to rows with Gibbings. 'Mr Gibbings was not very good at printing my rather black wood-engravings. He used a lot of ink. We ended hardly on speaking terms. The paper was practically impossible.'[35] His views of the problem were exaggerated, but the choice of paper was indeed not good as the solid black areas of his figures suffer from the laid mark of the paper showing through.

In August, Gibbings's own book which he had promised as a result of his trip to Tahiti, appeared. *The Seventh Man, a True Cannibal Tale of the South Seas* was told in '15 wood-engravings and precisely 189 words' — it hardly constituted a piece of serious literature, but this was technically his first published book as an author. This small and slight book was certainly a very original concept; Gibbings retold in his own words the story he had heard on the dockside at Papeete. Delightfully humorous and uncomplicated, it is a book that Gibbings clearly enjoyed making. What gave him the idea for such a simple form — one squared up illustration per page with just one or two lines of text above or below — is uncertain. The almost comic strip approach has appeal and simple charm and it was a format that he was to return to later. Following the example of Hester Sainsbury, Gibbings designed an appropriate cover paper with a repeating pattern, but this time combining a palm tree with a human skull printed in black on a deep red — Gibbings was developing a taste for colourful bindings. He had also been working on engravings for a new story by Coppard, *The Hundredth Story of A. E. Coppard*, which was announced for publication in the next year as a uniform edition to *Count Stefan*. The last book to be printed that year was *A Journey from This World to the Next* by Henry Fielding, with etchings by Denis Tegetmeier, uniform with *Tristram Shandy*.

Over seventy books had been produced by the Press since 1921, and a full bibliography was published to accompany an exhibition of Golden Cockerel books, held by the booksellers J. & E. Bumpus Ltd at their premises in Oxford Street, between April and May 1930. Virtually all the books were marked as being out of print, but a note from Bumpus in the catalogue advertised that they had copies on their shelves.

IN THE AUTUMN OF 1930 Gibbings was looking for a suitable book on which to collaborate with Eric Ravilious. Ravilious suggested an edition of Shakespeare's *Twelfth Night* which, after careful consideration, Gibbings agreed was a 'very feasible proposition'. Gibbings ordered three hundredweight of new Golden Cockerel type with which he proposed to set the text in galley proof and then they could design the book together: '... we can chop it about and paste up to taste and then you can carry on with the whole book. As far as I can see we could pay you about £200 for the job which I hope will be agreeable.[36] Plans for *Twelfth Night* progressed over the following months. Robert and Moira invited Ravilious and his new wife Tirzah to stay at Waltham for a weekend at the end of November to discuss the project in detail: 'We are daily expecting delivery of the new type and hope to have some pages set up by the time you come down.'[37] The two couples got on well and Moira and Robert enjoyed their visit and were looking forward to them 'coming along to camp in the orchard hut in the spring'.[38]

Eric Ravilious and Tirzah had married that summer. She was an ex-pupil of Eric's who had taken on some part-time teaching, and was a talented artist and printmaker in her own right. Gibbings had hoped to find a suitable commission for her too, without success,[39] but had been very pleased by some patterns she had designed for printing onto binding cloth. A repeating star pattern devised by Tirzah became a regular feature of the Press's bindings over the next few years. The design incorporated the initials of the Press but for each new book the pattern was adapted to include the initials of each author.

The regular visits from Gill continued and as usual discussions about work ended with relaxed and sociable evenings. On one visit in June, Gill completed

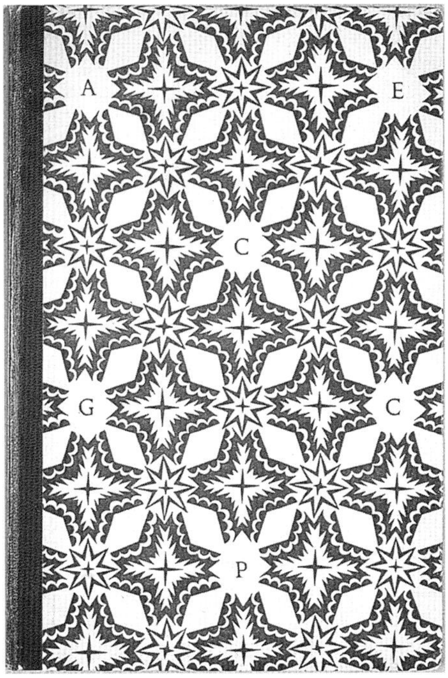

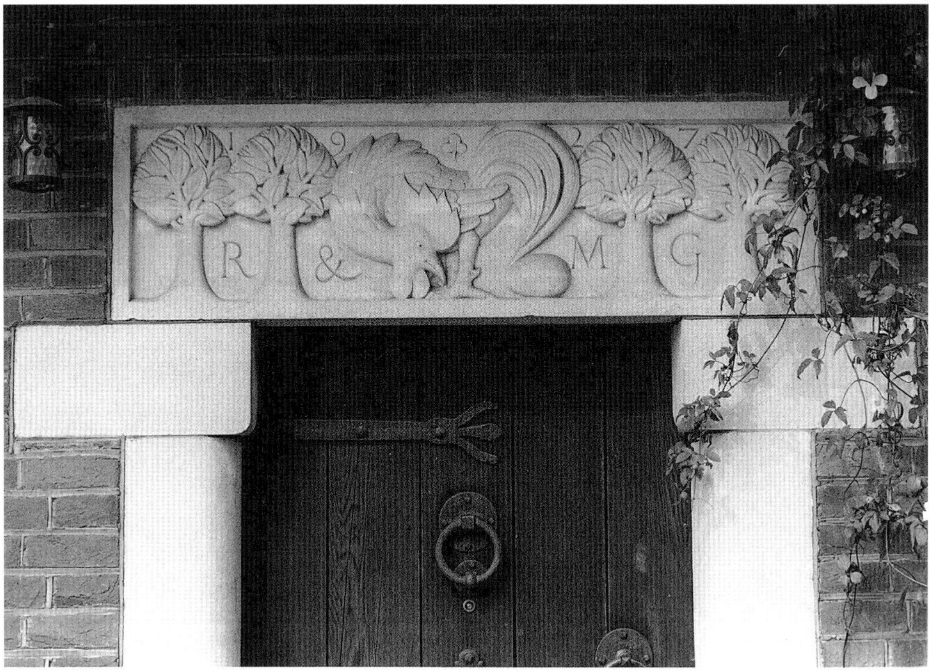

122 *above* Design used on the binding cloth of the Guinea Series from an engraving by Tirzah Ravilious. This example is *The Hundredth Story*, 1931, by A. E. Coppard and his initials and those of the Press are incorporated in the design. Reproduced by permission of the Golden Cockerel Press Ltd.

123 *above right* Relief carving by Eric Gill on the lintel stone over the doorway at Four Elms. Photograph taken in 1989.

the relief carving on the lintel stone over the doorway at Four Elms during a day punctuated by games of nude tennis, quoits and sunbathing. Not long after this Gill appropriately began work on 'an essay on the nude' which the Press published the following year as *Clothing Without Cloth*. Busy as ever, Gill was still working on *The Canterbury Tales* throughout the summer and on another typeface which he named Joanna, after his daughter Joan. In September he experienced a traumatic breakdown which took the form of an attack of temporary amnesia; he became so ill that at one point his life seemed in danger. Fiona McCarthy has analysed this crisis and has looked for possible causes in the contradiction between Gill's religious and public life and his extraordinary private sexual behaviour and domestic life. The diversity of his talents brought about its own pressures and confusion over his identity as an artist. After so many years of intensive work together, both men seem to have run out of steam at the same time. Gill's crisis led to a period in hospital, the pressure on Gibbings led to an ever increasing desire for change and escape.

Once over the worst, Gill seems to have rather enjoyed his stay in hospital being administered to by nuns. News of Gill's illness had been a shock to Robert and Moira and Gibbings sent his best wishes in the form of a chatty note scribbled on a postcard. To amuse Gill, Gibbings had drawn the outline of a curvaceous nude woman on the card and fitted his message within her figure: 'I will keep all the tit bits of news, till we meet.'[40]

Up until publication in November 1931, *The Four Gospels* occupied a great deal of Gill's time and also that of the Press. The pressures of administration and the day-to-day running of the Press were relieved to some degree by the arrival of a new member of staff. George Churchill was taken on as a general assistant in January 1931; previously he had established his own Fulcrum Press[41] which had become a victim of the economic slump that was beginning to bite following the Wall Street crash in 1929. One of his first tasks was to help organise the *Spring Prospectus*. In February, with the presses occupied with other jobs, Gibbings had decided to approach John Johnson at the Oxford University Press about off-loading the printing of the prospectus. Despite the short notice, Johnson replied that he was happy to oblige: 'You know very well that I will do this and more for you. Therefore I look forward to the coming of Mr Churchill ....'[42] On 9 February, Churchill arrived at Oxford University Press bearing galleys of type and woodblocks engraved by Ravilious and Gibbings and some initials by Gill. The text had been set at Waltham in Golden Cockerel type, but rather than printing from the original engravings, electrotype duplicates were made and substituted in the forme when the pages were imposed. Proofs were sent to Churchill a week or so later and the final run of just over 4,000 copies was printed and bound in March. Rather than apologise for the necessity of going outside for printing, Gibbings turned the fact into a selling point: 'Owing to the brevity of life and the fleeting of time', the prospectus was proclaimed as 'unique in being the only printed pages ever issued ... not entirely the product of their own workshops'.

Major productions tied up capital for long periods and with increased staff and the regular payments going to the bank for the loan and mortgage, sometimes Robert and Moira were desperately short of money. Neither of them really had any interest or ability in business matters and even though things became a little better organized with Churchill's input the situation was bad. Coppard, too, was always there with support and together they realised that what was needed was a series of short books with the potential of a quick turnover to generate cash. The idea emerged to produce a series of autographed first editions of work by living authors, to be sold at a reasonable price, with appeal to a wider collecting market. The first in the new 'Guinea series' was *The Hundredth Story* by Coppard, published in January 1931, with five engravings of birds and butterflies by Gibbings. This sold well and Coppard suggested contacting further authors with a view to signing them up. Gibbings was a great admirer of the work of the Powys brothers and approached T. F. Powys through Chatto & Windus. The result was the second book in the series, *When Thou Wast Naked*. Originally John Farleigh had agreed to do the illustrations but due to demands on his time from the Shakespeare Head Press he had dropped out and John Nash took up the commission. By March, flat sheets were ready for Powys to sign and the book appeared in July. Despite some printing errors, Powys was extremely pleased with the book and it too sold well. But there were problems when it came to settling up; Moira asked for a delay in payment due to 'the present unprecedented general financial crisis'.[43] When a cheque was finally sent it was for the wrong amount; Moira, embarrassed that it looked like 'sharp practice' hastily blamed 'domestic worries' for the error:[44] 'The fact is that our children have all been ill, we have had three operations in two months and now another imminent.'

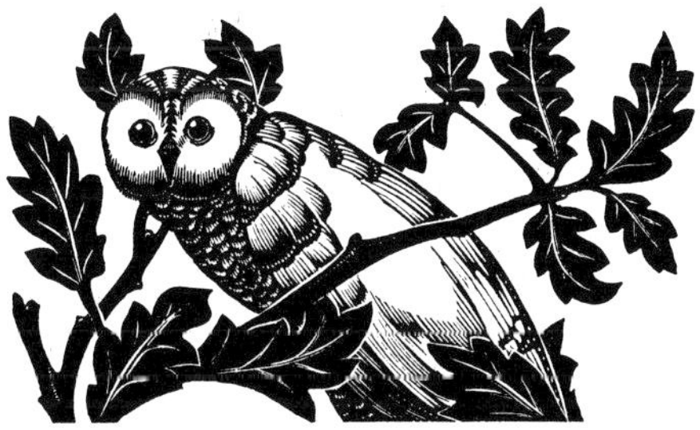

124 Illustration from *The Hundredth Story*, 1931, wood-engraving, 65 x 112 mm.

Early in 1931 Gibbings had started on a set of engravings for an edition of Flaubert's *Salambo* [*sic*] translated by Powys Mathers. This strange and rather cruel

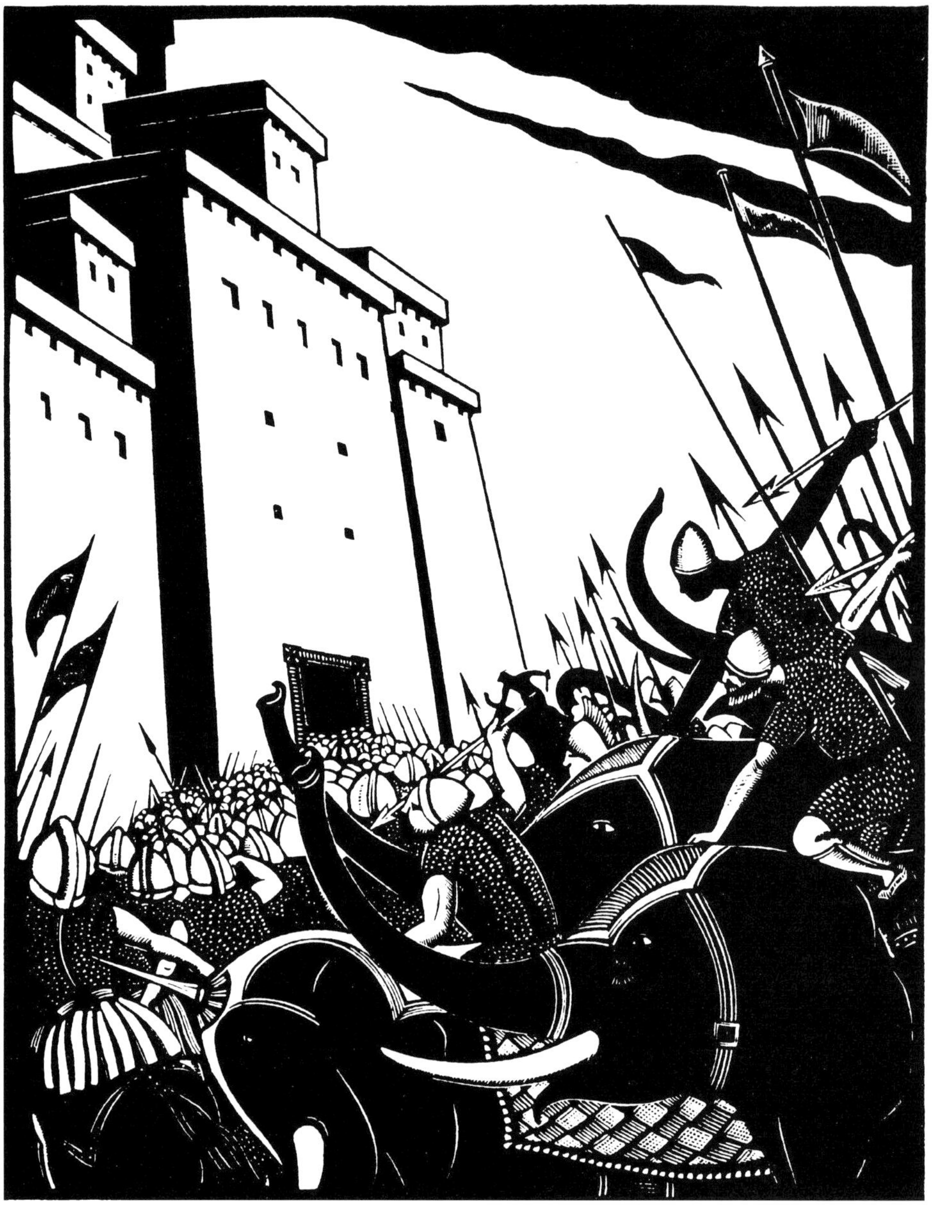

125 Frontispiece from *Salambo*, 1931, wood-engraving, 161 x 127 mm.

tale of the ancient world, full of battles and the siege of Carthage, gave Gibbings the opportunity to depict some dramatic scenes, but he was disappointed with the result. He felt the wood-engravings for *Salambo* were 'laboured' and he never liked them. This was harsh self-criticism for some of the illustrations are powerful and effective and the treatment of the chapter openings shows his concern for the integration of text and image. A review in *The Studio* was very positive:

Decorations in wood by Robert Gibbings are introduced in the form of a frontispiece and as headpieces to the chapters, each at once embellishing and symbolising the opening lines. The wood engravings thus take their places with an easy naturalness in the book and are not strained into the difficult rôle of descriptive illustrations to Flaubert's already sufficiently descriptive realism of words. They have, moreover, a dramatic boldness and grandeur in keeping with the vivid and sumptuous imagery of the text, and in colour-weight and arrangement consort with the type of the 'chapter-openings' to a degree bordering on perfection.[45]

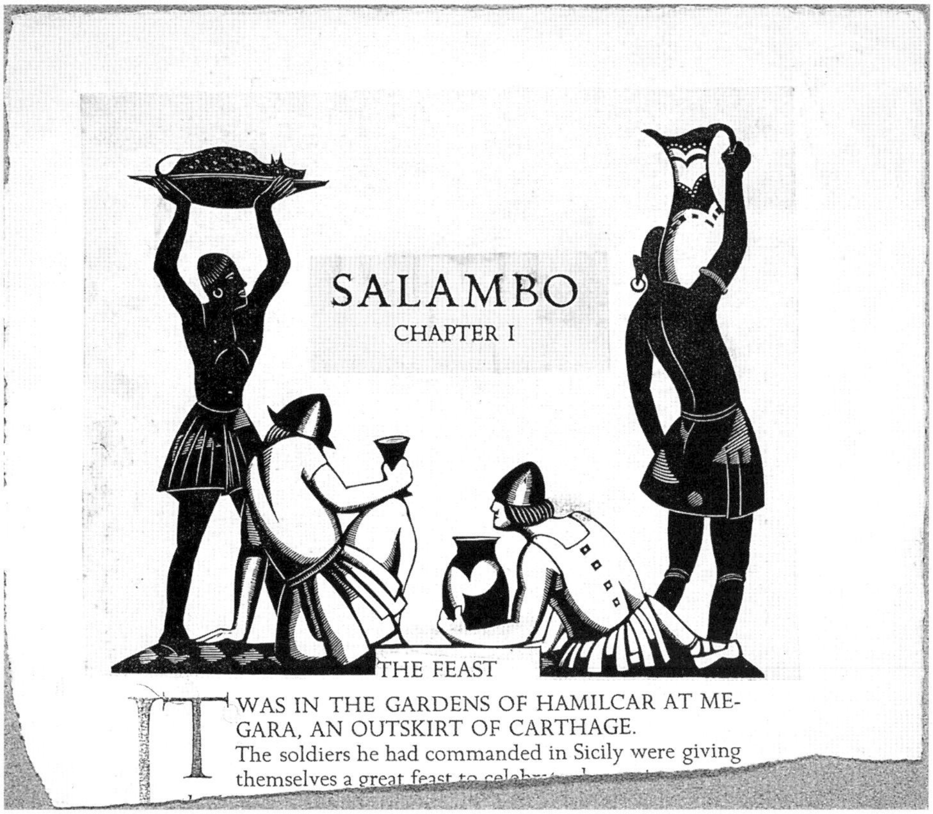

126 Proof of the opening of chapter one of *Salambo*, 1931. Examples of trial layouts show the working method; engravings and the title lettering were printed onto tissue paper so that the image and title could be laid over a proof of the text and adjusted until the balance was just right and then the tissue was pasted down. Albert Cooper Collection, RUL.

For months now, Gibbings had been waiting to hear from Norman Hall that he had completed his text for the book on Tahiti, but nothing had come. Then one day in the middle of this activity, a letter came from Houghton Mifflin:

> 'Hall finds he cannot do those essays,' it said. 'He is so tied up in a series about the mutiny on the *Bounty* that he cannot get his mind free. He wants to be let off. Can you suggest any other author who could write around your engravings?'
>
> 'The only author I can think of is not an author,' I replied. 'He is myself. I have letters that I wrote home and I have notes that I made while abroad, and if you like I'll see what I can do. No need for an agreement,' I added, 'till you see the MS. Then you can decide as you wish.'[46]

The publishers readily agreed and so now Robert was committed to yet another project — his first serious attempt to write.

Work on *Twelfth Night* continued throughout 1931, but in early February Gibbings had asked Ravilious to complete the illustrations for the title page so that it could be included in the *Spring Prospectus*. Gibbings was delighted with the result, which he thought 'absolutely spiffing': 'I think this is far and away our best title page yet and I hope very much the volume is going to set a new standard for us …'.[47]

Frequent letters passed between Gibbings and Ravilious about matters of detail but now Gibbings was able to send George Churchill to sort out more serious issues. Problems were again arising from the shallowness of Ravilious's cutting with the engraving tool which meant that there was a tendency for the fine lines to fill in with ink. Gibbings pointed out that the Oxford University Press had

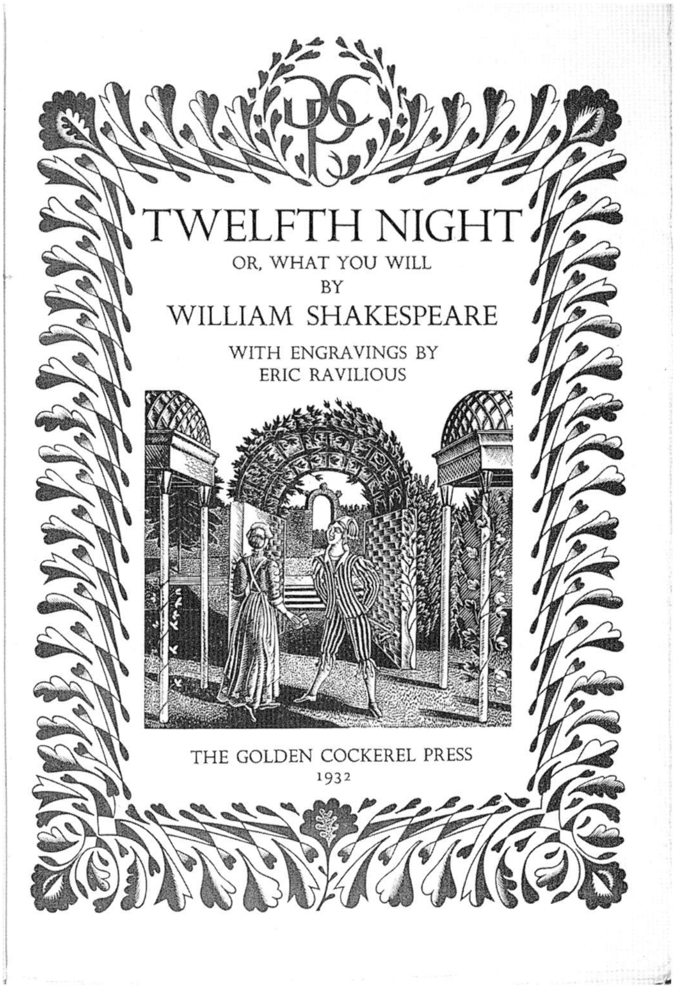

127 Title page from *Twelfth Night* with wood-engraving and decorative borders by Eric Ravilious, 1932, page size 337 x 235 mm. Reproduced by permission of the Golden Cockerel Press Ltd.

taken particular care with the printing of the prospectus, even making 'a special ink' to do justice to the blocks. Gibbings was aware that much of the problem was to do with the paper. He knew that printing on 'cheap pulp paper' would be easier but it would eventually 'discolour and fall to pieces' — Gibbings had a clear view: '... wot I sez is Let Posterity be our Motto'.[48] Tirzah's work caused the same problem but she was prepared to adapt her design for the binding cloth: 'I have cut it a little more since the print, the stars are a trifle smaller & the back ground is a little more cut away.'[49]

In a letter of 17 June, Ravilious discussed the possibility of a 'grey inking' to reduce the problem but felt he had been able to resolve the issue in the cutting of his later blocks: 'Of course the finer the cutting, the richer the result if it can be printed clearly, and perhaps with separate prints I might manage to cut more elaborately.'[50] Despite reporting good progress on the book the letter ended with an ominous comment from Ravilious that he was sorry to hear that '... the play doesn't seem to be selling as well as it might: there is something called a "depression" at work just now — May the Devil fly away with it'. Unfortunately this particular devil was to stay and the effects of economic depression were to have an increasing influence on the fortunes of the Press.

By September, Ravilious was very gently asking for a further interim payment for his work on *Twelfth Night* as his funds were low. In his reply Gibbings was anxious to help, sending twenty pounds on account, but he admitted 'We are going through a horrible crisis at the moment owing to shortage of capital and tightness of credit.'[51] Matters were worse as Gibbings went on to report on the state of subscriptions for the play: 'Now I have sad news about the Shakespeare. This slump has really begun to hit us hard and instead of orders coming in we get nothing but cancellations. In the case of Salambo published last week, we have over 100 copies unsold although a year ago it was fully subscribed and we were refusing orders.' Gibbings rejected the solution of reducing the size of the edition or the price and hesitantly put forward the suggestion of a lower fee for Ravilious: 'I hate to ask all this but I feel we are all in this soup or slump together. I have postponed for the time being any idea of the Milton [*Paradise Lost*] ... but I do not want if I can possibly help it to postpone the Twelfth Night.' He signed off the letter, 'With many regrets but not without hope.'

To ask Ravilious to reduce his fees must have been humiliating for Gibbings but he had not lost his sense of humour and was at least able to offer Ravilious another small commission to devise yet another version of the cockerel for the *Autumn Prospectus*:

> Do you know those comic cockerels they have on the round-abouts? We thought it would be fun to have one of these with a somewhat luscious nude lady on its back as shown in the enclosed very rough sketch. I think the bird ought to be definetly [*sic*] a robust animal with good strong legs, making a great noise, going at tremendous speed and with a naughty twinkle in its eye and its comb rather suggesting a drunken coronet. The lady should be very luscious and very beautiful à la Tintoretto; the banner she is waving might have my initials. Could you possibly do this for a fiver and the block which I can send you?[52]

In his usual generous manner, Ravilious, in his reply, spared Gibbings further embarrassment by accepting both the lower fee and the commission. Gibbings was grateful: 'Very many thanks for your sympathetic letter', but he went on to explain his financial plight in more depth:

> Our great difficulty is going to be between October and January. The Gospels, which has been our main work this past year, should with luck be published in the middle of December and then cash will begin to come in during the new year. Once January is over the cash ought to be coming in freely. ... though we will not be out of the wood till March. ... As regards the Twelfth Night, we hope to finish actual composing of the Gospels by the end of this month. Then we will get right down and concentrate on the Shakespeare and will work as quickly as you can keep us going.[53]

As a footnote Gibbings added: 'I am sending Tirzah a copy of our Salambo. I abominate all my engravings but her cover is nice.'

The *Autumn Prospectus* mentioned a title, *Preface to 'A Production'*, which never appeared. The project was to fall victim to the same financial crisis that had affected *Twelfth Night*. Oxford University Press had recently published *A Production*, a lavish and expensive folio volume of Edward Gordon Craig's theatre designs for Ibsen's *The Pretenders*. Through a mutual friend, Ellis Roberts, Gibbings had

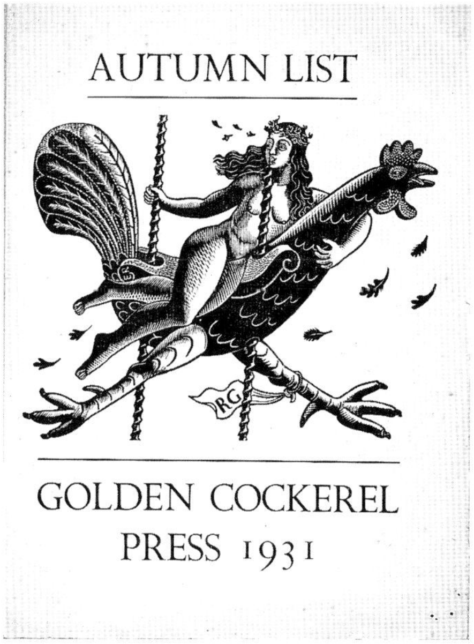

128 Cover of the *Autumn List* 1931, wood-engraving by Eric Ravilious, page size 250 x 192 mm. RUL. Reproduced by permission of the Golden Cockerel Press Ltd.

approached Craig about the possibility of publishing a preface to the volume, with a new introductory note by Craig and illustrated by some of his woodcuts. Craig, a figure of international reputation, was well known to the private press fraternity through his work with Count Kessler on the Cranach Press edition of *Hamlet* and his own book, *Woodcuts and Some Words*; to be able to add Craig to the list of Golden Cockerel illustrators would have brought further prestige. Craig, who now lived in Italy, was invariably in need of money and quickly agreed to the project and terms of fifty pounds to be paid a month after publication. He pleaded that shortage of time prevented him from cutting any new blocks but offered a choice of old blocks which he had to hand. Oxford University Press gave permission to use the text but demanded a fee of twenty-five pounds which, because the budget was so tight, reduced the amount Gibbings could pay Craig. Over the summer letters were exchanged about the selection of illustrations, as some of Craig's blocks were too wide to fit into the proposed page layout, and Craig's additional text. Writing to Craig in early July, Gibbings was feeling pressured: 'At the moment I am snowed under with visitors and every possible interruption, so that I can't think clearly on anything ....' Money was again the issue: 'At the moment we are a bit short of cash, being in the throes of publishing two books on which we cannot expect the returns to begin coming in for a little while ...' but he was able to offer Craig new terms: '... say we will pay you £15 on receipt of the new preface and the balance of £25 a month after publication? ... I am very glad indeed that our list is going to be honoured by the presence of your name'.[54]

Gibbings received the copy for the new preface at the end of August and managed to promptly pay the agreed fee of fifteen pounds promising another ten pounds on receipt of various blocks. The blocks had arrived by the end of September and Gibbings intended to send a cheque but explained his difficulties: 'At this particular moment we are most horribly short, awaiting one or two cheques due at any minute .... Our children are all being ill and life is rather hectic so excuse more at the present.'[55] But the cheque never arrived and Craig was forced by his own desperation for funds to prompt Gibbings again in a pencilled footnote to a letter he sent a month later: 'And now tell me in private — is it utterly out of the question for you to let me have a fiver, although perhaps you cannot send the £10 you spoke of.' A few days later the response from Gibbings to Craig's request was negative: '... the news is not at all good concerning your book. For some reason or other the orders are not coming in as they should be for this item so that unless things improve I may have to cancel the project. In this case I would ask you to retain the £15 I sent you as combined fee for the extra preface you did for us and compensation for the trouble to which you have been put: but I hope when American orders come in that it may be possible to go ahead'.[56] Unfortunately matters did not improve and plans for the book were dropped.

Worries over the future of the Press were creating tension and it was inevitable that this should also affect the domestic situation. Living on top of the business

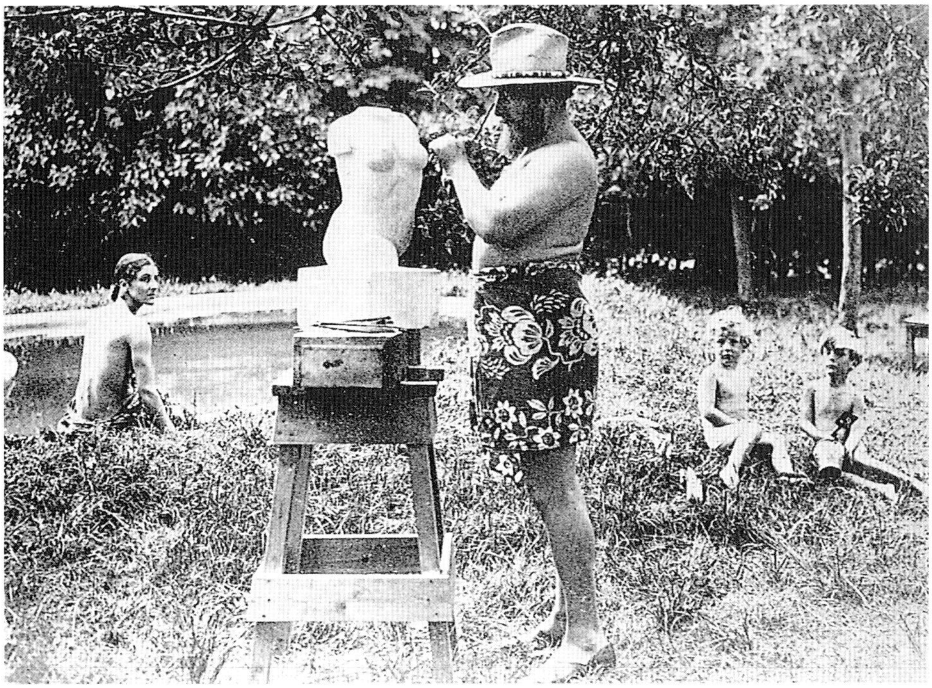

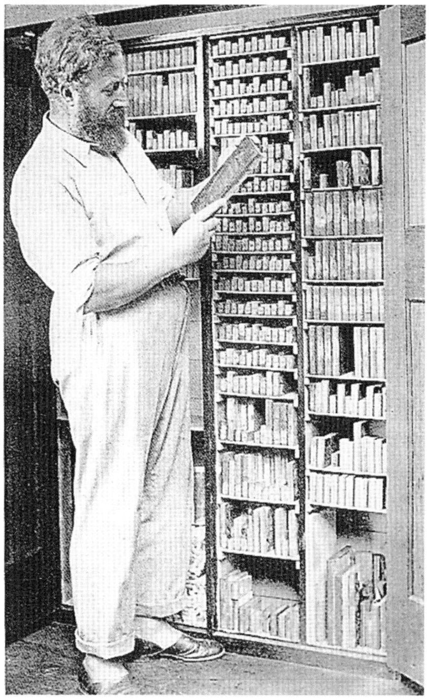

had its advantages but also its problems. Robert had complained of how 'hectic' things were at home and there was tension building with Moira; arguments became frequent and Robert's constant desire to get away could only have made matters worse. But on the surface the public image that the Gibbingses presented was of peace and harmony in a rural idyll. Writing to Gibbings in August 1931, Craig remarked that he had seen '... some jolly pictures of you and your kiddies and printers and nymphs and trees and pools in a newspaper — and I thought you looked like William Morris come to life again'.[57] Craig was referring to a full page feature article of photographs of life at Waltham which appeared in *The Graphic* the previous month under the heading 'Arcady in Berkshire, South Sea Dress and Freedom in the English countryside'.[58] Two photographs concerned the Press; Gibbings had been photographed scrutinising an engraved block, and another image showed Cooper hanging a printed sheet from *The Four Gospels* up to dry, the caption giving the misleading impression of a relaxed atmosphere: '... the printing processes are done in leisurely fashion by hand'. The remaining images conjure up a vision of idyllic family life. Photographs show Robert carving, sketching and hay making, surrounded by Moira and the twin boys naked and soaking up the sun in the gardens at Four Elms and carefully posed relaxing by a bathing pool that Robert had partly built himself.[59] Robert's modesty was preserved by a Tahitian pareu, or native cloth wrap, printed with bold patterns, which had become his favoured garment when weather permitted; his noble frame (he now weighed eighteen stone) was topped by a wide brimmed straw hat with a band of threaded shells. The scene was staged for the camera and the sculpture Gibbings is shown carving was the female torso of the acrobatic dancer he had completed some time before, yet there was also a reality to the picture. Robert's belief in the joy and health to be found in naturism had

129 *left* Gibbings carving by the swimming pool at Four Elms observed by his twin sons and Moira. Gibbings is wearing a native pareu which he brought back from his trip to Tahiti. The photograph was used as an illustration in a feature entitled 'Arcady in Berkshire' which appeared in *The Graphic* in 1931.

130 *right* Gibbings standing in front of a wall-case full of wood-engraving blocks at the Golden Cockerel Press, 1931. RUL.

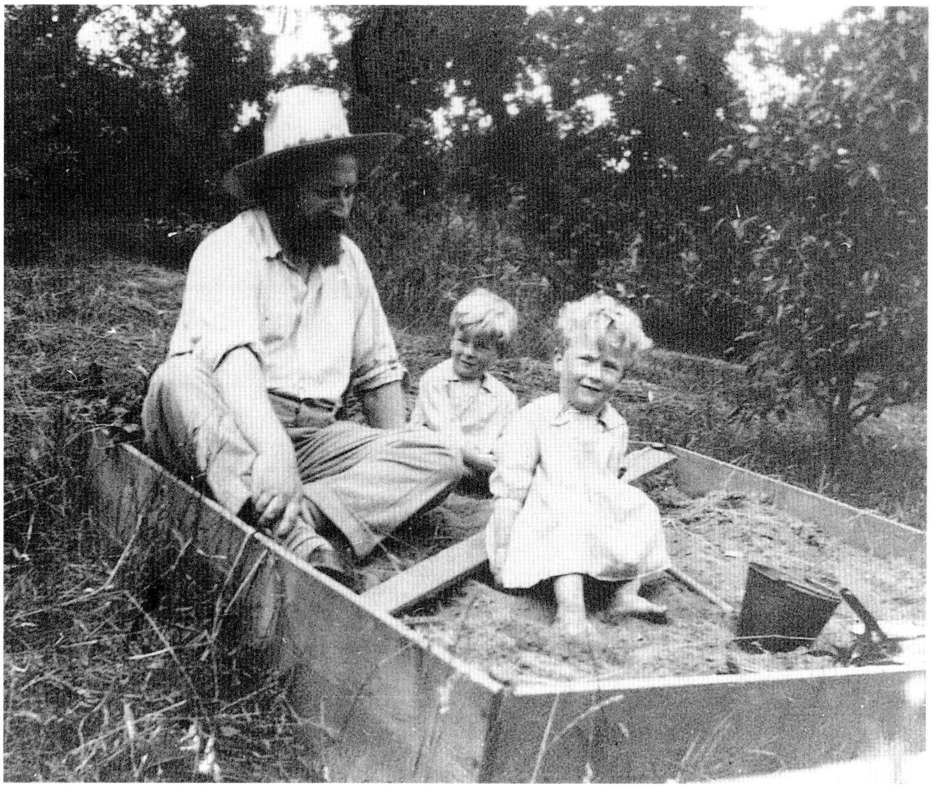

131 Gibbings playing with his twin sons in a sandpit in the gardens at Waltham, *c.* 1931. RUL.

developed beyond the confines of his private garden and, following his visit to a nudist camp in Germany, he had become increasingly involved with the pioneering nudist movement in this country. In his letter, Craig also mentioned that he thought Gibbings had been seen at 'Bedales'; summer conferences and camps were held in the grounds of the public school by the naturist organisations. In the year following, 1932, Gibbings was to publicly associate himself with the movement by signing a letter supporting naturist aims and ideals, which was published in *The Times*.[60]

The article in *The Graphic* shocked some of his more conservative acquaintances but Gibbings was unashamed: 'Very glad you were amused by the photos in the paper. Many tell me I am like William Morris, others think I am more like Neptune or Bacchus. ... The pictures have had the good effect of wiping out all my respectable friends. They know the sort of fellow I am! my name must not even be mentioned. A great relief to me.'[61] The general public had also been given a glimpse of working life at Waltham when the Golden Cockerel Press featured in a *Pathé News Pictorial*. On 10 September a Pathé crew spent the day filming Robert and the printing staff — avoiding anything of a more risqué nature![62]

EVEN WHILE RECOVERING in his hospital bed in October 1930, Gill had begun noting ideas for a new book. 'Typography as it is affected by the conditions of the year 1931' was to be the subject, and the conflict between industrialism and 'ancient methods of handicraft'[63] was its basic theme. Gill's experiences working

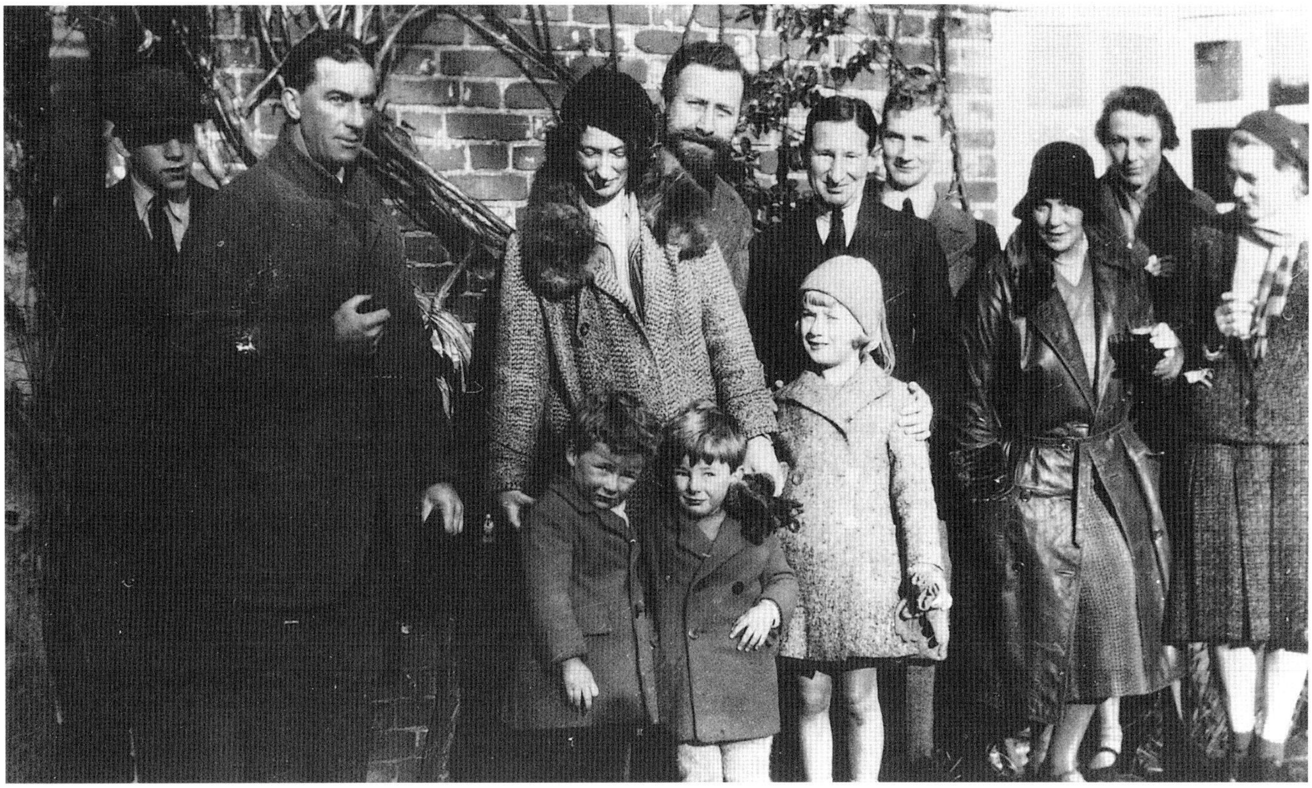

132 A gathering of visitors at Four Elms. Moira, Robert, Brigid and the twins are in the centre. To Moira's left is A. E. Coppard. The other guests or staff are unidentified, c. 1931. RUL.

with the technicians at Monotype and with Gibbings at the Golden Cockerel Press helped to form the background to his views. *An Essay on Typography* was set in Gill's Joanna typeface and printed by René Hague and Gill, on the press they had set up together at Pigotts in June 1931. In the same month, Gill's essay on the nude, *Clothing Without Cloth*, was published at the Golden Cockerel Press as the first of a series of 'saddle-back' Cockerels.[64] Gill was pleased with the design of the book but unhappy at the way his blocks had printed: 'You seem to have had gt. difficulties with that paper (very nice paper too) & that ink (can't bear the ink — why do you use that shiney stuff?) & consequently the blks [blocks] aren't very successful wh. seems a pity but the typographics are v. good &, as they say, "a book is a thing to *read*"'.[65] Yet another essay, *Clothes*, had gone to press at the Cambridge University Press but Gill still found time for a major commission. The BBC had asked him to carve the figures of Prospero and Ariel over the entrance to their building in Langham Place. Writing to Desmond Chute in February 1931, he was clearly enthusiastic: 'The building is commendably plain & machine made in appearance .... This job will occupy all 1931 and as it is well paid we are in luck ...'. Gill ended the letter with a significant comment: 'I am about to begin engravings for GC. Press Four Gospels.'[66]

Chapter Nine
The Triumph Before the Fall 1931

AT A TIME WHEN both men were under pressure, Gibbings and Gill were working on a book that was to be the supreme achievement of their collaboration; the perfect embodiment of their aims and beliefs about book design. *The Four Gospels* was to become recognised as one of the masterpieces of book production in the twentieth century. In retrospect, Gibbings saw his previous work at the Press as preparation, the building up of experience which enabled him to achieve this pinnacle. If harmony between text and image was the goal, then what better chance was there of achieving this aim than when the same hand and eye had designed both the typeface and engraved the illustrations? After seven years of working together the relationship between Gill and Gibbings had matured into one of mutual trust and respect, they understood each other's views — it was the 'ideal' partnership.

The Four Gospels was a project conceived on a grand scale. For two sons of clergymen, the text could not have been of greater significance, and the book was to be of majestic proportions. Views on the design of the book had evolved since it was first announced; the original intention had been to adopt a similar approach to *Troilus*, which featured decorative borders. However, perhaps in the light of some critical comment on the over-elaborate treatment of these borders, the *Spring Prospectus* for 1930 announced a change in concept: '... instead of floreated borders to every page as previously announced it has now been decided to decorate the book with a large number of engraved initials, printed in red, blue or black, many of which will contain pictorial devices illustrating the themes of the narrative'. Eventually, as the strength of Gill's engravings became apparent, colour was deemed unnecessary and dropped for the purity of black and white. Since their childhood both men had grown up with an intimate knowledge of Bible stories and their views on how to approach the text had not changed from that stated in the *Spring Prospectus* of 1928:

> While it is, of course, the intention of the Golden Cockerel Press and the engraver to avoid anything which could justly be called flippant or irreverent, nevertheless it is their aim to present in this book a lively and even amusing view of the grandest story in the world, lively because the central figure in that story came 'that he might give life'; amusing because, while it is easy to take things too seriously, it is not possible to take them too cheerfully. Nevertheless, the spirit of this edition will not be merely eccentric;

on the contrary the orthodox and traditional interpretation of the story will in all respects be followed.

John Dreyfus has written a most authoritative and thorough account of the creation of *The Four Gospels* in his book *A Typographical Masterpiece*, which is invaluable as a source.[1] But Gibbings wrote his own brief but illuminating version of events in the article entitled 'Memories of Eric Gill' already referred to. Written many years later in 1953, his recollections had no doubt been changed and idealised by the passing of time, but they still provide an interesting insight into their working method.

The first decision was which version of the Bible to use, and once again religious differences came to the fore:

My earliest memory of the making of this volume concerns the text. Eric, as a Catholic, suggested that we should use the Douai translation. I said that as a non-Catholic I would prefer the Authorized Version.

'Authorized by whom?' asked Eric.

'King James,' I said.

'What authority had *he*?' asked Eric.

Eventually Gill agreed to follow the King James version but they argued again over an important typographical decision:

Eric left the format and the typography entirely to me, his only suggestions being that we should print the poetry in verse form and that the lines of prose should not be justified. His argument in favour of the latter course was that even spacing between the words, and hence even colour on the page, more than compensated for the ragged right-hand edge of the unjustified lines. While agreeing about the poetry I was doubtful about the other proposition, and I am now sorry that I agreed to it; but Eric felt strongly on the matter and, as he had designed the type, I thought it only fair that he should have his way. But there was no serious argument. I remember our standing together in the press room at Waltham Saint Lawrence, he in his home-made smock and with a home-rolled cigarette in his hand, and each of us urging that the decision should be according to the other's wishes.

'You are the printer,' said Eric. 'It is only a suggestion of mine, it is for you to say.'

'You are the artist,' I replied. 'If you would like that form of setting then it must be so.' And Eric, always gentle in his manner even when his feelings were strong, pressed me again to have my way, and I in turn reiterated that it must be as he wished.[2]

On a number of previous occasions Gibbings had expressed his own preference for unjustified text and had eloquently argued the case for even word spacing. But his reluctance and eventual regret at setting the prose in this style suggests that Gibbings was not confident in breaking with convention, especially when dealing with such a revered text; it was Gill who led the way and was more original in his thinking. But if Gill led in terms of vision, it was still a true collaboration; everything was discussed and it was Gibbings, 'the printer', who was responsible for implementing the typesetting and page layout.

Before the setting was begun we went through each Gospel together, planning where the emphasis of illustration should fall. We felt that the opening pages of each Gospel must have a large if not a full-page block. We felt that at least one Crucifixion, and such subjects as the Entombment in St Luke and the Risen Lord in St John, should be similarly treated.

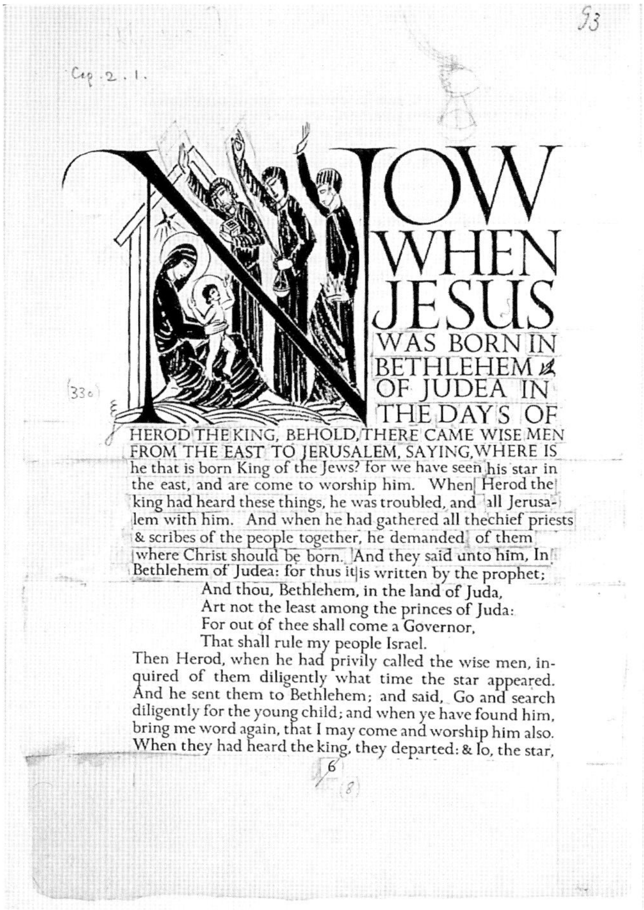

133 Gill's original drawing for the initial letter and opening three words of the Epiphany showing how the proof of the text was cut and pasted in designing the layout of the page. Sheet size 328 x 223 mm. Department of Printing and Graphic Arts, The Houghton Library, Harvard College Library.

He asked that I should allot about half a page to such passages as the Entry into Jerusalem and the Agony in the Garden in St Matthew, the Feeding of the Five Thousand and the Dancing of Salome in St Mark, the Annunciation and the Carrying to the Sepulchre in St Luke. He mentioned other places where if the type fell right he would like to do a smaller ornament. If two of the more important subjects came rather close together in one Gospel, then one of them could be left over to a succeeding narrative.[3]

Following his usual practice, galleys of the text were printed and then cut and pasted as rough page layouts to act as guides for the illustrator to plan the engravings by drawing or pasting proofs of the blocks into position.

The next stage in the work devolved entirely upon me. Before any blocks could be cut the type had to be set, for type is an austere and unyielding medium. With only three sizes of capitals, its potentialities of manoeuvre were more limited than usual. From the beginning we both realized that the type must be in command of the page.[4]

Thus the design of *The Four Gospels* evolved in an organic way, artist and printer changing and adapting their ideas in response to the demands of the text. The resolution of problems arose from the way the text fell on the page generating inventive and original solutions:

... I would spend hours with the compositors while they worked out the chapter headings or other occasions for decoration. Generally we would begin on the right of the page with a few words in the 36 point, set in short lines of perhaps half or a third of the measure. From the 36 point we would drop to the 24 point for another few short lines, and then having achieved a blank shape on the left of the page that seemed to offer possibilities to the artist for his initial letters we would continue for a few full lines in 18 point capitals. From then on it would be straightforward capitals and lower case until we reached the next site for decoration. We had no rules for the putting together of these varied sizes of capitals. We allowed the type almost complete control, improvising the tune according to the notes suggested. It came about, therefore, that almost every blank space left for the artist was different and that is one reason, I believe, for the liveliness which runs through the book. ... When the pages of type had been set up as I have described, I would send him proofs and on those he would build his designs, fitting his figures to the spaces determined by the type and following his fancy to spread into any quarter that offered itself. In the beheading of John the Baptist in St Matthew's Gospel, the sword of the executioner fits close outside the type area, the leaf in Salome's hand fills the narrow niche between the two paragraphs. Unless the type had been set first we could not have achieved such accord.[5]

Frequently Gibbings contributed creative ideas which Gill was happy to adopt:

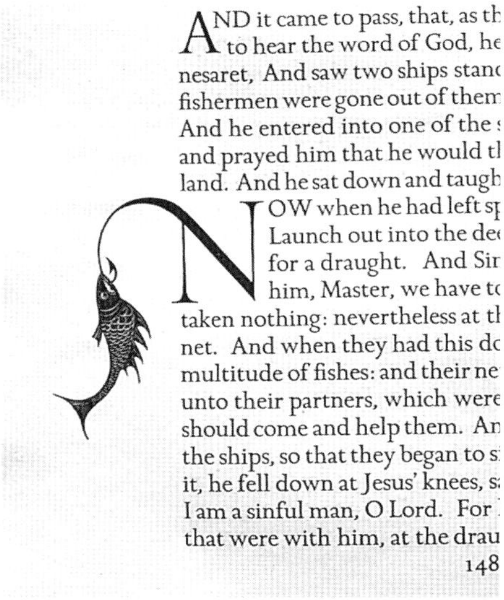
AND it came to pass, that, as th
to hear the word of God, he
nesaret, And saw two ships stan
fishermen were gone out of them
And he entered into one of the
and prayed him that he would t
land. And he sat down and taugh
NOW when he had left sp
Launch out into the de
for a draught. And Sir
him, Master, we have t
taken nothing: nevertheless at t
net. And when they had this d
multitude of fishes: and their ne
unto their partners, which were
should come and help them. An
the ships, so that they began to s
it, he fell down at Jesus' knees, s
I am a sinful man, O Lord. For
that were with him, at the drau
148

134 Opening of *The Four Gospels* at The Miraculous Draft of Fishes (detail). Reproduced from a copy in the Reading Local Studies Library, with permission of the Golden Cockerel Press Ltd.

Like many another man who is supreme at his job, Eric was essentially modest, and was always ready to listen to another's ideas. When, for example, I suggested that, for the Miraculous Draft of Fishes, a capital N with a fish hanging from the prolonged serif of the letter might be an appropriate accent of colour, he jumped at the idea and developed my simple pencil scratch into a delightful engraving.

The setting of the pages was by no means straightforward. Again and again it needed considerable manoeuvring to develop the spaces for decoration in suitable places on the pages. A verse that Eric specially wished to illustrate might fall at the foot of the right-hand page: if the block were put on that page it threw the relevant verses overleaf; if the block were put overleaf it was equally separated from its text. Almost the only course then was to work backwards over the pages and find a place where an extra block would push forward the right number of lines.

I had trouble with the pages immediately before the Agony in the Garden on page 69, as Eric wished to begin that passage with a large THEN on the top of a page. Unfortunately the verses just preceding finished a few lines from the bottom of their page, and because there was already a comparatively large block on page 66 I felt that any further engraving would overload the pages. Then it occurred to me that if with a small initial I put the words of consecration now used in the Communion Service into caps it would throw forward the text sufficiently to fill the page, and so it came about.[6]

Not wishing to be accused of false modesty, Gibbings admitted that he liked the book but as always he was self-critical: 'I am sorry that I did not make the pages just a fraction taller in proportion to their width my fault entirely.'[7] In retrospect, Gibbings never faltered in his admiration of Gill as an artist and craftsman and looked back to the period of their collaboration as 'idyllic' days. With hindsight it is obvious that Robert had only recalled the good things in his article. In fact, at the time he frequently felt dissatisfied with his way of life and there were warning signs of the impending financial problems which would eventually engulf the Press. For Gill too, life was difficult; the sculpture for the BBC was taking up much of his energy and the commission had generated a great deal of publicity and put him in the public eye. Committed to a punishing schedule for the engravings for *The Four Gospels*, he produced over sixty images, but the pace began to affect his health again. Writing to Gibbings in August 1931, Gill's wife, Mary, was concerned:

Eric is in town, working, and will finish one of the panels by the end of the week. He will then come home and continue your engravings — I was afraid last week he would have to give up all together — his head was getting bad again, and he also had lumbago .... I know Eric won't let you down with the engravings — but I *do* think he will have to slow up a bit — or he will burst — he was looking very worn and tired last week — and I began to think it was going to be a nursing home again. I just tell you this Robert my dear to give you a gentle warning, he does understand how much it means to you to get the book out ....[8]

The Four Gospels had been such a drain on time and money and for the future of the Press so much rested on speedy and successful publication. Dreyfus rightly makes the point that Gill could not have completed so many engravings in such a short time if it had not been for the help he was given from the 'exceptionally skilled hands' of R. J. Beedham. Beedham, trained as a commercial wood-engraver at the end of the nineteenth century, was in demand by many of the artist engravers, who valued his expertise. Gibbings regularly employed his talents and Beedham is frequently mentioned in correspondence with illustrators such as Ravilious for whom he provided 'technical support' and a 'clearing service' (cutting away and lowering surplus areas of the block around the image — a time consuming process).[9]

The announcement in the prospectus for spring 1930 had warned that the book would run to fifty more pages than originally planned. The price was raised to eight guineas, but if subscribers no longer wished to acquire the book at this new price 'early notification' was advised as the volume was already 'greatly oversubscribed'. By September, in a note to Gill, Gibbings expressed his concern that the position had been reversed: 'We find we have about 50 gospels over, due to recent cancellations. I don't quite know what is going to happen to anyone next year. Forgive note of melancholy!'[10] Gibbings's fears were thankfully unfounded; the economic climate had not improved but soon after publication, in November 1931, the edition of *The Four Gospels* had completely sold out. Even before publication the book had been declared their finest work; the *London Mercury*, quoted in an announcement printed earlier in 1931, proclaimed that Golden Cockerel books would 'stand comparison with any book printed in the whole history of mankind: lovely, solid, firmly printed, soundly decorated things which it is an abiding pleasure to possess'. With such hype and with the critical acclaim which greeted the book, collectors recognised quality and were eager to buy.

The significance of *The Four Gospels* was not only that the financial fortunes of the Press depended on its success, it represented an emotional and artistic investment too. As each sheet was printed and hung to dry, one can only speculate on the feelings of the workmen and the atmosphere in the Press. Gibbings repeatedly stated how much he relied on his staff and had always insisted that every colophon should list their names. They all had contributed so much and they must have been aware that this book was something special. For the compositors it presented a challenge; the open and fluid quality of Gill's blocks required patience and skill when being assembled with the type in the forme.[11] The blocks do not line up with the text, the limbs of letters and human characters overhang

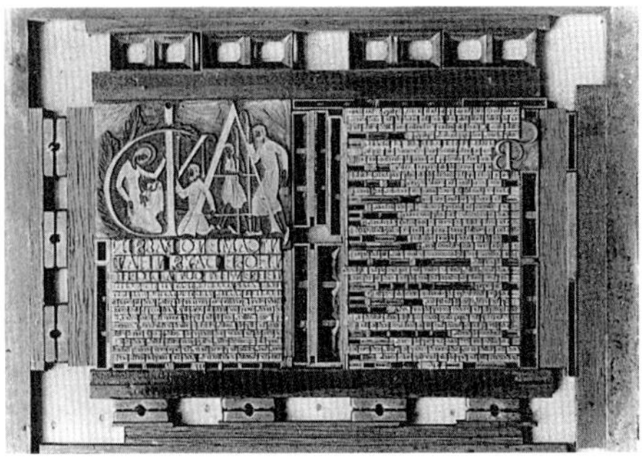

135 *above* Forme of type and wood-engraving by Eric Gill showing imposed pages 136 and 137, from *The Four Gospels*. RUL.

136 *right* Gibbings and Cooper examining a printed sheet. RUL.

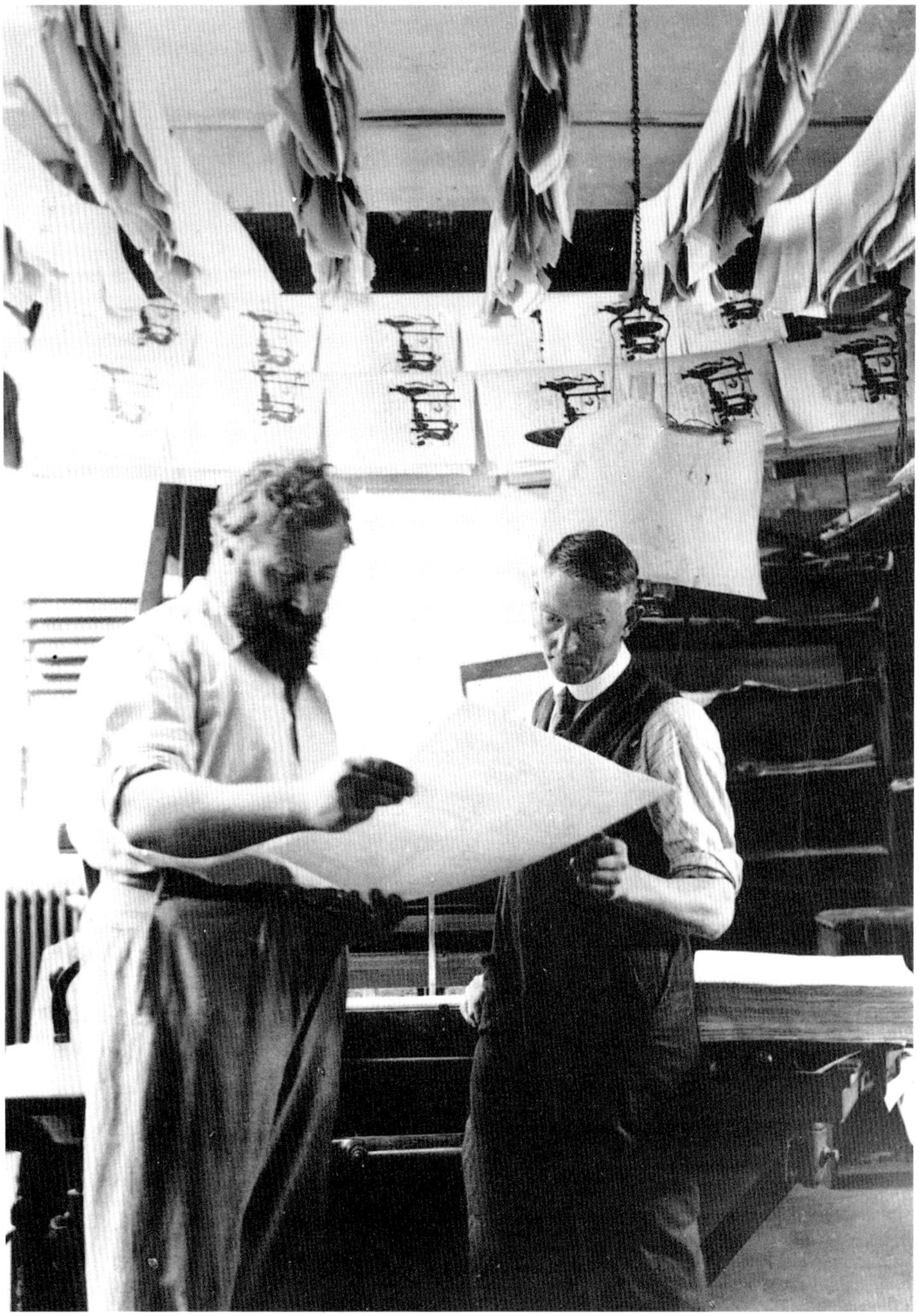

into the margins. Text and images fuse together, figures wrap themselves around the letters, and the letters themselves become scaffolding for the scene depicted. The inventive use of the limited range of typesizes and the careful letterspacing of the capitals is an example of the highest craftsmanship. From Cooper, too, it demanded all his skill as a pressman but also his visual sensitivity as an artist.[12]

Cooper later recalled his days at the Golden Cockerel Press; he enjoyed his work and felt that Gibbings was a kind and generous employer. For Cooper, the day started with a bicycle ride from his cottage in the nearby village of Ruscombe, arriving at the Press to start work at half-past eight; at one o'clock they would stop for lunch and in the summer Cooper would take a packet of sandwiches and

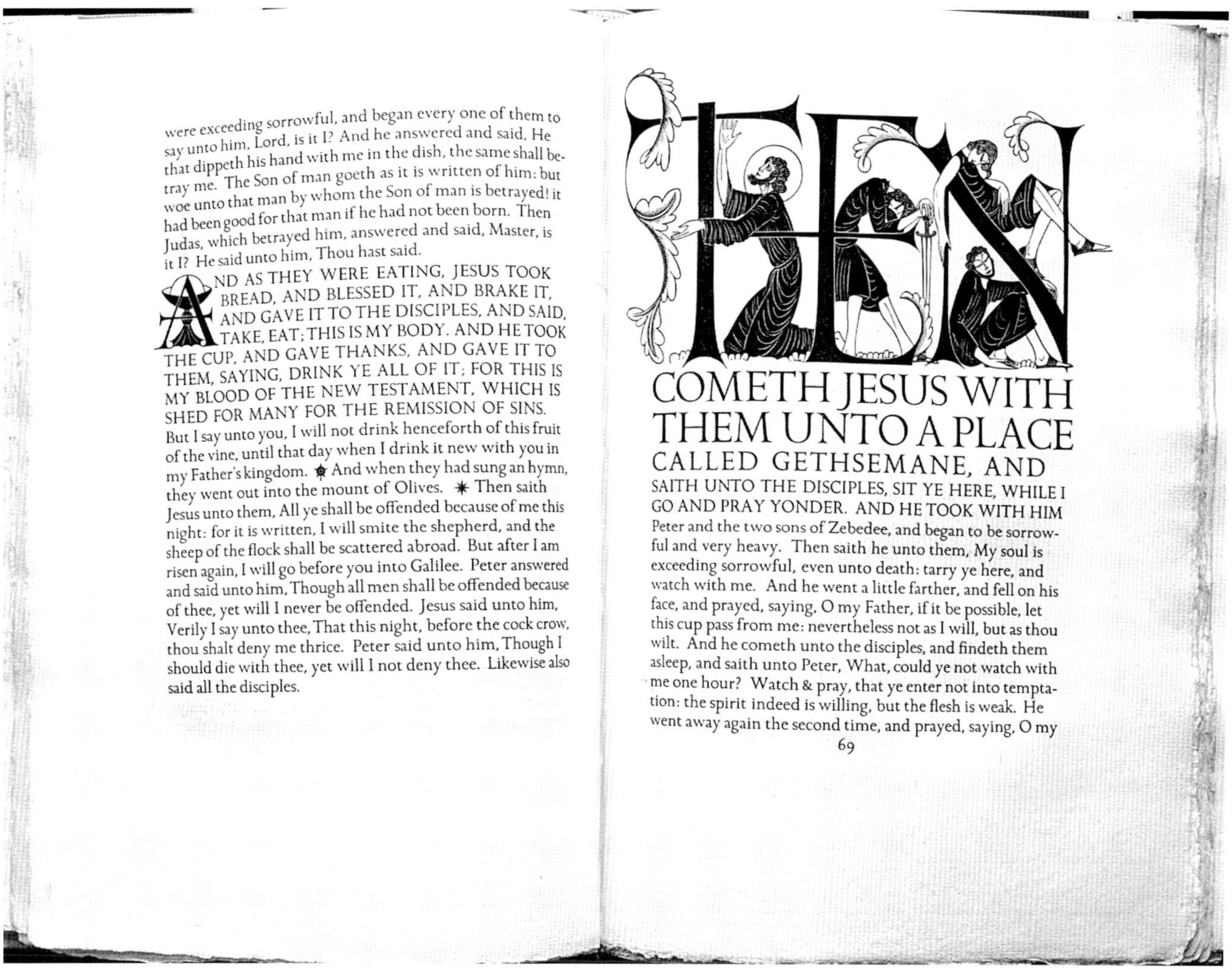

were exceeding sorrowful, and began every one of them to say unto him, Lord, is it I? And he answered and said, He that dippeth his hand with me in the dish, the same shall betray me. The Son of man goeth as it is written of him: but woe unto that man by whom the Son of man is betrayed! it had been good for that man if he had not been born. Then Judas, which betrayed him, answered and said, Master, is it I? He said unto him, Thou hast said.

AND AS THEY WERE EATING, JESUS TOOK BREAD, AND BLESSED IT, AND BRAKE IT, AND GAVE IT TO THE DISCIPLES, AND SAID, TAKE, EAT; THIS IS MY BODY. AND HE TOOK THE CUP, AND GAVE THANKS, AND GAVE IT TO THEM, SAYING, DRINK YE ALL OF IT; FOR THIS IS MY BLOOD OF THE NEW TESTAMENT, WHICH IS SHED FOR MANY FOR THE REMISSION OF SINS. But I say unto you, I will not drink henceforth of this fruit of the vine, until that day when I drink it new with you in my Father's kingdom. ✱ And when they had sung an hymn, they went out into the mount of Olives. ✱ Then saith Jesus unto them, All ye shall be offended because of me this night: for it is written, I will smite the shepherd, and the sheep of the flock shall be scattered abroad. But after I am risen again, I will go before you into Galilee. Peter answered and said unto him, Though all men shall be offended because of thee, yet will I never be offended. Jesus said unto him, Verily I say unto thee, That this night, before the cock crow, thou shalt deny me thrice. Peter said unto him, Though I should die with thee, yet will I not deny thee. Likewise also said all the disciples.

THEN COMETH JESUS WITH THEM UNTO A PLACE CALLED GETHSEMANE, AND SAITH UNTO THE DISCIPLES, SIT YE HERE, WHILE I GO AND PRAY YONDER. AND HE TOOK WITH HIM Peter and the two sons of Zebedee, and began to be sorrowful and very heavy. Then saith he unto them, My soul is exceeding sorrowful, even unto death: tarry ye here, and watch with me. And he went a little farther, and fell on his face, and prayed, saying, O my Father, if it be possible, let this cup pass from me: nevertheless not as I will, but as thou wilt. And he cometh unto the disciples, and findeth them asleep, and saith unto Peter, What, could ye not watch with me one hour? Watch & pray, that ye enter not into temptation: the spirit indeed is willing, but the flesh is weak. He went away again the second time, and prayed, saying, O my

69

137 Double-page spread from *The Four Gospels*, 1931, with wood-engraved letters and decoration by Eric Gill, page size 331 × 229 mm. Reproduced from a copy in the Reading Local Studies Library, with permission of the Golden Cockerel Press Ltd.

rest under the apple trees in the orchard. The working day finished at half-past five and according to Cooper they were rarely asked to do overtime.[13] In conversation, Cooper confirmed that Gibbings was very much part of the team in the workshops, and recalled that 'He used to work hand in glove with the staff', and closely supervised production: '... he used to come and read the proofs, and pass the sheets for printing .... Then he'd say, perhaps, I don't like *that*, or, I think that perhaps we'll have an initial put in'.[14]

Cooper printed *The Four Gospels* on the platen press which had replaced the Wharfedale that Gibbings had taken over from Hal Taylor. The edition consisted of 488 copies printed on handmade paper with a GCP watermark, designed by Gill, which had been specially made by Batchelor & Son in Kent, and twelve copies printed on vellum and hand bound in white pigskin. Cooper's account of the Press's procedures gives a clear picture of how books were printed:

The reams of paper were ordered from the mills double the size that the platen press would take, and cut in half by the guillotine so as to get one straight edge to feed up to the gauges in the printing press for good register of the printing of the other side of the sheet. The remaining deckle edges of the paper were preserved to be bound up in the completed book.

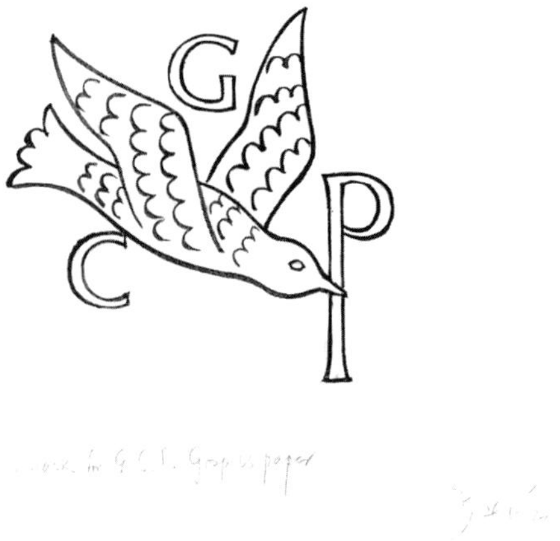

138 Original ink drawing by Eric Gill for the GCP watermark used in specially made paper by Batchelor & Son in Kent. RUL.

> The number of sheets required for the edition with the necessary overs in case of spoils were counted out and these were taken in batches, usually five sheets, and immersed through a bath of clean water and laid on specially made one-inch-thick boards a little larger than the sheets of paper. Then four dry ones were put over these, then another batch of five put through the bath, and then again four dry ones over them, and so till the whole pile was done, finishing up with a damped sheet; then another thick wooden board was placed on top of the dampened pile. This was done in the late afternoon so that the moisture would have time through the night to permeate with equal dampness to the whole pile of paper. The pile was put in a very large and strong press (similar to a copying press) and a little pressure was put on the paper. In the morning it was taken out and gone through by hand to straighten out any wrinkles caused by the expansion of the damp paper, which should be equally damp all through. It was then put back in the press for an hour or more, and the press screwed down very tight to make the sheets nice and flat and ready for printing.
>
> On the machine platen the inking was automatic from a trough of ink at the top of the machine. Small piles were printed at a time to avoid any set-off on reverse side, damp sheets of antique paper being placed at top and bottom of each pile to stop them drying out till the other side of the sheet could be printed. When it came to printing the other side of the sheet it was necessary to interleave with a thin sheet of ordinary paper placed underneath the hand-made sheet to stop any set-off from the first printing. (The pages were usually printed four-up in a forme. If the pages were bigger, I mean folio size [as with *The Four Gospels*], we printed two-up.) After a day the interleaves were taken out and the completed printed sheets were hung up in small lots on lines to dry the damp out of the paper and dry the ink. When the whole edition was completed, the sheets were packed flat in a strong box and sent by a local carrier to a high-class binder in London, Sangorski & Sutcliffe.[15]

Printing on vellum called for even more care as each sheet varied in thickness and the different surfaces on either side of the skin printed in different ways. The vellum was printed dry but each sheet had to be felt to 'see where the thin part was, and you had to pack it'. This meant that the pressure on the thin parts of the

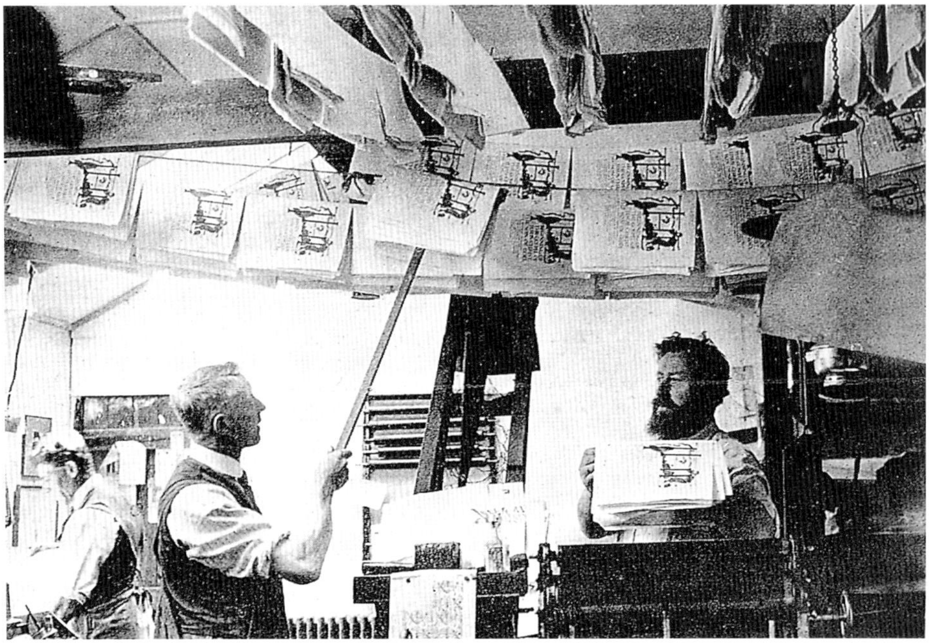

139 Cooper and Gibbings hanging up printed sheets from *The Four Gospels* to dry. RUL.

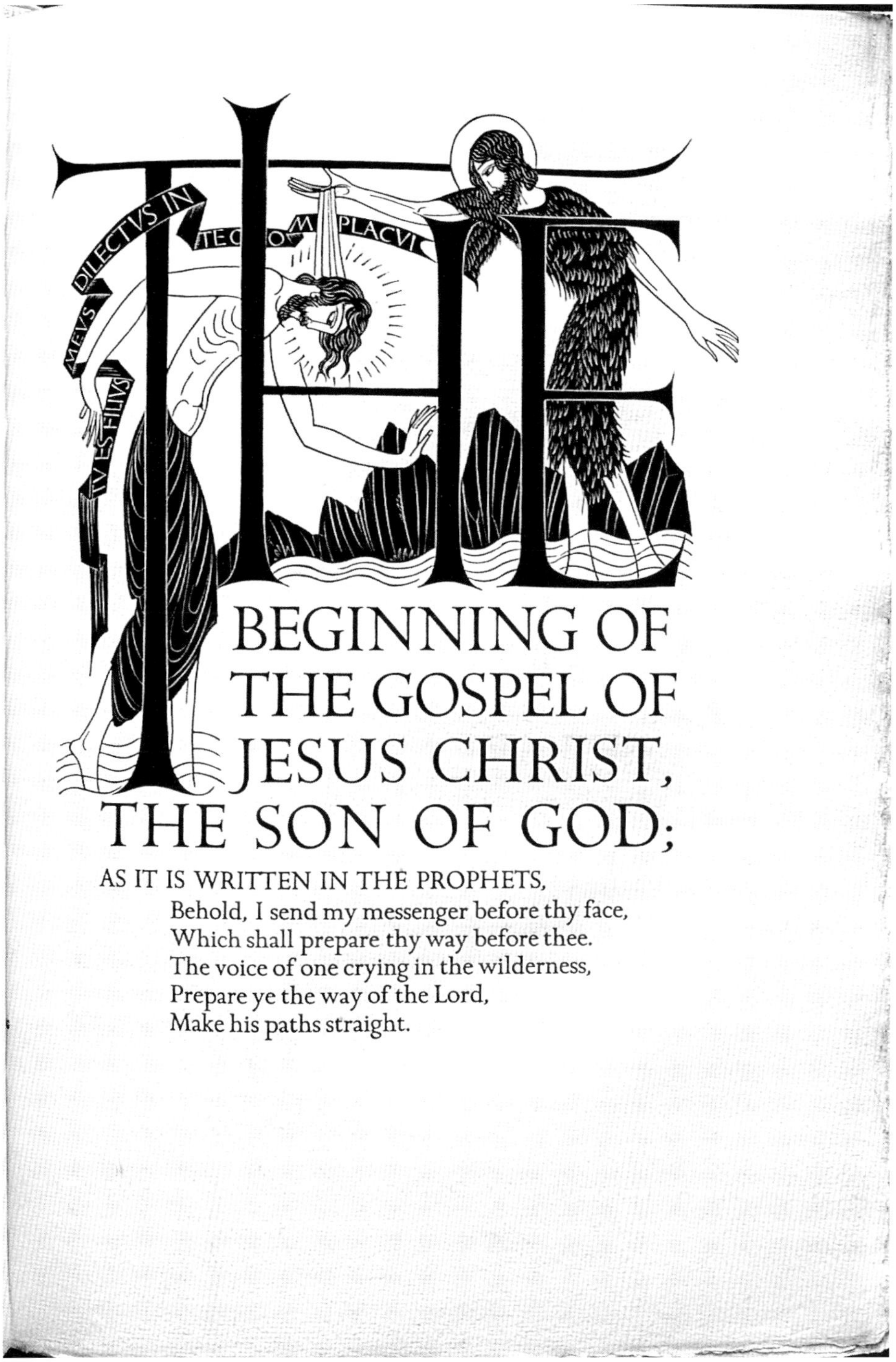

THE BEGINNING OF THE GOSPEL OF JESUS CHRIST, THE SON OF GOD;

AS IT IS WRITTEN IN THE PROPHETS,

Behold, I send my messenger before thy face,
Which shall prepare thy way before thee.
The voice of one crying in the wilderness,
Prepare ye the way of the Lord,
Make his paths straight.

140 *The Four Gospels*, 1931, opening page of the Gospel According to Saint Mark, page size 331 x 229 mm. Reproduced from a copy in the Reading Local Studies Library, with permission of the Golden Cockerel Press Ltd.

sheet had to be evened out by using patches of vellum (using spoilt sheets) to build up the thickness of the packing.

The edition had been limited to 500 books and thus there were few review copies available, but the publication of *The Four Gospels* was received with almost universal acclaim from critics in the national press and specialists in typography. Naturally it was Gill's contribution which attracted most praise and attention. Harold Child wrote enthusiastically about the book:

> It would be rash to say that this is the most beautiful book which even the Golden Cockerel Press has produced; but those who approach it with the very natural conviction that somehow and somewhere it is bound to seem unworthy, to jar, or to disappoint, are very likely to find that they are wrong. It is a book, first of all, that can be read. The type is superb .... Mr Gill has never done anything finer than these intensely dramatic woodcuts .... Of the workmanship of the book, printing, paper, binding ... it is only necessary to say that it is up to the standard of the Golden Cockerel Press.[16]

Gibbings must have been delighted and relieved at the success of *The Four Gospels*, but this did not alter his sense of being tied down by the Press. In December 1931, Christopher Sandford and his wife, Lettice, the artist and illustrator, came to stay at Waltham. Sandford, a fellow Irishman from Cork, was a partner in the Chiswick Press but had recently set up his own private press with his wife. He had suggested the visit because of his interest in fine printing and was keen to meet Robert and Moira — his father was a doctor in Ireland and had been a friend of Robert's grandfather, Robert Day, and knew his parents. Sandford had just read his copy of *The Four Gospels* and thought it '... one of the most beautiful books I ever saw. I don't think anyone is making such beautiful books as you. I like everything but the Paragraph stars & roses!'.[17] Following their visit Gibbings wrote to Sandford on Christmas Day expressing his frustrations:

> I was quite serious about wishing to sell. The point is that at present half my energy goes in making other artists do what I want & the other half goes in dealing with authors and booksellers so that I have none left either to do my own engravings in the way I wish to do them or to get on with my sculpture & painting which is really what I want to do. Of course it's great fun here and there's quite a comfortable living but it's not giving me quite what I am after. ... Last year, in spite of the bad times, was our best year yet so I'm not trying to get rid of a 'pup'. By the way keep all this to yourself as I don't want to sell to anyone who will exploit it commercially. I refused one offer last year on that acct.[18]

Although nothing was to come of his approach to Sandford for some while, the seed was sown.

Chapter Ten
Peaks and Troughs 1931–1932

INTEREST IN THE PRESS was being shown around the rest of the world as well as in America. In 1931 articles on the Golden Cockerel appeared in at least two continental journals. At home, Gui St Bernard warmly reviewed the annual exhibitions of the Society of Wood Engravers and their rivals, the English Wood Engraving Society, and wrote a spirited plea for British artists to be valued in the same way as their European counterparts. In November, Gibbings had contributed another article on the history and philosophy of the Press to the *London Mercury* and in the previous month *The Colophon* had published a longer and richly illustrated article by Gibbings, specially set in 14pt Golden Cockerel type. This article was much wider in scope and much of its content has already been quoted, but the analogies Gibbings used in the text show how his mind was fixed on his desire to pursue his art — even when discussing typography he constantly refers to sculpture:

> At the Golden Cockerel Press we endeavour to think of type as a means of artistic expression. The modelling of a page to a typographer should be as important as the modelling of a limb to a sculptor, and only when the decorator is in very close touch with the compositor can the best results be achieved.[1]

Gibbings argued that wood-engraving was a natural medium for book illustration:

> ... the design can be actually 'sculptured' on the wood in the same way as the punches of typefounders are sculptured from the metal. And a competent engraver can thus obtain a clean and incisive line exactly the same in quality as the type, having the same weight and the same relation of thick and thin. And it is only when all these points are fully considered that harmony can be achieved.

Finding artists who 'respected' type had been a problem for Gibbings; he felt most contemporary engravers would take 'any piece of wood & carve thereon any design that comes into their heads, with no idea of the scale of the page, proximity to type, or other problems, which confront the maker of books. The real artist has always accepted the limitations of his craft, and the book decorator must consider more and more the unit of texture of his type'.

Pursuing his interest in sculpture, Gibbings had applied at the end of November 1931 for permission to build a 'sculpture studio' in the grounds at Waltham. It was to be a large timber barn situated near the pool. The cost was partly

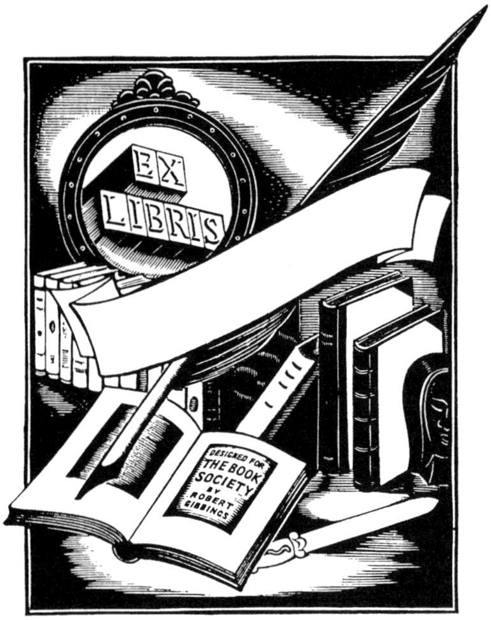

141 Universal bookplate designed for The Book Society, c. 1932, wood-engraving, 104 x 84 mm. Author's collection. A smaller version of the same image was used on a book mark for the Society – the words Ex Libris being replaced by the words 'Book-Mark of'.

financed by a loan from a friend, George Churchill's sister Lallah. An artist herself, Lallah was keen to try her hand at sculpture and occasionally helped Gibbings rough out his work.[2] Albert Cooper, a very thrifty man, saw the studio as an example of Robert's extravagance: 'When he had a bit of money (and you know, he was very lavish with his money) instead of paying his creditors, he'd have a studio built – he had a studio built in the orchard. He did a bit of sculpting there. When hard times came, he had nothing to back him up. He weren't as sensible as his pressman! He wasn't a businessman.'[3] Saving money and planning for long term security was not in Gibbings's nature; he wanted to live life to the full and live it now!

Gibbings had mentioned his plans to put up 'another shed' and 'concentrate more on stone' in a letter to his friend Margaret Pilkington. Gibbings was still a key member of the Society of Wood Engravers and very active on the committee. Since Moira's involvement had lessened, he had worked more closely with Margaret Pilkington and in November she had approached Gibbings about giving a talk on wood-engraving. He had written back declining the proposal: 'I'd willingly talk if I could think of any blooming thing to say but barring the application of woodcuts to type I have no ideas & as the Society aims rather at wall decoration, it would hardly be in line.'[4] This old argument over book illustration was still an issue — furthermore Gibbings was sensitive to the fact that it would be 'invidious' to concentrate on the work of the Golden Cockerel Press. But his main excuse was that he simply did not have enough time as all his efforts were directed at another project: '... all my "literary genius" is being concentrated on a South Sea Journal I have promised publishers in USA by the end of Dec.'

Since Houghton-Mifflin had agreed to Gibbings's own suggestion that he replace Norman Hall as the author of a book on Tahiti, he had been working on a text based on the notes and diaries he had kept on his visit. What emerged was a strange story, not a novel with a plot, nor a factual account of events, but a rather melancholic, reflective and deeply personal response to the experience — part fact, part fiction. Perhaps coloured by his own mental struggle and uncertainty, he expected to discover a paradise, but what he found was disillusionment over a lost Eden. Later, Gibbings commented on his own dissatisfaction with the work: 'Of necessity much of it is from imagination, and little of the truth that is in it is well recorded. I hope it will never be reprinted.'[5] Yet *Iorana! a Tahitian Journal*, as it was to be called, was written in the first person, and was based on his diaries — it has the ring of truth.[6] Perhaps, in later life, Gibbings regretted exposing so many of his inner thoughts and feelings and this led to him trying to veil the truth in the book by his dismissive comments. The opening paragraphs set the tone; after days at sea, the first glimpse of land reflects the glories of nature as the 'Pearl of the Pacific' draws 'closer every moment, purple mountains rising to a fantastic skyline, and up and down the coast an endless ribbon of white sand edging the emerald lagoon'; yet the cynical words of the ship's chief officer have already shattered any illusions:

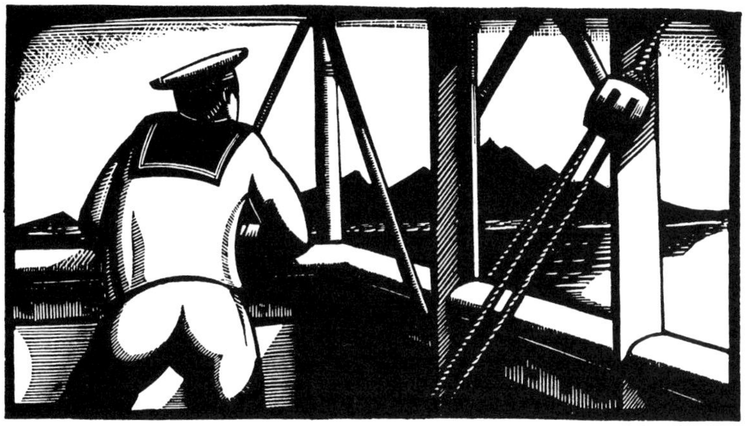

142 Illustration from *Iorana* of the ship approaching Tahiti, wood-engraving, 1932, 55 x 100 mm. All illustrations from *Iorana* are reproduced with permission of the publishers Gerald Duckworth & Co. Ltd.

Tahiti, he said, consists of a few rich Americans, a few poor Englishmen, some French officials, a great many Chinese, a great many half-castes, and three or four Tahitians. He says there's good rum punch at the Cercle Bougainville, and all the girls are obliging though dangerous, and there's a lot of elephantiasis and a good deal of leprosy; the mosquitoes are bad, and the place is full of land crabs. He never goes ashore.

What follows is a collection of anecdotes and observations about the characters he meets; frank and graphic descriptions of their way of life; vivid pictures of the landscape and the flora and fauna and observations of daily life and customs, all interwoven with accounts of barely connected episodes recorded by the narrator as entries in a journal. The book is divided into two parts; the dominant theme for part one is the corruption and pollution of this paradise in the Pacific by white culture; bars filled with drunken colonials, the native inhabitants losing their innocence and dignity by being seduced by western values — producing a listless and stagnant society. The narrator is an artist and the reader sees through his eyes; his descriptions appeal to the senses — vivid colour, evocative smells, the observation of minute details, scenes described as if composing a painting. One of the characters in the book lays the blame for the corruption of this Eden on the missionaries. Before white people came the islanders were 'innocent'; conversion to Christianity meant convincing them of sin so that they could be redeemed – sins that had to be invented:

... and the result, a race dying of white men's diseases, a race robbed of all desire to live because all enjoyment in life has been taken from them.

Syphilis and exploitation are the lamps we have lit for them, and for every humane human sacrifice that we have stopped we have slowly murdered thousands. Not content with our own daily human sacrifices in the mines and factories at home, we must drag our misery of mind and body into the lives of these people whose greatest mortal sin was eating greedily of a turtle or a pig's head.

So now these children of the sun parade in stiff collars and patent leather boots, the women in mother-hubbards and hard straw hats like an English charity school, and, without understanding any of it, they subscribe to a religion founded on poverty and humility, whose leaders cannot live on five thousand a year.[7]

These words are spoken by one of the characters in the book but surely reflect Gibbings's own views, as do the words of the narrator:

God Almighty! I'm lonely; why did I ever come to this blarsted [*sic*] island of decay? It's too ineffective; nothing ever gets made; all the time disintegration. There isn't a white man whose eyes aren't falling out with sadness or drink. Sad, sad beyond all comprehension. The natives are dying — there's hardly one left — and the sons of chiefs are picking leaves from millionaires' lawns. There's nothing left except the lagoon. Old Liza's gramophone is playing ' Show me the way to go home.'[8]

In an unexplained reference in the book, Gibbings quotes a letter from someone simply referred to as 'M' but who is surely Moira: 'Paint exactly as you want to. Do exactly as you wish, so that you can best express things.' Gibbings goes on to quote Havelock Ellis, adding his own thoughts:

... when a man completely changes his belief he must of psychological necessity attack and persecute those very fortresses which a short while before he had defended. I think in something the same way an artist is himself his greatest hindrance to finding himself. Puritan ancestry plays hell. What I want to paint is not nude but naked women, yet every day I go out drawing palms, drawing fish, drawing pirogues.

There's no nudity on Tahiti; no one will even pose. The missionaries *have* done wonders!! The amoeba grows around the cell of its desires and then multiplies by fission. An artist should envelop and absorb his inspiration, and then split his very soul in creation.[9]

Gibbings was reflecting and reassessing his own life, in a new world with different values, free from the ties of wife and family. In writing the book Gibbings seems to have been exploring his own mind; it was some kind of therapy and he was able to voice ideas and confront issues through his characters that he could not express as himself. In later life Gibbings hardly ever spoke about his war experiences, only referring to the basic facts of his wounding and never mentioning his deep psychological injuries, either in writing or conversation. In *Iorana* he is able to confront these suppressed memories by putting the words in the mouth of another. He describes the sensations of being shot with all the vividness with which he had privately described his feelings in letters to his father at the time. But now he is able to go beyond this, and under cover confront his mental anguish and the full horror of his own memories. Describing the days after he was shot, he writes:

Throughout the day he lay delirious amongst the wounded and dying, and that night was taken off the peninsula and shipped to Lemnos. But all the time he was tearing through innumerable trenches and always getting back into the same enormous dug-out, through the trenches again and then back to the same vast empty crater.

For days he could not eat, drink, or speak. They tried to find the bullet in his arm, but had no chloroform. His neck was so foul that he asked to have the latrines moved, not knowing it was the stench from his own wound.[10]

The narrator longs to draw and paint naked bodies; he desires a woman, and the book is full of sensual descriptions of Tahitian women. Eventually his sexual frustration is satisfied by a local girl who slips into his bed but any guilt is absolved: 'What saved the situation was the knowledge that she would do the same to anyone else'. He uses her body but that is all, he feels nothing for her personally: 'The women here affect me as the prostitutes in Paris — decorative as objects, but beyond that, nil. Sensuousness is not enough'[11] Did this notion come from his own experiences in Paris? Gibbings was in a state of confusion about his wife and his marriage. The narrator comments: 'Lonely — God! how lonely one can be; the happiest married artist in the world is more lonely than the only white man on Puka Puka. No one can understand — he does not understand himself; if he knew what was in labour in his soul he could give birth'.[12]

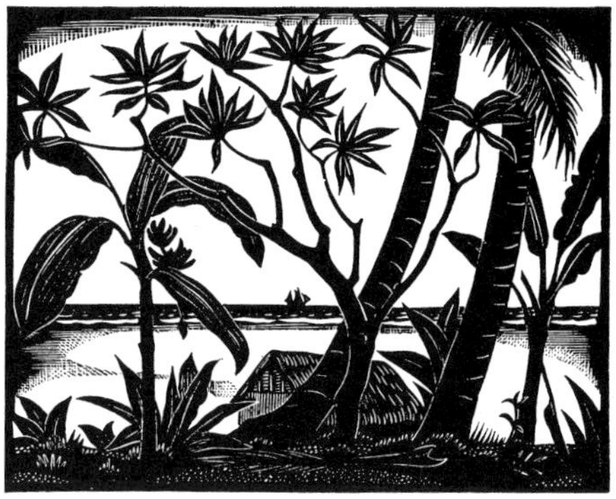

143 Illustration from *Iorana* of a native hut on the shore, wood-engraving, 1932, 81 × 104 mm.

Many passages in *Iorana* illustrate Gibbings's newly found talent, not only an ability to create pictures with the graver, but a natural ability to create pictures with words in a lyrical and sensitive way. Many people were captivated by the gentle Irish lilt of his voice and the colour and richness of his conversation, which flowed with such ease; now he was to extend this ability to the written word. At one moment the narrator is moved by nature and at the next he is despairing at what man has done to the Tahitian society:

A wonderful sunset this evening; the tide was unusually low, the purple sand appeared above its surface in dark ridges, which, seen against the tiger yellow of the water, gave the appearance of some great beast's skin stretched out to dry.

Everything that belongs to the island is glorious, everything imported is horrible. The mynah bird, a kind of rather ugly starling, was imported to eat the wasps, but it hadn't touched them; instead, it had practically driven out all the native birds and had increased to an alarming extent. So with the Chinese; imported first as cheap labour, they have now practically driven out the natives, and soon the island will belong to them. The natives are unbusinesslike; they run up accounts until their land is fully mortgaged, then it changes hands, and soon the true Tahitians on the island will be as rare as the little rose-breasted rice birds.[13]

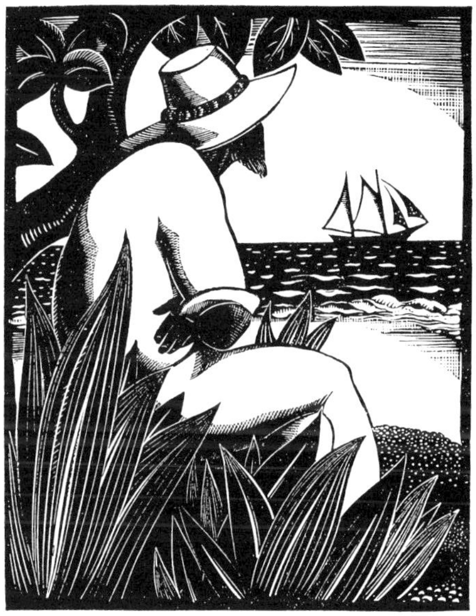

144 Illustration from *Iorana*, wood-engraving, 1932, 126 × 100 mm.

Gibbings was living in a traditional native hut, but he bemoans the fact that, in the part of the island in which he was living, few genuine bamboo huts, thatched with pandanus, have survived, being replaced by almost suburban tin-roofed bungalows. What still remains is the 'astounding ... luxuriance' of the vegetation. The dramatic outline shapes of leaves and grasses made perfect subjects for wood-engraving and Gibbings made endless sketches to be cut on his return. Human beings made less easy subjects — the narrator records in his diary: 'Made some pencil notes of palm trees and schooners. The people are self-conscious; if they see themselves being drawn they will giggle and move away. For that reason most of my sketches seem to be back views.'[14] The depressing mood that pervades the book must in part have been the product of Gibbings's imagination and his narrative purpose. In reality he had enjoyed many aspects of his stay on the island. Later he recalled some happy occasions:

There were parties, of course: yes, plenty of them, and I'm not suggesting that I turned in to a lonely cot, at nine o'clock in the evening, when the moon was rising over the banana groves and the drums were beating out a rhythm for swaying hips; neither do I pretend that I refused all invitations to picnic in the valleys or bathe in the streams that cascaded down from the hills ....'[15]

If the first section of the book describes a corrupted and lost world after the fall, then the second part of the book represents a glimpse of an earthly paradise — the garden of Eden itself. According to the journal, the narrator has moved away from the populated area to a remote peninsula. Here he discovers the

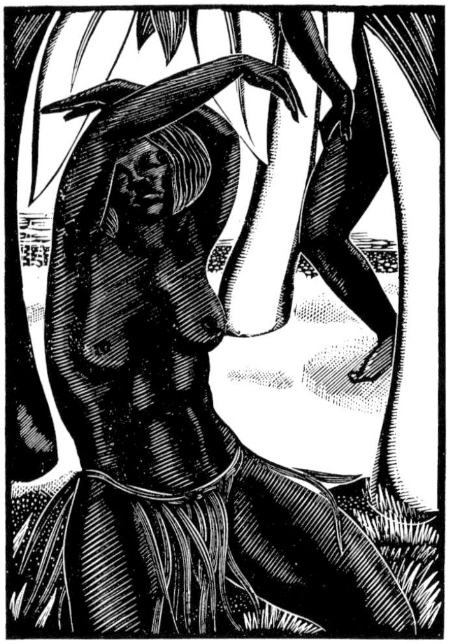

145 Illustration from *Iorana*, wood-engraving, 1932, 140 × 100 mm. Gibbings made an oil painting of the same subject which is in the Gibbings Collection, RUL.

untouched and innocent world of Tahiti that he thought had disappeared. He falls in love with a native girl, Pua, the niece of the woman who has lent him a simple hut, and the story then follows their romantic affair. It is a tale full of sensuality and passion, surrounded by the backdrop of mist-covered mountains and exotic vegetation. With warmth and shelter and food in plenty from the abundant fruits and fish, they resemble Adam and Eve. The story is interspersed with details of the folk-life, customs and ceremonies of the locals; descriptions of pearl diving and shark fishing. Eventually, after capsizing their canoe on a sketching expedition, the narrator and Pua, now naked as the result of losing their native pareus in the sea, discover a deserted 'white man's disused residence', which becomes their secret love nest. Pua, however, is constantly troubled by the advice from her aunt that 'like all the other whites' her lover will go away when he is tired of her. The narrator promises to stay as long as she wants him; he argues to himself that he 'can do engravings equally well here as at home. If I sell an occasional painting to a tourist there should be enough to keep us both'. England is very distant and 'everyday England grows more vulgar; only through a fog of poison can her cities seem romantic'. Eventually he is forced to face reality and accept that he must return. Back in the town of Papeete and dressed once again in western clothes, he hankers for the life he has left: 'I want a pareu and I want Pua in a pareu'. In its closing pages, the story reverts to the earlier theme; returning to the town by car 'it bumped its way home through all the luxuriance and decay, past millionaires' pleasure houses, past Gauguin's old hut. Everywhere decay of mind, decay of body; tuberculosis, elephantiasis, syphilis'.

Gauguin, and his life as a 'noble savage', must have been something of an inspiration to Gibbings, who could well have visited Roger Fry's Post-Impressionist exhibition as a student to marvel at his paintings of Tahiti.[16] Gibbings gives no other account of his stay in Tahiti. How much of *Iorana* is a truthful record of his stay will remain open to interpretation, but he was never to write like this again. There is little of the lightness, humour and convivial style of his later books; *Iorana* is uncompromising, slightly bitter and often dark. The style is frequently naive and sometimes crude, very much the work of an inexperienced writer, but the emotions are passionately felt.

One passage in *Iorana* describes Pua emerging from the bathing pool at their deserted hideaway:

> Pua comes from the pool, the water glistening on her body. Some day I will carve her in stone as a fountain. She will stand with feet apart and head thrown back and she will hold a bowl to her lips, and when the water over-flows from the bowl it will run down over her body, throwing out little cascades from her breasts or seeking out the hollows and following the inner line of her thighs to the pool at her feet. Blue fish will play in the pool.[17]

This description exactly matches a sculpture Gibbings began working on when his new studio had been built at Waltham. A massive female figure, over six feet in height, legs spread apart and head thrown back, was roughed out in Portland stone but never finished. He said the figure represented Earth: 'a woman, heroic

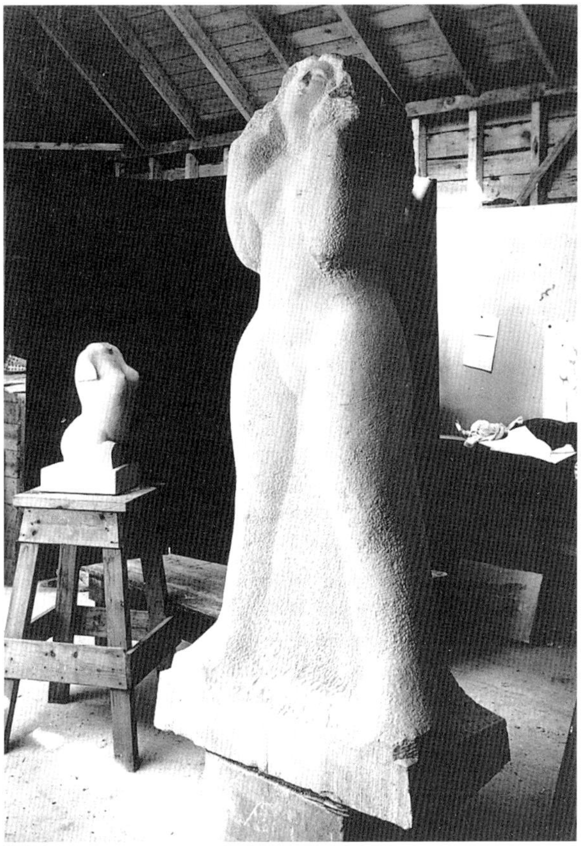

146 *Earth*, the unfinished sculpture standing in the studio at Waltham. The sculpture now stands in the grounds of the house belonging to Gibbings's granddaughter. RUL.

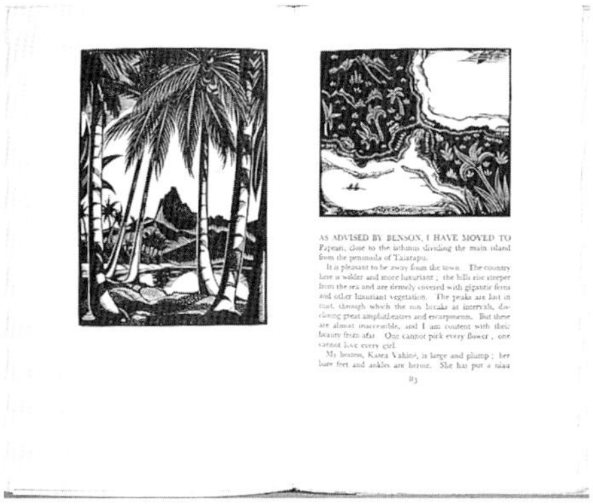

147 Double-page spread from *Iorana*, published by Duckworth in 1932. Page size 250 x 156 mm.

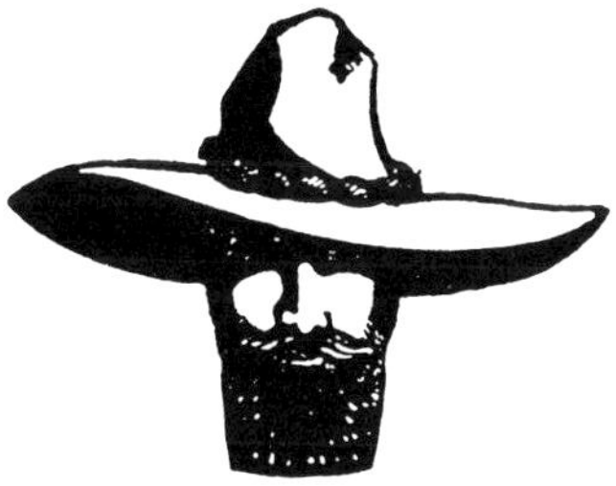

148 Small self-portrait of Gibbings used on the title-page of *Iorana*, wood-engraving, 1932, 24 x 30 mm.

in size, standing with feet apart, and hands and face upraised to catch the rain. Earth waiting to be fertilized'.[18]

Iorana was eventually published in September 1932, by Houghton-Mifflin in Boston, as a limited edition of 385 signed copies. The following month they brought out a much larger and cheaper edition (1,500 copies) and at the same time a similar edition was launched in this country by Duckworth. Gibbings dedicated his book to his intended collaborator, James Norman Hall. He kept control over the design of the book; the format was unusual, rather tall in shape with very generous margins especially at the foot, giving the book a very individual feel. Boldly cut engravings were fitted closely in the text area, balanced by heavy and generously sized type. The text was quite short and so the book was printed on a heavy weight of a soft cream cartridge paper. As well as bulking out the book, the paper was very sympathetic to the printing of the engravings, producing a good printed black. The cover boards were very dramatic and bold in design: he used a pattern derived from copra nuts laid out to dry, which was printed in brown on cream paper. The dust jacket was printed in green on a bright yellow paper. Despite Gibbings's own dismissive comments the book has, in its visual and literary content, a powerful unity. This was Gibbings's first serious book and in it he explored themes that would later dominate his writing. His passion for nature is evident in the detail of the book; it is a constant backdrop to events, and not just in relation to dry land — a fascination for marine life was beginning to develop.

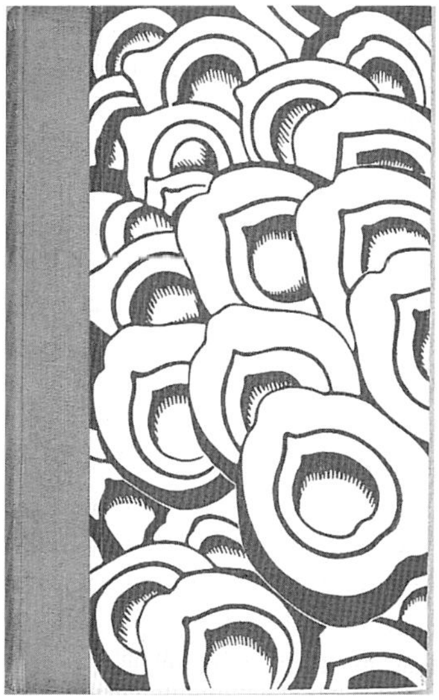

149 Decorative pattern derived from copra nuts used on the cover boards of *Iorana* printed in brown on cream paper.

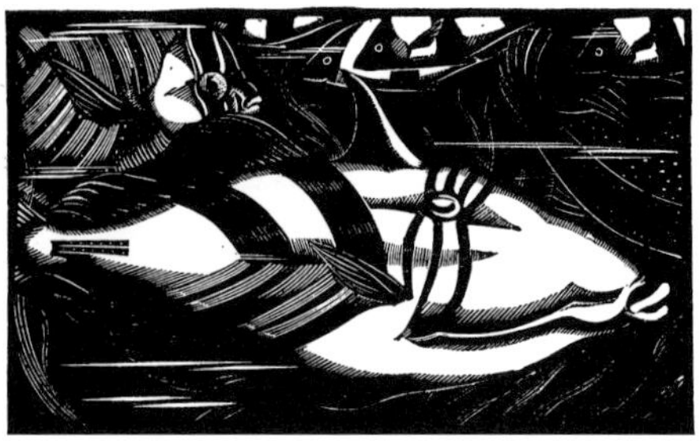

150 Illustration from *Iorana* of tropical fish, wood-engraving, 1932, 60 x 99 mm.

The typescript for *Iorana* must have been completed on time for at the end of January 1932 Gibbings again escaped the depths of an English winter and, apparently at a moment's notice, boarded a cruise ship for the West Indies. Feeling 'a bit weary', Gibbings had written to the Orient Line Shipping Company, for whom he had already undertaken some commissions, suggesting that there must be '... at least one spare cabin in their *Otranto*, due to sail a few days later on a pleasure cruise to the West Indies. Would not a few engravings on my part be *quids* for their *quo* of hospitality? A telegram saying 'Cabin reserved' was the reply'.[19] Once again Moira was left to keep things running at home. In his haste to get his trip organised, Gibbings had overlooked an appointment he had made with John Murray for him to make a social visit, with some friends, to view the press. It fell to Moira to make his apologies:

... my husband went off suddenly at a few days' notice on a 6 weeks cruise to the West Indies. Some people are super lucky — he was feeling horribly in need of a thorough change & was goaded into dropping a line to the Orient Line people ... asking whether they'd be prepared to swap a cruise in exchange for a few blocks, & they simply leapt at it. So he went off in a cloud of dust last Tuesday ....[20]

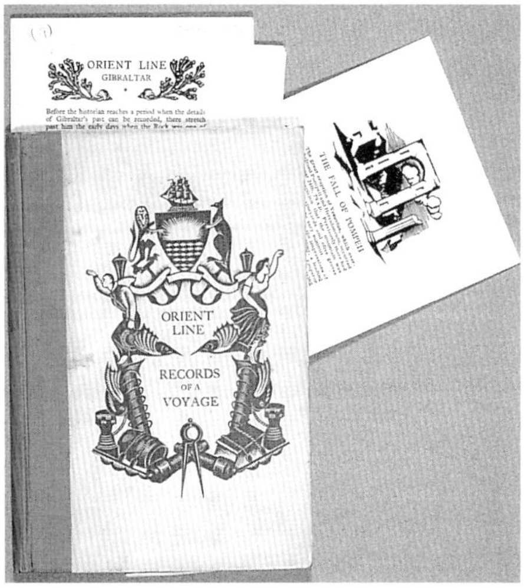

151 Cover design by Gibbings used on a folder containing the voyage records produced by the Orient Line as a souvenir for passengers on their cruise ships, 1932. Cover size 225 x 150 mm, printed in green on a buff cloth with spine in pink cloth. RUL.

The Chairman and the board of the Orient Line company were discerning patrons of the arts and commissioned artists, such as Lynton Lamb and McKnight Kauffer, to illustrate promotional material and a range of ephemera, including menus and dance cards, to use on board their ships. Gibbings produced a range of wood-engravings which were used to decorate menus and information leaflets about each port, contained in a souvenir folder or voyage record, with a cover

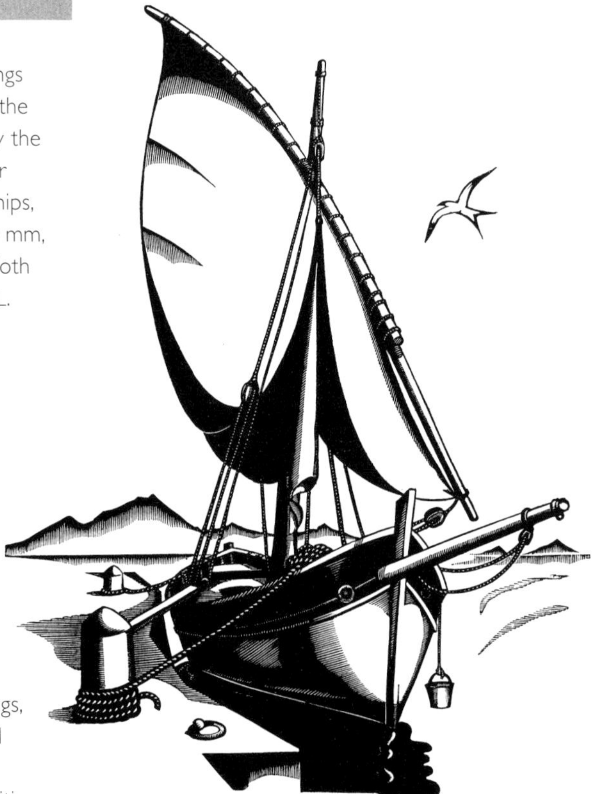

152 *Mediterranean Calm*, from *Fourteen Wood Engravings* by Robert Gibbings, 1932, 205 x 150 mm. Based on drawings Gibbings had made on his journey to Tahiti.

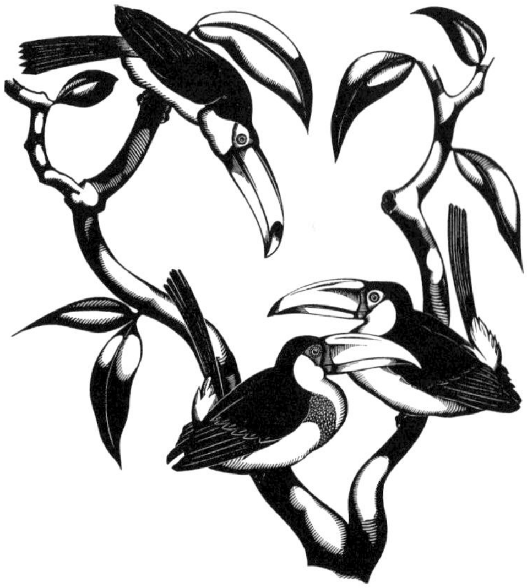

153 *Toucan (one can't) La Guaira*, from *Fourteen Wood Engravings*, 1932, 200 x 183 mm.

design which he also engraved. Of his own cruise, no detailed account exists. On his return Gibbings produced a series of large, vivid engravings based on drawings he had made on his previous voyage to Tahiti, also on the *Otranto*, and on his cruise around the Caribbean islands. Scenes of Italy, Egypt and Tunisia were amongst those illustrated in a bound volume of prints published by the Golden Cockerel Press in October 1932, entitled *Fourteen Wood Engravings*.[21] One of the images, of a gentleman named Hezekiah Brown Esq. sitting on a park bench, was later transformed into a large coloured image and used by the Orient Line on a poster advertising their West Indian cruises, which 'brightened many a platform on the London Underground.' Another piece of publicity for the company was produced at about this time but remains something of a mystery. A small publicity booklet, entitled *Thus we go to Australia* appeared, describing a fictitious voyage to many of the places Gibbings had visited.[22] Illustrated by wood-engravings that are definitely by him, the lettering on the cover uses decorative capitals from the Golden Cockerel Press. The text also seems to be written by Gibbings but the title page gives the following attribution: 'Described and illustrated by Patrick and Moira Edwardes and offered to the Orient Line after a very happy trip'. Published by the Orient Line but undoubtedly printed at the Golden Cockerel Press, it seems strange that Gibbings used such a complicated pseudonym rather than his own name which would have added prestige to the document — perhaps he now considered himself a serious writer and thus did not want to be associated with such trivial publications; he may have felt that it would amuse his son to see his name in print.

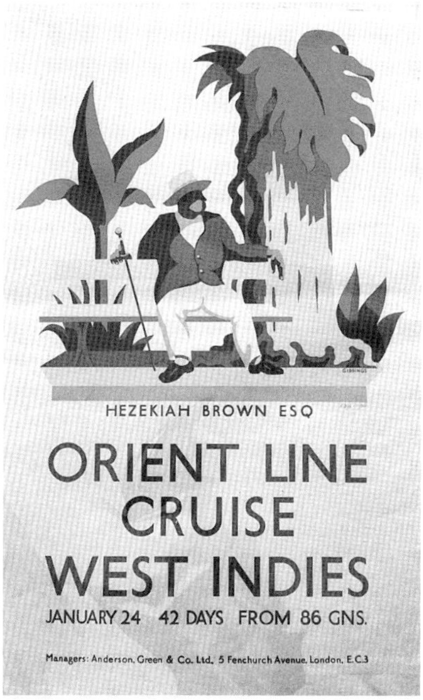

154 Poster for the Orient Line, c. 1933, illustrated by a coloured version of a wood-engraving of 'Hezekiah Brown Esq.' that was published in *Fourteen Wood Engravings*. Poster in private collection.

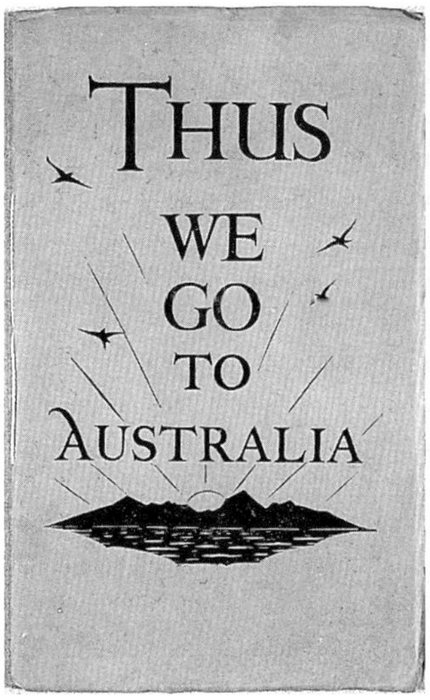

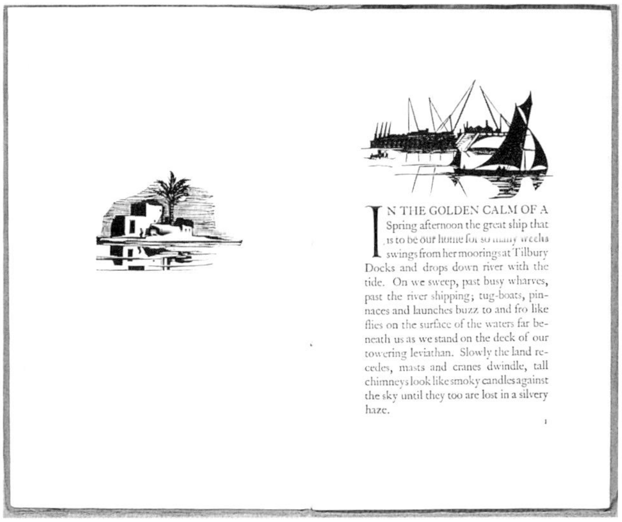

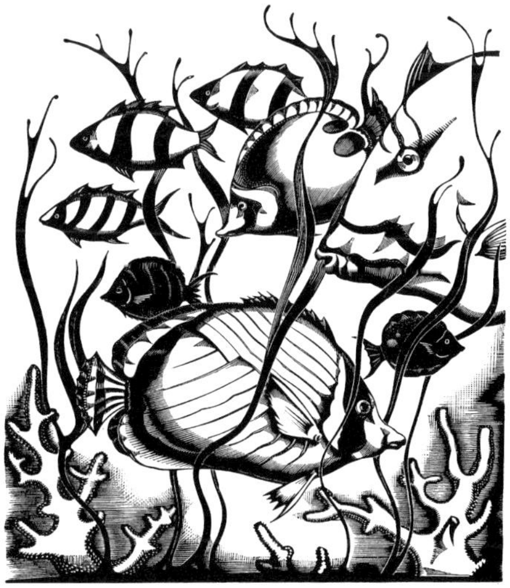

155 *left* Cover of *Thus we go to Australia*, c. 1932, 228 × 142 mm. A small publicity booklet apparently written by 'Patrick and Moira Edwardes' and 'offered to the Orient Line after a very happy trip', but really written and illustrated by Gibbings and printed at the Golden Cockerel Press. RUL.

156 *right* Opening pages of *Thus we go to Australia*, c. 1932, page size 228 × 142 mm. RUL.

157 *Mid Coral Caves, Bermuda*, from *Fourteen Wood Engravings*, 1932, 185 × 163 mm.

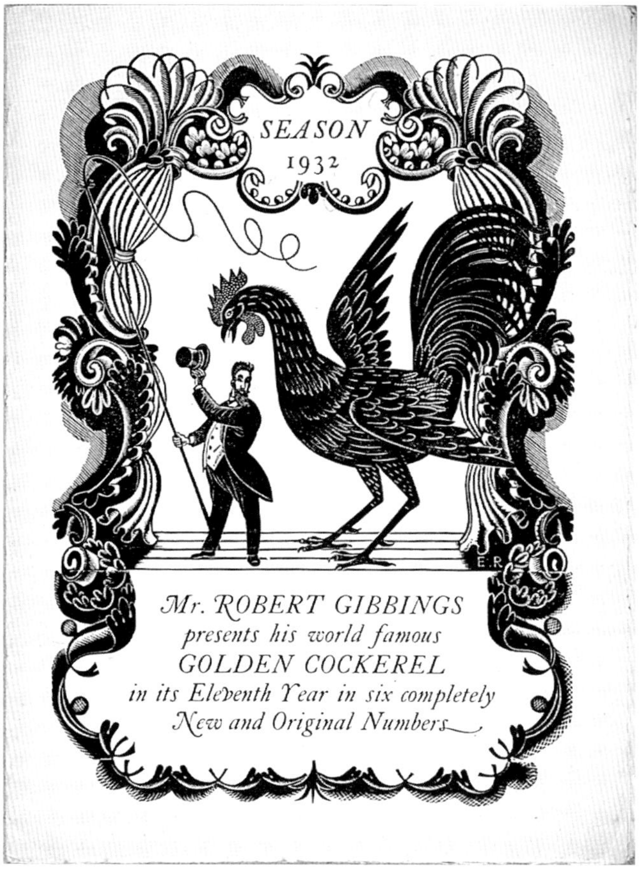

158 Cover of the *Prospectus* for 1932, page size 252 x 190 mm. Illustrated with a decorative wood-engraved design by Eric Ravilious. Reproduced by permission of the Golden Cockerel Press Ltd.

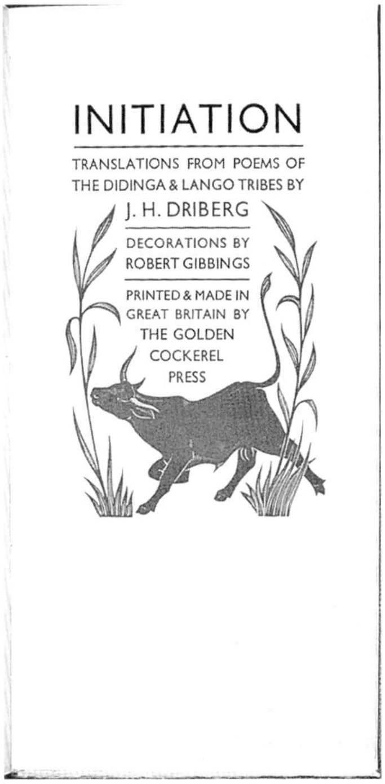

159 Titlepage from *Initiation* by J. H. Driberg, 1932, page size 228 x 114 mm. Designed and illustrated with eleven wood-engravings by Gibbings, printed in colour. This is an early example of a book set entirely in the typeface Gill Sans. Reproduced by permission of the Golden Cockerel Press Ltd.

FOR THE COVER of the Golden Cockerel Press prospectus for 1932, Eric Ravilious provided yet another of his humorous and highly decorative engravings. Gibbings was depicted on the cover as a ring master in top hat and tails, dwarfed on stage by a gigantic cockerel. 'Mr Robert Gibbings presents his world famous Golden Cockerel in its Eleventh Year in six completely New and Original Numbers'; in fact the prospectus featured all ten of the books that had been, or were yet to be, published that year in addition to the *Fourteen Wood Engravings*. One project announced was a book of essays to be entitled *Sermons by Artists*, which was later postponed and did not appear until 1934. The printing of bookplates was also advertised in the prospectus. Holding in the region of one thousand woodblocks by the leading artists of the day was an asset not to be ignored in these times of financial strain. Gibbings offered to print 250 bookplates, at a cost of five guineas to subscribers, using any block selected from the Press's publications.

The first book to be printed in 1932 was a collection of poems by J. H. Driberg called *Initiation*. A tall slim volume, uniform with Gill's *Clothing Without Cloth*, it was entirely set in Gill Sans and must be one of the first examples of a complete book using this typeface.[23] The design of the book is sensitive; Gibbings engraved eleven blocks which were printed in subtle colours of blue-grey, terracotta, and sepia. Although small, *Initiation* is a beautiful little book and is an example of Gibbings's more adventurous typographic design. A new translation of Ovid's elegies by Powys Mathers entitled *The Amores of P. Ovidius Naso*, was published in March with engravings on copper by J. E. Laboureur, followed by *A German Idyll*, by H. E. Bates with wood-engravings by Lynton Lamb.

After well over a year working on the engravings for *Twelfth Night*, Ravilious finally completed the work and the play was published in April. It was a handsome book, uniform in format with *The Four Gospels*, and Ravilious's engravings were among his best. Gibbings had made the brave decision to print the blocks in colour, either a sepia or a blue-grey, but Ravilious was disappointed when he saw the result. In July two more companion volumes were published, *The Life of Mr Jonathan Wild the Great*, to accompany Henry Fielding's *Journey from this World to the Next*, again with etchings by Denis Tegetmeier, and *Crotty Shinkwin and The Beauty Spot* by A. E. Coppard, produced in the same format as Coppard's *Hundredth Story*, with wood-engravings again by Gibbings. In addition to *Fourteen Wood Engravings*, four more books appeared at the end of the year.

Sales were down and, in an attempt to build up new markets, it was decided to try publishing a limited edition of a particular book while at the same time printing a popular unlimited edition on machine made paper in 'an attempt to produce cheap Cockerels for small purses'. Two titles were published in this series in October 1932; both were light and humorous books based on parlour games. The first was a 'complete story' but one which was written adopting the format of the game 'consequences', which became its title. Nine different authors were asked, in turn, to write a chapter. Coppard had contacted a number of

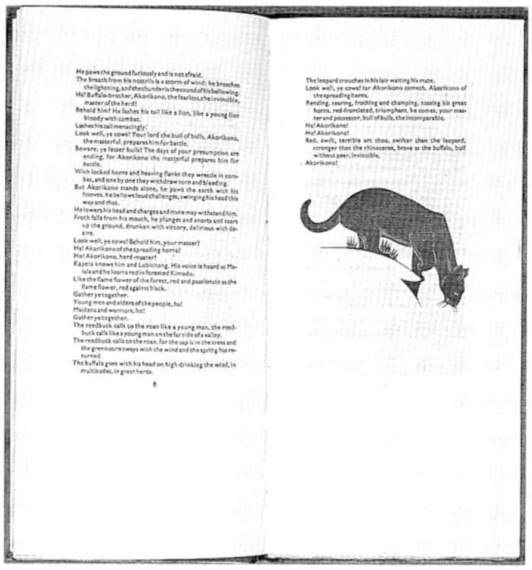

160 Double-page spread from *Initiation*, 1932, with a wood-engraving by Gibbings printed in a terracotta colour, page size 228 × 114mm. Reproduced by permission of the Golden Cockerel Press Ltd.

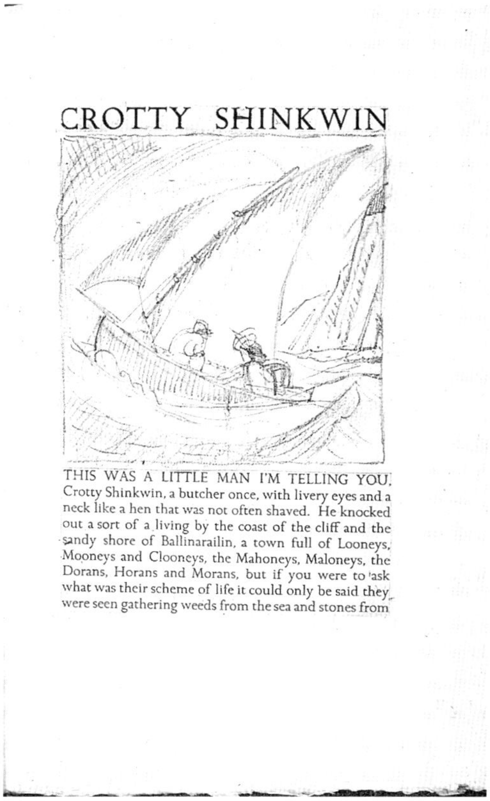

CROTTY SHINKWIN

THIS WAS A LITTLE MAN I'M TELLING YOU. Crotty Shinkwin, a butcher once, with livery eyes and a neck like a hen that was not often shaved. He knocked out a sort of a living by the coast of the cliff and the sandy shore of Ballinarailin, a town full of Looneys, Mooneys and Clooneys, the Mahoneys, Maloneys, the Dorans, Horans and Morans, but if you were to ask what was their scheme of life it could only be said they were seen gathering weeds from the sea and stones from

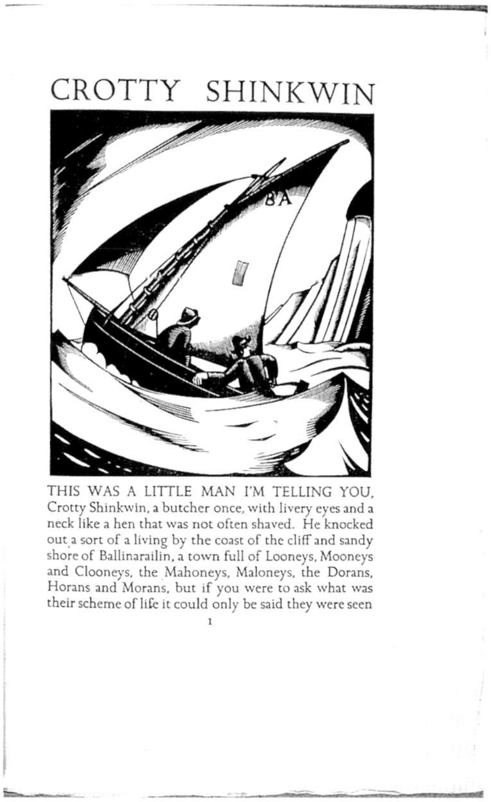

CROTTY SHINKWIN

THIS WAS A LITTLE MAN I'M TELLING YOU. Crotty Shinkwin, a butcher once, with livery eyes and a neck like a hen that was not often shaved. He knocked out a sort of a living by the coast of the cliff and sandy shore of Ballinarailin, a town full of Looneys, Mooneys and Clooneys, the Mahoneys, Maloneys, the Dorans, Horans and Morans, but if you were to ask what was their scheme of life it could only be said they were seen

1

161 *left* A rough layout for page 1 from *Crotty Shinkwin*, with a pencil sketch showing the position for the engraving and proofs of the text cut up and pasted down by Gibbings. Author's collection.

162 *right* Page 1 from *Crotty Shinkwin* by A. E. Coppard, 1932, page size 241 × 153 mm. Illustrated with seven wood-engravings and border by Gibbings. Reproduced by permission of the Golden Cockerel Press Ltd.

eminent authors to collaborate on the project such as Siegfried Sassoon, Walter de la Mare, Evelyn Waugh, David Garnett and Osbert Sitwell,[24] but eventually a group of talented but less well-known writers agreed to contribute.

> John van Druten described 'the man,' G. B. Stern described 'the woman.' A. E. Coppard told 'Where they met.' Sean O' Faolain told what 'He said to her,' and so on via Norah Hoult, Hamish Maclaren, Elizabeth Bowen, and Ronald Fraser to Malachi Whitaker, who recounted what 'The world said.' The book, edited by A. E. Coppard, was a great success.[25]

The only illustration was a splendid frontispiece by Ravilious of the authors sitting around a table perched on top of an iced cake. Two hundred copies, on hand-made paper and signed by the authors, were priced at two guineas, the cheap edition at six shillings.[26]

The second title in the series was the amusing and eccentric book called *Rummy*. The tale was mainly told in words by Coppard, but with protests and interjections by Gibbings. The story, if story it could be called, recounts a family holiday shared by the Gibbingses and Coppards in the 'mountain fastnesses of Cork and Kerry'; but the book is also about the 'noble game' that gives the book its title. Weather was an ever present factor on a holiday in Ireland and Gibbings and Coppard, grounded by the rain, had entered into an extended bout of playing cards; for a few weeks, with the added excitement of bets, the game became an obsession. Illustrated with delightful caricatures of the two men, Coppard wrote an extremely colourful and funny account of the rivalry between the two competitors. Despite a feigned ruthlessness over their titanic battle with the cards, the book is full of affection and friendship. Memories of Gibbings's theatrical role as God were evoked in a witty portrait of Robert and his friendliness with his native people:

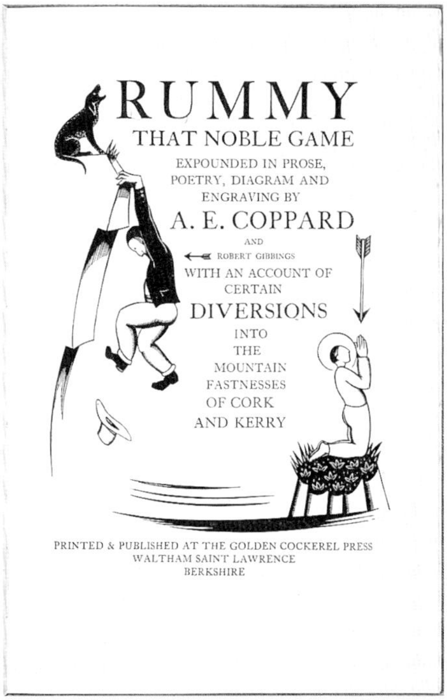
RUMMY
THAT NOBLE GAME
EXPOUNDED IN PROSE, POETRY, DIAGRAM AND ENGRAVING BY
A. E. COPPARD
AND
ROBERT GIBBINGS
WITH AN ACCOUNT OF CERTAIN
DIVERSIONS
INTO THE MOUNTAIN FASTNESSES OF CORK AND KERRY

PRINTED & PUBLISHED AT THE GOLDEN COCKEREL PRESS
WALTHAM SAINT LAWRENCE
BERKSHIRE

163 Title page from the popular edition of *Rummy* printed on machine-made paper, 1932, page size 241 × 160 mm. Illustrated with fifteen wood-engravings and a diagram by Gibbings. Reproduced by permission of the Golden Cockerel Press Ltd.

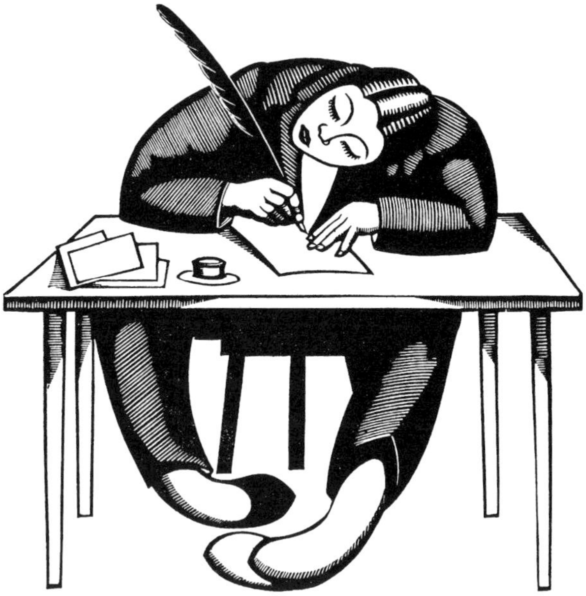

164 and 165 Portraits of Coppard the writer, 96 x 97 mm., and Gibbings the artist, 115 x 75 mm., from *Rummy*, 1932. Wood-engravings by Gibbings.

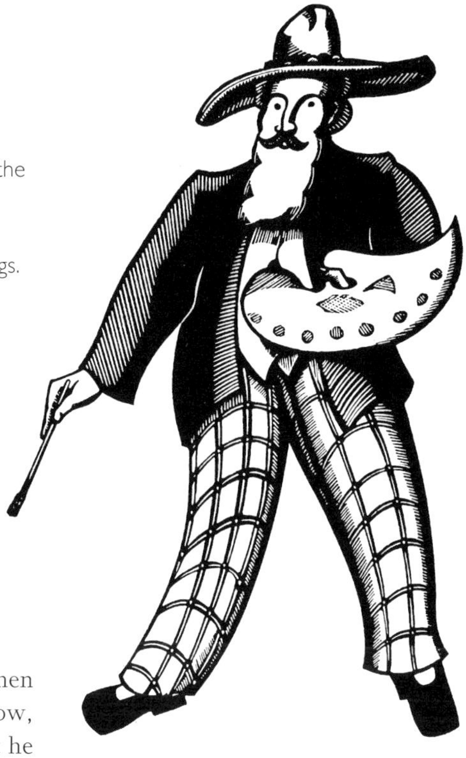

... Gibbings came from Cork, so he is Irish to the backbone, and calls a sod a sod when he means it is a tuft of grass. ... As you may see, he is a large man. I declare now, solemnly, that I have nothing much to urge against largeness merely *as* largeness, but he has a beard also to match, which gives him the aspect of the Great Personage reproduced so often in the engravings of William Blake, and so when we drifted into the fair at Bantry the whole market — drovers and tramps and the girls in the bars, even the old round-shouldered farmers sagging asleep on angular nags that were probably sleeping too — the whole market I might say woke up or stopped its business just to look at him, to talk to him, to shake hands with him, to recall deeds of his ancestors, and to predict great things of a man with such a holy appearance on him.[27]

On the next page, Coppard gave a vivid word picture of Gibbings at work:

Well, as the man is shaped, so are his arrangements. He has two or three studios — and I declare to God they are all as large as gymnasiums — and you could see him sitting in one or other of them quietly drinking his beer, his whisky, his rum, his gin, his brandy, or whatever, as happy as a child at the breast, and squinting through a magnifying glass to carve his little pictures on a wood block no bigger than a ham sandwich.

Coppard recalled breaks from the game to walk along the sea shore with the Gibbings twins, defying the weather:

These two fair-haired youths of the age of three were wandering alone with me one day over the rocks that stretch in places half a mile out to sea, and as it was stormy we were in our macintoshes, our gumboots, and our sou'-westers, slipping and staggering on sea-weed or gazing at sea-urchins and anemones. Of these two little imps it may be said that taciturnity is their birthright. Incapacitated by spray, bewildered by rain, quaking with cold, or in some sort of speechless communion with the elements, they took these enjoyments with an appearance of misery that reft me to the soul ....[28]

The book was dedicated to 'the finest hotel in the world, Cronin's of Gougane Barra', where they stayed for most of their holiday. The Cronins were great friends of Robert and the hotel was situated on the shore of a lake called Gougane Barra, surrounded by precipitous mountain sides — a peaceful and atmospheric place to which Robert would return. The hotel was remote and at that time somewhat primitive, but a place flowing with gossip and tales, jigs, reels, hornpipes, fiddles and Gaelic airs. There were moments when the weather was kinder and Coppard gave an account of an outing to the mountains:

> The day was bright and warm, and our track grew steeper as the region began to quarry out in vast crescents of rock and bog. By and by Mr. Gibbings, who is normally a personage of spiritual tone although his physical contour is as generous as the outline of a map of Africa, removed some parts of his costume. At intervals, as we travelled higher into the beguiling privacy of nature, he removed the whole; and in beard and shoes only, trousers under arm, bestrode the ridges like a shameless Greek colossus, murmuring: 'Damn the flies!' or 'That was a snipe, that was!'[29]

Daisy Matthews and Three Other Tales, published in November 1932, was a collection of short stories by the Welsh writer Rhys Davies, with engravings by Agnes Miller Parker. Since 1930 Agnes and her husband William McCance had been employed by the Gregynog Press in Wales. McCance was the 'controller' of the Press and Agnes was paid a retaining fee as a wood-engraver. They shared the work with Blair Hughes-Stanton, who was 'chief artist' and his wife, Gertrude Hermes, who was also an illustrator. By 1932 tensions were mounting at the Gregynog and Agnes had responded with relief to a request from Gibbings that she should do some engravings for the Golden Cockerel Press.[30] Writing to Gertrude Hermes, Agnes referred to the offer: 'He'd got some stories that he thought would suit me .... What I'm so pleased about is that he told me what he could afford and said he was sorry he could not be more generous.' Even in his own times of financial crisis, it would appear Gibbings 'exceeded the rate paid by the miserable Gregynog management'.[31] Agnes produced four delicate engravings for the book which demonstrated her masterful draughtsmanship. As with so many of the new generation of engravers, Agnes used fine and shallow cutting on her blocks, which presented the usual challenge to the printer. Gibbings's own engravings became progressively finer and more detailed but he was always clean and decisive in his cutting — he had learnt from his difficulties with printing certain blocks at the Press. Gibbings advised Agnes to take an edition of numbered proofs from the blocks before she sent them to the Press. This was his own habitual practice and one he recommended to all his artists — the prints could be sold separately and provided a much needed source of extra income.

Apple Trees, the last book to be printed that year, was a collection of four autobiographical pieces written by Hugh Walpole about his childhood and early days in literary London. Walpole had written the first of his reminiscences while visiting Carthage on holiday at the beginning of 1932 and had finished the remaining stories while enjoying a stay on the island of Sark that summer. Wood-engraved illustrations had been supplied by Lynton Lamb and the book was rushed into production to meet the Christmas market. Walpole was surprised by 'a marvellous notice of it in the Express today ...', written by an old adversary, the critic James Agate. Unfortunately Walpole was notorious for being hopeless at spelling and punctuation and he relied on professional proof-readers to correct his typescripts; perhaps due to their haste, Gibbings and his team 'let a shoal of anomalies through the net'.[32]

When Gibbings had returned from the West Indies in early March, he had written to Eric Ravilious to thank him for his design for the prospectus: 'Each one you do gets more magnificent and this one is superb.'[33] His tone was full of optimism as he reported that he had 'Just got back from a splendid trip in the sun feeling full of energy'. But at home the situation had got worse. The slump had really taken a grip on both sides of the Atlantic and with everyone anxious to hang on to their money, sales of luxuries such as expensive books slumped too:

> But clear days at sea were a prelude to clouds ashore. I came home to find that times had grown difficult: the slump was upon us. Then some panic-stricken statesman got up in Parliament and told the nation that it must buy nothing it did not use: all luxuries must be renounced. Next morning, and for weeks on end, it was cancellations instead of orders that were piled upon my desk, and soon I was wellnigh renouncing necessities.[34]

But the crisis was behind the scenes. On the surface the Press had reached a peak; in the past year it had published some of its most prestigious and beautiful books and its reputation for quality had never been higher. Articles in the press continued to appear in many parts of the world; the *Cape Argus* in South Africa published two articles on the Press and in May 1932 a checklist of Golden Cockerel prospectuses, compiled by George Churchill, appeared in the American journal *The Book Collector's Packet* of New York. A short introduction about the Press praised the originality of their work:

> Lack of timidness in design is another characteristic of the books they produce. New conventions and striking innovations in typographic arrangements are constantly being used. So their books seem fresh and contemporary and this strain is also felt in the design of their announcements and prospectuses.[35]

Notes on the Press, written by Moira, had been published in *A Catalogue for Typophiles* and Clare Leighton had included examples of Gibbings's wood-engraving in her influential instructional book, *Wood-Engraving and Woodcuts*. Commenting on his technique, Leighton stressed his 'exceptional cleanness of outline'. Referring to his print *Pandanus Grove, Tahiti* that had appeared in *Iorana*, she felt that it typified his style: 'His simple masses of black and white have extra solidity given them by the cross-hatching work with the graver (*vide* the tree trunks) which merges the black into the white with a grey. All his greys have a definite shape by being cut off along their edges by the whites. This means that his white and his black masses also are definite.'[36]

IN EARLY SUMMER, Gibbings had heard from the 'angel from Skibbereen', Mary O'Sullivan, that she had given birth to a little girl, and that she wished Robert to be a godfather. In July, he sent her a christening gift:

> I'm sending you today by registered post a little bit of a present for the child so that if she wasn't born with a silver spoon in her mouth (and *you* ought to know best) at least she can have one soon after.

If the devil wasn't not only twisting my tail but stamping on me as well, I'd have sent the girl something worth having. But as this is the only bit of personal silver I was ever given I'd like the only God child I've ever had to have it. It was given me by my Godfather John Day 43 years ago so its in the family nearly as long as yourself!![37]

Sadly his own family life was coming to an end. At the end of the year Moira left Waltham for South Africa, where she had family, taking Brigid and the twins with her. The tension between Robert and Moira had been building up, resulting in frequent arguments. Perhaps Moira resented the way Robert felt entitled to desert the Press and home when he felt like it — leaving her to take all the strain. Despite efforts to recognise her contribution (her name always appeared jointly with Robert's on the colophon in Golden Cockerel books), she must have felt that it was Robert whose name was always linked with the Press. She was a very strong and independent woman and perhaps was no longer prepared to play a supporting role. The reason for leaving given to the younger children was that Larry had contracted TB and needed the sun and fresh air of South Africa for his health. Even if this was part of the truth, Moira never returned to live permanently in England; she came back briefly in 1936 to finalise a divorce. On arrival in South Africa, the children were sent off to stay with an uncle on his farm, while Moira set about finding a means of making a living. Her mother was already living in South Africa and gave her financial support, enabling her to buy a seaside hotel near Durban, where the children later joined her. Patrick, then aged twelve, stayed behind with his father to continue his education at St Piran's Independent School in Maidenhead.[38]

At this time of reflection and upheaval, a new personality appeared who was to have a profound effect on Robert's approach to life:

It was one Sunday morning in the early part of December 1932 that a knock on my studio door brought me face to face with Llewelyn Powys for the first time. I was then running the Golden Cockerel Press in the garden of my home in Berkshire, and about a fortnight before this appearance Llewelyn had sent me the MS of his essay, *Glory of Life*. I had replied to him by return and with enthusiasm ... from the first moment I saw him and gripped his hand I knew that there could never be anything but agreement between us, that indeed though neither of us had known it there had never been anything but affinity of thought in the past. ... I do not remember a word that he or Alyse [his wife] or I spoke to each other that morning, I only remember the radiance that they brought into that almost suburban abode.[39]

Powys had attended a luncheon at Merton College, Oxford, the previous evening and wrote to a friend describing the event and his meeting with Gibbings the following day: 'On Sunday we went to the Golden Cockerel Press to see Robert Gibbings. He appeared out of his printing house all bearded and golden like a printing Vulcan in the cold winter fields. He is going to bring out an essay of mine in the same magnificent format as his Gospels.'[40]

Llewelyn Powys, the writer and bard, came to represent the embodiment of the 'Glory of Life' — he was a mystic figure. Tall and thin, he had a white beard and a thick mop of crispy white hair like a 'silver halo' and often dressed in a flowing cape. He was photographed holding a crudely wrought iron ankh, the Egyptian symbol of enduring life and generative energy, a motif that he used as his own and incorporated into the design of his books. He later gave Gibbings an ankh, made by a local blacksmith, which he treasured. Gibbings reflected that although he had met Llewelyn no more than a 'dozen times', he seemed a 'life long friend'. Robert had difficulty identifying with organised religion but the all-powerful belief in nature and life that radiated from Llewelyn was almost priest-like, and deeply moved Robert. On the last day of 1932 Gibbings visited Llewelyn at his house near Chydyok, 'set high in the folds of the Dorsetshire Downs'; at that time Gibbings did not know that Llewelyn was a sick man:

> Next day he and I wandered over the Downs, making our objective the grave of Caractacus high above Lulworth Cove. I did not understand then the full measure of anxiety in Alyse's eyes as we set out lest he should overtire himself. I did not understand the strength of the spiritual flame that nourished his frail body.
>
> Rich fertile ploughlands, poor flint-strewn pastures, reed-fringed boggy pools; lapwings wheeling, a snipe or a grey owl rising, each brought its exaltation. Nothing was too small to escape his notice; in every pebble he saw a miracle, in every flower a sacred mystery. He was realising the very words that some time later he put in a letter to me: 'We should live every day as if we had been suddenly let out of our graves where for two centuries our diet had been dust and darkness.'
>
> When we reached that mound under which the great Welsh king lies buried, Llewelyn took off his hat and stood in silence and in reverence.
>
> Again it was dark when we reached Chydyok and again as we sat over the big fire that evening there was love and worship of life. A kitten was frisking and playing at our feet and we laughed at its antics and wondered at its agility.[41]

His meeting with Llewelyn had renewed Robert's flagging spirit but the truth was that his life had reached a turning point. Moira and Robert had been through so much together during the years of struggle to make a living from the Press and Robert's art. The marriage had been a sexually open one and both partners had shown tolerance towards each other. But by nature the artist has to be single-minded and has to take priority; this inevitably brings about a conflict with the constraints and responsibilities of parenthood and family life. Now, with his marriage over, Gibbings had to contemplate his future and the future of the Press.

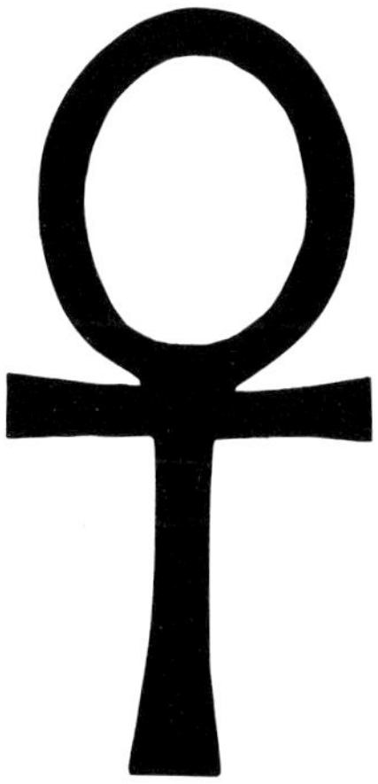

166 Representation of a metal ankh given to Gibbings by his friend Llewelyn Powys and made by a local blacksmith. Author's collection.

Chapter Eleven
An End and a Fresh Start 1933–1935

In January 1933, Eric Ravilious had sent Gibbings a sketch for yet another cockerel for the cover of a spring prospectus. He had enjoyed engraving the last one so much that he was keen to do another but Gibbings had replied that he had decided 'to run the G. C. on very much quieter lines' that year. Rather than producing one large prospectus, he had planned to issue separate leaflets for each book: '... especially as we are going to reduce our number of publications by about half in order to meet the distressful times'.[1] There was an ominous ring to his words, but Ravilious responded with a typically generous offer; on 1 February he wrote to Gibbings that he was sorry he was not printing a prospectus:

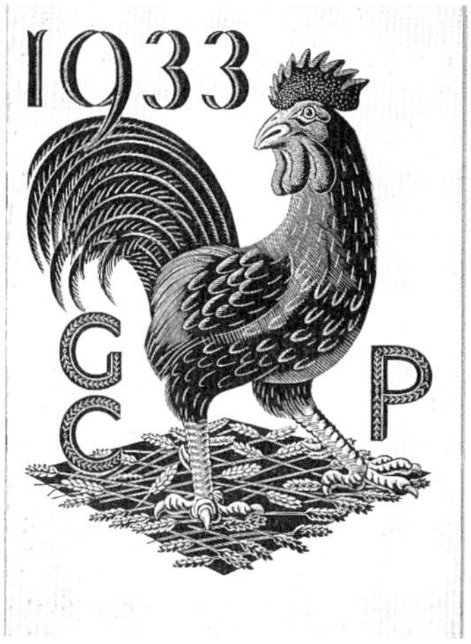

167 *Golden Cockerel Press Prospectus*, 1933, wood-engraving by Eric Ravilious, page size 250 x 184 mm.

> An idea: I shan't be going away for a week or two yet at least. I like doing these Spring Lists you publish every year, besides I feel they are by now an institution — one I would miss very much.
>
> That being so, if you like to pay Beedham for clearing the ground for me, I'll make you a present of the rest.
>
> All this in case you have not finally made up your mind about separate leaflets — I know a large prospectus must be an expensive item.[2]

Gibbings gladly accepted his offer and insisted on paying for the wood and sending 'a few books as very small appreciation'.[3]

At the beginning of the New Year there were still a number of publications in progress. Gibbings had recently printed and illustrated a wine list for the Crown and Thistle Hotel in Abingdon-on-Thames;[4] in February, *Lord Adrian: A Play* by Lord Dunsany appeared with eight wood-engravings by Gibbings. The illustrations were of wild creatures including badgers, a fox, a hare and otters, and are particularly lively and well drawn; his more usual style of heavy black and white was relieved by the use of a mid-tone for the animals' fur, achieved through a stippled use of the graver. *Lord Adrian* was the last book to be published by the Press under the direction of Gibbings at Waltham.[5] When the *Spring Prospectus* was finally ready the opening paragraph was a poignant message from Robert to his faithful subscribers:

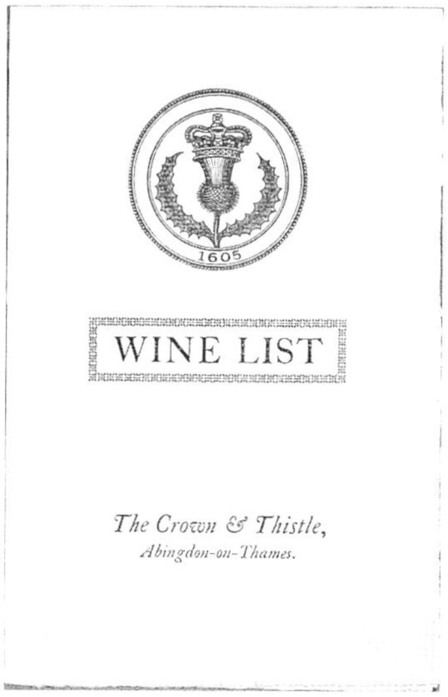

168 Wine list for the Crown and Thistle, c. 1933. Illustrated with wood-engravings by Gibbings and Farleigh, page size 207 x 138 mm. RUL.

> From Gibbings, R., to his well beloved clients, Greetings! Whereas the urge to carve stone has now succeeded the desire to model type, it has seemed good unto me that the mantle of Golden Feathers should fall upon one Christopher Sandford, born of the same noble city of Cork, late owner of the Boar's Head Press and a Director of the Golden Hours and Chiswick Presses. But don't be thinking that it's all his own way he'll be having, for Francis Newbery, a fellow-director of the Chiswick, will be his partner, and Owen Rutter,

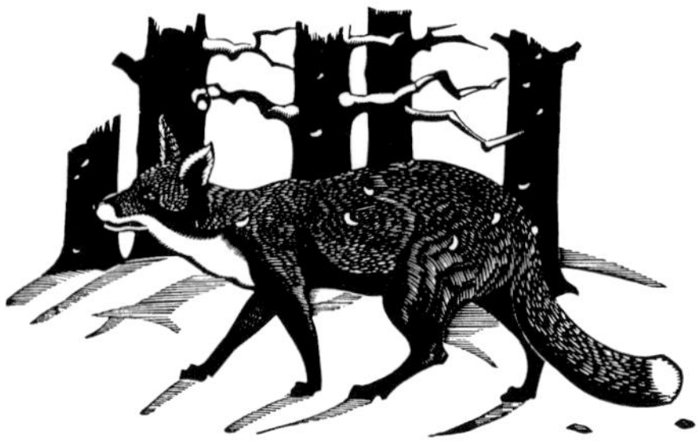

169 Illustration from *Lord Adrian*, 1933, wood-engraving, 55 × 88 mm.

writer of many admirable works, will supervise the literary adventure, and indeed I'll be there myself just on and off.

So after nine years I'm saying goodbye, and don't be sad or lonely, for I don't know of anyone who could take better care of me poor little bird; and anyway you'll be hearing lots about me in all their lists, and there are grand days still to come!

In a letter to Sandford following his visit to Waltham in December 1931, Gibbings had insisted that he 'was quite serious about wishing to sell'. Sandford's reply expressed his regret that he had been unable to find a partner to join with him to raise the money to purchase the Press. Gibbings responded in a letter in March that he was 'sorry and at the same time glad'. He said that he was 'really fond of the blessed old bird', but, 'On the other hand', he continued, 'it does take a lot of my time that I want to devote to stone etc. so if you ever feel like it again I'm always ready to be tempted'.[6] Sandford clearly did tempt Gibbings again, as on 18 April, he replied to a letter from Sandford giving an outline of the financial position:

I've written you a long letter but cant [*sic*] make up my mind to send it. I could not step out in my shirt so to speak under £5000 for the Press & £3000 for the house & land, the latter is freehold & was valued at that figure before we spent about £300 in improvements.

If these figures make it at all possible for you let me know & we can go into it further. But in any case treat them as strictly *confidential*. I will also reply to your other letter in a few days. I've been having a burst of wood and stone cutting and find it hard to get back to pen and paper.[7]

Sandford must have expressed interest in a deal for only ten days later Gibbings wrote another letter giving details of his assessment of the current position.

Right! let's leave it till we have a talk in the summer. If times were normal you should have no difficulty whatever in making £1000 P.A. making full allowances for the work I throw in. Although our books are few in number they are [?] and last year we sold over £7000 invoice value. I am not attempting anything like that this year although English sales are holding up very well indeed.

While I have the advantage of throwing in engravings you would presumably be able to save on Secretaries, Churchills & what nots & then again you would have your missis who would presumably throw her work in. But I would really much rather leave the matter over. Everything in the world is too unsettled to form any idea of real value & I don't want to DO !! or be done by !! a friend. If the world goes to blazes we are all in the soup, if it recovers this is a jolly good show.

It would never do to 'farm out' that would ruin everything. No page of our *books* has ever been printed anywhere but here; our lists, yes! but not books.

So lets [*sic*] leave it till the weather gets warmer. Come down then & have a swim.[8]

But the matter was dropped until the next year. Gibbings and Sandford kept in touch and Sandford had even suggested that the Press might publish some of his poems but Gibbings declined. Sandford eventually revived the issue of the sale of the Golden Cockerel in May 1933. In his response, Gibbings assured him that he had not sold it yet but he had had various offers:

Many thanks for your letter. No I haven't sold the G.C. yet as I did not think it would be possible to work in with those particular publishers. Now I have had a definite offer from a private individual but I'm inclined to think that my acceptance would make it necessary for me to give more time to the show than I wish. What I am most anxious to do in life is sculpture and I want to plan my life so that I have at least half time for same. I am quite prepared to sell the press either as a going concern or merely the name and goodwill with the small stock of books, etc. I have no particular wish to be in it myself though if necessary I would be prepared to accept *part* time job at a salary. Supposing I should decide eventually not to sell the name and goodwill at all and merely disband, what figure would you be prepared to offer me for all rights in the G.C. type. Caslon hold the punches of the following

36' Caps 24' Caps
18' " and l.c. Roman.
14' " " " "
14' l.c. Italic.

and we have in stock about 2300 lbs mostly in 18 pt. and 14 pt. A great deal of it is practically unused and some has never been in the cases.

Let me know what you think, also come and sunbathe.[9]

The negotiations had been open and friendly, Sandford and Gibbings had a great deal in common, but Sandford was much more experienced and astute when it came to business matters. Notes scribbled at the end of Gibbings's letter by Sandford show that he had remembered Robert's optimistic statement of turnover — he was very conscious that these figures were based on the Press's most successful year of 1930. Aware of the effects of the slump on values, he drafted a letter which was much more cautious and realistic:

It is rather hard to answer your letter or make offers for your type etc. since everything is at a stand-still & there are no 'market-values' on which to base offers, everything depending on what the vendor-bloke will accept for his stuff.

As to the type & punches I expect these cost you £300 or £400 at least but you have used the type in several books so that it has lost all its value in newness & must therefore just be considered a good proprietary type (that is the 18pt & 14pt l.c. are proprietary but the 'Perpetua' Caps. seem all to be on the open market.) *As metal* of course the whole is only worth about £17. I think it would be best if you could say (supposing you decided to disband) the lowest *you* would take for it.

After your recent negotiations you have probably now made up your mind what is the amount you count to clear for 'name & good-will and type'. If you could let me know this also I should see if I could do anything, though I have nothing *specific* in mind. It all depends on whether you are not too ambitious in what you want, & as you are anxious to concentrate on sculpture anyhow, I expect you would not be too exacting.

We adore sun-bathing but are frightfully busy at the moment changing house, but some other time we shld. love to come.[10]

Selling his entire interest in the Press was one solution but, with Barclays Bank pressing him to keep up with payments, Gibbings had to consider other ways to carry on. One possibility was to take on another partner who could carry some of the administrative and financial burden. An offer of support and help had come from a friend, Owen Rutter, who lived close to Waltham at Wargrave-on-Thames. Rutter was an author of remarkable versatility but not always of the highest quality, many of his books being of a popular nature — full of mystery, horror and adventure.[11] But above all Rutter was a traveller and in 1933 he had published a travel book about the West Indies, and no doubt he and Robert shared stories about their adventures. Rutter was to be very supportive to Robert over the break-up of his marriage, but Gibbings was unsure whether his offer to help at the Press would work:

> ... even if you did half the work at the press I should still have too much to do. Your offer of help is much appreciated, but the queer thing is that though I've been thinking for months I don't see how I can delegate part of the show ... I think my only plan is to clear out altogether & if required act merely in some advisory capacity for a small salary ... All I really want in this world is a small income & TIME to get on with my own job ....[12]

Since meeting with Norman Hall, Gibbings had been fascinated by the story of the mutiny on the *Bounty*. This interest was shared by Rutter, who had already published, in 1931, a book on the Court Martial of the mutineers. Throughout 1932 they had been collaborating, with Rutter as editor and Gibbings as illustrator, on an account, based on contemporary journals of the ship's Master, of the remarkable voyage to safety that Captain Bligh and eighteen of his companions made in the ship's launch. The book was announced for publication by the following spring in the prospectus for 1933. During the summer of 1932, the two men had also explored various commercial ventures including working on advertisements, this time with Rutter as copywriter and Gibbings producing the artwork — and they had even tried to set up a contract with the gas industry. But Rutter still nourished a long-term desire to get involved with book production, so when he and Sandford were introduced to each other by Gibbings, a new possibility arose. Sandford, although very comfortably off, could not afford to purchase and run the Press by himself; he needed partners, and Rutter, who could also offer wide contacts with the literary world and editorial expertise, was an obvious candidate.

With his family gone and his financial problems increasing, Gibbings finally gave in to pressure and in August 1933 sold out to a consortium consisting of Sandford, as principle partner, Rutter and a third person, Francis J. Newbery, who was a director and manager of the Chiswick Press. Much to Gibbings's disappointment it had been decided to move the Press to premises at 10 Staple Inn, London, and for the books to be printed by the Chiswick Press (in which Sandford was also a director) and as David Chambers has observed, the Golden Cockerel from then on 'became more a private publishing house than a private press proper'.[13]

But, owing to his desperate need to sell the Press quickly, Gibbings had had to settle on a price far lower than he had hoped; he received £750 straight away which was enough to clear his immediate outstanding debts, followed by another £300 paid in instalments. The deal covered stock, plant, copyrights and goodwill, but other items, such as framed prints and other sundries, were purchased separately. It must have been a shock for Gibbings to accept a mere fraction of his asking price, but, to be fair to Sandford, the slump had brought about such a collapse in the market for limited edition books, and the state of the Press's finances was becoming so dire, that it was a very risky investment and one that might not show a profit for some time.

If circumstances were hard for Gibbings then they were equally difficult for his staff, who were now without jobs. Cooper had been laid off since early spring and in May Gibbings wrote to him to explain the situation: 'I am afraid there is little chance of our doing any more here than completing those two books we have already set up and perhaps printing a small job for America. … I am terribly sorry about this and I hope very much you will get a regular job soon. I will try and complete the printing of the books in hand at some time convenient to you.'[14] Unfortunately no more books were printed at Waltham, but Gibbings had made efforts to find other employment for Albert, and had written a note of introduction to the Co-operative Society Printing works in Reading. This job failed to materialise and Cooper was out of a work for a year before getting a job as a draughtsman for the GPO — he never worked as a printer again. Harry Gibbs, the compositor, was more fortunate and got a job at the Chiswick Press and in September moved with his family to New Southgate in London. He wrote to Cooper to explain that he was enjoying his new job and that the future there was optimistic especially as his new 'boss', Mr Newbery, was a 'hard-headed business man, just the opposite to our old friend Bob, but none the less a very nice fellow' (Gibbings was known as Bob to friends and family).[15] What happened to Frank Young immediately after the Press closed is unknown, but in 1936 he took a post as a printing technician in the department of Fine Art at Reading University, where he stayed until retirement.

Gibbings felt that he had been forced to sell the Press too cheaply and at the end of July, even before the sale was completed, he had replied to a letter of sympathy from John Johnson at the Oxford University Press expressing his disappointment over the sale and also seeking work: 'I do not think that I got a price anywhere near what the show is worth but these are difficult times and I want to be free. If at any time you want some engravings done I will be only too glad to have a job, as from this on I expect to depend on my wits; but there is plenty of life in the old dog yet!!'[16] Johnson had always made efforts to support Gibbings as he greatly admired his abilities. Gibbings had regularly sent examples of the Press's work to Johnson, who was a keen collector and wanted to promote its work. In February 1933, Johnson attended a lecture given by Gibbings on the working of the Press and he wrote a warm letter of appreciation, congratulating him on his performance:

> I have seldom in my life enjoyed a lecture so much as yours. The simplicity of it and the directness of it and the truth of it just caught us who were unconscious how and why we were being caught. It was a triumph of the simple method. And it was the simple method for no other reason than that you are [a] craftsman and were telling us how you do it. I get just the same sense of things from Emery Walker and from no other.
>
> And you could not have pleased me more than by sending me this handsome gathering of your work. Thank you very much indeed.[17]

Johnson was concerned for Gibbings's future and in August had sent him a notice of a possible post at the Gregynog Press. William McCance and Blair Hughes-Stanton had recently broken with the Press and the Gregynog was in need of a new director, but Gibbings wrote to explain why he was not interested in the job: 'Very many thanks for sending me news of the Gregynog but I think

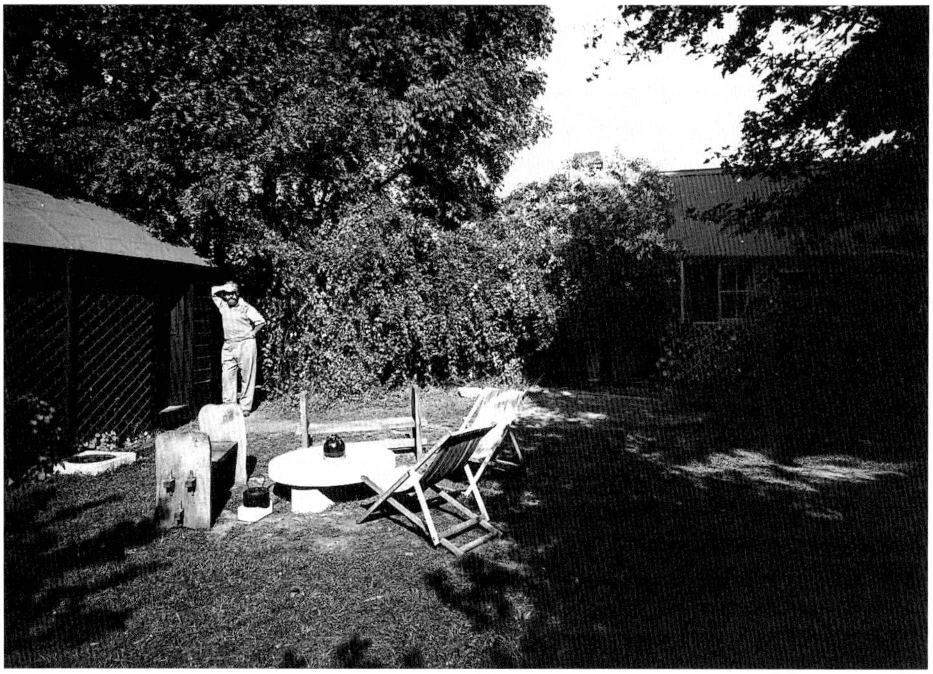

170 Gibbings standing by the huts in the orchard at Waltham, c. 1933. The stone table was made by Lallah Churchill and the ceramic pot was the work of Katharine Pleydell-Bouverie. RUL.

I want to keep quite free of any regular work other than my own engraving & sculpture and I do not suppose the new buyers of the Cockerel would like me to take on another show of the same kind.'[18]

Concern and support had also come from Mr Mackenzie, a wealthy collector of Cockerel books, who owned a large house and estate, Fawley Court, near Henley. Replying to a letter from Mackenzie inviting him for a visit in April 1933, Gibbings explained his situation:

> ... I have been going through a very difficult time financially, domestically & every other way as well. Now I am living in the orchard hut where I fend for myself & where I prove the truth of your remark 'either a castle or a cabin'. I've certainly known more peace this past ten days than I've realized for many months, I almost said years & if I can dispose of the house, life will be very much easier'.[19]

But by May his mood was less buoyant: 'Just now life is *very* difficult in more ways than one & though I try & forget it in the orchard there are dark moments when the sun is heavily obscured.'[20]

The house and grounds had not been part of the sale but as an economy Gibbings had moved into one of the huts in the orchard near his sculpture studio, and in a later letter he told Mackenzie that he hoped he had found some 'old friends to take the house'. His son, Patrick, then aged twelve, had his own hut for use during weekends at home and in the vacations from his boarding school. For Patrick, despite feeling the loss of his mother, it must have been a glorious state of affairs and it must have impressed his school friends that he lived in his own cabin! During those times together, Patrick and Robert grew very close. In later life, Patrick would recount how he looked after his father and even cooked for him: 'Conditions were basic and primitive. My father had no money, and yet every week, I don't know how, he arranged for a hamper from Fortnums'.

Gibbings sold his car and resorted to a bicycle for transport but life was not without some pleasure and he regularly cycled to the Hind's Head at Bray at the invitation of his friends Barry Neame, the manager, and Charles Gardiner, the owner. As a welcome guest he was provided with a splendid lunch with good wine, convivial conversation and good company — Patrick often accompanied his father and was known to fall asleep under the table as the debate and chat extended into the evening.

Released from the burdens of the Press and free at last from routine, Gibbings had time to reflect. Although he was a very gregarious character with a wide circle of friends, Gibbings also enjoyed solitude and he was content to be alone with nature. Recalling those months living by himself in the orchard, he wrote:

> It was spring, and after a year of disintegration in worldly affairs I was once again among living things; apple-trees all around me, a maple-tree throwing out its golden inflorescences, everything budding into new life. In my seclusion clothes were unnecessary. My feet grew hard, my skin brown. Gradually my whole body became alive and perceptive, and I found a new and fuller consciousness. Instead of regarding the trees and the wild creatures of the woods as beings separate from each other and from myself, I came to consider that they and I were related as closely to one another as limbs of the same body or as branches of the same tree.
>
> Though living alone I was rarely lonely. The grass was full of daffodils, and I planted cowslips, foxgloves, and the yellow mullein. A flower bed held nasturtiums for midday gaiety and night-scented stock for evening fragrance. Gradually the birds lost their shyness. Two turtle doves came daily to my door, a pair of grey flycatchers made their nest in the gutter above my window, swallows came and built inside my studio.[21]

The intensity of these feelings seems to have some of the inspiration of Llewelyn Powys; Gibbings was working on engravings for his book *Glory of Life* which was still to be published by the Golden Cockerel under its new management.

Gibbings still had a living to earn and throughout 1933 he kept things going with small commissions. In May *The Roving Angler* by H. E. Palmer was published by J. M. Dent & Sons Ltd, for which Gibbings provided a frontispiece and a

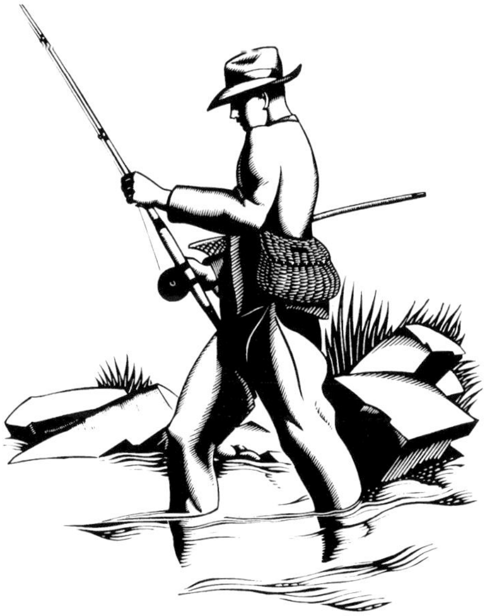

171 *left* Illustration from *The Roving Angler*, 1933, wood-engraving, 112 x 90 mm.

172 *right* Cover of Dent's *Descriptive List* for the Everyman's Library, c. 1933, wood-engraving, page size 218 x 141 mm. Another of the commissions for Dent that Gibbings undertook around this period. Printed in black on buff card with a blue border. RUL.

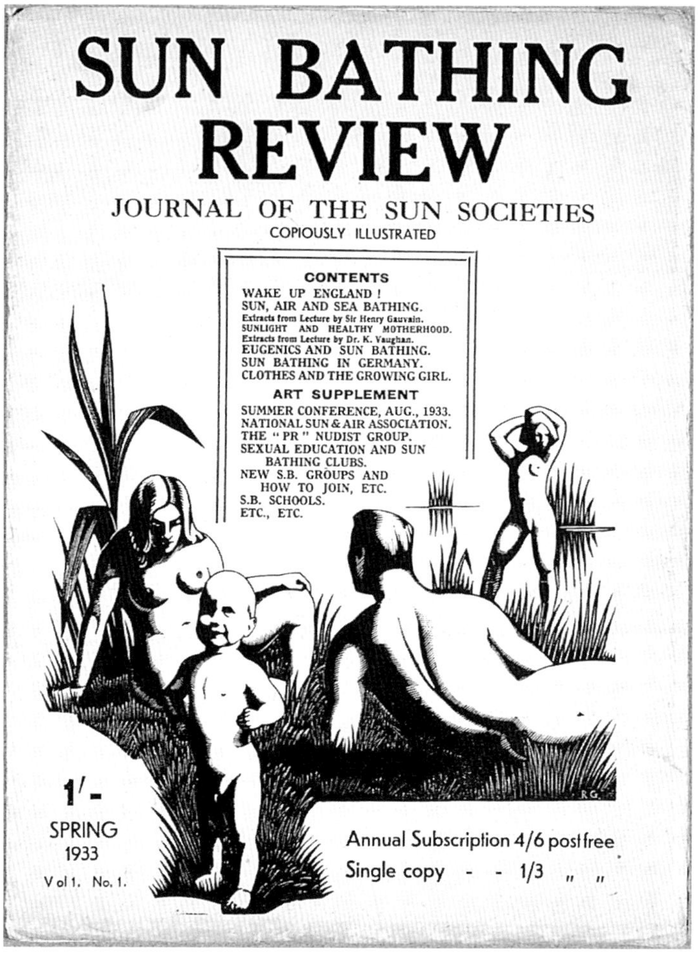

173 The cover of *Sun Bathing Review*, 1933, 257 x 194 mm. Editions were printed on a variety of coloured stock – the copy is on yellow paper. Reproduced by permission of David Knott.

The Wright Encyclopaedia of Gardening, frontispiece – see colour plate 5c.

number of small vignettes and tailpieces. This was an important introduction to a publisher that was to play a significant part in his later life. In October, another commission from Dent for a highly colourful frontispiece to the *The Wright Encyclopaedia of Gardening* was published. He had also been writing; he contributed an article on the revival of wood-engraving to the journal *Discovery* in October[22] and earlier in the year he had helped to launch a new magazine for British naturists called *Sun Bathing Review*. Gibbings engraved an illustration for the cover of the magazine of a group of naked sunbathers relaxing at the water's edge. Issue number one appeared in May 1933, and his design was used for the first eight issues. The first edition contained a report on the movement's first public appeal which had been published in *The Times* on 18 March 1932. The idea had been to elicit the signatures of 'eminent medical men and women, scientists, psychologists, educationalists, authors etc., in the sure belief that their support would lend weight and authority to the movement'. The list of twenty-two signatories included Bernard Shaw, Vera Brittain, Beverly Nichols and Winifred Holtby; Gibbings signed too, along with his friends Coppard and the writer Naomi Mitchison. The first article he wrote for the magazine was a humorous piece about the absurdity of wearing 'a garment for sun bathing'.[23] The article came about because Sun Lodge, one of the first camps to be opened in Upper Norwood

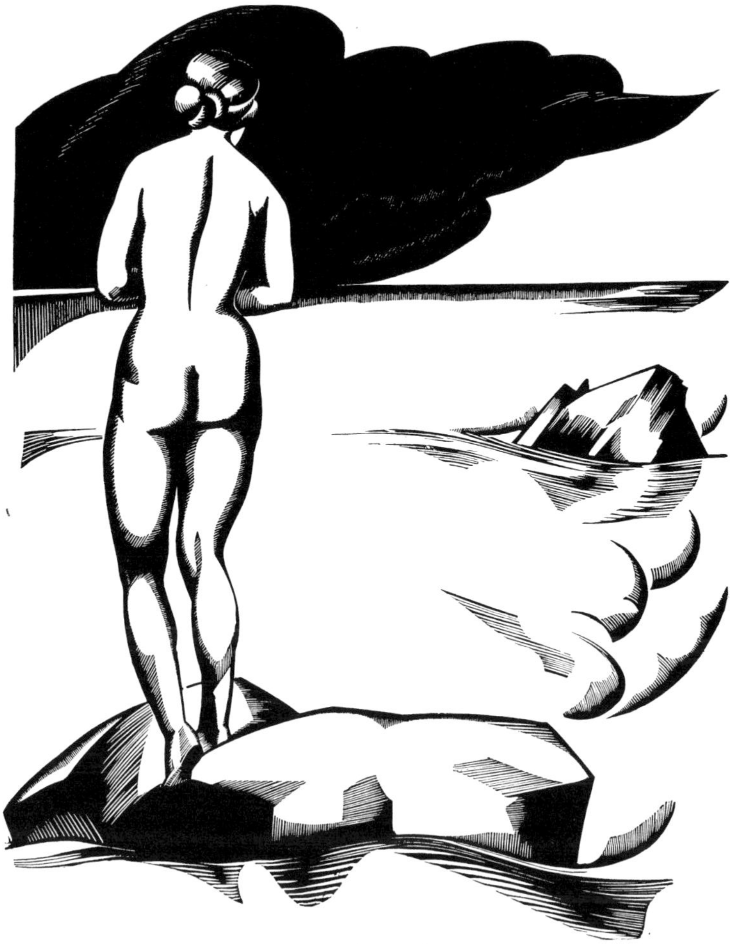

174 *The Sun Bather*, 1933, wood-engraving, 237 × 187 mm. In the third issue of *Sun Bathing Review* this full page engraving was published, supposedly drawn from life and modelled by one of the members of the recently established Yew Tree nudist camp.

in 1929, initially had a 'moderate' policy of advocating minimal clothing, and as a designer Gibbings had jokingly been asked to design a suitable garment; in 1931 another camp, Yew Tree, was founded near Croydon and became completely nudist. Over the coming years he wrote a number of articles, including an account of his earlier stay at the Motzenmuhle camp in 1928. Gibbings was a familiar figure at the early Sun Bathing Society's Summer Conferences: '... his noble bulk distinguishing him from the lesser men around him' — he was particularly effective at the end of the line in the tug-o'-war![24] He became friends with many of the leading personalities in the movement who valued his involvement, feeling that his presence added to the movement's credibility.

N. F. Barford had founded the Sun Bathing Society in 1927, and had set up the early camps; his son remembered Gibbings's visits to Sun Lodge and Yew Tree: '... he was a big, robust, hearty man; enlivening all around him with his jokes and good fun. He could be heard everywhere at Sun Lodge'. Gibbings seems to have really enjoyed the mixed social nature of these gatherings. He had already commented that all pretensions of class and the differences of social background were stripped off along with clothes. Away from artists and literary folk, with people he had little in common with other than a love of the sun, he could relax with no thought of reputation or what people expected of him. Gibbings had given Barford a copy of *Salambo* in 1933, but another leading figure in the movement, Alan Warwick, who was a writer and journalist, also had an interest in printing and books. Warwick regularly visited Waltham to join Robert in sunbathing in the garden 'where the sun was trapped at the corner of a thick hedge':

> ... he the while, as likely as not, fiddling with a pencil and a pad of paper, making rapid and delicate drawings of figures and flowers and blades of grass that caught his attention. To enjoy and capture the beauty of life was the begin-all and end-all of his own existence.
>
> Sometimes he would sun bathe in the garden of his enduring friend, A. E. Coppard. He would at all times sun bathe where and when he could.[25]

Through the Sun Bathing Society Gibbings again came into conflict with Bernard Shaw. Barford had written to Shaw, a keen naturist, about a remark Shaw had made about people 'insisting on the fig-leaf'. Barford, always seeking publicity for the movement, had suggested a debate over the issue, putting forward Gibbings to uphold the opposing view: '... our friend Gibbings, (Golden Cockerel Press); who is another magnificent Irishman both in mind and stature, hotly contests the idea ...'.[26]

Eric Gill and Coppard, who was the first editor of the *Sun Bathing Review*, also contributed articles to the magazine, but Gill never formally joined the movement. Since publication of *The Four Gospels*, Gill had spent less time at Waltham. With no new projects planned the two men had begun to drift apart. Gill was heavily preoccupied with his major project for the BBC, but in June 1933 he had visited Waltham to discuss the sale of the Press with Gibbings and to buy back all his blocks for the sum of £200. Neither Gibbings nor Gill ever mentioned any falling out between them, but in his autobiography Gill makes no reference to his collaboration with Gibbings or to their friendship. Fiona MacCarthy has given one explanation of Gill's behaviour:

> It is one of those queer ironies with which Gill's life is littered that their summit of achievement, climax of collaboration, saw some subtle changes in his attitude to Gibbings. He could act like the child impelled to kick down his prize sandcastle, and there are some clear signs that, by the time they started to work on *The Four Gospels*, the closeness of their friendship was already on the wane. ... Perhaps their intimacy had its built-in time-clock because it had been in a sense a young man's friendship; and by this time Gill and Gibbings were both ageing visibly.[27]

In a letter to Owen Rutter in February 1934, Gill declined an offer to 'take on the continuation of the Bible' claiming he was too busy, but he also made a cryptic comment about *The Four Gospels*: 'I am, for reasons I could explain better in conversation, not really very satisfied with the GCP Gospels.'[28] Gibbings remained loyal to their friendship and was generous in his lasting admiration and praise of Gill's work. Gill retained his affection for Moira; writing to her in 1937 he apologised for his long silence and continued 'dear Moira I do love you still & I do want to see you again.... We've neither heard nor seen R & Co since we saw & heard *you*. Poor R. You know — but no, its impossible to judge justly in this world. I wont [*sic*] try. You two have cut apart — we must accept that & forget the rest. But oh, how I wish you could have made a do of it & that you were still a happy family at W. St. L. ...'.[29]

Although restricted by space and lack of transport, Gibbings retained a social dimension to his life in the hut, and villagers must have been rather intrigued by the new domestic arrangements of their popular but rather bohemian resident. The daughter of a local landlord who ran a public house on the London road remembered that it was Robert's habit to drop into the pub for a whiskey — her father kept a special bottle of his favourite Irish brand behind the bar. The pub was a dropping off point for the bus from the city and it was the daughter's duty (and pleasure) to drive Gibbings the few miles to Waltham. She recalled that to her, at the impressionable age of seventeen, Gibbings was an exciting and very attractive figure. She knew of his reputation as a local celebrity and he was the subject of gossip when he came into the bar with his groups of sophisticated and 'arty' friends; the women dressed in long skirts with open-toed sandals. She was captivated by his charm and happily accepted an offer from Gibbings to see his sculpture in the studio. Despite her crush on him, Gibbings remained a 'perfect Gentleman'.[30]

Gibbings's reputation as an established artist and local resident had spread to the Department of Fine Art at Reading University and occasionally art students would make the journey to Waltham to seek inspiration and advice. Gibbings happily welcomed their visits, offering hospitality and tea, especially if they were attractive young female students and were willing to sit and be drawn. To impressionable students, Gibbings must have seemed a very romantic figure, the very essence of an artist. It was as a result of one of these visits that Gibbings was introduced to a young woman who was to become his second wife. One fine art student at Reading was friendly with a fellow undergraduate, Molly Empson, who was studying English. Molly was the eldest of five sisters, the daughters of Arthur Herbert Empson, a cousin of the eminent poet and critic, Sir William Empson. Herbert Empson was a man of independent means and the family lived in a rambling old house called Box Farm, in the village of Winkfield Row, about ten miles south east of Waltham St Lawrence. After their initial visit, Molly called on Gibbings again and before long he became acquainted with other members of the Empson family. Patience Empson, the fourth daughter, was just twenty and enjoying life in London, working in an art gallery in Kensington. Returning home for weekend visits, she visited Robert on several occasions but did not know him well at that time. She remembered that Gibbings was not always domestically organised but nobody minded — it was all part of the charm of Waltham and, like everyone else, Patience would lend a hand preparing food. On one occasion, Gibbings presented her with a signed proof of one of his engravings for *The Glory of Life* on which he had been working — he inscribed it 'For cutting Beans'.[31]

Molly also introduced another sister, Elisabeth, who was a few years older than Patience. Elisabeth loved animals and in particular, horses; art and literature were of little interest to her but she shared Robert's affinity with nature and the outdoors. Elisabeth began to visit Robert more regularly, often riding over on a horse she was exercising for a friend. Like her sisters, Elisabeth was tall, athletic and

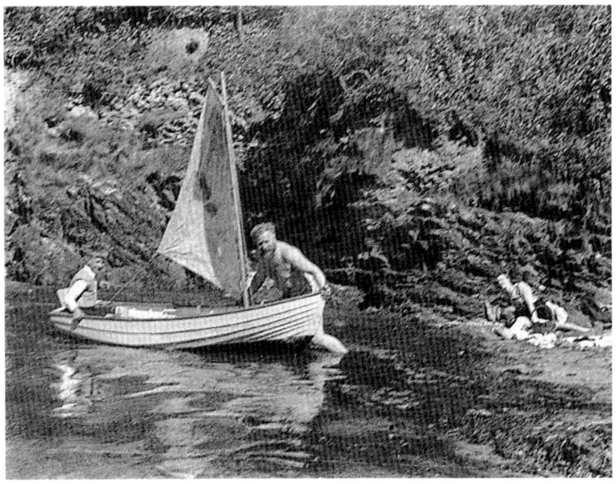

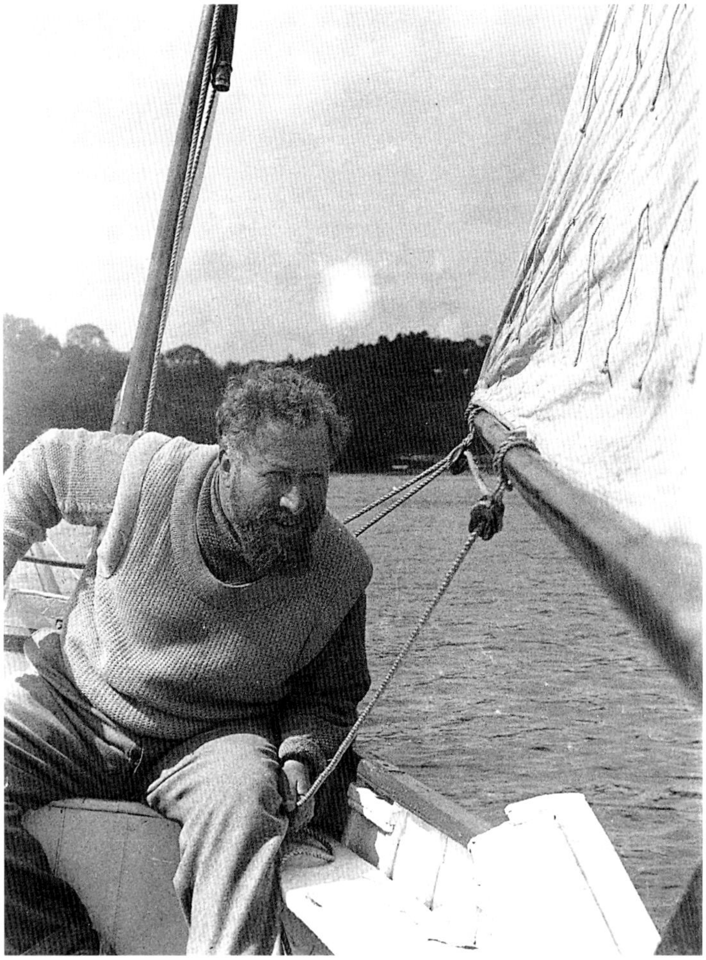

175 *above* Elisabeth, Robert and Patrick enjoying the Cornish seaside, *c.* 1934. Patrick shared his father's love of sailing. RUL.

176 *right* Gibbings at the helm, *c.* 1934. RUL.

handsome — she was also head-strong; Robert was physically attracted to her and although he was over twenty years older, the attraction was mutual. The result was that early in the new year of 1934 Elisabeth discovered she was pregnant. The response of her parents was deep shock; the Empson family was a warm and caring one but conservative and highly respectable. Their father was rather Victorian in his views and was outraged when he heard the news. He had made it clear that he disapproved of Robert's lifestyle; he was suspicious of 'artists' and would not be pacified even when Robert presented him with a copy of the Golden Cockerel *Psalms*. In the years to come he would never fully accept Robert as part of the family, but Elisabeth's mother eventually became reconciled and warmed to him.

The immediate problem was made worse by the fact that although Moira and Robert had separated, she had not agreed to a divorce and proceedings had not been started — so it was impossible for Gibbings to do the 'honourable thing' and marry Elisabeth. Nearly all that Gibbings possessed had been sold to repay the loans on the Press and now he was virtually penniless. He had even insisted that Moira should have the collection of Cockerel books which had been shipped to South Africa.

Elisabeth could no longer live at home but the couple could hardly live in Robert's primitive hut, however romantic; this problem at least was soon solved when a friend offered to lend Gibbings a holiday cottage in Cornwall. The offer came from Lieutenant Colonel Goodden, who had met Gibbings on a troop ship during the war. They had kept in contact over the years and Robert had always sent him a copy of each new Golden Cockerel book as it was published. He owned a cottage called Tresue in Maenporth, a small coastal village midway between Falmouth and the mouth of the Helford river.[32] This remote and beautiful spot offered Gibbings a chance to break free from his life at Waltham and the uncomfortably close presence and disapproval of Elisabeth's parents. He could hardly have planned this new relationship but he had to face his responsibilities and treat it as a fresh start.

FOR THE PAST FEW MONTHS, Gibbings had kept body and soul together with several small commissions and Christopher Sandford had been true to his word and had asked him to illustrate a number of new books and to finish blocks for projects that had been in the pipeline when they took over the Press. In January 1934 *Glory of Life* by Llewelyn Powys was published by the Press at their new address at Staple Inn. Although Robert had not seen it through production, he had done the planning and design. It was a book of great personal significance, which is reflected in the magnificence of the title page and frontispiece. The design is on a grand scale; Sandford commented that it was 'Probably the finest example of Robert Gibbings' book illustration. His magnificent title-page engraved in wood was an innovation ....'[33] The vigour of Gibbings's large engraving of a seagull is beautifully balanced by the big, bold titling letters, cut by Gibbings and printed in red. The edition was small, 275 were quarter bound in vellum with cream cloth boards and printed on hand-made paper; two copies were printed on vellum with a white pigskin binding.

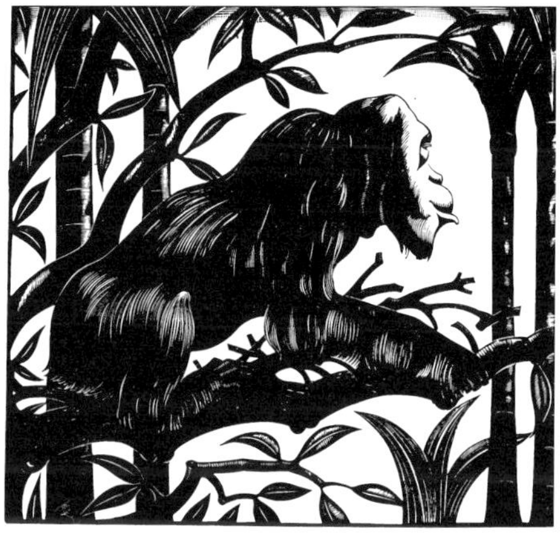

177 Illustration from *Glory of Life*, 1934, wood-engraving, 140 × 153 mm.

Soon after he had moved into the cottage in Cornwall, Gibbings sent a specially bound copy of *Glory of Life* to Hugh Walpole, who was an enthusiastic art connoisseur and collector of fine books. In a letter that accompanied the gift, Gibbings explained that he considered that the 'new G.C.P. had put a rotten casing on the edition', and that he had had a copy bound for Walpole in a style 'uniform with our Gospels' which was 'good workmanship by Sangorski & Sutcliffe'.[34] By chance, Walpole had bumped into Gibbings in London the previous May. They had not met since Gibbings had published *Apple Trees* in 1932, but Walpole was taken by his presence: 'He is like the reincarnation of William Morris, huge and burly with bright blue eyes and a beard. He is a great nudist, very charming, honest.'[35] Walpole had been in London seeing his friend the opera singer, Lauritz Melchior and 'supporting a young friend through the divorce court; buying a new Alvis and a new Epstein'. Undoubtedly Walpole was attracted to Gibbings and enjoyed his company. Gibbings needed wealthy patrons and must have been delighted when Walpole commissioned him to carve a sculpture for his garden at Brackenburn, his house in the Lake District. Only a photograph of a back view

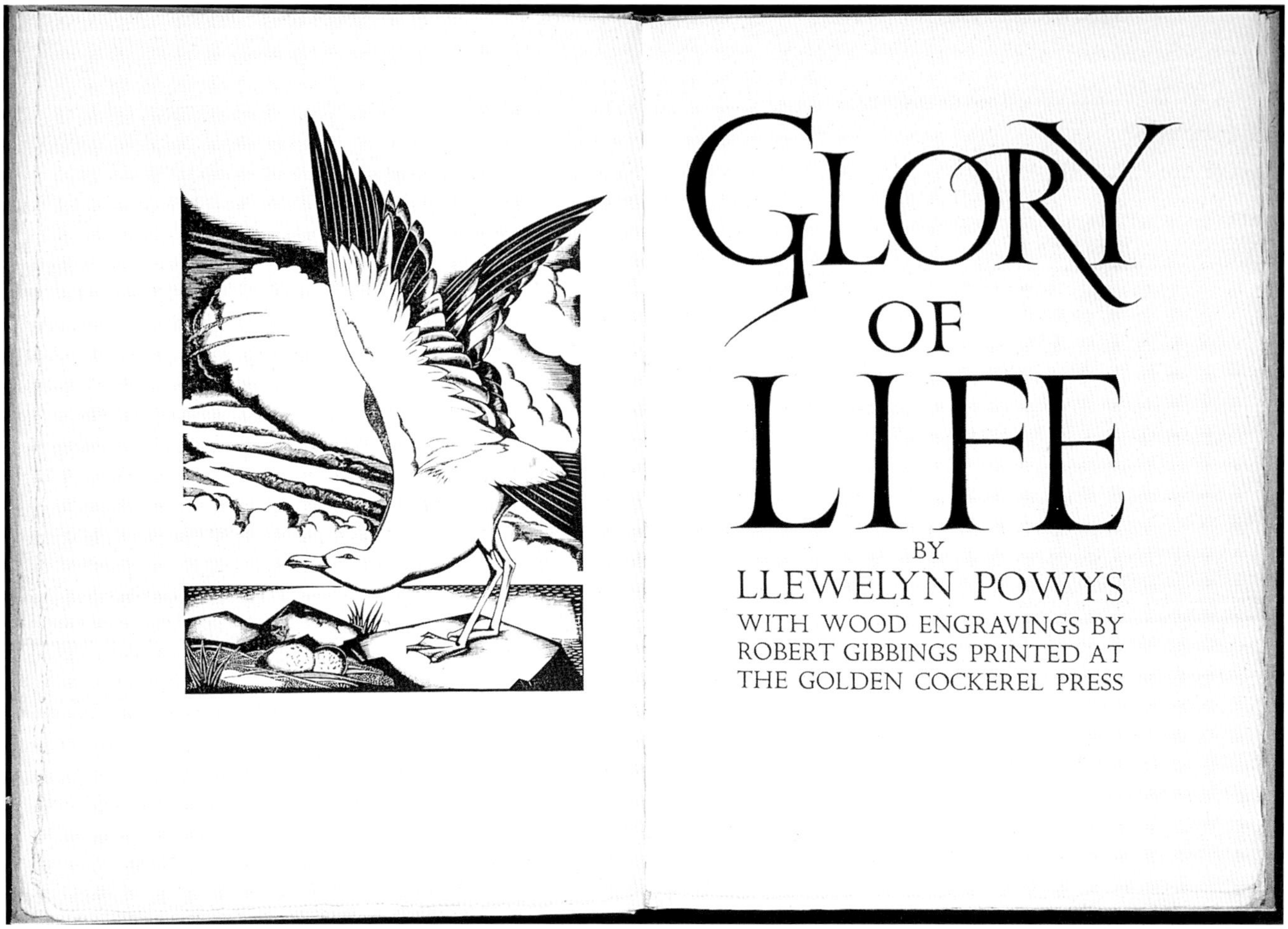

178 Title page and wood-engraved frontispiece from *Glory of Life*, 1934, page size 317 x 228 mm. In *Chanticleer* there is a note that *Glory of Life* is probably 'the finest example of Robert Gibbings' book illustration. His magnificent title-page engraved in wood was an innovation, and titles of this kind would enhance the beauty of many publisher's books'. Reproduced by permission of the Golden Cockerel Press Ltd.

of the resulting sculpture has survived — the original work was sited in Walpole's garden for many years but is now lost. The subject or title of this work is unknown; the photograph shows a male figure standing in tall grass, arms raised and clenched fists held to each side of the head.

Walpole was a benefactor of struggling artists and was generous with financial help as well as giving spiritual support and advice. It would seem that Walpole had been taken into Gibbings's confidence over his relationship with Elisabeth and her pregnancy.[36] In the letter that accompanied *The Glory of Life*, Gibbings had sent love from them both and continued:

> I dated it [the book is inscribed and dated on the inside cover] the day we came down here because that was the day I sent the sheets to the binders in addition to the other momentous facts. A day or two ago I found Elisabeth putting out food for a mangy old rat that hangs about our back door. I asked why she did that & she replied 'Well he's there & after all he must live'. Christ or St Francis might have said that but not many others.
>
> We are well & very happy, the sea is blue & the hedges are rich with celandine, stitchwort [...?] & blue bells, the rocks are covered with campion & pinks. My 'holy' sister writes that 'Sin is Sin'!! but E's father recovers and begs forgiveness for his early letter. I am working *very* hard & send for your portfolio a few rough proofs.

Gibbings's 'holy' sister was probably May, his elder sister and a very religious woman who became a missionary. These first few weeks in Cornwall were like being on honeymoon; in July Robert reported to Owen Rutter that his plans were to stay there until at least the spring:

As I expect you have gathered I came down & am living with the girl I love but I had to be vague & non-committal before I left both for her people's sake & her own.

Life is wonderfully happy though I've been a bit seedy owing to some sort of reaction after the strain of the past couple of years. I am anxious that for the present as few people as possible should know where I am as affairs with Moira are still very unsettled & unhappy. There is a certain amount of mud being thrown about too which is very disappointing.[37]

This had been a period of reflection and reassessment for Gibbings and this spiritual mood was reflected in the essay he contributed to *Sermons by Artists*; a book which had been announced in the Golden Cockerel Press prospectus for 1932, and was eventually published under the new management in April 1934.[38] The book consisted of a collection of essays by a group of ten 'artists, prominent as sculptors, illustrators, painters or cartoonists'. According to the foreword, this group felt that there was a common belief that artists were regarded as 'impractical dreamers'. As a challenge to this view, each artist was invited to choose a text from 'Holy Scripture' and 'to write thereon a Sermon expressive of their attitude towards life'. The impressive list of contributors included Paul Nash, Eric Kennington, Leon Underwood, Stanley Spencer, and Roger Fry. Gibbings had chosen St Luke, chapter two, verse fourteen, 'Glory to God in the highest', as his text. In his opening paragraph, Gibbings expressed his alienation from the formal church and its rituals:

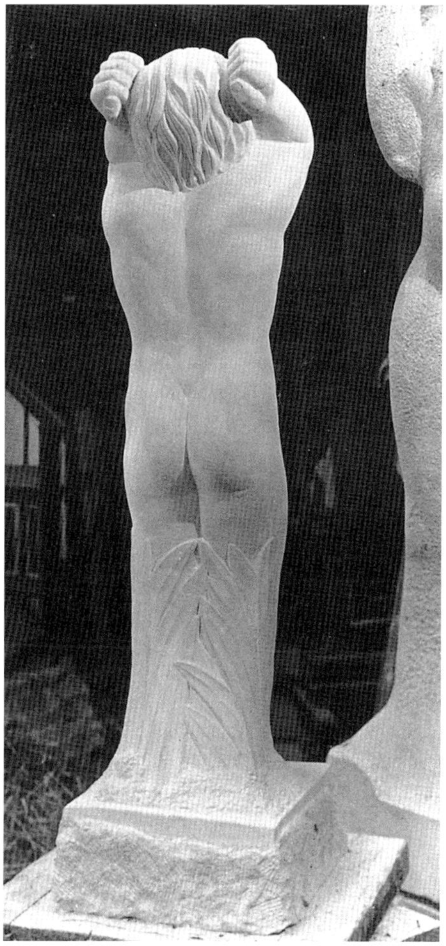

179 Male figure in Bath stone commissioned by Hugh Walpole, c. 1932, height 915 mm. Photograph, RUL.

Why don't I go to church? is that what you're asking? Am'nt [*sic*] I giving praise from the time I get up in the morning till the time I go to bed at night? What do I want when the whole vault of heaven is open before me? What do I want listening to jubilates, sung out of tune in the village choir, or chanted by paid mummers in the big churches? What do I want with the endless, lifeless repetition of the same words, when, outside in the fields there is a never-ending spontaneous paean of praise?

Describing how the demands and artificiality of modern life deny us the time to celebrate God by appreciating nature all around us, Gibbings went on to decry the arrogant sense of man's superiority and pleaded 'Let us be more humble ... God is obviously far greater than any concept of which the human mind is capable ...'. Gibbings asked:

How then can we of the cunning brain tune into the great orchestra? How can we find the wave length? only by contemplation. How can we contemplate? by leisure. How can we obtain leisure? by being satisfied with half our present income and one-tenth of our present possessions. Never mind about keeping up position.... Thus there can be time. The business man says 'Time is money', but the artist says money is time, time for leisure and contemplation which is worship ... therefore go into the sun and the wind and the rain. Learn to walk with gentleness so that wild life does not fly before you. Learn to think gentleness so that wild life need not fear you. Where the turf is smooth remove your shoes and let the grass touch your naked feet, that the current of life may flow into you. When the day is warm remove your clothes and let your whole body breathe.... Lie down flat on your back, spread out your arms, close your eyes and feel the earth tearing through space, think yourself into that space, remember that our earth is one star in the

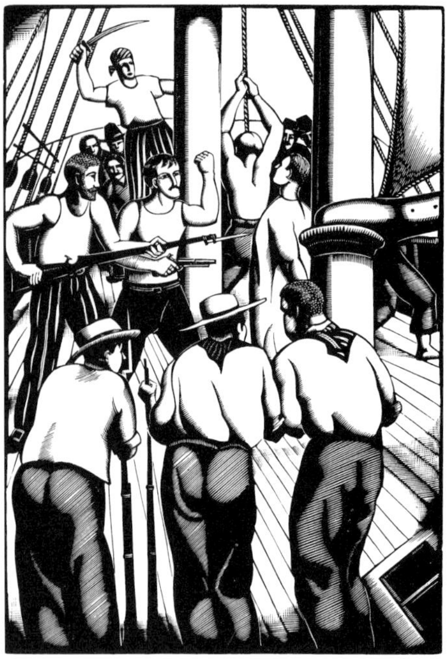

180 Illustration from *The Voyage of the Bounty's Launch*, 1934, wood-engraving, 173 x 119 mm.

milky way, and that we are no more distant from many of the other stars in that constellation than they are from each other. What matter then for the striped trousers you can't afford?

Sandford summed up Robert's philosophy as being 'simple, gentle, and pantheistic'. With love Gibbings 'turned nature into art. "When out of the forms and colours of nature the artificer is able to coordinate the elements of a more comprehensive design, then it is that for brief moments he reaches harmony with the universal spirit . . . ."'[39]

During the months spent alone in his hut in the orchard, Gibbings not only thought these thoughts, he lived by his words — but work and his new responsibilities had interrupted his meditation. *Sermons by Artists* had been planned by Gibbings at Waltham and originally the text had been set there in a small size of Caslon.[40] A note in *Chanticleer* states that the new partners were dissatisfied with this and had reset the book in 14pt Perpetua, which they had recently acquired. The following month *The Voyage of the Bounty's Launch* was published at the Golden Cockerel Press. Gibbings and Rutter had started work on the book in 1932, and this was the first of a series of books based on 'Sea Logs', which Gibbings illustrated over the next few years.

In May 1934 possibly his first article about a natural history subject was published by the magazine *Discovery*. In 'Exploring a Coral Reef' Gibbings vividly described his fascination for tropical fish and how he had studied them during his visit to the South Seas; the article was illustrated by his engraving *Mid Coral Caves, Bermuda*, renamed *The Reef*, from *Fourteen Wood Engravings*. He had visited London Zoo prior to his travels to 'gain some idea of what I was likely to see on my visit', but this had not prepared him for encountering the fish in their natural environment. Gibbings had obtained a 'water-box' and had floated over the reefs in a canoe, his face glued to his apparatus, captivated by the variety and colour of the scene below. Recalling his trip to Tahiti, he recounted a visit he had made to Tetiaro, an island north of Tahiti, famed for the fish in its lagoon:

> In that lagoon I have spent some of the most glorious hours of my life. Filling my mouth with cocoanut I would clamber along the reef until I had found a likely pool, then sitting on a ledge of coral immersed to the chin, I would chew the cocoanut into pulp and let it fall into the water.
>
> Sitting quite still the white cloud about me would soon be filled with a thousand fish, closer and closer they would dare until with confidence they would come and suck the morsels of nut from any part of my body where it had chanced to rest. In five minutes I would have seen a hundred species, from the little black swallowtails and the tiny zebras to torpedo headed Oiri with the Astrakhan patches on its stern and cobalt blue stripes across its head. The colours of most of these fish are prismatic and the artist's brightest pigment could scarce do them justice. The markings of many of them are as definite as the designs on camouflaged battle ships, some longitudinal, some horizontal, sometimes the same pattern with different colours, sometimes the same colours with different patterns.[41]

Disparaging of tourists whose glass-bottomed boats frightened the fish away, Gibbings supported the 'modest explorer' who, with a dugout and 'waterglass', could discover a 'world whose beauty no words can describe'.

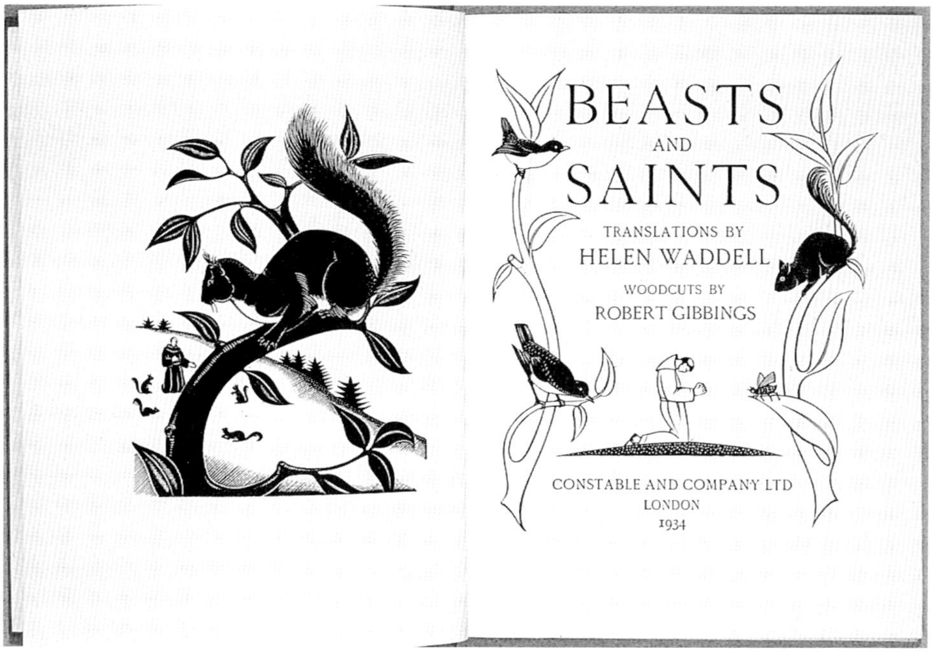
BEASTS
AND
SAINTS
TRANSLATIONS BY
HELEN WADDELL
WOODCUTS BY
ROBERT GIBBINGS
CONSTABLE AND COMPANY LTD
LONDON
1934

181 *left* Title page and frontispiece from *Beasts and Saints*, 1934, page size 203 × 152 mm.

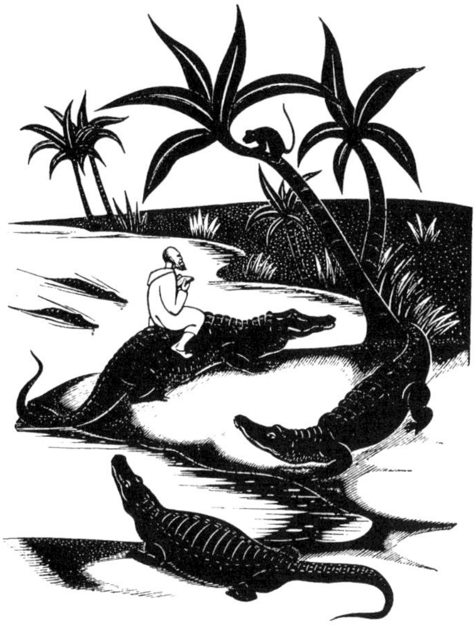

182 *right* Illustration from *Beasts and Saints*, 1934, wood-engraving, 120 x 90 mm.

Gibbings's touching anecdote of Elisabeth's saintly care for her fellow creatures, however lowly, was probably prompted by the fact that at the time he was engraving blocks for a book entitled *Beasts and Saints*. This was a collection of stories and folk tales on the theme of 'the mutual charities between saints and beasts', dating from the fourth to the twelfth centuries and translated from the Latin by Helen Waddell. The book was published in October 1934 by Constable and was illustrated by thirty-one engravings; the case was also blocked with an engraving and blind blocked with designs of foliage by Gibbings. This attractive book sold well; the first edition was 9,000 copies but by 1953 numerous impressions had been made totalling 30,430 copies. Gibbings was particularly satisfied with his work for *Beasts and Saints* and *Glory of Life*; he felt that 'My engravings in these two books were the best that I had so far accomplished, and gradually the sadness that I had felt at losing my Press was dissipated.'[42]

On 4 November 1934, Elisabeth gave birth to a daughter who was given the Tahitian name of Vahine. Robert had immediately ordered cards to be printed announcing the birth, illustrated by an engraving of a stork. On one card he proudly scribbled '9½ lbs, lovely baby wonderful mother very happy father'. Hugh Walpole, who had been a good friend to Gibbings during his recent problems, took on the role of Godfather to Vahine, Robert perhaps hoping that this would provide his daughter with a certain financial security.

For Christmas 1934 the Golden Cockerel Press had produced a card, illustrated by Gibbings, with the text of the Canticle of St Francis of Assisi set in 14pt Golden Cockerel type, and the *Spring Prospectus* for 1935 announced another book in the Sea Log series entitled *The Journal of James Morrison*. Based on extracts from the journal of the *Bounty*'s boatswain's mate, it documented the story of the mutineers after they had cast Captain Bligh adrift, and their time on Tahiti. Again Gibbings collaborated with Owen Rutter, who edited the text, and the book was promoted as

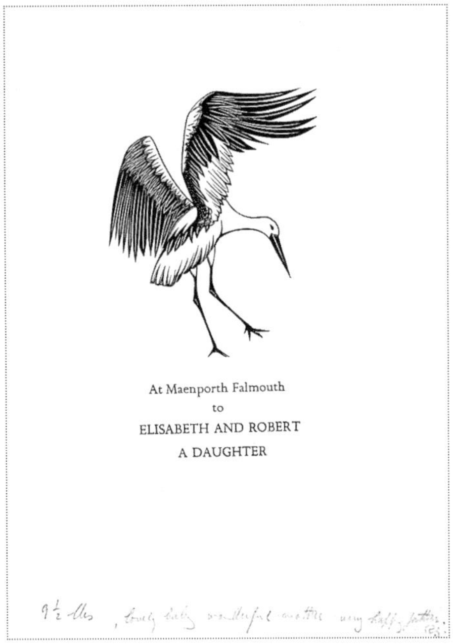

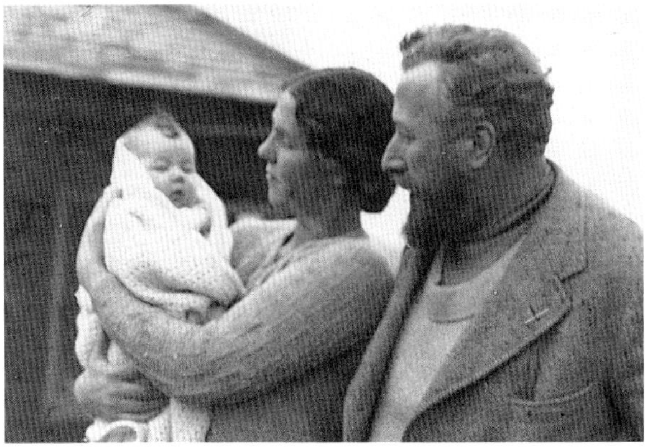

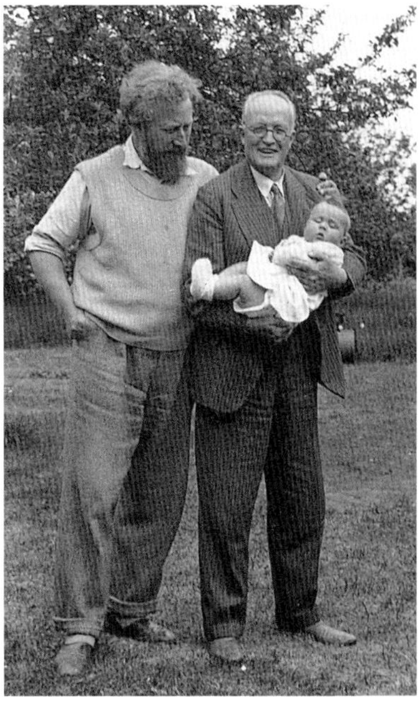

183 *left* Announcement of the birth of Vahine Gibbings, 1934, sheet size 217 x 158 mm. RUL.
184 *above* Robert with Elisabeth holding their baby daughter, Vahine, *c.* 1934–35. RUL.
185 *right* Robert, Hugh Walpole and Vahine in the orchard at Waltham, *c.* 1935. RUL.

'indispensable to all collectors of *Bounty* literature in particular, and of Australiana, pirate books, and annals of the sea in general'. Of the earlier *Bounty* volume, *The Voyage of the Bounty's Launch*, *The Times Literary Supplement* had commended it as 'a book of which the typography and make-up are those of the Golden Cockerel Press at its best, a pleasure to read even if the content were less enthralling'.

A more bloodthirsty and swashbuckling account of villainous pirates in the China sea was their next collaboration; Rutter edited the narrative of one Richard Glasspoole who was captured and held for ransom by pirates in 1809. *Mr Glasspoole and the Chinese Pirates* was a smaller format to the previous book, and Gibbings

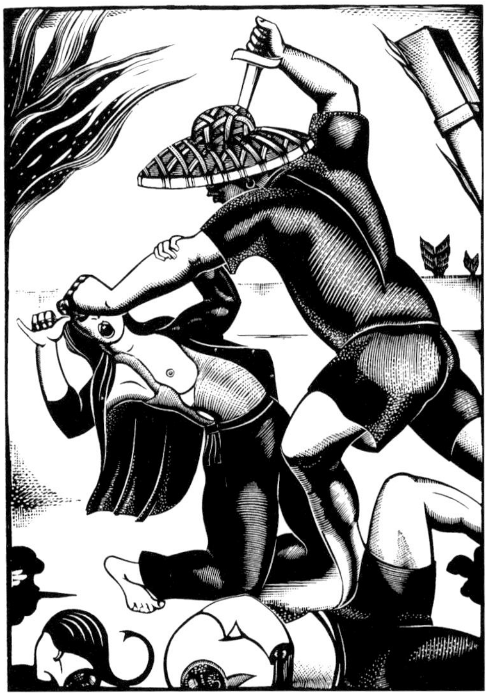

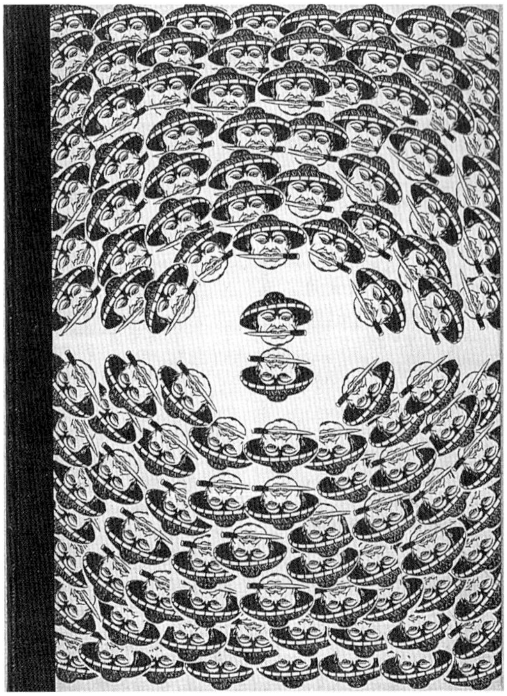

186 Illustration from *Mr Glasspoole and the Chinese Pirates*, 1935, wood-engraving, 142 x 103 mm. Reproduced by permission of the Golden Cockerel Press Ltd.

187 Decorative binding cloth on the cover of *Mr Glasspoole and the Chinese Pirates*, 1935. Reproduced by permission of the Golden Cockerel Press Ltd.

produced some gory illustrations as well as designing a pattern of a dangerous looking Chinese pirate clenching a knife in his teeth for the binding cloth.

For *The Journal of James Morrison*, Gibbings designed an impressive title page with the type fitting in to the sails and rigging of the ship. These commissions provided important income for Gibbings and his new family but they also appealed to his own passionate interest in seafaring tales. *The Journal of James Morrison* was published in March, and in October yet another volume in the series appeared, entitled *The Wreck of the Whale Ship Essex*, which was based on the journal of Owen Chase, the second mate of the *Essex*. Gibbings had unearthed the journal himself as he had begun to find time for his own literary research and, as well as illustrating the book, he wrote an introduction and edited the text. The *Essex* had been attacked and sunk by a gigantic sperm whale, and Gibbings felt that in his introduction he had shown that 'here was the germ of Melville's *Moby Dick*'.

Gibbings had not yet exhausted the material from his own trip to Tahiti. Working with Owen Rutter had brought his experiences vividly to mind and in February 1935 he had negotiated with the publishers Faber and Faber the possibility of

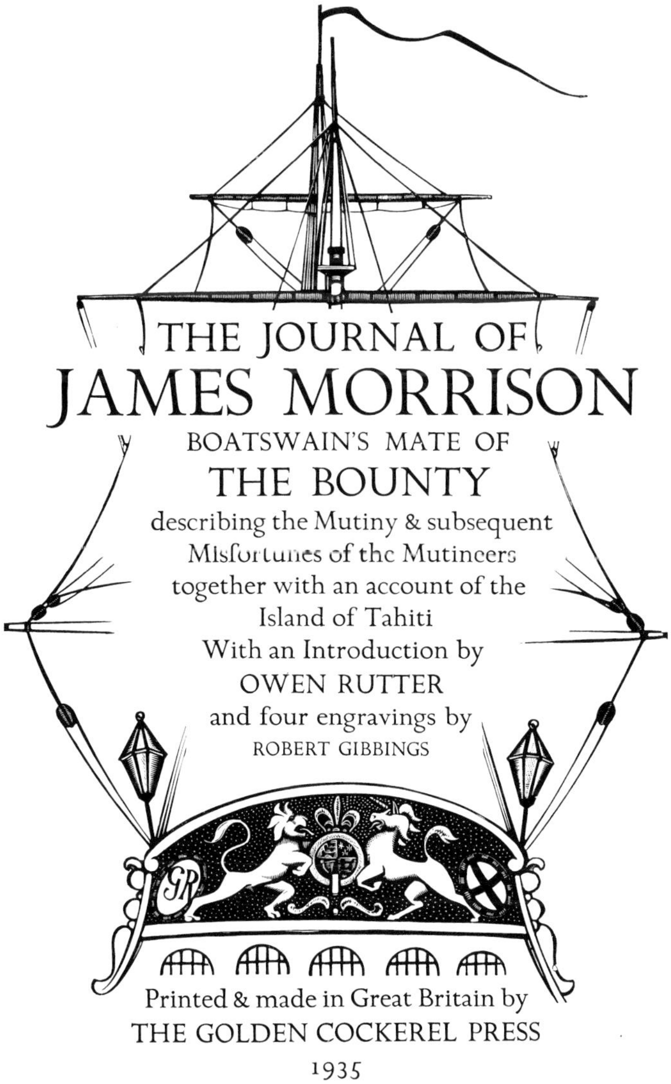
THE JOURNAL OF
JAMES MORRISON
BOATSWAIN'S MATE OF
THE BOUNTY
describing the Mutiny & subsequent
Misfortunes of the Mutineers
together with an account of the
Island of Tahiti
With an Introduction by
OWEN RUTTER
and four engravings by
ROBERT GIBBINGS
Printed & made in Great Britain by
THE GOLDEN COCKEREL PRESS
1935

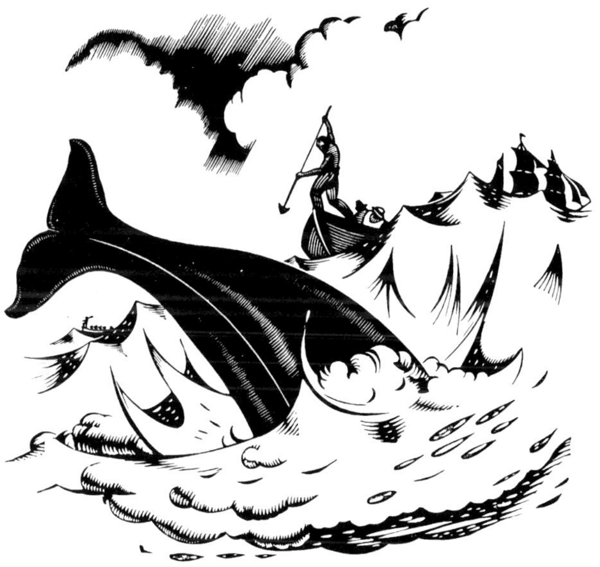

188 *left* Title page from *The Journal of James Morrison*, 1935, page size 317 x 191 mm. Reproduced by permission of the Golden Cockerel Press Ltd.

189 *above* Illustration from *The Wreck of the Whale-Ship Essex*, 1935, wood-engraving, 100 x 108 mm.

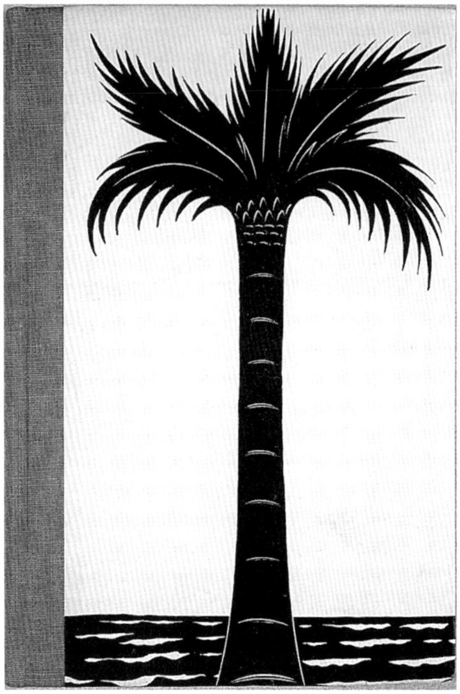

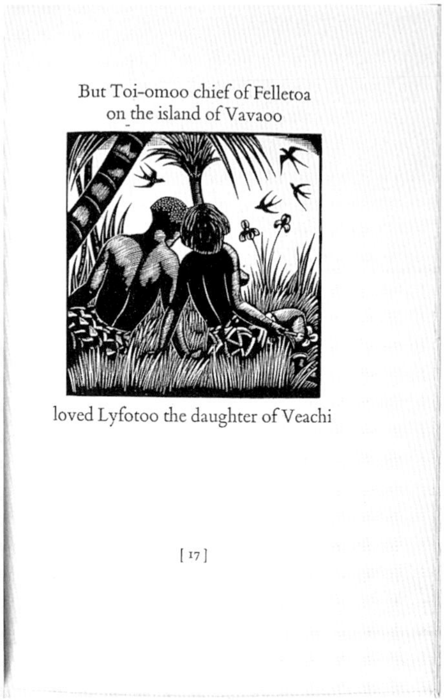
But Toi-omoo chief of Felletoa
on the island of Vavaoo

loved Lyfotoo the daughter of Veachi

[17]

190 *left* The cover of *A True Tale of Love in Tonga*, 1935, 208 × 135 mm. The wood-engraving of a palm tree was printed in black on a strong yellow paper.

191 *right* Page from *A True Tale of Love in Tonga*, 1935, page size 203 × 134 mm.

them publishing a little book, very similar to *The Seventh Man*. Based on a Tahitian folk tale, *A True Tale of Love in Tonga, told in 23 engravings and 333 words*, was published in October 1935. Dedicated to his daughter, Brigid, who was with her mother in South Africa, this simple but affecting story told of the love affair of a Tahitian chief with the daughter of the chief from another island whose family had been condemned to death for treachery, her escape and rescue and her eventual marriage and happiness. About this time, Gibbings had been introduced to the literary agents Pearn, Pollinger & Higham, possibly by authors such as H. E. Bates, who knew Robert and were already represented by the firm. He became particularly friendly with one of the partners, Laurence Pollinger, who was in turn a friend of the director of Faber and Faber and might well have recommended Gibbings to the publishers.[43]

In addition to bookwork, Gibbings also managed to get commissions for commercial work. The General Post Office produced a publicity booklet called *The Post Office in Pictures*, for which Gibbings engraved a lively collage of objects associated with the GPO as an illustrated cover design. At the beginning of 1936 the GPO issued the second in a series of Greetings telegrams, designed by Gibbings and printed in three colours. Around this period he was also commissioned by Shell-Mex to engrave a series of images to be used for advertising purposes and blocks of six decorated introductory words for use in publicity for the Orient Line.

Despite these commissions Robert's income was still precarious; having shed the ties of the Golden Cockerel, his family responsibilities meant that he needed a more secure future. At the end of March 1935, Gibbings wrote to John Johnson at the Oxford University Press, asking for a reference, as he was thinking of applying for the post of head of the Central School of Art and Crafts.

> I would not be writing to you now but for all the nice things you said about me that night I spoke at New College. I am wondering if you could put a few of them down on paper? The point is, I hear that the headmastership of the Central School of Arts & Crafts, in London, is falling vacant & with all due modesty I'm inclined to think I might be a suitable bloke for the job. They concentrate a great deal on book production which was more or less my job but in addition I've done stone carving, posters, oil painting, and of course engraving.
>
> Could you possibly say that you've known me & my work for several years (I think our actual 1st meeting was about 8 years ago) & that you have heard me lecture on your own subject .... If you can think of any other pleasant attributes of mine which might make me a suitable guide (or inspiration!!) to the young I'll promise to hide my blushes behind my beard.[44]

Johnson happily obliged and wrote a glowing testimonial:

> Mr. Gibbings is not only a man of arresting personality, who would catch the imagination of his students. He is also a man who would be the ideal colleague for his subordinates and an ideal subordinate for his own Board.[45]

He continued by comparing Gibbings's approach to book design with that of William Morris and expressed his view that 'the future will single out the Kelmscott Press, the Doves Press, and the Golden Cockerel Press as the outstanding presses of their respective times, each showing great difference of treatment'. Expanding on his admiration of Gibbings as a lecturer, he recalled the talk which he had attended:

> The address left on my mind an impression, which has lasted ever since, of magnanimity (in the true sense of the word) combined with simplicity which would inspire any gathering of any kind, and would be calculated especially to stimulate the young. And even when mischievous undergraduates of the College (rioting after some Boat Race) fused the lights of the College there was not even a titter. Mr. Gibbings in darkness was still the dominant force of Mr. Gibbings in light.
>
> The appointment of Mr. Gibbings would be no experiment. Its success would be assured by the character and history of the man.

Gibbings was flattered and grateful when he read a draft of the generous reference and wrote to thank Johnson for his support. He opened his letter with words which have a strong resonance in the light of world events: 'I think your letter is a masterpiece & if Hitler or Mussolini retire I'll apply for their job!' Although he had no experience of teaching, Gibbings felt he had something to contribute: 'If I got the job I can at any rate put a certain amount of energy into it & having floundered through the mill myself I would greatly like to help along some of those who are now starting on the same course.'[46]

If he did submit an application for the job it was unsuccessful; Johnson, writing over a year later, observed 'Yes, I think you were born to be a free man in your art; so that perhaps it is all for the best that you are not to be chained to the Central School but they are the losers.'[47] Gibbings had ended his letter of 5 April 1935, by giving Johnson a new address: 'After Tuesday my permanent address will be The Hut, Waltham St Lawrence, Nr. Reading ....' Elisabeth's mother had to some extent come to terms with her daughter's relationship and

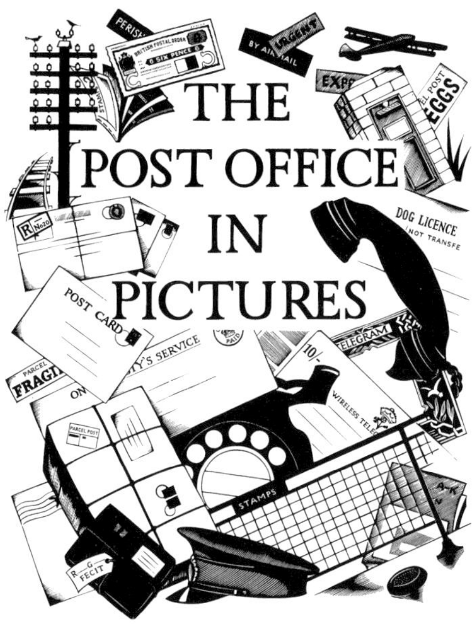

192 The title page of *The Post Office in Pictures*, 1935, image size 244 x 194 mm. RUL.

193 Greetings telegram, 1936, 164 x 214 mm. Gibbings had also designed a new golden envelope to match the telegram but it was never used. The idea for specially designed 'greetings' telegrams was new to the UK and the various motifs depicted were meant to indicate the variety of purposes that the telegram could be used for. They were to prove very popular with the public – for the year 1936–37 an average of 48,000 telegrams were sent per week. Author's collection.

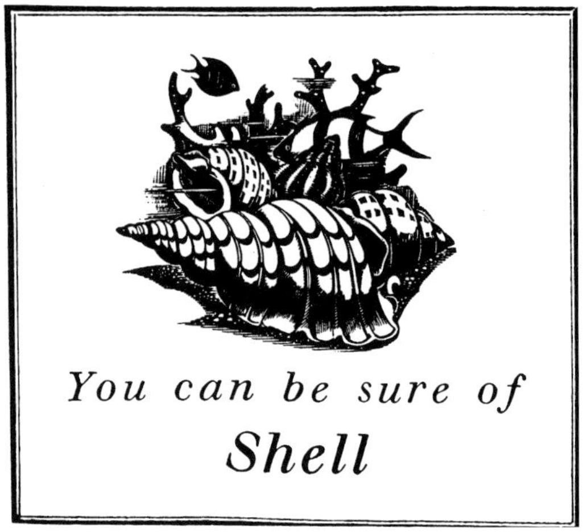

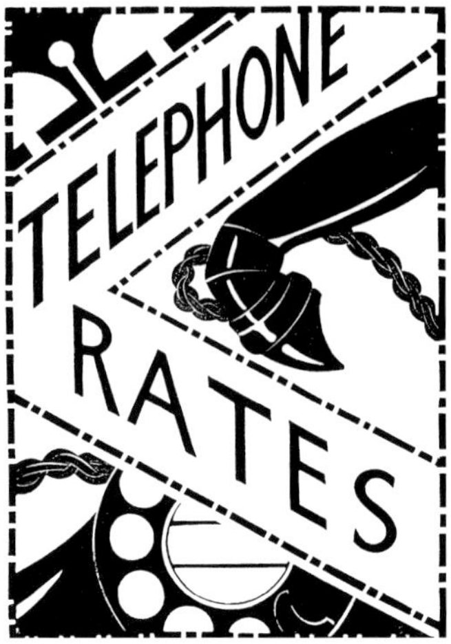

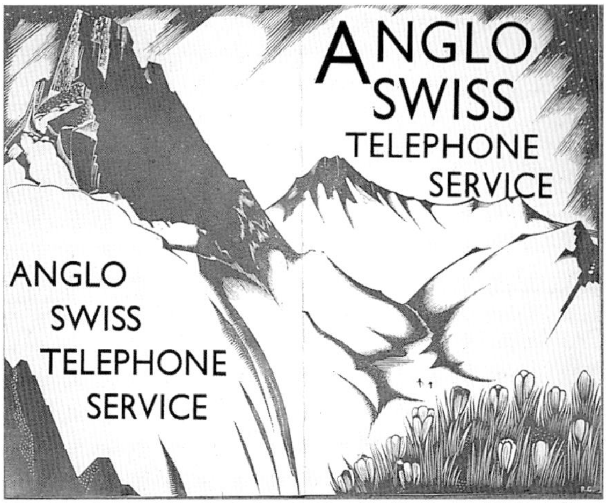

194 *left* Wood-engraving used for advertising purposes by Shell, *c.* 1935, image size 52 x 63 mm.

195 *centre* Cover design for a pamphlet giving information on telephone charges commissioned by The General Post Office, *c.* 1935, 135 x 94 mm. RUL.

196 *right* Cover design for a pamphlet giving information on the Anglo-Swiss Telephone Service, *c.* 1935, 192 x 237 mm. RUL.

now that she had a grandchild, she gave the couple the money to have a small bungalow built, part timber and part brick, in the orchard at Waltham. The building was much more substantial than a hut and would provide a satisfactory home for the family and very soon the name of 'The Orchard' was decided upon.

Back in Berkshire in their new home, the family's financial security was enhanced further when Robert was approached by Professor Betts from the Fine Art Department at Reading University. Betts offered Gibbings some part-time teaching at the university — Robert, having already contemplated teaching as a possible career, jumped at the chance.

197 *right* Two of six designs of decorated introductory words for use in publicity material by the Orient Line, *c.* 1935, wood-engravings, 40 x 57 mm. RUL.

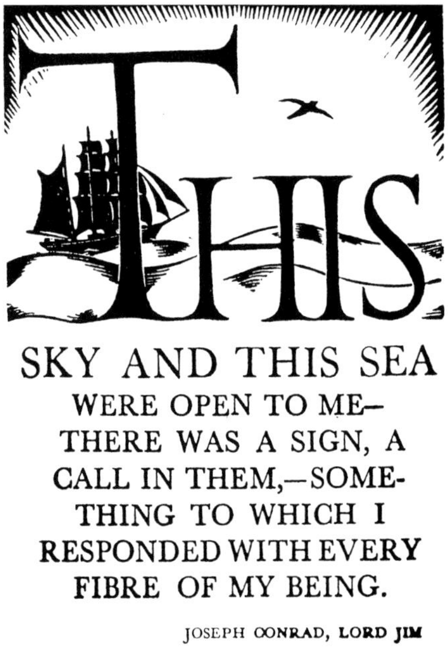

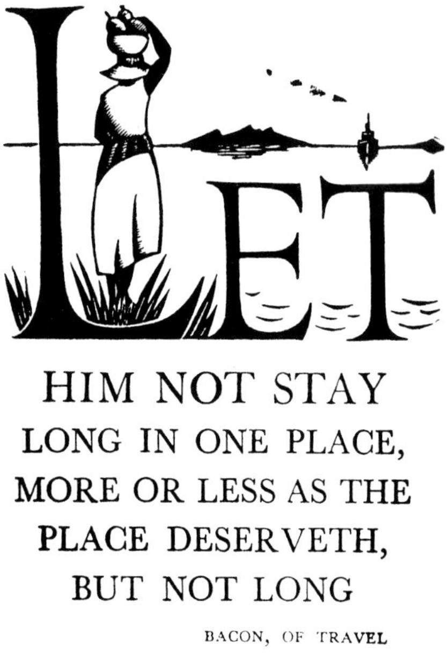

Chapter Twelve
University Days 1936–1940

ROBERT'S ENTRY into academia at The University of Reading has been described as 'a most enlightened and adventurous appointment for an academic body to make'.[1] Professor Anthony Betts, who had taken over as the Head of the Art School in 1933, was ambitious in his ideas for developing new courses and keen to build up prestige by bringing in younger artists of reputation to teach. Many of the existing staff had been there for a long time and had become tired and, according to one former student, 'old pedagogues'.[2] The department was in a rut and run down; Betts was determined to breathe new life into the place. A painter and inspirational teacher of drawing, Betts was aware that the school had a strong illustration and printmaking tradition and he was anxious to develop this area of study and was very conscious of the fact that printing was one of Reading's most important industries.[3] Gibbings was an ideal person to take on such a task and the University was not slow to exploit his presence. For Gibbings the offer of a steady job came at a fortuitous time.

A memorandum from the Registrar, only a year after Betts joined the University, revealed plans for the development of his department: 'An important development in the near future will be the formation of highly specialised classes in Pictorial Design, Book Production and General Lay-out Design.'[4] There were even suggestions that Betts had long term intentions of setting up a University Press, but lack of money and equipment scuppered this.

An announcement in the *University Gazette* of 19 March 1936 recorded Gibbings's appointment as 'Sessional Lecturer in Typography, Book Production and Engraving'. The Finance Committee recommended that 'Mr. Gibbings should receive a stipend of three pounds per day "for services rendered on one day per week for the Lent and Summer Terms".'[5] This limited appointment must have suited Gibbings as he was heavily committed to a number of commissions and was also engrossed in writing another book of his own — a children's adventure story set in the South Seas.

With a part-time job at the University Gibbings had plenty of time for freelance commissions. Following *A Roving Angler*, Dent had asked him to engrave fifteen bird illustrations for *A Bird Diary* by Godfrey Harrison, which was published in March 1936. A favourite subject for Gibbings, the engraving used on the title page showed evidence of his mature style — the stems and leaves of the rushes are cut with fineness and delicacy, very controlled and clear. In May *The Insect Man*

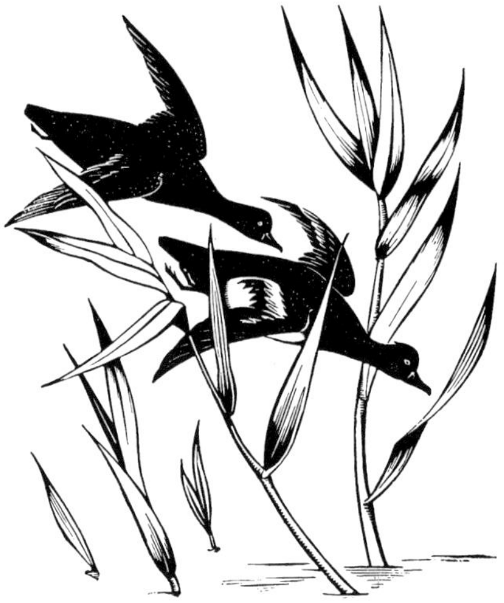

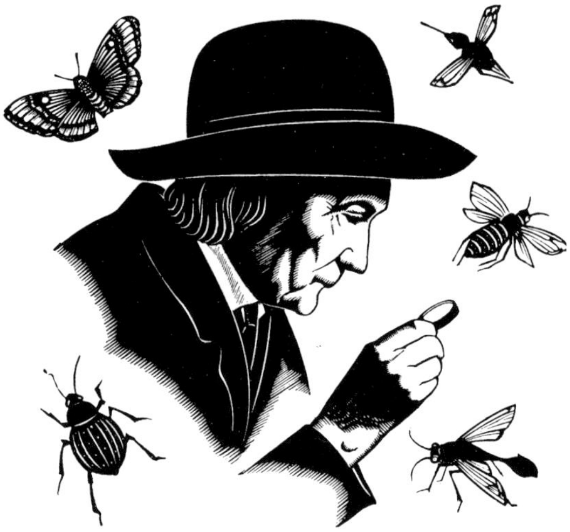

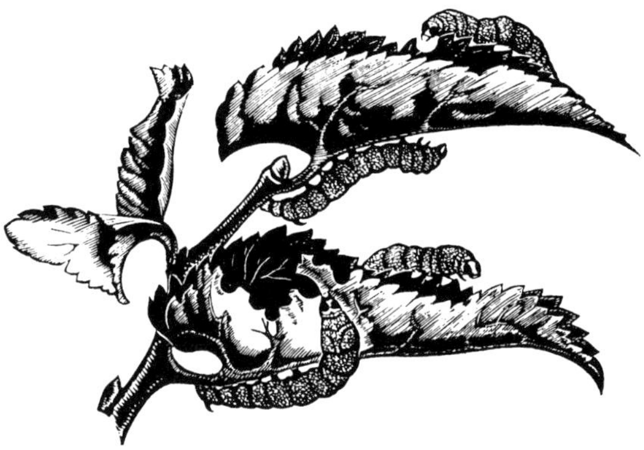

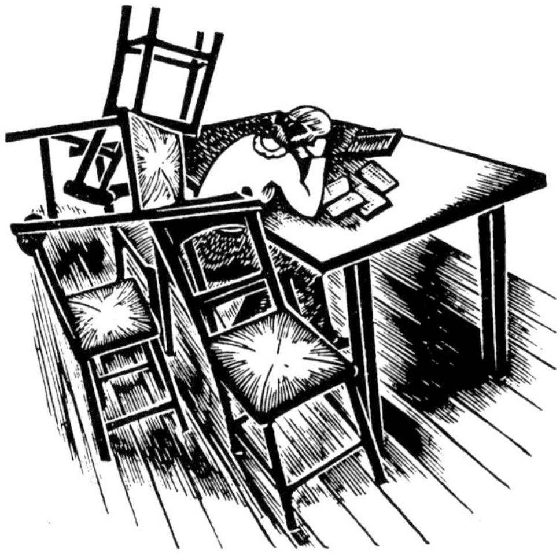

198 *top left* Illustration from the title page of *A Bird Diary*, 1936, wood-engraving, 90 × 76 mm.

199 *top right* Frontispiece from *The Insect Man*, 1936, wood-engraving, 88 × 96 mm.

200 *bottom left* Illustration from *The Microbe Man*, 1938, wood-engraving, 65 × 95 mm.

201 *bottom right* Illustration from *The Radium Woman*, 1939, wood-engraving, 63 × 63 mm.

was published by W. Heffer & Sons Ltd of Cambridge. Gibbings described the author Eleanor Doorly as 'one of my earliest supporters'. She was headmistress of King's High School, Warwick, and the book was a tale for children about the life of the naturalist Jean Henri Fabre. Walter de la Mare provided an introduction in which he praised Doorly's skill for writing directly and not talking down to children. *The Insect Man* was the first of a number of books written by Doorly and illustrated by Gibbings; *The Microbe Man*, a life of Louis Pasteur, appeared in 1938 and in 1939 William Heinemann published *The Radium Woman*, a life of Madame Curie. With typical modesty and some justification, Gibbings, as so often, felt dissatisfied with his work: 'Alas, through *force majeure* these engravings had to be hurried, and for the most part I was left only with regrets.'[6] Despite his own reservations, the publishers Appleton Century of New York, perhaps as a result of seeing his engravings for *The Insect Man*, commissioned Gibbings to illustrate Fabre's book *Marvels of the Insect World*, which appeared in September 1938, with eighteen engravings which were perhaps more refined and successful.

In November 1936 a 'sumptuous' three-volume boxed edition of Malory's *Le Morte d'Arthur* was published by George Macy of the Limited Editions Club of New

York, profusely decorated with wood-engravings by Gibbings. The book was printed by the Golden Cockerel Press and, according to a note in a letter from Gibbings to John Johnson, Macy had approached Gibbings about a possible collaboration in July 1933. But Gibbings, then busy negotiating the sale of the Press, had commented that he was 'leaving it to Sandford & Co. to make a deal with Macy ...'.[7] The book was decorated on every page; sixty-three engravings were made and repeated in various combinations throughout the book. This was a prestigious and substantial job for Gibbings and was well paid. It also gave him the opportunity to indulge in designing fluttering banners and heraldic devices with charging knights — images flowing around the text and interacting with the words. Gibbings had accepted his part of the ambitious commission in April 1934 and began by carrying out historical research, 'taking a few weeks off' to work on his illustrations for *Beasts and Saints*.[8] Initially he was daunted by Macy's idea that each page should be decorated but devised a scheme whereby certain blocks could be used repeatedly in different combinations. At the end of May, Macy was pleased with his progress: '... the work you have done is magnificent. ... superlative terms might only make you blush. The engraving itself is glorious'.[9] Macy's delight made him agreeable to a request from Gibbings for interim payments — he was short of cash due to his difficult circumstances and the need to pay creditors after the sale of the Press. By October 1934, he had finished fifty blocks and in the New Year Macy wrote to Sandford with his reaction to the finished engravings. Although he still thought them 'admirable' he admitted some disappointment as he had visualised a book that was 'highly floriated' in the style of Gill's work on *The Canterbury Tales*. Despite his original intentions, he felt that Gibbings had not produced enough 'units' that could be combined to make varied decorations for each page.[10] Gibbings accepted the criticism and agreed to produce ten or so more units making them as 'non illustrative' as possible. With the completion of these extra blocks in February 1935, Macy was satisfied and Sandford began work on page proofs, but the production was to take over a year.[11]

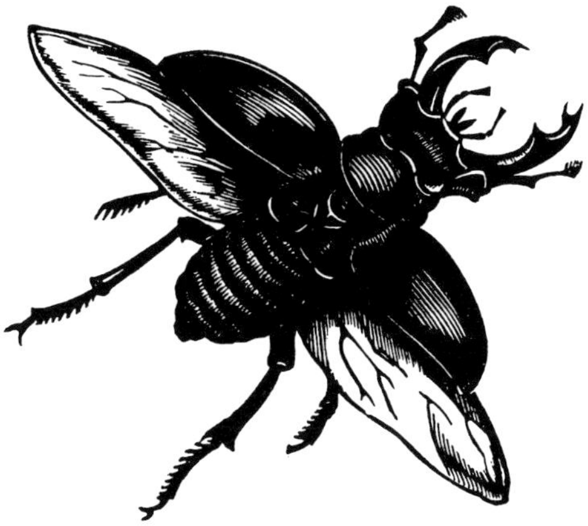

202 Illustration from *Marvels of the Insect World*, 1938, wood-engraving, 52 x 62 mm.

At the end of 1936, Gibbings was working on four engravings for a tiny and delicate edition of Pushkin's *The Tale of the Golden Cockerel* which was published by the Golden Cockerel Press in December. A month or so earlier, Sandford had also commissioned him to engrave the coat of arms for the City of Manchester which was used to decorate the title pages of four volumes of the Roll of Honour of the Manchester Regiment 1914–18, and was printed at the Press.

Perhaps it was through his aquaintance with Eleanor Doorly that Gibbings had the idea to write his own children's adventure. No doubt, too, his close relationship with his son Patrick and his thoughts for Brigid and the twins, now in Africa, prompted the idea to write a story for them. The book was originally to be called *Motu-Marama* but was eventually entitled *Coconut Island* and dedicated to Patrick and Penelope, Elisabeth's younger sister who was close to Patrick in age.[12] It was an exciting tale of two children and their 'artist' uncle, who set sail to meet a scientist friend of their uncle's who was studying fish on a Polynesian island. As a

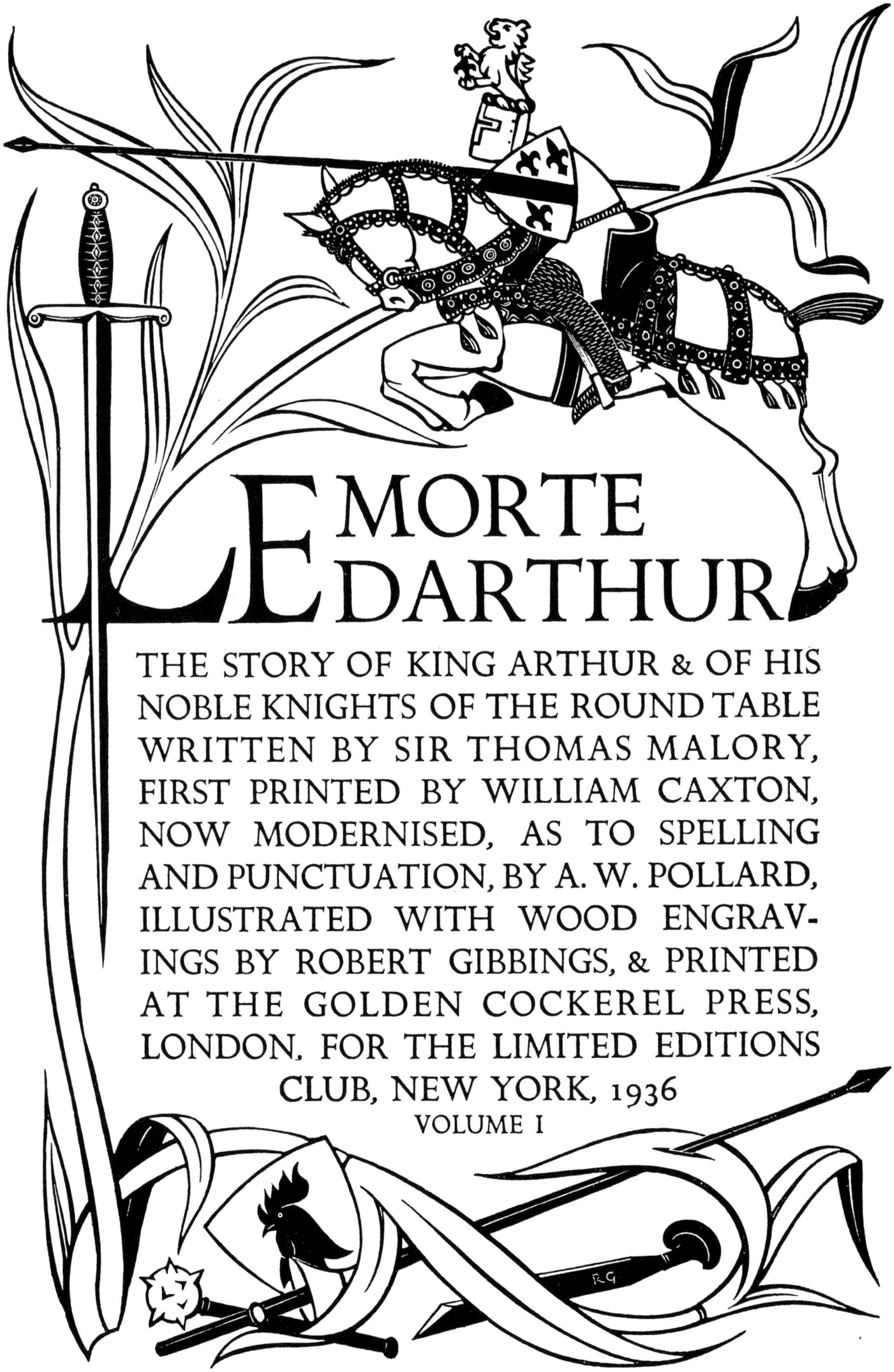

LE MORTE DARTHUR

THE STORY OF KING ARTHUR & OF HIS NOBLE KNIGHTS OF THE ROUND TABLE WRITTEN BY SIR THOMAS MALORY, FIRST PRINTED BY WILLIAM CAXTON, NOW MODERNISED, AS TO SPELLING AND PUNCTUATION, BY A. W. POLLARD, ILLUSTRATED WITH WOOD ENGRAVINGS BY ROBERT GIBBINGS, & PRINTED AT THE GOLDEN COCKEREL PRESS, LONDON, FOR THE LIMITED EDITIONS CLUB, NEW YORK, 1936

VOLUME I

consequence of a freak wave during a storm, the children are separated from their uncle and ship-wrecked on a deserted tropical island. Discovered there and befriended by a native, the children are initiated into the art of catching coconut crabs, pearl diving, building a house and acquiring the necessities for survival. Escape leads to further adventures in search of a hoard of pearls in a sunken wreck, in the company of pirates and a ruffian ship's captain. Full of details of flora and fauna, the book gave Gibbings the opportunity to include facts and anecdotes that fascinated him, but in a context that was engaging for young children. He was to become very adept at recycling stories and ideas and in *Coconut Island* he reused parts of his material from *Iorana*. Obviously the young heroes, Patrick and Penelope, were based on his son and sister-in-law but there are disguised references to other members of the family and his own life, put in to amuse his children. Elisabeth became an 'Aunt' who lived at Box Farm, noted for her excellent pies and puddings; Vahine is the name of a native girl; their Uncle John had many aspects in common with Robert himself, although a thinner version. Gibbings added another amusing reference to himself as a father:

> Patrick, fair haired and blue eyed, was tall for his thirteen years, and slight. Thanks to an irresponsible father, now dead, his education had been somewhat erratic, but his lack of knowledge from books was amply made up for by his self-reliance and ability to do other things of at least equal importance. He thought nothing of bicycling alone across England or sailing his own dinghy in the open sea in weather that brought the bigger yachts inshore for shelter.[13]

Gibbings had bought his son a sailing dinghy while they were in Cornwall and Patrick was to share his father's passion for sailing for the rest of his life; Gibbings had also encouraged his son to cycle by himself and in later years Patrick proudly recounted the story of a journey he made at thirteen, travelling to Cornwall from Waltham on his bicycle. With ironic humour, Gibbings made the physical appearance of 'Uncle John' almost the opposite of himself — medium build, bald, 'The quietest and the soberest man', he had the fortunate knack of making himself inconspicuous in any company.' Robert's own growing ambitions, soon to be fulfilled, are hinted at in the success of Uncle John: '... being an artist, he had filled countless notebooks with sketches made in strange places and had become one of the leading illustrators of travel books'.[14]

203 *opposite page* Title page from *Le Morte d'Arthur*, 1936, image size 236 x 158 mm. Gibbings incorporated his own family's coat of arms on the knight's shield, a cockerel's head at the bottom of the page, together with an engraving tool. Reproduced by permission of the Golden Cockerel Press Ltd.

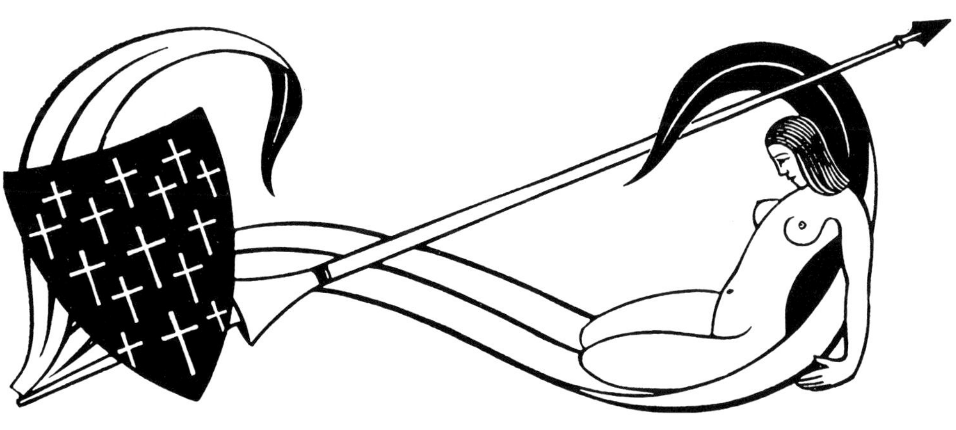

204 *this page* Decorative block from *Le Morte d'Arthur*, 1936, wood-engraving, 53 x 130 mm. Reproduced by permission of the Golden Cockerel Press Ltd.

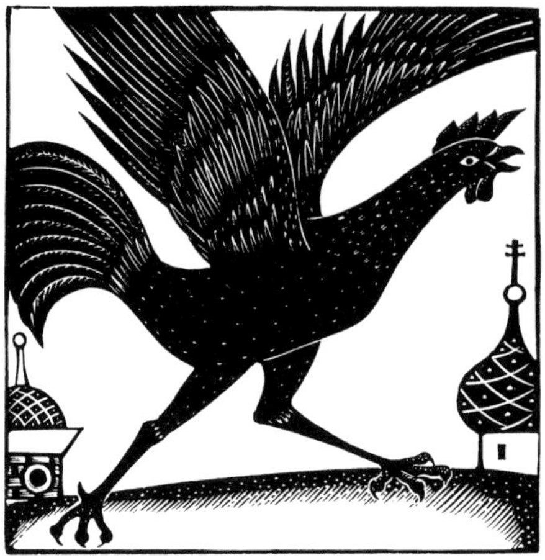

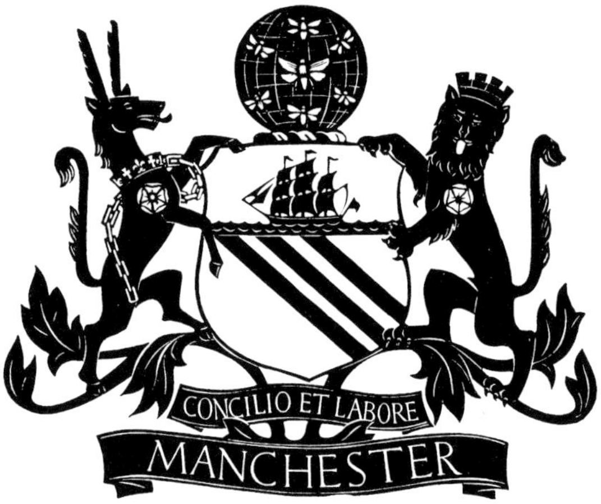

205 *above* Illustration from *The Tale of the Golden Cockerel*, 1936, wood-engraving, 63 x 63 mm.

206 *above right* Coat of Arms of the City of Manchester, 1936, wood-engraving,

207 *centre right* Illustration from *Coconut Island*, 1936, wood-engraving, 46 x 92 mm.

208 *right* Illustration from *Coconut Island*, 1936, wood-engraving, 50 x 92 mm.

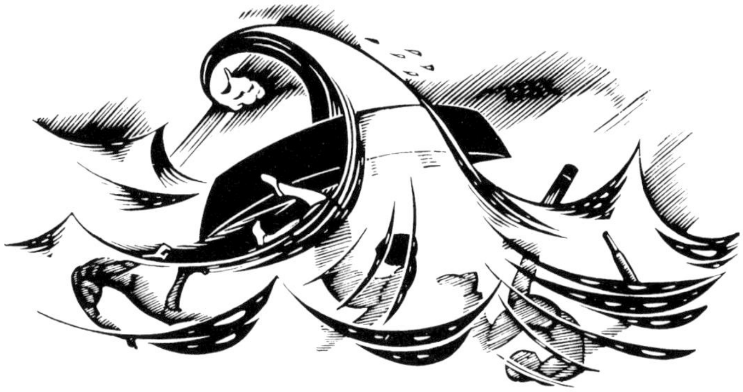

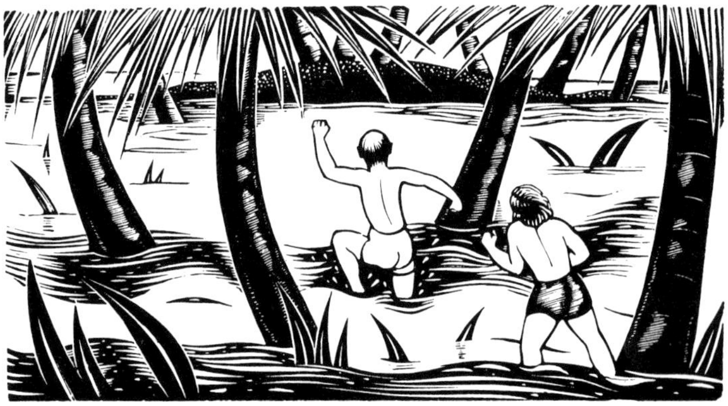

In *Coconut Island*, Gibbings even managed to work in a reference to his favourite corner table at the Café Royal — on the left of the entrance. Light-hearted though the book is, there is a more telling personal reference in the text: one of the fierce looking ruffian sailors the children encounter is described by a mate as really being as 'gentle as a lamb ... he's killed a few in his day, but only when he had to'. Penelope asks if this was during the war but the reply was unexpected: 'No, didn't kill anyone in the war; never fired a shot. He says the Turks very nice fellows, didn't see any reason to kill 'em. When he took a prisoner he used to give him a packet of fags ....'[15] Gibbings's memories of the war were still with him —perhaps he was making a veiled confession, working out his feelings in print. His writing style was rather faltering at the start of the book but improved as the adventure unfolded. Modern tastes would find the book dated and rather obviously 'educational' in parts and certainly his references to the natives would not be 'politically correct' today. But Gibbings clearly admired and identified with the self-sufficient way of life of the people he wrote about.

The book was illustrated with over seventy lively and often informative wood-engraving by Gibbings. Following *A True Tale of Love in Tonga*, Faber and Faber published the first edition of 2,215 copies in November 1936 and a second edition of 1,500 in June 1939. It was a modest success but later many other editions would be produced. Penguin brought out an edition of 50,000 copies in 1945 as a Puffin Story Book and in 1949 Dent brought out a revised edition which was reprinted twice, making a total of 11,600 copies; the book was also translated into French and published in Paris and Brussels in the same year.[16] One claim to fame was that in May 1937 the book was reported to have been banned in Germany 'on the grounds of excessive sentimentality'.[17]

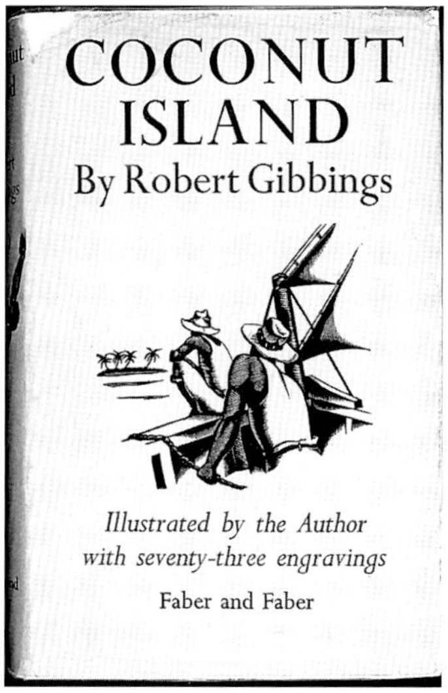

209 Cover of *Coconut Island* published by Faber and Faber in November 1936.

HAVING ENTICED GIBBINGS onto the staff, the University was anxious to exploit his presence and increase his involvement by developing a new specialist course. In October 1936 the Vice-Chancellor put before the University's Council a detailed memorandum on the '... proposed institution of a special advanced course in Design applied to Typography and Book Production. It would be the essential purpose of such a course to bring instruction in design into the closest possible relation to the practical processes of wood-engraving and fine printing'.[18] Gibbings's reputation and achievements 'both as an artist and as an expert in the processes of fine printing and book production'[19] were put forward as a major factor in favour of establishing the course. By January 1937, conditional approval had been granted for the course and Gibbings was appointed full-time Lecturer in Typography and Book Production from February at a salary of £500 a year. His contract stipulated that he would 'undertake whole-time duties in the School of Art on three days and evenings per week throughout the Session as required'.[20] A grant of £200 was allocated for type, type-cases, cabinets and sundry equipment, to establish the course and as a supplement to the meagre resources of a small amount of type and an Albion hand-press already in the print room. The post of compositor and printing technician was also created at a wage of four pounds per week, and it was soon filled by Frank Young, lately the compositor from the Golden Cockerel Press. Before long, Gibbings persuaded the University to grant him the money to buy a powered press and Anthony Betts later recalled scouring London with Gibbings for a second-hand Victoria platen press.

Classes began at ten o'clock, broke at one for an hour and resumed with an afternoon session running from two to four; in the evening additional classes were held for part-time students. Most students studying Fine Art were required to undertake a basic foundation course in typography and wood-engraving, as part of a programme that included the usual study of drawing from life and the 'antique', perspective, anatomy, composition, commercial design and modelling, as well as academic elements such as the history of art and architecture. The

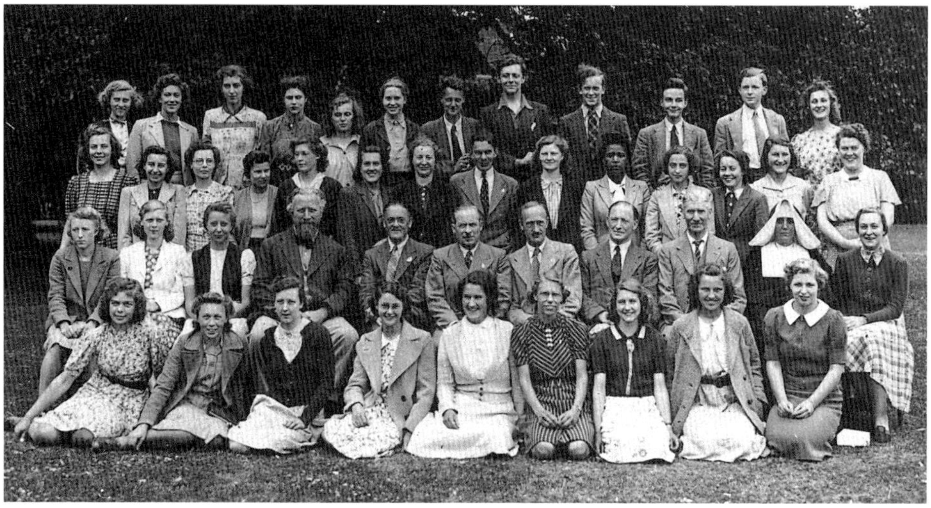

210 The Department of Fine Art at the University of Reading in 1939. Gibbings is fourth from the left in the second row from the front, next to him is Harry Carter, who taught sculpture, then Professor Anthony Betts, RUL.

typography course consisted of one class a week for a year and was a practical workshop. Students were then able to specialise in this area if they wished and Gibbings soon established a small group of enthusiastic students who concentrated on illustration and wood-engraving. Gibbings favoured small classes that allowed him to work on a one-to-one basis with students rather than teaching in a more formal manner.

Gibbings got on well with students; they were aware of his growing reputation as an artist and author but were never intimidated or overawed by him because he proved to be a patient teacher, taking a supportive approach. He was able to communicate his own passion and enthusiasm for his subject, working with the students rather than teaching at them. He was more like a genial GP, running a surgery offering personal consultations to sort out individual problems. Despite his physical stature his voice was soft and his attitude gentle, but he was firm and forthright in his criticism of students' work — his comments were encouraging rather than caustic. Having set a project Gibbings let the students start the work on their own. He quietly carried on with his own activities, either engraving or working on his own writing, proof reading or correcting scripts, sitting at a large roll-top desk and responding to students when help and advice was needed. Thus students could see him engraving and he was happy to demonstrate his own techniques and explain how he would approach the translation of a student's drawing onto wood, often referring to examples of his own work or that of other artists from the Golden Cockerel Press.[21] Gibbings insisted on peace and quiet in the workshop, partly, no doubt, to allow him to concentrate on his own work, and he insisted on discipline and 'good manners'. An amusing booklet of 'rules' entitled *Notes for Would-be Engravers* was printed in the department and distributed to students:

No one who TALKS while at work can be a good wood-engraver
Any one who WHISTLES while at work disturbs the whole class
Any one who SINGS during hours is a blue-pencil nuisance
Any one who HUMS forgets that other people want to think
THE MACHINE makes all the noise that is necessary in the WORKshop of R.G.[22]

In 1939, Gibbings had a visiting student in his class. Margaret Levetus was a student at the London Central School of Art and Crafts, but owing to the war the Central had closed for the Autumn term and so she spent that term at Reading, studying with Gibbings. The following extracts are from Margaret's diary which give a glimpse of the workshop and her working relationship with Gibbings — they also document an interesting divergence of views on their approach to wood-engraving:[23]

Monday October 9th

Mr Young (our tame compositor) set up some type for me. In this place, the type is not kept locked up in a den, guarded by a dragon ... Gibbings told me how helpful & enthusiastic all the people were at Reading; members of each department doing their best to help others. He said it was all one happy family ...

Tuesday October 17th

Gibbings & I had a slight controversy on the way to prepare a drawing for engraving. His method is to make the drawing look as much like the finished engraving as possible. I told him it was his passion for being more than one person (viz: his speech at the Arts & Crafts Society meeting held at the Central about 2 years ago, in which he described himself as 'Quads:- author, artist, printer & publisher') that led him to become first a designer & then an engraver, instead of merging the two arts into one (as Farleigh does, for instance, & as I have tried to do up till now). I agree that precision is necessary, & vagueness to be avoided in wood-engraving, but I do like to let the graver find its own way a bit, otherwise the thing is liable to look stiff & strained — dry & devoid of 'feeling'. Even some of Gibbings's work suffers a little from this in my opinion, while I admit some of Farleigh's shows weakness in the opposite direction. I must steer a middle course somehow.

Monday October 23rd

Started engraving. Rubbed powder into my block — a device which, for some reason, is never practised at the Central. But Lucian Pissarro does it so it must be all right.

Tuesday October 31st

Gibbings & a classical chap are doing a book of old Greek legends, translated by them into modern Anglo-Irish. Gibbings read one of them (Pan & Syrynx) aloud to us. It was hilariously funny.

Thursday November 23rd

Gibbings produced his Bermuda conch-shell & blew a blast on it. He says I can take it & try to make holes in it & play a tune on it.

Friday November 24th

... felt fed up with my illustrations & everything & biked off to draw some pigs that Gibbings told me about.

Thursday November 30th

Bought some re-surfaced blocks from Gibbings at 1d per square inch ...

Gibbings could be fun; his conversation was full of anecdotes and stories and he must have amused and impressed the students when he wore his wide-brimmed straw hat with a band of threaded sea shells. At the University's annual festival Gibbings appeared at a dance with a red rose tucked behind his ear — in the South Seas this was a sign of being available and looking for a sweetheart! Margaret recorded in her diary on 28 March 1940 that she attended one of a series of lunch-time concerts given by the University Orchestra. On this occasion Gibbings was guest conductor for a performance of Haydn's Toy Symphony:

He made a startling & picturesque entry, attired in a flat velvet cap (black) & a voluminous gown (cream-coloured with crimson sleeves) [another student at the time recalled that on turning round to face the orchestra, Gibbings had an 'L' plate pinned to his gown.]. He conducted with a hefty knobbly walking-stick. His conducting was more vigorous than accurate, but fortunately the orchestra was well-trained & took no notice of him. They played the last movement again for an encore, & then a girl placed a laurel wreath round his neck & he made a pretty speech in broken English.

Gibbings had borrowed the academic dress from a colleague but he was entitled to wear it. On joining the staff at the University, Robert had been sensitive to his lack of formal academic qualifications but in the academic year of 1938–39 the University College, Cork, had conferred an honorary degree of MA on him in recognition of his achievements.[24]

The first project set for students joining Gibbings's class was the engraving of a design incorporating the word 'In' as initial letters for the opening verses of the Old Testament. The type was set by Frank Young and then adjusted to fit with the block produced — the occasional 'typo', poor spacing, and evidence of loose type on the proofs suggests that the students themselves might have fitted the page into the chase. They were then involved in taking proofs under the guidance of Gibbings and Young. Naturally much of the work had echoes of the style of the Golden Cockerel Press and, as might have been expected, emphasis was put on exploring the relationship between illustration and text.

Particularly successful work was put on public display in the Buttery and reproduced in the University students' magazine *Tamesis*. The influence of Gibbings can be seen in the many wood-engravings used as illustrations in the magazine, both in style and subject matter, and Gibbings himself occasionally contributed a

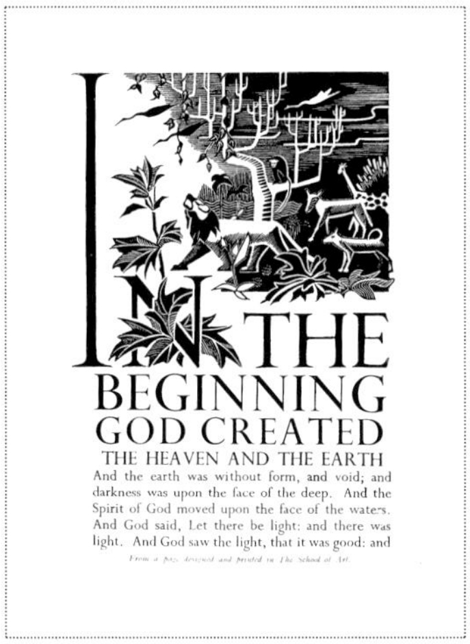
IN THE BEGINNING GOD CREATED THE HEAVEN AND THE EARTH
And the earth was without form, and void; and darkness was upon the face of the deep. And the Spirit of God moved upon the face of the waters. And God said, Let there be light: and there was light. And God saw the light, that it was good: and

From a page designed and printed in The School of Art.

211 *above* The opening page of the Bible designed and printed in the Fine Art Department as a student project under the supervision of Gibbings. Reproduced in the University students' magazine *Tamesis*, vol. 34, no. 2, 1935–36, page size 230 × 175 mm.

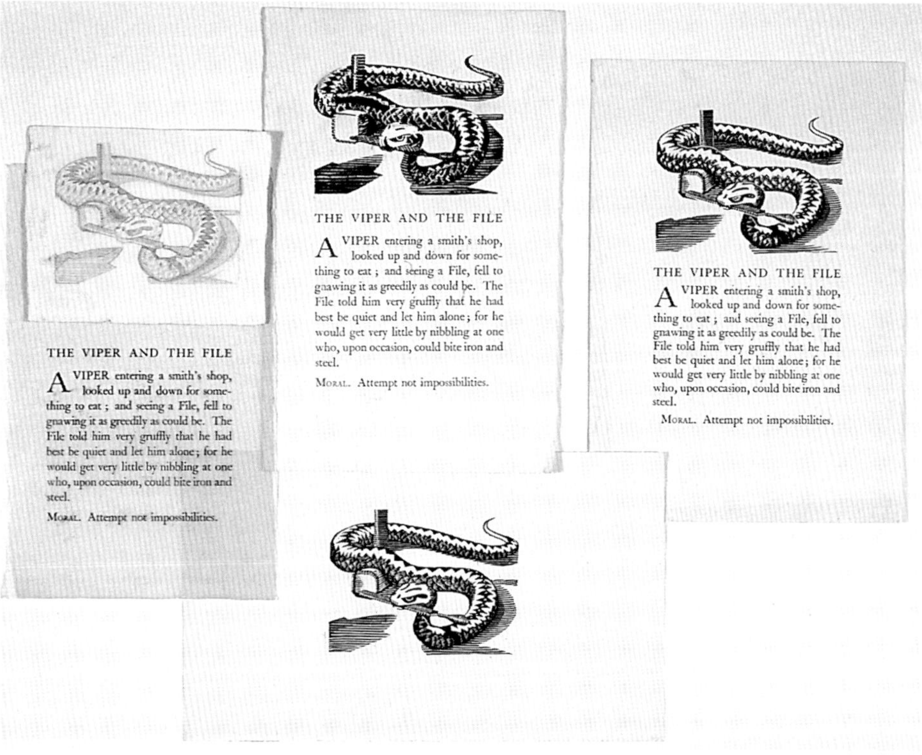
THE VIPER AND THE FILE

A VIPER entering a smith's shop, looked up and down for something to eat; and seeing a File, fell to gnawing it as greedily as could be. The File told him very gruffly that he had best be quiet and let him alone; for he would get very little by nibbling at one who, upon occasion, could bite iron and steel.

MORAL. Attempt not impossibilities.

212 *right* A student project by William Wilder showing how Gibbings encouraged his students to ensure a balance between the text and wood-engraved illustration by working on proofs of the type and overlaying the image on tracing paper. Page size 204 × 136 mm. Reproduced with permission of Joan Wilder.

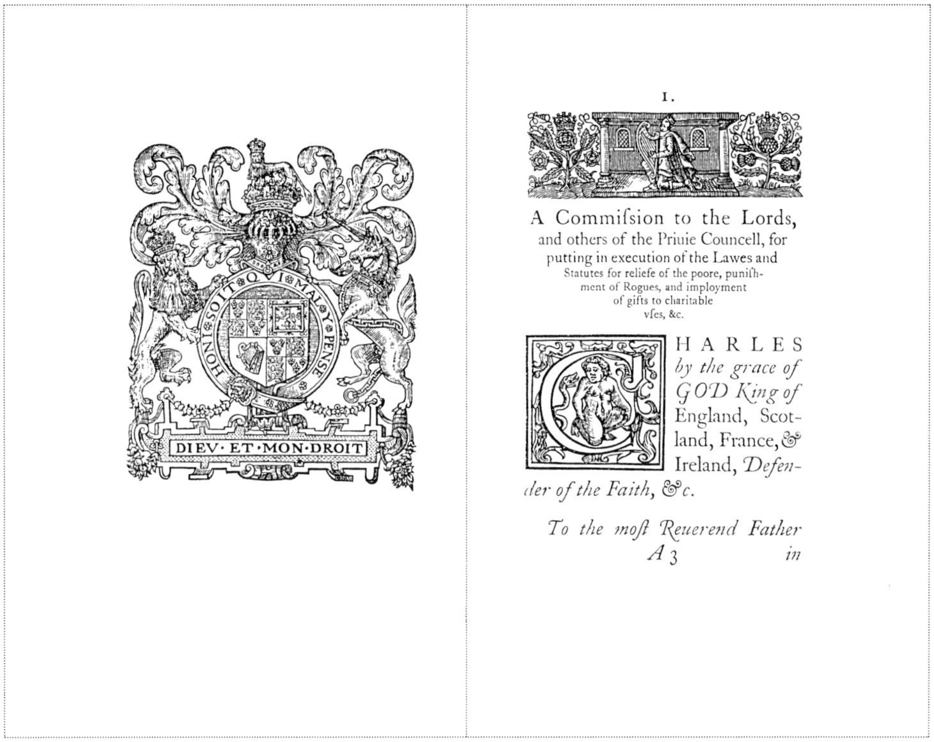

1.

A Commiſsion to the Lords, and others of the Priuie Councell, for putting in execution of the Lawes and Statutes for reliefe of the poore, puniſh-ment of Rogues, and imployment of gifts to charitable vſes, &c.

CHARLES *by the grace of GOD King of* England, Scot-land, France, & Ireland, *Defen-der of the Faith, &c.*

To the moſt Reuerend Father
A 3 *in*

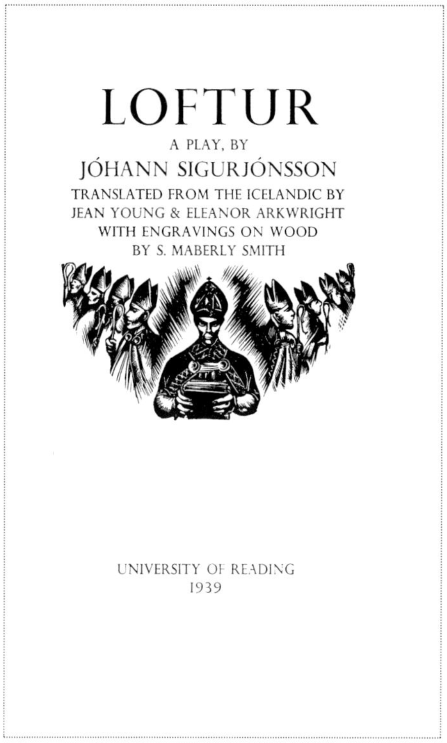

LOFTUR
A PLAY, BY
JÓHANN SIGURJÓNSSON
TRANSLATED FROM THE ICELANDIC BY
JEAN YOUNG & ELEANOR ARKWRIGHT
WITH ENGRAVINGS ON WOOD
BY S. MABERLY SMITH

UNIVERSITY OF READING
1939

213 A fascimile edition of *The Book of Orders 1630–31* printed at the University in 1940 with wood-engraved frontispiece and decorations faithfully copied from the original by Ralph Beedham. Page size 187 x 125 mm. RUL.

214 Title page from *Loftur*, an Icelandic play printed by Gibbings at the University in 1939 with wood-engraved illustrations by S. Maberly Smith who was one of his students. Page size 250 x 160 mm. RUL.

block. He also developed a programme of printing and publishing limited edition books, encouraging students to provide illustrations. The first of these was *Fatherless Oberlus* which was printed during the Summer term of 1936. The text was taken from yet another 'journal', this time that of Captain David Porter, 1822, and was an account of the adventures of Patrick Watkins on Charles' Island in the Galapagos. A group of the most promising students each contributed an engraved illustration and the cover paper was also printed with an engraved design of an iguana.[25]

In addition to student projects, Gibbings, assisted by Young, produced some fine editions of early academic texts. *Observationes Anatomicae Selectiores Amstelodamensium*, 1667, was printed in March 1938 and in 1940 *The Book of Orders*, 1630–31, which was a line-for-line reprint of the original edition, beautifully bound in full leather. Both books demanded wood-engraved illustrations of the highest technical standard and, in particular, those in *The Book of Orders* needed to be faithful fac-similes of the original blocks. Certainly no student would have had the ability, nor was Gibbings experienced in such work, so Ralph Beedham was commis-sioned for the project and produced engravings that demonstrated his immense talents as a reproductive engraver.

The scale of production never reached a level that could be described as a University Press but the range of short pamphlets and books published was varied.[26] In 1939 the publication of *The Diary of W. Lashly*, a record of the return journey of the supporting party on Captain Scott's expedition to the South Pole,[27] was followed by *Loftur*,[28] a translation of an Icelandic play, and *The Log of the 'Sea Bird'*. This last book was an account of a dramatic seafaring adventure based on the journal of a voyage undertaken by two young men to Bermuda, with an introduction by Gibbings.[29] This was a very short single section book with paper covers, and a similar format was used in 1940 for *The Man Who Saved Two Hundred*, an account of war-time heroism written by Ralph McCarthy and printed for Barry Neame. In 1941, a talented student, Margaret Webb, produced twenty-eight wood-engravings for an edition of *The Shepherd of Banbury's Rules*, which consisted of observations on forecasting weather by John Claridge, shepherd; their most ambitious project to date, this book was reprinted by the Sylvan Press in 1946. All these books were illustrated with wood-engravings by students and proved to be very successful; so much so that in a report to the University's Council in May 1940, the Vice Chancellor noted that 'in every case the cost of production has been covered by subscriptions before the work was undertaken'. These publications were taken sufficiently seriously for a committee to be appointed to 'select books for future production and to control their publication'.[30] Profits were ploughed back into new projects and the purchase of type and equipment.

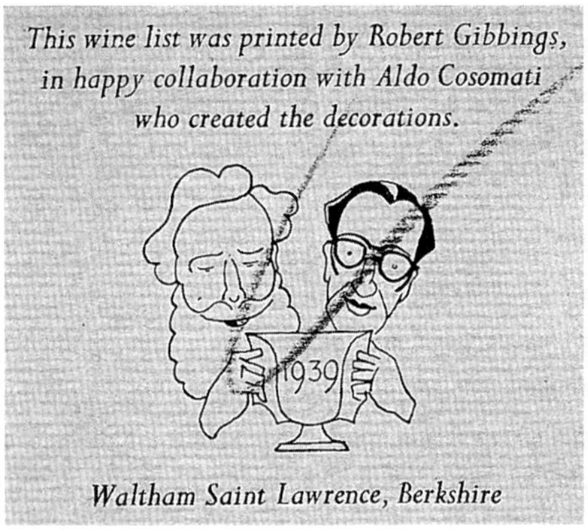

215 Imprint on the back cover of a wine list printed for Barry Neame at the Hind's Head Hotel in Bray-on-Thames. The list was decorated with lively line illustrations by Aldo Cosomati and produced at the University. This illustration comes from a proof copy of the list in the Gibbings Collection, Department of Typography & Graphic Communication, The University of Reading, and has been ticked off in blue pencil by the printer.

Gibbings built up the range of equipment and, together with the technical expertise of Frank Young, they organised an efficient printing unit. They took on a certain amount of jobbing printing for the University but were very careful not to offend the Unions or appear to be taking work away from printers in the town. Prospectuses were produced for a number of their books but more ephemeral material was also printed; menus and invitation cards for University functions, a wine list for Barry Neame, Christmas cards and postcards. For the war effort, Gibbings used a block from *The Log of the 'Sea Bird'* to illustrate a printed notice requesting a collection of unwanted books to donate to the 'Seafarer's Library'.

One of the major projects that Gibbings regularly set for his students was to illustrate a book of their own choice. The brief gave the option for students to write their own text or research and select material from an existing work. The length of the text and the number of engravings differed greatly according to the skill and interest of the student, but two of the more successful efforts were by Elisabeth Geddes and Margaret Webb. Both students were enthusiastic pupils of Gibbings and worked closely with him. Elisabeth Geddes produced such a distinguished piece of work that Gibbings was able to persuade Christopher Sandford to publish it. The book consisted of twenty-four original humorous verses about a variety of creatures, each illustrated by a wood-engraving. The little book was entitled *Animal Antics* and was published in August 1937 as a 'Christmas frivolity', a 'cheerful little gift-book' which would 'make everyone chuckle'; *Animal Antics* was dedicated to Gibbings in recognition of his help and encouragement. Margaret Webb selected and brought together a collection of fifteenth century recipes for which she engraved numerous illustrations. *Early English Recipes* was also published in 1937, but this time by Cambridge University Press.

Gibbings was always looking for opportunities to further the careers of his students by getting their work published and this extended to part-time students attending evening classes. He had been impressed by the engravings of one such student, Russell Leslie, who was head-gardener for a wealthy landowner near Reading. Leslie's particular skill was in cultivating alpine plants and Gibbings suggested that he should use these as the subject of his engraving. The results received high praise; so much so that in 1940 Lindsay Drummund published a book by Russell Leslie entitled *Alpines I have Grown*. Gibbings contributed a foreword expressing his admiration for Leslie's work: 'He knows every stage in their growth as a father knows the growth of his own child. That is why he has engraved them with the hand of a master.'[31]

Gibbings had time in the working week free of teaching and was also able to carry on his with his own projects while supervising the workshop. As well as encouraging others he was busy with freelance commissions but most of all he now found himself with time to develop his own writing.

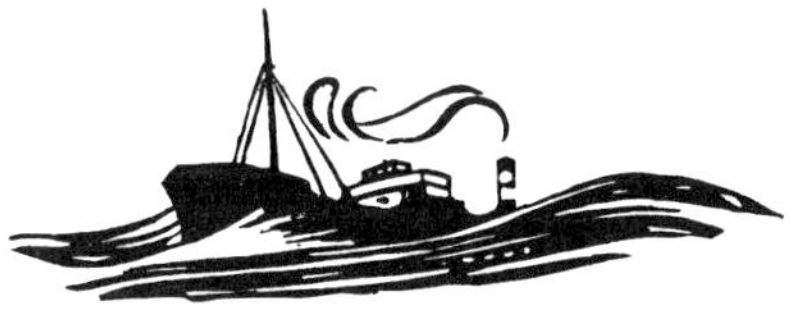

THERE MUST BE MANY BOOKS on your shelves, Penguins and others, that you do not really need. I am collecting for "The Seafarers' Library." Any volumes left in my room will be forwarded direct to headquarters from whence they will be distributed to ships of the Merchant Navy.

ROBERT GIBBINGS

216 A notice printed by Gibbings asking for contributions for The Seafarers' Library illustrated by a wood-engraving from *The Log of the 'Sea Bird'* by M. E. Mills who was one of his students. Gibbings Collection, Department of Typography & Graphic Communication, The University of Reading.

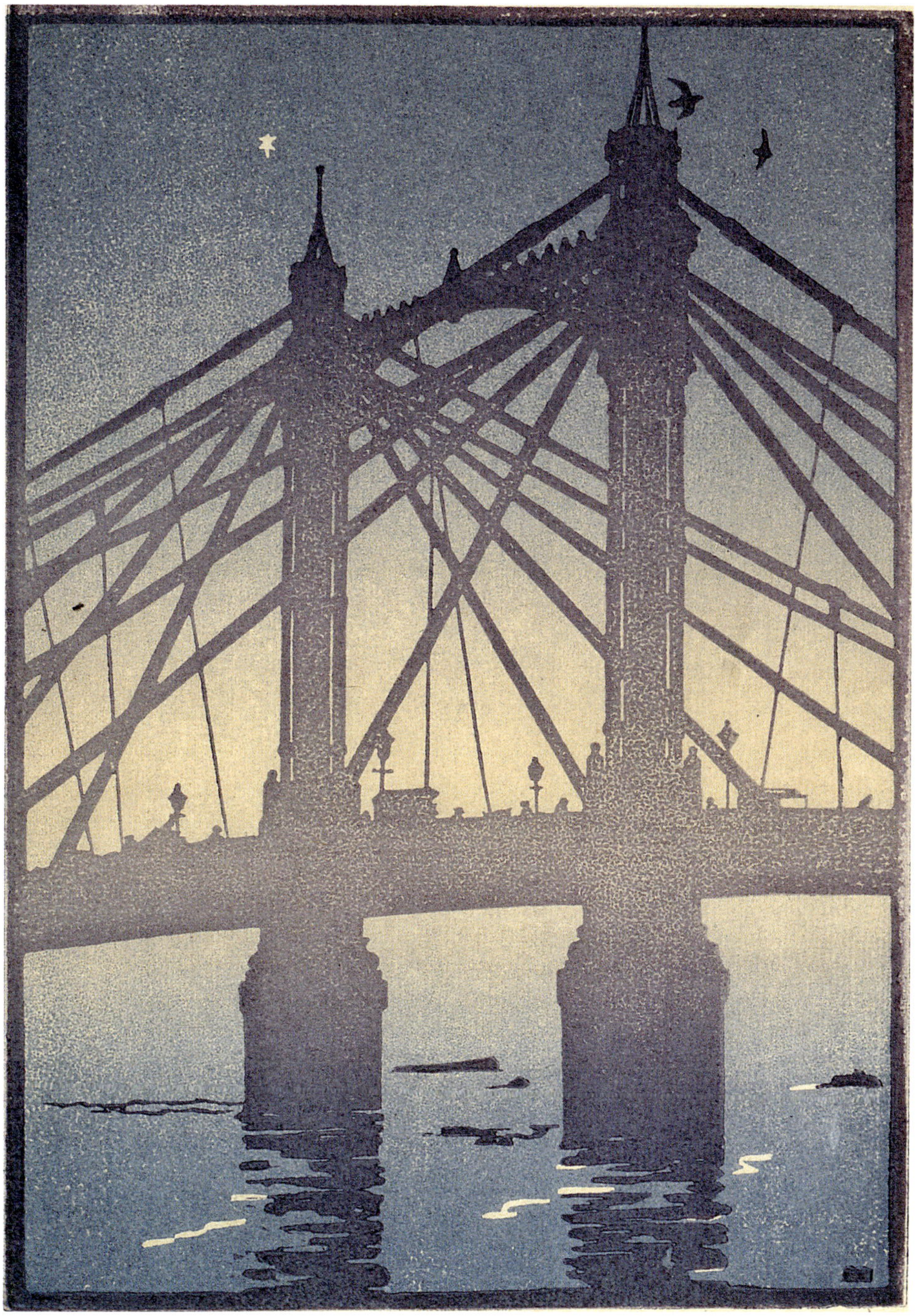

Plate 1 *Albert Bridge*, Chelsea, 1919, coloured wood-engraving, 180 × 128 mm.
Reproduced with permission of the Central St Martin Museum and Study Collection.

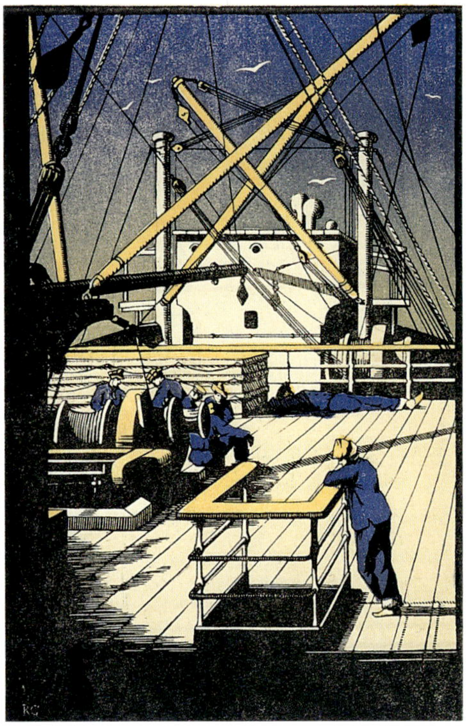

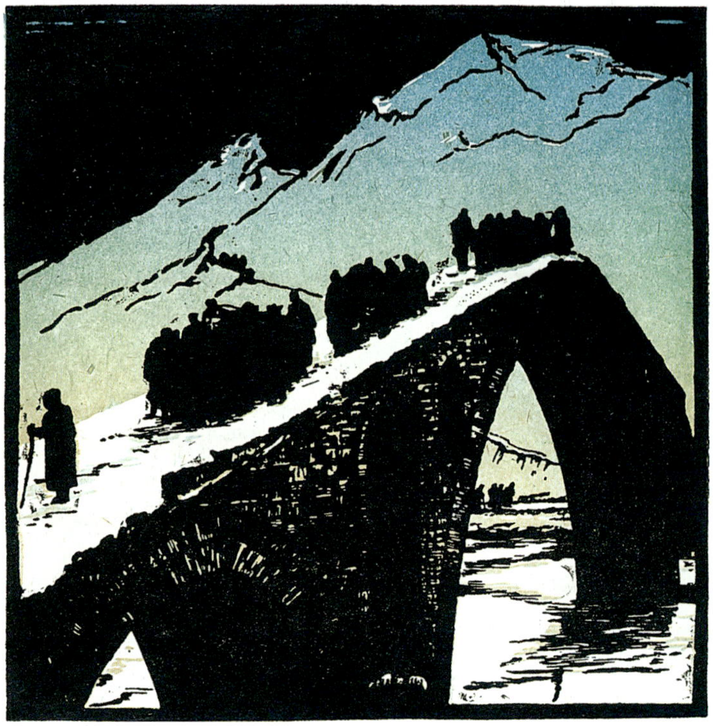

Plate 2a *above* *Llandovery Castle*, 1918, 190 x 127 mm. A wood-engraving in three colours of the hospital ship on which Gibbings returned home from Malta. The image is based on drawings he made during the voyage.

Plate 2b *above right* *The Retreat from Serbia*, 1916, 180 x 180 mm. A coloured wood-engraving based on a photograph Gibbings had seen in the *Illustrated London News*.

Plate 2c *right* *Sunset over Lemnos*, 1919, oil on canvas, 750 x 546 mm. This was based on a view near 'W' beach with *HMS Triumph* and *HMS Swiftsure* in the middle distance and with a foreground of scrub and barbed wire typical of the terrain. Commissioned by the Imperial War Museum, the painting was initially rejected; it was felt that the subject matter was too general and differed from the composition that Gibbings had put forward. Gibbings argued that the foreground was indeed simpler than originally intended but the inclusion of a road and Dressing Station, as first proposed, ruined the composition and distracted the eye away from the ships – and he also admitted he had insufficient drawings on which to base these details. The painting was finally accepted in January 1920 at a reduced price. Reproduced with permission of The Trustees of The Imperial War Museum, London.

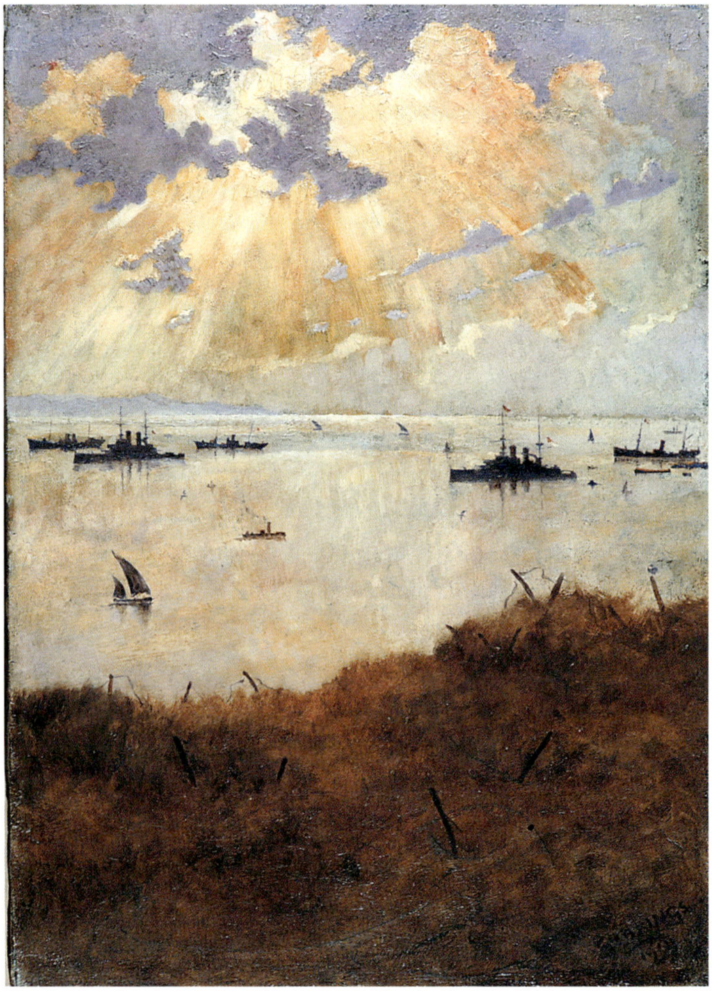

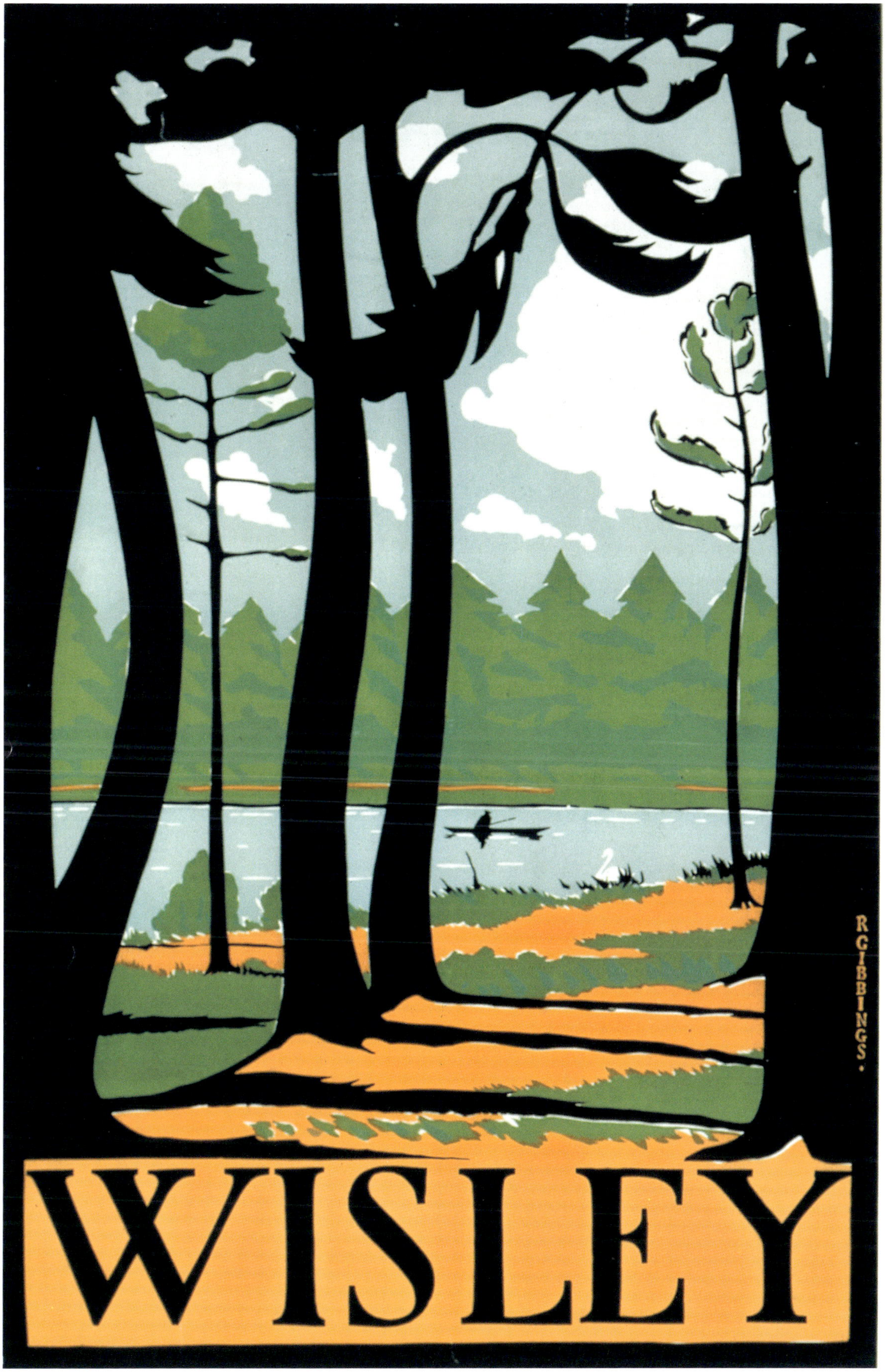

Plate 3 Poster advertising Wisley gardens, 1922, 762 x 508 mm. (double crown). This poster is a rare example of a woodcut made by Gibbings. Probably his largest image, the poster was commissioned by the Underground Electric Railway Company (London Transport was not formed until 1933) and was probably displayed on the front panels of buses on either side of the destination board. Gibbings may have found it easier to work out a design and the colour separations on wood; the imprint at the bottom of the poster states that it was printed direct from woodblocks by Sanders Phillips & Co. Ltd at the Baynard Press. However, it was a practice at that time to take proofs from the blocks and transfer the separations to lithographic plates to be printed by offset litho. The original wood-blocks are now in the collections at The Museum of Reading. Reproduced with permission of the London Transport Museum.

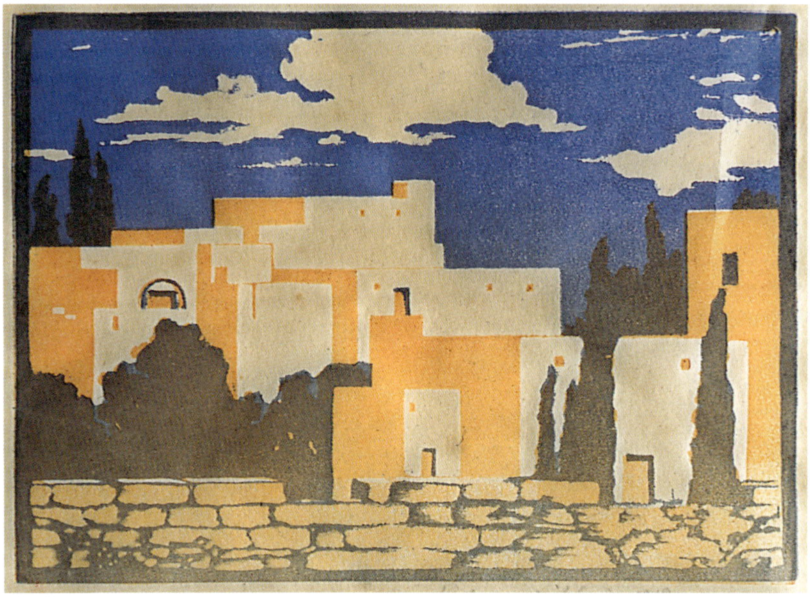

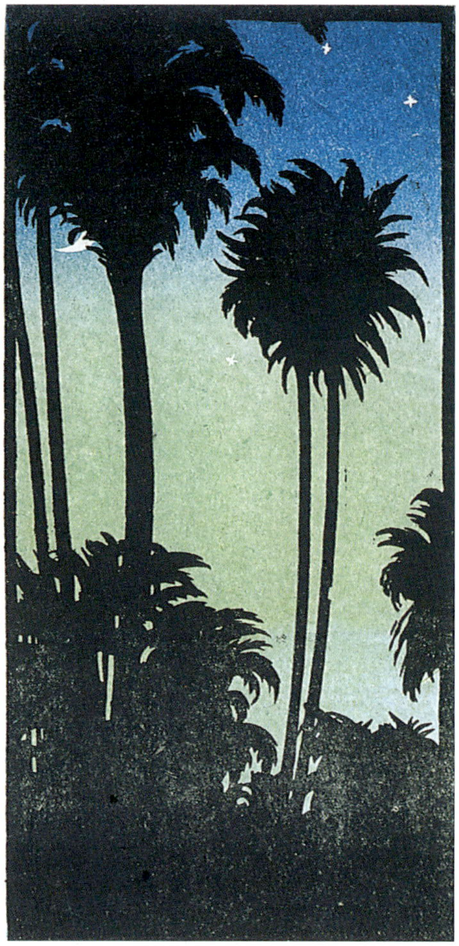

Plate 4a *above* *A Corner in Malta*, 1918, coloured wood-engraving, 94 x 133 mm. Salaman described the colour scheme of this print as 'suggestive of hot sunlight, revealed in a pattern of three tints printed from two blocks'. Author's collection.

Plate 4b *above right* *Evening at Gaza*, 1918, coloured wood-engraving, 131 x 270 mm. The art critic Malcolm Salaman commented '... its romantic beauty of blue night in a grove of palm-trees, is a reminiscence of "somewhere" in the neighbourhood of Alexandria ...'.

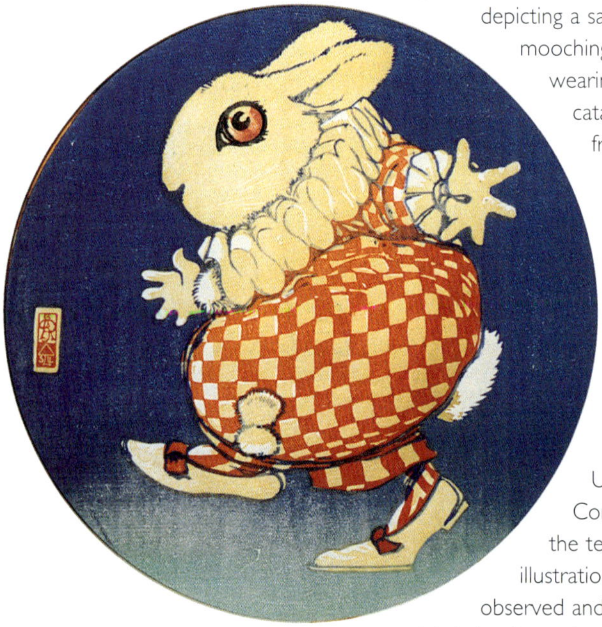

Plate 4c *below* *Play*, coloured wood-engraving of a comic rabbit, *c.* 1918, diam. 258 mm. This unusual subject for Gibbings was intended as decoration for the nursery. It is signed on the block with Gibbings's initials and S J – attributed on the print at the V&A to 'Serj Lapin'. A similar print, depicting a sad and guilty looking dog mooching along on his hind-legs, also wearing baggy trousers with a catapult and dead bird dangling from his belt, was produced to make a pair. Private Collection.

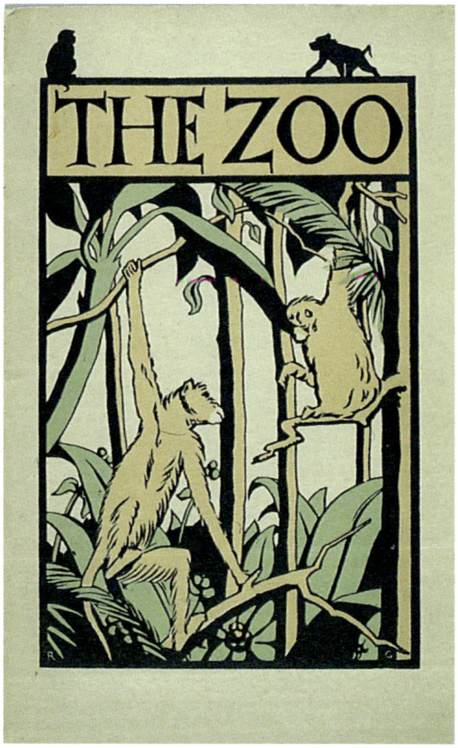

Plate 4d *right* Cover of a booklet illustrated by Gibbings and written by himself and his wife Moira, 1922, 243 x 156 mm. Produced to advertise London Zoo, it was printed at the Baynard Press for the Underground Electric Railway Company. The humorous nature of the text is carried through into the illustrations which are bold, well-observed and frequently framed by a heavy black border and printed over solid blocks of colour, creating a strong graphic feel. The copy reproduced here is from the collections of Cal Hyland and originally belonged to Tom Balston. This is a very rare item but a number of copies are in the collection of the London Transport Museum.

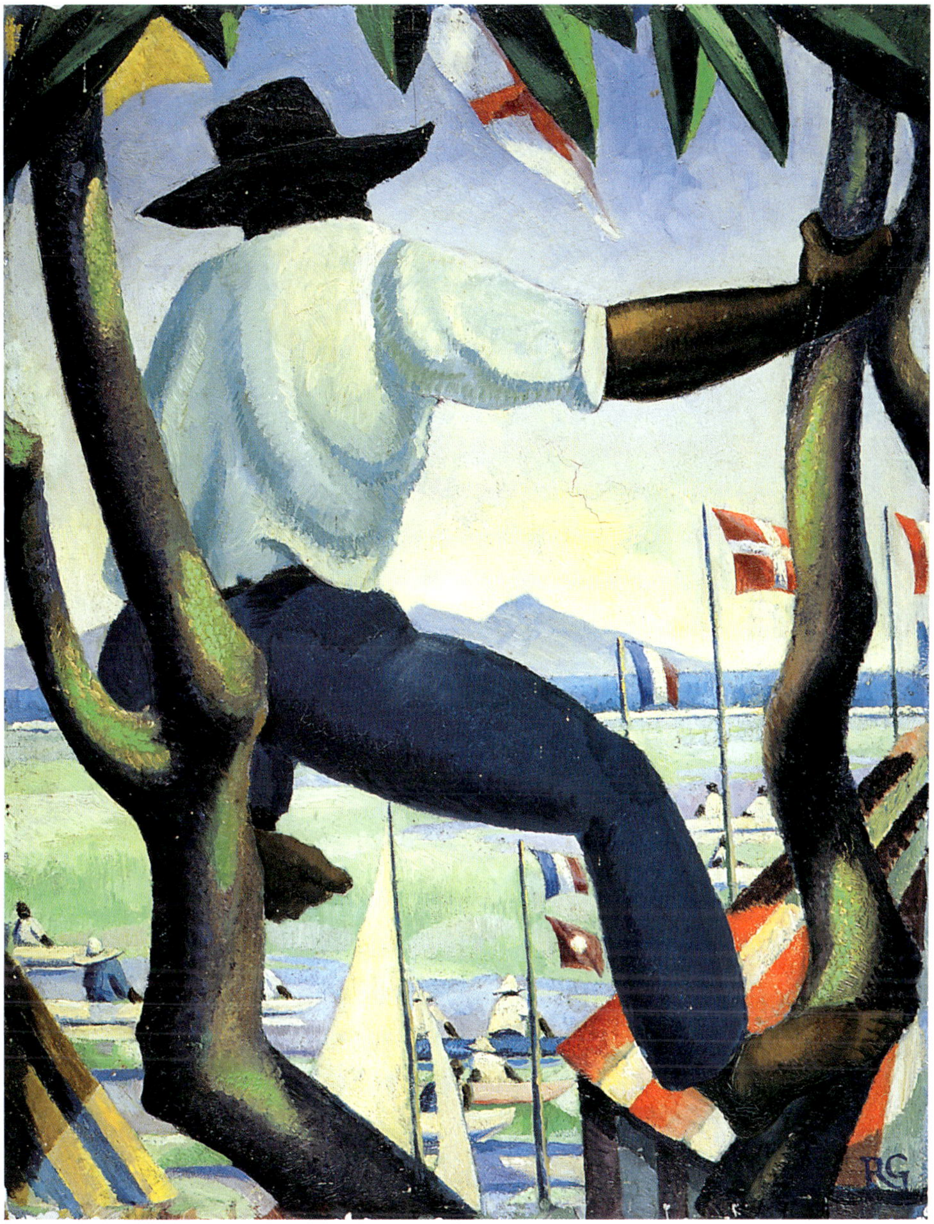

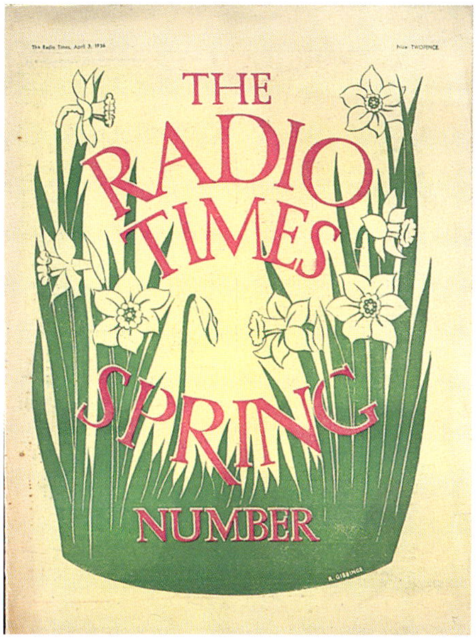

Plate 5a *above* Man in a tree, *c.* 1928, oil on panel, 509 x 403 mm. Although the precise date of this painting is unknown, it is based on drawings that Gibbings made during his first visit to Tahiti and appears to be a scene of a regatta – probably held close to the port of Papeete. It is possible that it was painted some years later. RUL.

Plate 5b *above right* Cover of *The Radio Times*, 3 April 1936. RUL.

Plate 5c *right* *The Wright Encyclopaedia of Gardening* published by Dent in October 1933, coloured wood-engraving, image size 150 x 110 mm. RUL.

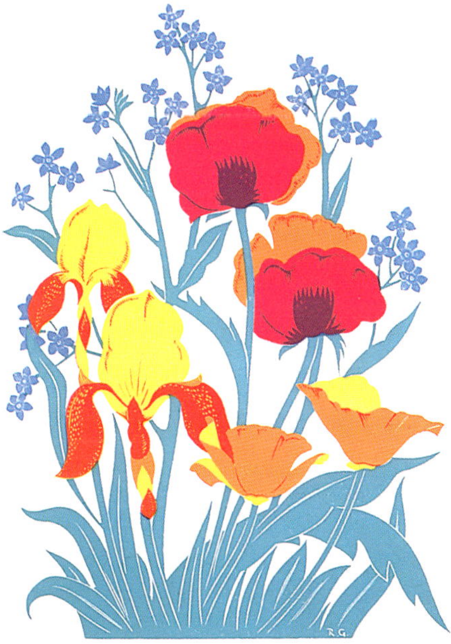

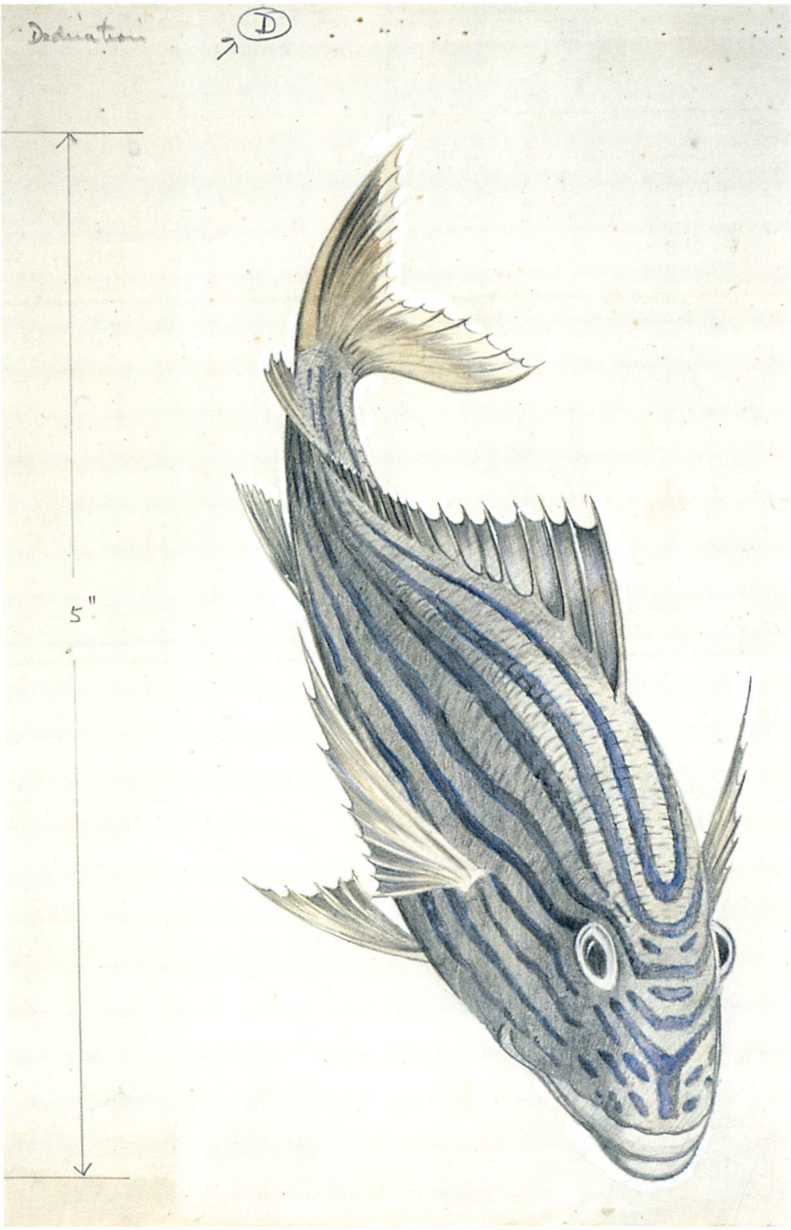

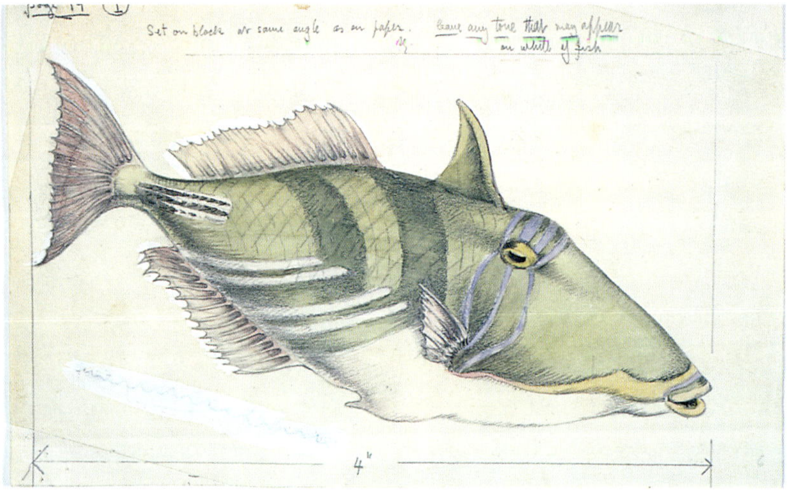

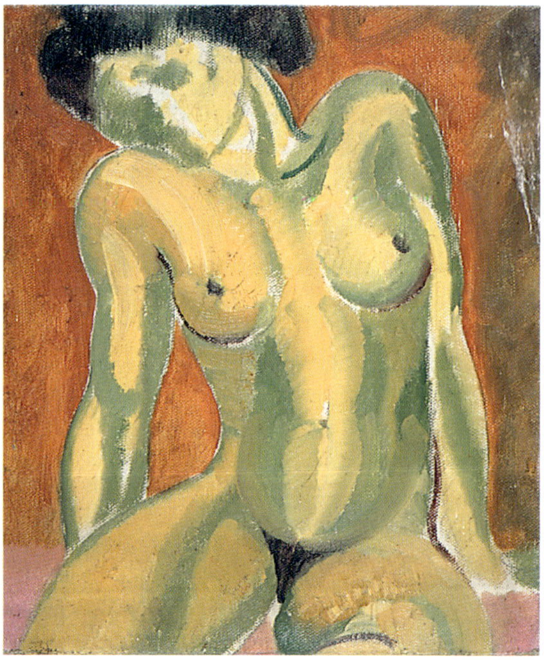

Plate 6a *left* Tropical fish, *c.* 1938, pencil and watercolour, image size 240 x 120 mm. Gibbings based a number of engravings on this drawing and a version, printed in two colours, was used as the frontispiece to *Blue Angels and Whales*. Private Collection.

Plate 6b *below left* Tropical fish, *c.* 1938, pencil and watercolour, image size 100 x 200 mm. Private Collection.

Plate 6c *below* Female nude, *c.* 1954, oil on canvas, 400 x 355 mm. One of a number of unfinished experimental paintings of the female nude that were stored in the studio at Footbridge Cottage until 1994, when they were given to the Gibbings Collection, RUL.

Plate 7a *opposite above The Harbour of La Flotte on the Île de Ré*, *c.* 1953, oil on board, 215 x 265 mm. This painting was reproduced in *Trumpets from Montparnasse*. Private Collection.

Plate 7b *opposite below left* Female nude, *c.* 1954, oil on board, 350 x 270 mm. RUL.

Plate 7c *opposite below right* Seascape, *c.* 1955, oil on board, 220 x 270 mm. Gibbings inscribed this painting 'To PAE'. Private Collection.

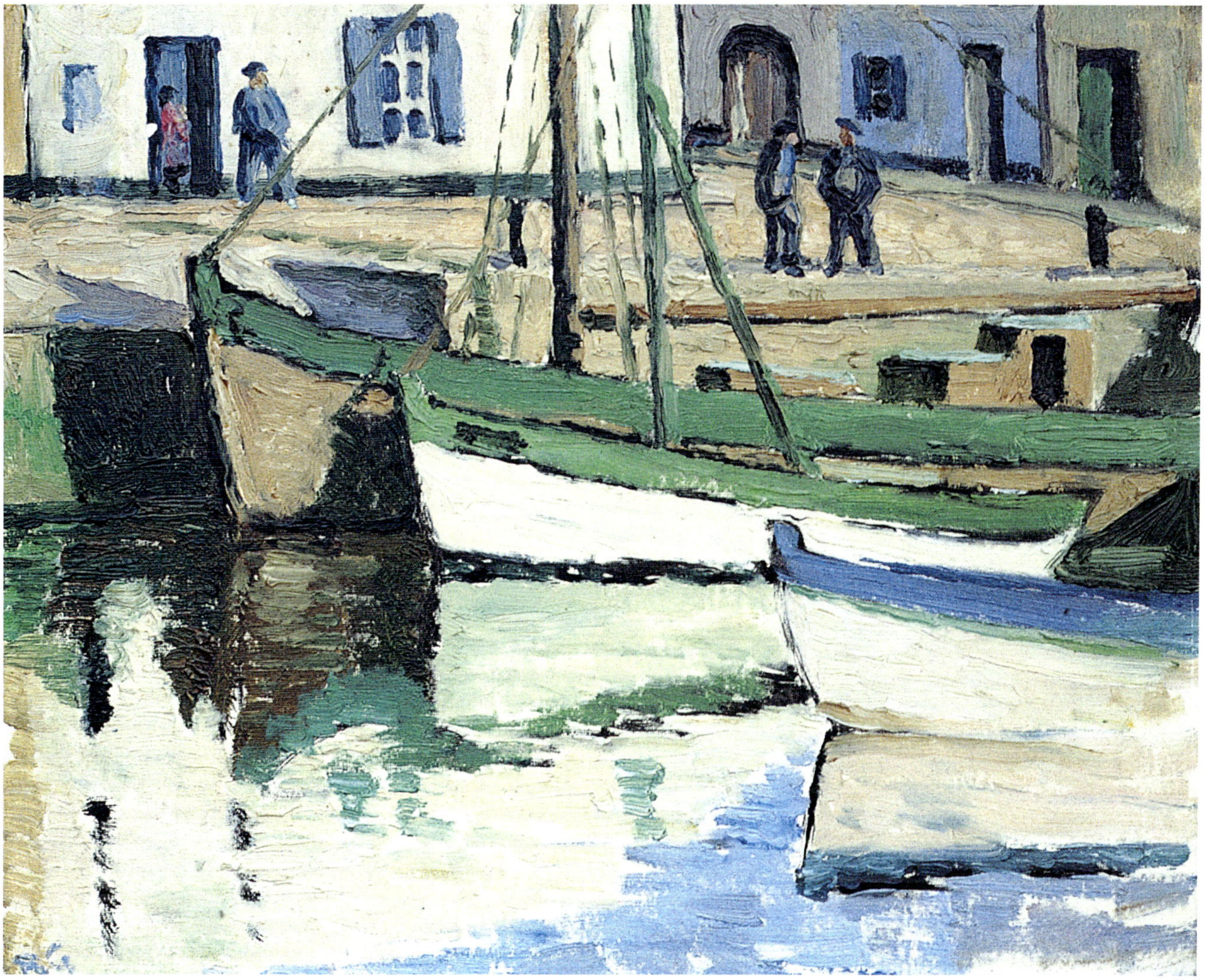

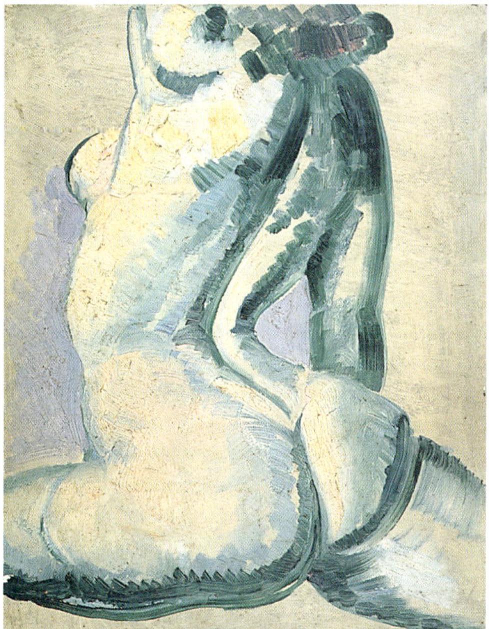

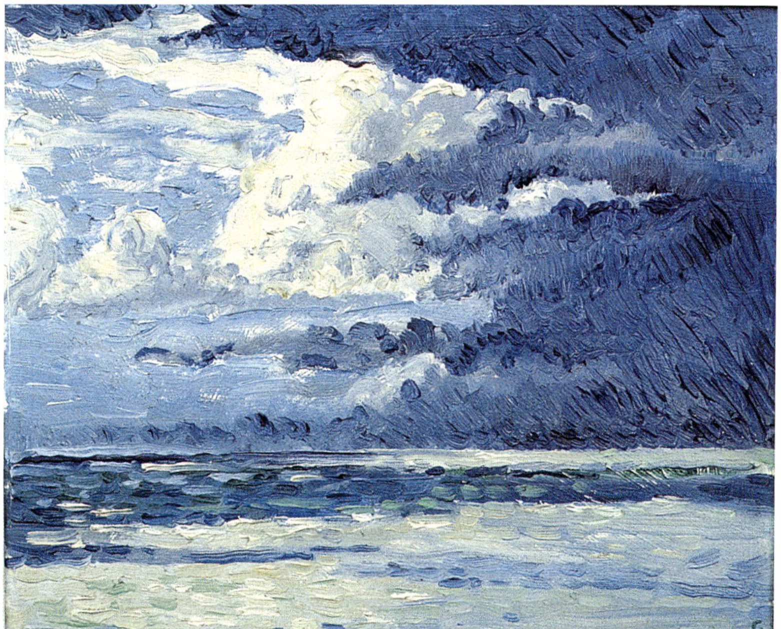

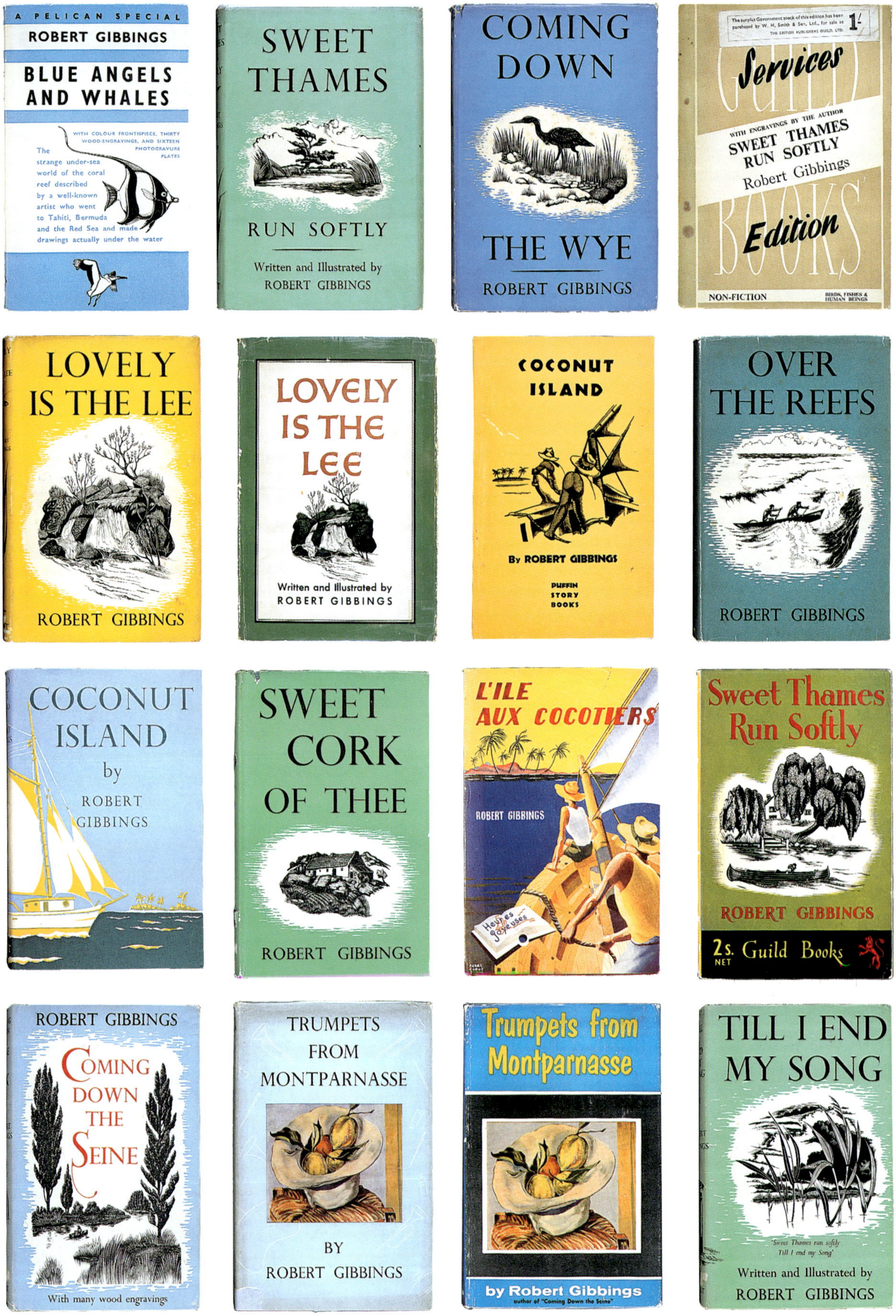

Plate 8 Covers *from left to right*

a *Blue Angels and Whales* published as a Pelican Special in 1938.

b *Sweet Thames Run Softly*, 1940.

c *Coming Down the Wye* published in December 1942.

d The Services edition of *Sweet Thames Run Softly* published by for Guild Books (The British Publishers Guild) by J. M. Dent & Sons Ltd in 1944. Paperback.

e *Lovely is the Lee* published in December 1944.

f The American edition of *Lovely is the Lee* published by Dutton in November 1945 which was made the Book of the Month Club Dual Selection in December. Dutton frequently made changes to the design of their editions of Gibbings's books, using different typefaces and cover designs to appeal to the tastes of the American market.

g *Coconut Island* published as a Puffin Story Book by Penguin Books Ltd, 1945.

h *Over the Reefs* published by Dent on 28 October 1948.

i Dent's edition of *Coconut Island* published on 6 October 1949.

j *Sweet Cork of Thee* published by Dent on 14 June 1951.

k A French edition of *Coconut Island* published by Editions De L'Amitie, G.-T Rageot, in 1949.

l An edition of *Sweet Thames Run Softly* published for Guild Books (The British Publishers Guild) by J. M. Dent & Sons Ltd in 1953. Paperback.

m *Coming Down the Seine* published by Dent on 10 September 1953.

n *Trumpets from Montparnasse* published by Dent in October 1955.

o The American edition of *Trumpets from Montparnasse* published by Dutton in November 1955.

p *Till I End my Song* published by Dent on 3 October 1957.

Chapter Thirteen
A Time to Write 1936–1939

IN 1936, AT ABOUT THE TIME when he joined the University, a friend and collector of his work, A. Crooks-Ripley, wrote to Gibbings: 'I'd like to give you a present,' he wrote; 'is there any special book that you are in need of?'[1] The previous day Robert's attention had been drawn to a copy of *The Wreck of the Stirling Castle* in a bookseller's catalogue. With his usual passion for such accounts, Gibbings instinctively felt that this book might offer a suitable subject for his own writing and, taking up his friend's generous offer, he ordered the book. His imagination was immediately fired by an account of the life of an Irish youth, John Graham, who had been transported to Australia in 1824 and sentenced to seven years for the trivial theft of some hemp for rope-making. While there, Graham had rescued the widow of the captain of the *Stirling Castle* from a tribe of aborigines, the captain himself having been murdered by the tribesmen. Feeling for the plight of his fellow Irishman, Gibbings became fascinated by the tale and immediately undertook research to authenticate and flesh out the story. Although in his youth Robert had been bored by academic study, in the pursuit of a subject that stimulated him he was meticulous in his research and anxious to be accurate in all aspects of factual detail. He wrote to the curator of the Mitchell Library in Sidney and was delighted to receive copies of documents relating to the period, from when Graham arrived in the penal colony to when he was granted a free pardon as a reward for the rescue.[2] Encouraged by this, Gibbings consulted many other authorities and reference books to piece together not just the facts of Graham's life but the background and context of the period — the grim social history of life as a prisoner sentenced to transportation.

Writing and research occupied much of his spare time that year but in August 1936 Gibbings started planning another book by Llewelyn Powys, *The Twelve Months*, a collection of poetical essays on the months of the year which had originally appeared in the *Daily Herald*. The Bodley Head was to publish the book and had approached Gibbings about illustrations the previous year. Powys was delighted at the possibility of another collaboration with his friend: 'I like well to think that our names will always be so associated and I honour and admire your art more than anyone's, to say nothing of your personality towards which my spirit leapt, when I saw you first, like a fish back to its native stream.'[3] As well as providing wood-engravings to illustrate the text, Gibbings was involved in the production of the book. Lindsay Drummond at The Bodley Head had consulted

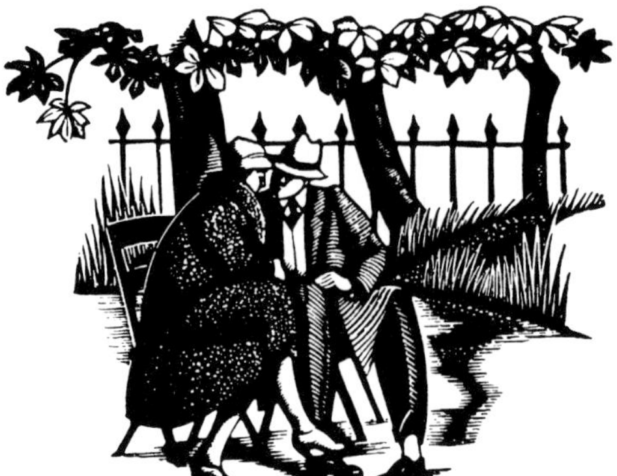

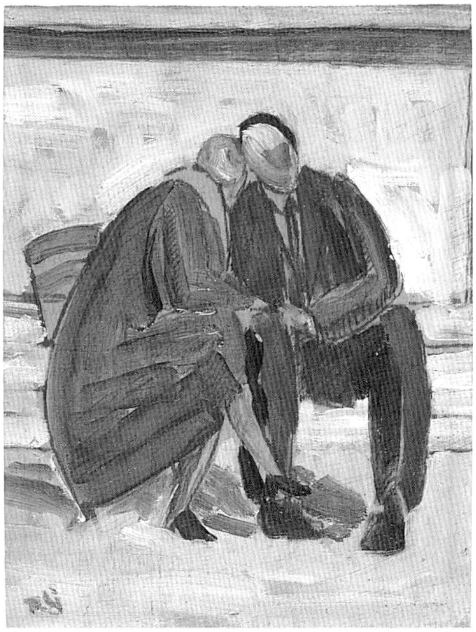

217 *above* Illustration from *The Twelve Months*, 1937, wood-engraving, 50 x 64 mm.

218 *right* *Lovers on a bench*, *c*. 1937, oil on board, 200 x 154 mm. The illustration from *The Twelve Months* (*above*) is clearly based on this painting. Private collection.

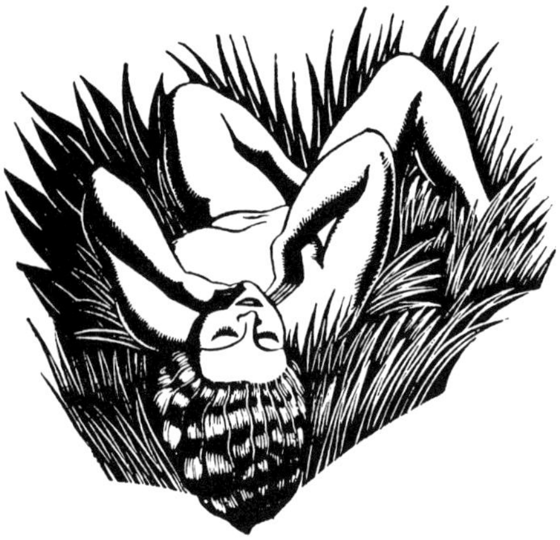

219 Illustration from *The Twelve Months*, 1937, wood-engraving, 56 x 60 mm.

Gibbings on a suitable printer for the job and he had recommended Oxford University Press, knowing from his previous experience that they would be co-operative and welcome his intervention. Gibbings was able to oversee the project, deciding on the layout of each page with John Johnson, but not all his ideas were implemented.[4] Gibbings engraved twenty-eight head- and tail-pieces for the book, which came out in March 1937.

At the Golden Cockerel Press, the long awaited edition of *Paradise Lost* was finally published, with all the engravings, apart from Gibbings's title page, by Mary Groom. A prospectus for *A Croppe of Kisses* appeared with a cockerel by Gibbings on the sample title page and a prospectus for a range of Christmas cards printed at the Press included eight designs by him (a number of engravings were used on Christmas cards for the following two years). In October, Methuen had published a collection of verses by George Scott-Moncrieff called *A Book of Uncommon Prayer*, with nineteen engravings of birds and animals by Gibbings.[5] That same month his own book, *John Graham, Convict*, was published by Faber and Faber. This was an historical account but much of the skill and imagination in Gibbings's writing came through his use of dialogue — he captured the colour and lilt of the Irish accent and turn of phrase.

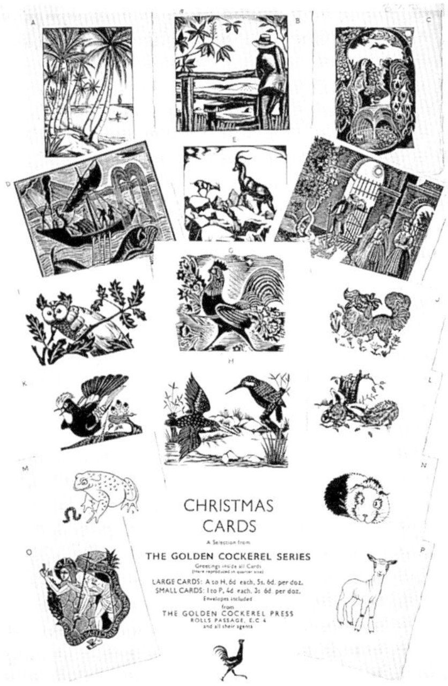

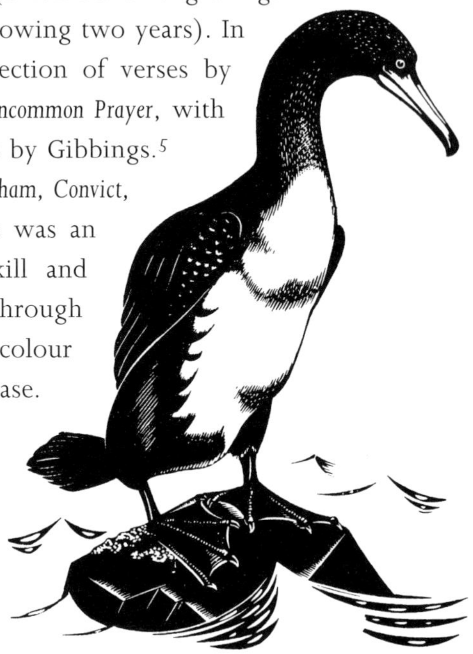

220 *left* Publicity sheet for the Golden Cockerel Christmas cards, sheet size 304 x 213 mm. RUL.

221 *right* *The Cormorant*, frontispiece from *A Book of Uncommon Prayer*, 1937, wood-engraving, 112 x 85 mm.

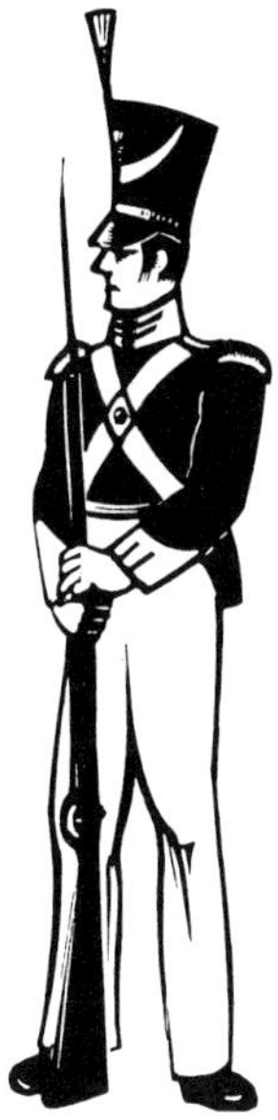

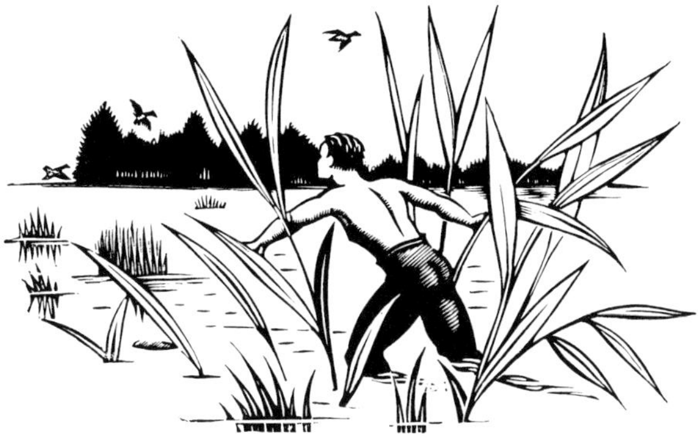

222 *left* Illustration from *John Graham, Convict*, 1937, wood-engraving, 74 × 18 mm.

223 *above* Illustration from *John Graham, Convict*, 1937, wood-engraving, 48 × 78 mm.

The book was well received by the Press: 'A brilliant reconstruction' in the words of a review in the *Glasgow Herald*; Ivor Brown wrote in the *Observer* that the narrative was 'no less vivid than his illustrations … told with a sense of drama which enlivens the characters but never works for cheap effects. Mr Gibbings's luminous prose throws light on some of the darkest corners in the bleakest of all human houses'; *The Times Literary Supplement* described the book as 'a cameo of history'. Gibbings had engraved forty-one blocks to illustrate his text but had reservations about their success: 'I fear my illustrations were not up to the interest of the story',[6] and indeed a number of the engravings were rather ineffectual.

Working at the University had advantages; Gibbings seems to have revelled in being part of the social and academic life of the University — then a fairly small

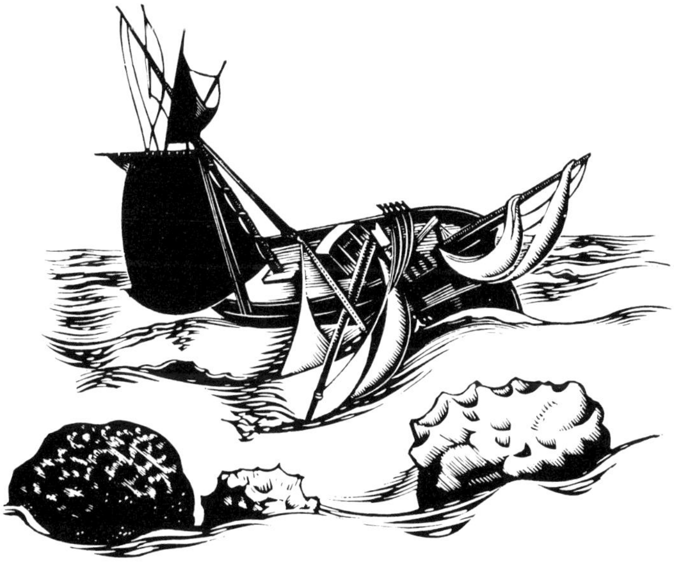

224 Illustration from *John Graham, Convict*, 1937, wood-engraving, 75 × 90 mm.

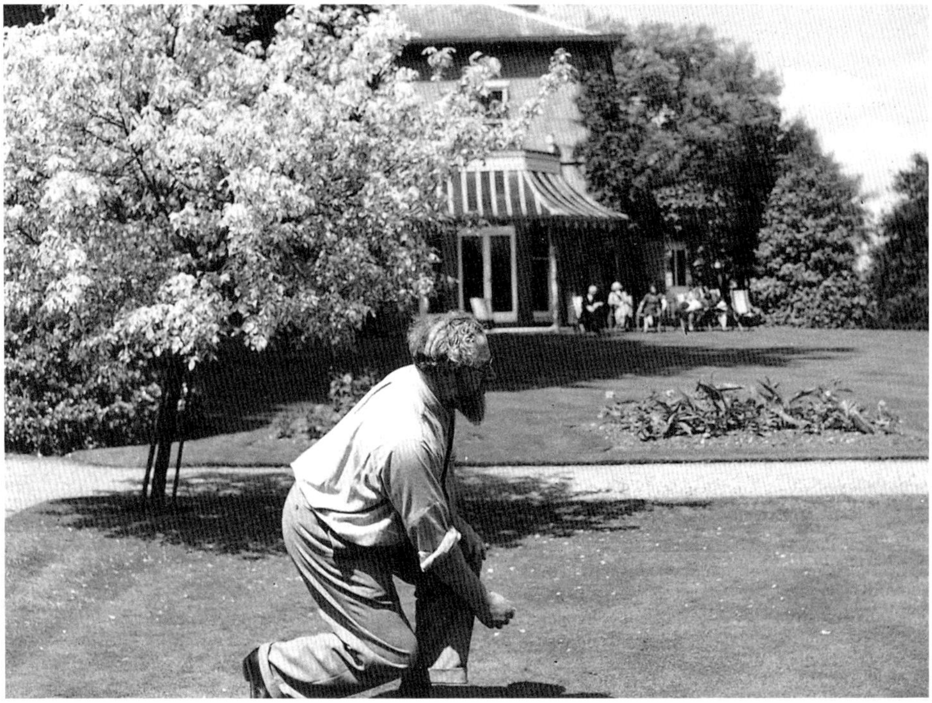

225 Gibbings playing bowls on the lawn of Acacias, the Senior Common Room, June 1939, The University of Reading at London Road. RUL.

community in which it was possible to know everyone. Certainly everyone seems to have known him, and he was well known as both a great conversationalist and a canny listener. Gibbings had an extraordinary capacity for absorbing information and anecdotes which he was later able to use to rich effect in his books. Perhaps, above all, the University was an ideal place for him to extend his already impressive knowledge of natural history.

Around the time that he was offered the post of lecturer, Gibbings had reluctantly turned down the proposal from a London publisher of a further visit to Tahiti: 'If it had not been for the cares of a family I should certainly have gone, but much against my inclinations I decided that it was my duty to stay at home and attempt respectability.' Despite his disappointment he recognised that University life offered compensations: 'I soon learned, however, that tropic islands are not the only places with wide horizons, and that even university cloisters can be avenues of romance. Faculties, Departments, or Schools of Agriculture, Zoology, Botany, Geology, Geography, Physics, Chemistry, Philosophy, all within a few steps of my door, and their professors and lecturers ready to hand out information with oriental lavishness.'[7] Leisurely lunch hours were spent in the Senior Common Room which was housed in 'Acacias', an elegant neo-classical house which had been the home of one of the Palmer family. The smooth lawns to the house were the perfect surface for the game of bowls which was a popular pastime amongst the staff. Gibbings made many friends and gained the respect of his colleagues for his range and depth of knowledge, acquired from his life-time of observation and his ever inquisitive approach to the world of nature. He was particularly close to Charles O'Donoghue who had recently left a post as Professor of Zoology in the University of Manitoba, and had joined the staff at Reading in a similar capacity, and another lecturer in Zoology, Dr Ian Crichton. Gibbings frequently dropped into the laboratories to observe experiments in progress which added to both his awe of nature and his excitement.[8]

For Gibbings, another advantage of holding an academic post was that he had the time and opportunity to undertake major projects in the vacation. In the summer of 1937 he set sail for Bermuda. Family obligations notwithstanding, he had been commissioned by Penguin Books to write about his interest in marine life in tropical waters — another chance for travel and adventure could not be refused. How Gibbings had been introduced to Allen Lane and Penguin Books is uncertain. He had already worked for The Bodley Head and Lane had become chairman of that publishing company in 1930, following on from his distant relation, 'uncle' John Lane, who had died in 1925. In 1936, in addition to the engravings for *The Twelve Months*, Gibbings had been commissioned to design and engrave a new device for the firm and a Christmas card for Allen Lane and his brothers, Dick and John.[9] The year before, Allen Lane had broken away from the family business, which had been failing for some time, to set up Penguin Books. He was a well known figure in literary circles and a great party-goer and it is probable that Gibbings met him socially as Lane also enjoyed the hospitality of the Hind's Head at Bray. An introduction might have been made through Laurence Pollinger, Gibbings's agent, who had close contacts with Lane.

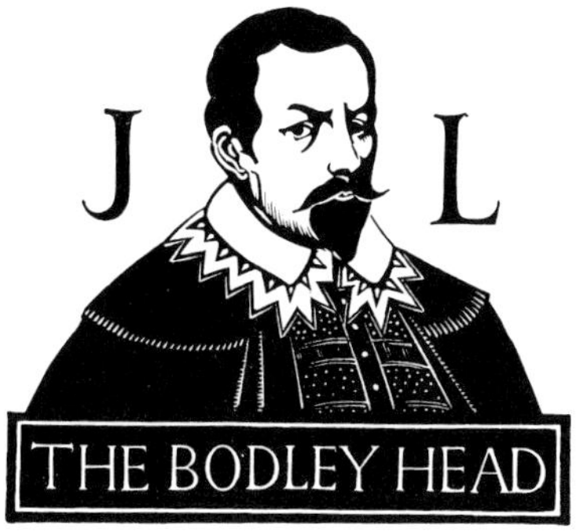

226 Publisher's device designed for The Bodley Head, 1936, wood-engraving, 44 x 50 mm.

Gibbings had approached Penguin Books with a proposal to write a book for their new series of Pelican Specials and at about the same time had discussed the idea of publishing a series of paperbacks illustrated with wood-engravings.[10] Gibbings was desperate to travel again and when Allen Lane agreed to commission the book he made plans to depart as soon as the University term ended. Gibbings was a prolific letter writer, and his growing fame meant an ever increasing post. One correspondent was a hopeful poet who had sent his work to Gibbings for comment; Gibbings, determined to avoid any obligations on his trip, had politely refused to correspond:

> Now as regards a letter from Bermuda I am going to be churlish & refuse because I am hoping that whatever happens I can at last get away without any obligations to do anything but go comatose & absorb sunlight & beauty much as an amoeba absorbs its protoplasm or whatever it is that it feeds on. I've had nearly 4 years without more than 3 consecutive days holiday & I write by hand an average of 8 or so letters a day. So please forgive me. By this time next year I hope there will be on the market 264 pp of text & engravings dealing with coral reefs; for the price of a tanner![11]

On his previous trip to the South Seas, Gibbings had been both excited and frustrated by his experiences studying marine life. He had been taken over by a passion for the underwater world:

> Of course, I knew absolutely nothing about these fish except that they were beautiful. They appeared more gorgeous than anything I had ever seen in my life, their shapes, their markings and their colours seeming to vie with each other as to which could be most bizarre. Every morning while the surface of the lagoon was still unruffled, every evening when the trade wind had died down, I would spend hours drifting in the canoe, watching with amazement the under-water panorama which unfolded below me.[12]

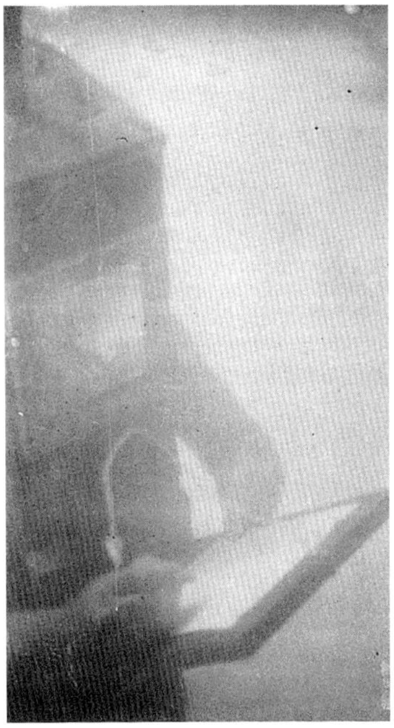

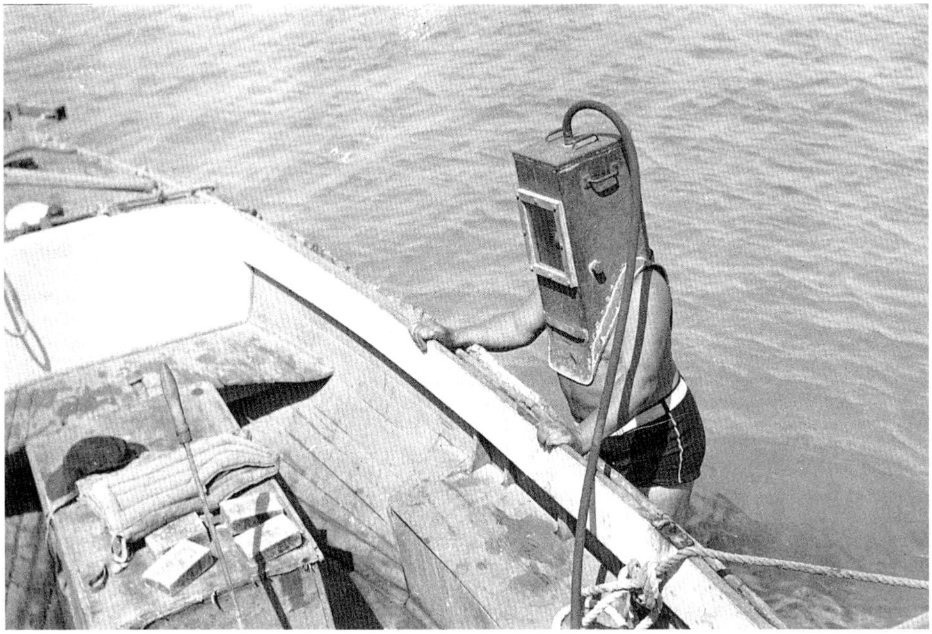

227 *above* Gibbings making an underwater drawing on xylonite in the sea off Bermuda, 1937. RUL.

228 *right* Gibbings testing the diving gear in shallow waters in Bermuda, 1937. RUL.

But this was observation; drawing from dead specimens that had faded in colour was hopelessly inadequate, as were attempts at drawing specimens caught by local fishermen, swimming around in an 'old enamelled basin'. What Gibbings wanted was to draw marine life in its own environment or as he wrote: '... it was my ambition to get on closer terms with the fish, and to meet them on their own level.'[13] One of his main reasons for choosing Bermuda for his expedition was that he had been offered the use of diving facilities belonging to the Marine Research Station on the island. This would enable him to explore the reefs, but how to draw under water was the problem and it was a colleague at the University who suggested the solution. Gibbings's first thoughts involved drawing on copper-plates prepared with a wax coating for etching but a better solution was suggested by Cyril Pearce, lecturer in Design and Composition at the School of Art. He proposed that Gibbings should try drawing on sheets of xylonite, a waterproof celluloid-like substance which, when roughened with sandpaper, would accept the marks of a pencil as well as paper, even under water; instead of pencils, sticks of graphite were fitted into rubber tubing.

When he arrived in Bermuda he found that the diving apparatus was very simple: a helmet, a hose pipe and an air pump. Air was continuously pumped into the weighted helmet by an assistant in a boat above, the air pressure keeping the water out of the helmet loosely sitting on Gibbings's shoulders. A pair of bathing shorts and thick-soled shoes completed the outfit and, thus equipped, Gibbings attempted his first experimental dive:

The sea was rough, the water was cloudy and there was a strong current running. As I stepped off the ladder and staggered into the deeper water the noise of the air pump echoing down the hose pipe seemed deafening, and the waves splashing against the window of my helmet prevented me seeing anything either above or below the water. I wondered why I had ever left home and heartily wished I had not done so. Then a couple of steps took me completely below the surface, and I entered a new world. My ears ceased throbbing, I breathed easily, I forgot the noise of the pump. It was like being in some great cathedral lit by pale-green glass ....'[14]

His only problem was that buoyancy meant that he could not get a good grip with his feet to propel him along. This was corrected by a belt of 20 lbs of lead piping which weighted him down sufficiently to walk about with ease. When he tried drawing he found that it was difficult to make 'elegant sweeping lines' because of the pressure of the water and that his visual perception had changed:

The strange thing was that when I came to the surface I found that during my time below I had forgotten all rules of perspective and other dicta of the art schools, and that I had drawn everything in the proportion of its importance to me. ... Under the water all these adjustments vanished, and if a particularly interesting small fish passed in the distance, I found that in my drawing it was depicted as very much larger than some dull fellow twice the size who happened to be near at hand. This suggests a parallel with primitive art, where objects were drawn on cave wall or canvas according to their importance to the artist, and not according to mathematics and laws of optics.[15]

The technique worked and, to his delight, now he had entered their world, the fish were completely unafraid of his presence and crowded around him in their hundreds:

There were Blue Angels and Yellow Grunts, Sergeant Majors, Trigger Fish and Porgies, Four Eyes and Demoiselles. The Angels came and looked through the window of the helmet, the Porgies and Slippery Dicks swam between my legs, and the Sergeant Majors nibbled at my shoulders.[16]

Gibbings travelled to various locations amongst the numerous islands that surround Bermuda seeking more remote places such as Cooper's Island, which were free from tourists:

It was good to be alone and to know that in whatever direction I cared to look there would be no sight or sound to remind me of humanity. Nothing but the bo'sun bird imitating the cry of the sirens as he circled overhead, reflecting the emerald green of the sea from his breast.[17]

On his return, Penguin Books were anxious to gain as much advance publicity as possible to promote the forthcoming book. In their newsletter for Autumn 1937 there was a note referring to articles about Gibbings's expedition that had appeared in national newspapers. Eager to point out that this was to be Penguin's first 'commissioned' book, they reported that Gibbings had written to them that he was 'working like hell, and everything going according to plan. My scheme for drawing under water is a huge success and I've completed several highly valuable works in about 20 feet of water. If I'm not diving or drinking I'm drawing specimens ...'.[18]

Gibbings had arrived home in England two days late because the engines of the cruise liner that he had joined for the return journey had broken down near Havana. But Gibbings was not troubled:

... bless your soul I didn't care, what did I pay my 2/6 for a deck chair for! I remained faithful to Chilean wine & particularly to an even better brand of which a bottle was presented to me by a very charming Chilean lady. In Bermuda we kept to rum, at 16/- a

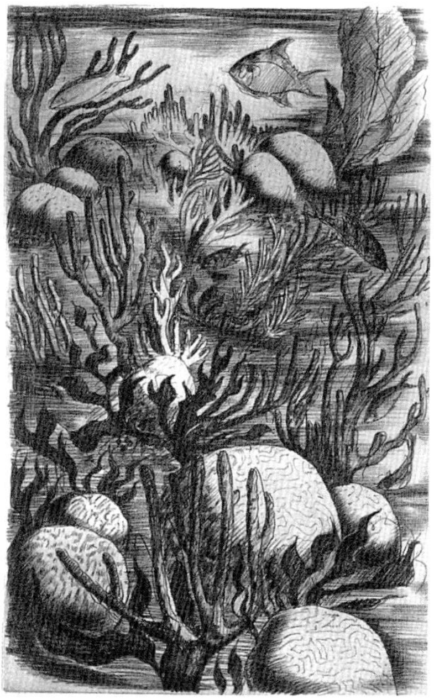

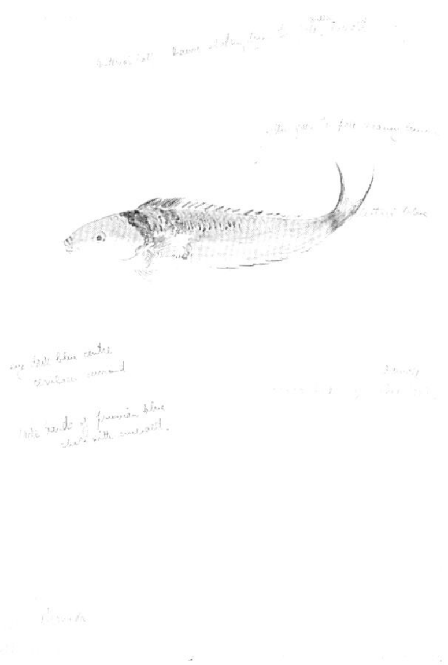

229 Xylonite drawing, 1937, 320 x 205 mm. RUL.

230 A tropical fish, pencil and watercolour sketch from Gibbings's note book, Bermuda 1937, image size 55 x 140 mm. RUL.

Tropical Fish – see colour plates 6a & 6b.

gallon one could go a long way for 30/-. I have designs on the Red Sea next spring & the Great Barrier Reef in the summer but I've got to sell a lot of John Graham to get me to either.[19]

Despite the overall success of the trip, on reflection Gibbings felt disappointed with what he had seen in Bermuda. The fish were not so brilliant nor the corals as interesting as those he had seen in the Pacific. When he was in Tahiti he had met Dr Cyril Crossland, a coral specialist, who had told him that the Red Sea was one of the richest areas in the world for varieties of coral. Crossland was then in charge of the Marine Biological Research Station at Ghardaqa, a branch of the University of Egypt, on the banks of the Red Sea, about seven miles from the port of Hurghada. Gibbings had written to him about the possibility of his continuing his research into marine life there. Crossland had replied positively but pointed out that he was leaving his post that June and so the visit would have to take place during the Easter vacation. He could provide the use of a launch, diving gear, and equally important, a canoe with 'special personnel to watch for sharks'.[20] The only problem now was to find the money. Gibbings decided to apply for a research grant. In January 1938, he applied to the University's Research Board, having calculated that the whole trip would cost about £75. He asked for a grant to cover a second class return fare of approximately £50, informing them of his future publication and his wish to produce a series of 'at least fifty' large engravings to be printed on the University presses in 'de luxe form' and perhaps

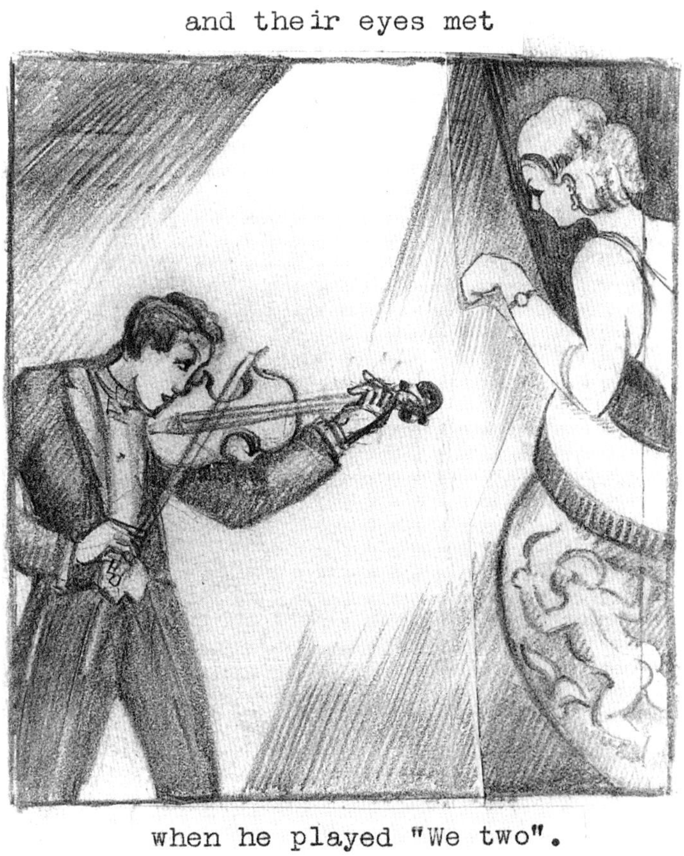

231 *The Violin Player*, 1938, pencil, image size 110 x 98 mm. This is a page design for another book, similar in style to *The Seventh Man*, that was based on a story Gibbings heard on board a ship to the Red Sea. The story was never published. Clark Library.

issued by the University itself.[21] Gibbings had also made an application to the Leverhulme Foundation for a grant to continue his study during the autumn on the Great Barrier Reef in Australia. The latter appears to have been unsuccessful but in late March 1938, Gibbings set out on his travels again — this time to the Red Sea via the Suez Canal.

Travelling overland through the Rhone Valley, he picked up a P&O ship, the *Strathallan*, at Marseilles which took him as far as Suez. For once he seems not to have enjoyed the journey; only being able to afford to travel tourist class he was confined to a small cabin in the 'uttermost bowels of the ship'. He found most of the company soulless but one or two of his fellow passengers attracted his attention: 'A fanatical evangelist with a *lovely* wife. He has tried to convert me to his beliefs, I have tried to convert her to mine, so far no score on either side'.[22] One of the more memorable encounters had been with a girl who had told him the tale of her shattered romance with a violinist:

> It seems that she saw him first from a stage box, that he was tall and slight, that his dark hair waved and 'he played *divinely*.' She had leaned from her box when he played 'Moonshine' and their eyes had met when he played 'We two,' and when the curtain fell he had sent her a bouquet 'To the girl in the box with the beautiful eyes. Would she dine next night?' And she did, and he talked about his art and himself, and about himself and his art, so that her heart went out to him and she asked *what* was his greatest ambition. Then he had said that 'he thought — that it probably — was — to keep a pub.'[23]

Gibbings later attempted to adapt this rather funny and pathetic tale for yet another of his books in the format of *The Seventh Man*. He sketched out his ideas in a series of delightful drawings but the book was never published.

Writing to the staff at Penguin Books on 28 March, Gibbings reported on his voyage: 'Well my lads & lasses sitting comfortably in your offices while I am braving unknown dangers in uncharted seas. I reach Port Said at 4 am. on Wednesday. There's hardship! How would you like to be up & dressed at that hour in the morning.'[24] The final leg of his journey was on a small oil tanker, sharing a cabin with the third engineer, who was of 'uncertain origin'. Arriving at Ghardaqa it was not long before Gibbings was stepping into the sea for a test dive. Again they had initial trouble in adjusting weights to counter the buoyancy of Gibbings's big frame; there were problems too with changes in water temperature — in some areas he could only spend twenty minutes below before suffering from chill. Despite these difficulties, Gibbings was not disappointed by the coral:

> Besides the multitudinous hard corals which branched around me there were the alcyonaria whose delicate tasselled heads formed bell-like flowers as they opened and closed in their search for food. Some of them were biscuit-coloured, others were every shade of lilac, some were rich and lustrous like those growing on the pier at Hurghada, others seemed fragile as thistle-down.[25]

Gibbings's exploits excited public interest and not long after his return the *Observer* ran an article with the intriguing headline 'An Artist under water: "studio" in the Red Sea'. Gibbings was quoted as remarking: 'Compared with Bermuda, the first dive ... was like visiting the Chelsea flower show after looking

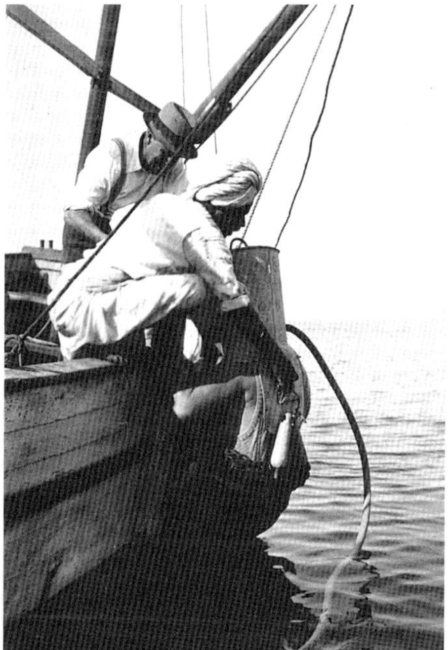

232 Gibbings being hauled over the side of the boat to start one of his dives in the Red Sea, 1938. RUL.

at a London window-box.'[26] Drama was added to the article by the mention of a '... certain apprehension of sharks, although the popular idea of their ferocity is probably exaggerated. One of the boatmen at Ghardaqa had deep scars on his legs from a ten-foot shark which seized him ...'.

Cover of *Blue Angels and Whales* – see colour plate 8a.

The finished book appeared in November 1938 in an edition of 50,000 copies and was called *Blue Angels and Whales*, partly after the fish and partly after a buxom, cocktail-sipping blonde — nick-named 'Blue Angel' — he had encountered in the ship's bar on his outward voyage. 'She did *so* admire artists. Did I understand? She did so admire tall men, and men with beards. Did I only draw fish? Did I ever draw people? She would like to be drawn. Did I understand?'[27] — Gibbings was in the habit of including the occasional discreet but risqué anecdote amongst the serious material of his books — perhaps consciously realising this would increase his popularity.

Dedicated to his wife Elisabeth, the book was illustrated by thirty-three wood-engravings and reproductions of his xylonite drawings and photographs of Gibbings on location. Before setting out on his travels, Gibbings had spent many hours in preparation at the Natural History Museum. He read widely around the subject and although the book is full of colour and vivid description, Gibbings also took care to refer his readers to important reference books and acknowledged authorities. One chapter was dedicated to the story of the reckless voyage of the 'Sea Bird' and how it became wrecked; the boat's log book for the voyage was published as a student project at the University the following year.[28] But over and above the anecdotes and adventure, Gibbings wrote in a serious way about the natural world he had so closely observed. He had a particular ability to capture the interest of his readers and convey his own enthusiasm and fascination — his book was both informative and entertaining — he had found a way to make natural history popular. The concluding chapters of the book were detailed studies of topics that particularly engaged him; the astonishing range of techniques used for camouflage by fish and creatures of all kinds, and the geology of the surrounding landscape and the rich deposits of fossilised remains of living creatures. Both chapters are full of factual material but told in such a way that the subjects come alive creating in the reader an emotional response; stimulating the visual imagination and the intellect. Gibbings could convey his own awe of nature and sense of human history:

> Inside the pass, peaks rise up, on the one side granite, sharp and crystalline in form; rose, crimson and lavender in colour: on the other side turbulent slag heaps of gargantuan size, broken black basalt, as if cast up from Vulcan's own kitchen. Afar, beyond the porphyry mines once worked by the Romans, the road stretches again across the desert towards the setting sun, towards the Nile, towards Luxor and towards the glory that was Egypt.[29]

The image of this huge man sitting on the sea bed, sketching a swirling mass of sea-life, with the ever present threat of attack by sharks, was so colourful and bizarre, that it made an ideal story for the media and resulted in widespread publicity. Newspapers and magazines were eager to cover the story but those in the fledgling medium of television were also quick to see the potential. Only two

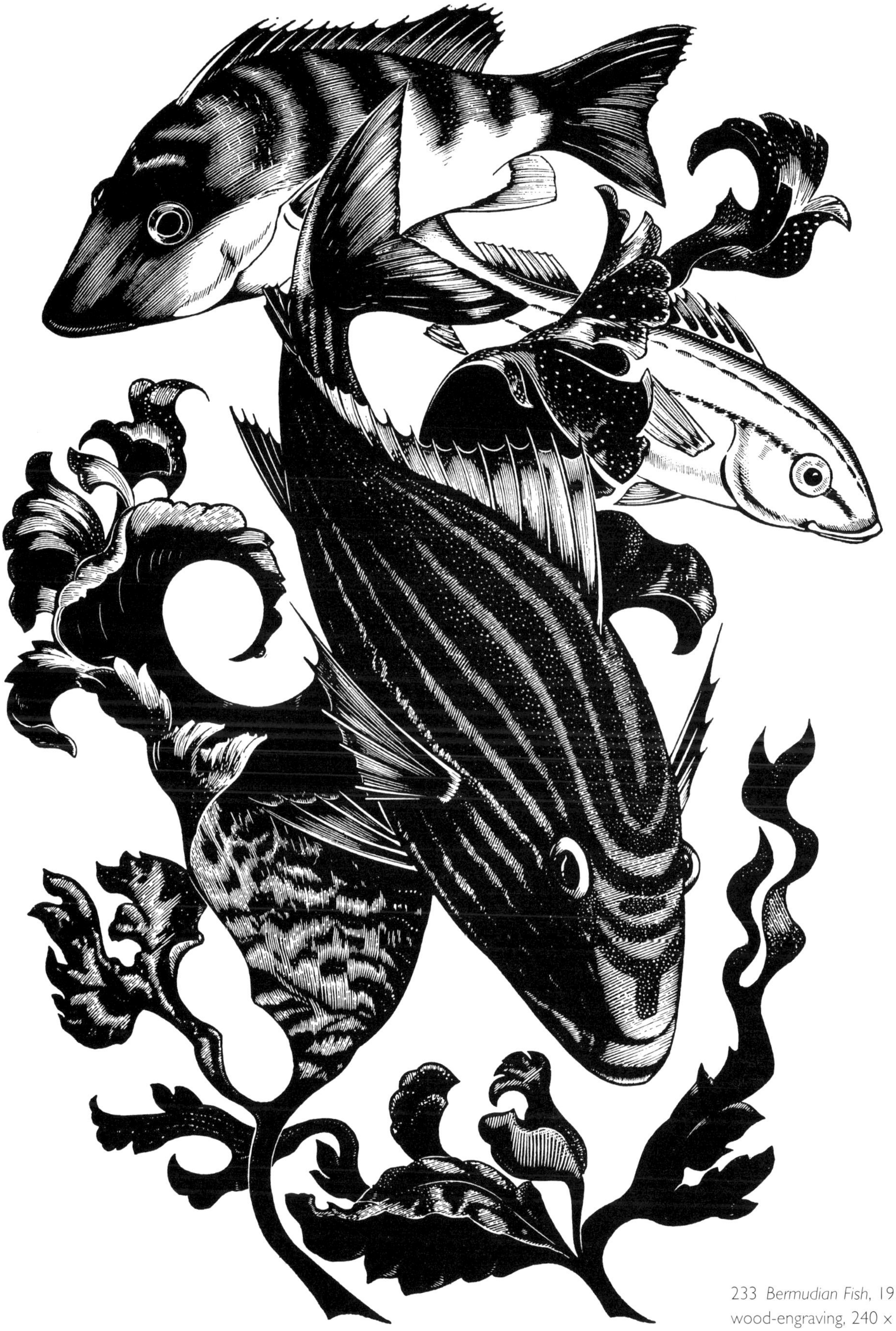

233 *Bermudian Fish*, 1938,
wood-engraving, 240 × 165 mm.

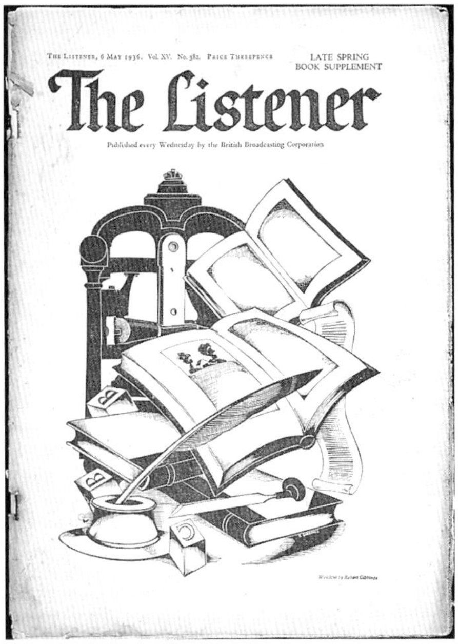

234 Cover of *The Listener*, 6 May 1936, vol. 15, no. 382, illustrated by a wood-engraving by Gibbings, page size 332 × 240 mm.

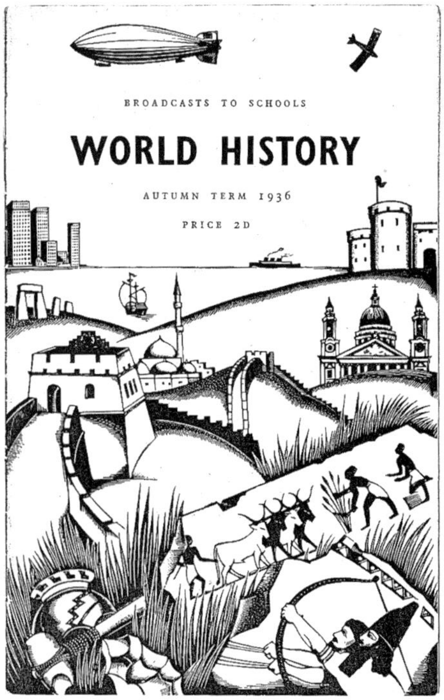

235 Cover of the BBC's teachers' pamphlet to accompany the programme 'World History' broadcast for schools, 1936, 210 × 135 mm.

years after the BBC had begun regular television broadcasts from Alexandra Palace Gibbings made his first appearance on screen.

In his capacity as an illustrator, Gibbings had already worked on publications associated with the BBC. In April 1936, the *Radio Times* had used a line block of daffodils by Gibbings which was printed on yellow paper in two colours (unusual as most editions were printed in black and white at this time), for their special 'Spring number'.[30] The following month on the cover of *The Listener* was a large and splendid wood-engraving of a montage of images representing aspects of book production for a special 'book supplement'.[31] This was the first of a number of cover designs that he was to undertake for the magazine. In the Autumn of 1936, Gibbings designed and engraved a clever composition of images depicting the development of human civilisation for the cover of a pamphlet, aimed at teachers, to accompany a programme on 'World History', broadcast to schools. *The Listener* for 25 May 1938 included a short summary of an interview with Gibbings on 14 May in which he gave a relaxed and graphic account of his diving adventures in Bermuda.[32]

In July he appeared again, bringing viewers up-to-date on his latest trip to the Red Sea. As a broadcaster, Gibbings was a gift to producers; not only had he good stories to tell but he was also a natural communicator. In a review of his latest appearance, illustrated by photographs and engravings, which also appeared in *The Listener*, Peter Purbeck observed: '... Mr. Gibbings happens to possess the type of personality ideally suited to transmission over the ether. He has just that natural, intimate manner which makes us forget that he is broadcasting to an audience of many thousands, and makes us feel that he is talking expressly for the benefit of ourselves and the circle of friends gathered round our receiver'.[33] In these early days of television the BBC were trying out different formulas for programmes and the review discussed whether a talk such as that given by Gibbings had added value on television over radio broadcasting or the public lecture. The conclusion was that 'Of course, the answer to that is the pictures. What Mr. Gibbings had to show was fully as important and as fascinating as what he had to say ... Mr. Gibbings' talk last week was much more like asking in to dinner a friend who had just returned from a strange and fascinating enterprise ... and looking at the drawings and the photographs as he handed them around'.

In November 1938, Gibbings made yet another contribution to *The Listener*, but this time, as well as using one of his engravings on the cover, he wrote a lengthy article entitled 'Sharks Permitting', again describing his underwater experiences and illustrated by his xylonite drawings.[34] His writing style was well suited to journalism and he was easily able to adapt material from his books; in March 1939 *The Listener* published another article, 'Under the Coconut Palm', which drew on anecdotes and material from his trip to Tahiti and his book *Iorana*.[35]

Blue Angels and Whales had brought Gibbings to the attention of the general public. Having gained such a reputation in the arguably elitist world of the private press, he was now making a name through the popular paperback. His association with the pioneering days at Penguin was made stronger when, at about the same time as he was negotiating over his own book, Gibbings was appointed Art Director of yet another new series, The Penguin Illustrated Classics. Whether or not it was Gibbings who had made the suggestion to Allen Lane, the proposal was a courageous one. Given that Allen Lane had been trained in the traditions and values of The Bodley Head, it is not surprising that he took up the idea with enthusiasm. John Lane had always striven for excellence, printing small editions of carefully selected texts, which were beautifully produced and often illustrated by the leading artists of the time. Now Allen wanted to bring the same values to the mass market. Gibbings was an excellent choice as art director — through his association with the Society of Wood Engravers he had good contacts with a range of contemporary illustrators; he had also been active in promoting and popularising the medium of wood-engraving. The decision to produce editions of the 'classics' was made partly with the intention of exploiting the out-of-copyright market with which the World's Classics and Everyman series had already found success. It was decided to publish nine titles simultaneously (*Robinson Crusoe* came in two volumes); the books selected were a mix of traditional classics by Jane Austen, Laurence Sterne, Edgar Allan Poe, Jonathan Swift, Robert Browning and Daniel Defoe, with a number of more unconventional choices such as work by Herman Melville, Richard Jefferies and Henry David Thoreau. The publication of a second selection of a further ten classic titles was proposed but depended on the reception of the first series. Gibbings also approached his friends and fellow engravers from the days of the Golden Cockerel Press. Each artist was to receive £50 per book for a minimum of twelve engraved illustrations.[36] In a letter to Lynton Lamb dated 9 June 1937, he wrote:

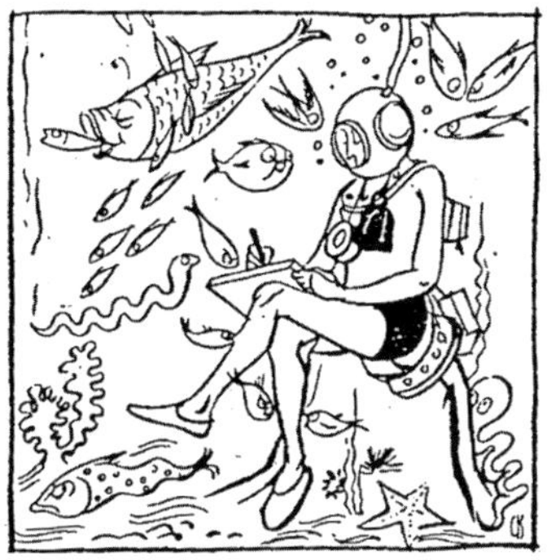

236 Cartoon of Gibbings (a much slimmer version) drawing under the sea from *The Listener*, 25 May 1938, vol. 19, no. 489, p. 1114.

Cover of the *Radio Times*, 3 April 1936 – see colour plate 5b.

> How would you like to illustrate, decorate, illuminate or generally speaking glorify an edition of 'Religio Medici & Urne Burial' (one vol.) .... As I see it, it's up to us wood-choppers to give the best value we can because this is a venture which may have far reaching and very beneficial results for all of us. I have persuaded Penguins to put £1000 into our pockets this year and if all goes well they'll do the same again next. ... editions anything from 50,000 to 150,000.[37]

Gibbings had the foresight to recognise the huge potential for this new approach to publishing and was anxious that illustrators should secure their share of the work. For the first series Gibbings gathered together well established wood-engravers such as Gwendoline Raverat, Douglas Percy Bliss, Ethelbert White, and Iain Macnab to illustrate particular volumes, but also included some younger and more challenging engravers; Gertrude Hermes, J. R. Biggs, Helen Binyon and Theodore Naish joined the team. Naish had been one of Gibbings's students who had only recently graduated from Reading University; he had illustrated *Gulliver's Travels* as a student project and Gibbings, having been impressed by his talent, had generously recommended him to Penguin as an illustrator.

Gibbings selected Herman Melville's *Typee* to illustrate himself, providing a handsome frontispiece and palm leaf decorations for the title page as well as illustrations in the text. Melville's account of his survival on the Marquesas Islands was just the kind of book to appeal to Gibbings. He was working on the

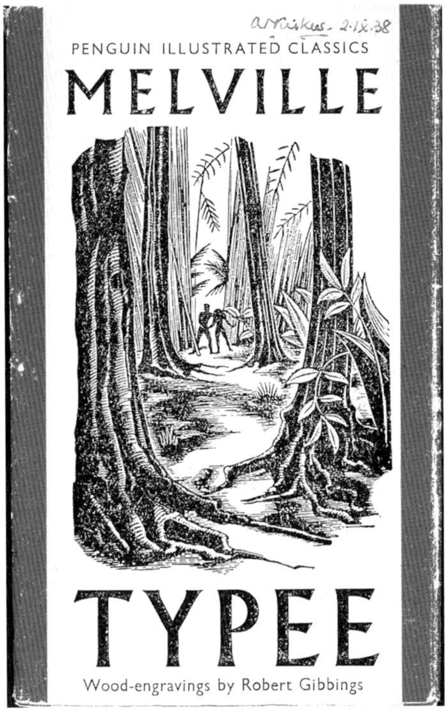

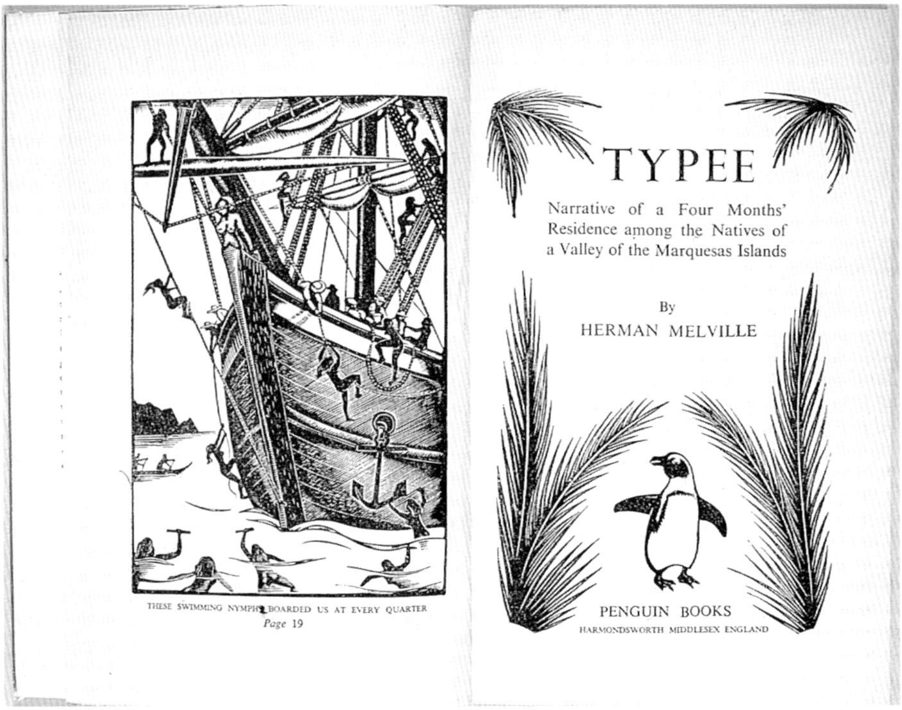

237 *left* Cover of *Typee*, 1938, with wood-engraved illustration by Gibbings. One of a series of Penguin Illustrated Classics, of which Gibbings was Art Director.

238 *right* Frontispiece and title page from *Typee*, 1938, page size 180 x 114 mm.

Illustrated Classics over the same period of time as he was writing *Blue Angels and Whales* and Gibbings readily used references to *Typee* in his own book, theorising about the parallels between the camouflage of fish and the tattooed patterns used by native warriors.

The first Penguin paperbacks were wrapped in dust jackets which were identical in design to the book cover itself; for the Illustrated Classics, Penguin Books adopted the same idea but a wood-engraving was prominently placed on the front cover. The familiar Gill Sans typeface used for the title lettering on the general books was replaced by a large size of the distinctive typeface, Albertus, which gave the Illustrated Classics a strong identity. Edward Young was in control of the overall design of Penguins at the time and Gibbings was very satisfied with the covers of the new series: 'I must say, though I says it myself, those first ten vols seem to me ruddy fine & I only hope they create a revolution. Young's arrangement of the covers is *masterly*, & I can't help feeling they'll make a grand display on the bookstalls.'[38] On the flap of the dust jacket emphasis was put on the importance of the illustrator by including a photograph of the artist with a short biographical note.

Gibbings had become excited by the prospect of a long publishing association with Penguin; he got on well with Allen Lane and they became friends. They were both involved in public speaking and at the beginning of May, Lane suggested a meeting in Reading before he gave a talk to a gathering of the John O'London's Literary Circle. A few days later, Gibbings invited Lane to a meeting of the University Dining Club: 'We are just a group of about a dozen of "the hearties" who meet for food, wine & chat. Except for dinner jackets there are no formalities, or speeches. I do hope you can come. Apart from pleasure I think it might be useful in other ways for they are all likely lads in their own line.'[39] Lane obviously had plans for the future as Gibbings went on in his letter to express enthusiasm for illustrated books: 'I am frightfully glad you like the idea of short contemporary books with heaps of illus. There's no reason why, barring paper, they shouldn't be absolutely "de luxe" & if they are thinner presumably the paper could be better. By Golly there's no end to where this may lead.'[40]

The first ten Illustrated Classics were launched at a reception on 18 May 1938 and were heralded by a publicity campaign.[41] The company's publicity newsletter, *Penguins Progress*, issued a special number which was almost entirely taken up with promotion of the Illustrated Classics. Profiles of the careers of 'Robert Gibbings & his brilliant team of artists' filled a double spread. An introductory paragraph extolled the virtues of woodcutting and engraving as media for book illustration and championed their revival: 'The Penguin Illustrated Classics, we hope, show what a magnificent medium wood-engraving can be, and provide at the price of sixpence, a long-needed contact between the modern artist and the man-in-the-street.'[42] More independent reviews were also encouraging; Bernard Newdigate's survey of a decade of book design published by *The Studio* illustrated a selection of cover designs and praised the series: '... the Penguin Illustrated Classics ... show how art and good craftsmanship may be devoted to a series published at the lowest possible price.'[43] However, despite all the optimism and high ideals, the series was not a commercial success. Morpurgo suggested that 'the choice of title was almost too obvious; their newly created British audience expected from Penguin something more original ...'. He went further to explain the reason for the failure of the series:

> But the venture was damned as much by its technical inadequacies as by any failure in editorial judgement or by indifferent perception of the market potential. The charming wood engravings commissioned for the series, some by artists of high repute such as Gwen Raverat and Robert Gibbings, had about them all an outmoded refinement, as if they had been prepared by tired disciples of the old John Lane school of book illustrators. Their extravagant elegance did not match either the bustling, youthful vigour of Penguin or the starkness of a world hurtling towards war. The weaknesses of illustration were exacerbated by the indifferent paper and by the Penguin format, seemingly too cramped to carry illustration.[44]

The criticism is harsh but it is true that narrow margins, dense type area, cheap thin paper and mass production, all worked against that kind of illustration. Given the strict house style and format, Gibbings had little control over the design issues he cared about. All his concerns about the choice and weight of type harmonising with the engravings were impossible to uphold. The engravings in *Blue Angels and Whales* had worked because they were factually informative and related closely to the text. Illustrations concentrating on artistic merit to embellish novels and poems that stood well enough on their own, had little point in the genre of cheap mass production. The 'weakness' of illustration in itself would not account for the failure and in fact many of the engravings were good — it was just a poor choice of titles and the principles behind the series were honourable but misguided.

Artists had been chosen to illustrate the second group of titles in the series; the team included such eminent names as John Farleigh, Eric King, Lynton Lamb, Clare Leighton, Agnes Miller Parker and Blair Hughes-Stanton. Anthony Betts, Gibbings's Head of Department at the University, had also agreed to illustrate a volume — a strange choice of artist as he was not known as a wood-engraver. But the second batch of Illustrated Classics never appeared and the series was dropped. Two of the proposed titles, Isaak Walton's *Compleat Angler*, illustrated by Gertrude Hermes and Gilbert White's *The Natural History of Selborne*, illustrated by Clare Leighton, were eventually published as part of the 'miscellaneous series', in colour coded yellow covers.

Busy though he was, the appreciation of Gibbings's engravings for *Le Morte d'Arthur* led to another prestigious commission from the Limited Editions Club of New York, for six full-page wood-engravings for an edition of Shakespeare's *Othello*; the book appeared in August 1939. Macy had invited him to join an impressive list of leading illustrators he had compiled at the beginning of 1936.

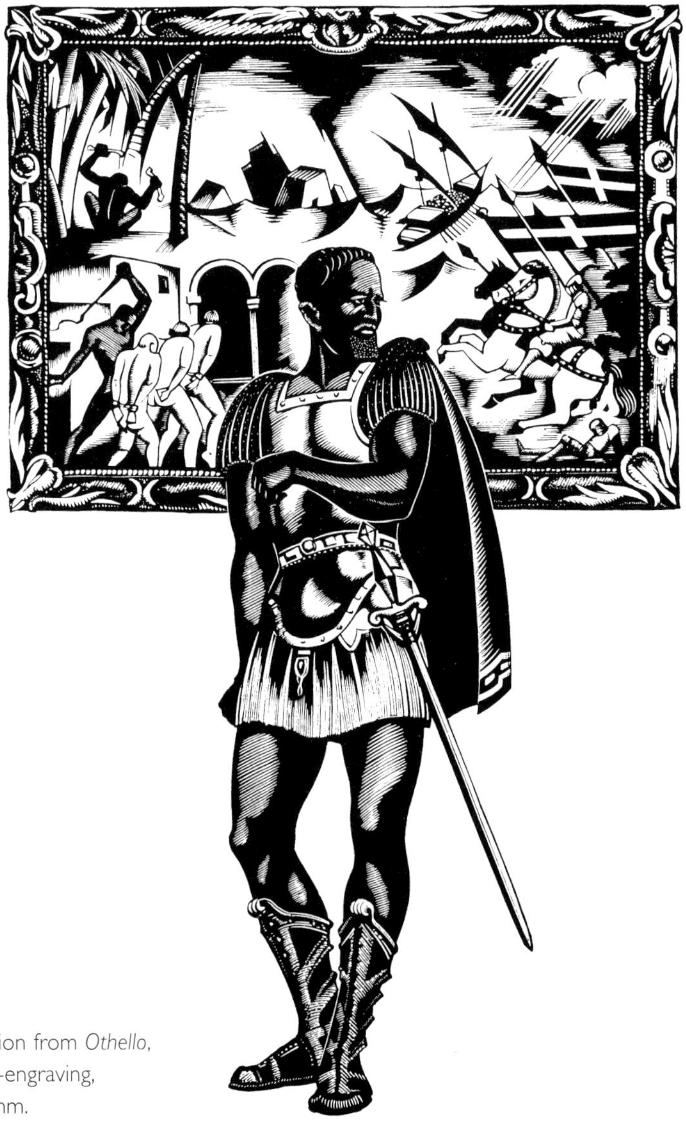

239 Illustration from *Othello*, 1939, wood-engraving, 226 x 140 mm.

The intention was to publish a complete set of Shakespeare's work as 'the most ambitious publishing venture of our times'.[45] The typography was to be by Bruce Rogers and Gibbings readily agreed to the commission and asked that *Othello* be earmarked for him. When he saw the sample pages he was shocked by the size of the blocks needed and asked for an increase in fee. Macy agreed but Gibbings needed further help:

Can you help me out? With two missus, five children & the hell of an overdraft, not to mention John Lane going bust, I find the 'half year' most depressing. I'm hard at work on Othello & have some promising designs. Could you send me an advance of say $150 just to encourage me & quieten the – – – bank.[46]

Gibbings hoped to have the blocks ready by the new year but the project slipped and in March 1937 he was promising the blocks by June. However, in July Macy was becoming agitated that no blocks had arrived — he became angry when he found out that Gibbings was on his expedition to Bermuda:

I am considerably surprised to find myself in England and you in Bermuda. I suppose you are too far away for me to plunge a knife into your throat? So I can only send you a letter to tell you that I expected to have the blocks for Othello from you; and I wonder whether you will tell me when I am going to have them?[47]

Elisabeth later confessed to Macy that she was rather pleased that Robert had got away as he was very tired and not able to do his best work. Gibbings apologised and Macy soon forgave him and the printing schedule was reorganised. At the end of the year he was working flat out on Macy's blocks but he was having difficulties: 'The trouble is that this bloke Shakespeare is no mean author & he cannot be treated lightly!'[48] The blocks completed, Macy allowed a short time to lapse before he wrote to Gibbings, in March 1938, to tactfully suggest that apart from the frontispiece and illustrations for acts three, four and five the remaining engravings were 'not done with your usual verve ... you have permitted a wooden quality to come into the composition ...'.[49] Gibbings was sorry that Macy was disappointed but he had done his best and taken trouble over the blocks; he did not want to be too dramatic or vulgar. He explained that he would have preferred to have integrated the text and image; he disliked the use of 'plates' and felt this might have added to the woodenness. Gibbings had written on 22 March on the day that he left for the Red Sea.

The following year, on 16 April, he sent a biographical note and the draft of a short essay about his approach to his designs for *Othello*, to be used to promote the series:

I have always been prone to put decoration before illustration partly because I find decoration the easier of the two but also because I feel that only in the rarest cases do illustrations, as such, help the text. ... my mind immediately jumped to 'Othello' because ... I saw a pleasing contrast of dark and light skins, and at the same time a richness of texture in the tessellated pavements of the Mediterranean setting. ... Perhaps our minds are becoming affected by the cinema for I certainly felt the need of sequence rather than stills![50]

Othello was finally published on 23 August 1939.

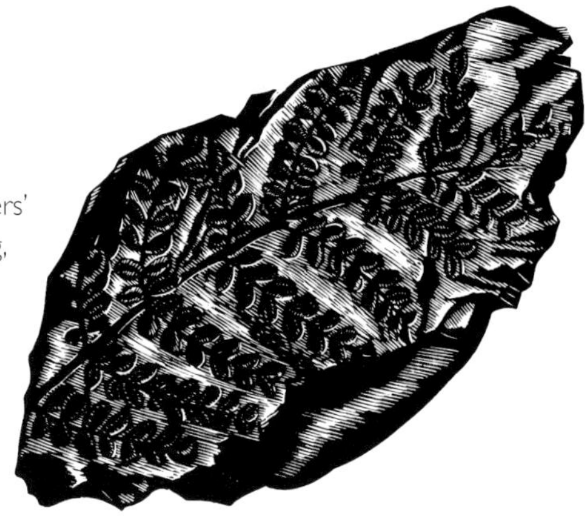

240 Illustration for a booklet for the Coal Owners' Association (unpublished), 1939, wood-engraving, 55 x 62 mm.

His work rate never eased and so Gibbings was only too happy when Geoffrey Holme, the editor of *The Studio*, asked if he could use a number of his earlier prints as illustrations in his book, *The Children's Art Book*, published in 1938.[51] Following his *Othello* he began engraving over thirty illustrations for a glossy booklet commissioned by the Coal Owners' Association to promote the privately owned coal industry. The engravings illustrated the formation of coal as well as the history and process of its extraction, but owing to the outbreak of war, the project was dropped and the blocks were never used. Gibbings had made the drawings while staying with a friend, the Rev. W. J. McAdam, in the Leeds area. He was invited to be a guest speaker at a luncheon club during his stay; his popularity as a speaker led to a demand for the public talks and lectures that were to become a feature of his life.

Gibbings was contributing regularly to exhibitions. In addition to shows organised by the Society of Wood Engravers, in December 1937 he exhibited work alongside that of his colleagues in the University's Fine Art Department, in an exhibition of paintings by the Chiltern Group held at Reading Museum and Art Gallery. The same gallery put on a one-man show in June of the following year entitled 'Twenty years of Engraving' which included a representative selection of one hundred and fifty engravings and a small number of Gibbings's underwater drawings which attracted the usual media attention. Early in 1939 a complete exhibition of his xylonite drawings was held at the Stafford Gallery, St James's Place in London, which also excited the imagination of the Press; an enthusiastic reviewer commented 'They are delightful pictures as well as valuable documents. ... But the shapes are new beyond the dreams of surrealism, the setting has a sense as well as a reality of extent that is more impressive than a mere aquarium glimpse'. However, some reviews were less enthusiastic. Herbert Furst reviewed the exhibition in the arts magazine *Apollo* and felt that 'the romantic side of his venture has traduced Robert Gibbings's artistic purity'. Furst, a strong supporter of wood-engraving, felt Gibbings would have done better if the sketches had been used as a basis for engravings — '... in the genesis of engravings he would probably have made a triumphant success of his original attempt. As it is we just get a glimpse of rhythmic and varied black-and-white patterns; the primary importance of the drawings now being only their curiosity value'. What also detracted from his enjoyment of the drawings was that Gibbings openly admitted that the rough sketches made under the water had been subsequently 'touched up'. Contrary to Gibbings's aims, Furst felt that 'Any one of us can get more thrill out of the under-water "landscape" by merely visiting the Aquarium in the Zoo, where we see Nature with its colour and its movement.'[52] At the end of the year Gibbings contributed work to an exhibition of the Arts and Crafts Society at the Royal Academy — a colleague, Valerie Bayford and Miss Stephanie Maberly-Smith, a student and illustrator of *Loftur*, also showed work.

Domestically the last few years had also seen changes. Eventually Moira had agreed to a divorce and as soon as that was finalised, Elisabeth and Robert were able to get married. The wedding was very quiet and informal, taking place at the Registry Office in St Pancras on 26 May 1937, with Elisabeth's younger sister, Patience, and the family friend Lallah Churchill as witnesses. On the 19 December that year, Elisabeth gave birth to a second daughter, who was given another Tahitian name, Tiare.[53] Although settled in The Orchard at Waltham, the demands of his career meant that Robert was unable and perhaps reluctant to become as committed to family life as Elisabeth might have wished. Long hours were spent at the University beyond his contracted day — returning to Waltham in the late evening. Not long after the wedding day Robert had set out for Bermuda, leaving Elisabeth to cope with pregnancy and the home. Success brought new demands on his time and Robert must have found it hard to relate to domesticity and a young family; he was forty-eight and Elisabeth was twenty-seven. Robert was spending less and less time at home and his relationship with Elisabeth was becoming stormy. To some extent duty had led to the marriage; beyond physical attraction, their personalities and temperaments were less suited. Tension was building up in the marriage — Elisabeth was at a time of life where she wanted to build a family, Robert's motivations were elsewhere.

With a regular job at the University, financially their affairs should have been more secure, but the shadow of the crisis over the loss of the Press still hung over Gibbings. However optimistic his life was on the surface, in fact Gibbings was suffering from enormous stress as a result of debts that he had accumulated at the collapse of his business. He had sent money to Moira for the children when he could but now he had another expanding family to support. Throughout most of 1938 and the beginning of 1939 he was in bitter dispute with Barclays Bank, and drafts of his angry letters to the Bank survive which reveal the desperation which had begun to affect his health. In the letters, Gibbings explains that when he had approached the Bank for a mortgage on Four Elms Cottage in 1929 and a loan to buy the Press, it had been the Bank itself that had taken the initiative and offered him an additional loan and overdraft, making the financial judgement that they would prosper from his growing and profitable business. Unfortunately the slump, which Gibbings was at pains to point out was 'NOT due to the artists of this world but to the financiers', dramatically changed prospects — interest rates went up and business collapsed. Gibbings's bitterness resulted from a sense of violated innocence and feelings of injustice. The Bank had voluntarily entered the partnership, taking a risk on their judgement, yet it was he who had lost everything: 'I sold everything I had including household effects, books, carpets, chairs even to my signet ring in order to pay off the loan.' The Bank lost nothing but simply charged higher interest rates. By 1938 his overdraft had mounted to over £1000, yet he had paid more than that in interest and Bank charges. The regular nagging from the Bank to pay not only the interest but the capital as well had worn Gibbings down and he was at the point of break-down:

> Now it is more than I [can] stand & I've been ill from sheer overwork & worry. How the hell can I concentrate on my work at the University or anywhere else when I have to drug myself to sleep at nights & fill myself with tonics by day in order to keep going. The jeer of one of your directors that I look too healthy & that you are worried because it will be some time before you can claim life insurance does not help matters.[54]

Even at this time Gibbings always appeared to be genial and charming in public; it was not an act, this was genuinely part of his character, but he felt it his duty to perform and he did not let his public down — underneath was a darker and insecure self which rarely showed. Whether the final letters that followed these drafts were ever sent is not known. Some of the more extreme comments probably had a useful therapeutic effect, even if on reflection they were considered too intemperate to be sent, but they show something of his state of mind: 'You would Kill a man for a few hundred pounds — if you could get away with it. … I hereby refuse to accept your miserable standards or to be bound by your self consecrated rules. Do what you like I am finished with you all & I despise you utterly.' Gibbings threatened liquidation; in more responsible moments he offered to cash in a life insurance policy to pay off some of the capital. Eventually the Bank offered to drop interest charges for a year '… on the understanding that you make every effort to reduce the principal amount owing'. This compromise gave Gibbings a breathing space which he used to great effect. His next project was to dramatically change his financial fortunes.

Chapter Fourteen
Sweet Thames Run Softly
1939–1941

SINCE HIS CHILDHOOD when he lived near the banks of the Lee, rivers had always held a special attraction for Gibbings; they offered solitude, peace, and a place to reflect, as well as adventure and constant interest. He had a great affection for the Thames in particular: '... that quiet stream obedient to every lock and weir, where "in the late evening there is scarcely a murmur save the munching breathing of cattle or the churring note of a warbler in the reeds"'.[1] After so many years living at Waltham St Lawrence and now with his association with Reading, he naturally gravitated towards the river Thames and its tributaries that flowed through the town. He often joined in field excursions organised by the biological departments. On one such occasion in the summer term of 1939, he accompanied Professor Tom Harris and a group of students to the River Kennet to study 'riparian and aquatic vegetation' and also to take a dip in the reed-fringed weedy pool near the lock; the occasion was affectionately remembered by one of the students: 'Gibbings wore a wide-brimmed black hat, scarlet shirt, and voluminous khaki trousers — truly a Garibaldi figure! But to cap it all, besides carrying his swimming gear, he carried a 2lb jam jar held by a handle of string tied round the rim, such as a child collecting tiddlers uses!'[2]

Despite his protests at the onward march of suburbia, his long association and love for the Thames and its valley gave him an idea for his next book:

> Having travelled more than fifty thousand miles over salt water, and having visited the five continents of the world, it occurred to me that it might be fun to explore the river Thames, in whose valley I had lived for fifteen years. It seemed to me that it would be a neat and compact little journey within clearly defined limits.[3]

Gibbings decided to take his proposal to a publisher and John Hadfield, then a senior commissioning editor for J. M. Dent & Sons Ltd, recalled his first appointment:

> ... there strode into my office a vast, silver-bearded figure, who looked like one of the more jovial Old Testament prophets, in tweed cap and sky-blue pullover. ... 'I've been wearing a diving suit and drawing underwater pictures of fishes in the West Indies,' he told me. 'In the last year or two I have lived in Tahiti, travelled round Australia, and spent a while in the Red Sea. Now I've come back to the placid valley of the Thames. I want to

disguise myself as a willow and drift down the river, seeing, recording, and drawing whatever comes my way.'[4]

This first meeting with John Hadfield was to have great significance in Gibbings's career and was the start of a long working association with the publisher. Hadfield immediately took to Gibbings and the feeling was mutual; they were to become firm friends. Hadfield remembered that he felt something special about the Thames project; he had a hunch that it was going to be a success and would capture the mood of the times as a complete contrast to the insecurity and foreboding of the threat of war. It would be a boost to morale and offer an escape from the disasters about to be inflicted by humanity on the world of nature and the English countryside.

Gibbings's unfinished memoir 'Some Recollections' ends with the following paragraph:

> In the early days of 1939 there arose in me a great desire to find peace beside a river. I wanted more than ever to get that same closeness to nature to which I had referred in my early poem. So, on the floor of my studio I chalked out the shape of a flat bottomed boat.

In order to collect his material Gibbings wanted to travel down the river at his own pace, abandoning the use of guide books and human companionship. He required a special kind of boat with a flat bottom in order to negotiate the shallow and stony parts of the river, and one which was stable and large enough to sleep in and provide storage for apparatus such as microscopes, as well as the paraphernalia of living. Although it was to be punt-like, the boat was to be propelled by oars — Gibbings had been brought up by the sea and had 'an instinctive scorn of "prodding the mud"'. Enquiries about a boat of this sort were fruitless and Gibbings was left with one alternative — to build the boat himself.[5] To many people the idea of building a boat would seem a formidable task and not many would be in a position to undertake it. Gibbings was fortunate in that he could make use of certain facilities at the University and had access to knowledge of boat building from tradesmen in the town; he also had the determination to follow the project through.

Gibbings managed to persuade Hubert Davis, then teacher of woodwork construction in the Fine Art Department, and his assistant Norman Howard, to do the work with himself and his son Patrick as willing assistants. In a notebook Gibbings admitted that 'Davis was in charge. I was no more building this boat than I had set the type of the Golden Cockerel books which bear my name as printer. He and Howard were the builders and my son and me to supply unskilled labour'.[6] The carpentry workshop was in a room close to the typography and wood-engraving studios and it was here that work began on the construction of the boat at the beginning of the summer vacation in 1939.

Although Davis and Howard had never built a boat before they were both very accomplished craftsmen. Undaunted by their task, they had no worries about the actual construction, but they were aware of certain technical difficulties, above all the question of what makes a boat float. To get the answer to this they contacted

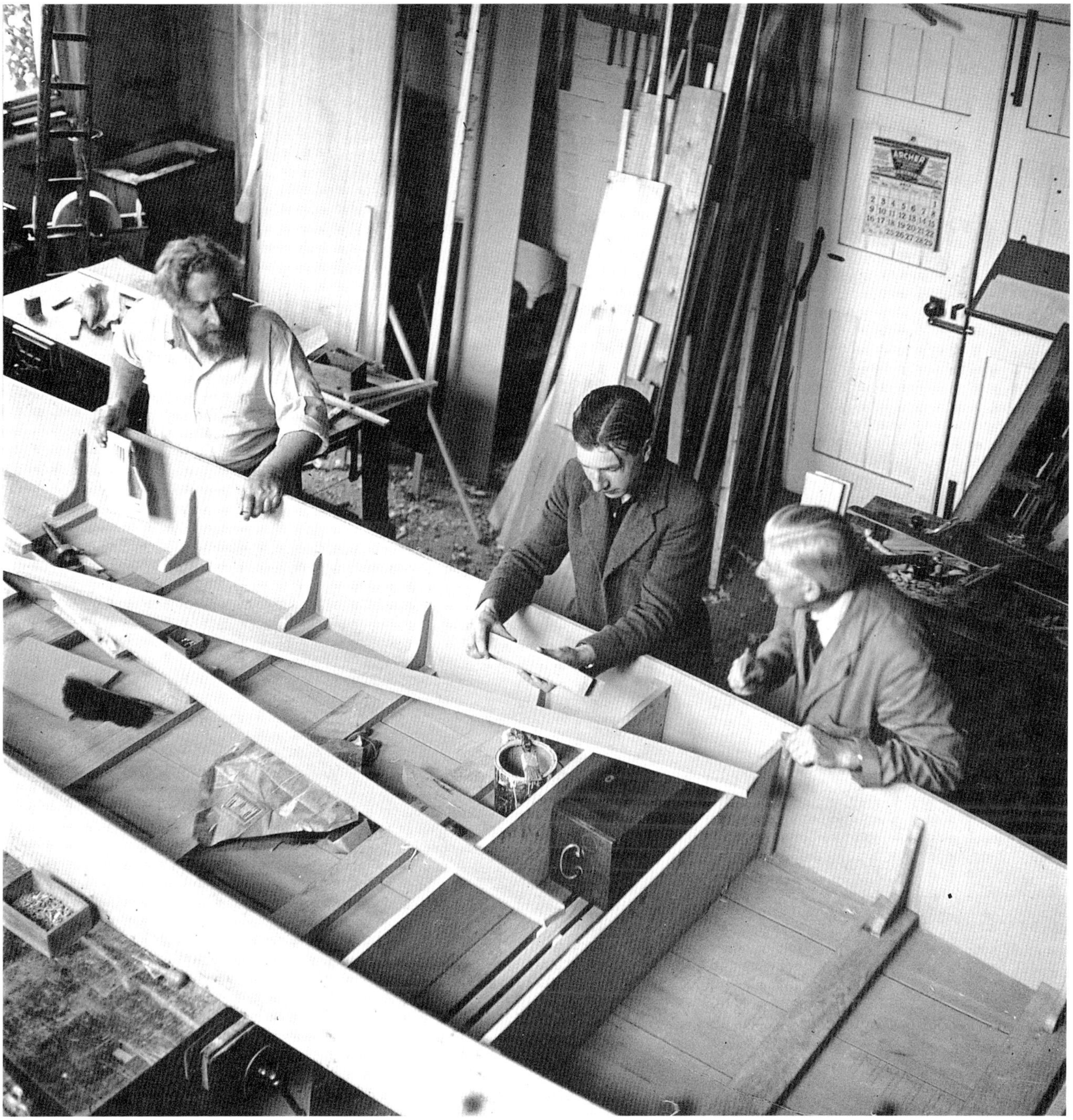

H. J. Isaacs and Frank Pearce of Moss's boat yard near Caversham Bridge and from them learnt that caulking was the secret of a floating vessel. This was the bruising of the edges of the planks of the bottom of the boat so that when immersed in water the wood would expand and prevent water seeping in. Gibbings designed the boat to suit his needs. Being of a large frame he had to have a large boat — its width was therefore determined by his own. He wanted a long boat, about the length of a punt, but this was ultimately determined by the size of the room in which it was built. He was totally unaware of technical factors, as is evident in this extract from his notebook:

241 Gibbings, his son Patrick, and Hubert Davis discussing the construction of the *Willow* during the summer vacation of 1939. RUL.

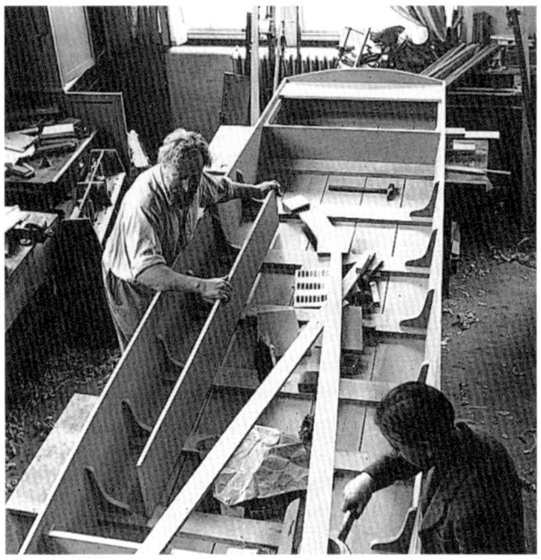

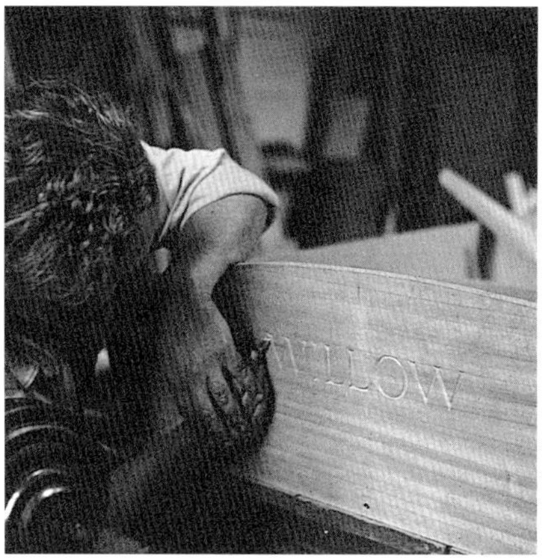

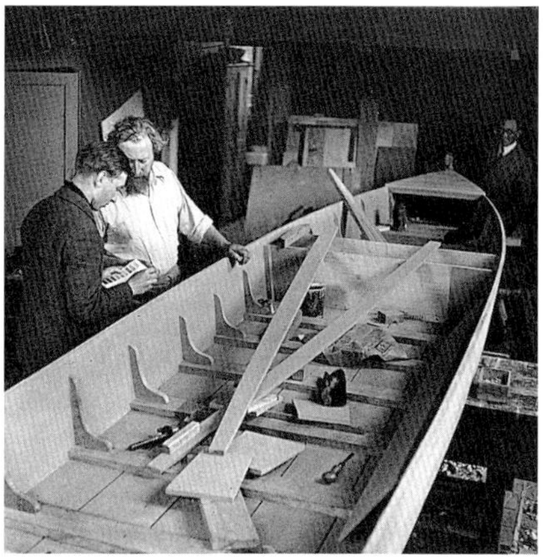

242 *left* Patrick and Robert fitting the lockers to the *Willow*. RUL.

243 *centre* Gibbings cutting the name *Willow* into the stern of his boat. RUL.

244 *right* Patrick and Robert choosing colours. RUL.

When I first thought of building the boat myself it seemed to me that all I need do was fasten two long boards at one end to form a bow, join them at the other end by a stern board and push out the centre to whatever width I wished by means of a thwart. Then it would only be necessary to nail on the bottom and the hull would be complete.

The wood had already been ordered; obechi for the hull, chosen for its lightness and comparative cheapness, and oak with a specially twisted grain for the shoulders and stem. The pieces for the hull were ordered from London and Patrick cut the shoulders on a bandsaw. Davis and Howard made the rest.

The first thing that Gibbings learnt was that a flat-bottomed boat was not constructed as such, but with a camber at each end of roughly four inches in twenty feet, and that the sides should not be vertical but sloped out at an angle of seven and a half degrees. These two factors were important in getting the correct curvature of the boat. The cross-members or formers were made first and the bottom, which had been caulked, was fixed to these. The floorboards were placed a quarter of an inch apart to allow for drainage and expansion.

The only parts of the boat that Gibbings made himself were the stem, which he carved from oak in the shape of a scroll or ram's horn, and the lettering on the back panel. He called the boat the *Willow*, a name with no special significance, but which seemed very appropriate as pollarded willows are a common feature along the banks of the Thames. In order that a tarpaulin could be pulled over in bad weather and for shelter at night, five bamboo hoops were placed at intervals down the sides. Finally, Patrick and his father painted the *Willow* eau-de-nil green. The internal fittings consisted of lockers in a U-shape that ran across and around the middle of the boat to contain food, drawing equipment and other essentials. Between these was a gap wide enough for Gibbings to sleep in; the surrounding weight meant that he could sleep safely without fear of the boat turning over if he moved too violently. Additional lockers were in the bows and the stern, that in the latter being notorious for containing his liquid refreshment!

Within fourteen days the *Willow* was ready for launching. They were now left with the problem of how to remove her from the woodwork room. Because of her size, the only solution was to take a window out of its frame and manoeuvre the *Willow* through the opening; it was not an easy task as she had to be pushed through on her side, the window being too narrow. Once through the window, the *Willow* was loaded on to a lorry and driven to Moss's boat yard at Caversham Bridge, where she was put into the water at two o'clock. At eight-thirty that evening Mr Howard was able to report that she had not taken in a single drop of water.

The next test of the *Willow* was to make sure that she could take a substantial amount of weight. The building of the *Willow* had caused considerable interest in the School of Art and Robert, Patrick Gibbings, Davis, Howard and other members of staff and students went to Caversham Bridge to see her float. The test came when Gibbings suggested that half a dozen people should get into the boat to see how she held. Six stood in the *Willow* and there was very little change in the level of the boat. Everyone was therefore convinced that she was safe.

Gibbings set out on his trip on 29 July 1939, a start somewhat rushed owing to the imminence of war which might at any moment have thwarted his plans. Logically enough, the journey was to start at the source of the Thames and Barry Neame hired a motor launch to tow the *Willow* upstream to Lechlade. Other members of the farewell party were Elisabeth, Vahine and Patrick, who accompanied Gibbings to Shillingford Bridge where they enjoyed a picnic and toasted the voyage in champagne. Patrick then towed his father the remaining miles.

Originally Gibbings had intended his boat to have a glass bottom through which he could study the underwater life but the Thames did not offer the same possibilities as Bermuda or the Red Sea. The idea had to be abandoned because of fears that he would put his foot through it and Davis thought that there might be difficulties in making it watertight. Gibbings used instead a glass bottomed box made by his son. He could put the box over the side when he wanted and observe the fish and life on the river bed. Later, in words and images, Gibbings was able to describe a dimension of the river not often considered with the enthusiasm and fascination he had had in more exotic places:

> In rhythmic accompaniment tendrils of the Canadian pondweed, tufts of hornwort, and the threaded whorls of milfoil sway to the same ebb and flow, while sticklebacks dart here and there, and solemn perch pursue their dignified excursions. Beetles, too, some of them burrowing in the mud, others charging about with self-important urgency, and red water-mites paddling their busy way in search of small crustacea.[7]

Such rich descriptive passages were constructed from the multitude of notes and observations that Gibbings scribbled down in a series of small ring binders; he could then shuffle his notes around to order and bring his ideas and sources together in a finished piece of writing. This system was to become important, for as his accumulation of material grew and his publishing increased, he needed to be able to reference and keep track of ideas — partly to make sure he did not repeat material he had already used.

Leaving the *Willow* moored at Ford's boatyard in Lechlade, Gibbings went by road past Cricklade to the source of the Thames. He was disappointed to find that the traditional 'Thames Head' was a dried up Roman well, full of stones. But he was not down-hearted:

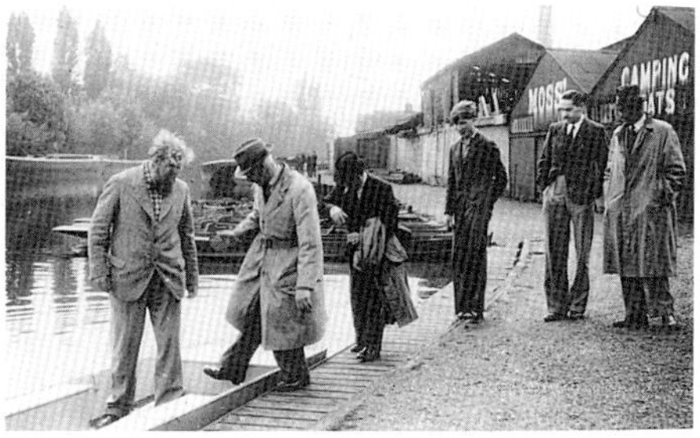

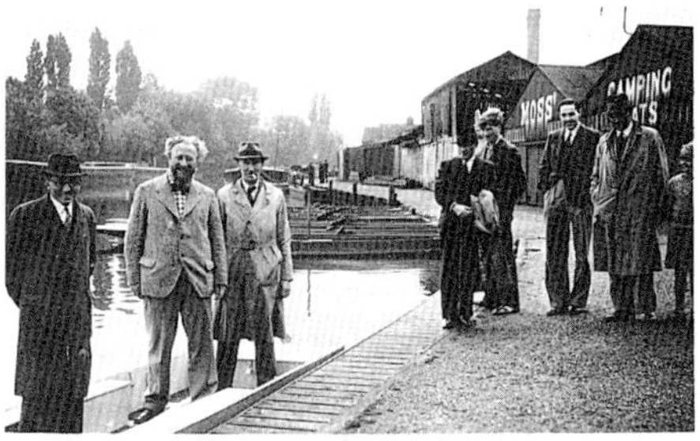

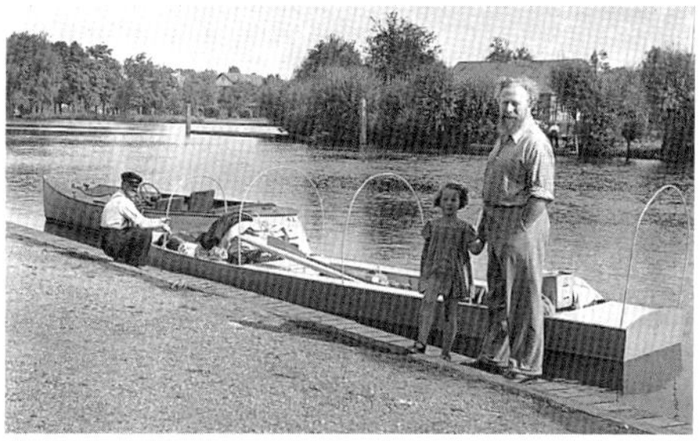

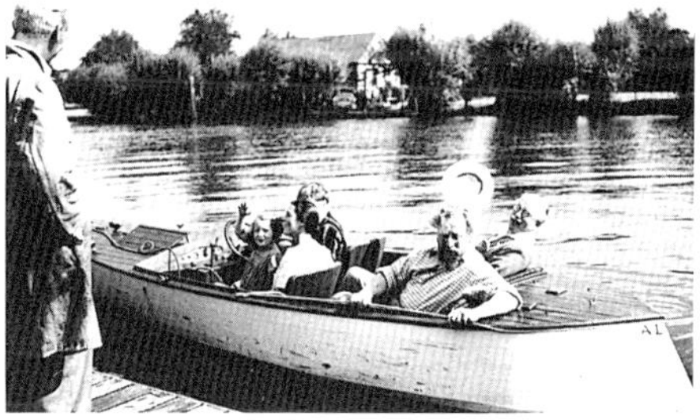

245 Testing the *Willow*. This sequence of photographs was taken by William Wilder who was a student in the Department of Fine Art at the time. RUL.

246 Mr Howard, Robert Gibbings and Mr Davis afloat. RUL.

247 Robert with his daughter, Vahine, in front of the *Willow*, loaded for the trip, just before he set off on his voyage. RUL.

248 Barry Neame, Robert, Elisabeth, Vahine, and Patrick at the wheel as they cast off to start on the journey to the source of the Thames. Neame's motor launch was used to tow the *Willow* to Lechlade. RUL.

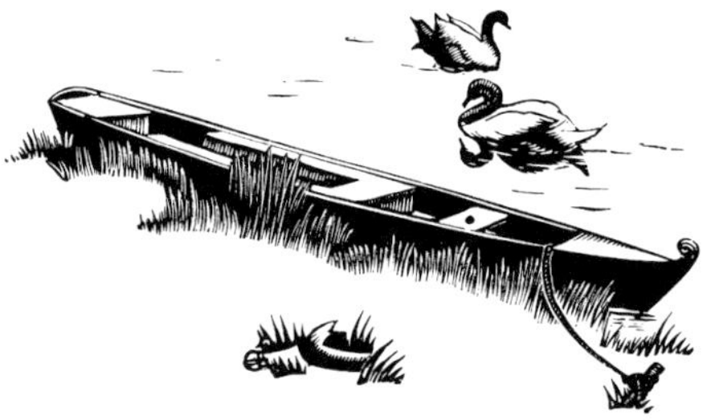

249 The *Willow*, 1940, wood-engraving, 45 x 75 mm. Illustration from *Sweet Thames Run Softly.*

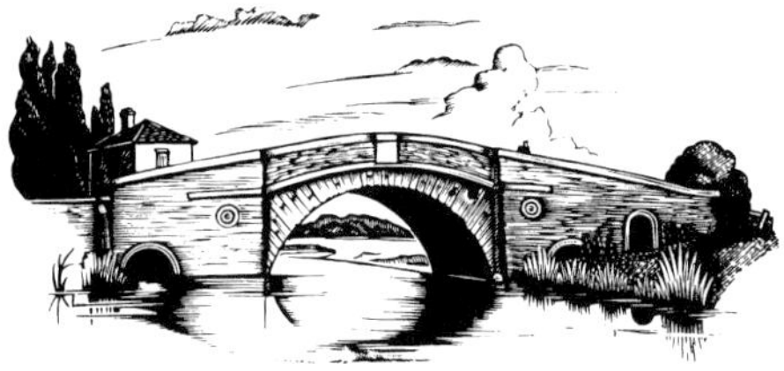

250 Halfpenny Bridge at Lechlade, 1940, wood-engraving, 47 x 100 mm. Illustration from *Sweet Thames Run Softly.*

251 *below* Gibbings making notes in his boat the *Willow*, on his journey down the Thames in 1939. RUL.

So now I was at the head of the river, and my travelling was to be downhill all the way. I don't for a moment agree with Swinburne when he suggests that rivers grow weary on their journey to the sea. On the contrary, it seems to me that they have a very easy and joyous time wandering through flowery meadows, dancing over weirs, eddying round pools, and lazing for long hours in the sun.[8]

The next morning Gibbings set off on foot to follow the river back to his boat at Lechlade. He was to spend the next weeks drifting down the Thames, his nights spent under canvas on the boat:

During the six weeks I spent in my boat last summer I carried neither clock nor calendar, preferring to forget those two tyrants of modern life. When it was dark I went to sleep, and when it was light I woke up, and when I was hungry I prepared myself some food, and so I lived as peacefully as any old fox in his earth.[9]

It was not a continuous journey; detours were made up tributaries, time was spent visiting historic sights and buildings, many public houses were also visited and, if the mood took him, he would stay for a few days in one spot to explore or just observe and contemplate. He had time for conversation and tales told to him by the folk he encountered on the way were noted and stored away for later use. Like his journey, his book was not to be a continuous narrative but a patchwork of wide ranging and almost random thoughts, facts, observations and anecdotes that were woven and linked together, the River Thames being a common thread holding it all together.

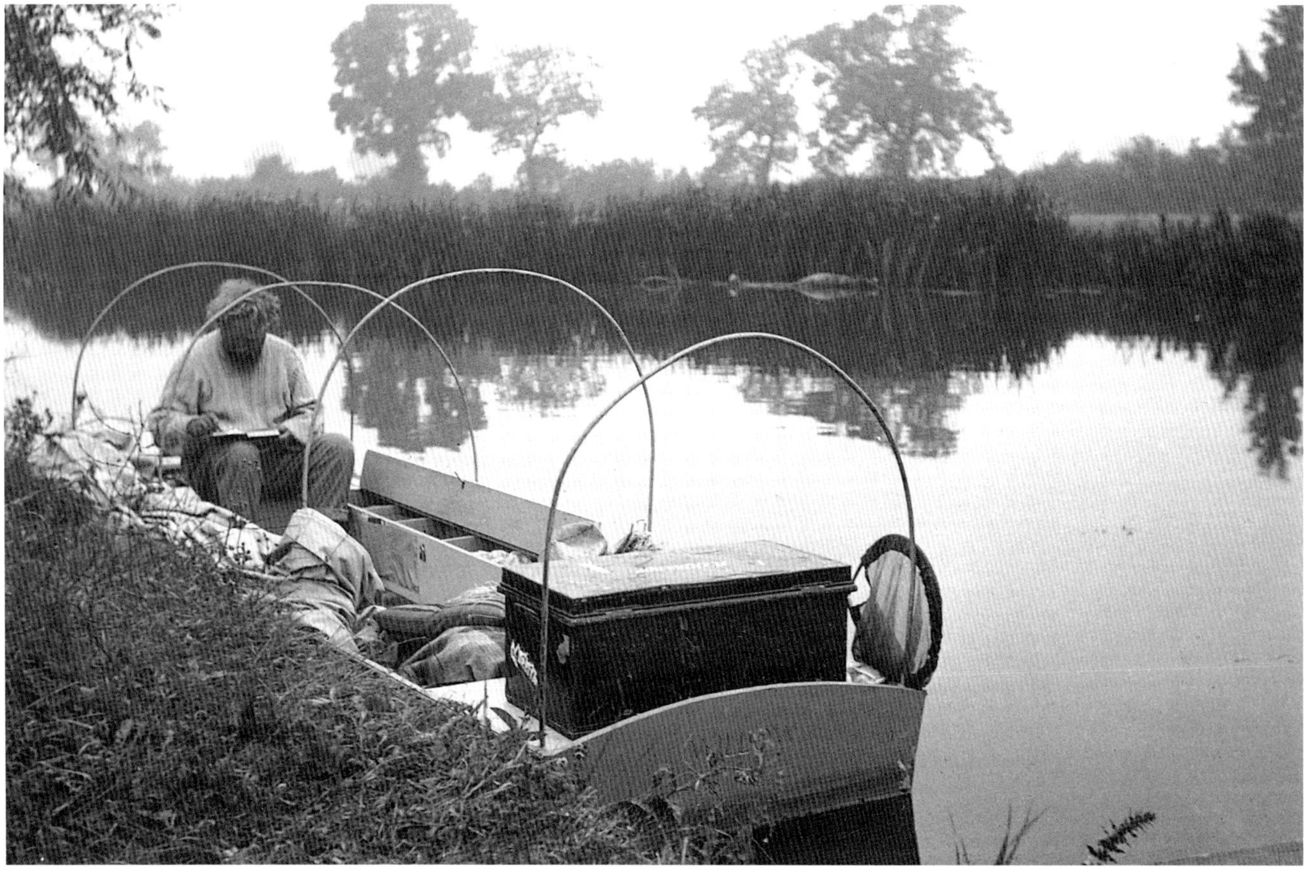

For six weeks things went well and Gibbings made good progress. On a particularly scorching hot day he reached Oxford, spending a day browsing in bookshops. He was a little disconcerted to discover the window of Blackwell's bookshop full of authoritative books and maps on every aspect of the Thames — it made him feel rather unsure of his own abilities and he questioned the need for yet another book on the topic. He was somewhat calmed by the words of Mr Blackwell himself:

> 'The last time I saw you you were stripped to the waist, bronzed, wearing a sarong, and looking like a river god,' said Blackwell himself, emerging from his door.
> 'And now I'm pale, in a puce sweat, and feeling like a water-rat,' I said. But, as ever, he was kindly and encouraging. He seemed positively anxious to see whatever I might write, and he even suggested that these very pages might some day appear in his window.[10]

His confidence was given a further boost when he was recognised in the street by a passer-by who had seen him on the television — he then noticed other people looking in his direction with their hats off: 'Damn it!' I said to myself. 'I can't be as famous as all that'; looking up the street Gibbings could see a hearse coming along covered with wreaths![11] He drifted on over the next few days past Nuneham Park and Abingdon, enjoying one of 'the rarer moments in life' as the full moon lit the 'falling waters' of Sutton's Pool by Sutton Courtney. The next day he sketched the little church at Appleford and carried on through Clifton Hampden, stopping at the Barley Mow, a thirteenth-century cruck-framed inn, famous for being the hostelry where Jerome K. Jerome wrote *Three Men in a Boat*. Gibbings would have 'enjoyed its hospitality for some days, but the threat of war had become too acute'.[12] He felt he had to push on to Reading but first he managed to count the one hundred and twenty-eight house martins' nests that were glued under the arches of Clifton Hampden bridge. Taking in the historical sights in Dorchester, he went on to Shillingford where he anchored mid-stream to draw the bridge, and then through the Goring Gap with 'some of the grandest scenery on the river'. Gibbings commented on the many 'vistas' between Streatley and Mapledurham, feeling that it was all too perfect, too close to the idealised pictures in the Royal Academy: '... like a Victorian drawing-room it is too rich and comfortable to engender thought'. Approaching Reading, Gibbings felt that the 'face of the country' was 'blemished by the marks of man'. He had reached the town and home just in time; on 3 September war was declared and he was forced to abandon his journey and return to his family and to his duties at the University.

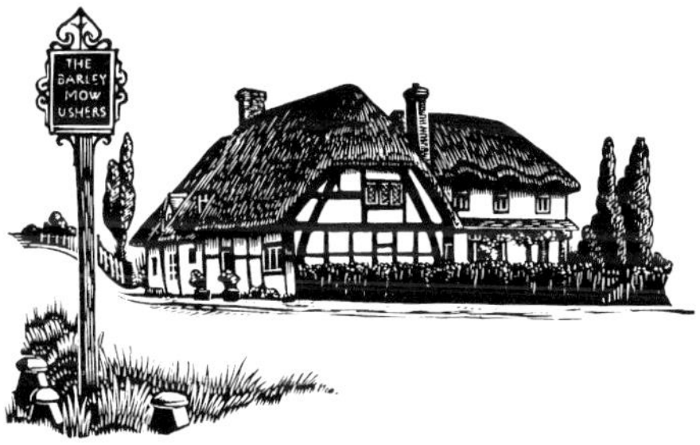

252 *The Barley Mow*, 1940, wood-engraving, 50 x 81 mm. Illustration from *Sweet Thames Run Softly*.

His recent experience messing about in boats prepared him for his own contribution to the war effort, the manning of the River Patrol, with his friend H. A. D. Neville, Professor of Agricultural Chemistry. At fifty, Gibbings was too old for active service, and his experiences in the last war would have made it inappropriate, but he was anxious to be of use. In a news bulletin for members of the Society of Wood Engravers, sent out later in the war (Autumn 1941), a report on members' activities was given and Gibbings's war contribution was outlined:

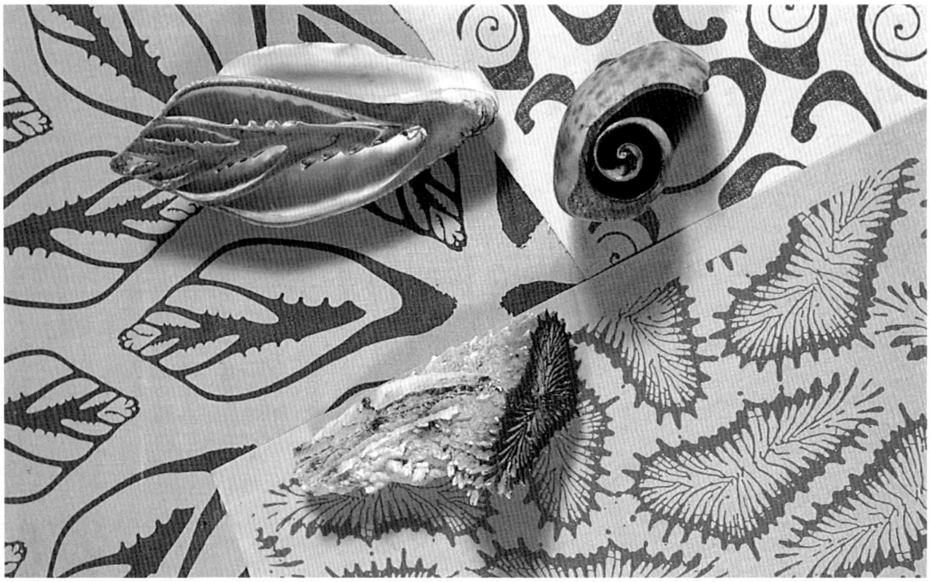

253 Designs for binding cloth based on seashells. Gibbings enjoyed using strong patterns and colour on the bindings of books. An entry in the *University Gazette*, vol. 12, no. 2, 1939, p. 31, reported that examples of binding cloth printed in colour and designed by Gibbings had been purchased by the Victoria & Albert Museum. The designs had been taken from sea shells, brought back from his various expeditions, cut in half to form printing blocks. The samples of binding cloth and the shells are now in RUL – the shells were found in the studio at Waltham when it was cleared before sale in 1989.

As none of the Services seemed to want men of 50 with waists of 40 he continued writing. After a period with the Home Guard (Army), armed with a blackthorn, he transferred to the River Patrol (Navy), armed with a rook rifle, and was served out with a chauffeur's cap to look nautical. In due course, the University needed his services in their private fire-brigade, so he became a fireman but has not yet been used for testing ropes.[13]

Formal applications to join a camouflage unit and an offer to make drawings from submarines were turned down, but, together with some of his colleagues from the Fine Art Department, he was later able to help with camouflage in the local area and thus able to pursue his fascination for the subject in a practical and unexpected way. His printing department at the University was also kept busy by work generated by the war.

In August 1940 the war had a major effect on Gibbings's family life. The University of Toronto had set up a scheme offering the families of University staff in Britain accommodation and support in Canada. Elisabeth had relations in Toronto and with two small children it made sense to seek safety and take advantage of the offer — the Canadians were to take on all expenses. The security of the family was the prime motivation for their acceptance but the strains in the relationship between Robert and Elisabeth must also have made a temporary separation more acceptable and may have been a factor in their decision.

Writing to an American collector and enthusiast for his work, Ralph Hartman, in July 1940, Gibbings commented that he was '... labouring to complete my next book entitled "Sweet Thames Run Softly". It is mostly about natural history on the river but it is difficult to concentrate on such things with enemy planes overhead'.[14] He explained that his wife and children were shortly sailing for Canada but he felt concern for the future: 'I think we are in for a tough time but as I said in a broadcast the other day this is the greatest day in our history & it's grand to be alive for the fight ... give us all the help you can & *quickly* & we'll put those liars where they belong. I think the more sinister thing in the whole business is their absolute disregard & disdain for anything approaching a word of honour'.

Elisabeth, Vahine and Tiare left England in August and tenants were found for The Orchard. Gibbings moved into rooms in St Patrick's Hall, an all male hall of residence, and began to settle into a bachelor life again. Writing to his American friend again at the end of August he explained that Elisabeth was staying for a few weeks in Ontario, near to his friend's home, and was feeling lonely: 'I am quite sure she would appreciate any gesture you can make for it's her first time away from home & the Atlantic is a wide stretch of water.'[15]

The family had left at the height of the Battle of Britain; Gibbings reported that they were '... all feeling cheerful over here after the last week's air battles. They came down like flies. Pray heaven it continues'. In the midst of this tension Gibbings was hard at work on his book: 'I am working against time and have nearly got writer's cramp.'[16] Ian Crichton, who had joined the staff of the Zoology Department in 1938 as an assistant lecturer, had rooms next to Robert and they shared a bathroom and kitchen. They had been friends before Gibbings moved into Hall and often sat in deck chairs on the lawns sipping tea together and indulging in long chats. Crichton remembered Gibbings's room being full of mementos of his travels and that he would don his 'pareu' when weather permitted. In May 1940, at the time of the Dunkirk evacuation, the two had sat in the residents' garden watching Hurricanes and Spitfires flying to the front-line airfields. Crichton sympathised with Gibbings's decision to evacuate his family to Canada but later reflected that in retrospect it might have been a mistake, as he saw the family losing touch.[17]

Although much of the extra-curricular activity at the University had been curtailed in war-time, Gibbings made efforts to take advantage of the social life on offer. Once again he took to the stage and he gave a memorable and superb performance as Noah in André Obey's play of that title; he had already had to 'loom' large as Dr Johnson in a small play he had helped to produce in 1938. He gave talks to the Art Society and on one occasion rather shocked a more conservative student by wearing a bright blue shirt, red tie and yellow socks. Gibbings had also encouraged students to write to Eric Gill and invite him to talk but Gill declined, claiming he was too busy. As a member, and later a Steward, of the Senior Common Room, Gibbings was known for his munificence, particularly with the whisky bottle. He was a member of the Dining Club, a select body of fourteen members which met three times a term to entertain distinguished guests with good food, wine and conversation — Gibbings was noted on these occasions for his ebullience, his expansiveness and the ability to talk about and be interested in any subject.

As a well known artist, Gibbings's presence had also come to the attention of local art groups in the town of Reading itself. The Chiltern group, with whom Gibbings had already exhibited, was a 'breakaway' group of the more professional artists who were members of the flourishing Reading Guild of Artists. In

1940 Gibbings was invited to be the guest 'critic' at the Guild's annual show. He endeared himself to members by being generous in his praise, justifiably so as standards were high, and when the Chiltern Group was dissolved the following year, Gibbings joined the Guild himself. His membership was to last only one year due to the demands of his writing, but he exhibited three of his engravings from *Sweet Thames Run Softly* in the annual exhibition.[18]

The declaration of war had interrupted his journey on the Thames, and having explored the upper reaches, Gibbings now had to make shorter trips, fitting in with his other commitments, to explore the rest of the river. In early October he visited the river Colne, which joins the Thames above Lechlade, noting the onset of autumn and the abundance and variety of berries in the hedgerows; a fortnight later he was in the woods near Henley 'marvelling at the lemon and gold of the beech leaves suspended over the dark evergreen undergrowth of box trees and red-berried yews'.[19] In May he was moored in the *Willow* at Shiplake, hoping to glimpse the great crested grebes which nest there. Hambledon Lock, Medmenham Abbey, the suspension bridge and church at Marlow, Cliveden and Maidenhead were all visited in 1940. Rowing past the Hind's Head at Bray, scene of many a memorable dinner, he could not resist stopping for lunch on the lawn. Gibbings, as a valued guest and famous raconteur, recalled one special dinner in his book when he met a fellow compatriot from Cork, Maurice Healy KC, for the first time:

> That was a night, the night we met. Forty strong men sat down to dine at eight o'clock and did not rise again till a quarter past one next morning. There was every sort of guest, from a member of the royal family downwards, including soldiers, sailors, a member of Parliament, a second-hand bookseller, writers, and other artists; and over them all brooded our host, Barry Neame, shedding a genial warmth among the company. Wines flowed like the water over Marlow weir: the sort of wines that a Frenchman would cross the Channel to drink. Lafite 1924, Haut-Brion 1924, Margaux 1920; imperials, magnums, jereboams of them.[20]

Further down the river, Gibbings was impressed by the grandeur of Windsor Castle, the sight of it prompting him to think of Malory's description of the death of King Arthur and he quoted the passage in his book. From Windsor he took a 'quicker mode of conveyance', a Salter steamer, in order to help him past 'the increasing number of architectural disfigurements on either bank'.[21] Past Hampton Court Palace and on to Kew, where in the glass houses the 'paw-paws and mangoes, the frangipani and hibiscus, and the hot sweet smell of tropical forests', brought back memories of his own travels.[22] Memories of his youth and early days as an artist were evoked on passing Chelsea. At Blackfriars Bridge he stopped for a while at Captain Scott's ship *Discovery*, at which point Gibbings was able to introduce material he had gleaned from his correspondence with William Lashly about his exploits on the polar expeditions.

Back in his rooms in Hall, Gibbings re-worked his notes and added linking passages to make his writing seem like an effortless flow of prose. An observation, a comment in conversation, or a reference in a book could prompt him to a stream of apparently related ideas or subjects. Often the connections seem tenuous or at least eccentrically personal, but Gibbings's skill was to make it all work and carry the reader along with his train of thought as if engaging in conversation. With the theme of the river as a background he was able to cover a range of topics from folk lore and potions for curing rheumatism or cleansing flesh wounds, to Dr Merryweather's invention of the Tempest Prognosticator, to the legend of St Columba, to Crystology, to theories about pre-natal influences, giving by way of example extracts from love stories by Heliodorus, the Bishop of Tricca in Thessaly in 400 AD — he even managed to include a gently erotic encounter with a female nude bather. His intensely personal account was full of his own reflective thoughts and philosophy; references to his own life and experiences and incidents and personalities from his childhood in Ireland were affectionately recalled, often with great humour. Folk tales and anecdotes overheard in public houses or in conversations with characters he bumped into on his journey were hurriedly noted and then retold in his book, using dialogue which tried to capture the accent and character of the speaker. But above all it was in his observation of nature and his descriptions of the mood and atmosphere of the open air and the landscape, ranging from the evocation of a dramatic sunset to the detail of a dew drop on a blade of grass, that his writing was at its best. His style was not that of the intellectual, it came from the spirit, a mixture of poetic evocation, intense observation, factual detail and, above all, a sense of enjoyment and love of life.

Gibbings sent his manuscript drafts to a Mr McLachlan in St Leonards for typing, and then went over the typescript making amendments. As in the past, he wanted

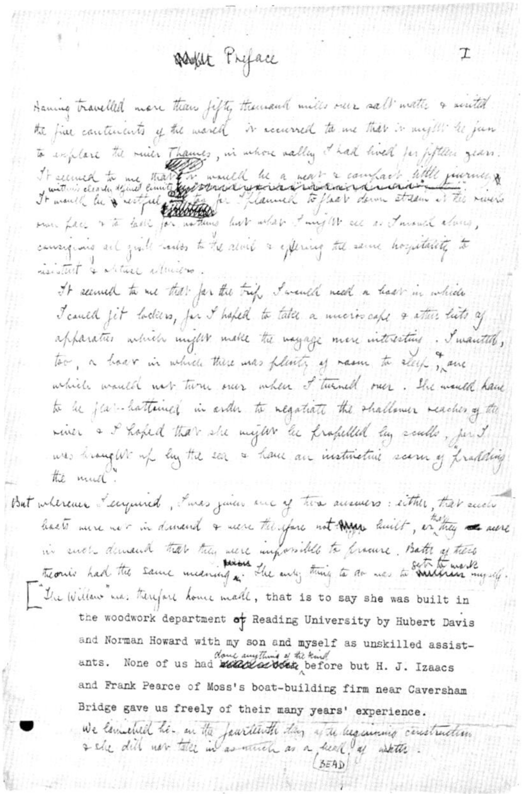
Preface I

Having travelled more than fifty thousand miles over salt water & visited the five continents of the world it occurred to me that it might be fun to explore the river Thames, in whose valley I had lived for fifteen years. It seemed to me that it would be a neat & compact little journey within clearly defined limits. It would be restful [illegible] for I planned to float down stream at the river's own pace & to look for nothing but what I might see as I moved along, consigning all guide books to the devil & offering the same hospitality to [illegible].

It seemed to me that for the trip I would need a boat in which I could fit lockers, for I hoped to take a microscope & other bits of apparatus which might make the voyage more interesting. I wanted, too, a boat in which there was plenty of room to sleep, & one which would not turn over when I turned over. She would have to be flat-bottomed in order to negotiate the shallower reaches of the river & I hoped that she might be propelled by sculls, for I was brought up by the sea & have an instinctive scorn of "paddling the mud".

But wherever I enquired, I was given one of two answers: either, that such boats were not in demand & were therefore not built, or they were in such demand that they were impossible to procure. Both of these theories had the same meaning. The only thing to do was to set to work myself.

"The Willow" was therefore home made, that is to say she was built in the woodwork department of Reading University by Hubert Davis and Norman Howard with my son and myself as unskilled assistants. None of us had done anything of the kind before but H. J. Izaacs and Frank Pearce of Moss's boat-building firm near Caversham Bridge gave us freely of their many years' experience.

We launched her on the fourteenth day after beginning construction & she did not take in as much as a bead of water.

(BEAD)

254 The first page of Gibbings's handwritten draft for his preface to *Sweet Thames Run Softly* with typed alterations pasted in. RUL.

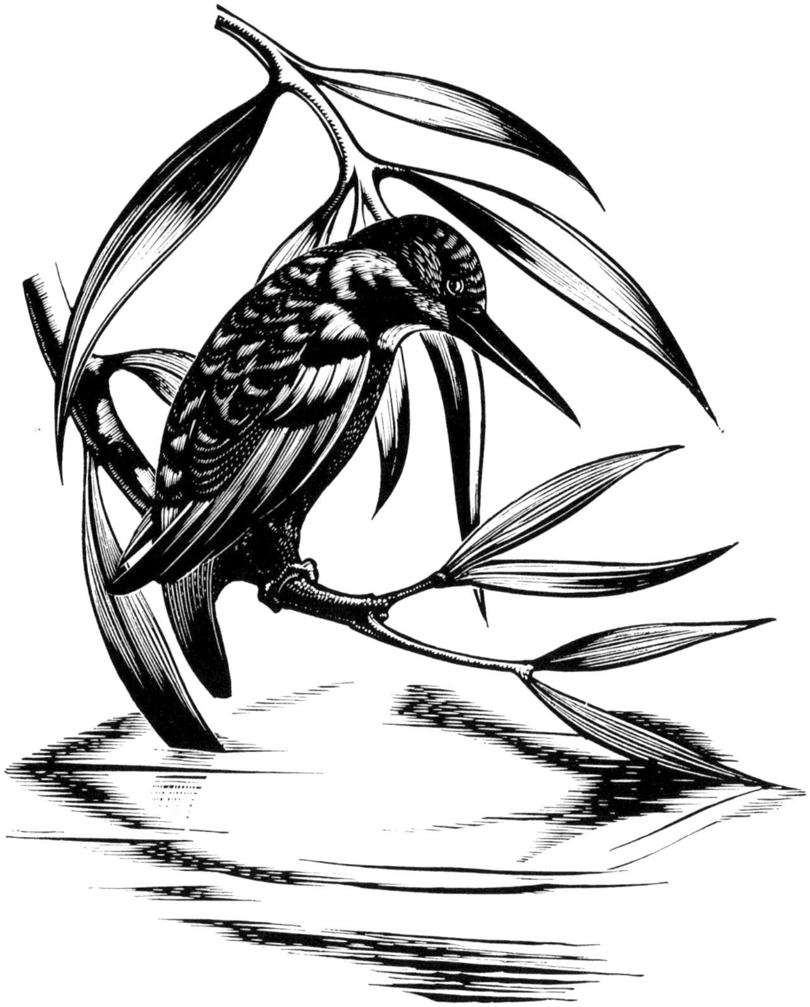

255 *right* *Kingfisher*, 1940, illustration from *Sweet Thames Run Softly*, wood-engraving, 132 x 110 mm.

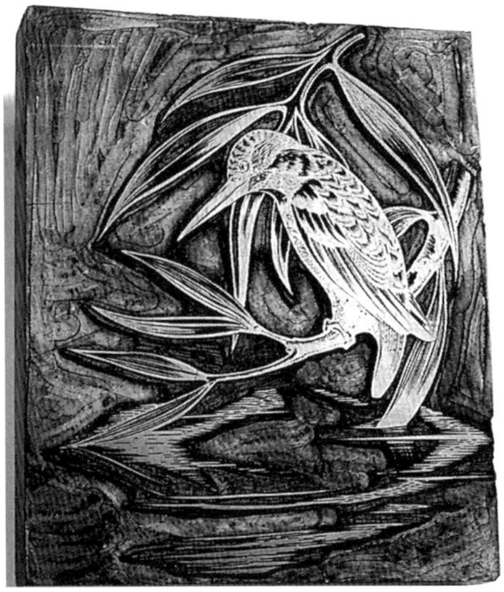

256 *below* Engraved woodblock used to print the image *right*, 134 x 114 mm. The original block was not used to print the book, as this could have resulted in damage and wear, so an electrotype copy was made from the block. Blocks for *Sweet Thames Run Softly*, *John Graham, Convict*, and *Till I End my Song* are in RUL.

An electrotype is made by taking an impression of the original block in a form of wax and then coating the surface of that mould with a conductive graphite powder. A thin film of copper is deposited on the surface of the mould through electrolysis. This copper skin is then supported and given strength by being backed by a layer of metal similar to that used for type and the resulting plate is mounted on a wooden block which makes the printing surface the same height as the type. This duplicate of the original block is so accurate that in the final printing it is usually impossible to tell that the image has been printed from an electrotype.

to control as much of the design and production of his books as possible. His friendship with John Hadfield and other directors and managers at Dent meant that he was allowed much greater involvement than was normally given to authors. The typeface chosen for the book was Gill's Perpetua, and as the text was relatively modest in length, a generous size of type was used. Once the text had been set as galleys, Gibbings was then able to introduce his wood-engravings and by cutting and pasting the proofs of the illustrations and the text together he created a 'dummy' of the book. It was an organic process; Gibbings considered each spread individually, adjusting the position and distribution of the engravings. Where necessary, he altered the text itself, adding or removing engravings until he was completely satisfied with the relationship of text to image from both visual and informative points of view. The book was broken up into a multitude of short chapters, sometimes only four or five pages long, each chapter dealing with a particular topic or story. Because it was not a continuous narrative Gibbings could even shuffle and reorganise the order of chapters or parts of chapters, provided it did not upset the linking theme of his journey. The completed dummy then became a specification for the printers.

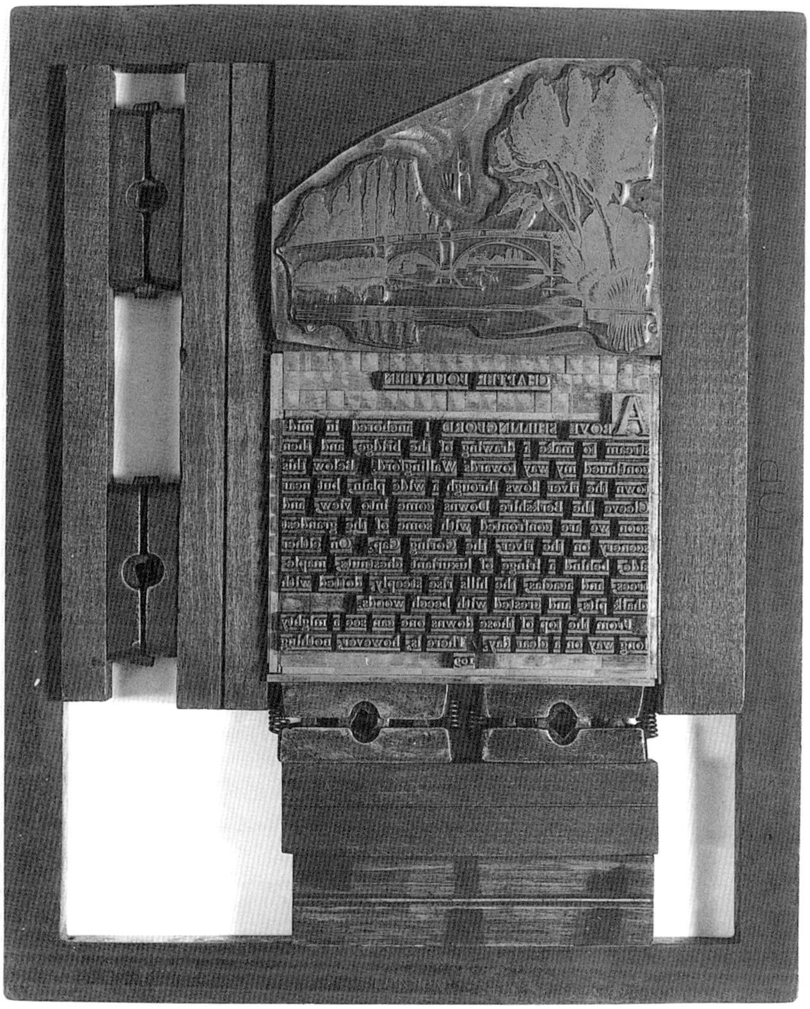

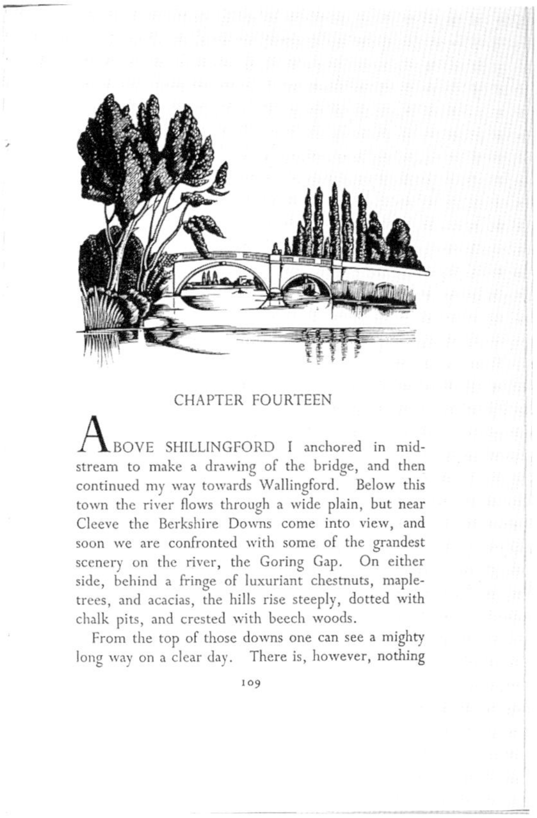

CHAPTER FOURTEEN

ABOVE SHILLINGFORD I anchored in mid-stream to make a drawing of the bridge, and then continued my way towards Wallingford. Below this town the river flows through a wide plain, but near Cleeve the Berkshire Downs come into view, and soon we are confronted with some of the grandest scenery on the river, the Goring Gap. On either side, behind a fringe of luxuriant chestnuts, maple-trees, and acacias, the hills rise steeply, dotted with chalk pits, and crested with beech woods.

From the top of those downs one can see a mighty long way on a clear day. There is, however, nothing

109

While gathering material on his journey Gibbings made visual as well as written notes. Back in Reading, he selected drawings he wanted to make engravings from and made new drawings in black ink, refining and interpreting the loose pencil marks of his sketches into a tighter design suitable for engraving on wood. The drawing was then photographed onto the block ready for Gibbings to cut. For practical reasons the final book was printed using electrotype copies made from the original blocks, but Gibbings made sure that he took editions of prints from the wood on quality paper before sending the blocks off.

A working title of *Disguised as a Willow* had been used on the contract with Dent and Gibbings had agreed to engrave a minimum of 30 illustrations and write 50,000 to 70,000 words, all to be ready for printing by 31 January 1940. In the event, he produced fifty engravings and *Sweet Thames Run Softly* appeared on 28 November 1940. When Hadfield had read the completed typescript a year after his first meeting with Gibbings, his original impressions of the project were confirmed; Gibbings had found his perfect medium. But initially he had reservations:

257 *left* A forme of page 109, the opening of chapter fourteen, from *Sweet Thames Run Softly*, specially prepared for Gibbings by the compositors at Dent's printers, The Temple Press, Letchworth, for use as a visual aid in his public lectures. The block is an electrotype copy taken from an engraved woodblock depicting the Shillingford Bridge Hotel. The forme is now in the Gibbings Collection, RUL.

258 *right* The opening page of chapter fourteen of *Sweet Thames Run Softly*, page size 224 x 150 mm.

When the first chapters of this book reached me, I was bewildered by its apparent inconsequence, which led its author's thoughts from dragon flies to pre-history, and from riverside pubs to the South Seas in the course of a page. Then I realised that here was something new and delightful — a man of multitudinous interests 'talking on paper,' and illustrating his words with wood-cuts of exquisite sensibility and flawless technique. 'Sweet Thames' was published in the second grim winter of the war. It was unquestionably the book of the year. ... A war-worn Britain responded to it as soldiers respond to the song of a thrush amid gun-fire ....[23]

The mixture of light-hearted adventure, rich anecdote and story telling, a sensitive eye for detail and a passionate love of nature and history all blended perfectly. Gibbings had reached a level of control and detail in his engravings that matched his words; it all worked together. The reader was presented with a book of quality, almost recreating the feel of a private press book with wood-engraved illustrations, which must have seemed a reminder of luxury in such utilitarian times. *Sweet Thames Run Softly* was priced a little higher than the average novel but was still an immediate and surprising success. Published at 12s. 6d. in an edition of 2500 copies it was reprinted three times in December 1940, in February and November 1941, then in 1942, 1943, 1945, 1946 and 1948, making a total of 40,950 copies. Many special editions were published by such organisations as the Readers Union and Guild Books (Services edition), reaching a grand total of over 134,000 copies sold by 1953 — a major publishing success. This was a winning formula: neither Dent nor Gibbings had set out to create a series but there was a demand for more. For Gibbings it was the turning point of his career. From now on writing was to be his main source of income, and in the meantime it helped to solve his pressing financial problems.

Cover of *Sweet Thames Run Softly* – see colour plate 8b.

Cover of Guild Books Service Edition of *Sweet Thames Run Softly* – see colour plate 8d. Another paperback edition was published by Guild Books in 1953 – see colour plate 8l.

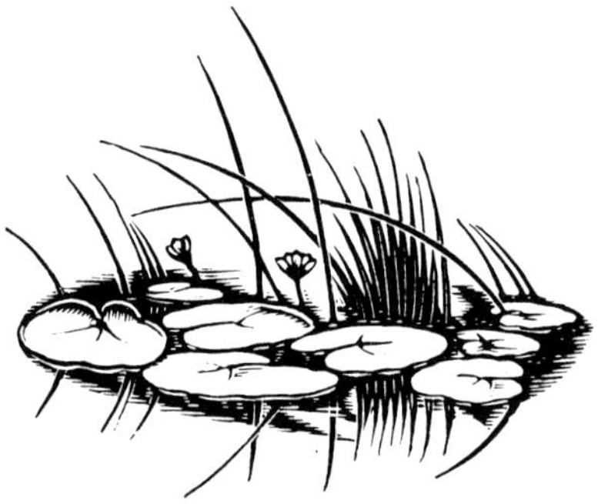

259 Illustration from *Sweet Thames Run Softly*, 1940, wood-engraving, 61 x 76 mm.

The realities of the war however were always present. In a letter to Hartman of 6 May 1941, Gibbings reported that 'There has been a good deal of thumping & window rattling & one day I actually saw the bombs leave a plane but they fell at least a mile away'.[24] Expressing his appreciation for America's support in the war, Gibbings was 'convinced that such evil as comes out of Germany cannot win in the end ...'. He recounted incidents which conveyed the attitude of the British people and had deeply impressed him. One of them was when he asked some of his students how they were going to spend their vacation and they had replied that they were going to London to relieve some of the shelter wardens — several were bombed out of their quarters more than once. Later in his letter he commented on the recent success of *Sweet Thames Run Softly*: 'It went into its 5th printing in under five months. Now I have fixed up with Duttons in New York & they are bringing out a U.S.A. edition in June.' The scale of his success, however, was not to be so great on the other side of the Atlantic. Dent had an arrangement with Dutton of New York to release books in America, but editions of *Sweet Thames Run Softly*, published in 1941 and 1945, only ran to 7000 copies.

But in Britain the book was received with acclaim and newspaper reviews were very positive: 'The narrative is exquisite, the illustrations are superb. "It's got everything"' was the comment from C. B. Rees of Allied Newspapers; 'For the soul's refreshment read and keep this book. It is wise, kindly, and full of lovely things' from *The Sunday Times*; 'A lovely, lingering, babbling, sparkling and endlessly refreshing book' from the *Manchester Evening News*. His friend Hugh Walpole was equally warm in his review for the *Daily Sketch*: 'It is a lovely book. Gibbings took a boat, sailed down the Thames, made drawings, and then wrote as he breathes, so naturally ... that it scarcely seems to be written at all'. Publicity for the book was widespread and the publication date was timed to meet the Christmas market — *Sweet Thames Run Softly* made an ideal present. A full page review in *The Times Literary Supplement* praised the 'splendid' engravings: 'The whole of the upper Thames is focused into the picture of a tall poplar on an island, summer days are put down in the lines of cows and elms and willows, and winter flood is concentrated into a picture a bare two inches square'. Generally the review was more restrained in its praise than some of the others, commenting on Gibbings's 'excursions and discursions' and that 'the Irishman in the author cannot resist an anecdote on any subject under heaven ...'.[25]

Sweet Thames Run Softly was by no means unique in its focus on the countryside and use of illustration. It was part of a genre that was generally enjoying popularity at the time. Writers such as Mary Webb with her story *Precious Bane* had established a market for 'countryside books' (an illustrated edition had been published in 1929). Publishers were quick to exploit the demand and Collins had published *A Wiltshire Village*, written and illustrated by Heather and Robin Tanner in 1939, and Victor Gollancz had had great success with *Country Matters* and other books written and illustrated with wood-engravings by Clare Leighton, in 1937. In the same year, and using the same format, Gollancz had also published *Down the River*, written by H. E. Bates, with eighty-three exquisite wood-engravings by Agnes Miller Parker.[26] This book covered very similar ground to that of *Sweet Thames Run Softly*, yet despite being of high quality and well received, did not achieve the popular success of Gibbings's book. These books were all large in format and were more like collector's books or 'coffee table' books in modern terms and perhaps this approach limited their market. *Sweet Thames Run Softly* was hardly bigger than the average novel and the style and tone of Gibbings's writing and the charismatic force of his personality that came through his words made his book accessible to a wide audience. However charmingly dated and curiously sentimental his prose style seems today, in the context of the times his writing had great appeal.

Gibbings was skilled at making the most of his material and before publication of *Sweet Thames Run Softly* he had contributed four articles to *The Listener*, based on notes and passages from his manuscript and illustrated by engravings he had already completed. An enlarged line-block taken from an engraving was used to illustrate the front cover of *The Listener* in February 1940.[27] Not only did this bring in useful income but it also added to the public interest and anticipation of his book. In the opening paragraph of one of these articles, 'Peace on the River', Gibbings expressed his feelings about the war which might also throw light onto why the book had such appeal — a reminder of the stability and indestructibility of nature was a comfort:

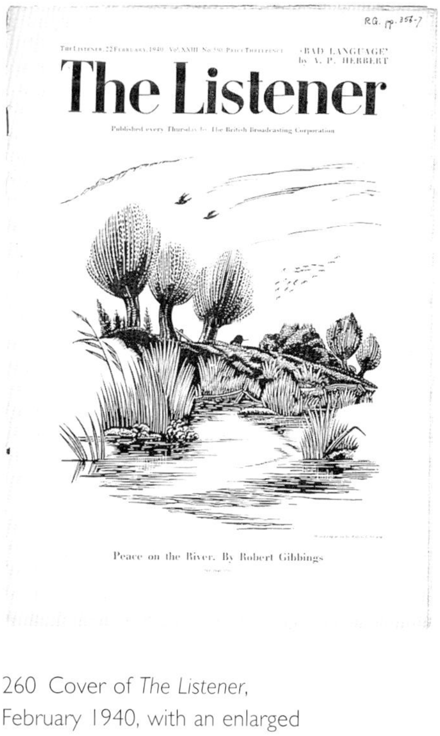

260 Cover of *The Listener*, February 1940, with an enlarged illustration of a wood-engraving by Gibbings from *Sweet Thames Run Softly*, 332 x 234 mm.

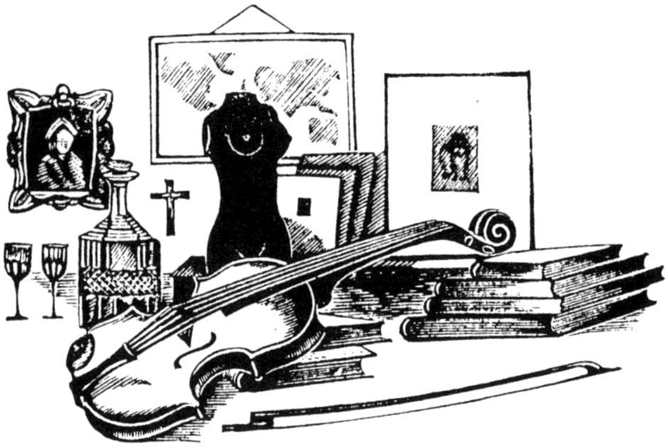

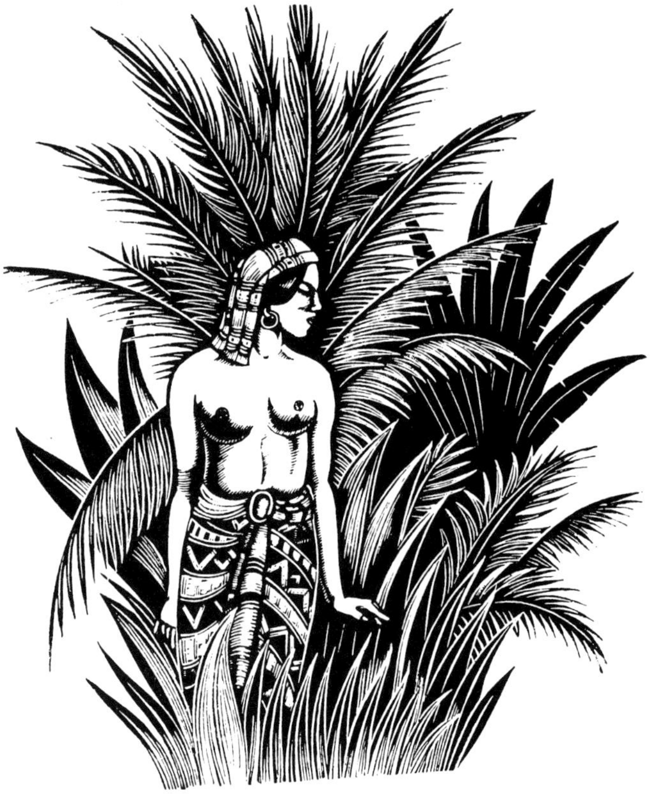

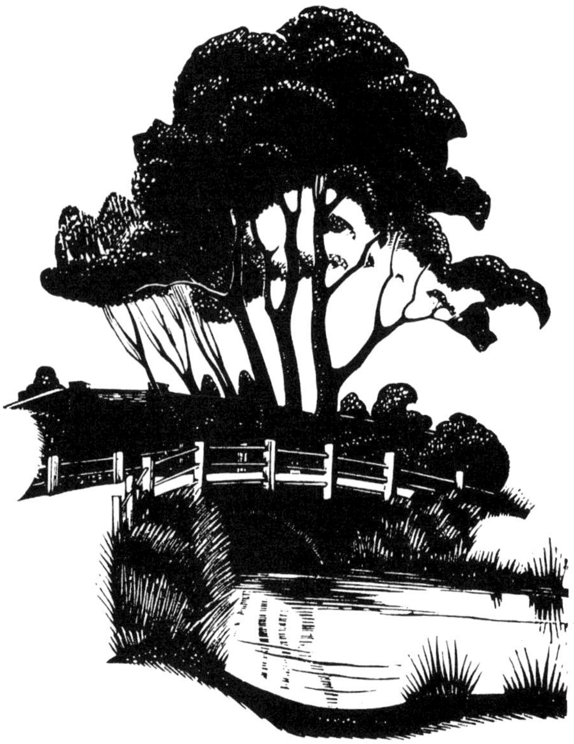

261 *top left* Illustration from *The Art of Living*, 1940, wood-engraving, 50 × 89 mm.

262 *left* Frontispiece from *A Summer on the Test*, 1941, 115 × 90 mm.

263 *above* Wood-engraving used on the title page of *Illusion in Java*, 1940, 104 × 85 mm.

In these times of anxiety it is perhaps refreshing to realise that if it is human folly which has brought about the present catastrophe, it is for the most part only human beings who are paying the price of this madness. The world of nature continues unaffected. Flowers still bloom, cattle graze and give their milk, birds sing, swallows and even butterflies continue their migrations, and rivers wind slowly towards the sea.[28]

Although preoccupied with writing his book, Gibbings still had time to take on a commission from the English Universities Press for twelve wood-engravings to illustrate a collection of essays entitled *The Art of Living* by André Maurois and seven engravings for an edition of *A Summer on the Test* by John Waller Hills for Hodder and Stoughton.[29] Dent had commissioned an engraving to decorate the title page of a book written by Gene Fowler entitled *Illusion in Java*. He also contributed an article to the *Sun Bathing Review*[30] and, rather unusually, an article on his underwater exploits entitled 'Fleet Street to Tahiti' for the 1940 *Penrose Annual* (a review of the graphic arts which more usually contained material of relevance to the printing industry).[31] The Carnegie Institute in Pittsburgh USA published an article by Gibbings on the English Society of Wood Engravers in an edition of their magazine to accompany an exhibition of the Society's work held there from May to August 1940.[32] Several blocks from *Sweet Thames Run Softly* were used for a series of postcards printed for Basil Blackwell by the print room at the University.

Ten engravings by Gibbings were used as decorations in the *Kynoch Press Note Book*, their diary for 1941. The blocks had originally been cut as illustrations for Kinglake's *Eothen: or Traces of Travel Brought Home from the East* (1844), the text of which was going to be used for a type specimen book produced by the Press. Unfortunately the project had been postponed because of the war but Gibbings's blocks were considered too good to remain unused and so were printed in the *Note Book*.

Gibbings seems to have had an almost tireless enthusiasm for new projects. In January 1941 he wrote to Allen Lane reporting that he had been in touch with Noel Carrington about one of his students illustrating a Puffin book and putting forward his own idea of a series of books focusing on particular places such as Malta and Abyssinia which were 'going to be red-hot news for some months to come. Malta is a scrumptious place with its harbours & medieval bastions & all the sort of places and bits of history that boys would adore to read about — crusaders firing Turk's heads as cannon balls etc.'[33] Gibbings even had authors in mind and a student to engrave the illustrations, but nothing came of the idea. A month later Gibbings wrote to Allen Lane with yet further suggestions; a Puffin on 'Deep Sea Monsters' and a book on tropical fish in the King Penguin series — Gibbings was yearning for his hut under the palms on Tahiti again! But in the same letter, Gibbings reported that he was busy on his next book, *Coming Down the Wye*. To build on the success he had had with *Sweet Thames Run Softly* and use the same formula for another book on a river was an obvious move and so Gibbings looked west to the Welsh border country for inspiration.

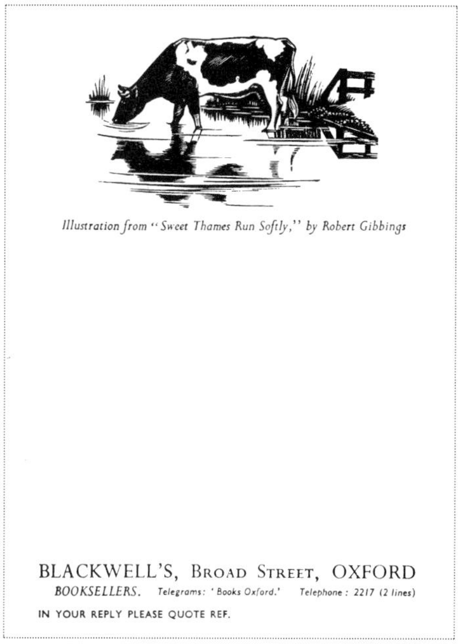

264 Postcard for Blackwell's bookshop of 50 Broad Street, Oxford, illustrated by a wood-engraving from *Sweet Thames Run Softly*, card size 140 x 102 mm.

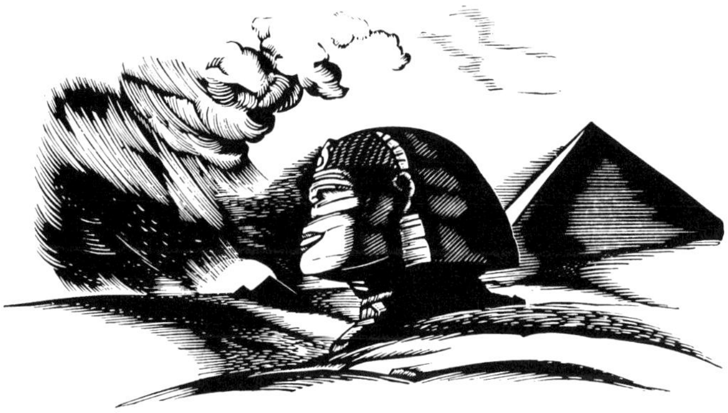

265 Illustration from the *Kynoch Press Note Book* for 1941, wood-engraving, 48 x 90 mm.

Chapter Fifteen
The Wye and the Lee 1941–1945

At the end of the summer term of 1940 Ian Crichton had volunteered for the RAF, and in March 1941 had been sent for initial training as a navigator at a camp in Aberystwyth. On the 28th of that month Gibbings travelled to Wales to spend a weekend with his friend and then spent the rest of the week in the National Library of Wales carrying out research into the river Wye. Crichton had hunted around the local garages earlier in the week and had found a 'Triumph "Gloria" which was on hire with driver at 6d a mile'.[1] Gibbings had expressed a desire to climb the mountain of Plynlimon to find the source of the river Wye. He had attempted the search in the previous winter but had been beaten back by a sudden blizzard; now in early spring he hoped to do better. The two men set out in their hired car the next morning. Gibbings later described their day together in the opening of his book, omitting all mention of Crichton's presence, and giving the impression that it was a solitary expedition, which suited the narrative. On this day the weather was kinder: '... diamond clear, with tufts of high white cloud throwing purple shadows over spur and combe ...'.[2] They drove to

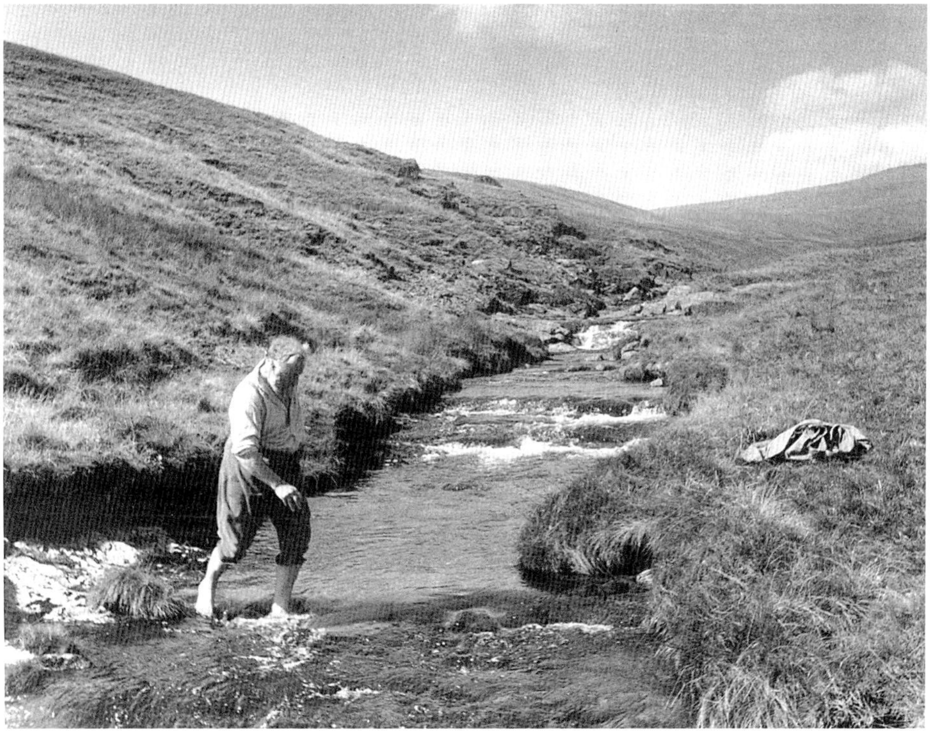

266 Gibbings crossing the river Wye near to its source on Plynlimon. This is one of a series of publicity photographs taken to illustrate an article on Gibbings published in *Picture Post*. RUL.

the highest point on the road to Llanidloes where it was less than three miles to the summit of the mountain. The climb was slow but not too arduous as the ground was good. Crichton recalled: 'As Gibbings weighs nearly twice my weight he does have to pick his way rather more carefully. Plynlimon is not an imposing hill because there are no steep crags & the surrounding ground is all high, but there are fine views ....' They must have made an incongruous couple as Crichton was notably tall and thin. After two hours they reached their goal; unlike the source of the Thames, the Wye had a fitting beginning:

> After a gentle murmuring underground the water welled up, brushing aside the young spring grass, to form a pool no bigger than a bowler hat. Then gently it glided between rich tussocks of moss and rushes still bent from their load of winter snow, until it tumbled like a shower of sequins over the black velvet of a peat face. The pool below this was wider and deeper, and with every yard of its flow the strength of the rivulet increased. Small streams from successive dells and dingles joined in, and so, between thick felts of sphagnum moss starred with cotton grass, and over rocks long since worn smooth, it frisked and dived towards its first main tributary a thousand feet below.[3]

On the summit they sat down and enjoyed a picnic lunch but then a north westerly wind blew up and it became bitterly cold; pausing to take in the magnificent view across to Cader Idris, they started their descent. The evening was spent in the convivial atmosphere of the hotel in which Gibbings had quickly become a popular guest. He insisted on paying for drinks and dinner: 'He has been most generous in all this entertaining .... His excuse was to celebrate the success of "Sweet Thames" and we have done that thoroughly.'

The journey down the Wye did not start in earnest until the summer vacation. In midsummer he returned to the source again:

> Then it was ecstasy, ecstasy unbelievable. I was one with the earth, one with the shale and the shingle washed clean by the winter springs. A warm wind swept over the hills, combing the short grasses, caressing everything it touched. I was alone, utterly alone, and for as long as I wished. A gull soaring in the valley was the only moving creature, a sheep bleating from the shadow of a rock the only sound except the wind, the wind in the grasses. ... And the great mountains heaved and swelled; and the river, a thin silver stream, sprang from gigantic thighs.[4]

From the source he set out on foot, whenever possible walking the towpath of the river. His first stop was the village of Llangurig and the hostelry, the Black Lion, where he immediately felt at home. Dai Rees was the landlord and Gibbings eventually dedicated his book to him, but he became equally fond of the local characters with their 'quick wits and kind faces', who frequented the bar. Although the final book reads as a continuous journey, in reality Gibbings used the Black Lion as a base for expeditions out into the hills. Writing to John Hadfield on 9 July he described his preparations: 'To-day I am sorting out luggage & boiling eggs & tomorrow I start for "the top" putting in a few hours with a fox shooting party en route. Shearing & hay making just beginning.' He had invited the Hadfields to join him for a few days at the pub: 'Do bring Anna because in Welsh mythology there's a lady in every lake & I need models if I'm to make the book a real success.'[5] The following week Gibbings was disappointed that the

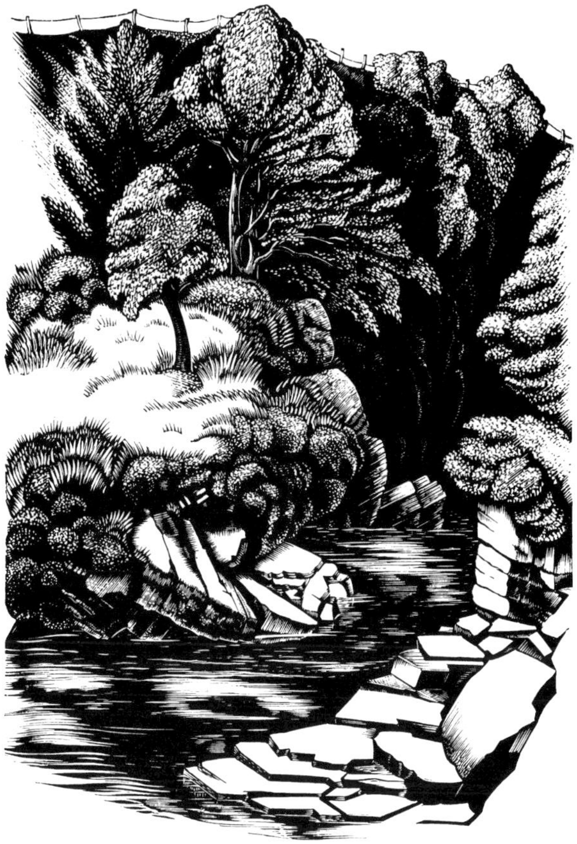

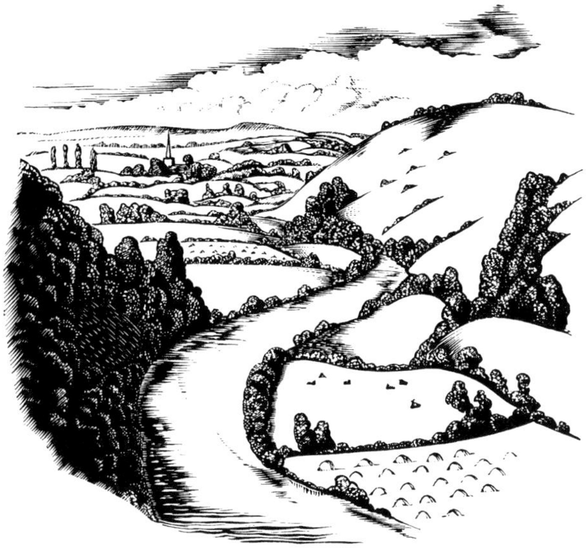

267 Illustration from *Coming Down the Wye*, 1942, wood-engraving, 158 × 108 mm.

268 Illustration from *Coming Down the Wye*, 1942, wood-engraving, 60 × 105 mm.

Hadfields were unable to get away but reported that he had spent a night on the top of Plynlimon:

It was so fine & clear at 10 pm that I didn't bother to put up my tent. It was the same at midnight but at 2 am I woke up to find everything soaked in fine rain. Next morning the mist was so thick I could hardly see my own feet & I had to slither down about 800 feet before I could see more than a few yards ahead of me. ... This afternoon am going poaching, tomorrow I'm haymaking. Have got half a dozen drawings & many pages of notes. Everyone very busy with shearing. I was just too late for the turf cutting. I expect to be here at The Black Lion for another week at least as it is an excellent centre from which to work.[6]

The poaching episode resulted in ten 'sizeable trout in two hours, nine of them tickled, one speared' — other anglers in the hotel were less successful:

It is really damn funny that a man with bare fists can do more in 10 minutes than another with £20 worth of Hardy's tackle in 10 hours. Don't for Gawd's sake say anything about this anywhere or I'll be destroyed for ever. I'll work it in tactfully in due course. It'll make a grand page of copy.[7]

In planning his journey that summer, Gibbings considered that the river Wye broke naturally into three sections:

... the first from its source to Boughrood, a few miles above Hay, where it is all the time a torrent tumbling joyously from the hills, whispering, sighing, singing in the shallows, tossing tumultuous at the falls, seething and swirling in the pools; the second where it winds calm and leisurely through the wide valley whose soil is red as the flesh of salmon;

the third after Goodrich when with accumulated energy it cuts its way through one majestic gorge after another until, finally, joining its sister the Severn, it gently merges into the sea.[8]

Until he reached just below Boughrood Gibbings had been able to walk 'the whole watercourse on foot', but then the weather deteriorated; rain and the fact that private boundaries impeded his way forced him to seek other paths and roads. Up to that point he had 'travelled slowly and sedately as any old heron, peering into rapids, pondering over pools, and straying but short distances from the river bank when it became necessary to seek the wherewithals of life'.[9] At Hay-on-Wye Gibbings had anticipated hiring a boat to row the rest of the river to the sea but unfortunately all the local boatyards only hired boats 'by the hour'. In the middle of August he booked into a hotel in Ross-on-Wye and wrote to Hadfield expressing his frustration:

I need a collapsible canoe & a non-collapsible girl. Can you supply both? ... I *must* get in touch with the water. It's no damn good walking a few fields & then doing a mile by road & then another field or two & so on. I have therefore decided that after reaching Monmouth in a weeks time I must go back to Hereford, find my canoe waiting for me & then do one really elegant chapter as a finale in which I rush down the whole way to Chepstow ....[10]

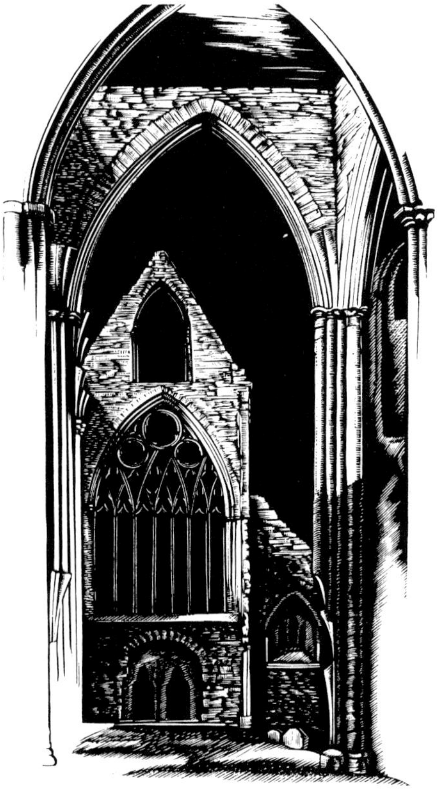

269 Tintern Abbey, 1942, wood-engraving, 126 × 72 mm. Illustration from *Coming Down the Wye*.

His scenario for the rest of the book was later to change and he was thwarted in his attempts to find a canoe. Despite letters to Gamages, Harrods and the Army & Navy stores he failed to find a supplier. Gibbings describes how in desperation he made a hurried visit to London to buy a collapsible canoe, but, much to his embarrassment, he was just too large to fit![11] He decided to stay in Ross-on-Wye for a few more days and then move on to the Royal Hotel in Symonds Yat. He was concerned that he '... must sustain this idea of being on & of the river & I must do a bit of sleeping by the stream which is impossible when I have to lug all my gear'.[12]

He confessed to Hadfield that 'My spirit is cracking & my clothes are giving out, I don't like hotels & I can't get near the river. Therefore I think seriously of coming back for a week's rest'.[13] Earlier in the summer he had visited Llangorse Lake and taken a boat out onto the water to investigate the legend of a drowned city; caught in a sudden squall, the effort of keeping the boat afloat had brought on lumbago — a medical problem which was to recur in the years to come. War regulations meant that it was not possible to transport a boat by rail and Gibbings did not feel fit enough to row against a flood current caused by the torrential rain. He therefore abandoned any idea of travelling by water.

Back at St Patrick's Hall in Reading, Gibbings wrote to Hadfield in September that he was in need of a 'complete holiday with no thought of work'. He had just returned from a 'few days hard work at Tintern'; the abbey had inspired him: 'The full harvest moon was clouded over but I waxed poetic the night before & I made a drawing the day after'.[14] According to his account in *Coming Down the Wye*, when he finally reached Chepstow and the sea the weather was changeable with sudden downpours. Cold and wet and in need of a stiff drink, he was relieved to book into his hotel. In the bar he met an acquaintance he had made in Llangurig who offered him a lift in his car back to the starting point of his trip. The next day, as the car pulled into the yard of the Black Lion at Llangurig, he was greeted by his drinking companions. In conversation Gibbings heard about a remote cottage that was to let beside a small lake, Marsh's Pool, at the foot of Plynlimon.

It belonged to Mrs Hugh Lewis and was mainly used by the brother of Eiluned Lewis, the writer and journalist on topics of the countryside, as a fishing cottage. Inaccessible by road, its beautiful location offered Gibbings all the peace and solitude he wished. At the end of November he wrote to Hadfield:

> ... I've found a cottage & if I can get it I'm going to be a Holy Hermit. It is over 1000 feet up in the mountains, by the edge of a scrumptious lake, surrounded by bog. ... If I can get it I'll go back next week & spend the six weeks vac there, ditto the 4 weeks at Easter & twelve in the summer. ... There'll be wild duck on the lake & snipe paddling round my door. There's a waterfall for the morning bath & a dingle for romance.[15]

The surrounding countryside of water, woods and hills was rich with a diversity of bird life and it was the ideal location for Gibbings to live once again with nature and study the changing seasons:

> The closer I am to nature the happier I am. I love to be alone with the winds that come up from the other side of the world, to be alone with these hills, some of the oldest on our planet. I like to feel the seasonal rhythm, to be conscious of the rising sap in spring, the maturing of the growth in summer, the tonic of the autumn, the sleep of winter.[16]

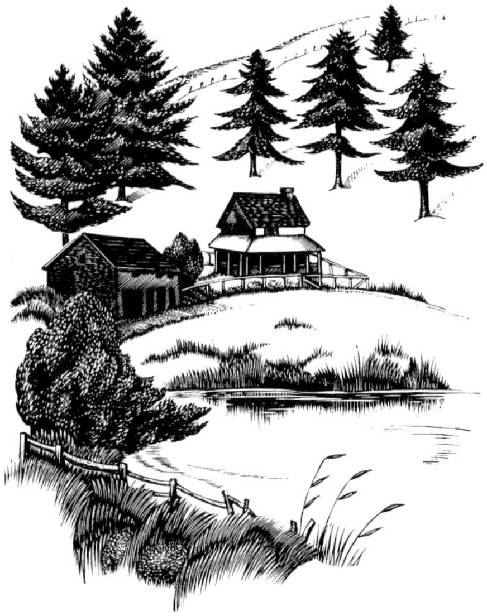

270 Cottage at Marsh's Pool, Plynlimon, 1942, wood-engraving, 126 x 104 mm. Illustration from *Coming Down the Wye*. The cottage was Gibbings's base while working on his book.

Gibbings respected Hadfield's editorial advice and at the end of November had sent him draft chapters for comment: 'I now send you some more great literature .... Looking at it with a fresh eye I can see that it needs the hell of a lot of adjustment but if you regard it, as I do, as a collection of material to be licked into shape, amplified & polished you will not be as disappointed as I was when I saw it in typescript.'[17] On 29 November he wrote again announcing to Hadfield that he had secured the cottage at a rent of 'Ten quid per year'. He had also been working on how to manipulate the story and structure of the book. He had decided to divide it into two parts; the river and the lake:

> The river starts off, as you know ... & I think I can keep it fairly interesting for say 50,000 but after Chepstow I am going to get fed up, as I was, with tea shops & char-a-bancs & I will bolt back to Llangurig where I find the cottage waiting for me. In between dawns dusks middays midnights hail rain sunshine mist & solitude there will be the human side of life in those hills ....[18]

Although the cottage was very remote, Gibbings soon made friends with his distant neighbours on the other side of the mountain. The local community were welcoming and, in the spirit of survival in the tough conditions of the mountains, were anxious to help: 'Is it the loan of the horses to fetch a load of coal from the town four miles away? Is it a bit of wire for the fence? Is it a few boards to make bookshelves? Why, to be sure! Aren't we neighbours now?'[19] His possessions were transported as close to the cottage as possible on a neighbour's wagon driven by his friend Cobbler, the postman and village odd-job man who had appointed himself Robert's personal attendant — the car he was using had

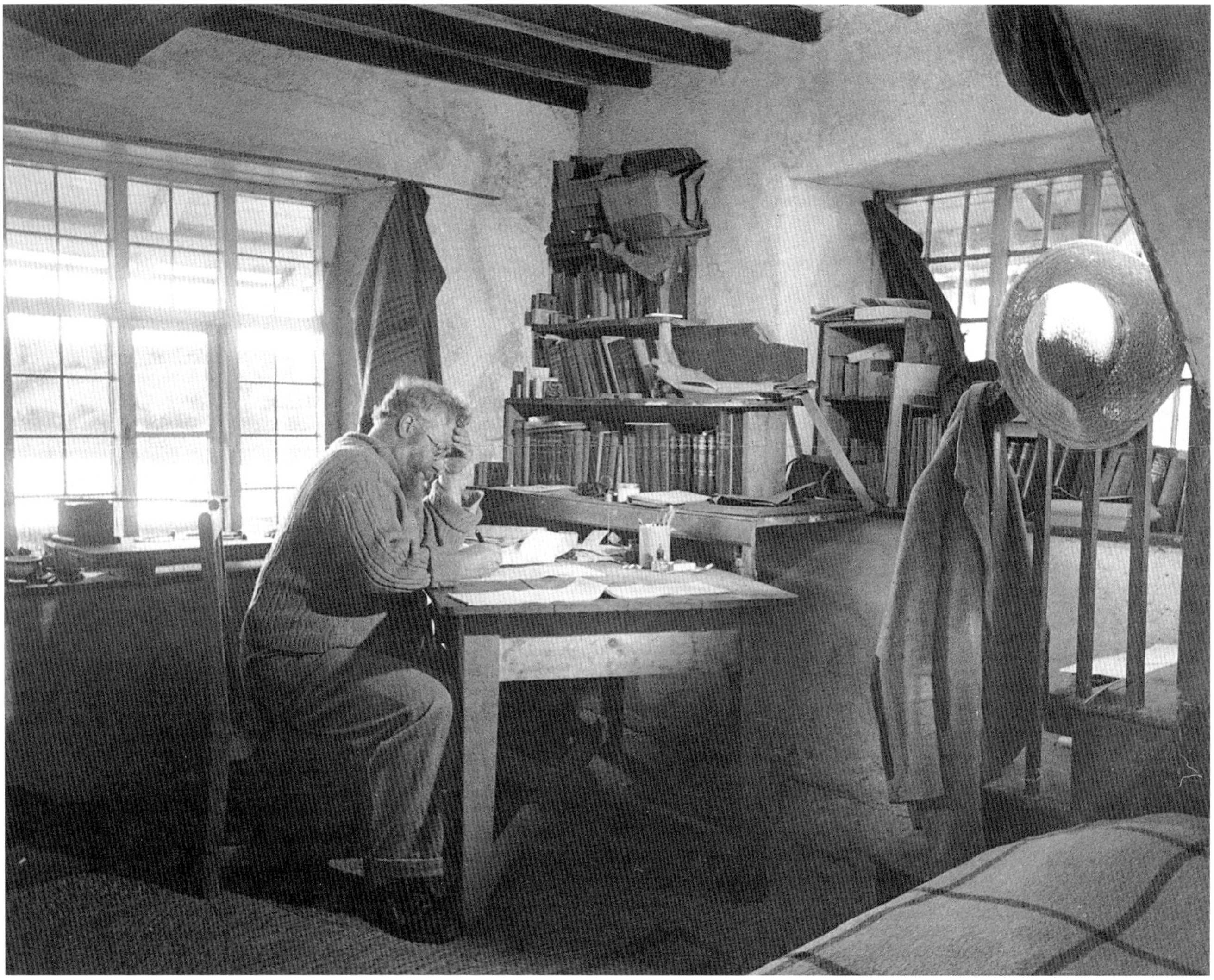

271 Gibbings writing up his notes in the cottage at Marsh's Pool. This photograph was published as an illustration to an article on Gibbings in *Picture Post*. RUL.

become stuck in mud! Gibbings also very quickly became a popular 'regular' at the bar of the local pub, where as usual he captivated his audience with his own stories but also listened intensely to theirs — gathering ideas for his book.

Gibbings was happy here and he was in love with the place — it was special. On his first evening there, after rain had cleared, he contemplated the sunset:

> I watched the sun drop behind lavender clouds in a saffron sky. The rushes were still; even the old dried thistle stalks did not quiver. A heron honked. A crow called 'kr-raw kr-raw,' another answered 'ke-way ke-way.' A magpie cackled. A blackbird's last notes came down the hill. The day was done. Owls would soon be stirring. Foxes would be sniffing the scents that hang heavy in the night air. Indoors there was only the sound of the fire. I closed my eyes and listened to its music. It seemed to me then that I had come through a curtain of rain into a land of faerie ....[20]

Gibbings stayed in the cottage over the Christmas vacation to experience the winter months: 'At twelve hundred feet above sea-level, in winter, when the lake is silver with ice and the red bogs dusted with snow ... it may be picturesque, but it is cold. ... When there is snow the hills are like the flanks of some great

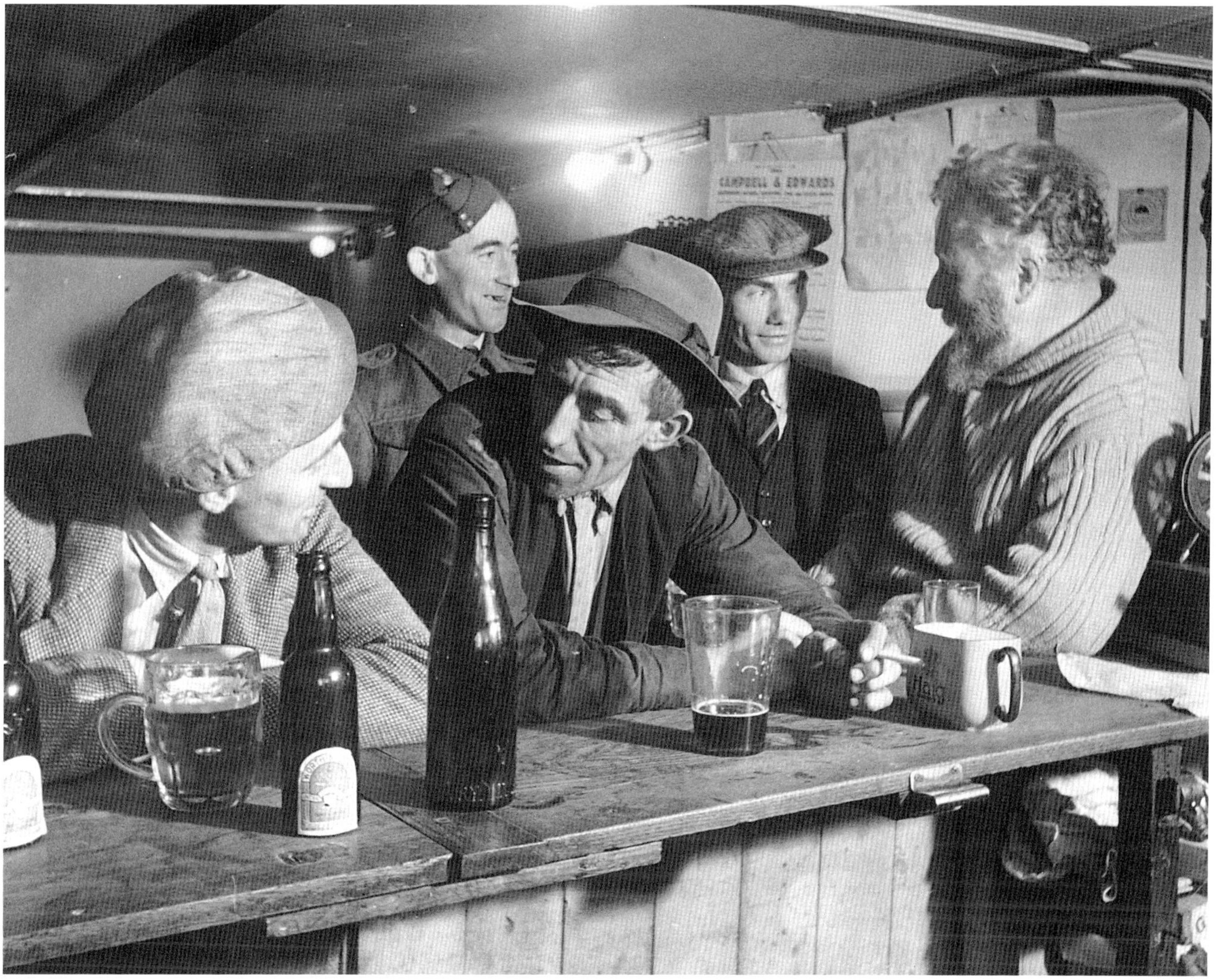

272 Gibbings chatting with the locals in the bar at the Black Lion at Llangurig. This photograph was published as an illustration to an article on Gibbings in *Picture Post*. RUL.

polar bear, and the fox and the hare leave their tracks for all to follow ....'[21] Despite the severe conditions Gibbings wrote to Hadfield:

For Heaven's sake sell all that you have & come & live with the poor. This is the most staggering entrancing spot you could think of in your wildest dreams. As I wrote those words, six goosanders swam along the near side of the lake. After diving one of them had difficulty with a big fish & had to sit up straight on his tail & flap his wings violently before he got it down. ... Now a heron has come along & is scratching his chin. There's a frame of glass out of the window so I can watch in comfort through my glasses.[22]

Writing again a few days later he was 'fair dizzily drunk with delight & I haven't moved 100 yards from the cottage barring ½ a mile for a bottle of milk. ... I can't do any work — because I can't take my nose from the window'.[23]

Solitude was what attracted Gibbings to the place, seeking the peace it brought: 'And so I lived for a time, grudging each moment when a fellow human drew near, counting only those moments happy when I was alone, until the last day of the year.' That New Year's Eve farmers and shepherds with their wives and daughters came and sat around his fire and sang song after song in their native

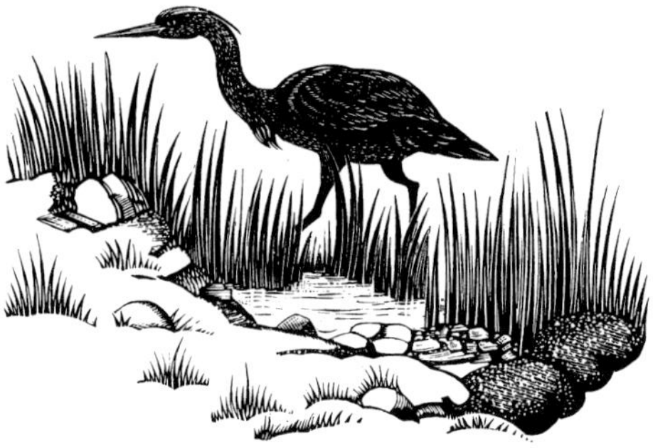

273 A heron, 1942, wood-engraving, 68 × 104 mm. Illustration from *Coming Down the Wye*.

tongue: 'Then I realized that they were born of the same soil as the reeds and the rushes, and that their voices were the spirits of the wind and the rain and the sun that shines golden on the snow. Then I realized too that I need no longer be alone or lonely ....'[24]

But even in his isolation the everyday problems in life had to be faced. Robert and Moira had kept in touch with the occasional letter concerning practical issues but their correspondence was short and curt and often bitter in tone with accusations and implied insults. In June 1941 Moira was complaining that some maintenance cheques had gone astray — Gibbings replied that it was '... entirely due to war conditions as the bank has had instructions for some considerable time to send you a cheque at the end of each month'.[25] But their personal squabbles were overshadowed by their mutual concern about their eldest son. Patrick had been to naval college and, following Robert's brother Maurice, had joined up with the Royal Navy. During his active service he had suffered a problem with his ears which had been affected by the noise of the guns and Robert's concern had led him to arrange a consultation with a Wimpole Street specialist. Patrick had also recently suffered a narrow escape; the day he had left on leave, two bombs had hit his ship, killing eleven seamen and wounding fifteen more. Perhaps their mutual relief at their son's escape gave the couple a new perspective because in December 1941 a letter from Robert to Moira suggests some degree of reconciliation:

> I was awfully glad to get your letter of Nov. 3rd. yesterday. It was good of you to say what you did. No, don't let us wipe out *all* the past but just the unpleasant bits, then we will have some pleasant memories.
>
> The fact is that we are all drawn by forces far stronger than ourselves. Thank you again and again for your letter.[26]

The letter continued with a reference to Gibbings sending out sums of money for his children's Christmas presents — he had left arrangements rather late because in the middle of term he had been in hospital to have his tonsils out after suffering for some time with sore throats. But his good news was that he had now resolved his financial problems: 'With your letter yesterday came one from my publisher saying that my book "Sweet Thames Run Softly" continues to sell ... I am at last seeing my way out of the financial mess in which I was neck deep for some years ....'

He was able to increase his maintenance allowance and felt he could sustain the payment at that level for the foreseeable future. He also told Moira of the cottage and his new book: 'I hope to spend Easter & summer here too as the country is wild & there's a lake right in front of the cottage with wild duck, herons etc. which I can watch & draw. It is the kind of life that gives me greatest happiness.' The letter closed with a poignant reminder that he had lost touch with his first family: '... drop me a line sometime and tell me how you are, let me know too what the children are doing & what the boys are going to be — forgive me if I seem to intrude'.

But at the end of the vacation Gibbings had to return to start a new term in Reading: 'For ten weeks I was away from the Wye. I walked the cloisters, and wore a gown at dinner. Then, at last, towards the end of March, I got my collar off in the hills.'[27] He returned in the spring and also for the summer vacation of 1942. For the summer months Gibbings decided he needed a horse or pony for transport: '... a nice quiet old horse that I can ride, one that will stand still if I want to watch a bird, one that will mind its steps if I want to look at the country'.[28] A suitable pony was found, called Betty, and he spent the next weeks roaming the hills in the saddle. Betty proved to be steady, patient and strong but one day she was startled by some flapping white drawers on a washing line beside the road — Robert was thrown and concussed. He was taken to a local hospital with a broken rib and a dislocated shoulder. He stayed a fortnight, enjoying the luxury of a warm bed, regular hot meals served on trays and being clean, before returning to the basic and rather spartan conditions in the cottage — with no electricity or running water. For the remaining weeks of his stay he continued to explore with Betty, collecting material and working on his engravings and manuscript. That a well known author and artist was living in the hills soon became the subject of local gossip, and, apart from the welcome he gave to neighbours, unwanted visitors began to be a problem. His landlord and friend told his sister Eiluned Lewis what happened when the locals heard about Gibbings:

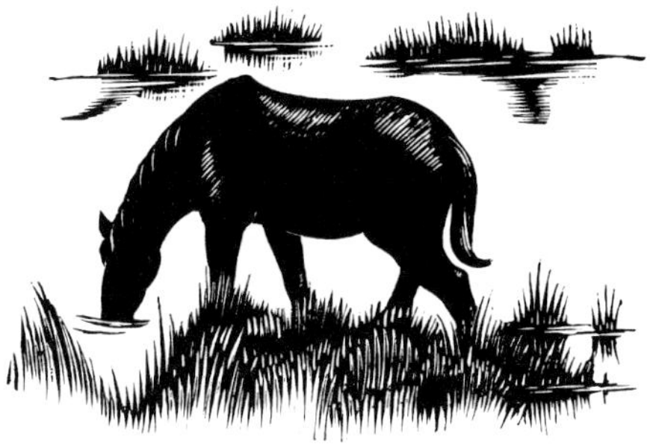

274 Gibbings's pony which he called Betty, 1942, wood-engraving, 48 x 64 mm. Illustration from *Coming Down the Wye*.

> ... they came on foot from farms and cottages, crossing the whaleback hills and bogs to stare through uncurtained windows in rapt admiration at the great man writing by candle-light at his table. The hospitable Gibbings, knowing how far they had travelled, would ask them in for a drink. Finally the situation became impossible. He had to abandon cottage, lake and mountain and return to England.[29]

This is probably an exaggeration of the situation but clearly public interest was beginning to intrude. Maintaining his tenancy, Gibbings had to return to the University for the autumn term. The next few months were spent putting the final touches to the text and engravings and working on the paste-up of the book.

This time most of the manuscript had been typed by Patience, Elisabeth's sister. Patience was at that time employed as a secretary and administrator on a research project at the Wingfield-Morris Orthopaedic Hospital in Oxford. Knowing of her considerable abilities in this capacity, Robert had asked her to help out with his book and sent portions of his rather messy scripts written in his scrawny handwriting to her home, Box Farm. Patience became extremely adept at sorting out Gibbings's manuscripts, using her own meticulous knowledge and standards of grammar and style. On more than one occasion Patience stayed with Robert in the cottage at Marsh's Pool for a weekend, sleeping on a camp bed in the attic bedroom, while Robert slept on a bunk downstairs. She rather enjoyed the spartan life, happy to rough it in basic conditions. One day Robert wanted to concentrate peacefully on his writing and suggested to Patience that she go to the other side of the lake and draw the cottage in its surroundings; Patience had some artistic ability and Gibbings later adapted her drawing for one of the engravings in the book. She even suffered crawling around measuring and copying the exact pattern of the beautiful cobbled floor on which Gibbings then based an

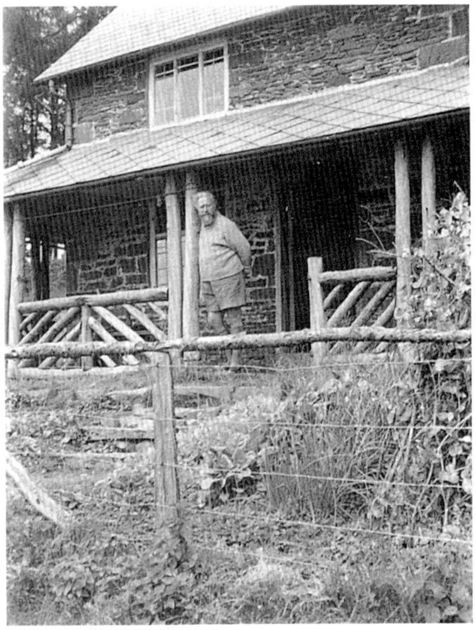

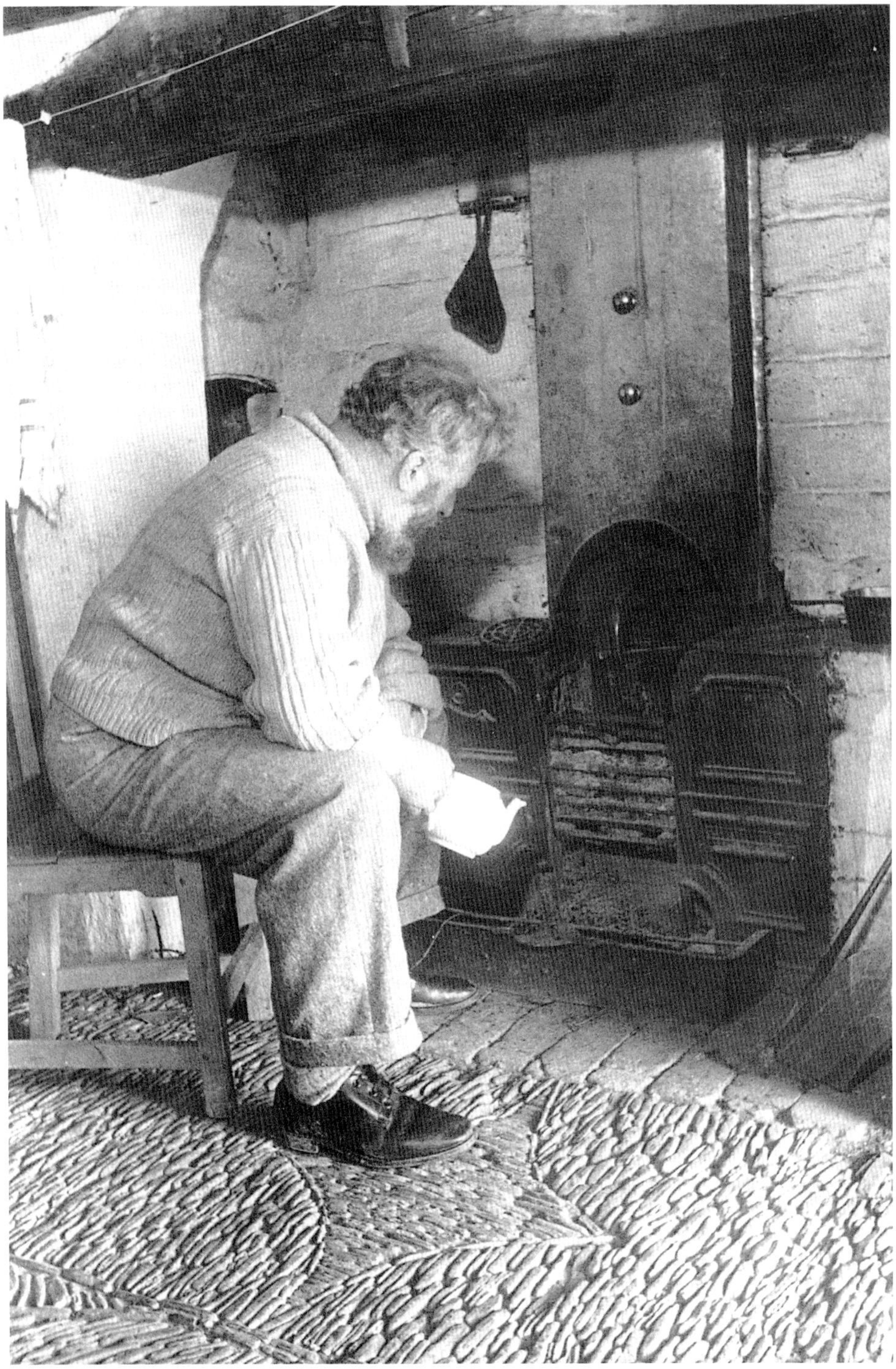

275 *above* Gibbings outside his cottage at Marsh's Pool. RUL.

276 *right* Gibbings by the kitchen range in his cottage at Marsh's Pool. The cobbled floor became the subject of an engraving and featured in *Coming Down the Wye*. RUL.

engraving. Gibbings greatly appreciated her assistance and their friendship increased.

Gibbings completed fifty-nine wood-engravings and three maps as illustrations for *Coming Down the Wye*, which Dent published on 3 December 1942 in a first edition of 11,000 copies. Following the pattern of *Sweet Thames Run Softly*, it was reprinted twice in the next year and three more times by 1955. Again there were large editions for the Readers Union in 1943 and for W. & G. Foyle's Travel Book

Cover of *Coming Down the Wye* – see colour plate 8c.

Club in 1946. Dutton published an American edition in September 1943 but, despite reprints in December 1943 and October 1945, sales were only modest in comparison with Britain.

The ingredients were much the same as for *Sweet Thames Run Softly* and the formula worked once more. Critical comment was just as appreciative; *The Times Literary Supplement* commented: 'Mr. Gibbings has with rare understanding captured the essence of this haunted, nostalgic country. It is richly illustrated with his own wood-engravings, which catch to perfection the inner spirit of their text.'

In the acknowledgements at the beginning of *Coming Down the Wye* Gibbings ended by mentioning the University: '... and to my colleagues at Reading University I say Hail! even as at this same moment I say Farewell.' The success of his first two river books had been sufficient for Gibbings to contemplate making a living from writing alone, without the obligations and duties of his University post. He resigned and, giving up a steady income, took a gamble that he could repeat his success. He now had time and freedom to concentrate on his writing and wood-engraving and go wherever his inspiration took him. But he had taken on a new pressure — he now depended on producing books regularly to maintain his income and support two families as well as finance his travels.

BY THE END OF DECEMBER 1942 Gibbings had decided on the subject for his next book and in a letter to Mary O'Sullivan he outlined his plans:

> A line in haste as I'm in the middle of packing for Ireland. I'm going over in a few days to do my next book on 'The Ould Country'. I've left the University in order to get more time for writing. My book 'Coming Down the Wye' has been a great success even better than the Thames. I'll probably go to Cork first & then on to Kerry & up to Clare & Galway. ... What fun it will be walking the roads of Ireland again.[30]

He had been pleased to hear that his godchild was getting on well and reported to Mary that Patrick was now a Sub-Lieutenant in the RNVR and was out in the Indian Ocean. During a visit to South Africa, Patrick had visited his mother and the rest of his family and reported that all were well; news had also come from Canada that his second family were 'getting on grand too'.

Gibbings was to spend most of the next year roaming around Ireland gathering material. The account of his travels that was finally published shows he rearranged the order in which he visited parts of Ireland, starting out in Galway and finishing in Cork. But it is difficult to be certain about the true sequence as Gibbings felt at liberty to change events if it suited his narrative purpose; his books were clearly based on autobiography but they also had elements of creative reinvention.

Crossing to Dublin and then taking the train to Galway via Mullinga, he booked into the Royal Hotel; within minutes he was in the bar being bought a drink and engaging in conversation with a local who was deep in thought: 'His elbows rested on the counter and his chin was sunk in his fists. ... He seemed to be weighed down with some great mental problem. ... "I'm a man of few words. Tell me, in one sentence, in one sentence only, what's wrong with the world?"'[31]

And so Gibbings began his stay in Ireland. He felt he was at home; everywhere he went he received warm hospitality from the people, especially ordinary working folk for whom he had such respect and affection. After so many years away and having travelled around the world, he was exhilarated to be back in the land of his birth, re-discovering the landscape and culture that he held so dear. For the reader there is perhaps a feeling of Robert's almost obsessive desire to identify with the Irish way of life; in truth Gibbings was an Anglo-Irish exile and in England he spoke with only a soft Irish lilt to his voice — in Ireland his accent became much stronger. But he seems to have been readily accepted by the Irish and he was very anxious to recount how he was continually recognised by family friends and acquaintances.

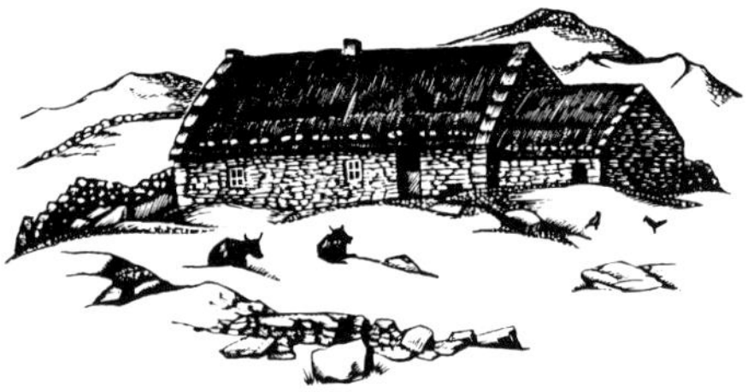

277 Illustration from *Lovely is the Lee*, 1945, wood-engraving, 37 x 75 mm.

From his base in Galway, for some months Gibbings explored the surrounding countryside, visiting Connemara and taking a bus to towns and villages such as Ballynahown, on the south coast, to Clifden and Ballyconneely in the west and further south to Ennis in County Clare. From there he visited Spanish Point on the coast where his aunt owned a holiday cottage and where Gibbings had taken his own family for a holiday, renting a 'lodge' nearby, and joining his aunt and cousin Kathleen at Maam Cross and Glendalough among the mountains, for a few weeks together in the summer.

An invitation from Patrick Flannery of Ballinrobe, a small town on the banks of the river Robe which flows into the nearby waters of Lough Mask, and the offer of a boat, tempted Gibbings to leave Galway and take the bus north. Patrick Flannery had arranged rooms for him at the local Moran's Hotel and Gibbings was to spend the next six weeks there. He had not met Flannery previously but had corresponded with him and Flannery had told Gibbings one of the stories he had used in *Sweet Thames Run Softly*.

The men soon became friends and together they walked the landscape and the ancient archaeological sites in the area. Gibbings also visited some of the many islands in Lough Mask, fascinated by the historical tales and legends that are associated with them, and wandered over the ruins of early monasteries, chapels and castles. They spent quiet moments too, afloat on the waters of the Lough: 'That evening Lough Mask was without a ripple. Land and water were drowned in light. Save for the splashing of mergansers in the distant creek, the water was unbroken. We took the oars into the boat. Flannery lit his pipe. We sat without talking, watching.'[32]

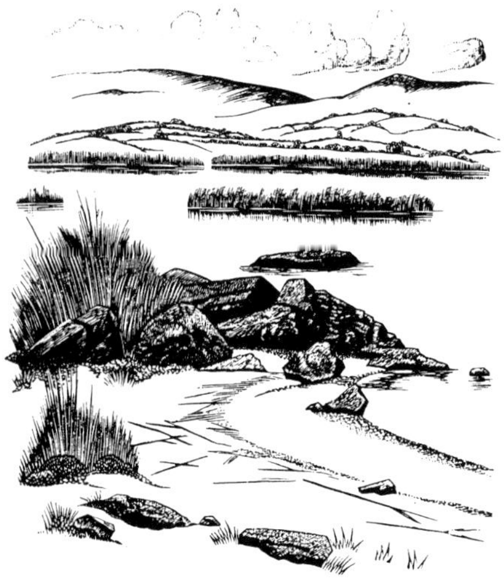

278 View across Lough Carra, 1945, wood-engraving, 112 x 102 mm. Illustration from *Lovely is the Lee*.

In the middle of May he took advantage of an offer from another friend, Robert Ruttledge, of the freedom of his boat and island in Lough Carra. Ruttledge had an isolated house on the island, but Gibbings preferred the solitude of living under canvas and being in the open air. Here he absorbed nature around him but also investigated a nearby island which appeared to be man-made; on closer inspection it proved to be a 'crannog' or artificial island created for the dwellings of the early Christian inhabitants of the area. He organised his own archaeological dig, assisted by Ruttledge's children and a local farm worker — much to their excitement they found some early worked timbers, nails and bones which were sent to the National Museum for identification. He visited other islands on Lough Carra and Castle Bourke, standing on the mainland at the head of the lake, imagining the life of the inhabitants. From Lough Carra he ventured out to sea and, on the recommendation of a local doctor who knew his family, he visited the island of Inishbofin, four miles off the coast of Galway. For four days his crossing to the island was prevented by storms and he stayed in a hotel in Clifden, taking trips into the hills of Connemara to do some bird-watching. The crossing to Bofin proved to be a very rough one and Gibbings was marooned on the island for some weeks. Cut off from the mainland by storms, Gibbings stayed in the Priest's house on the island with the doctor who had accompanied him. A monastery had been founded on the island by St Colman, who had left the Abbey of Lindisfarne after a disagreement in AD 664. Tradition has it that students once flocked to Bofin to learn the arts of calligraphy and illumination; Gibbings visited the remains of the monastery building, now covered by nettles. When the seas were calmer, he ventured out with the doctor and some islanders in a sailing boat to do some fishing. Gibbings's passion for boats comes across in his account: 'The spray strikes one's eyes. It is salt on one's lips. The water around is black. White flecks of foam pass to leeward. We dip into a trough and almost lose way as we rise to the next wave. ... The sail flaps. I let her head away and again she is sailing.'[33]

His friend from Lough Carra, Robert Ruttledge, joined Gibbings on Bofin. Also a keen ornithologist, he was in search of 'Leach's fork-tailed petrels', thought to be nesting on the island. Their search for the birds led them to cross to the neighbouring island of Inishshark and to spend a night on High Island, much to the dismay of the locals who believed it to be haunted! Leaving his companions, Gibbings next visited the Aran Islands. He wanted to see the ancient ruined forts on the islands, and in particular Dun Aenghus, which he considered 'the most magnificent barbaric monument in Europe'. Ancient churches, round towers, Celtic high crosses and holy wells were also objects that fascinated Gibbings and were to be found in abundance on the islands. From Aran he had been rowed to the islands of Inishmaan and Inisheer in a traditional local boat, the curragh.

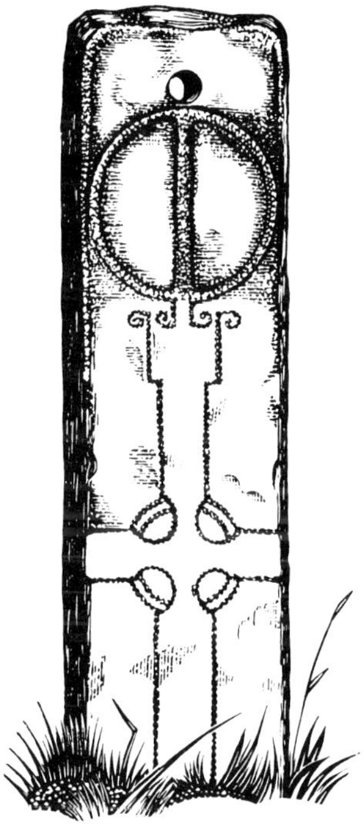

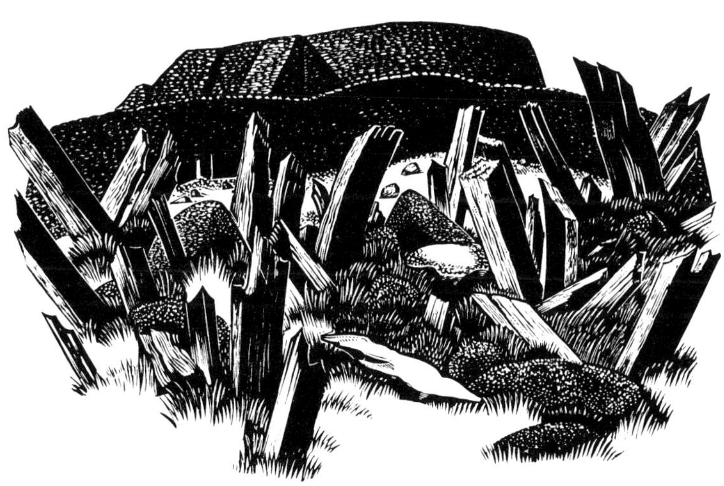

279 *left* The ancient fort of Dun Aenghus on one of the Aran Islands, 1945, wood-engraving, 60 × 95 mm. Illustration from *Lovely is the Lee*.

280 *above* Celtic cross on Inishmore, one of the Aran Islands, 1945, wood-engraving, 90 × 40 mm. Illustration from *Lovely is the Lee.*

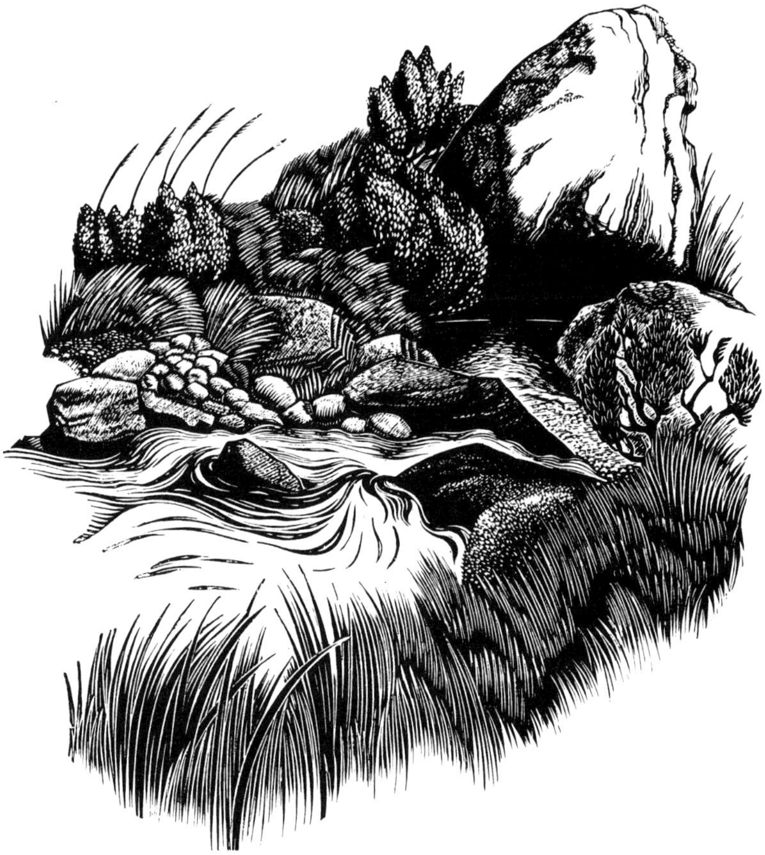

281 Illustration from *Lovely is the Lee*, 1945, wood-engraving, 110 x 103 mm.

Back in Galway Gibbings went to 'The Races'. The town was packed with people; for this special event crowds arrived daily from Dublin, Limerick, from Cork and all over Ireland. Before long Gibbings had been recognised by friends and acquaintances from his home city of Cork and the village of Carrigrohane where he had grown up. Moved by reports that, knowing he was in Ireland, his friends had all been asking after him, the pull of his beloved city was too much: 'Don't say another word,' he said, 'I'm going back tomorrow.'[34]

Gibbings's views on Cork were simple and biased:

> Cork is the loveliest city in the world. Anybody who doesn't agree with me either was not born there or is prejudiced. The streets are wide, the quays are clean, the bridges are noble. Two wide channels of the river reflect the glittering limestone buildings. … It is such a friendly city, too. People that you have never met in your life stop you in the street to say that they knew a relation of yours.[35]

From Cork, Gibbings returned to the familiar haunts of his youth and the valley of the river Lee. Naturally this prompted him to recall and note down stories about the characters and places he had known as a child and memories of his family and home life. For three miles above Cork the river ran slow and smooth: 'Pleasant meadows border the stream, meadows in a wide valley …. There are no man-made barriers in the fields beside the Lee. … You can walk the full length of the river without seeing a notice board.' Above Carrigrohane the river is narrower and more lively: 'There is a sprightliness, a spring-like gaiety in its flow.'[36] Exploring a tributary, the Shournagh, Gibbings visited the famous Blarney Castle on its banks. Continuing his journey upstream, he described the changing nature of the landscape and the character of the river, passing many bridges, castles and standing stones, each with a significant story attached. In early September he visited Inchigeela where the country changed abruptly: 'No longer the swift river among broad meadows; now it is wide lakes and wild moorland, with crowded mountain peaks on all horizons.'[37] Yet further upstream, at Ballingeary, the river altered again: 'The wide-spreading lakes have gone. Now it is a mountain torrent, cascading over natural weirs, sluicing under rocks, lingering a moment, then whirling on again. On all sides boulder-strewn moor, heather and gorse, holly, rowan, and birch, royal ferns, meadow-sweet, and broom.'[38]

Five miles above Ballingeary is Gougane Barra, a lake surrounded by mountains and a place that had a deep attraction for Gibbings, and here his exploration of the Lee ended:

> Gougane Barra, a valley withdrawn, a garden enclosed, the holiest place I know. Here, by this quiet pool, where, for a thousand years, tired souls have prayed, there is the peace that passes understanding. Mountains on all sides rise twelve hundred feet above the lake, forming a vast amphitheatre whose floor is silver. Small emerald fields dot the margin of the lake. Above them gigantic boulders split from the purple hills pile high. Above those boulders cliff upon cliff.[39]

For much of his remaining time in Ireland Gibbings stayed in a hotel run by the Cronins on the shores of the lake — he was already a familiar guest and had dedicated his book *Rummy* to the owners. In fact there were two hotels run by two brothers and Gibbings knew them both well: 'Sometimes of an evening I sit in Connie's kitchen, sometimes I visit Denny's.'[40] Gibbings was welcomed into this remote community and it was to provide rich material for his book. He was so content with life in the valley that his stay stretched on: 'The weeks since I

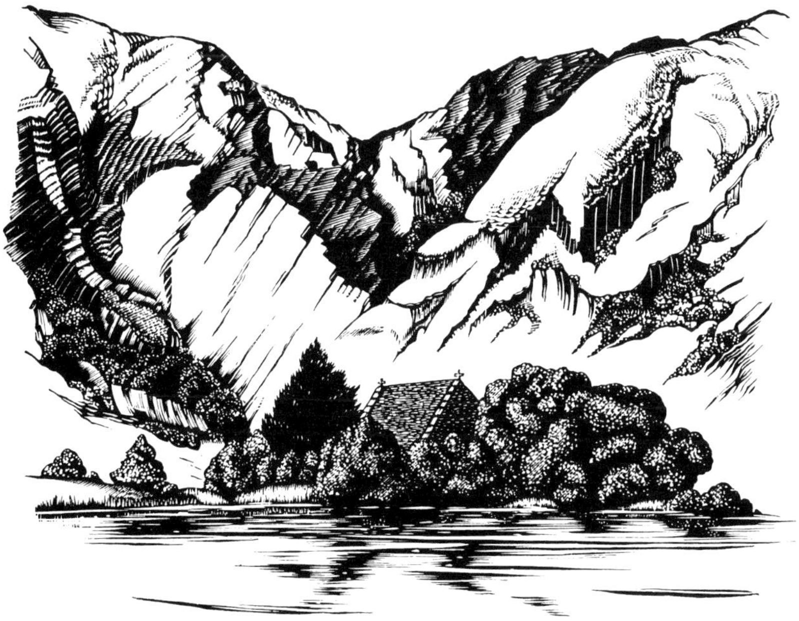

282 The lake at Gougane Barra, 1945, wood-engraving, 80 x 108 mm. Illustration from *Lovely is the Lee.*

reached Gougane had run into months and now the months began to look as though they might soon be a year.'[41] Reluctantly Gibbings recognised that he would have to leave. A farewell party was arranged and the next day as he left both brothers offered him a home; Denny promised 'Come back as soon as you can and I'll give you an acre of land over-right the river, and you can build away as grand a house as ever you like.'[42] After over a year gathering material in Ireland he now returned to The Orchard at Waltham to work in earnest on his manuscript and engravings.

Patience typed out numerous drafts, which Robert worked on, adapting and rearranging his material and checking on detail. His books give the impression that he always travelled alone and that his journeys and explorations were for long, unbroken periods. The reality was that even while gathering material in Ireland, Gibbings had frequently returned to England for short breaks. Sometimes it was to give a lecture or for a business meeting with his agent and publishers, other times it was just to have a quiet retreat and a chance to regain his energy. Friends frequently joined him, particularly when he was at Marsh's Pool, but these visits are never mentioned in his books or allowed to interrupt the flow of his narrative.

Cover of *Coconut Island* – see colour plate 8g.

Even in such a remote place as Gougane Barra, Gibbings had not been totally cut off from life back in England. Penguin had decided to publish an edition of *Coconut Island* in their Puffin Story Book series. Negotiations had begun early in 1944 and on 18 February Gibbings replied to a letter from Eunice Frost, Allen Lane's personal assistant:

> I was delighted to hear from you but unfortunately I only got your letter when I got back here yesterday after 3 weeks in the wilds. Now I am packing up with the idea of returning to England early in March .... When I get back it is going to be pretty hectic for a few weeks ....[43]

Eunice Frost had asked Gibbings to engrave a new block as an image for the cover of their edition, but Gibbings suggested using an existing block from the book as he was going to be too busy on his return. Not knowing what address to give, Gibbings suggested that Frost should write to him care of Box Farm. Gibbings ended the letter by pointing out how much publicity he had given to *Blue Angels and Whales* through public talks — clearly hinting that a reprint might be necessary:

> And by the way I continue to give endless publicity to *Blue Angels and Whales* & it's all on barren grounds. I must have given at least 100 lantern lectures on the subject during the past couple of years & with an average of a couple of hundred, no with *at least* a couple of hundred in each audience (there were about 700 at the Royal Dublin Soc. last Dec.) there should surely be half a dozen to buy copies of the reprint. I'm not sure the time hasn't come for a "fine edition".

Gibbings's public profile as an author was given a timely boost when a month or so before the publication of *Lovely is the Lee*, as his new book was to be called, a four page feature article on his writing and engraving appeared in *Picture Post*. The article was called 'A man of hills and rivers', and was written by his friend John Hadfield, who, as a past editor for Dent, had commissioned *Sweet Thames Run Softly*.

The article summarised his career as an author to date and concentrated on the time spent with the people and scenery of Montgomeryshire and the Wye valley. The article was illustrated by numerous atmospheric and evocative photographs of Gibbings at work against a backdrop of the landscape, and included portraits of the local characters and locations featured in the book — Gibbings and his 'cronies' in the bar of the Black Lion, the poacher 'tickling' trout, 'Cobbler' the postman. Hadfield, and his wife Anna, had stayed with Robert in the tiny cottage at Marsh's Pool as he was putting the finishing touches to *Coming Down the Wye*:

> Into this book he breathed the spirit of the hills and the generous friendship of the hill-dwellers. We lay still amid the bracken while for hours he trained his field-glasses on the redstart nesting in a gorse-bush. In the evenings, while a saucepan of soup simmered on the hob, we sat round his cobbled hearth and talked about the ghosts that rose from the lake, the ways of herons and salmon, the rich scholarship of the blacksmith at Cwm Belan, the magic of the 'conjurer' in a distant valley who had an infallible cure for rheumatism. Throughout his conversation and throughout his books, Gibbings' enthusiasm for all living things, for all that is strange and curious and beautiful, rushes and ripples like a fast-flowing stream. Everything he says and writes is lit by a rich Irish humour, a zest for the fun and enjoyment of common things.[44]

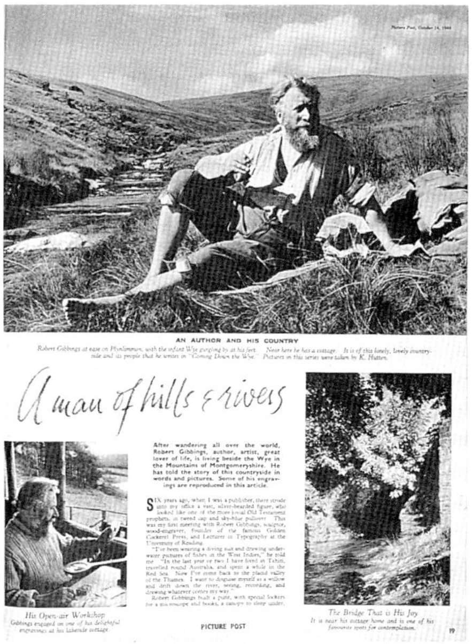
AN AUTHOR AND HIS COUNTRY

Robert Gibbings at ease on Plynlimmon, with the infant Wye gurgling by at his feet. Near here he has a cottage. It is of this lonely, lovely countryside and its people that he writes in "Coming Down the Wye." Pictures in this series were taken by K. Hutton.

A man of hills & rivers

After wandering all over the world, Robert Gibbings, author, artist, great lover of life, is living beside the Wye in the Mountains of Montgomeryshire. He has told the story of this countryside in words and pictures. Some of his engravings are reproduced in this article.

SIX years ago, when I was a publisher, there strode into my office a vast, silver-bearded figure, who looked like one of the more jovial Old Testament prophets, in tweed cap and sky-blue pullover. This was my first meeting with Robert Gibbings, sculptor, wood-engraver, founder of the famous Golden Cockerel Press, and Lecturer in Typography at the University of Reading.

"I've been wearing a diving suit and drawing under-water pictures of fishes in the West Indies," he told me. "In the last year or two I have lived in Tahiti, travelled round Australia, and spent a while in the Red Sea. Now I've come back to the placid valley of the Thames. I want to disguise myself as a willow and drift down the river, seeing, recording, and drawing whatever comes my way."

Robert Gibbings built a punt, with special lockers for a microscope and books, a canopy to sleep under,

His Open-air Workshop

Gibbings engaged on one of his delightful engravings at his lakeside cottage

PICTURE POST

The Bridge That is His Joy

It is near his cottage home and is one of his favourite spots for contemplation.

19

283 Opening page of an article on Gibbings by John Hadfield entitled 'A man of hills & rivers', published in *Picture Post* in October 1944.

A caption to one of the photographs in Hadfield's article mentioned that Gibbings had just finished a book on the river Lee and had plans to return to the South Sea Islands.

The article was published on 14 October 1944 and at about that time Gibbings visited Dent's printers, The Temple Press, in Letchworth for a few days to help supervise the production of his latest book. It was very unusual for an author to have any involvement or even interest in printing and the staff and pressmen at the works were both impressed by his knowledge and inspired by Gibbings's appreciation of their skills and he in turn was able to oversee the printing of his engravings. By the end of November he had been sent an advance copy of his book and he was 'well pleased with the production'. With the experience of the two previous river books, Dent produced a bigger first edition of *Lovely is the Lee* of 21,750 copies which appeared on 18 December 1944. The proportions and margins of the page for the first edition were less generous than with his previous books and the quality of the paper was inferior. This was as a result of the increasing restrictions and shortages brought on by the war and books now had to conform with the 'Authorized Economy Standards'. As before, sales were good and the book was reprinted in 1945, 1947 and 1949. Press reaction was again enthusiastic and, although the formula was similar to his previous books, the public had not tired of his style. Once more, the book was issued for Christmas and people were now collecting his latest offering to go with his previous books. In *Coming Down the Wye* Gibbings had concentrated more on the broad description of buildings, towns, villages, and landscape in the first section; when he moved to the cottage at Marsh's Pool he had focused on birdlife. *Lovely is the Lee* had all the usual nature observations but concentrated more on the early history, myths and legends associated with the ruins and ancient stones that are scattered with such abundance over the countryside. A deep sense of continuity with the past

Cover of *Lovely is the Lee* – see colour plate 8e.

pervades the book. The most dominant aspect was Gibbings's desire to convey his love of the people and their language, attempting to give accurate portraits of the characters he met and their conversations and ways of thinking. The promotional copy on the dust jacket emphasised Gibbings's Irishness: 'He moves and talks and writes like a man at home.' Although Gibbings never became involved in politics and indeed had a distinct dislike of politicians and party politics, ironically others could see a political dimension to the book in that its very neutrality made it a useful bridge. Gibbings was seen as 'an ambassador of genuine good will, who sees the best of both sides of the Irish Channel. His new book is bound to rouse feelings of mutual friendship and understanding'.

But the greatest significance *Lovely is the Lee* had on Gibbings's career was that this book made the break into the American market. After Dutton's publication on 26 November 1945, the book was chosen as Book-of-the-Month Club Dual Selection for December which resulted in a dramatic increase in the edition to 46,294 copies. This was a huge breakthrough. Relations with the American publishers became very warm, as reflected in a reply to a letter from Gibbings by Elliott B. Macrae, President of E. P. Dutton & Co. Inc., dated 22 August 1946:

Cover of American edition of *Lovely is the Lee* – see colour plate 8f.

> As far as I know, this is the first letter I have had from you, Mr Gibbings, and I want to reiterate what I have said in my previous letters and cables: how delighted we are to be your American publisher! I am glad that we had the courage of our convictions in keeping faith with you. Our editorial reports on *Sweet Thames Run Softly* and *Coming Down the Wye* were so enthusiastic that we hoped that there would be a fair sale of these books in the United States. Such was not the case, and even though the editorial reports on *Lovely is the Lee* were just as enthusiastic, I must say we were somewhat doubtful of putting the book over in the way we wished to do it. Then the Book-of-the-Month Club came through with their offer, and Robert Gibbings and Dutton's are well repaid for their good work.[45]

This letter reached Gibbings care of the Bank of New Zealand, Apia, Samoa, for in August 1945, Gibbings had sailed to Polynesia to collect material for his next book.

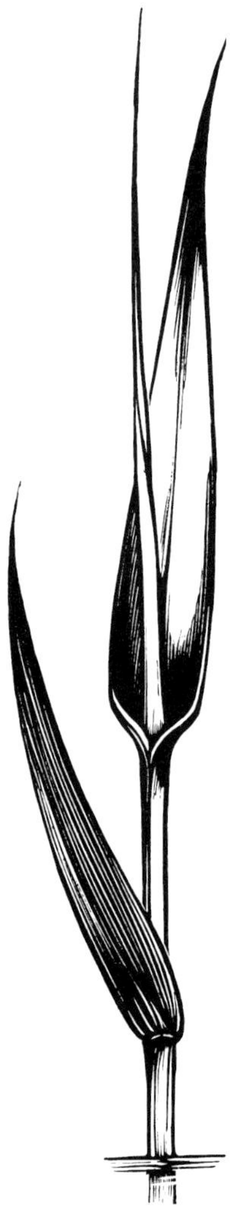

284 *Lovely is the Lee* was dedicated to Patience Empson and this image of a rush appeared on the dedication page and later was used for her bookplate (a smaller version was also engraved and used for the same purpose). Wood-engraving, 134 x 30 mm.

Chapter Sixteen
Over the Reefs 1944–1947

BY 1945 THE FINANCIAL SUCCESS of *Lovely is the Lee* had enabled Gibbings to be more ambitious in the scope of his subject material and allowed him to indulge his ever present desire for exotic travel. He was to spend much of the next two years exploring the South Sea Islands, using the same formula of anecdote, diary and observation, but against a background of the colourful people and landscape of Polynesia. Research for this book was to take longer. He had managed to research, write and illustrate a book every two years since 1940 — a work rate which undoubtedly generated pressure. The public had created a demand for his books which he had to satisfy.

On his return from Ireland, Gibbings stayed for a short time with his mother-in-law at Box Farm. Mrs Empson had grown very fond of Robert and, since her husband had died, he was very welcome in the house. During his absence The Orchard had been rented out and Gibbings had to wait until the lease had expired before he could move in. He was uncertain about his immediate plans as his expedition to the South Seas depended on the course of the war, and in October 1944 he had heard from Elisabeth that there was a possibility that the family might return at any moment. In early November he was able to move back into The Orchard but was shocked to find that the last tenants had left the house in chaos. The roof had started to leak, the garden was a wilderness, paintwork and electrical fittings had been damaged and generally it was a mess. Gibbings's priority was to put things right before the return of his wife and children. He felt unsettled and conscious of the fact that he had spent much of the last four years living out of suitcases — he had been looking forward to coming home and had been thrown by finding it in such a state. Finding labour in war-time was difficult but eventually he employed a builder to mend the roof and decorators to repaint the interior. By the end of November the work was done and he had even managed to employ a charlady.

Robert's mail now included many letters of appreciation from enthusiastic readers of his books and he tried to reply to them all. Occasionally his correspondence developed into a more lasting friendship, as was the case with Mr and Mrs Lennard Jones. They had written to Gibbings not long after his return from Ireland and from October 1944 letters were exchanged regularly for many years. The letters were mainly from Mrs Lennard Jones but before long formality was forgotten and Robert began to address them as Cathleen and George. As their friendship grew their letters became increasingly intimate — even flirtatious! Cooking had become difficult in The Orchard due to a problem with blocked flues; when Cathleen heard of his plight she sent him cooked pheasant and even a Christmas pudding. Cathleen clearly admired Gibbings's books but he was modest in return concerning his skills as an author:

> People tell me that my books are 'revealing', though I never can quite see how or why. I try to write of things as they occur to me. I never attempt style. If I can get away with my ignorance of grammar I am well satisfied. I am not a bit intellectual, really, or even educated, though I seem to give that impression. I work entirely from the waist-line instead of the hat-line. When I feel things very strongly I try to put them down. That's all there is to it.[1]

Gibbings was now established as one of Dent's leading authors and they were anxious to encourage him to write more. They fully backed his plans to return to the South Seas but, with the war dragging on, transport was too difficult to arrange. In the meantime, Dent had obtained permission from Penguin to publish an edition of *Blue Angels and Whales*, revised and redesigned to conform with their other Gibbings books. Over Christmas and the New Year Gibbings was working on additions to his text and selecting some new illustrations; it had been decided to drop his original wood-engraved illustrations and replace them with half-tone reproductions of the drawings he had made on location, adding a number of new images to explain more fully topics in the text.

Conditions in The Orchard were cold and damp over the winter months. Gibbings had spent Christmas with his mother-in-law and made the most of the home comforts but in February, with snow on the ground, he had suffered from bouts of flu. Hopes for the return of his family from Canada had been frustrated by advice from the shipping companies that conditions were still unsafe for women and children to travel.

In March 1945 he spent some weeks on the Isle of Man at the Marine Biology Station to research the sea-life of British waters for an additional chapter in *Blue Angels and Whales*. Unfortunately the weather was too cold to allow him to adopt his usual method of lying on his stomach staring into rock pools: '... of course a fish that likes to lurk in dark crevices is not going to be anything but "self-conscious" in a highly lit aquarium'.[2] He was also a little disappointed that the scientists were more interested in specimens that needed to be viewed through a microscope. There were difficulties in trying to draw while looking through a lens and he was aware that the results were not really interesting to the general public; he had been intrigued, however, by the acrobatic antics of a half-inch sea slug in a bowl of water. He had also been greatly interested in the 'antiquarian remains' on the island which were very similar to those he had found in Ireland.

At the end of March he returned once more to Waltham. His plans for the trip to the South Seas were beginning to take shape, as the High Commissioner for New Zealand had offered help with his passage and the necessary permits. He intended to make the island of Samoa a base and travel on to the other islands from there, and had hopes that he might get away in July or August. In a letter to Cathleen Lennard Jones of 12 April, Gibbings reported that:

> Yesterday I was starring for Pathé. The other one, Pictorial No. 30, in which I appeared for a few seconds is now showing at The Monseigneur in town & is quite successful. But this new one is a sort of 'day in the life of R.G.' I'm drawing at an easel in the studio, I'm writing under the apple blossom in the garden; I'm wandering, soulful, by the river. We have yet to do another day at it in which I'm to muck about in my boat.

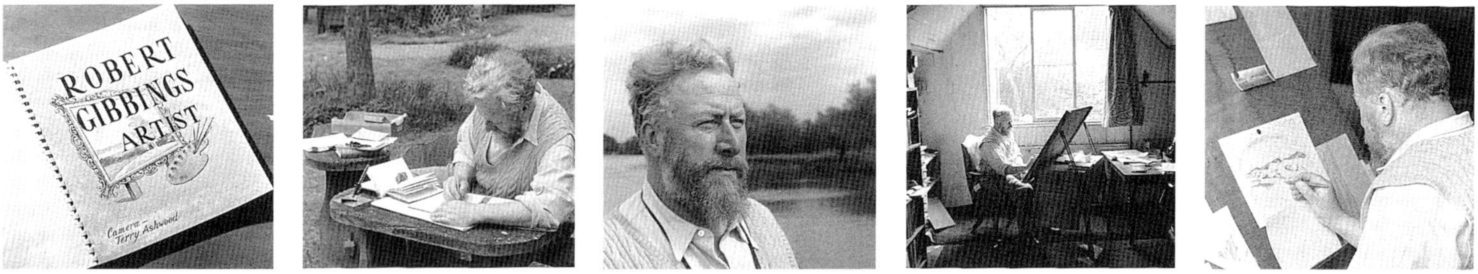

285 Stills taken from a Pathé newsreel film made about Gibbings in April 1945. Reproduced with the kind permission of Pathé News who retain a copy of the film in their archives. He is shown writing in the orchard at Waltham St Lawrence, walking beside the Thames and preparing a drawing to be photographed on to a woodblock in his studio. Author's collection.

In rather flirtatious and flippant remarks to Cathleen, Gibbings speculates that his film stardom should hopefully result in a 'few proposals'. The final Pathé film was cut to just over three minutes and entitled 'Robert Gibbings, Artist'. The black and white pictures were accompanied by the usual rather stilted and formal commentary; Gibbings himself remained silent.[3] The film was shown widely in Britain but also got a viewing in distant parts of the world. As a youth in South Africa, Larry Gibbings, one of the twins, was suddenly amazed to see moving pictures of his father on the screen of a local cinema — he had not seen him for over ten years.

By May, Gibbings was preparing for his voyage and making frequent trips to his tailors in London, to be kitted out for the tropics, and to his publishers — he even managed to meet Cathleen Lennard Jones for lunch at the Café Royal. While researching themes and ideas for his new book Gibbings became interested in supernatural phenomena. Reading about the early missionaries in the South Seas he found that they had repeatedly referred to the actions of poltergeists and Gibbings had approached the Society for Psychical Research for further information. He shared his new interest with Cathleen and they swapped accounts of psychic experiences in their letters.

With an almost certain departure date in mid July, Gibbings was feeling unsure about what to do with the house and whether and when Elisabeth was returning. He had finished his work on *Blue Angels and Whales* but still had to make a paste-up dummy of the book for the printers before he left. He wrote to Cathleen, who also shared his passion for natural history, asking if she could look after some of his reference books during his absence. Elisabeth's plans were still uncertain; the Germans had surrendered to the Allies in May and she had written to him at the end of that month suggesting that he should travel out to meet her in British Columbia. He had decided that this was impossible and went ahead with his own plans. In the event, Elisabeth did arrive home just a few weeks before his departure; that Gibbings could contemplate leaving his family within weeks of their

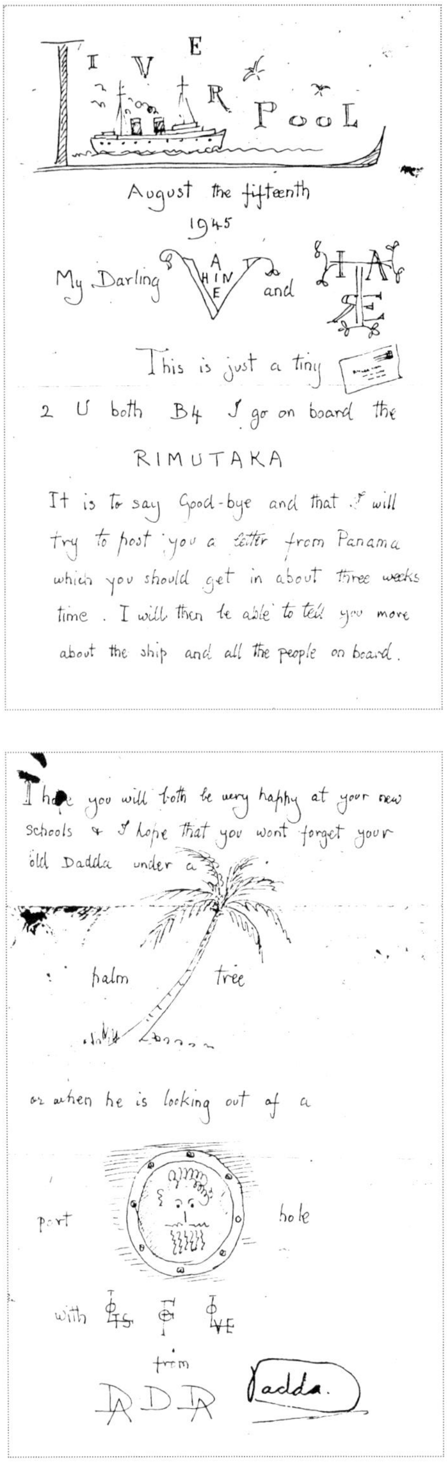
LIVERPOOL

August the fifteenth 1945

My Darling VAHINE and TIARE

This is just a tiny
2 U both B4 I go on board the
RIMUTAKA
It is to say Good-bye and that I will try to post you a letter from Panama which you should get in about three weeks time. I will then be able to tell you more about the ship and all the people on board.

I hope you will both be very happy at your new schools & I hope that you wont forget your old Dadda under a palm tree or when he is looking out of a port hole with LOTS OF LOVE from DADDA Dadda.

286 Letter from Robert to his daughters, Vahine and Tiare, sent from his hotel in Liverpool on 15 August 1945, while waiting to sail to New Zealand. Private collection.

return, after nearly four years apart and knowing that he intended to be away for over a year, must imply a great deal about their relationship.

Elisabeth was a difficult person to get on with — even her family found her so — and although reunited, Robert found it hard to contemplate their living together. He was delighted to be with Tiare and Vahine — even for such a short time. In a letter to Cathleen he declared that he 'was quite in love with the two daughters. The little one is going to break many hearts, elf-like in form with the most lovely eyes & full of fun. The elder is more stately & serious, but I think intelligent, & most affectionate'.[4] It must have been very confusing for the two little girls to be saying good-bye to their father after so little time together. Whatever the state of their marriage, Elisabeth had developed a strong desire for another child and Gibbings, perhaps to detract from the anxiety of his imminent departure, agreed to try for a baby. Other family matters had to be attended to before he left, as on 25 July Patrick had married a Wren after a whirlwind and romantic courtship of a few weeks. For the honeymoon, Robert had arranged for them to have the cottage at Marsh's Pool. He wrote to Cathleen that he liked Patrick's bride very much: 'She matches him well in size, colour & age and seems of a bright & happy temperament. The Lord knows what they are going to live on when they are both demobbed but if they are not worrying why should I!' Much to his relief Gibbings also reported that he had received letters from Moira in South Africa '… "making up" all past differences & seeing things as I always hoped that she would'.[5]

His departure was eventually delayed until August and even then the ship developed engine trouble and almost immediately had to return to the docks at Liverpool. Gibbings was booked into the Adelphi Hotel, along with the other passengers, to await repairs or a replacement ship. Bored, he frittered away the evenings with concerts and the theatre. He saw a performance of *Lady Windermere's Fan* but did not enjoy it: 'Wilde always leaves a bad taste in my mouth'.[6] After a few days he decided to take up an offer from Evan Gill, Eric's brother, to stay at his home in the city. Each day Gibbings reported in and collected his mail from the hotel and, after a week or so of delay, he finally sailed for New Zealand. The war was over and he was about to return to his beloved Polynesia, but he had left his young family in Waltham and Elisabeth was pregnant again.

Gibbings arrived in Auckland in late September 1945 after an excellent voyage — 'a good ship & good weather'. He was surprised to find himself treated as something of a celebrity. A government car had been put at his disposal and 'every possible kindness had been shown'. Shortly after his arrival he gave a broadcast interview which was subsequently published in the *New Zealand Listener*, and an article, head-lined 'Famous Illustrator-Author goes to Samoa', outlined his proposed expedition in the *Pacific Islands Monthly*.[7] Three weeks after his arrival in New Zealand he set out for Apia in Samoa. Writing to friends back home he reported his first reaction:

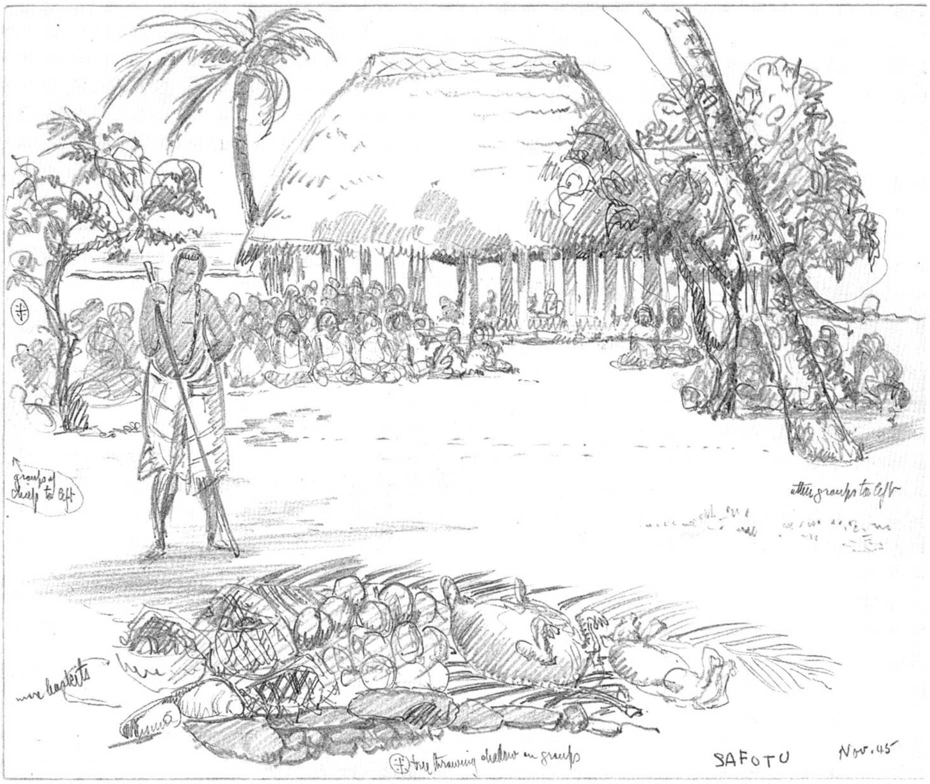

287 Pencil sketch of a village welcoming ceremony, Safotu, 1945, 203 x 253 mm. In the foreground are baskets of fruit and roasted pigs prepared for a feast. Gibbings frequently drew on thin, buff card which was punched with holes for storage in ring-binders. Author's collection; a collection of other sketches is in RUL.

Here I am with a blue lagoon before me, palms and bananas all around & brown figures in lava-lavas passing silently to & fro in bare feet. To add that I am sweating behind mosquito netting & that it has hardly ceased deluging with rain for days may spoil the romance but there it is.[8]

With temperatures well in excess of eighty degrees, Gibbings was finding it difficult to adjust to the conditions.

His anxiety about the delays and late departure from England was partly because he wanted to experience a natural phenomenon concerning the palolo worm:

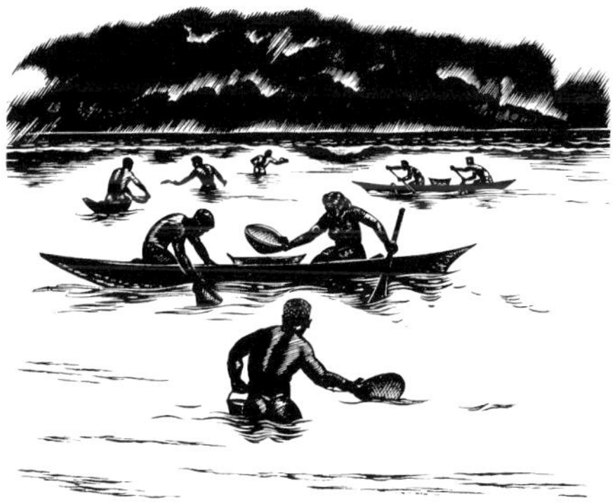

288 Fishing for the palolo worm. Illustration from *Over the Reefs*, 1948, wood-engraving, 82 x 102 mm.

It is a stringy creature that on one or two nights in the year rises to the surface of the sea. It comes up in clouds & the natives gather them for food, considering them a great delicacy. I set out from here with a bloke called Grattan, motoring 20 miles along the coast. We then marched 7 miles along a bush track in tropical sunshine most of the way. Was I hot?!! A guide met us outside the village & led us to the guest house which was decorated like a bridal bower, garlands of sweet smelling flowers & ferns everywhere … 4 chiefs came & welcomed us with much ceremony. We drank Kava & they presented me with tappa cloth, fruit, & a pig roasted whole. Next morning we were out at 3.30 am while it was still dark in company with nearly 100 canoes. Unfortunately the rise was disappointing but we got enough for breakfast. When cooked with coconut cream they resemble spinach & have a pleasant taste, reminiscent of oysters — some say more like the reef at low tide, but they are philistines! It poured, a real tropical downpour, the whole way home, after which I retired to bed for 18 hours. The next jaunt will probably be in search of a fish that climbs waterfalls, & then I hope to get on a schooner & go up to the Tokelau islands for a few weeks. Later I hope to get on a plane & visit the Cook Islands.[9]

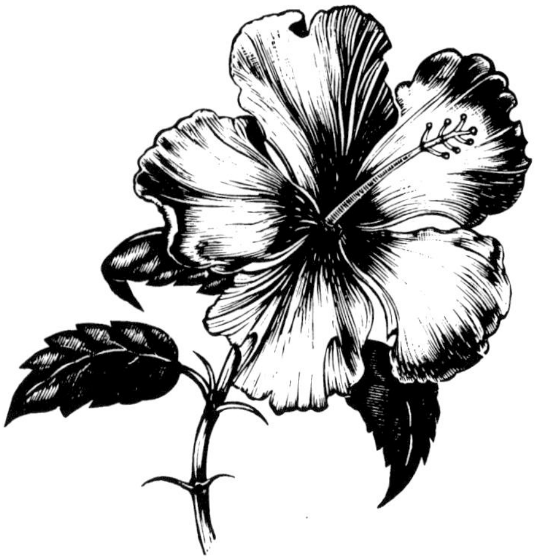

289 Hibiscus, a sweet smelling flower which commonly grows wild on the islands of Polynesia. Illustration from *Over the Reefs*, 1948, wood-engraving, 63 x 63 mm.

When his book was eventually published, a map of the Pacific islands was printed on the endpapers and Gibbings's route from island to island was marked out for the reader to plot his progress as they read the text. However, this was very much the author's device to give a coherent and logical structure to his narrative — in reality his travels were much more chaotic. Gibbings had to take advantage of opportunities to hitch lifts on boats when they were offered; he needed to find suitable bases to spend weeks writing up his notes, so, as with his other books, the real experience was much more haphazard than the version that finally appeared. Accounts of incidents, observations and locations were all true, but the sequence and circumstances under which they happened was re-organised in such a way as to make the book work.

Gibbings had been astonished to find how, even in this remote part of the world, his books had found their way to the islands. He was even more pleased to hear the news that *Lovely is the Lee* had been made Book-of-the-Month in the USA — although not so pleased at the thought of paying more tax! Gibbings was impressed by the friendliness of the local people who gave him the name 'Tusitala', which meant 'a teller of tales', a name usually associated with Robert Louis Stevenson. In contrast to the rationing and shortages at home, food was in abundance and, even though prohibition was in force, alcohol was available under the heading of 'medical comforts' and Gibbings made sure of his supply of whiskey and rum: '... I can get 4 bottles a month of the best at about 14/- a time'. He was impeded to some extent by the language barrier and as he wanted to get close to the people, he struggled to master some basic words. On his expedition in search of palolo he had taken an interpreter.

In the new year he wrote to John Hadfield and his wife Anna, feeling a little dispirited after a lonely Christmas, but making progress with the book:

> Greetings from Samoa & a happy new year to you both. I hope you had a better Christmas than I did, with a boil under my coccyx. No white man within 20 miles. Spent Christmas day with the young native medico probing round my arms with hypodermic needles. Oh, didn't we 'ave a merry time! But in spite of such [?] complaints I am getting quite a spat of work done, especially in the way of drawings. The difficulty with the text is that not knowing the language it is almost impossible to achieve any intimacy. The only real way to learn a language doesn't appeal to me; they've all got lice in their hair. Even so I've got the makings of a few chapters. ... Did a 10 day tour with the [?] & saw much in the way of native ceremonial. Damn impressive it is too. Much song & dance too but neither of these very impressive, the dancing being mainly posturing of the body with movements mainly of the arms & hands. Nothing whatever of the hula about it. Apart from cricket & church services, which are more or less continuous performances, this island is largely 'unspoilt'. In this village, almost any day, one can see them weaving mats & beating the tappa [*sic*]cloth. The big drum in the centre of the 'green' calls to church or any other assembly. Tattooing is still almost universal among the men and I hope to see some of it in operation next week. The Kava ceremony remains one of the most important rituals of the community life. But the missionaries have got a *frightful* hold over the people ....'[10]

Gibbings planned to go to Fiji in February for a few weeks and then travel on to Tonga if a passage was available. Sometime in April he hoped to be able to get to the Tokelau group of islands and then travel on to the Cook Islands; at that time, he intended to end his tour of Polynesia in Honolulu and the Hawaiian islands. But for the next few weeks he explored the island of Savai'i, visiting the crater of a volcano which had devastated the area in 1905 and a lava field still smoking and giving off sulphur fumes. Despite the heat and humidity, Gibbings had undertaken some serious walking along bush tracks that were heavy going. He had also visited outlying islands including a small island which was the summit of a volcano, a single village nestled in the centre of the crater, entered through a gap in the crater wall. Gibbings was fascinated by the geography, describing it as an example of the 'sunken-island-atoll-to-be-type', the creation of which he had theorised about in *Blue Angels and Whales*.[11]

Pursuing his passion for marine life, Gibbings had been observing a 'wonderful' reef in front of the house in which he was staying. In his letter to Hadfield he wrote:

> I float about in goggles & try not to gasp with astonishment. Have done little but draw fish these past few days. Managed to get quite a number into the 'studio'. So you see it is the same old story of toiling & moiling for the good of the cause! ... At the moment I could do with some Roederer 28, off the ice; I'm drinking tepid whiskey & it's giving me prickly heat. Haven't had a cool drink for a month. I think I hear my ruffianly 'man Friday' by name Sione. He lived for a time in Apia & is a thorough going pimp, though his church attendance is phenomenal. He can't understand why I don't want his services in getting me a series of girls. Apparently the U.S. Marines set a fairly virile standard here as elsewhere. But Sione gets things done which is rare in Samoa & now he is coming to be drawn in his canoe.

In February he reached Tonga and visited the shores where Captains Cook and Bligh had landed and he even 'sailed the waters where the Bounty hunting had occurred'. By April he was back in Apia on Samoa, hoping to pick up a schooner which was due to sail to the islands of Tokelau, 300 miles north and not far from the equator. Before leaving England he had promised a number of his male friends that he would send postcards of the beautiful local girls — he kept his promise and on a postcard of a bare-breasted maiden sent to George Lennard Jones, Gibbings reported that despite some hardships he was 'getting quite a bit of work done & "the field" is opening up well. But I doubt if I'll be home before 1947'.[12]

On the 10 May, Gibbings wrote to George Lennard Jones asking for help with some 'Serious anthropological, ethnological, literary research'. Gibbings had been annoyed at a reference in a nineteenth century book by a 'fat-headed B.F. "Scientific" traveller' who had been surprised that the natives of Tonga had no word for high numbers such as a million. Gibbings objected to the author's assumption that this meant that their culture was 'behind' that of Europe. He wanted George to carry out some research on 'less educated labouring men' in England to see if they had any better concept of what a million really was. Gibbings was anxious to get accurate results: 'Try to make an *exact* note of their replies in the vernacular, "danged if they ain't ..." etc. The only way to remember the exact wording & phrasing is to carry paper & pencil — I find a blank P.C. the best — & I write it down the moment their back is turned.' Today, Gibbings's

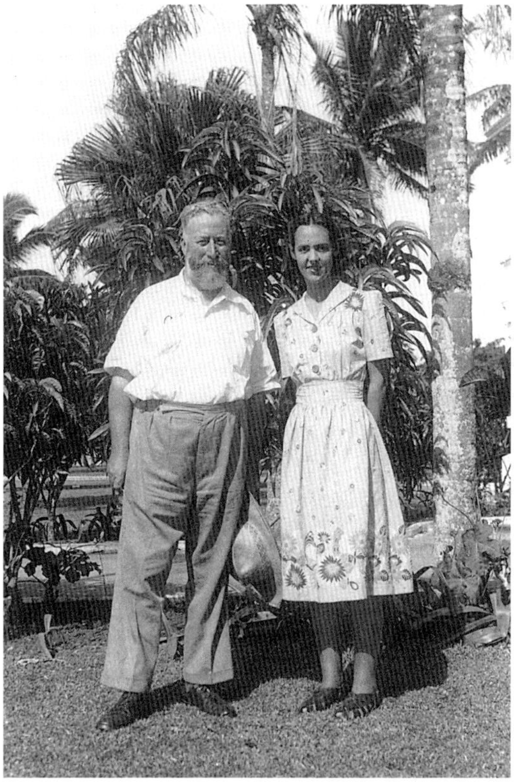

290 Robert and Patience photographed shortly after her arrival on Fiji in May 1946. RUL.

attempts to reproduce 'vernacular' may seem rather patronising but he clearly wanted to achieve authenticity in his dialogue. He went on to report that he was again suffering from the heat: 'Yesterday, a month after the cool season should have set in the temp. was over 90 degrees in the cool rooms of the house. Because I want light mine is a hot room. Even now, at six o'clock in the evening, & wearing next to nothing, I'm pouring sweat'. A fortnight earlier he had returned from his trip to the Tokelaus. On the voyage he had shared a cabin, nine foot by five foot, with the doctor; the only ventilation was a port hole eight inches in diameter. The schooner was alive with cockroaches — Gibbings noted that as they lay on their bunks he could not tell whether it was the cockroaches running over him or sweat pouring off him. On his return to Apia he had had to attend the local hospital to have treatment for boils that had started from septic bites of the roaches.

The previous month Gibbings had heard that Elisabeth had given birth to a son on 14 April.[13] They had decided to name the baby Shaun and an announcement duly appeared in the press. Gibbings was imminently expecting more news from home but this time directly from his sister-in-law, Patience. On 16 April Patience had sailed from Tilbury in the ship *Rangitata*, bound for Wellington in New Zealand, via Melbourne.[14] From Wellington she flew, in a rickety RAF Dakota, to Auckland and then on to Fiji where she arrived on 30 May to meet up with Robert.[15] Gibbings had organised his passage to Fiji in the middle of May and had visited some other islands on the way; he was also hoping to take the opportunity to cool down in a hotel in the mountains of Fiji. In a letter to John Hadfield,

Gibbings had stated that it had been Elisabeth's idea that Patience should join him on his travels as an assistant — later she was to become very difficult over the arrangements.[16] Writing to George Lennard Jones he confessed he was finding it difficult to handle all his material on his own: 'The scope is so vast that it is almost impossible for me to deal with it, without help.' Patience had already proved her worth and Gibbings appreciated her qualities: 'She is a trained secretary, most efficient, & well read & has helped me with my last two efforts. You'll be thinking I'm intelligent, again, when my next appears, & half of it will be hers!'[17] Robert's first thought, when he realised he needed help, had been to employ a secretary from New Zealand, but he was delighted with the alternative; he enjoyed Patience's company and she would also be in a position to help him deal with the increasing fan mail that he was receiving via his postal address, care of the Bank of New Zealand in Apia. He ended his letter to George with a description of his living conditions: 'At the moment there is a guitar twanging downstairs, & several copra bugs, upstairs, crawling over ME. There's also a lizard on the writing table which though a nice little fellow is distracting to the thoughts, so forgive incoherence.'

For the first weeks of June, Gibbings and Patience explored Nukualofa and the other islands around Tonga on a small cargo and mail ship, the *Matua*, returning to Apia on 12 June.[18] On their arrival the weather deteriorated and they were bombarded by gales and deluged with rain. They were staying in a ramshackle house with broken glass in the windows that hardly kept out the elements. The humidity was so intense that books and clothes all felt damp and sticky and it was a battle to keep them free of mould. But soon the weather returned to glorious tropical blue skies with a gentle breeze. By the end of the month Gibbings had found better accommodation; he had taken over a suite of two bedrooms and a large office in a house on the outskirts of the town on the shores of the lagoon. The rooms were on the first floor with doors that opened onto a balcony that ran around the whole house and had views across the water, only interrupted by a

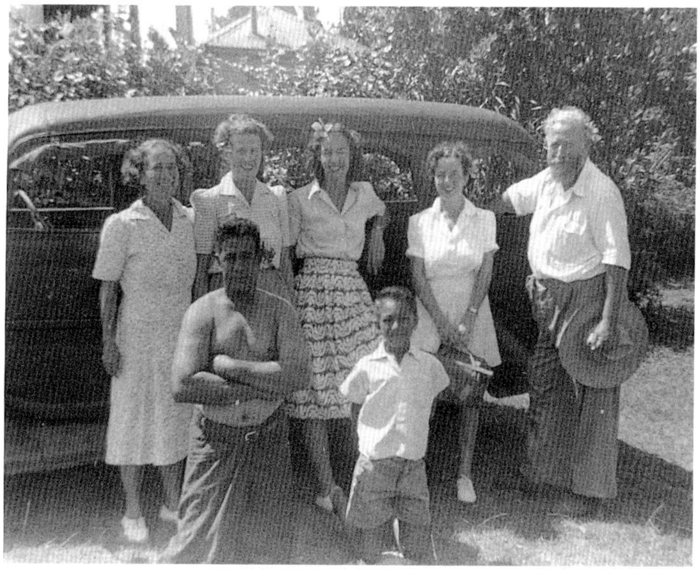

291 Robert and Patience with friends and Tina McCrory, their landlady, and other members of the household outside their lodgings on the island of Apia in Samoa. Back row: Tina, Rosemary Jack (a nurse from New Zealand who was to become Patience's travelling companion), Patience, another friend who was also a nurse, Robert – front row: their regular taxi driver and friend and a local boy from the village. RUL.

fringe of palm trees. It was a quiet place and the 'office' consisted of a large table in the centre of the room with two dilapidated wicker chairs, a chest of drawers, an old iron bedstead, and an aged, crumbling piano; but with large maps of the South Seas pinned to the walls and the typewriter unpacked it was an ideal, if eccentric, place to work. The landlady, Tina McCrory, ran a well organised establishment and was an attentive hostess; Robert and Patience were made comfortable and welcome: 'Instead of being a headquarters, the house very soon became home.'[19] With a glass of rum beside him, he wrote to Cathleen that things were 'moving fairly well .... My S. in-law (unmarried &, selfishly, I hope she remains so) met me in Fiji & we are down good, hard, & solid on the work. Already 5000 are in typescript & my office is wonderfully tidy'.[20] At the end of June he was expecting an expert anthropologist from New Zealand to come and stay as a guest. Having spent a number of years on the islands, his guest was to be a guide and interpreter on a month-long expedition around Apia. 'With him as A. D. C.', Gibbings wrote, 'my S-in-law as secretary, two "Talking Chiefs" — which are a necessary part of such an entourage[21] — & at least half a dozen carriers for the luggage I shall feel like an Eastern Potentate trekking through the jungle.'[22] Patience was proving a great help — not just as a secretary 'but in her own observations of the life here. Her aptness of phrase is grand & I have already incorporated many of her thoughts & words'.[23] They had sent off the first four chapters of the book 'all complete and beautifully typed'; by September Gibbings had sent a draft of the first 8,000 words to Pollinger and he had received a letter from E. F. Bozman, editor at Dent, to say he was 'highly delighted' with it.

Their few months were spent visiting remote native villages in Samoa, experiencing the way of life and observing the landscape and wildlife. Feasts were

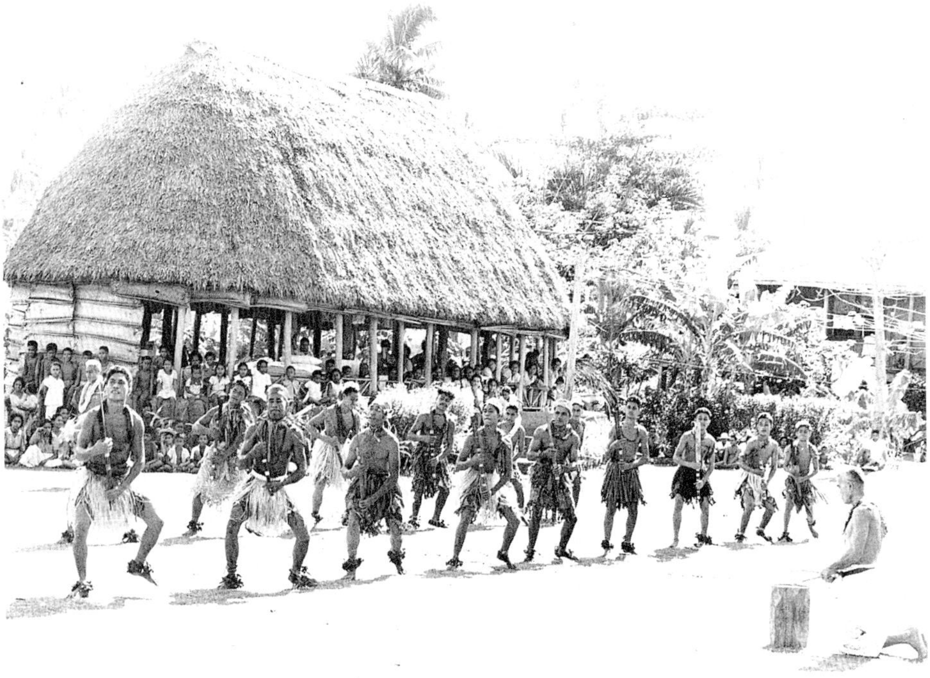

292 A Samoan ceremonial dance. One of many photographs Gibbings took or bought depicting the life and landscape of the islands. He frequently made use of these images as references for his engravings. Author's collection; a collection of other photographs is in RUL.

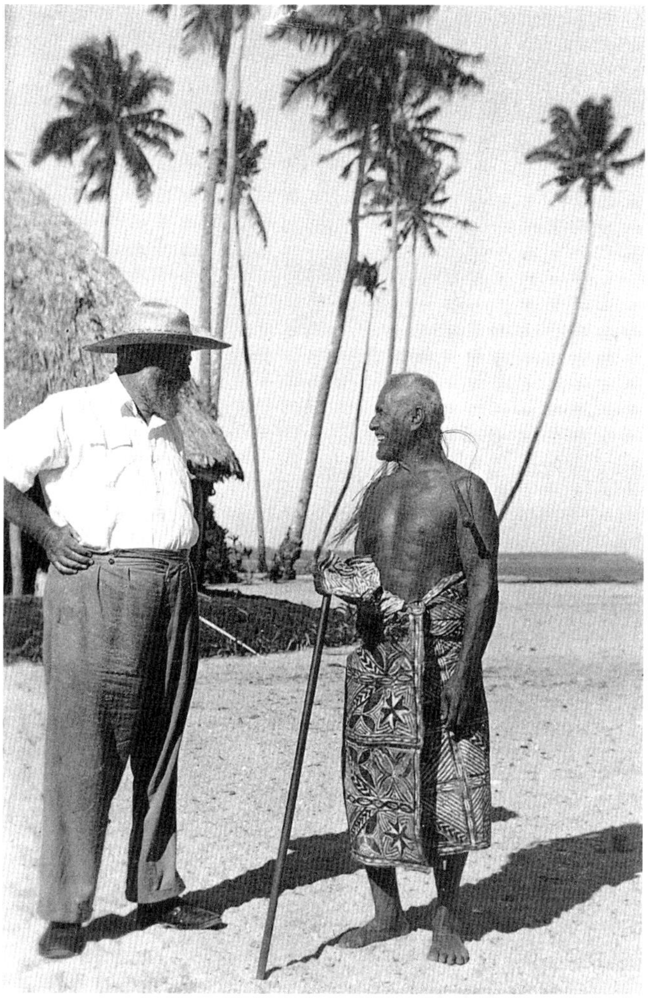

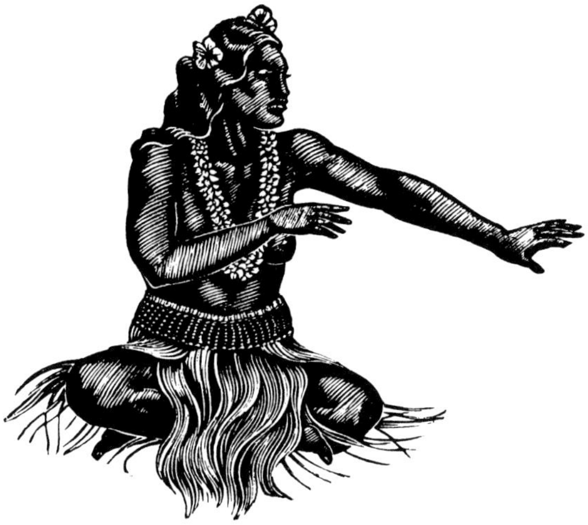

293 *left* Gibbings in Samoa with his host, a village chief, who is wearing a piece of traditional tapa cloth. RUL.

294 *above* Traditional dancer. Illustration from *Over the Reefs*, 1948, wood-engraving, 64 x 73 mm.

295 *below* Patience and Robert outside a traditional village hut. Author's collection.

organised in their honour — vast quantities of food; fish, lobsters, chicken, pigeons, roast pig and every kind of native vegetable were laid out on banana leaves and followed by ceremonial dancing. It was usual that the villagers would prepare and decorate a guest hut for their stay – an open-sided thatched structure festooned with flowers. However enjoyable, the long sessions of feasting and entertainment caused Robert and Patience some discomfort; etiquette required that they sat cross-legged with their backs straight against the upright poles of the hut for long hours. Robert found such contortion difficult to achieve but even Patience suffered from stiffness. Frequently they were asked to name new-born babies as an honour but their own names and titles soon ran out and one of the later arrivals was named 'Aialani' which is Samoan for Ireland. Patience's name translated as 'Onosa'i' and she was given the formal title of 'Failautusi' which means 'maker of letters in a book'; Robert was always called 'Tusitala' but he was frequently mistaken for a missionary, which troubled him, as he was conscious of how western religion and culture had influenced the traditional way of life.

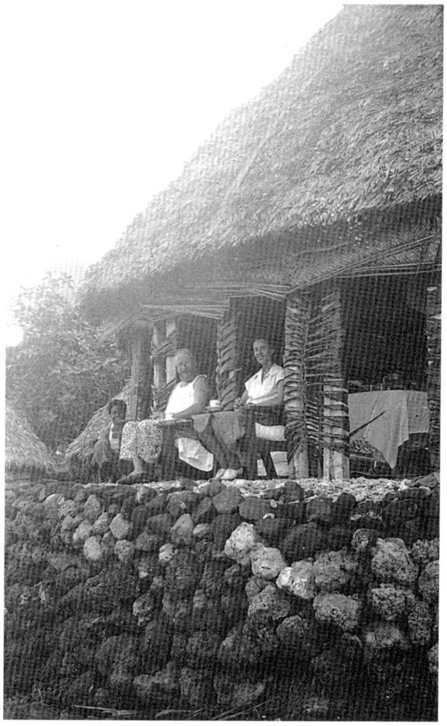

At the end of August they visited the tiny island of Manono. While staying with the villagers, observing their customs and ceremonies, the local elders had decided to honour Gibbings with the title of High Chief. He enjoyed describing

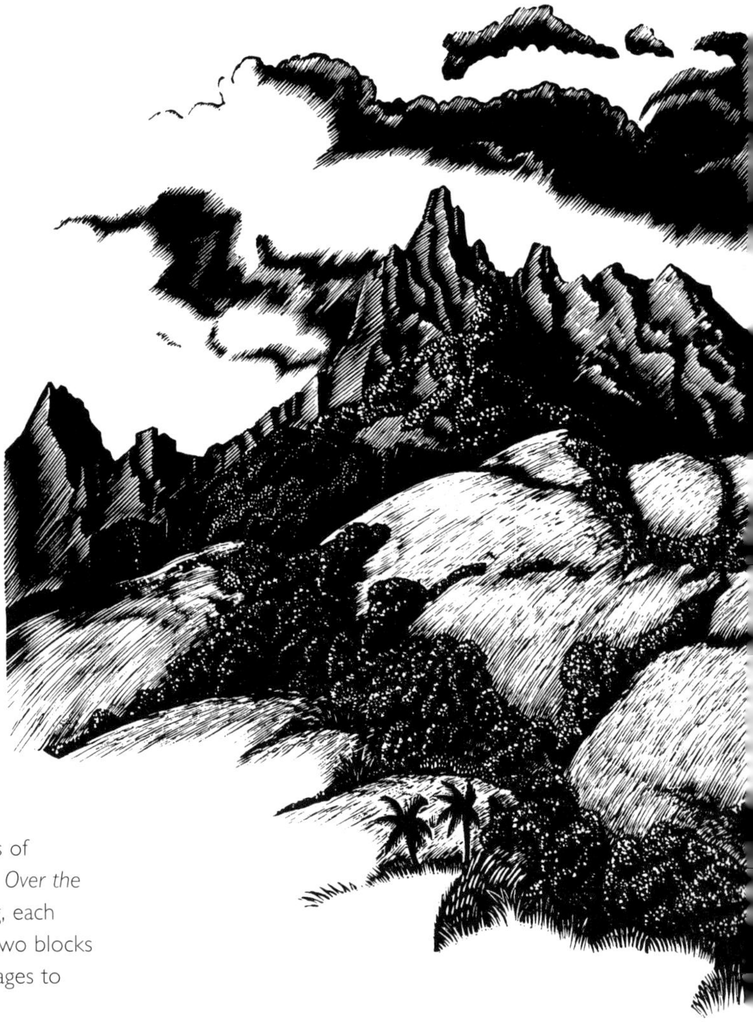

296 The high volcanic peaks of Rarotonga. Illustrations from *Over the Reefs*, 1948, wood-engraving, each image 130 x 102 mm. The two blocks were printed on opposite pages to form a panoramic view.

the ceremony which had begun with him being prepared for the event by dressing in the traditional sheet of tapa cloth:

You'd have laughed a lot if you'd seen me in one a few weeks ago when I was being installed High Chief of the island of Manono. I had been led away (not astray) by three old women who stripped me to the pants & then oiled me all over (almost). Then they wound a sheet of this tappa [*sic*] about my tummy, put a garland of flowers about my neck, wristlets of leaves on my arms & a red hibiscus behind my ear. Thus accoutred I was led into the presence of 23 chiefs & 'orators'. After much speech-making & drinking of Kava, with presentation of pigs roasted whole, coconuts & fish, it was assumed that henceforth I would be known as Tamafainga, a former king of all Samoa. I was told that he had been a wonderful warrior, uniting all the nations of Samoa & bringing peace to the world, as I was going to do with my pen. I hear since from Europeans that he was a notorious cannibal & ravisher of women. But Europeans will never understand native customs.[24]

Patience was involved too; she was made a 'taupou' or ceremonial virgin and was also oiled and similarly attired — all in view of the old village chief who sat close by observing the proceedings.

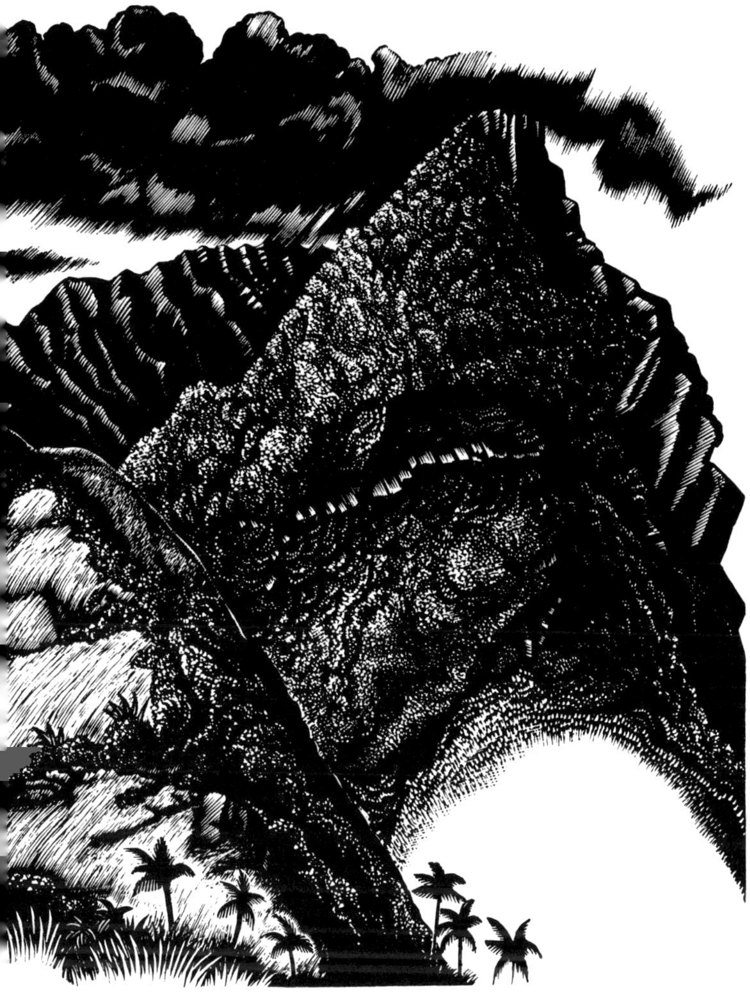

On 20 September, Gibbings and Patience flew the eight hundred miles to Rarotonga in the Cook Islands over volcanic peaks and landed on a strip of land cut in the belt of luxuriant vegetation that followed the shoreline of the island. They had delayed their departure as the writing was going so well in the comfort of their rooms in Apia. Earlier, the intense heat and humidity had made Gibbings feel low and he had suffered from a series of debilitating boils — for a man of fifty-seven the last months had been very physically demanding. He had been hoping that the cooler atmosphere of Rarotonga would revive him but as his condition had improved and the temperatures had dropped they had stayed on in Apia.

Gibbings was disappointed to find that, however spectacular the landscape of Rarotonga was and however comfortable the climate, the people had become sadly 'Europeanised' and, unlike the Samoans, had believed the 'white man's way of life' to be better. He had hoped to find a schooner to take them to the outlying islands and at the end of October the *Tiare Taporo* sailed into the port; she was to be their home base for nearly the next five months. The *Tiare Taporo* was a romantic

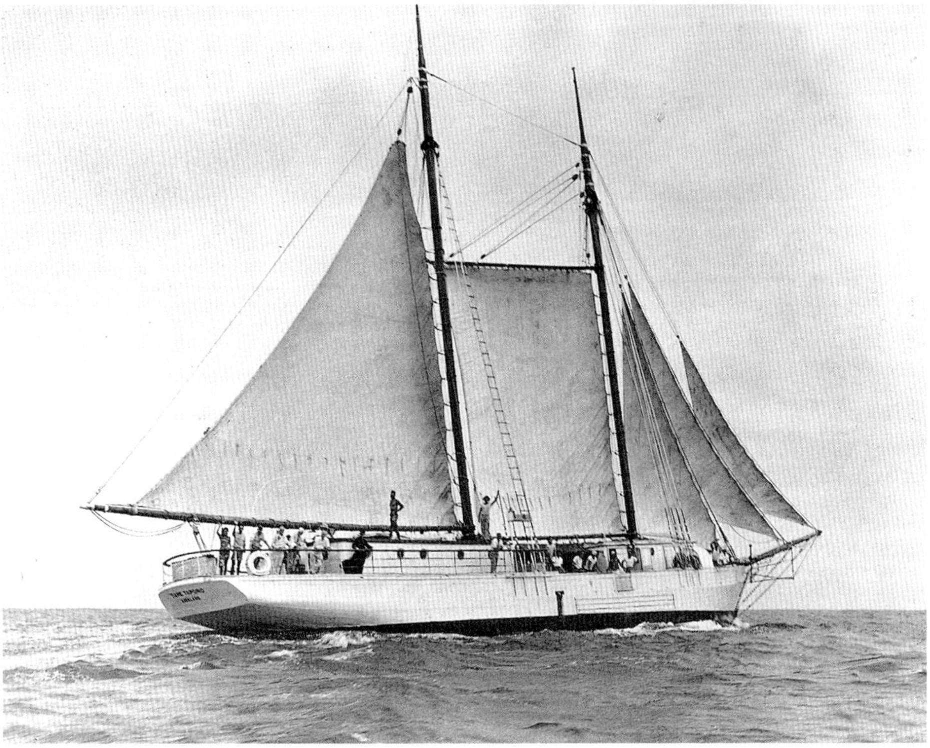

297 The *Tiare Taporo*, a trading schooner that became the temporary home for Robert and Patience on their travels to the islands of Polynesia. RUL.

looking schooner with graceful lines, but it was a working ship, loaded with goods of all descriptions, which plied a route between the islands transporting supplies and collecting pungent smelling copra. Gibbings, with his eye for boats, thought her 'a good schooner, but at times over-sensitive to the wind, like the "flower of the line" from which she takes her name.' The Captain, Andy Thompson, was an American who had married a native girl — he was an entrancing man with a mouthful of gold teeth and an endless fund of racy conversation; Gibbings immediately took to him and they became almost like blood-brothers. The *Tiare* was perfect from Gibbings's point of view: an island hopper which gave him the opportunity to get ashore on many of the smaller islands. The welcome at each port was such that Robert and Patience were soon exhausted from parties and dancing that went on till late at night. Many of the islands were coral atolls so getting ashore was a problem. Taking to canoes and smaller boats, the reefs had to be negotiated by riding a big wave over the treacherous coral, hence the eventual title for his book, *Over the Reefs*. Living conditions on the *Tiare* were cramped; only the Captain had a private cabin and Patience and Robert had narrow bunks either side of the main saloon above fixed benches around a central table — under which other passengers slept on the floor. Many locals travelled in even worse conditions as 'deck cargo' packed together on the open decks at night — but they travelled free.[25]

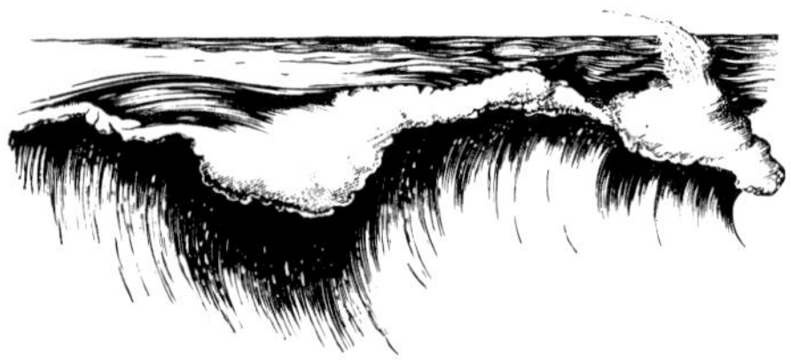

298 Wave over the reef. Illustration from *Over the Reefs*, 1948, wood-engraving, 44 x 104 mm.

Calling at Atiu, Mitiero, and Mauke, Gibbings and Patience were finally dropped off on the island of Mangaia and stayed for over a month. The local newspaper heard of their arrival and Gibbings asked them to publish a request for information about a much respected and well-known missionary in Tonga, who

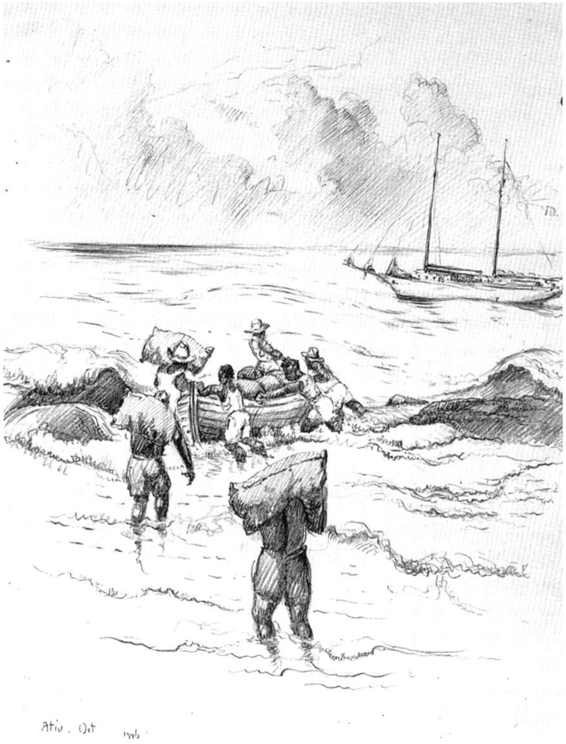

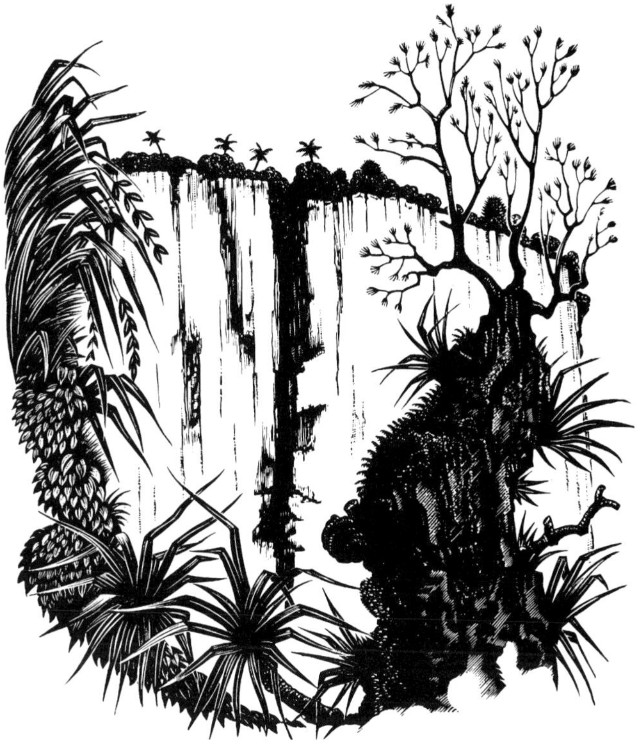

299 Loading cargo at the island of Atiu for transportation by the *Tiare Taporo*. Pencil drawing from Gibbings's sketch book, 250 x 195 mm., dated October 1946, on which he based a wood-engraved illustration in *Over the Reefs*. From a collection of negatives taken of drawings Gibbings made in Polynesia before the drawings were later sold or dispersed. RUL.

300 Cliff-face and vegetation on the island of Mangaia. Illustration from *Over the Reefs*, 1948, wood-engraving, 120 x 105 mm.

had lived on Mangaia for many years, known locally as Gillirua. This was Eric Gill's grandfather, the Rev. George Gill, and Eric's brother, Evan, had asked Gibbings to find out whether his grandfather was still remembered.

The return of the *Tiare* had been delayed but on the morning of 18 December a beating drum announced that she had been sighted. On board once more, the next day they off-loaded supplies at Mauke and then sailed on to Aitutaki, via Atiu. They sailed again on 21 December but ran into wild weather and for one day the wind blew them around in circles and ripped the mainsail. Things improved and a beautiful Christmas day was spent aboard the *Tiare*: 'Christmas day on the schooner was uneventful for every one on board but the poor pig. That night we dined on fresh pork.'[26] The following day they reached Manihiki, but a heavy swell made landing supplies impossible so the *Tiare* sailed on to the island of Rakahanga, leaving Robert and Patience marooned on Manihiki until their ship reappeared. It was a lovely island — a superb land-locked lagoon, six miles across, surrounded by a series of palm-clad islets. They befriended one of the few Europeans on the island, who quickly had a house made ready for them; it was built on a pier of coral rock that jutted into the waters of the lagoon. They spent the New Year there, sitting on the veranda in the moonlight drinking gin and coconut milk (drinking water was scarce) and thinking of the very different festivities at home. Celebrations had to be restrained, as earlier in the day an old man had died in the village nearby and the air was filled with the sound of wailing and moaning. After attending a church service to usher in the New Year with 'the ringing of bells and much embracing', Gibbings returned to the veranda:

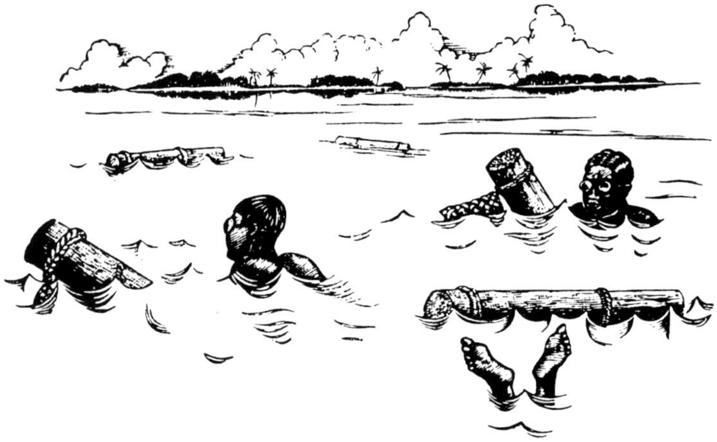

301 *right* Pearl divers. Illustration from *Over the Reefs*, 1948, wood-engraving, 58 x 96 mm.

302 *below* A pair of pearl diver's goggles, a fishing hook, a basket used to collect oyster shells, a carved wooden figure, and early stone tools – some of the souvenirs Gibbings brought home from the Polynesian islands. From the author's collection and the Gibbings Collection, RUL.

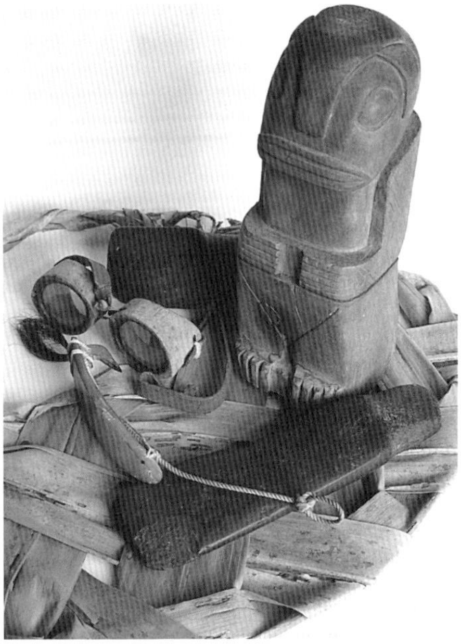

By now the wind had dropped completely. Every star was clearly reflected in the lagoon. The moon was low behind the palms. I thought of the people who, in stuffy clothes, were welcoming the New Year in crowded buildings. Standing on the veranda, I dropped my *pareu* and dived into the lagoon, to meet the New Year among the reflected stars.[27]

The heavy seas had continued to pound the reef but eventually the *Tiare* returned during a short period of calm and was loaded quickly and sailed for the island of Penrhyn, a larger version of Manahiki. They stayed for ten days; one day they had an all-day picnic on one of the islets, uninhabited except by sea-birds, and ate an enormous meal all caught and cooked on the island — sea-birds, fish and shell fish, with breadfruit and coconuts. They went fishing by moonlight in the open sea, and by the light of coconut torches in the lagoon. They watched pearl divers working all day, resting between dives on logs with baskets attached to collect the shells: the first diver they watched handed them the shell he had brought up and when Robert opened it they found a pearl!

On 16 January a fair wind arose and the *Tiare* set sail once again, this time for Tahiti, passing the islands of Borabora, Tahaa, Huahine and Moorea. It was important to reach a safe harbour before the hurricane season and many boats congregated in the port of Papeete in Tahiti for shelter. The weather was very hot and the only relief was provided by the occasion deluge of rain — everyone would rush on deck with only a pareu on and soap themselves madly — there were no facilities on board. With no refrigeration and a scarcity of fresh food it was a tremendous relief to reach Papeete, an outpost of French civilisation, and Robert and Patience revelled in gorgeous salads, fruit, fresh bread and firm butter and iced drinks.

On reaching Tahiti, Gibbings was disappointed to find that his friend James Hall was in America. It was eighteen years since Gibbings had last been in Tahiti but Hall had been true to his word and in his house Gibbings found a letter: '"The House that waited" is still waiting: use it and everything that is in it as your own ....'[28] The waters of the lagoon lapped the shores just a few feet from the simple thatched house; the walls were lined with books of every description and, best of all, there was a gramophone with a collection of classical records. After months on board the *Tiare* and after hearing no note of music except guitars since leaving England, this was blissful; the perfect place to recuperate and concentrate on writing up his copious notes. By now Gibbings had collected a vast quantity of material and, having someone else to do most of the note-making, he had more time and energy to concentrate on drawing and was particularly pleased with the quantity and quality of what he had produced. He was even thinking of organizing an exhibition of his drawings at Bumpus or The Times Book Club in London.

For Patience, domestic duties were lightened by the presence of an excellent cook, a local woman who also helped with the housekeeping. Strangely, essential supplies were harder to get in Papeete. Being a relatively sophisticated town, with a wealth of cafés, luxuries were in good supply but basic goods were less available and some items were rationed. In England, people were still suffering from strict rationing and throughout their travels, Patience and Robert had sent home parcels with tins of sugar, stockings and other scarce goods.

Long term plans were continually changing and Gibbings was now uncertain when he would return to New Zealand. There were a few islands which he still wanted to visit, the most important being Raiatea, known as the 'holy island' and the ancient centre of Polynesian culture. He expected to stay on Tahiti for two or three months; the shipping company had informed him that there was a ship going direct to New Zealand some time in May. He also had plans to return to England via South America to get material that might be useful in future books. However, the weather on Tahiti changed for the worse and torrential rain caused serious flooding — the island was even hit by a hurricane. Even when this had passed the atmosphere was damp and oppressive. Gibbings soon became disillusioned with Tahiti; the glamour of the harbour at Papeete was superficial and lacked traces of true native life so that he found little new to draw; he was also disappointed not to find old friends or the circle of artists and writers that had

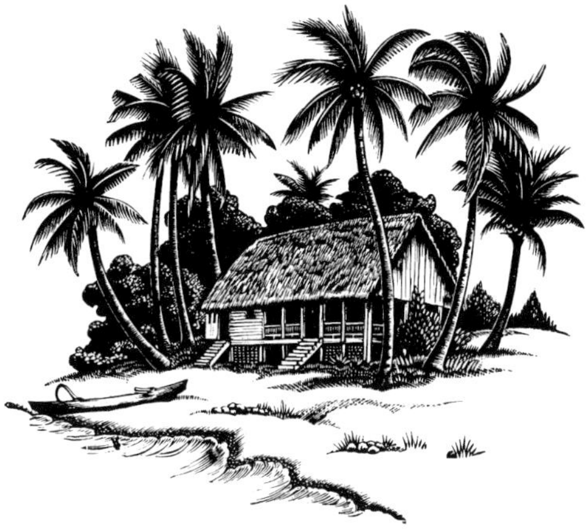

303 *above* 'The House that waited' – a guest house belonging to James Norman Hall that he built on the shores of the lagoon on Tahiti and lent to Gibbings for his stay on the island. Illustration from *Over the Reefs*, 1948, wood-engraving, 77 x 88 mm.

304 *below left* Photograph of a waterfront in Tahiti with trading boats and locals gossiping. Author's collection.

305 *below right* Pencil drawing of the mountains on the island of Moorea, dated 19 February 1947, 253 x 178 mm. Author's collection.

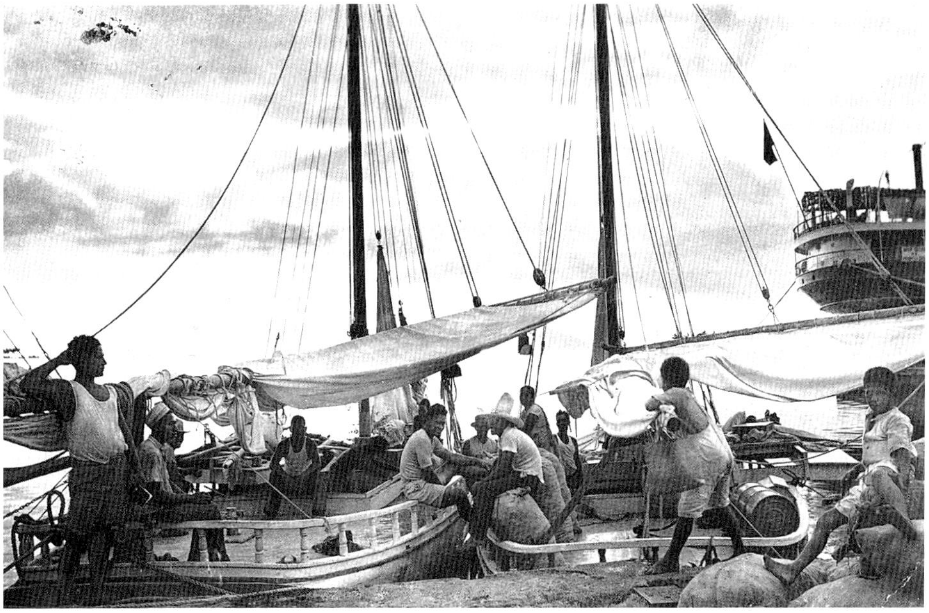

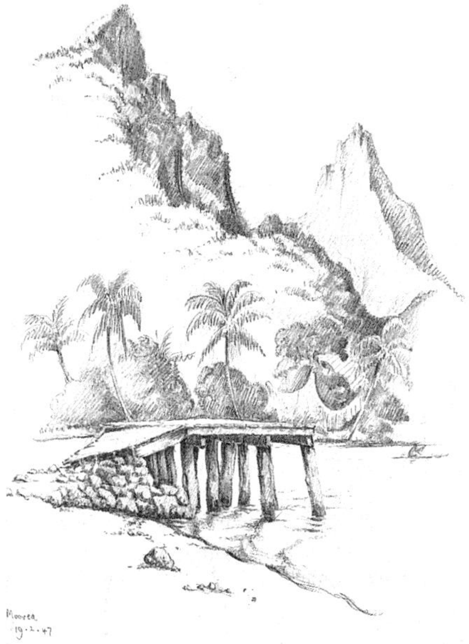

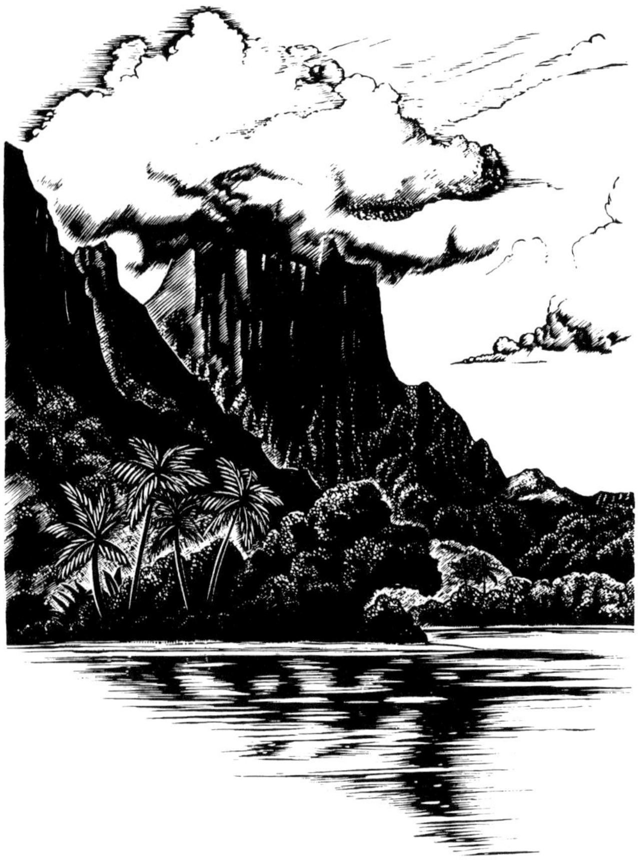

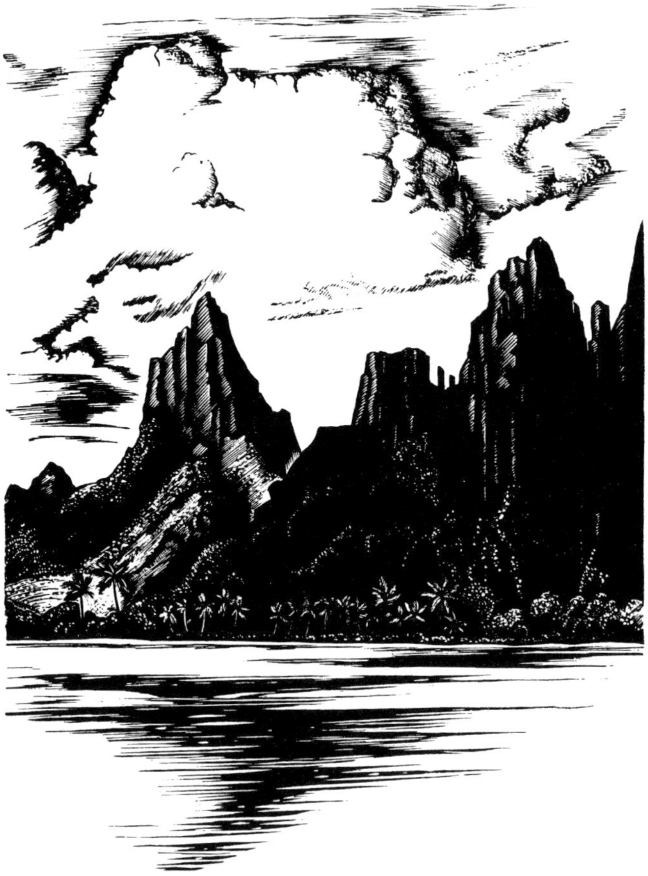

306 Papetoai Bay, Moorea. Illustrations from *Over the Reefs*, 1948, wood-engraving, each image 135 x 102 mm. Another example of two blocks printed on opposite pages to form a panoramic view.

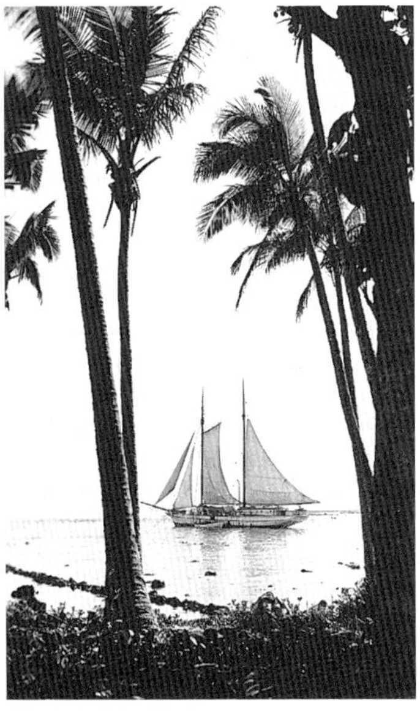

307 The *Tiare Taporo* at sea. RUL.

existed in the past. As a result of his feelings plans changed again, and, at the end of February 1947, passage was booked on the *Wairata* back to New Zealand.

A delay in the arrival of the ship meant that Gibbings and Patience had time to visit the island of Moorea and its beautiful Papetoai Bay. He was overwhelmed by the landscape and visual stimulation:

> Here on all sides were subjects offering themselves, not only to the sympathetic brushes of oil and water-colour, but to that austere weapon of book decoration, the burin. Everything is crisp and clear-cut. Even the tenuous mist that creeps through secret aisles, revealing hidden spurs and coombs, or the vaporous clouds that tumble like waterfalls from a ledge, are all precise and definite in form. It is a valley of silhouettes, dark shapes on light, light shapes against dark, each with its own enriching patina.
>
> The grandeur of the hills is the grandeur of gargantuan architecture. From the drowned amphitheatre rise pillars, buttresses, and broken arches; jagged outlines suggest fragments of a frieze. Everything is to scale; mosses and lichens have become giant ferns, swallows have changed to terns, and, instead of field-mice, land-crabs scuttle and scramble.[29]

He was inspired to do a burst of drawing which would provide a final flourish to his book.

In early March, Gibbings and Patience were on board another schooner, the *Hiro*, heading east for the island of Anaa. On their return to the port of Papeete they were just in time to watch from the quay as the *Tiare* sailed away. This was the end of the adventure; on 27 March they boarded the *Wairata* bound for Auckland via Samoa.

Chapter Seventeen
... And Far Away 1947–1949

FOR THE NEXT SIX MONTHS Gibbings made Wellington his base, renting a small bungalow in Eastbourne overlooking the harbour. He began the enormous task of bringing all his notes together while Patience spent her mornings checking factual details in the city library and evenings at the typewriter. Occasional evenings out included cocktails with Sir Patrick Duff, the High Commissioner, who had become a friend. At the end of June Gibbings had to move house, and while waiting for the new place to be ready he went to Wanganui for a couple of days and then on to Napier where he had arranged to meet Mr F. D. Robson, who was an expert on the kiwi, a bird then practically extinct. Robson, curator of the Acclimatization Farm, had raised four of the birds in captivity and Gibbings thought that his knowledge ought to be recorded and published. A booklet entitled *Kiwis in Captivity* was eventually published by a local museum in Napier.[1] Back in Wellington, Gibbings was kept busy with public talks and radio broadcasts as well as working on his book. Articles about his exploits were published in the *New Zealand Free Lance*, with a photograph of Patience and Robert together, and in the *New Zealand Listener*.[2] He had been invited to give a lecture by the University of Otago in Dunedin on the South Island, with all expenses paid, and took the opportunity to spend a few days in Christchurch on the return journey.

On 3 December 1947 *The Cog*, Dent's house magazine, published a letter to the editor from Gibbings, clearly intended to enhance his already friendly and close relationship with the managers and workers. Writing on 16 September, he opened the letter with an announcement: 'Yesterday morning I added the last paragraph to my new book, counted up to 80,000 words, and said to myself: Ready for Dent's.' By coincidence, a recent edition of *The Cog* had just reached him in New Zealand and had provoked him into writing:

> After all the sea air that I've had it gave me quite a longing for a good sniff of ink and glue. Then it occurred to me that as I am one of 'the family' it might interest readers to hear of some of the pre-chapel stages of a forthcoming book.
>
> It is just two years since I left New Zealand, and since then I have visited about thirty islands, from Fiji to Tahiti, covering about twelve thousand miles. Sometimes I went by mail-boat, sometimes cargo-boat, sometimes plane, sometimes schooner.'[3]

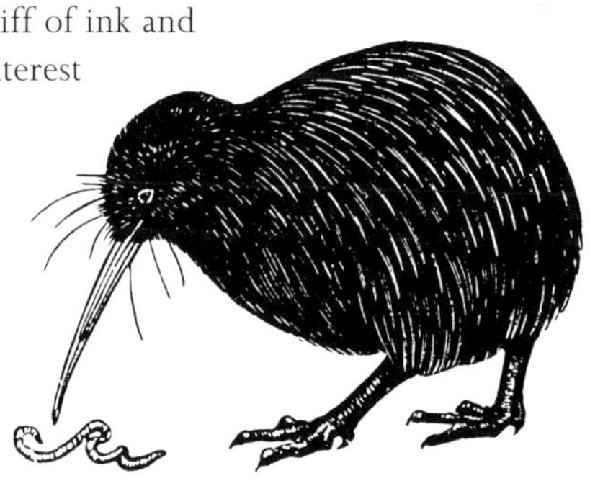

308 A kiwi. Illustration from *Over the Reefs*, 1948, wood-engraving, 40 x 55 mm.

There followed a description of some of his colourful adventures and he ended the open letter: 'Now, with my text completed, I have only to get home, and put in about six months on engraving the illustrations, and then I'll be dropping down to Letchworth to see old friends.'

He had booked his passage home on the *Athenic* which sailed on 23 October and reached London a month later. Patience stayed behind in New Zealand and together with another young woman, with whom she had made friends in Christchurch, spent a further year travelling throughout New Zealand and South Africa.[4] Patience's mother felt that it would be improper for her to return with Robert.

Once back in England Gibbings needed accommodation in London. He had written to his friend Charles Spencer from Wellington asking if by chance he and his wife were in a position to rent him a room; he wanted a place he could use as a studio and a sleeping apartment: '... it must be quiet and it must be well lit so that I can engrave ...'.[5] At that time he wanted a room to lease for two or three years as his permanent 'headquarters' while he travelled around and where he could 'leave everything lying about in my usual tidy way'. Although only vague, his plans were that after years in 'wild places' he hankered after the cultural centres of London, Paris and other European capitals, which he intended to be the subjects of his next book; his new 'abode' would form '... the nucleus from which my adventures radiate'.[6] This was a reason for having a base in London but it also suggests that his marriage was over. With the success of his last few books Gibbings was at last making money. He had to be careful about tax but income from royalties meant that he could pass on some financial security to Elisabeth and the children. While in Polynesia he had sent cheques for substantial amounts to be invested on their behalf, but there seemed no possibility of them living together again permanently.

On 15 October, Gibbings wrote to Spencer thanking him for agreeing to rent him a 'back room' at his house at 113 Cheyne Walk in London. His expected arrival on 23 November 1947 was well timed as he was grateful that he would miss the fuss of the Royal Wedding, but he was anxious to confirm arrangements:

> I think my best plan will be to send you a wireless from the ship, when we draw nigh to the shores of Albion, in which I will tell you when to expect me. I would like to come along direct from the ship together with my mosquito net & tropical whites which will be so damn useful to me in the winter!! ... It will be great fun to be back in the old home.[7]

Having installed himself in his new digs Gibbings quickly got down to the hard work of engraving blocks based on his drawings. Relations had not completely broken down between Robert and Elisabeth and over Christmas that year Gibbings split his efforts between London 'working like the devil against time' on his engraving and Waltham '... where I'm being a father to my offspring'[8] — it was the first meeting with his new son. He had delivered his manuscript and the verdict from his publishers was 'Best yet!' but he faced the daunting task of completing over one hundred designs that could be photographed onto blocks in the next four months. By the end of January 1948 he had completed fifty-six designs and was '... struggling to complete 60 by the 25th which is 60 days since I came

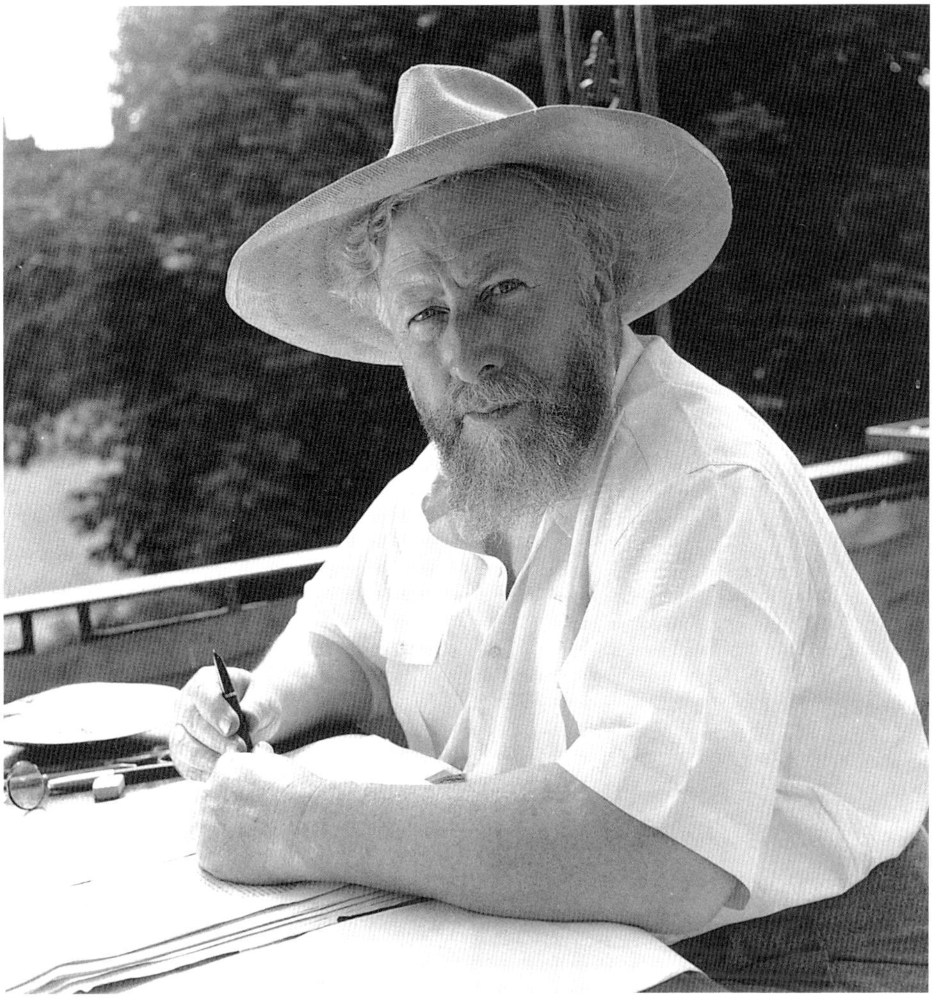

309 Gibbings writing on the balcony of his flat at 91 Warwick Road, London. RUL.

ashore'[9] —an exhausting rate. He had been reporting on his progress to Cathleen Lennard Jones when they had occasionally met for dinner and lunch dates in town. He complained to her about the smallness of his room: 'At the moment I have to take the *News Chronicle* because in my small quarters there wouldn't be room for *The Times* & me.'[10] His room overlooked the Thames but he could not help contrasting the 'crystal clear shimmering water' around the islands with the 'thick brown soup through which you couldn't see an inch' of the river.[11] By the end of February, he reported to George that he had decided to move out of Cheyne Walk into 'an elegant flat at 91 Warwick Rd. SW5'. He also reported that he had completed seventy-one designs and twenty-four engravings; with twenty-four designs and seventy-one engravings still to go he was half way![12]

He moved to Warwick Road in the middle of March. The flat had been organised by his sister Aimée, who was now living in Chelsea after a particularly eventful war.[13] Aimée had become well known as a singer and as the 'Irish contralto' had travelled the world giving concerts and broadcasts. She found the flat and helped furnish it with old family pieces and basic second-hand items, to which Robert added souvenirs of his travels. Now, with a permanent home, he was in a position to ask for the return of his collection of reference books from the

Lennard Joneses. It was a two bedroomed flat with a comfortable sitting room, with french windows that opened onto a balcony overlooking a tree-lined garden, providing excellent light for his engraving. Accommodation was not so easy to find in London as so many buildings had been damaged or destroyed by bombing — many of the surrounding houses in Warwick Road had missing roofs or smashed windows and there were gaping holes where buildings had completely gone. But Gibbings could forget this:

> ... when I sit on my balcony and close my eyes the roar of London traffic is not unlike the booming of the surf on the reef, and the sweet scents of flowers wafted up to me from the garden below are like the sweet scents that blow among the islands. For this balcony of mine is at the back of the house, away from the street, and it looks over a large public garden. Two big chestnut trees close beside me remind me of breadfruit trees and a tall evergreen tree might well be a mango but there is nothing at all that calls to mind a coconut palm. There is no sound that has the gentle rustle of the palm fronds. There isn't even the occasional thud of a falling nut.[14]

By the middle of June Gibbings was planning a visit to Letchworth to oversee the imposition of the book:

> It is absolutely essential that I should be there to put each block in its place & decide how many more blocks are necessary to put the 72 that I have completed in their place. E.G.,I have done a tail-piece for a chapter that is 2½ inches in depth. When the chapter is 'paged up' there may only be 2 inches left for the tail-piece. That means that either I have got to cut out a few lines of my most elegant prose or sweat my soul in another paragraph to throw the ending on to the next page. The same applies to the fitting of an illus. to its text. It is no good putting a dancing girl beside a deacon — not in a book, anyway![15]

Proofs of the text were arriving in batches and Gibbings was busy with corrections and amendments. At the beginning of July, later than anticipated, he spent a week in Letchworth working with the production team. Eventually eighty-four blocks were used, ranging from tiny tailpieces to panoramic images of a mountainous landscape, cleverly organised into two blocks printed on facing pages but combining to give a wide view. Over the summer months Gibbings was preoccupied with the final stages of production and giving the occasional public talk and lecture. In October he needed a break and considered a trip to Paris for a few days but was then tempted by a visit to Cathleen and George. Writing to Cathleen he commented: 'Now instead of the Folies-Bergères you will be able to put on a show for me — I always do prefer the more intimate Cabarets!'. Gibbings followed this flirtatious request with a more down-to-earth question: 'Are you by any chance short of tea or sugar? I have plenty and could bring some' — rationing was still having an effect![16] Unfortunately neither trip was possible as Robert came down with 'flu. A few weeks later he decided to 'hop off to Brighton where the air is supposed to be good';[17] the effect was beneficial and he was soon 'fit as a flea again'. On 28 October 1948 *Over the Reefs* was published.[18] The following day an article appeared in a Letchworth local paper, and was later reproduced in *The Cog*, which emphasised the close relationship Gibbings had with both his publisher and printer:

Cover of *Over the Reefs* – see colour plate 8h.

Residents may have seen in Letchworth recently a massive figure of a man, with a flowing beard and merry blue eyes. He is Robert Gibbings .... He has been visiting Dent's printing and binding works quite a bit in the last few months seeing his new book, *Over the Reefs*, through the press.

Dents have been the publishers of all Gibbings's best-selling 'river' books, from *Sweet Thames Run Softly* onwards, and they have all been printed and bound at Dent's works at Letchworth. Robert Gibbings has taken a practical on-the-spot interest in the production of each of these books. Gibbings at one time ran the Golden Cockerel Press, and for some years was Professor of Book Production at Reading University, so he knows something about printing. It is not surprising, therefore, that, with his rich personality and his enthusiasm for the craft, the printers and binders at Letchworth have come to welcome especially a new book by Gibbings, and the visits from the author-artist that his new book entails.[19]

In many ways *Over the Reefs* was Gibbings's most ambitious book to date. It had been three years since his last book and over that period he had accumulated a vast amount of material. It is a very dense book, an evocative and factual account of all aspects of the Polynesian culture and way of life, and at the same time the exotic location gave Gibbings the opportunity to fully develop the richness of his descriptive writing. For his readers he had experienced what to most people is never more than a romantic dream; in late middle age he had escaped on his own (there in no mention of Patience in the book) to another world, drifting from island to island on a tropical sea; exotic adventure, an underlying erotic mood of the hypnotic dancing of the women — these were powerful ingredients. Yet the book is also a serious anthropological study based on sound research and first hand observation — details of ceremonies, legends and folktales, traditional crafts and skills such as house building and fishing fill the pages of the book. Once again Gibbings had written a book with wide appeal. *Over the Reefs* received excellent reviews in the press and was reviewed on the BBC Third Programme.

Research and writing had dominated Gibbings's time for the last few years and he had had little time for commissions to illustrate any books but his own. In 1945 he had contributed three tailpieces to a collection of essays entitled *Voices on the Green* which was illustrated with blocks by most of the prominent wood-engravers of the period, but Gibbings's engravings were old images that had been previously published.[20] Since 1945 he had concentrated almost entirely on engravings for his own books. He was only deflected from this task by a request from his old university in Cork for a new design for their coat of arms to replace the etched version he had produced as a student in 1914 — a commission that he could hardly refuse.

Gibbings's life had been rich and full to date, but recognition and fame on a national and international level had come relatively late in life. On his fifty-ninth birthday Robert wrote an affectionate letter to his son Larry on his twenty-first birthday:

I am now sending you a small cheque, to celebrate your 21st. birthday. Needless to say it takes with it every possible good wish for the future. To-day is my own birthday, the 59th., which puts me into my 60th. year — another solemn thought! I am not much good at giving fatherly advice but as I said to Finn last night I'm sure that the only way

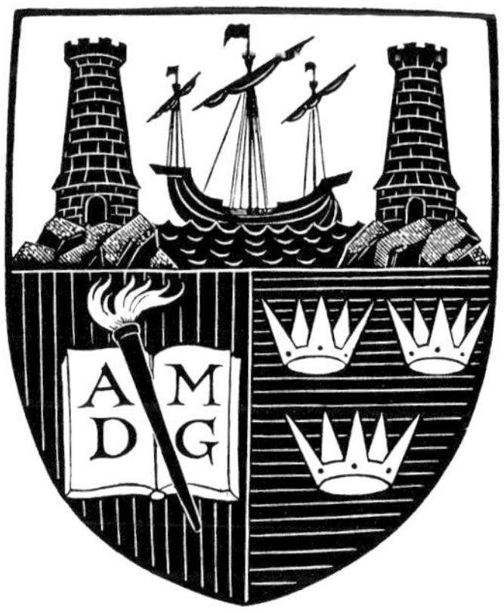

310 Coat of arms for University College, Cork, 1948, wood-engraving, 98 × 83 mm.

to get anything done worth doing is to follow your own star. Don't be misled by the miserable people who will want to give you advice — most of them people who have never done much themselves. Stick to what you really believe in & go for it with full energy. Of course if you want expert advice by all means seek it from an expert but that is different to being influenced by people with little real understanding. Even at my age people keep telling me what I ought and ought not to do! I do hope that life will bring you much interest & happiness. I often think to myself that one's code of life should be rather like that of wine drinking. If one drinks poor wine there is little enjoyment & next day one has a headache but if one waits for the good vintages & then partakes of them with aesthetic sensibility there are no regrets.[21]

The advice was sincerely meant and Robert had lived his own life following this philosophy, but it was at a cost. The artist has to be single minded and pursue his vocation no matter what, but others often have to pay the price. However inspirational Gibbings was, for the twins and his younger family, he was to be a remote figure and the loss of him as a father and a husband had brought pain to both his families and himself.

Radio and television were becoming an increasing part of his life. Since his return to England he had appeared on a children's television programme and had made several contributions to a series called 'Picture Page', in which he had demonstrated the art of wood-engraving. In April 1948, he received a letter from the Talks Producer of the BBC's Pacific Service asking him to contribute a piece for their series 'Calling the Islands', a programme specially broadcast for the islands of Fiji, Tonga, Solomons, New Hebrides and Gilbert and Ellice Islands but also received by many others in the south western Pacific. Gibbings readily accepted and soon became a regular contributor to the programme. In his first broadcast he established a personal rapport with his listeners, comparing his experiences of island life with that back in England. He was a familiar voice to them and Gibbings enjoyed sending his greetings to old friends.[22]

In December 1948 he began working on a revision of *Coconut Island* which was to occupy much of the next few months. Also that month, Tom Balston wrote an important article on Gibbings's writing and illustration which was published in *Alphabet and Image*. Profusely illustrated with wood-engravings, the article was an enthusiastic and perceptive analysis of Gibbings's river books and as a friend of many years Balston was able to reveal much about Robert's approach to his work and life:

Robert Gibbings hates slovenly work. He took to wood-engraving because 'the technique is austere and there are no happy accidents'. He is 'one of those who need a strict discipline from their medium' and, finding that even wood-engraving *per se* was not strict enough, he threw himself heart and soul into the even stricter discipline of engraving for books.[23]

Balston observed that 'The illustrator's, for the most part, is a subordinate, even a servile, job'; he argued that 'no illustrator of other people's works can hope more than once or twice in a lifetime to achieve that mating of his mind with the author's which will inspire the highest work of which he is capable.' But Gibbings had 'burst the bonds and started to illustrate his own writings or, perhaps, to write to his own engravings'. Balston felt that the underlying reasons for the popularity of his books was that people suffering from war longed for the simple life and that Gibbings was a 'modern Thyrsis'. His longing for solitude had led to an apparent desire to return to primeval days before man populated the world. Yet later he had been able to 'rejoice in his contacts with unsophisticated folk, their pleasures and their crafts'. Balston points out that unlike artists who find beauty in industry and machinery, Gibbings refused to 'accommodate himself to the nightmare *tempo* of a life based on telephones and telegrams and taxi-cabs. He draws and writes and lives in the rhythm of an earlier age ....' Gibbings had put much of this down to his own 'innate laziness' which is in such contrast to his insistence on discipline in his engraving and his amazing output of work. Balston was eager to deny that this disciplined approach could result in work that was 'cold and intellectual'; quite the contrary, he claimed that Gibbings's first inspiration was 'essentially emotional' and 'it is just because the emotion aroused in him by almost every form of physical or moral beauty is so strong, that he has found it necessary to put his art in a strait-jacket'. His engraving style had undoubtedly reached a level of technical perfection; the control over the marks he used to render texture and elements in his composition had become formalised and his engravings became increasingly 'designed'. Every mark was carefully considered and used for a purpose, with no free expression. They are not sterile and the engravings have a strong individuality but, with certain subjects, could very occasionally appear somewhat lifeless and contrived. The later delicate engravings, with such fine lines, were lighter in feel than the heavier images he had produced at the Golden Cockerel Press which had to harmonize with robust typefaces printed on damped handmade paper. His mass produced books were set in Gill's Perpetua typeface — creating a lighter feel to the page which Gibbings matched in his engravings. But these images are illustrations to decorate or amplify the text and he was never to return to the powerful visual statements of his earlier prints.

The material from his books adapted easily to scripts for broadcasting and for public talks. During 1949 he gave lectures to the Royal Anthropological Society and the Royal Geographical Society, of which he had been elected a Fellow in February 1944. One such talk, 'Politeness to Sharks', was broadcast and subsequently published in the *Listener*.[24]

Dutton published the American edition of *Over the Reefs* in March 1949, but with the extended title of *Over the Reefs and Far Away*.[25] Initially Dutton had proposed to set their edition in a typeface called 'Fairfield' but eventually they tried to match the English edition. However, the weight of type in the final version was a little light in Gibbings's view. Writing to Nicholas Wreden, the Vice-President of Dutton, he commented:

> I am neutral about the type page because, I suppose, I had planned the whole thing originally of a slightly darker colour; but that is not grumbling, and I am mighty grateful to you all for the trouble you have taken. I have only two adverse criticisms: (a) the somewhat saw edges to the pages, which I think make them a little difficult to turn over

and suggest an imitation deckle of which my high moral principles do not approve, and (b) the printing of the double blocks, pp. 230–1, which in several of the copies you sent me have got rather smothered in ink.[26]

Apart from these small gripes Gibbings was delighted with the edition.

Cover of Dent's edition of *Coconut Island* – see colour plate 8i.

June saw the publication of the new edition of *Coconut Island*, published by Dent, who were sufficiently pleased with the result to try to tempt Gibbings to write another children's book: 'There is a great lack of robust accurate factual boys' books at the present time; they have any amount of wildly improbable adventure stories, but not straight sensible stuff ... and the librarians are seeking for the latter.'[27]

Nicholas Wreden was a good friend of Robert's but also of John Hadfield. In his letter to Gibbings Wreden had said how sorry he had been to hear that Hadfield had been ill. Hadfield was now Director of the National Book League[28] but at the end of 1948 had suffered an attack of TB. By October 1949, Hadfield had recovered enough to be actively involved with the organisation of the official opening for an exhibition entitled 'Wood-engraving in Modern English Books', which had been arranged by Tom Balston for the League and was held at their premises in Albemarle Street in London. Balston had written the introduction to the catalogue for the exhibition, in which he made many references to Gibbings as an engraver and typographer.[29] Gibbings had been invited to give the opening address on 19 October, and a number of talks and demonstrations of wood-engraving as part of the exhibition programme over the following weeks. The

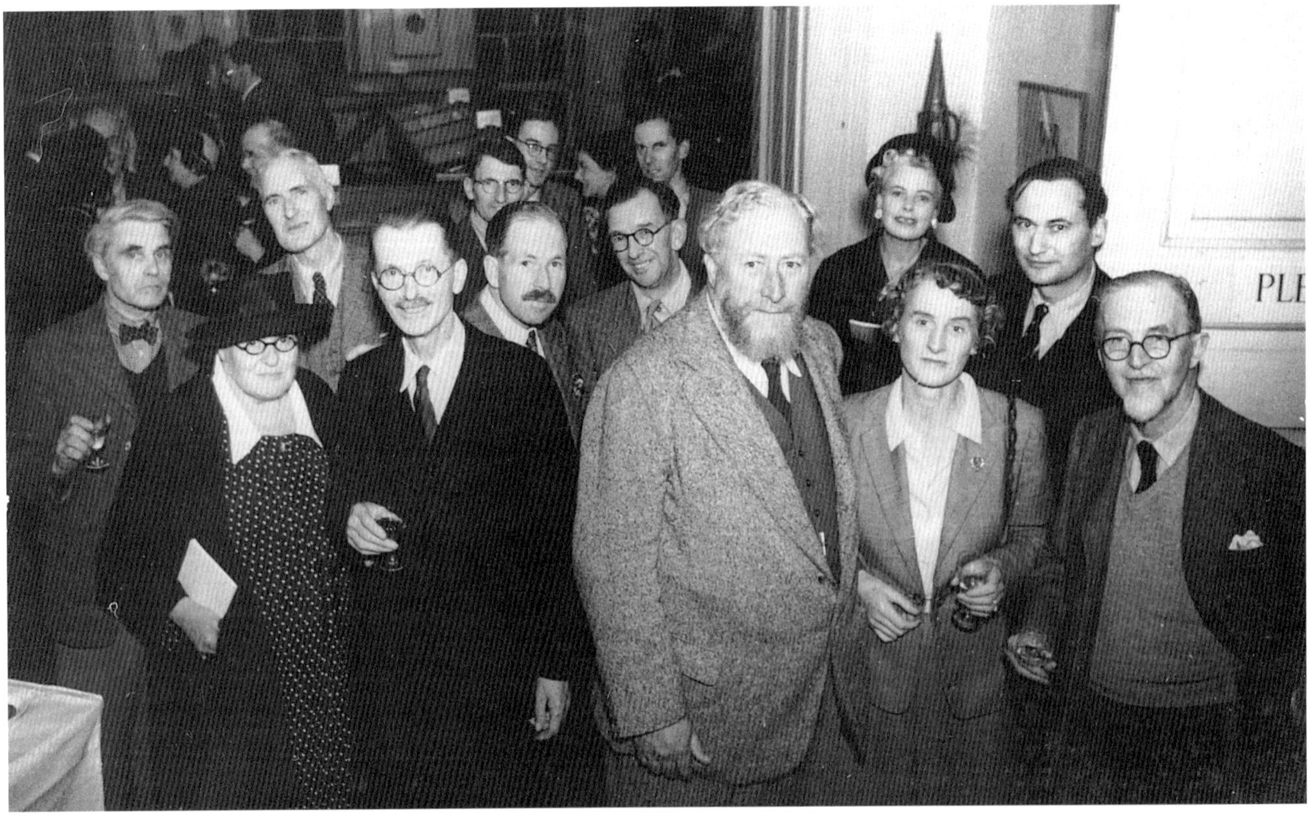

exhibition attracted an unusual amount of publicity as, mainly due to Gibbings's popular appeal, a national daily newspaper published a two-page feature on wood-engraving:

... the *Daily Graphic* chooses to break new ground in popular journalism by presenting this illustrated feature about English wood-engravers because this newspaper has faith in the ever-rising standards of the people's taste. We believe that there is a growing number of people who realise that there is something more to life than a constant preoccupation with material needs, with strategy and with strife. More and more people — especially young people — are coming to a knowledge of the beauty and wonder that is still to be found in our troubled world.[30]

Today these words seem patronising but perhaps they reflect post-war idealism and the article shows the public interest in the revival of wood-engraving. The article was given the headline 'The man in the hat isn't wasting his time' as the text was arranged around a photograph of Gibbings wearing his familiar large straw hat. As well as outlining the history of the art and illustrating work by leading exponents, the process of engraving was explained through a series of photographs showing Robert at work, accompanied by a description written in a tabloid style:

Robert Gibbings, aged 60, is Britain's tallest (6 feet) and heaviest (20 stone) wood-engraver. Besides that he is a wit, a sculptor, a naturalist, an authority on book production and a one-time lecturer on typography.

In the last ten years he has produced 300 wood-engravings for four books which have been read, and are still being read, by millions on both sides of the Atlantic.

He rises at dawn in his London studio and works on the engravings for two hours — 'any longer and my eyes hurt.' He engraves under natural light and uses a magnifying glass. Besides the tin of baby powder which shows up each engraved line like a thumb-print, and the duster, he uses six edged tools .... He sharpens them himself.

The largest engraving Robert Gibbings has made measures 10 inches by 8 inches; the smallest was about the size of a postage stamp. He usually spends a week on two or three

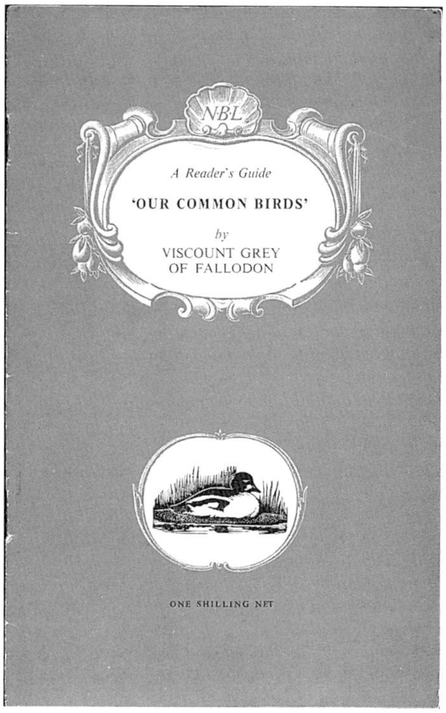

312 *Our Common Birds* by Viscount Grey of Fallodon. Booklet published by Cambridge University Press on behalf of the National Book League, 1949. Page size 215 x 140 mm. Author's collection.

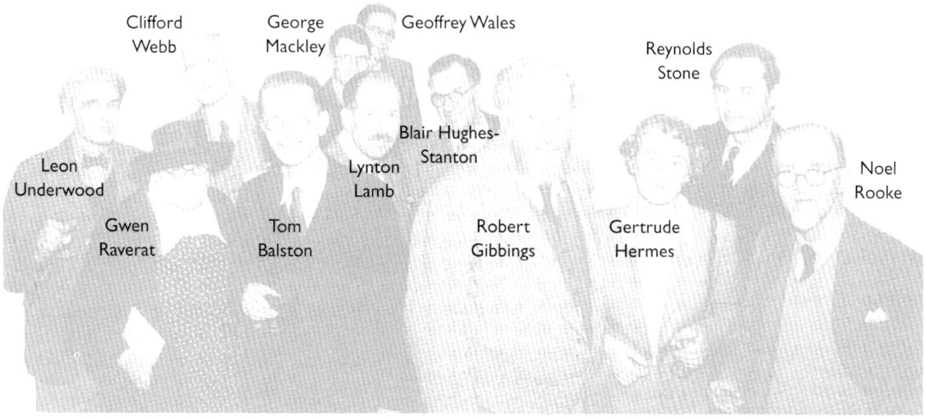

311 *opposite* Gibbings, surrounded by friends from the Society of Wood Engravers, at the opening of the exhibition 'Wood-engraving in Modern English Books' arranged by Thomas Balston at the National Book League, Albemarle Street, in October and November 1949. Gibbings remained an active member of the Society all his life. He regularly exhibited work at their shows and worked closely with Margaret Pilkington, organizing events and serving on the committee. RUL.

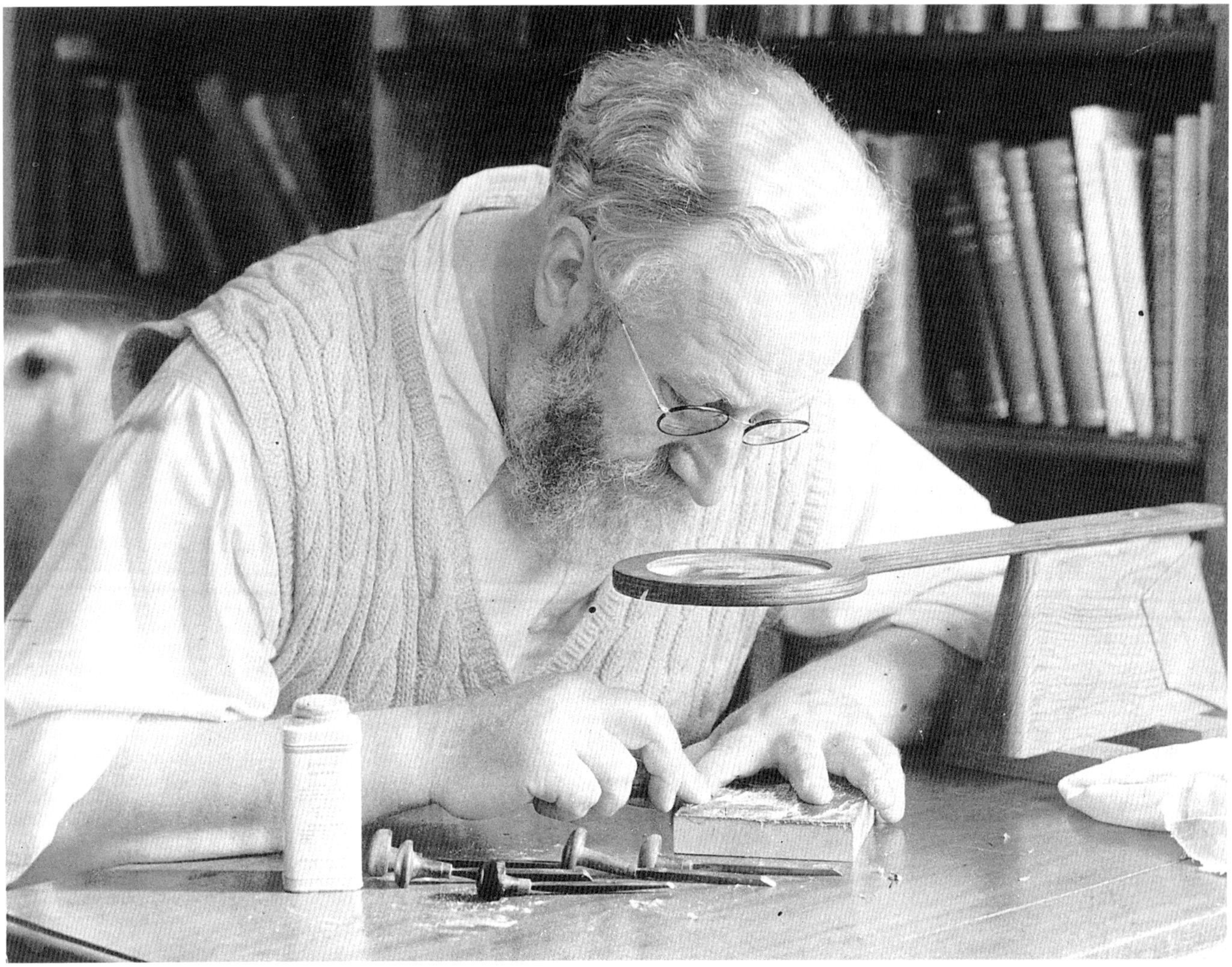

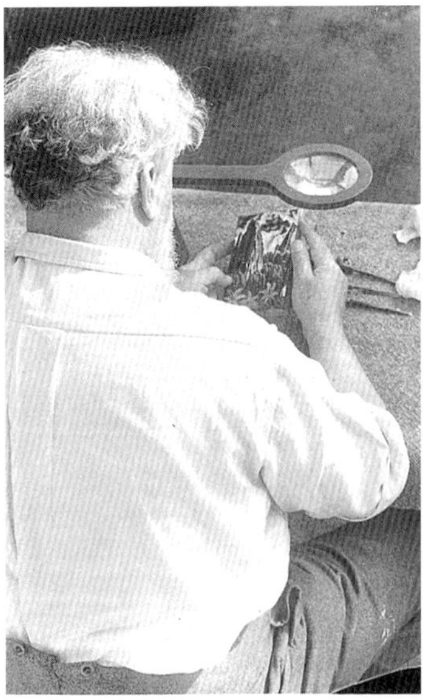

blocks, although he has taken as much as a fortnight on one and only two hours on another.

The wood he uses for the blocks is boxwood from Venezuela and South Africa. ... To see how the engraving looks at each stage, Robert Gibbings takes proofs on an old-fashioned hand press — 'the older they are the better I like them,' he says.

Balston had also been working on a book dedicated to Robert's engraving which was to be part of a series of small format books on various artists published by Art and Technics. A tribute to his friend, the book contained an outline of Gibbings's life based on conversations the two friends had had together in preparation for the book. Permission was obtained from publishers to reproduce a representative selection of over one hundred of Gibbings's engravings. As part of his introduction, Balston wrote a critical survey of his illustrative work and engraving style and technique. He described the engravings from *Over the Reefs* as showing that Gibbings had now reached a 'consummate' mastery of his art. During the period from 1923 to 1936 he saw Gibbings's approach to bookwork as being more about decoration than illustration; once he began to engrave for his own books his aims changed. Balston felt that *Coconut Island* had been 'inspired

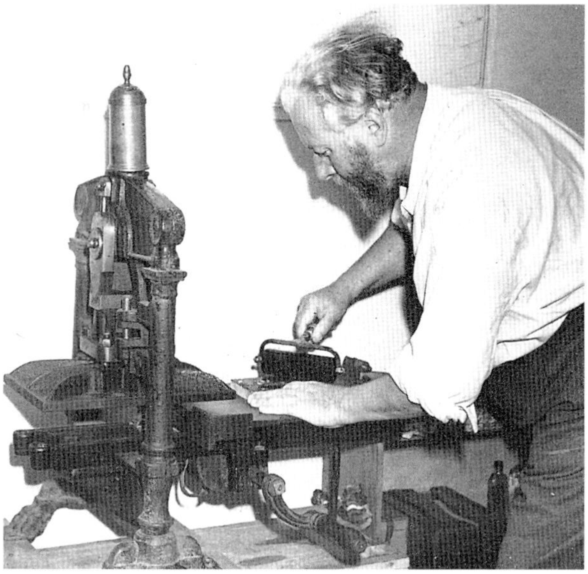

313 *opposite page and left* Photographs of Gibbings wood-engraving and taking a proof, published in the *Daily Graphic* on 20 October 1949, illustrating an article entitled 'The man in the hat isn't wasting his time'. He preferred to cover the working surface with a piece of Irish tweed cloth as in the photograph bottom left on opposite page. Unlike most engravers, Gibbings did not use a round leather pad or cushion on which to rest the block. The talcum powder was used to dust the block to show up his working. Copies of these photographs and a length of the tweed cloth Gibbings used to engrave on are in RUL.

by an impulse to write, and the engravings in it, though their decorative function is never overlooked, were primarily designed to elucidate the text where words alone would have proved inadequate.'[31]

Within a few weeks of the publication of *Over the Reefs*, Gibbings was already developing ideas for his next project. He had abandoned his plans for a book about European cities and the previous years abroad had, for the present, satisfied his lust for distant travel and adventure. Soon after his arrival in Samoa in 1945, a letter from a wealthy American admirer of his work had reached him with an offer of an all expenses paid trip to Nova Scotia with the intention that he should write a book on that province.[32] Gibbings declined; totally absorbed by his current project, he wanted to remain uncommitted. Now he was looking forward, in a more gentle and reflective mood, to regaining a sense of his roots and had decided to write once more about his homeland, Ireland. Even the offer of a trip to Mexico suggested by Nicholas Wreden could not tempt him. In a reply, dated 6 December 1948, to a letter from Wreden, Gibbings wrote:

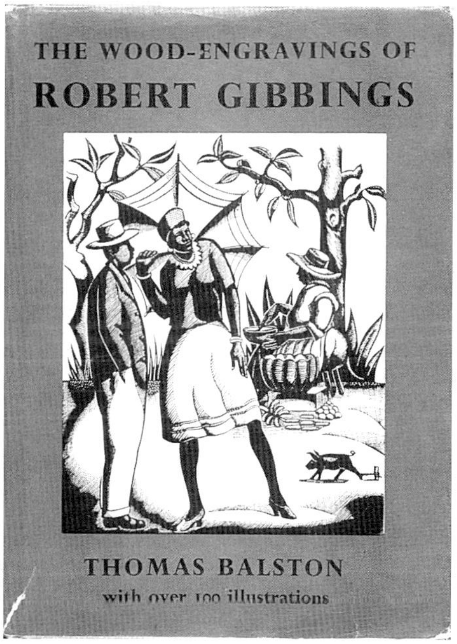

314 Cover of *The Wood-engravings of Robert Gibbings* by Tom Balston published by Art and Technics in 1949. Page size 183 × 135 mm.

> As to future plans, I have had any amount of talks with both Dents and Pollinger, and it really does seem best that I should go back to Ireland, where I belong, and do my next book there. I thought a lot about your kind offer and your suggestion of Mexico. But I cannot help feeling that it would be rather an effort on my part just now, to tackle a completely new country with a completely new language. In Ireland I know the idiom as well as I know the people, and they all know me, and will be only too anxious to help. I think that if I went to Kerry and concentrated on Killarney, perhaps even calling the book 'Killarney,' it might well be as successful as the 'Lee'.
>
> It is superb country all round there, to my mind the finest in the world — and of course, as you know, I speak without prejudice. So the present arrangements are that I should go over there in March, and spend most of the next two years in those parts, coming back here at intervals just to brush up my English.[33]

Gibbings was now fixed in his intention to return to Ireland. Over the next two years he spent long spells collecting material and finding the shape of the book.

Chapter Eighteen
Sweet Cork of Thee 1949–1951

IN A RECORDING made for the Pacific Service of the BBC on 11 July 1949, Gibbings opened his talk:

I wrote the whole of my last book, 'Over the Reefs', at Eastbourne in New Zealand. As I looked up from my table there, I could see across Wellington harbour to Somes Island, Karaka Bay, and Seatoun. Now I am beginning my next book in Ireland, at Gougane Barra, where I wrote 'Lovely is the Lee', and I am working in the same room overlooking that silver lake, in its setting of purple mountains. Apart from a small cottage across the lake there is only one other building in sight, the shrine of St. Finnbarr, patron saint of Cork, who lived here on a small island in the middle of the lake during the seventh century.[1]

This 'room with a view' was in the hotel owned by Connie and Joan Cronin. Being a friend of long standing, Gibbings had this particular room reserved for him whenever he visited them. This was his base, and his stay was punctuated by occasional breaks in England and wanderings around the countryside seeking material for his next book.

In order to solve the problem of accommodation on these wanderings and to give him the freedom of the road, Gibbings hit upon the idea of a vehicle that was fitted out for him to sleep in. Mr Morrissy of the C.A.B. Motor Company in Cork recommended a Ford van and Mr O'Reilly in the works reckoned on three

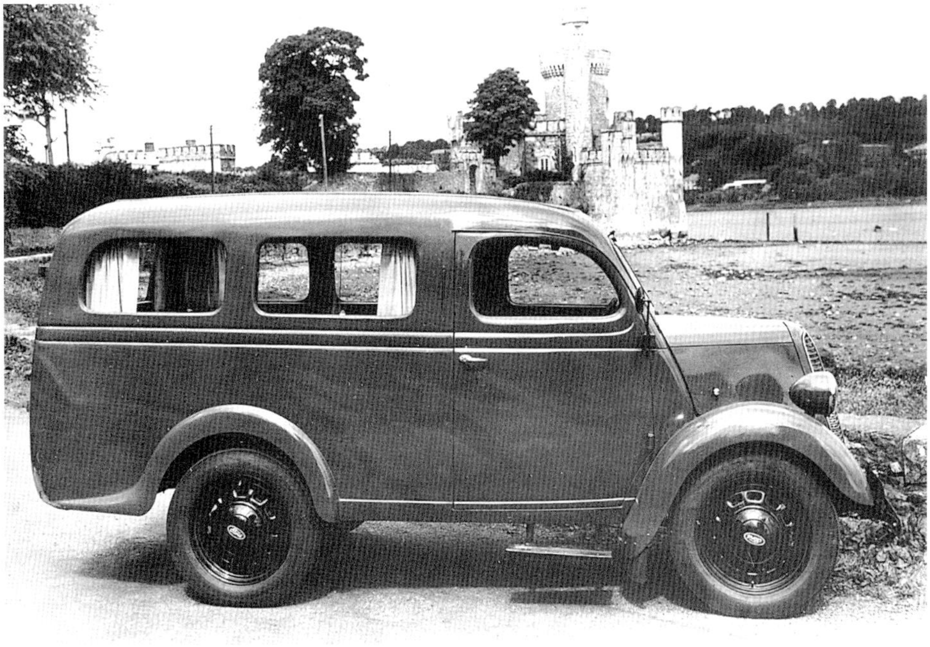

315 A Ford van which was fitted with a mattress and curtains to provide mobile living quarters while Gibbings roamed southern Ireland, collecting material for his book. RUL.

weeks to fit it out. Writing to Nicholas Wreden again on 29 March 1949, he explained his plans:

> ... since I last wrote to you I have spent a month in Ireland, making arrangements for the next oeuvre. I have bought a Ford delivery van, in which I am fitting *a single* mattress, and from the depths of my repressions I hope to give vent to a few expressions that may read well in print. I propose to make my head-quarters in the van, wandering among the mountains and lakes of West Cork and Kerry, according as my allowance of petrol permits. I think that, apart from descriptions of the scenery, natural history, etc., I could bring in quite a bit of autobiographical detail, told more or less by other people, which might be of interest to readers. There is no doubt that there is a wealth of colour, both in speech and language, over there, and somehow it seems to come easily to me to record it — I suppose because it is 'where I belong'. My idea is to spend the greater part of the next two years over there, living in out-of-the-way places and 'thinking aloud'. I will come back here occasionally for a change, and next winter I will probably spend some months here working on my notes, in particular those for the engravings, which I have made up to date.[2]

He did indeed spend much of the next two years travelling and collecting material but the reference to the mattress was later to have an unfortunate significance for Gibbings. On 25 June 1949, an advertisement appeared in the *Irish Times* for 'O'Dearest' mattresses, manufactured by a local firm, which consisted of a caricature of Gibbings reclining on a mattress in a caravan, with a rhyme that opened: 'When I am tired of sitting at the wheel I go inside into my boudoir on wheels and take a rest on my O'Dearest.' The verse was attributed to 'Bob Gibbings to Kees Van Hoek,[3] The Way of the World, *Irish Times*' and the rather poor piece of doggerel continued:

> 'In a caravan writing,' said Bob,
> 'Can at times be a wearisome job,
> Then it's nice to enjoy,
> One's O'Dearest nearby,
> So completely cut off from the mob.'

This was one of a series of advertisements which featured a number of famous Irish personalities, including Bernard Shaw. But the firm had not consulted Gibbings; the quotations had been entirely made up and his mattress, which had been specially made to suit his large frame, had been made by a different firm. Gibbings had not given his permission for his name to be used in this way; the result was that he decided to take the company to court. What really offended him was the implication that he was seeking financial gain by exploiting his name in a way unworthy of his status as an author and artist, that he considered himself superior to his fellow men and was anxious to avoid association with them.[4] Gibbings never felt superior to his fellow man, quite the contrary; he loved company and he drew much of the material for his books from his conversations with everyday folk. His legal advisors claimed he had been 'exposed to public contempt and ridicule and had suffered loss and damage'.[5] Gerald Goldberg, a local solicitor, represented Gibbings in the case and called upon a number of well-known local people to testify as to Gibbings's character and reputation.

Among these was Seamus Murphy, the sculptor and a friend of Gibbings. However, the case was ill-advised and it failed, but it did receive a great deal of publicity and a *Summary of Evidence* was published as being 'of interest to every advertiser and publisher'.[6] Gibbings had sent a copy of the advertisement to the secretary of PEN (the international association of Poets, Playwrights, Editors, Essayists, and Novelists) in September 1949, and had explained his embarrassment and concern over the affair. After the verdict, he wrote again expressing his outrage over the outcome:

> The case took five days last week in Dublin .... I had six reputable witnesses ready to swear that they had seen the advertisement and had thought the less of me for allowing my name to appear (as they thought) in such a form, and for so crudely (again, as they thought) selling my word. The Judge refused to hear any evidence of that kind from them, and left the decision to a jury most of whom, I imagine, knew little and cared less about art and literature.[7]

In solidarity, the Dublin branch of PEN held a protest meeting the evening after the end of the case.

The financial implications of the verdict were serious and the costs were high. Although his books had made money, Gibbings rarely hung on to it for long but spent generously and ploughed the money back into both funding his travels (two years in Polynesia had been expensive) and supporting his family. Gibbings feared that the costs of the case would leave him so short of money that he would be unable to provide financial support for his son Larry's further education:

> I wish I could help towards a University course but I fear that at present it is absolutely impossible. I've just been involved in a law-suit which has almost cleared me out. Added to that royalties are down to half what they were last year due to the general conditions. The law-suit was in Ireland — an action for libel that I took against a firm of mattress makers .... As I was using a different mattress in my van & everybody knew it, it looked as if I'd been paid highly to sell myself to a rival firm. Everyone thought I was sure of a verdict but the judge was biased from the start & refused to hear any of the witnesses that we had brought into court. I haven't heard what the 'costs' are going to be but I fear they will use up everything that I had saved. It is all rather depressing.[8]

Gibbings could not afford presents that Christmas and sent, as a greeting, copies of Balston's book about his work commenting that it had not been well produced — some images had suffered from being reduced and the detail on others had filled in.[9]

Gibbings managed to make a preliminary visit to Ireland in February 1949 but set off for his first lengthy stay in Gougane Barra on 7 April. His fame in Cork was such that the *Cork Examiner* carried a photo and brief note of his arrival, claiming him as a 'Cork author, artist and lecturer'. Most of May, June, July and August was spent researching, apart from brief visits back to England to give lectures or record programmes for the BBC, and to attend the opening of an exhibition of the Society of Wood Engravers held at Heals. Summer over, Gibbings returned to his London flat to write up his notes and work on drawings for the engravings. He had to attend the court case in Dublin in early December but apart from a short trip in January 1950, to lecture to the Hibernian and the Royal Dublin

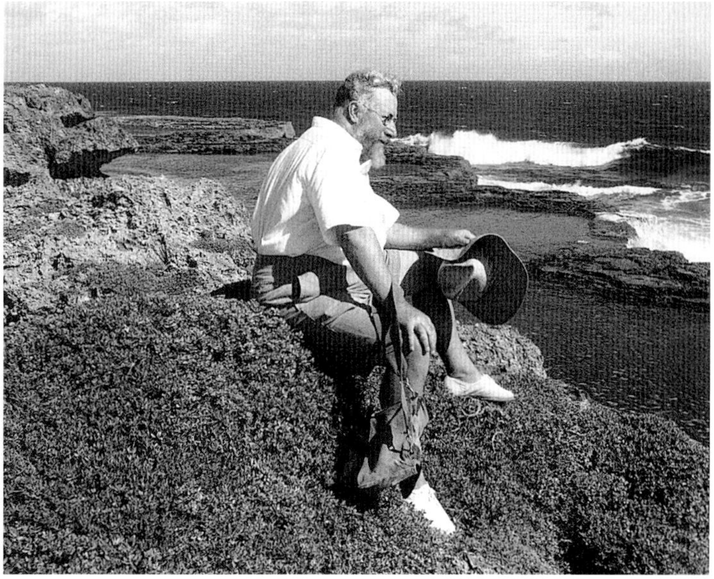

316 Gibbings on the coast during his journeys around southern Ireland. RUL.

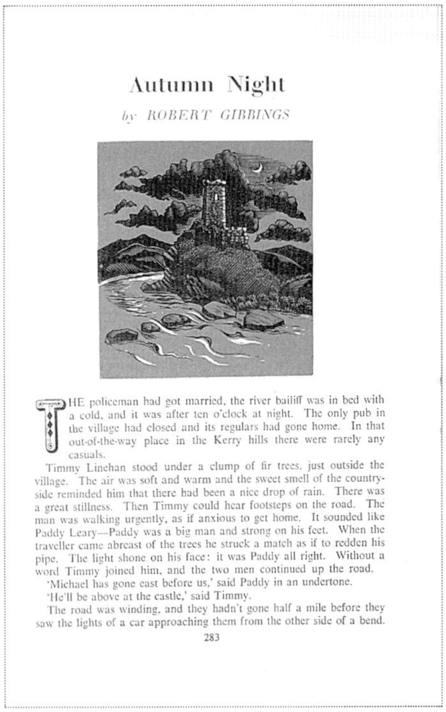

Autumn Night

by ROBERT GIBBINGS

THE policeman had got married, the river bailiff was in bed with a cold, and it was after ten o'clock at night. The only pub in the village had closed and its regulars had gone home. In that out-of-the-way place in the Kerry hills there were rarely any casuals.

Timmy Linehan stood under a clump of fir trees, just outside the village. The air was soft and warm and the sweet smell of the countryside reminded him that there had been a nice drop of rain. There was a great stillness. Then Timmy could hear footsteps on the road. The man was walking urgently, as if anxious to get home. It sounded like Paddy Leary—Paddy was a big man and strong on his feet. When the traveller came abreast of the trees he struck a match as if to redden his pipe. The light shone on his face: it was Paddy all right. Without a word Timmy joined him, and the two men continued up the road.

'Michael has gone east before us,' said Paddy in an undertone.

'He'll be above at the castle,' said Timmy.

The road was winding, and they hadn't gone half a mile before they saw the lights of a car approaching them from the other side of a bend.

283

317 Opening page of an article by Gibbings published in the *Saturday Book* in 1950. The article was illustrated by a wood-engraving printed in two colours. Image size 76 x 72 mm. Used by permission of The Random House Group Limited.

Societies, he waited until the spring for his next long visit. For much of February and March he was preoccupied with work on perhaps his most ambitious television project to date — a series of programmes called *Private View* which featured a behind-the-scenes look at the treasures of the British Museum, with Gibbings acting as guide and host.[10] He was enjoying the experience but found it tiring:

> The interesting side is hearing the facts about the objects under discussion but the exhausting part is 'lifting' the experts. Half of them get into a state of dither & shake all over during their appearances. If by any chance I ask a question out of turn they nearly faint! I did my third in the series last night & have now called off all further appearances until the autumn, at earliest, as I go back to Ireland on the 4th & expect to spend the summer there working on the new book. I don't seem to have quite the energy I had & this book is taking longer than the others. I suppose at 61 I must expect to slow down![11]

The series received mixed reviews. The programmes were closely scripted and Gibbings found this uncomfortable and artificial, hampering his genial and conversational style. A particularly upsetting review appeared in the *New Statesman* but judgement was balanced by more favourable comment from Harold Hobson in the *Listener* who described the programme as 'enchanting'.[12]

Although busy working for the BBC and producing his book, Gibbings could no longer afford to turn work away — especially work which appealed to his enthusiasms.[13] Charles Ede of the Folio Society wrote to him in December 1949 asking him to write an introduction to their edition of *Typee* by Herman Melville, which, with much of the research being done by Patience who had returned from her travels, occupied him over the following month.[14] In February Leonard Russell had also approached him for a contribution to *The Saturday Book*; fortunately Gibbings was able to provide a short story entitled 'Autumn Night', an Irish tale from the Kerry hills, which he had just completed, originally intending to use it as a chapter in *Sweet Cork of Thee*.[15] In the middle of March he flew to Dublin and then to Belfast to give lectures but also managed to find time for socializing —

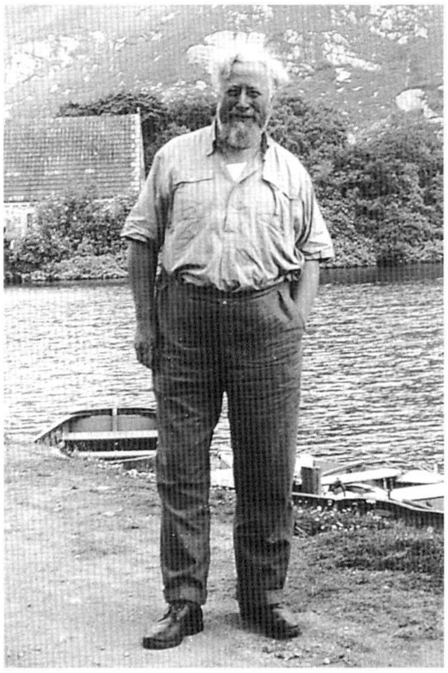

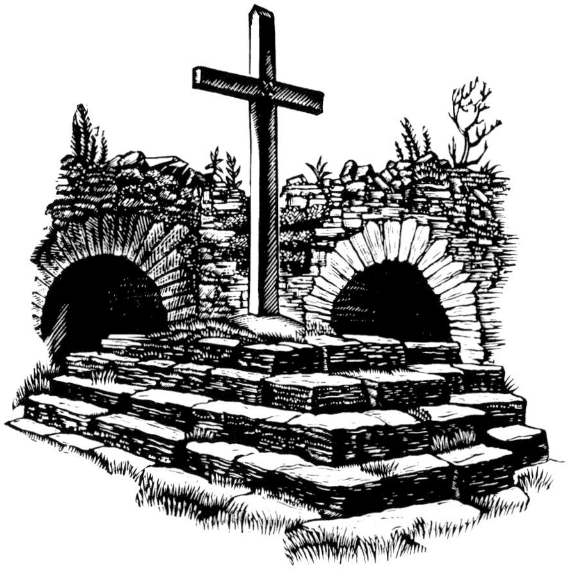

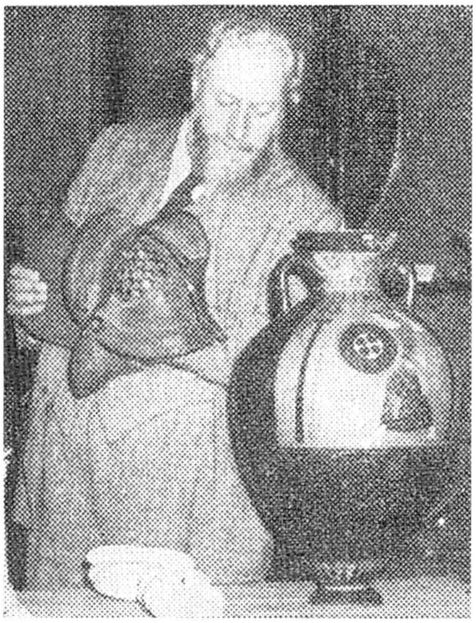

318 *left* Gibbings on the lakeside at Gougane Barra. One of the boats moored might have been the *Willow* which was reported to have ended its days on the lake. RUL.

319 *middle* The ruins of the hermitage of St Finnbarr, the patron saint and founder of Cork city, on the shore of the lake at Gougane Barra. Illustration from *Sweet Cork of Thee*, 1951, wood-engraving, 74 x 76 mm.

320 *right* Gibbings performing as the host on the programme *Private View*. This was a behind-the-scenes look at the treasures of the British Museum produced by the BBC; here Gibbings is seen in the King Edward VII Gallery with the famous Portland Vase. This episode went out at 8.30 pm on 28 February 1950. A cutting from the *Radio Times*.

he enjoyed a party held by the Golden Cockerel Press at Claridges on 22 March and a party held by Gertrude Hermes three days later.[16]

At the beginning of April, Gibbings returned to Ireland and at the end of the month was joined by Patience. Together they spent May exploring the counties of Cork and Kerry, all the while Gibbings avidly recording impressions and taking notes. For the first two weeks of June they were invited to share a holiday cottage in Dingle with Seamus Murphy and his family. Seamus, after a long apprenticeship as a stonemason, became well known in Ireland as a sculptor. Gibbings and Murphy became great friends and Seamus was to be a great source of Irish stories and anecdotes. Murphy was himself an author, capturing in his book, *Stone Mad*, published in 1950, the way of life and the true character and voice of the stonemasons he had met as a youth. Gibbings was a great admirer of this book and was influenced by Murphy's straightforward and truthful style and fascinated by his descriptions of tools and techniques. Gibbings wrote an enthusiastic review of the book, entitled 'Stones and Mud' in *John O'London's Weekly*.[17] Maighread, his wife, later remembered that Gibbings often dropped in for an evening during his time in Ireland, parking the van outside their house in Cork and sleeping in the sitting room — grateful for the company and a more comfortable bed.

As always, Gibbings took the research for this book very seriously. Historical notes and aspects of natural history were meticulously checked in reference books and he entered into lengthy correspondence with experts and appropriate societies.[18] Much of his 'research' took the form of a less academic process, engaging folk in chat in the comfort of the public bar, an environment in which Gibbings was in his element. He later described his technique:

> ... there is for the author an urgency in 'getting things down' while they are still vivid in his brain. Life passes with such kaleidoscopic changes that unless a word, a thought, a phrase, is recorded almost as it is born, it is lost. That at any rate is my experience. It is no good saying to myself, I'll write that down in the morning. By next morning it is gone for ever.

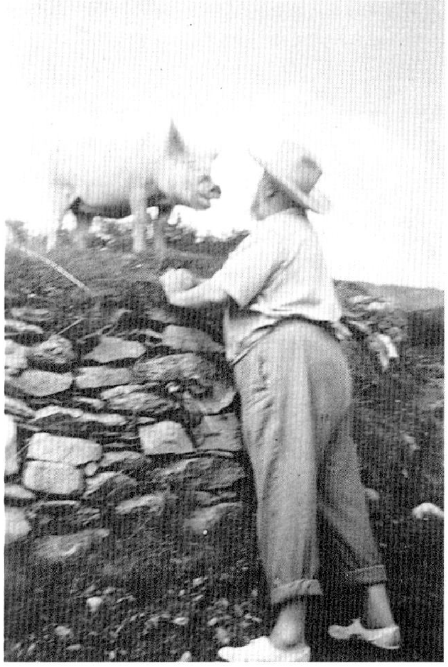

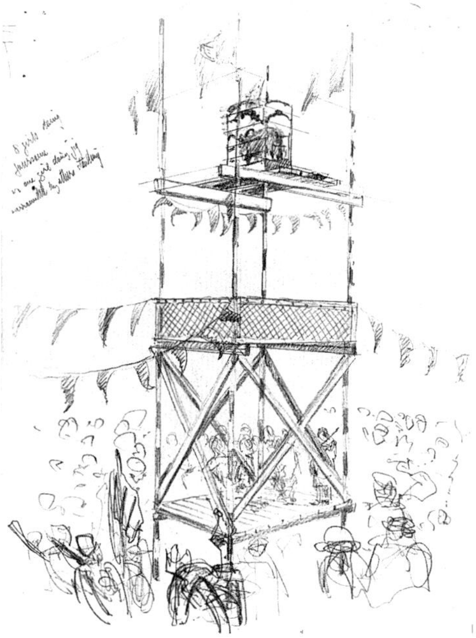

321 *left* Gibbings chatting to an unusual friend in Ireland. RUL.

322 *right* Annotated page from Gibbings's sketch book of a scaffolding tower, topped by a penned ram, with girls dancing on the lower platform, the centre-piece of the festivities at the Puck Fair. Clark Library.

> Here I will confess to a little bit of play-acting on my part which has got me over a few such difficulties in Ireland. With stories flying fast and furious of an evening, the only thing I could do was to develop 'a bit of weakness', or maybe 'a chill'. This would necessitate hurried exits from the scene of poetic narrative. 'Sorry, boys,' I'd say, with my hand to my waistline, 'I'll be back in a minute. Don't tell another story till I come back,' I'd say, and then I'd rush upstairs to my room and scribble like mad. And after I had come down again and there had been another good story, I'd rush off once more. 'My God, isn't the poor fellow bad?' I'd hear them saying as I hurried off.[19]

While gathering the material and making visual as well as written notes, Gibbings wandered the countryside. He would perhaps write an occasional descriptive passage but otherwise left the formal writing until he returned to London. Despite his apparent flowing and conversational style, Gibbings really had to work hard at writing. He would produce numerous hand-written drafts, adjusting the form and language until he felt satisfied. As before, the hand-written scripts were typed out by Patience, either being sent to her at her family home in Headington, Oxford (her mother had moved from Box Farm to a smaller house in 1946) or else she would travel to London to work in the Warwick Road flat. Two or three versions would be typed and corrected, Patience acting as a careful editor, offering criticism and suggestions. These typed versions would then be cut and pasted as the book developed.

During 1949, Gibbings signed an agreement with Dent which specified that the delivery of completed typescript and illustrations would be not later than 31 March 1951. In general, the terms were similar to those for his previous books. 'Not less than 50 (fifty) illustrations' were to be provided at a separate fee of 100 guineas, the publishers would have the option of publishing his next work and agreed to pay him the sum of £500 as a contribution to expenses in collecting material for the book. In the document, the title of the book is simply given as

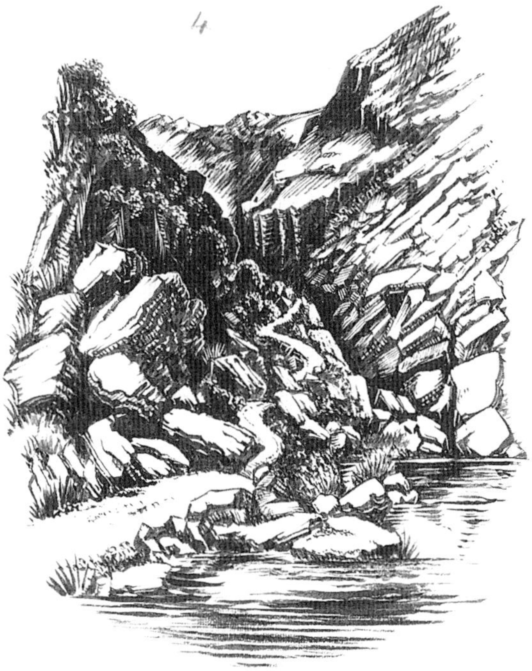

323 Ink drawing, with touches of process white, of a craggy river valley in Ireland. Designed for engraving and marked up to be photographed onto the woodblock, image size 190 x 152 mm (width marked to be reduced to 3 inches). RUL.

Kerry; it was some time before the final title was decided upon, *Sweet Cork of Thee* being a line from the song 'Bells of Shandon'.[20]

The completed typescript was presented to Dent well in advance of the agreed deadline and then Gibbings concentrated on the engravings. As well as using his drawings as a basis for his engravings, occasionally he had to look for other sources. Writing to a photographer in Dublin Gibbings requested help:

> Have you by any chance any photographs showing the rock formation on the Skelligs from which I could work for some woodcut illustrations in my new book about the south of Ireland? I would like in particular to get details of the ledges on which the kittiwakes nest, just above the landing place on Skellig Michael. I would very much like to have also a clear close-up of that magnificent rock arch on the south side of Little Skellig. Although it was a calm day when I was there, it wasn't possible to make a drawing from the boat.
>
> My sister-in-law, Patience Empson, who was there with me, has written an article for which she is anxious to get illustrations. Have you by any chance any photos showing the Little Skellig when the gannets are nesting? In her article, she compares the gannetry with one she visited in New Zealand ....[21]

Robert and Patience shared so many interests and he encouraged her to write — they were very compatible personalities and made an effective team.

Throughout the months prior to publication Gibbings was again heavily involved with the design of his book. Letters to and from the staff at Dent passed almost daily and show just how much control Gibbings was allowed in all aspects of production. In effect he now had more control than he had had at the Golden Cockerel Press, because he was now author as well as illustrator and designer and Dent encouraged him to oversee the printing. This was a rare and very special relationship between author and publisher and the spirit of the collaboration no doubt contributed to the success and quality of the product. Gibbings corresponded with many of the key members of staff at Dent, such as Martin Dent

(Chairman) and E. F. Bozman (frequently addressed as 'Boz') Editorial Director, who had become friends as well as colleagues, A. J. Hoppé (Director in charge of sales and publicity) and R. J. Hall (Production Manager). A letter from Gibbings to Martin Dent of 11 September 1950 illustrates how closely they worked together:[22]

I have promised to give a lecture on the making of an illustrated book in Manchester next month, and amongst other slides that I would like to show would be one of the big machines in your works, such as the 64 pager on which you print my books. Have you by any chance got such a photograph, or do you happen to have a photo of a 64 page forme, from which I could have slides made? Or any other relevant photographs? I am making the lecture a personal record of my experiences as printer, writer and artist.

Talking of formes, could you sometime during the next few weeks let me have back the small forme you lent me before, complete with block and type? I am also giving a lecture in the Isle of Man in December on the same subject, and would like to show it there as well as in Manchester. I think at one time we discussed the outright purchase by me of such a forme, and I think from the point of view of lectures it would be a good investment if you felt you could spare it.

As to the present book, I am glad to say that the two-colour frontispiece of fuchsias promises very well indeed; the design came nicely, and I am now awaiting the two blocks before I start engraving. If we are printing a four page separate for frontispiece and title page, the addition of the two colours on the title page will give a very rich opening. I have a design in mind but cannot get on with it until I see what space I have. Will it be possible sometime soon to let me have a pull of the title page? I suggest we keep it in the same style as the others, using as big type as possible in two lines for the title ....

The black and white blocks are coming on well. I have now about forty of them designed, and I think some of them are going to be the best yet.

I am presuming, by the way, that the type measure is to be 4" as in 'Over the Reefs', and not 4⅛" as in 'Lovely is the Lee' when paper supplies were shorter.[23]

The Manchester lecture took place on 24 October and Gibbings did indeed use a specially made up forme which he kept for such purposes. He had borrowed a copy of *The Four Gospels* from Christopher Sandford to illustrate his talk and Sandford wrote to him on its return: 'I am glad that the lecturing is going strong. It is good for people to hear you. Hubert Worthington told me how much you were appreciated when you opened the Exhibition of Books illustrated with Engravings in Manchester' — the exhibition had been the occasion for the lecture.[24] Commitments to the BBC and increasing requests for public lectures were a constant, although not entirely unwelcome, interruption and became a useful source of income. Talks about his travels were popular but he also lectured on his experiences in the world of books. He even proposed to Mary Adams at the BBC that one of his talks, on 'the making of an illustrated book', might be a suitable subject for a television programme: he intended '... dealing with the subject from the points of view of author, artist, printer and publisher, in all of which capacities I have served my time'.[25]

The demand for public speaking became so great that by 1953 Gibbings was signed up with at least two lecturing agencies, one run by Foyles and the other by Maurice Frost in the Charing Cross Road and his diaries became peppered with engagements from all parts of the country. At the end of December he gave a

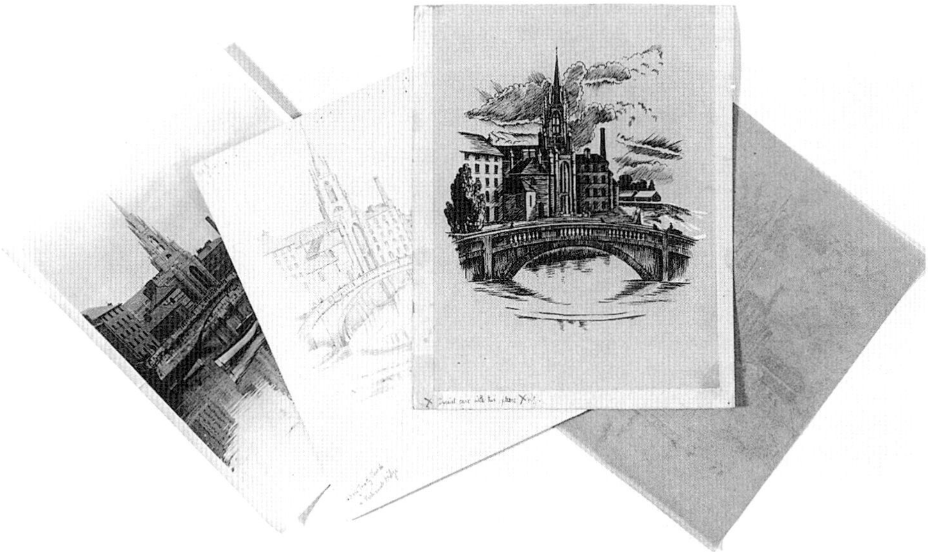

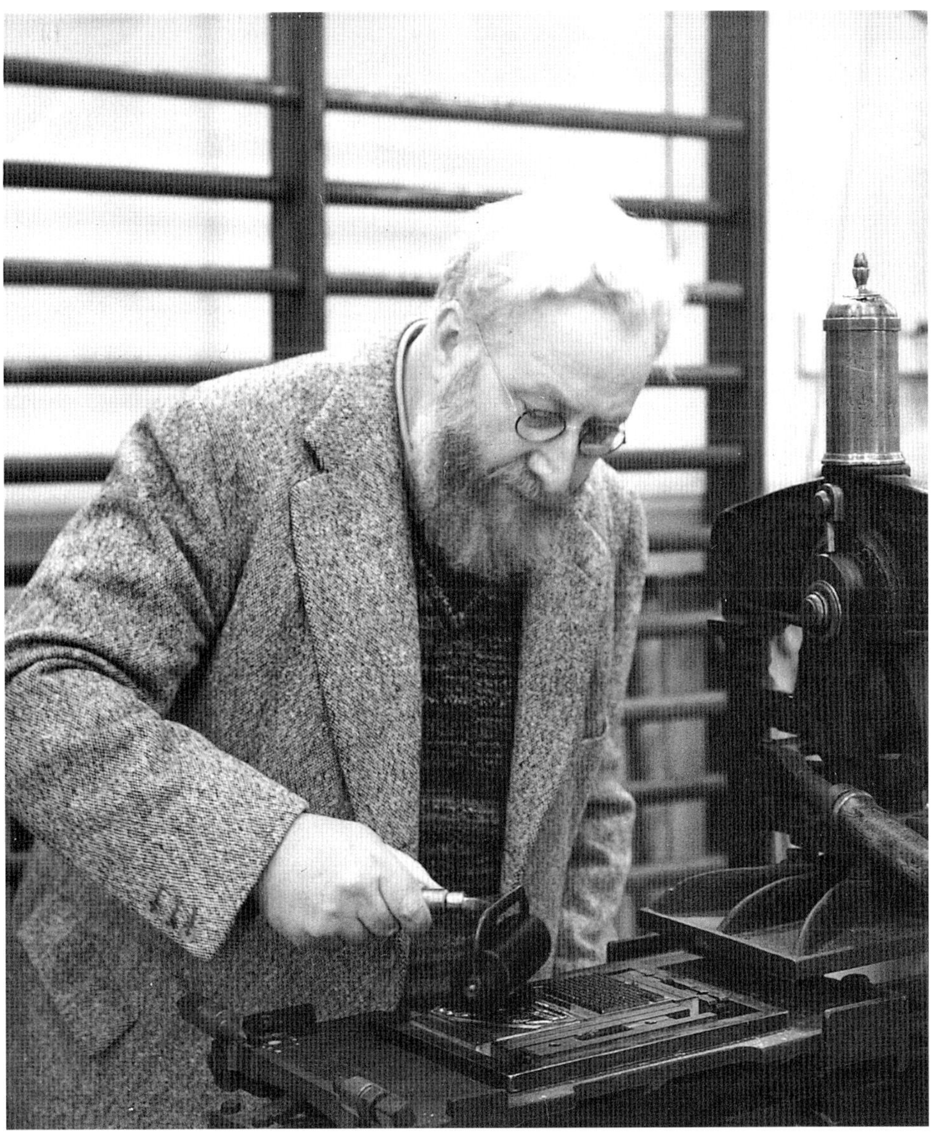

324 Photograph, pencil sketch, final design in ink with corrections in process white ready for photographing onto the woodblock and a tracing of Holy Trinity Church in Cork with Parliament Bridge in the foreground; all preparatory material to be used for a wood-engraved illustration for *Sweet Cork of Thee*. However, the engraving was never published; Gibbings wrote to Martin Dent on 25 February 1951: 'I am afraid that that full page which I had nearly finished for Chap I has proved to be a wash-out.' This was unfortunate as he had gone to some trouble over the accuracy of the image. He had written to Gerald Goldberg on 11 September 1950, asking if he could verify whether, at any time during the year, the sun rose behind the church – he had made his original sketch at midday but felt that a dramatic sunrise would improve the image. In return Gibbings promised to send a signed proof of the block as Goldberg was a keen collector of his work. Image size of the ink drawing 190 x 172 mm. RUL.

325 Gibbings taking a print from the forme, specially prepared for him by the compositors at Dent, of the opening of chapter fourteen of *Sweet Thames Run Softly* which he used for his public talks and demonstrations. RUL.

lecture in Wolverhampton and within a week he was lecturing on the Isle of Man. Earlier in October he was organizing the framing of three of his under-water xylonite drawings to be dispatched to the Munster Fine Art Club, for an exhibition to be held in November at the School of Art in Cork.[26] He then arranged for any unsold drawings to be passed on to the Royal Hibernian Academy for inclusion in one of their exhibitions.

In September discussions took place over the title of the book; Gibbings had provisionally called it *And Thus Grow Fonder* but Martin Dent had reservations: 'I never meant to give you the impression that I didn't like the title … as a title. In fact, I think it has great appeal. My point was that your other books have had a very definite title, and have been very successful, and that is always a good reason for continuing with "the mixture as before".'[27]

The pace at which Gibbings was now working was becoming relentless. Discussions were already taking place about the subject for his next book. A return to a river seemed appropriate but this time the country was to be France. In the middle of October 1950 Gibbings was already negotiating with Bozman:

> I have written to Pollinger asking him to get in touch with you about the 'Seine'. I am very happy indeed about the whole idea, and look forward very much to going over in the spring.
>
> Only one small and unimportant point has occurred to me, as a change in the agreement: instead of specifying not less than 50 engravings as in the last agreement, I suggest that we say that I will give the value in engravings equivalent to what I gave in the other books. This means that if I should find it possible to do some large blocks in

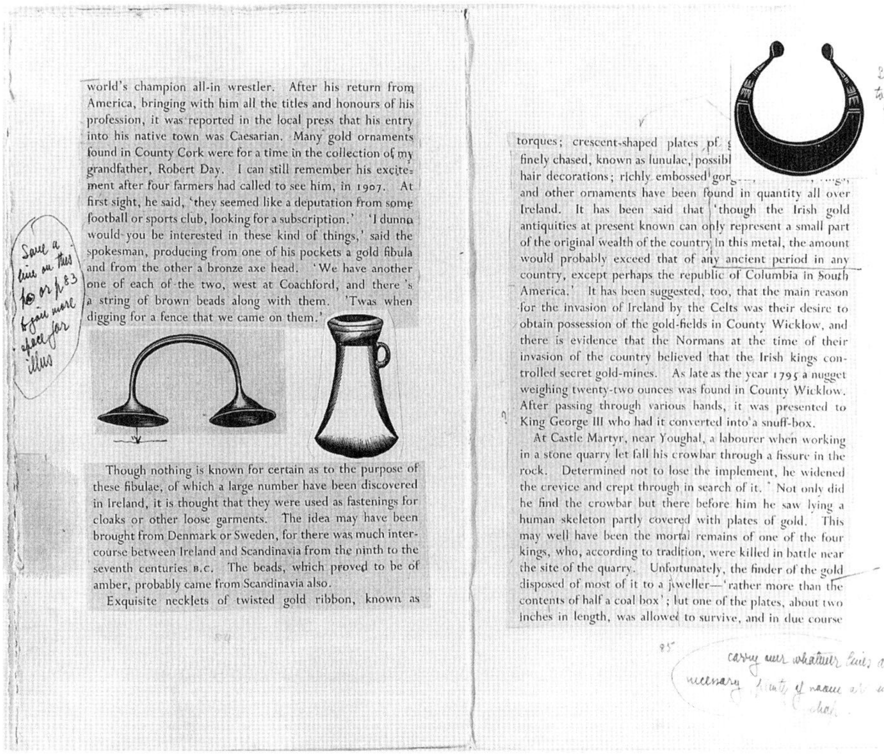

world's champion all-in wrestler. After his return from America, bringing with him all the titles and honours of his profession, it was reported in the local press that his entry into his native town was Caesarian. Many gold ornaments found in County Cork were for a time in the collection of my grandfather, Robert Day. I can still remember his excitement after four farmers had called to see him, in 1907. At first sight, he said, 'they seemed like a deputation from some football or sports club, looking for a subscription.' 'I dunno would you be interested in these kind of things,' said the spokesman, producing from one of his pockets a gold fibula and from the other a bronze axe head. 'We have another one of each of the two, west at Coachford, and there's a string of brown beads along with them. 'Twas when digging for a fence that we came on them.'

Though nothing is known for certain as to the purpose of these fibulae, of which a large number have been discovered in Ireland, it is thought that they were used as fastenings for cloaks or other loose garments. The idea may have been brought from Denmark or Sweden, for there was much intercourse between Ireland and Scandinavia from the ninth to the seventh centuries B.C. The beads, which proved to be of amber, probably came from Scandinavia also.

Exquisite necklets of twisted gold ribbon, known as

torques; crescent-shaped plates of g[…] finely chased, known as lunulae, possibl[…] hair decorations; richly embossed gor[…] and other ornaments have been found in quantity all over Ireland. It has been said that 'though the Irish gold antiquities at present known can only represent a small part of the original wealth of the country in this metal, the amount would probably exceed that of any ancient period in any country, except perhaps the republic of Columbia in South America.' It has been suggested, too, that the main reason for the invasion of Ireland by the Celts was their desire to obtain possession of the gold-fields in County Wicklow, and there is evidence that the Normans at the time of their invasion of the country believed that the Irish kings controlled secret gold-mines. As late as the year 1795 a nugget weighing twenty-two ounces was found in County Wicklow. After passing through various hands, it was presented to King George III who had it converted into a snuff-box.

At Castle Martyr, near Youghal, a labourer when working in a stone quarry let fall his crowbar through a fissure in the rock. Determined not to lose the implement, he widened the crevice and crept through in search of it. Not only did he find the crowbar but there before him he saw lying a human skeleton partly covered with plates of gold. This may well have been the mortal remains of one of the four kings, who, according to tradition, were killed in battle near the site of the quarry. Unfortunately, the finder of the gold disposed of most of it to a jeweller—'rather more than the contents of half a coal box'; but one of the plates, about two inches in length, was allowed to survive, and in due course

326 Pages of the paste-up dummy of *Sweet Cork of Thee* showing Gibbings's alterations and corrections. Clark Library.

two or three colours I need not put in so many of the small black-and-white ones. Of course this is only a figure of speech, and the whole idea will be to put in just as many as the book requires. I mentioned this point to Pollinger, and send you this note so that you will understand what I am getting at.[28]

But Gibbings was still busy with the production of *Sweet Cork of Thee*. By November he had reached the stage of making a dummy of the book. Writing to the production manager, R. J. Hall, he requested proofs:

I am now returning the marked galleys, which I thought perhaps you might care to work on.

I wonder if it would be possible to do so and to let me have a corrected set so that I can be quite accurate in my paste-up. A line here and there makes quite a difference, as you know, to where an illustration falls. In particular I would like clean pulls of the last two galleys: as you will see I have cut out quite a bit and it would be rather difficult to calculate exactly without seeing a revised version. Here especially I expect to have to make some rather careful adjustments.[29]

This was an activity that Robert and Patience particularly enjoyed. It was an extremely important part of the design process as the dummy would become a final specification for the printer; it was also immensely satisfying. Patience recalled spreading the material out on the floor of the flat, cutting and pasting, and where necessary altering the text until Robert was satisfied with the form and balance of the book.

Gibbings took proofs of his blocks before sending them off to Dent to have electrotypes made. This was done on a table-top Albion Press which he had set up on a stout work table in his bedroom at the flat.[30] The engraving of the blocks was progressing well but Gibbings explained to Hall the difficulties he was experiencing with the registration of the frontispiece, which was to be printed in two colours:

Herewith proofs of nine blocks, and under separate cover the wood. I hope you will like the frontispiece. When in place in the book it looks very much better than all by itself. As I have no tympan on my printing press, the only way I could attempt to register was by corner and side marks which I have left on the blocks in case they may be of use. They can easily be cut away before final printing. This is the best proof I managed to get, and I have since cut away a few touches to avoid some of the overlapping. I think the colours need to be a little brighter. Attached sample on H.M. paper gives more the quality of green I would like. The red should have a trace more crimson in it than on my proof.

I have no comments about the black and whites, except that many of them may seem very small. But the heavy guns are coming along in the rear ....

Now for the title page. ... Could you set up for me WEET ORK OF THEE in caps of as large a size as will fill the measure. Then I will cut the initials to fit. The tail of the S will reflect the motif of stamens of the fuchsias. As soon as I see the whole thing in type I will design the ornament of green rushes to fit. I think it might be a good idea to have OF THEE slightly smaller than the Sweet Cork. Perhaps I could have a few alternate pulls that I can chop up and play with.

The general situation re blocks at the moment is that I hope to send about another dozen in a fortnight's time, and another ten or so in mid December. Then I hope to take a much needed holiday in France for three weeks, during which I will make plans for the Seine adventure. Round about the 1st or 2nd week in Feb. I ought to be able to deliver

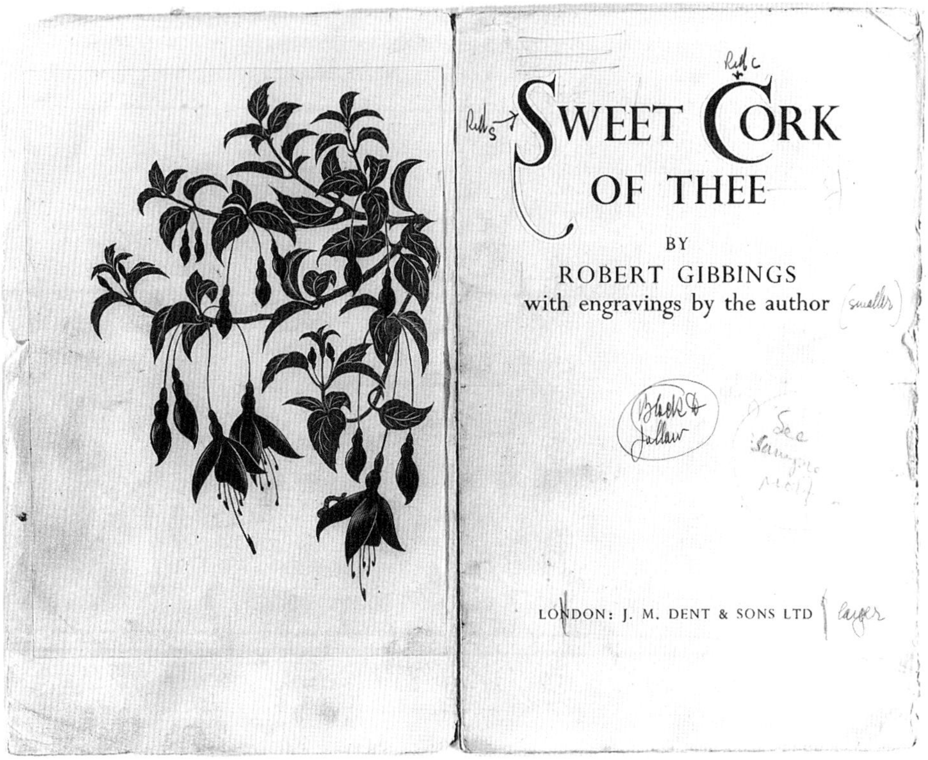

327 Paste-up of the frontispiece and title page of *Sweet Cork of Thee* annotated with comments by Gibbings. Clark Library.

the final 15 or 20, according to what the paste-up needs. Then I am at your service in any way you want me until I go to France again D.V. in the middle of March.[31]

Gibbings made an exploratory visit to France in the middle of January 1951. The weather was dreadful on his trip and a casual comment, to the effect that progress on his new book had therefore not been as great as he had hoped, led to an unfortunate misunderstanding with Bozman, who wrote to him in early February:

I am sorry I didn't have a chance of talking to you yesterday morning. You were presumably heading for your broadcast ....

I was rather disturbed by your account of the hold up in France, because the peculiar circumstances make it very important that there should not be the slightest hitch in this book, and it would ease things very much for me personally if I knew it was going ahead.[32]

Gibbings's uncharacteristically tetchy reply suggests that he was beginning to suffer from pressure:

I was a bit mystified by your letter of the 8th. What are the 'peculiar circumstances' that you speak of for 'the Seine'? The only ones that I know are that you want me to do in little more than one year what has hitherto taken me at least two if not three years.

There was no particular 'hold up' in France, except that on account of the bitter weather and a threat of 'flu I came back sooner than I expected. I got quite a bit of work done while over there and have been doing research since I came back — my broadcast on Wednesday was a translation I made for 'the Seine'. I cannot give full time to this until I have finished 'Sweet Cork'. As you know, I delivered the MS. of that six months before it was due, and two months before contract date I have delivered 60 blocks instead of 50, as well as a paste-up of the complete book and the design for the wrapper. Now I am doing an extra ten blocks, making about 70 in all, and these will be in your hands before even the paper arrives from the Mill. Why then the anxiety?[33]

On 13 February, Bozman wrote a brief and friendly letter apologising for the misunderstanding and expressing relief that the new book was progressing well.

As before Gibbings was involved with every aspect of the production of *Sweet Cork* including the design of the dust-jacket and casing. He was consulted on the colour and texture of the binding cloth and engraved designs for the gold blocked decoration for the spine and cover. On 18 March 1951 he wrote to Martin Dent with a suggestion:

When I got home after seeing you on Friday, I had the sudden idea that a string of bells is the obvious decoration for the spine, not only of the book itself but of the wrapper. I have, therefore, done a block of four bells, and I suggest you have two electros made from which you will cut one bell and use it as I have sketched on the enclosed paste-up. In gold on the blue-green binding it should look rather handsome and striking. It is important that eight bells should be used as that is the number in the Shandon chime.[34]

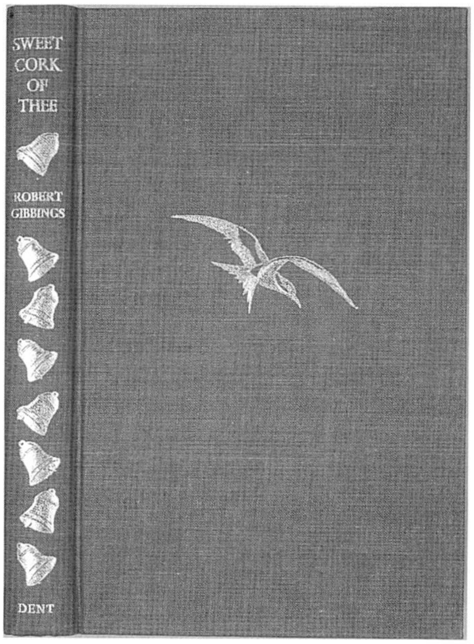

328 The binding of *Sweet Cork of Thee* with Gibbings's design of the bells of Shandon on the spine.

By the end of March the final touches were being made to the book and Gibbings was discussing the finer points of punctuation with Martin Dent:

I have gone through these proofs pretty carefully, and marked as few places as could be helped. I may seem a little inconsistent in the use of commas in expressions such as 'Oh then,' 'Well now,' but in Ireland these are really pronounced as one word, and any form of punctuation spoils the rhythm and sense. On the other hand, when I myself am using such phrases, there are times when they do need the slight break. …

I am sending you a new block of a water-lily for p.107; and as soon as ever I can manage it after this, I will send yet another small one of a corn stook for p.186. This, please God and Your Highness, will be the last and final one.

In general, I have marked the blocks at the heads of chapters to come close to the type. I rather stupidly forgot the running heads when planning the pages. I take it the spacing of the chapter numbers between the block and the first line of type will be adjusted accordingly.[35]

The book was ready for the press in good time but Gibbings knew that he could not keep up this rate of work and in a letter to Bozman he was anxious to renegotiate the terms for the next book:

On Monday evening I sent back to Martin the corrected page proofs, and now with the exception of one more small block which will be with him in a day or two, everything is ready for press. That is to say, you have everything in hand and can begin machining by the date agreed on for the delivery of the material. Not only that, but, instead of the 50 blocks mentioned in the contract, I have given you 74 which is practically 50% as many again. I am not saying this in any boastful way, or because I feel the advantages are going to be in any way one-sided: what is good for you is equally good for me. But I do mention it because I am seriously worried by the date to which you cajoled me into signing for the next book. The mere engraving of these last 70 blocks, apart entirely from gathering the drawings for them, has taken me a full six months. Several engravers who have seen them are staggered that I could do them in the time. I can only say that it has been at the cost of considerable eye strain.

If I am to spend as long over the next set — and I cannot possibly do them in less — it leaves me six months, speaking a foreign language, to gather all the material for the writing, to do the writing, and to make the drawings for the illustrations. It is an absolute impossibility. I have never been a quick worker: only the other night Noel Rooke, who has followed my work as an engraver for 40 years, mentioned that he had noticed that whenever I had been rushed there was a drop in the quality of my work. If I were to attempt to do the writing in six months it could only be journalese. It surely must be evident that if I am rushing from pillar to post I cannot get the atmosphere of leisure which is so important a feature of my books.

I do wish that we could leave it that, as regards dates, I will *do my best*. Ever since our last talks I have had a growing sense of irritation that I should be asked to do the impossible. Cannot you leave it to me to go to France in a happy frame of mind and write a happy book and let you have it as soon as I feel it is the best I can do? I haven't let you down with my last five books: why should I do so with the sixth?[36]

Bozman was understanding in his reply:

Thanks for yours. Yes I had already heard with pleasure of the extra blocks you have done and that Sweet Cork is now ready for press. Good work!

As regards your next book, in view of all you say there would appear to be no alternative to accepting your offer to *do your best*, and let us have it as soon as you possibly can. I agree that your best should leave us both satisfied.[37]

Cover of *Sweet Cork of Thee* – see colour plate 8j.

There were to be further minor corrections and finally *Sweet Cork of Thee* was published in an edition of 13,700 copies on 14 June 1951, followed by the American edition from Dutton on 2 November with a reprint in March, making a total of 12,190 copies.[38] Dedicated to his friends Anna and John Hadfield, by the end of December 9,850 copies had been sold.[39] The reception of the book was enthusiastic and subsequent letters include mention of possible appearances on television to promote it — Alan Melville hoped to cover it on one of his programmes.[40] Press reviews were very encouraging; Howard Spring, in *Country Life*, entreated the public 'Get this book, and read it and look at his pictures for

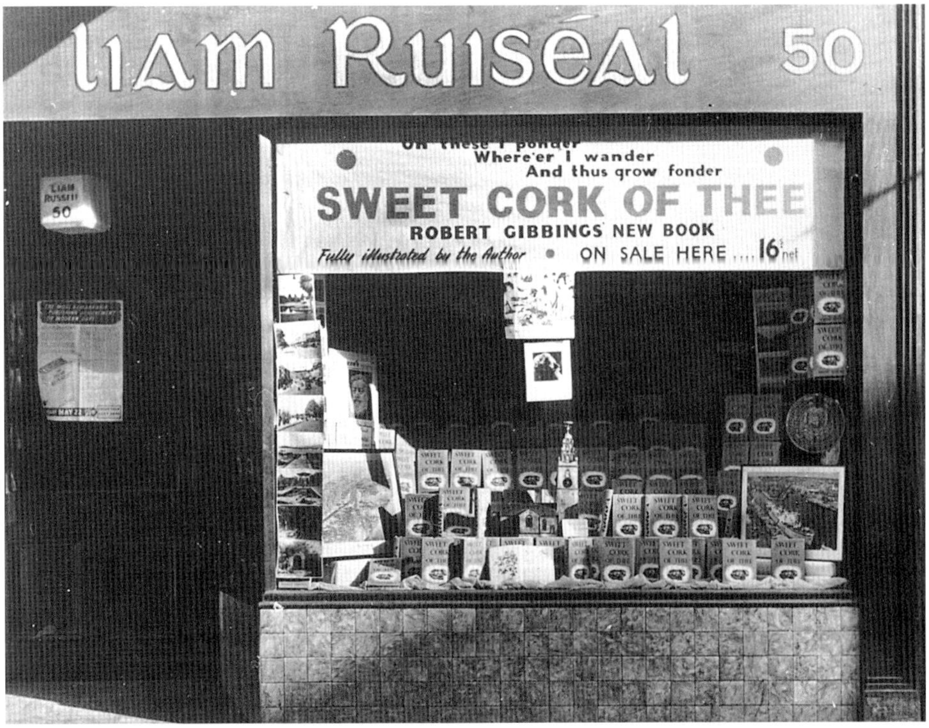

329 Shop window in Cork filled with a display of books for the launch of *Sweet Cork of Thee*. RUL.

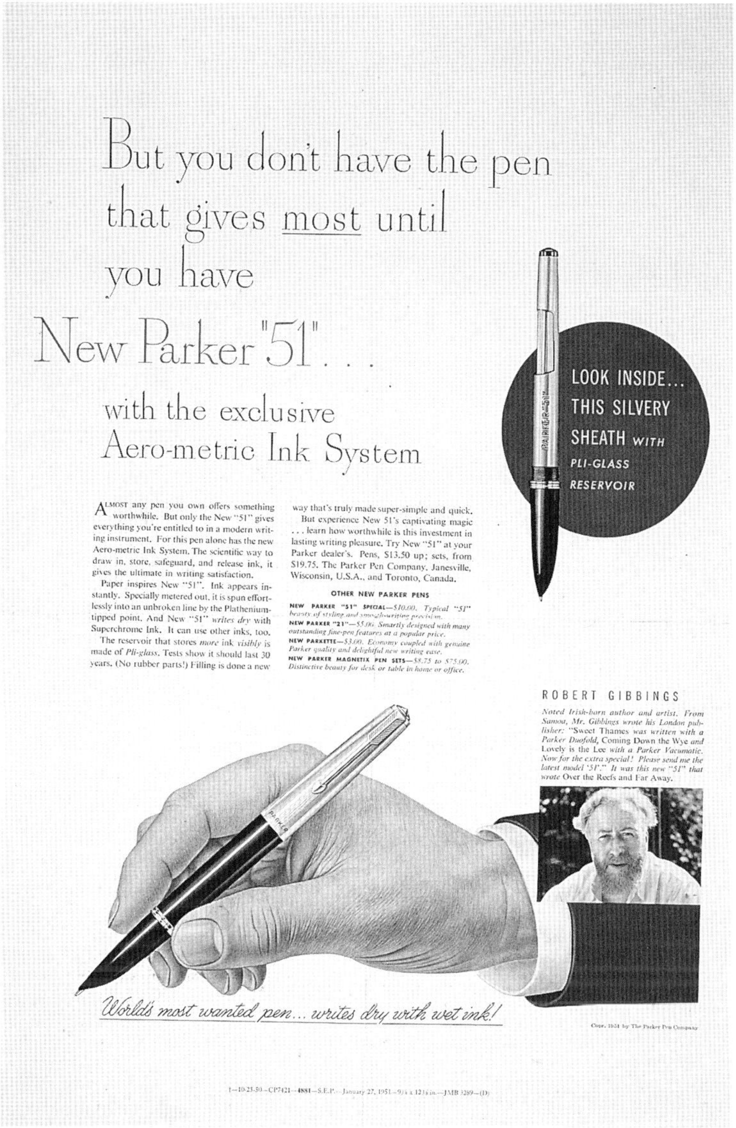

330 Advert for The Parker Pen Company, 1951, 465 x 358 mm. It is an indication of Gibbings's public appeal and reputation that he was used to endorse such products. The fee must have been too good to refuse as his other recent experience of the advertising world had been costly. RUL. Reproduced with permission of The Parker Pen Company.

your soul's good.' *The Times Literary Supplement* outlined the diversity and fascination of the book's content and concluded 'But it is in the description of the beauty of the country and the kindness and generosity of the people that perhaps the book's greatest charm will be found.'[41] One of the most significant reviews was written by David Marcus in *Irish Writing*, a magazine of contemporary Irish literature. Here Gibbings was being judged by a fellow countryman, but Marcus found the book sincere and truthful — Gibbings had found 'The real Ireland and the real Irish people ....' The quality of Gibbings's writing as well as his illustrations was praised:

> I submit, however, that there are passages of description in this book that are as haunting and memorable as poetry ... reminiscent, in its rhythm and idiom, of the best nature-poetry about Ireland left us by the pre-nineteenth-century Gaelic poets, and indeed Gibbings' 'oneness' with his subject at all times and the perfect aptness and joy of his style and stories remind me of no one more than of that other inspired recorder of the Irish countryside — the late Padraic O'Conaire.[42]

Chapter Nineteen
Coming Down the Seine
1950–1953

Recognition of Gibbings's qualities as a writer now paralleled the appreciation of his wood-engraving — Christopher Sandford described him as a 'grand "doyen" to the engravers'.[1] The significance of Gibbings's influence on book illustration and the art of wood-engraving was well documented in an essay on twentieth-century wood-engravers by Tom Balston, in a book entitled *English Wood Engraving 1900–1950*. Published in March 1951 by Robert Harling, as part of the Art and Technics series, it was illustrated with over one hundred engravings by prominent artists of the period — including two images by Gibbings.[2] The book was an adaptation of a special issue of *Image*, the quarterly journal of the visual arts, which had appeared in November of the previous year.[3] In a supplement to this edition of *Image*, Balston had written about engravers who were also authors, drawing attention to the quality of Gibbings as a writer. Balston was a good friend to Robert and had done so much to support the revival of wood-engraving — a fact that Sandford appreciated: 'I think Image 5 jolly good for the cause. We should all be very grateful to Balston for all he is doing. (It is primarily through love of you, I feel!).'[4]

Harling had written to Gibbings in February 1950, requesting two or three blocks to be made into electros for printing in the journal. Enthusiastic to support the project, Gibbings had obliged with a block illustrating a coral reef with fish and proofs of two engravings from *Glory of Life*. Subsequently he was angry to discover that Harling had used the original block for printing rather than electros and had serious concerns about wear and damage to the block which had shown signs of splitting along some of the joints.[5] Although letters remained polite, a heated dispute continued for some months, fuelled by the fact that Ethelbert White and Gwen Raverat were also rather shocked at the state of their blocks when they were returned.[6] In the event, the two engravings from *Glory of Life* were used in the book, printed from line-blocks with the image slightly reduced. But despite these problems the book was a splendid authoritative survey of contemporary wood-engraving and did much to promote the art.

More publicity came in the form of a flurry of exhibitions — mostly associated with the National Book League. 'British Book Illustration, 1935–1945', sponsored by the League, was reviewed in *The Times Literary Supplement*. Gibbings's pivotal role in promoting so many young engravers was acknowledged and his own work, especially that for the Golden Cockerel Press, was highly praised — the reviewer commented that 'it is fitting that it should have been Mr. Gibbings himself who took the original wood-block right down to the Penguin price level'.[7] Another exhibition, 'Books of Our Times', illustrating the renaissance of British book design and the quality of contemporary writing, was mounted in collaboration with the British Council, and an exhibition of books was held at the Victoria & Albert Museum from 5 May to 30 September 1951 as part of the Festival of Britain. Both exhibitions included work by Gibbings and the Golden Cockerel Press and mentioned him in the accompanying catalogues. Percy Muir compiled a catalogue for a touring exhibition, mounted by The British Council, entitled 'Private Presses and their Background', which was seen in many countries in Europe. Muir acknowledged Gibbings's influence on fine printing but explained that a commercial book, *Lovely is the Lee*, had been included as it had been printed under Gibbings's personal supervision and was 'exemplary of the direct influence of the translation into commercial terms of an experiment first worked out at a private press'.[8] In France, work by Gibbings and the Golden Cockerel Press was included in an exhibition entitled '*Le Livre Anglais*' held at the Bibliothèque Nationale in Paris, November to December 1951.

At the age of sixty-two Gibbings was a public personality and attracted media attention; earlier in the year he had been filmed at work on an engraving in his flat in Warwick Road for inclusion in a documentary made by the Crown Film Unit.[9] Sandford's description of him as a grand doyen was to some extent justified; the body of his work was substantial, indeed he had been prolific, and his achievement was widely recognised. Yet there was no let up in the pace of his life and work. In October 1950 Bozman was already writing to Gibbings, anxious to push his next book forward. They needed a title and some evocative outline blurb before Gibbings set off for France to begin his research on the Seine. Bozman pointed out that 'the Summer lists will be given to the travellers early next year and we want them to have as much time as possible to subscribe the book'.[10] Gibbings was still on the publishing roller-coaster so in January 1951 he made a preliminary sortie across the channel and his plan was to return in the spring and spend much of the summer in France.

Just before he left on his spring trip in April he wrote to his Aunt Suzanne — he was still finishing the blocks for *Sweet Cork of Thee*:

> I would have written before but that I was throwing in a few 'extra-late-final' blocks & have only just delivered them. Now the total is over 70 & my eyes are like lobsters', on stalks. But all that matters now is to hand over the flat to some New Zealanders who reach London to-day & then pack my bags & be off. Except for a few days in June when I have promised to speak in Dublin I expect to be away till October. ... When lecturing in Battersea a few weeks ago two old ladies came up in the queue for autographs. Each had a little black book & when they came near they opened them & said 'Would you recognise the writing?' One was in mother's hand & the other in father's & the books were Sunday School prizes given to them in 1902, in Kinsale.[11]

ON 14 APRIL 1951, Gibbings eventually managed to get away and establish himself in a first floor flat in the Boulevard Raspail in the Montparnasse district of Paris. The flat belonged to his friends Jacqueline and Gustav Kleinberg, who were only too happy to make it available to him on the frequent occasions when they were not in residence.[12] Patience joined him at the beginning of June and no doubt their relationship was more relaxed, as on 14 April the Decree Absolute had been granted and Robert was now released from his marriage to Elisabeth. Together they spent a week or so visiting museums and galleries and enjoying the best of Parisian cuisine. Robert was sketching and making notes for his book but even in Paris they could not escape the more tedious tasks of the author and spent time checking the galley proofs for the American edition of *Sweet Cork of Thee*.

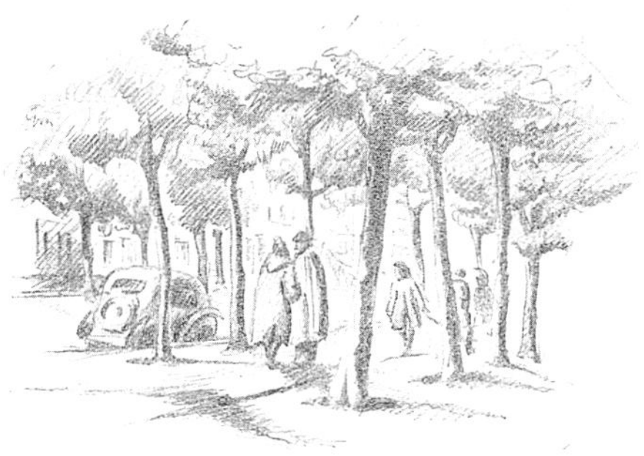

331 Drawing of the Boulevard Raspail reproduced in *The Saturday Book*, no. 12, 1952, image size 87 x 120 mm. Used by permission of The Random House Group Limited.

Towards the middle of the month Robert and Patience travelled to Dijon to investigate the source of the river Seine in a valley of the Côte d'Or. Patience noted in her diary that she had eaten snails for the first time while dining with Robert — an episode that Gibbings later expanded into a humorous anecdote in the book but described as if he had eaten alone. The weather was hot, very hot, but Gibbings wrote a romantic account of the visit to the source of the river: 'It was early summer when I visited the source; the roadside was vibrant with the colours of flowers, the air exultant with the songs of larks and the chitterings of cicadas.'[13]

The next day they caught a bus back to the source which is marked by a reclining statue of the Goddess Sequana which Gibbings sketched. But the weather was thundery and sultry and the following day Patience noted a 'terrific thunder storm' — the accompanying downpour was to prove an ominous portent for their summer explorations of the river. On the 14 June, the day that *Sweet Cork of Thee* was published, they took a bus to Saint Seine de l'Abbaye and during the following days visited Chanceaux, the village of Aisey, where they stayed at the

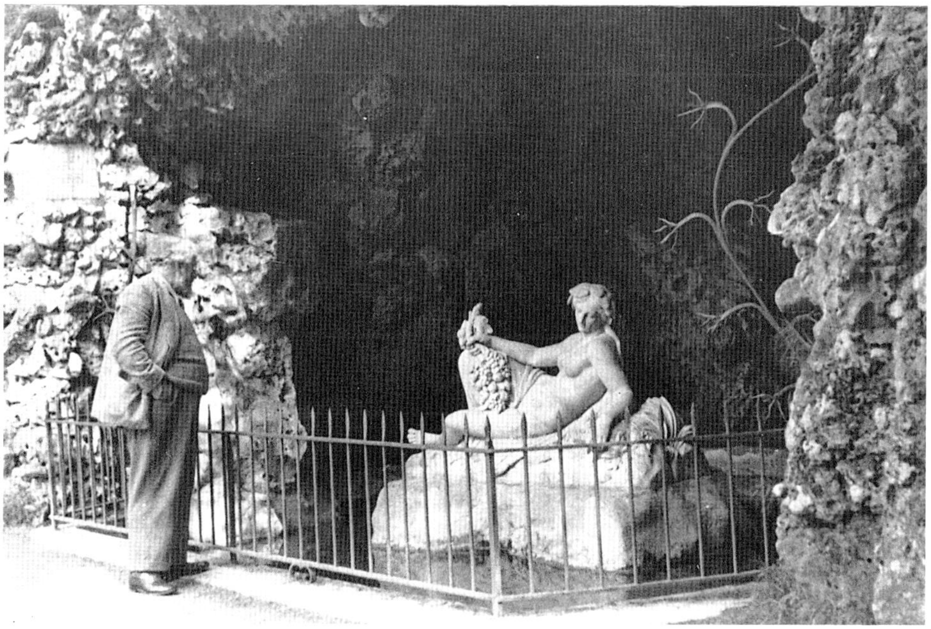

332 Gibbings visiting the statue of the Goddess Sequana at the source of the river Seine in June 1951. RUL.

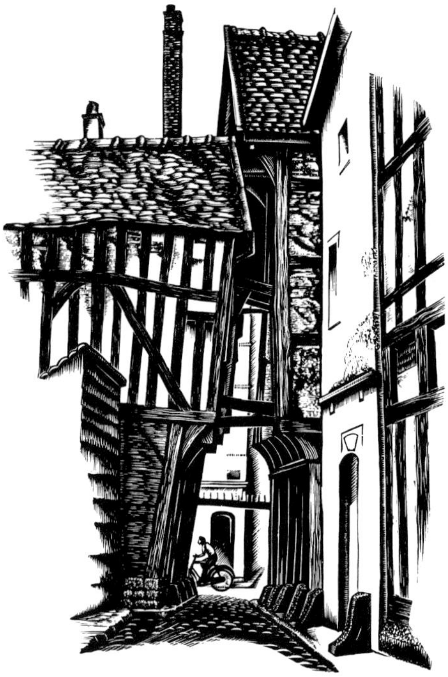

333 Street in the town of Troyes, 1951, wood-engraving, 138 x 92 mm. Illustration from *Coming Down the Seine.*

Hôtel Roy and enjoyed the epicurean delights served up by the patron Monsieur Chrétien. The next day there was another thunderstorm but they travelled on to Châtillon where Gibbings made a drawing of the source of the Douix, a tiny tributary of the Seine, while sitting in the rain. Their stay in France had to be a short one as Gibbings was due to be guest of honour and speaker at the banquet of the annual conference of the Booksellers Association in Dublin on 25 June. So they took the bus back to Troyes and the train to Paris where they picked up their post and packed up the flat before flying back to London.

A few days after his return from Dublin, Robert and Patience set out once again for France. The Kleinbergs lent them a car and Patience had her first experience of driving on the right as they set off on a round trip via Auxerre and Fontainebleau taking in the banks of the tributary rivers, the Yonne and Loing, and then on to Vézelay and Avallon before returning to Paris and the Kleinberg's flat. But the bigger plan was to row down the river Seine back to Paris and to that end, on the second day of July, they took a train back to Troyes where they had arranged for a boat to be delivered by rail. Gibbings had commissioned it from a boat builder in Tours but unfortunately when they arrived at Troyes there was no sign of it and so, frustrated, they settled to wait in the heat.

Three days later the boat arrived — a small wooden craft painted blue, only eleven foot six inches in length, with a flat bottom and an arrangement for a canvas awning to allow one person to sleep aboard — unfortunately this was stolen and substituted by an additional tent. They had brought a small scout tent from England and appropriate equipment to enable them to camp on the river bank. The first night they camped by a bridge at Riancy but slept in the open and woke very early to a perfect morning. They enjoyed a leisurely breakfast on the

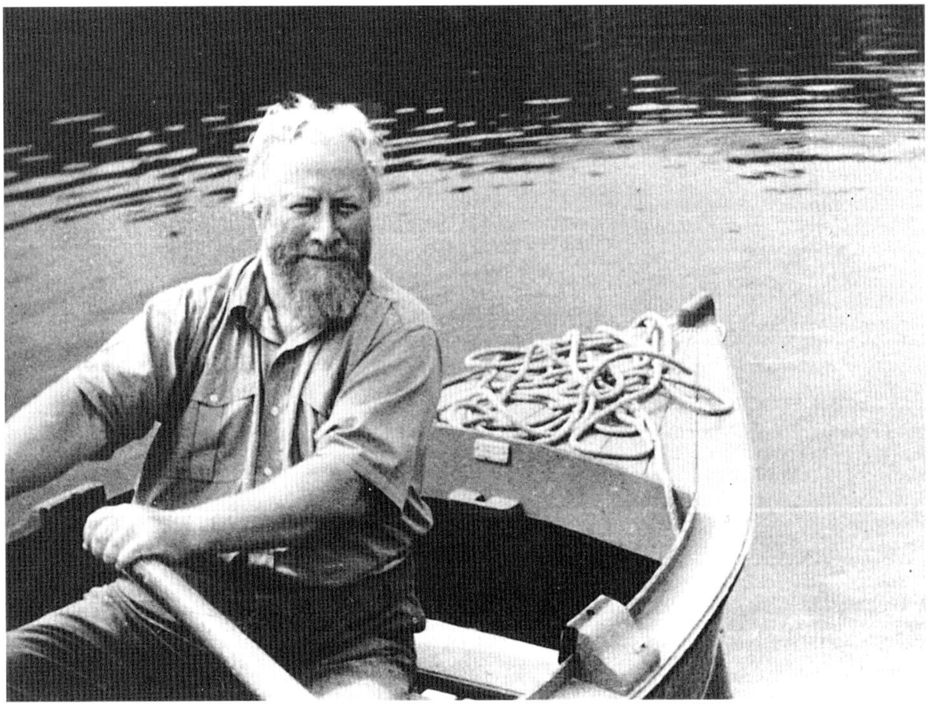

334 Gibbings in his boat at the start of his journey down the river Seine. RUL.

bridge before casting off for a blissful day meandering downstream. That night they camped at a bridge at Savières and a storm forced them to resort to the tents; the following night they pitched the tents under some lime trees outside the little town of Méry. Locks had to be negotiated and Gibbings quickly found that the boat was difficult to manoeuvre, particularly in the rapidly swelling waters. Bedding and tents were now soaking and needed to be dried out and so they moored at Sauvage and decided to return to Paris, via Moret, to write up notes and make some day excursions. Back in Montparnasse they went to dine at La Coupole, Gibbings's favourite restaurant in Paris, and then wandered the streets watching the dancing, as the city was alive with celebrations for the Bimillénaire de Paris; the following evening they enjoyed the colour and energy of a Latin American ballet at the theatre. They returned to the boat on 23 July but the weather broke once again and their start was delayed. By the time they finally set off the river was in flood. Patience recalled that it looked like a vast sea punctuated by the odd tall tree and telegraph pole. Bridges seemed isolated humps and, when seeking a dry sleeping place at night, Patience was acutely aware that she was sharing a place of refuge with many small stranded creatures — Robert slept in the boat! Other nights the weather was so fine that they could sleep ashore: '*à la belle étoile* — no need for a tent', as Gibbings recalled, 'My only regret as I lay down was the crushing of the grass — sad that you cannot take one step in a meadow without bruising some living thing.'[14] Looking back at the end of the year Gibbings described the conditions in a letter he wrote to friends:

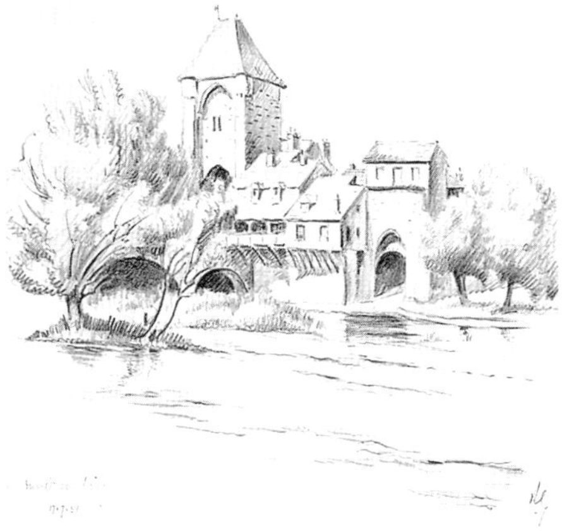

335 Pencil drawing of Moret-sur-Loing, dated 17 July 1951, which was later reproduced in *The Saturday Book*, no. 12, 1952, image size 150 x 174 mm. Author's collection.

> I'm working on a book on the Seine & was swimming & floating on & in & damn near drowning a few times most of last summer. ... I struck the highest flood in living memory & for five days was hurled through vast [?] forests never seeing dry land except at bridges. At most of the bridges it was easier to go over than under. I lost a stone in weight ... which shows you how artists have to struggle for their living.[15]

By the beginning of August they had covered about one hundred miles and had reached the town of Valvins where they left the boat and returned to Paris, hoping to complete the journey a few days later when conditions had improved. After the physical stress of the journey, Robert and Patience were only too ready to relax at the Kleinberg's flat. On occasions during their voyage they had been in real danger — swept along by fast currents, avoiding fallen trees and debris. Gibbings later recounted at least two incidents when he had nearly been crushed or impaled when passing under bridges with little room left by the swollen waters — at the age of sixty-two this was quite a physical test. Going through his post, sunk in an armchair at the flat, Gibbings had been amused by a review of *Sweet Cork of Thee* in the *Irish Independent*. Signed with the initials N. N., the article began: '"Mr. Gibbings is now turning sixty and ought to have sense instead of gallivanting around the queer places of the world." You're right, me boy, I said to

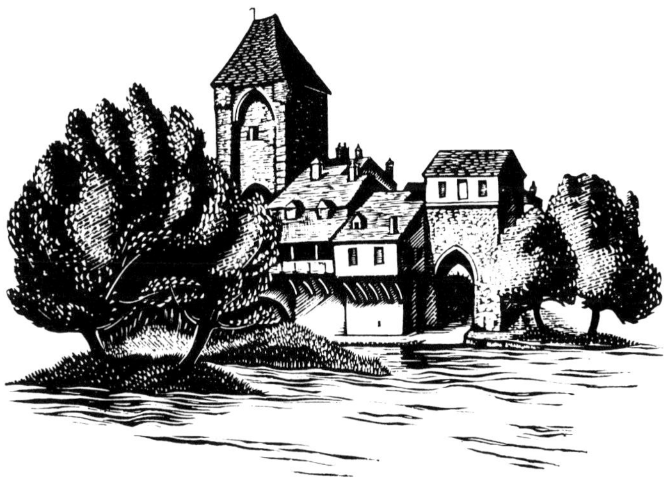

336 Moret-sur-Loing, 1951, wood-engraving, 62 x 90 mm. Illustration from *Coming Down the Seine*.

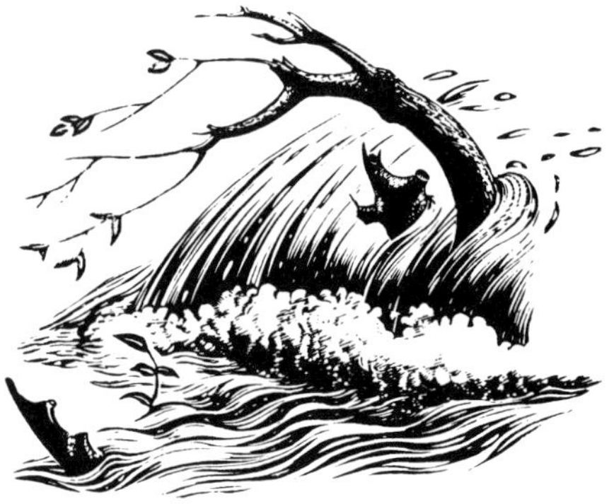

337 Flood waters, 1951, wood-engraving, 48 x 58 mm. Illustration from *Coming Down the Seine.*

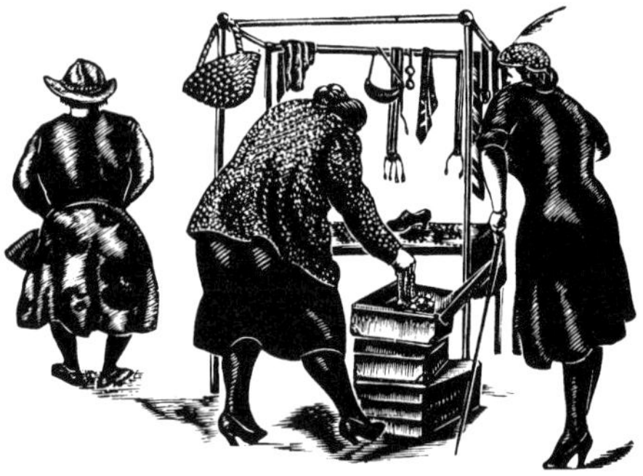

338 Street market in Paris, 1951, wood-engraving, 60 x 82 mm. Illustration from *Coming Down the Seine.*

myself, but whatever nom de plume nobility "N. N." stands for, it also stands for "now or never."'[16] Gibbings was feeling reflective about his increasing years — age was clearly beginning to affect him but he felt there was a positive side too:

There is great peace in old age; responsibilities have passed to others, anxiety about our choice of road in life no longer exists. We see, too, the inevitability in the sequence of many past events. What at one time seemed a climax to all adventure, was but a prelude to fresh enterprise. Unknowingly we had gone stale, had lost interest in the old activities; without realizing it, a new focus for our energy had appeared.[17]

The weather remained bad so Gibbings decided it was time to start writing and headed his paper 'Chapter One' — and then broke off to celebrate the beginning with a good lunch! The muse was with him until late afternoon when he suffered a writer's block; the next day was spent at the Louvre looking at Corot, Rousseau and Poussin. The next week was filled with Patience typing up notes while Robert wrote and sketched scenes of the river, busy markets, and people in the streets. Evenings were spent at the theatre and exotic ballets; Latin American and Spanish — the colour and energy appealed to Gibbings.

With no improvement in the weather conditions, the decision was made to abandon attempts to row from Valvins to Paris and Gibbings arranged to sell the boat to a friend, Professor Karaghensian of Melbourne University, along with all the camping equipment, for use by scholarship students staying in Paris.[18] To overcome the problem of completing the journey along the Seine to Le Havre, Gibbings had arranged to hitch a lift on a much larger vessel, the *Yarvic* — downstream from Paris the Seine widens into a major waterway easily navigable by small ships. The *Yarvic* had been built during the war for carrying ammunition to warships in harbour but in recent years she had been commissioned by Pan

339 Pencil sketch of a picture seller on a street in Paris, c. 1951, image size 123 x 144 mm. RUL.

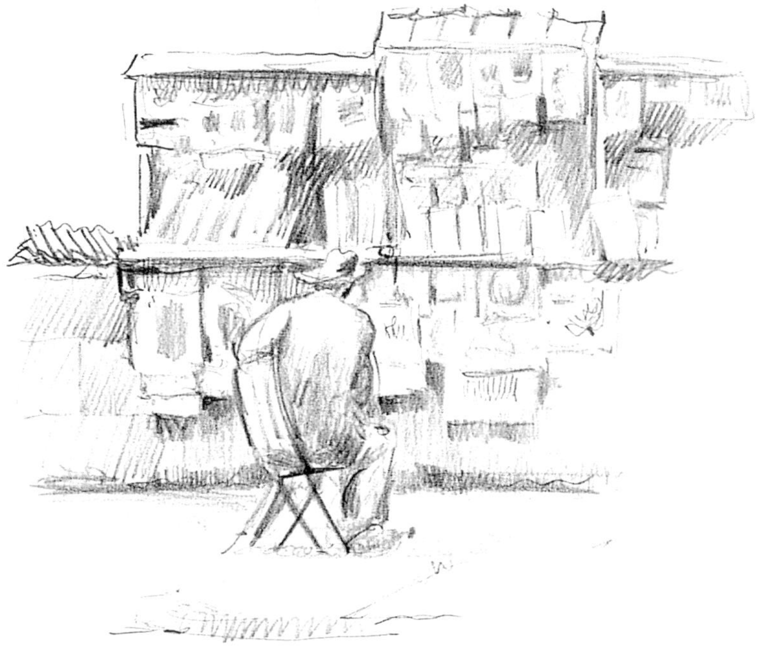

Books to sail from Paris to London delivering books — it was cheaper for them to print in France. Alan Bott of Pan Books had made the offer of a trip earlier in the summer and now it was timely to accept. The *Yarvic* set sail at 9 am on 25 August and Peter Boizot, the captain, gave up his cabin to his passengers. They reached Le Havre three days later after a colourful voyage which included going aground on a sand bank below La Mailleraye. Later that day they caught a train back to Paris and Gibbings immediately started writing up the voyage as a chapter in the book while the experience was still fresh in his mind.

Robert and Patience flew back to London in the middle of September but their hasty departure was mainly due to problems Gibbings was suffering with back pain. The day after his return to 91 Warwick Road, he wrote to Madame Rageot:

> I was so very sorry that I was unable to come in and see you again before I left France. My plans had to be changed daily owing to the bad weather, and during my last few days in Paris I had a bad attack of lumbago and neuritis so that I could hardly move out of a chair. However, I plan to return to Paris at the end of November, and will most certainly come and see you then.[19]

Madame Rageot owned Editions De L'Amitie, a publishing firm who had commissioned a translation of *Coconut Island* and had brought out a French edition in 1949. She had been organising an article on Gibbings's career and his adventures in the Pacific Islands for their house journal and Gibbings had provided photographs to illustrate the piece.[20]

As with all his books, Gibbings went to great pains to research and verify his material. His fascination for mythology and folk-lore had led him to join the Folk-Lore Society with the intention of making use of their library. However, with his increasing commitments, he had never been able to attend talks and lectures and the library proved unhelpful, having no subject index. He went as far as to write his resignation but was persuaded to withdraw it and now he was able to take advantage of his membership. In France he had collected some old anecdotes, about how the local clergy would banish common pests that attacked the vines by threatening them with excommunication. Gibbings wanted to use the stories but had the idea of adding a contemporary example. He asked the Folk-Lore Society for help and they began searching their records. Eventually it was the American Folklore Society who put him onto an account of the expulsion of rats from a house, published in the Society's journal, which Gibbings adapted and used in his book.[21] Gibbings also had a fascination for the paranormal and for a while was a member of the Society for Psychical Research. Although no longer a member, Gibbings wrote to the Society in October 1951, to report two strange incidents that had occurred in France and one on his return to London. Two of the happenings involved examples of coincidence; incidents that occurred soon after he had anticipated the event in a dream or thoughts — the other was when two girls seemed to disappear in the gardens at Versailles. These unexplained incidents made such an impression on Gibbings that he felt they were worth reporting and he had written down notes within hours of the events. In his letter to the secretary of the Society he reminded him of a previous incident:

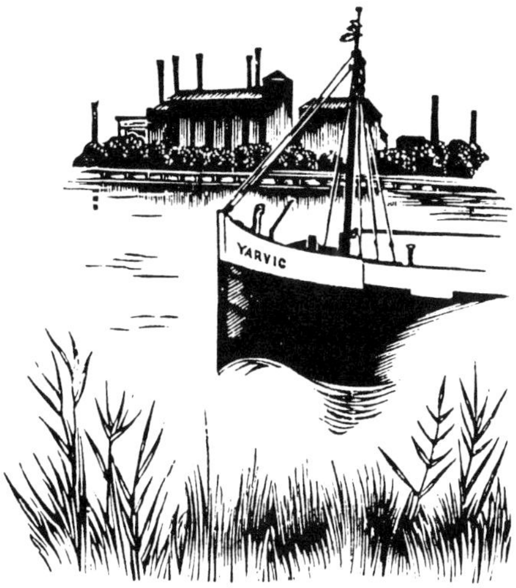

340 *Yarvic*, 1951, wood-engraving, 65 x 60 mm. Illustration from *Coming Down the Seine*. The ship was commissioned by Pan Books to transport books from France. Gibbings and Patience hitched a lift on the vessel from Paris to Le Havre.

Cover of the Editions De L'Amitie edition of *Coconut Island* – see colour plate 8k.

'You may remember that some little time ago I sent you a strange story of my sweating yellow when irritated by a yellow-haired man.'[22]

Gibbings was not really a 'club' or 'society' man by nature with the exception of the Society of Wood Engravers, of which he had faithfully remained an active member. He joined organisations in pursuit of information or because he supported their aims. However, he did enjoy the recognition of his peers in a more formal way and had been pleased to be nominated for membership of the Irish Academy of Letters the previous year. An old acquaintance from University College Cork, Professor Denis Gwynn, had been lobbying members on his behalf — he had even approached George Bernard Shaw. Shaw, a former president of the Academy, had replied with support for Gibbings:

> Resident as I am in England, I hardly feel qualified to interfere in the elections of the IAL; but as Mr Robert Gibbings is in the field I seize the opportunity to say that he shall have my vote because all such Academies as ours are desperately in need of members who do not, like poets and novelists, work in solitude without the necessary contacts that qualify men for business and politics, but are experienced in the various highly social arts that go to making books decorative and agreeable to handle and look at: typographers, illustrators, page designers, printers, binders, etc etc etc
>
> With this in view Mr Gibbings is the man for me.[23]

Gwynn also wanted a favour from Gibbings — he needed sponsors to nominate him for a seat on the University's governing body and as an Honorary MA and former student Gibbings was entitled to a vote. Gwynn had been active on his behalf in other ways, arranging his nomination for election to the Royal Hibernian Academy of Arts. To qualify Gibbings had to exhibit at the annual exhibition so he had arranged for three of his underwater drawings on xylonite to be entered after they had been shown at an exhibition of the Munster Fine Art Club at the School of Art in Cork; Gibbings was accepted as an Associate Member in October 1951. The following year he was invited to join the Royal Society of Arts but Gibbings politely declined nomination explaining: '... members of such a society should take an active part in its proceedings, and not be mere 'passengers' wearing idly the title of Fellowship. In my case I find it more and more difficult to keep up with present commitments, and all too often I find myself unable to give them the energy that I would like'.[24] But it was not just in the worlds of art and literature that he was held in respect; his contribution to the study of natural history and the understanding of other cultures and climes had been recognised by his being elected a Fellow of the Royal Geographical Society in 1944, and he was also a member of the Royal Zoological Society and the Royal Anthropological Institute of Great Britain and Ireland.[25]

While he had been away in France, talks he had recorded earlier for the BBC were transmitted on the radio and on his brief returns home he had frequently given public lectures and demonstrations. At the end of October 1951, he wrote to Hoppé at Dent to report that his writing was going well: 'The Seine flows along quite nicely, and I am now approaching the 25,000.'[26] A small distraction came in the form of a commission from the Naldrett Press to illustrate and design a dust jacket for a new book on the Pacific to be titled *The Midmost Waters*, written by John Fisher.[27] Instead of using wood-engravings to illustrate the book, Gibbings had shown the editor the sketch books he had filled with drawings during his trips to Polynesia. It was decided that these would make ideal illustrations which could be reproduced as half-tones. Gibbings was only too delighted to be able to reuse existing material rather than add to his workload, and Dent, anxious for him to concentrate on the *Seine*, readily agreed that using the drawings would not interfere with their claims on the wood-engravings used in *Over the Reefs*. Gibbings did commit himself to producing a finished drawing for the jacket before returning to France at the beginning of December. Eventually thirty-seven drawings were reproduced in the book which was published at the end of the following year.

Hours before he boarded the plane for France, Gibbings was hurriedly writing letters about another project which, much to his regret, eventually came to nothing. United Rum Merchants Ltd. had approached Gibbings offering to finance a trip to the West Indies and a commission to write and illustrate a book which they would use for publicity and to boost their image. The company had suggested that Dent might collaborate on the project with Muller, another publishing company. Gibbings's reaction was hesitant; he was rather daunted at the responsibility of a full length book, especially when he would be obligated to more than one master. His books to date had been a comfortable arrangement — any risk being shared between himself and the colleagues and friends at Dent whom he trusted. Yet he was tempted: '... I can't help a hankering for those West Indian isles, and it is certainly now or never for me. Although I put my reasons down as those of health and old age, I think that my chief inhibition is that I don't want to have the issue confused'. He was unhappy about too many bodies being involved but longed for another adventure: 'I am sorry if I seem vacillating but it does seem a pity to throw away this opportunity of a last skimander in the tropics.'[28] Eventually it proved difficult for all the publishers to reach an agreement and Gibbings was relieved to have the problem lifted — he hated the prospect of letting people down: 'One of my few virtues is that I am scrupulous regarding any promises I may make concerning MSS and their illustrations. Bozman will tell you that if I give a date I do my damnedest to keep to it ....'[29]

Gibbings spent most of December in France gathering more material and visiting Aisey again. For much of the coming year he was to be preoccupied with work on the book. He had let his flat in London to his friend John Harris[30] and from April until the beginning of June 1952 he was based in Paris and intending to travel further afield. In terms of the text he was already beyond the drafting stage and had started on the illustrations. He wrote to Martin Dent in February 1952 to organise the transferring of his drawings onto the surface of blocks using photography:

The battle is now beginning. I enclose eight drawings and eight blocks which I hope will fit when the drawings are reduced to the sizes marked on them.

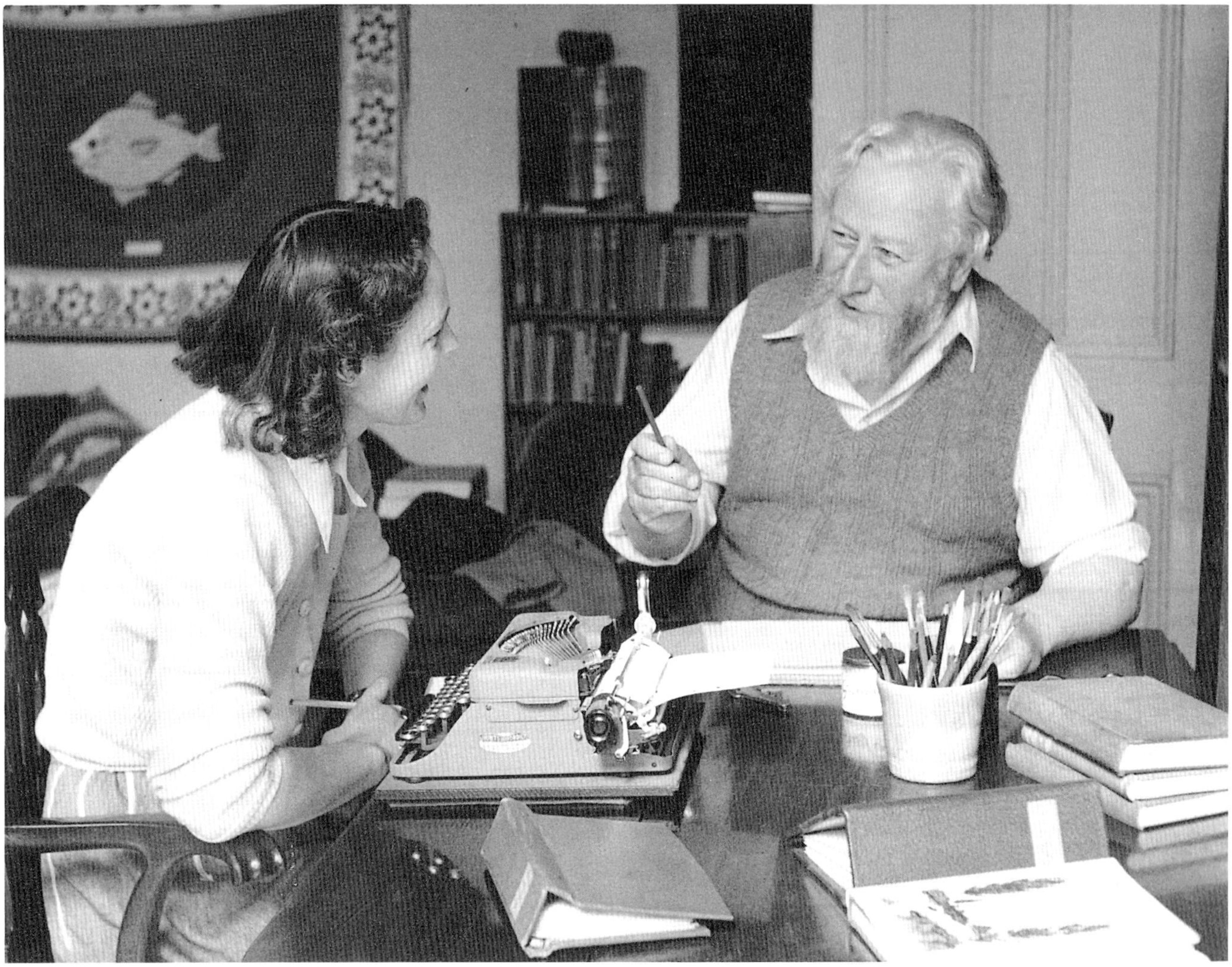

341 Patience Empson and Gibbings at work in his flat in Warwick Road, 1953. One of a number of publicity photographs taken just after the publication of *Coming Down the Seine*. In the foreground, on the table, are two of the small ring-binders in which Gibbings used to keep the copious notes he made during the research for his books. RUL.

It will be wonderful if they can make a good job of them for me. Before I went away in December I sent a few to the other bloke as there was no immediate hurry; I got them back in six weeks' time so badly done that one of them (the statue in the grottoe [*sic*]) I am now sending to you in the hopes of better results. The statue in the boat is the one I thought of for the frontispiece. Printed in a nice gin-bottle green with suitable initials on the title page it might look well. The block for it is a bare six inches but I have asked them to make it as near as possible to that size.

Perhaps you would emphasize to Odhams that though the drawings may appear rough they give me the details from which I can work. If by chance I have miscalculated the size of the smaller ones, a slight variation from my measure will not matter. I have put a number on the back of each block to correspond with the number on the drawings, and look forward very much to seeing the result.[31]

Just before he left for France in April, Gibbings had completed six blocks for the *Seine*. He sent them off to Dent but was anxious that electrotype copies should be made straight away: '... the summer will be coming along and one never knows these days what hot weather may do to the blocks ...'.[32] Heat could have the effect of warping woodblocks, especially as modern blocks tended not to be so well seasoned, thus rendering them useless for printing. By October his manuscript had been typed by Patience and delivered to Dent and the book had been given its final title of *Coming Down the Seine*. A month later Martin Dent was pressing Gibbings for ideas for the wrapper: '... will you consider whether you can let me have some sort of rough, indicating what this design is going to be ...' — he wanted something to show the travellers at a meeting at the beginning of January.[33] At the end of the year Gibbings had pasted up galleys and proofs of engravings for the first thirty-two pages. He had made some adjustments and had left a few gaps while waiting for blocks to be returned: 'As soon as I get the blocks for pp. 10 and 15 from Odham's, I will send you tracings so that you will know just what space is required; and within a few days I should be able to send the blocks. Odham's had the drawings early last week so they should be able to produce something soon.'[34]

PROGRESS ON *Coming Down the Seine* had been good but this was by no means the only writing that Gibbings had produced in 1952, as he had also managed to publish a surprisingly large number of articles. At the beginning of the year he was corresponding with Kenneth Hopkins, a long-time admirer of Gibbings's work, who, as a rather naive youth and aspiring poet, had been invited to tea by Gibbings at the Golden Cockerel Press. Hopkins had later become a commissioning editor for the magazine *Everybody's* in 1949 and had immediately approached Gibbings as a possible contributor.

Hopkins had written a very enthusiastic review of *Over the Reefs* in *John O'London's Weekly* which Gibbings greatly appreciated and he had readily agreed to write articles provided he was not entirely taken up with one of his books. In March 1951, he was implementing some editorial changes to a story for Hopkins entitled 'Drama in the Pacific' for which he was also to provide two or three illustrations. The revisions took a long time, for it was the new year before Gibbings posted off the new version. But he already had other ideas for further pieces, suggesting that a 'folk tale from Samoa, dealing with a girl and an eel, might be acceptable', the idea was to 'connect it up with the Eve and the Serpent story, and one or two other bits of comparative snake mythology'.[35] Although in January 1952 he was working hard on the *Seine*, he felt: 'Now is a good time for me if you have any ideas, as I am concentrating mostly on the engravings for my book, and have the other side of my brain comparatively free.' Eventually the article appeared under a new title, 'Lost in the Loneliest Ocean', in September 1952.[36]

Gibbings had also became a regular contributor to the popular arts, literature and music journal, *John O'London's Weekly*. His first piece for 1952 was an appreciation of his friend James Norman Hall and later in the year he wrote an article discussing Thor Heyerdahl's book *American Indians in the Pacific*. Gibbings felt a natural affinity with Heyerdahl as a writer and adventurer and was fascinated by his theories on the origins of the peoples of Polynesia. At first he was sceptical but was to become impressed by the evidence presented; later he reviewed the same book for *The Sphere*.[37] He became increasingly in demand as a journalist and was to be a regular contributor to these publications and to others such as

Everyman, *The Book Collector*, *Time and Tide* and the BBC's overseas journal, *London Calling*.

John Hadfield had given up his job at the National Book League and had taken over from Leonard Russell as the editor of *The Saturday Book* and at the beginning of 1952 was planning his first edition, which was to appear for the Christmas market. He shared Russell's tastes and the successful formula of a joyous miscellany of fascinating short articles, poems, and stories on every subject under the sun was to remain the same. Hadfield had a wide network of writers and themes to call upon for material and Gibbings fitted perfectly into the character of the books. On a visit to Gibbings's flat, Hadfield had by chance seen a number of preliminary pencil sketches, made as working 'notes' and sources for his engravings, and had persuaded Gibbings that they would reproduce well and could be turned into an article for *The Saturday Book*. To enliven the half-tones, Hadfield suggested that they be highlighted with an effect of a watercolour wash. The illustrations included a view of the Boulevard Raspail, a selection of views of the river, the towns and villages he passed en route, and sensuous sketches of a life model which he had drawn at the Grande Chaumière. 'An Artist on the Seine' was published in volume twelve and formed valuable pre-publicity for Gibbings's book.[38]

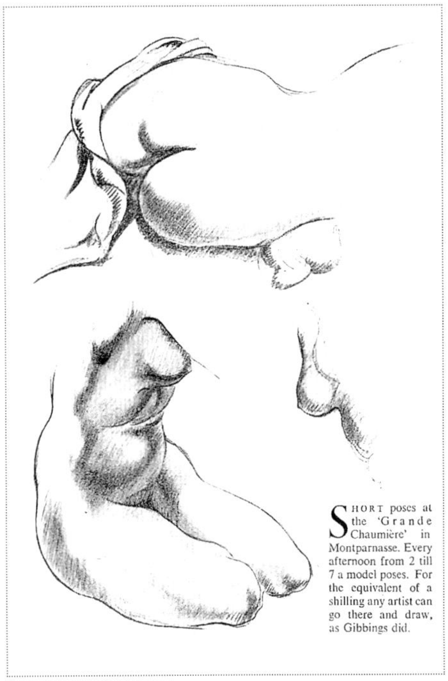

342 Reproductions of pencil drawings of the nude models at the Grande Chaumière in Paris illustrating an article entitled 'An Artist on the Seine' by Gibbings, published in *The Saturday Book*, no. 12, 1952, pp. 51–58. Used by permission of The Random House Group Limited.

Over the years the friendship with John Hadfield had become very close. They loved many of the same things; nature, good food and wine and beauty, especially beautiful women. John was one of the regulars who enjoyed the company at the Hind's Head Hotel at Bray. In March 1952, Gibbings was feeling a little tired and run down and booked into the Hind's Head for a couple of weeks rest. While resident there a birthday party was organised in his honour at which the Hadfields were amongst the guests, together with another friend, Patrick Campbell, the writer and television personality, who was also one of the convivial raconteurs who frequented the hotel.

During that year the Hadfields moved from their home in Hitchin to a Tudor manor house near Ipswich. They could only afford it because it was 'beautiful but decrepit', but an account of its restoration and the acquisition of a pair of peacocks for the lawn became the subject of a gentle and humorous book written by Anna Hadfield which included a reference to Gibbings. Not long after they moved in Gibbings had gone to stay for a few days. During a visit to an empty but interesting historical house nearby, Gibbings tried to gain access via a window and became wedged in the frame. Anna and John struggled to release him: 'We pushed and we pulled, but it seemed hopeless. We tried not to hear his cries of pain, intermixed with oaths, all in a rich Irish brogue. At last a concerted effort on the recalcitrant leg did the trick and he tumbled out. But he was not pleased, and claimed that a particularly tender portion of his anatomy had suffered irreparable damage.'[39]

With such pressure of work it was inevitable that some offers had to be refused. Gibbings had declined a commission from the GPO to design another greetings telegram for the Coronation period. At the beginning of the year Charles Ede had opened negotiations in an attempt to persuade Gibbings to illustrate a Folio Society edition of Trelawny's *Adventures of a Younger Son*. Discussions went on all year but in October Gibbings wrote that he just did not have the time, explaining that plans were already being developed for another book:

As soon as I have finished present commitments I shall almost certainly be going over to Ireland to start another book there, and that means that I shall be away for the greater part of next year, and after that I will again have to concentrate on the results of my travels.[40]

In March he had been discussing with Erskine Childers, the Irish Minister for Posts and Telegraphs, the possibility of designing a stamp:

I wonder if I might do you an experimental block. Here is a suggestion. Some years ago your Department invited me to take part in a competition to design a high value stamp — either five or ten shillings. The drawing had to be done in pen and ink which is not my medium, and eventually I only sent in my design with great reluctance. It was of a Irish piper coming over the hill, with a sunrise behind him. Now if you happen to have that drawing anywhere in your files and you could send it back to me I would carry it out as an engraving, say four or five inches in height. ... I have often wished that it were possible to have a set of really good pictorial stamps for Eire, and wished too that they could be carried out as wood-engravings which would give them a strong and distinctive character.[41]

It would seem that later the project was dropped.

A more ambitious project, which was started but also eventually came to nothing, was a sequel to *Coconut Island*. Dent were keen to publish the follow-up and plans were fairly advanced by the end of 1952; in fact Gibbings had written 10,000 of an estimated 50,000 words needed for the book. The intention was to finish the book by March 1953 and have it ready for Christmas, but for some reason it was never completed.[42] But the BBC had also shown interest in *Coconut Island* and a two part dramatisation of the book was broadcast as a schools programme in October.

Throughout the year Gibbings's diary was peppered with bookings for talks in towns as far apart as Battersea, Bristol, Monmouth, Nottingham and Hull. In a letter from Hoppé in October, reference is made to a lecture and demonstration of printing and book production to be given by Gibbings at the 'Five Hundred Years Exhibition' to be held at Hutchinson House in December. Dent were contributing a set of books, a framed set of engravings from *Sweet Cork*, and a selection of pages from the manuscript to represent Gibbings's work.[43] In the same week, Gibbings was guest of honour at a dinner held by the National Book League.

On 17 December, Gibbings contributed to the festive mood by taking part in an unscripted discussion programme on the topic 'Christmas in the British Isles' for the BBC series 'Calling the Islands'. For his own Christmas celebrations, Gibbings joined his eldest son Patrick and his wife Diana at their hotel and restaurant on Monkey Island, Bray-on-Thames. Patrick and Diana had tried their hand at the hotel business on leaving the forces after the war. After a short spell in South Africa learning on the job with Moira, Patrick's mother, who had set up a business after the break-up of her marriage to Robert, back in Britain they took on a number of public houses and small hotels. It quickly became apparent to this

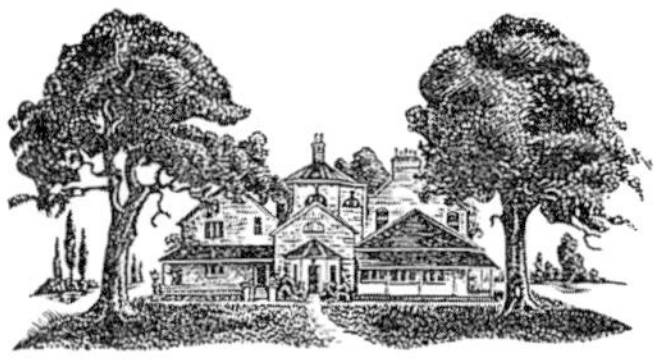

MONKEY ISLAND HOTEL

BRAY-ON-THAMES, BERKSHIRE

(*Maidenhead 849*)

PROPRIETORS:
PATRICK AND DIANA GIBBINGS

WHEN CHARLES SPENCER, *Third Duke of Marlborough, bought Monkey Island in the year 1738 in order to build himself a fishing lodge encircled by the Thames, the island may already have been called by its present name: earlier it had formed part of the lands of the neighbouring Abbey of Burnham, and so had been known as "Monks-eyot" (or islet), of which "Monkey Island" is possibly a corruption. There is, however, a wide belief that the name arose from the frescoes with which Andien de Clermont, the French artist employed by the Duke, adorned the ceiling of the pavilion—frescoes of monkeys in human dress diverting*

343 Publicity brochure for the Monkey Island Hotel run by Patrick and Diana. Illustrated with wood-engravings by Gibbings and printed at the Kynoch Press, 1952, page size 192 × 122 mm. RUL.

gregarious couple that they had considerable talent; Patrick as a chef and Diana as an organiser — they were ideally suited as hosts. Starting at the bottom, they had worked their way up, until in 1952 they managed to take over the Monkey Island Hotel. The place had a distinguished history; still grand but now rather run down. The young couple were determined to work hard and breathe new life into it. Patrick's reputation as a chef, very influenced by simple French cooking, and the welcoming atmosphere, soon made it a great success. Patrick was the only one of his children that Gibbings had really spent time with and father and son were particularly close; Patrick shared many of his father's tastes and his approach to life, as well as beginning to resemble him physically. Robert was anxious to encourage and do all he could to help his son and arranged to have a publicity brochure printed at the Kynoch Press for which he engraved three illustrations. Monkey Island was sufficiently close to London for Gibbings to visit regularly, staying in rooms in the hotel while Diana and Patrick inhabited an old barge which was moored close by. After so many years estranged from family life it must have meant something special to spend Christmas with his son and daughter-in-law and their young family. Gibbings was looking forward to the break as he explained in a letter to his Aunt Suzanne:

> Yes, I'm popping off to Bray for a couple of days & am hoping for a fairly cheerful time with Patrick & Co. I'll be glad of a break, however short, as I've been working seven days a week & about ten hours a day. Dents wanted the engravings sooner than I expected & I stupidly took on a job for Bovril ... I'm caught between the two. To add to the rush, the bloke who does my rough work is such an ardent vegetarian that he cannot even work on my blocks for meat-juice, so I've got to do it all myself! However I mustn't grumble, Dents reader reported that the Seine M.S. was 'Vintage Gibbings'. Although they are in a hurry for the blocks they won't publish till September. Meanwhile, as soon as I've got the wood out of my skull I've contracted to do another children's book — a follow on to 'Coconut Island'. Busy isn't the word for it but proceeds are needed. Thank heaven the domestic situation is now finally settled. The court have awarded E [Elisabeth] in maintenance almost exactly the figure that I was allowing voluntarily before proceedings started. It just means that I'm £200 out of pocket for legal expenses. However 'tis worth it to be free![44]

It was poor Ralph Beedham who felt so passionately about his vegetarianism and could not bring himself to do his usual job of clearing Gibbings's blocks. The commission from Bovril to illustrate a company history and promotional book had come unexpectedly and the time scale for the work was tight. Gibbings produced nineteen engravings and had spent many hours in the library and photographic collections of the Royal Geographic Society 'digging out the material from which I did the frontispiece and the Alcock and Brown plane. ... In addition, I had to do a bit of coaxing at the Admiralty to get the profile photograph of the destroyer'.[45] Christopher Bradshaw, of Newman Neame Ltd who produced the book, had farmed the design of the book out to his friend, the typographer and book designer, John Lewis. In retrospect Lewis was rather dismissive of the final product, which was published in 1953, finding it rather dull.[46] Some of Gibbings's engravings are a little stiff and contrived and the subject did not

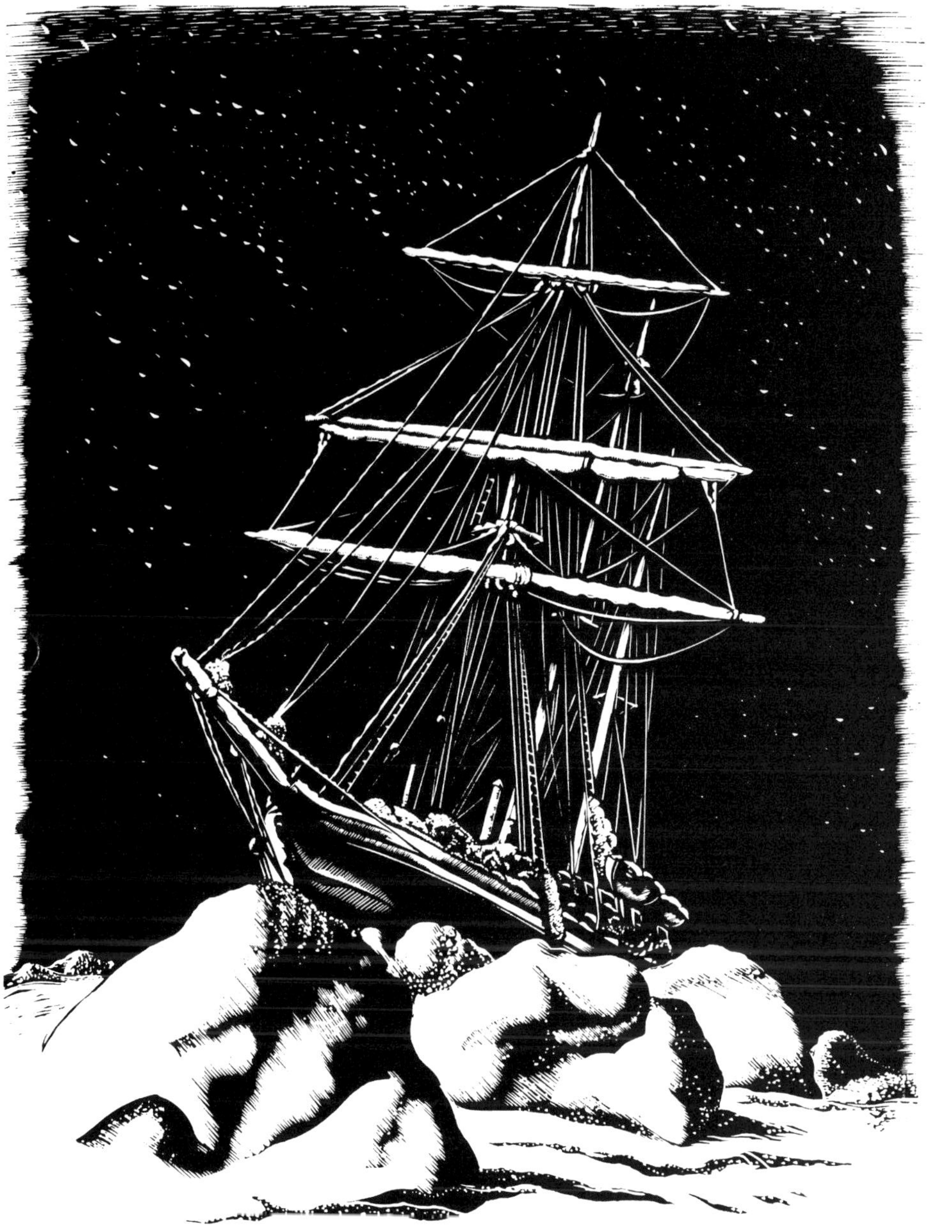

344 Frontispiece of the *Endurance* in the Antarctic from *The Story of Bovril* published in April 1953 and produced by Newman Neame Ltd for Bovril Ltd, wood-engraving, 182 x 140 mm. BOVRIL is a registered trademark of Bestfoods. Reproduced by kind permission of Bestfoods UK Ltd.

perhaps excite him but he was pleased with the dramatic frontispiece. He offered to produce a signed limited edition of the engraving on Japanese paper to be used for 'presentation to special clients of Bovril'. He needed a quick response to the idea: '... I would want to know about this pretty soon so that I could print them all by hand before I go abroad'.[47]

At the beginning of the new year Gibbings was approached by another film company wishing to make a short feature on him. The company were making a series of films on nature and outdoor life for worldwide cinema distribution. Made up in the magazine format of short items, subjects included 'profile' features on personalities and they wished to include Gibbings. One of the production team mentioned that they had a mutual friend in the artist Marshall Hutson, of the Cork Art School. Hutson, a talented but rather irascible character,

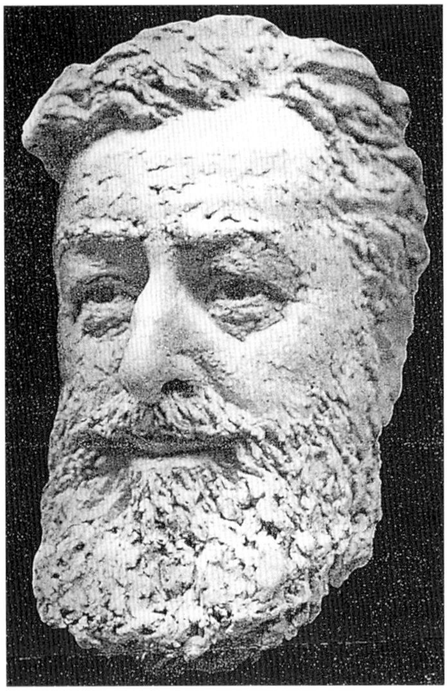

345 A bronze portrait bust of Gibbings by Marshall Hutson reproduced from a cutting pasted into an album by Gibbings's sister Aimée. The image appeared on the cover of the journal *Arts News and Review*, 16 December 1950. The album is now in the possession of Diana Gibbings – the whereabouts of the sculpture is unknown.

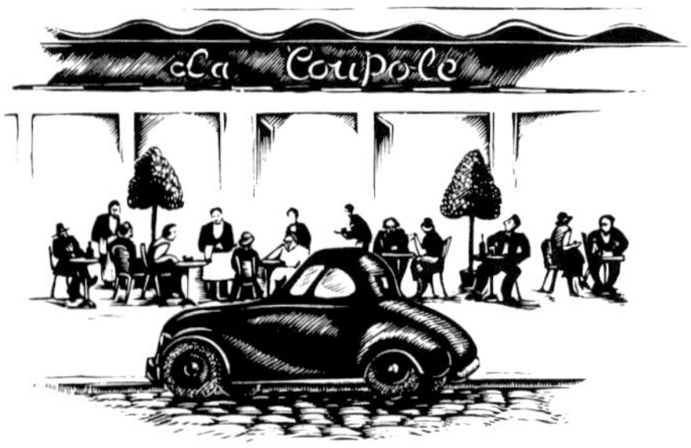

346 La Coupole, Gibbings's favourite restaurant in Paris, 1953, wood-engraving, 56 x 92 mm. Illustration from *Coming Down the Seine*.

was one of the artistic community in Cork and Gibbings had known him for some years. Hutson had made a bronze portrait bust of Gibbings which was exhibited at the Royal Academy in London but which has now been lost.

Gibbings responded favourably to the suggestion of a film:

> The only trouble as far as I am concerned is that if we are to do some country shots it may be difficult to fit it in at an appropriate time, as I hope to go abroad — either to France or Ireland — about the end of April, and will be away all the summer. I don't know how much you wish to concentrate on country subjects, but imagine that in any case you will want something of actual methods of work on the engravings etc. For the latter, any time now would be excellent because I am right in the middle of the engravings for my new book on France, and you could do actual blocks and all the rest of it almost as they sit in my room. These I hope to deliver by the end of the month at latest, after which we would have to concoct a semblance of similar work.[48]

Unfortunately, to date, no further record of the filming has been found.

The reference to the next book being set in Ireland suggests that some plans were already in the making but on 12 February 1953, Bozman noted at the end of a letter that 'the Shannon book' was off.[49] On the same day Gibbings wrote to Hoppé and Martin Dent that the last eight blocks for the *Seine*, apart from extras for the wrapper and spine of the binding, were ready but he was not pleased with the engraving of his favourite restaurant in Paris: 'I do think it would be better if the printing was not held up for the one of La Coupole, which I will certainly try to do. The trouble with that one is that it is not really a subject suitable for engraving but for painting, and it may be rather complicated to get the effect on the wood.'[50] To Martin Dent he tried to explain the technical problems he was having with the photography of the image onto the block:

> I am also sending back the block and the drawing which reached me from Odhams yesterday. As you will see, they have lost practically all the detail, so much so that it would be almost impossible to engrave through the photographic surface. I know that I am partly to blame in that the drawing is inclined to be uneven and also the board on which I pasted the tracing has cockled a bit which no doubt makes it difficult to get good focus in the photograph; but I feel that if they pinned the card down and then took rather more care, they could get something a good deal better than enclosed. There is a tendency at times to put rather a thick film on the block, and to over-print so that much of the detail is lost. It would be better from my point of view if the fault lay in rather a grey proof.[51]

Gibbings concluded the letter saying that he hoped that his 'engraving efforts' would be completed for a while.

By the end of March the subject and mood of his next book was decided. In a letter thanking Aunt Suzanne for her birthday greeting, Gibbings outlined his plan:

> Yes, I've been nearly smothered with work — 80 engravings in the past six months as well as quite a bit of writing etc. But the book is now in the press & my chief concern is preparations for the next. I still have a few articles to write, a couple of broadcasts to prepare & a book token to engrave but then I'll be free to pop over to France & begin again. This time it really is a beginning again for at last I'm to be a little painter & instead of following a river I am going to follow my brushes. As you know I have always wanted to work in colour & now at last the chance has come. The book will have a number of

colour illustrations, D.V., & the text while following the usual vein will I hope have more intimate studies of the people I meet & the places I visit. Instead of being hurried from place to place I'll be able to pursue a much more leisurely & selected course. To what extent I succeed as a painter does not matter greatly as the theme will really be my life-long ambition to be a painter & the problems in colours that arise as I go along.

'Coming Down the Seine' is to be published early in Sept. & a label for your copy has already been addressed.[52]

The comment, 'quite a bit of writing', alluded to, amongst others, a short article for his friend Tom Iremonger of the magazine *Overseas*, published by the Overseas League in March 1953. Gibbings had been asked to focus on the Pacific and somehow link the theme with the visit of Queen Salote for the Coronation. In the event Gibbings chose to focus on another Polynesian Royal, her son Prince Tungi, Crown Prince and Premier of Tonga, who had become a great friend of Robert's during his visit to the Islands.[53] Prince Tungi had invited Gibbings to his wedding but he had been unable to attend. Knowing of the Prince's great love of music, which he shared, Gibbings sent him one of his own favourite books — *The Oxford Companion to Music* — as a wedding gift.[54] Reference to his admiration of this book found its way into *Coming Down the Seine*. The following year Gibbings supplied a selection of blocks from his books on the Pacific to illustrate a book on Prince Tungi's mother, Queen Salote, who had made such an impact at the Coronation.[55]

Another friend of recent years was Evan Gill who had suggested to Philip Gaskell, editor of *The Book Collector*, that Gibbings would be the person to write an appreciation of Eric Gill's work for the Golden Cockerel Press. Gibbings was only too delighted, although later he became rather bored of being asked about Gill, and the result was the article 'Memories of Eric Gill', already quoted from. Despite the fact that Gill had virtually ignored him after the sale of the Press, Gibbings was both generous and warm in his description of their collaboration. Evan Gill was delighted with the result when Gibbings sent him the manuscript in late March:

What a pleasurable feelin' comes over one as one reads something with every word of which one is in whole-hearted agreement. I literally 'purred' as I read every word you have written under the title 'Memories of Eric Gill'. Forgive me for gushing like this .... You see, we have here most precisely exactly what we hoped for. You have set down in black and white what I, personally, had hoped I would some day see set down. ... Every word — every sentence, may I say it, is like the other tools you use, fit for its purpose.[56]

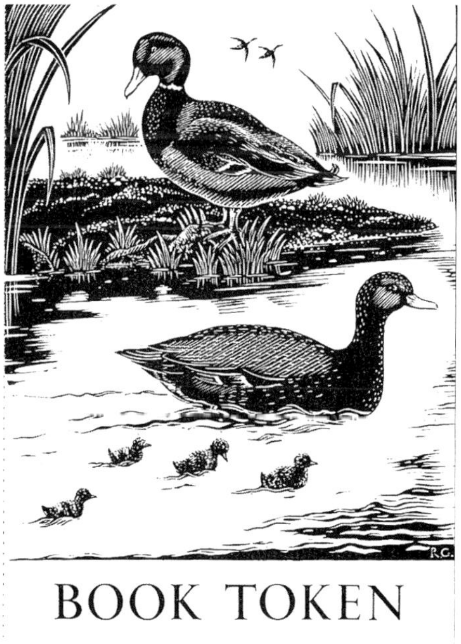

347 Book token, design no. 39, 1953, wood-engraving, page size 124 x 90 mm.

Gibbings's first trip to Paris to pursue the life of a painter as research for his next book was organised but he still had one more commission to fulfil: 'One more block before me now — a 'Book Token', wild ducks being the subject & then its grease to the gravers & oil to the brushes. The Treasury have granted me francs & tomorrow I ring up Air France to know if they want ballast.'[57] Once again his flat was let to John Harris and on 8 April Gibbings departed for Paris where he stayed until 23 June. From his base in Paris he travelled further afield in France, spending some weeks painting the harbour and boats of La Flotte on the Île de Ré on the west coast. It must have been confusing working on one book

Oil painting of the harbour of La Flotte on the Île de Ré – see colour plate 7a.

when the previous one was reaching the final stages of production. In May, Martin Dent wrote to Gibbings at 229 Boulevard Raspail. Adjustments were being made to the title page which was to be partly printed in red:

> I think your arrangement of alternate black and red lines, using the darker red, is a very happy one, and I propose to adopt it. ... I will start a hunt for a darker red cloth right-away. I think the book would have looked quite well in the New Temple Shakespeare colour .... I am glad to hear the new book is beginning to take shape. I can well imagine it needs a good bit of mental adjustment to see your subjects in colour instead of black and white.[58]

Martin Dent also raised the possibility of including some small illustrations in the text in the form of half-tones reproducing his pencil sketches, thus avoiding wood-engraving — this was to be a new and different book and drawings might complement the colour reproductions of his paintings.

Back in London Gibbings was busy with articles and scripts for broadcasts; Pippa Vincent, a BBC producer, had approached him with the idea of another series based on stories from *Sweet Cork*. On 15 September he had been invited to open an exhibition on the life and work of the wood-engraver, Thomas Bewick, mounted by the Victoria & Albert Museum at Bethnal Green. In reply to a request for a public lecture in Rochdale, Gibbings had politely refused; he could manage a talk already booked in Bridgewater on 2 December but after that he intended to 'hurry back to France' where he was negotiating to rent a painting studio — so far without success.

On his return from France, Gibbings managed to take a few days off and he borrowed his son's car to drive to Scotland to explore the valley of the river Tay — perhaps with a vague intention of making it the subject for another book. On his journey he passed the house of Cathleen and George Lennard Jones but, without notice, they were away. Rain stopped him from camping and although the landscape appealed, Gibbings returned to London sooner than planned. He wrote to Cathleen to apologise for not warning of his arrival and outlined his recent adventures on the Seine and his plans for his next book:

> I haven't got very far with it yet but I hope to go back about mid Sept & will spend the winter there if I can find a studio. I'm on the track of one now but it is on the 5th floor & there's no 'ascenseur' & I'm 23 stone .... I haven't really got fat, it's just that I'm filled out a little.

As a postscript he added a plea:

> It has just occurred to me, I suppose you haven't got a gamekeepers cottage that you would let to a 'clean friend'. I am very tired of London & after this next venture in France will buy a donkey & a bath chair & retire to the country for a quiet & contemplative senility. I want a small cottage with one room large enough to work in. I want a smaller room in which to hang my clothes when I'm not wearing them (there'll have to be a kitchen too I suppose) & equally important I want a stream & a wood within crawling distance. I'll promise not to poach![59]

Cover of *Coming Down the Seine* – see colour plate 8m.

On 10 September 1953, *Coming Down the Seine* was published in Britain and on 21 September Dutton brought out their edition in America. 10,000 copies were

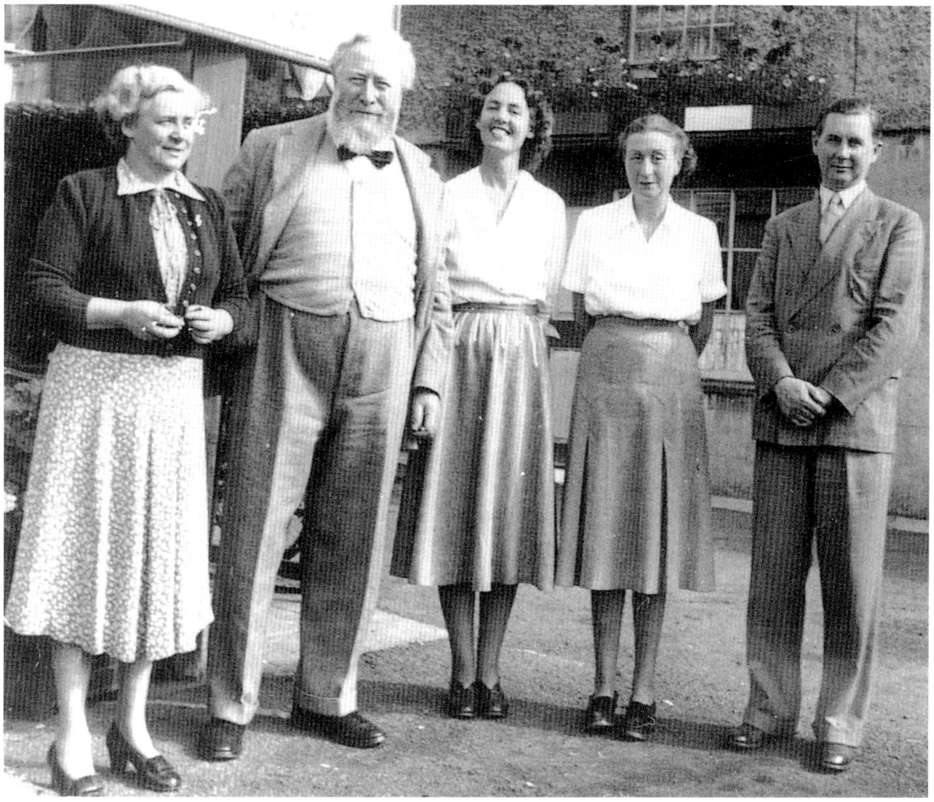

348 'Jim' Williams, Robert, Patience and Anna and John Hadfield outside the Hind's Head Hotel in Bray, c. 1953. RUL.

printed for the first edition but second and third impressions followed in October and December amounting to 17,500 copies in total. To celebrate the success, a dinner party was held at the Hind's Head Hotel, attended by most of the usual crowd — the Hadfields, Patience and Diana Gibbings, Patrick Campbell and his wife, and 'Jim' the manageress presided.[60] A special menu was printed listing sumptuous dishes and wines which liberally flowed: Batard Montrachet, 1950, followed by a Chateau Latour, 1924, and ending with a toast, 'Success to the Seine', with Chateau Filhot, 1945.[61]

Months before, Gibbings had been delighted by the report of Dent's reader:

I thoroughly enjoyed this delightfully written book on Mr. Gibbings's latest river journey — all four hundred miles of it! While it struck me as being rather more serious in mood at times than his last book, it loses none of its appeal because of that. The occasional pause for meditative comment or philosophic aside takes nothing from and, indeed, tends to enhance the characteristically light and facile touch. No opportunity for the humorous approach is ever missed, no opening for the apt story ever escapes, no 'character' ever fails to receive deft appreciation. From the source of the river to its mouth, there can be but very few places worthy of any note about which he did not find something interesting or amusing to relate, whether because of their historical importance, their artistic associations, their scenic peculiarities or their local legends, customs or industries. The dangerous nature of his journey in a flimsy little boat on the flooded river will be missed by none of his readers, despite his light-hearted way of describing it.

He has captured the 'atmosphere' of Paris with effortless ease — Paris of the bridges, the pavement cafes, the art schools and the ateliers — which after all is not very surprising! Recurring through the book are passages of descriptive writing of great beauty, rich in imagery – writing in fact of a high order.[62]

The book was given a boost when *John O'London's Weekly* chose it as their book-of-the-month and published an appreciative review by Richard Church. Church was perceptive about Gibbings's philosophy and also his personality. He speculated that Gibbings and Geoffrey Chaucer would have made 'congenial buddies': 'They share so much; not only wine, women and song, but the little feathered beauty of the English hedgerows, the fish, the nests, the pebbles, the shining things, the downy things, all things touchable and shapely.' On Gibbings's writing, Church commented:

> ... Gibbings carries that vast capacity for enjoyment, a Gargantuan appetite for pleasures that would not come within the consciousness of most pale men and women. And that enjoyment expresses itself in a prose as seemingly artless and free .... It seems that he is incapable of an abstraction. He lives in terms of the concrete, bringing to the world around him a capacity for true worship .... Thus a great wine, a standing tree, a nobly pregnant woman, a sky full of stars, a river sliding with all of nature's cunning down to the sea, are for him the symbols of a lasting sacrament.[63]

Gibbings was very flattered that Church, whose work and literary judgement he admired and respected, had found his writing so inspiring, and commented in a letter: 'I know that my books pass odd hours for stray old ladies, but the idea that such a man as you could find pleasure in any one of them leaves me "speechless".'[64]

Many positive reviews appeared and even four years later, in 1957, the book was still receiving attention when Godfrey Winn wrote a feature on it in *Woman's Illustrated*. Winn's article lavishly quoted extracts from the book interwoven with his own comments; they both obviously shared tastes — gastronomic adventures, landscape and the city — Winn enjoyed it all. He was fascinated and captivated by Gibbings's style of writing which he too rated highly: 'There is much to laugh at in this book, and a tenderness, a receptiveness to beauty in all its manifestations, that brings one to the brink of happy tears' — Gibbings's writing appealed to the broadest of audiences![65]

The need for a second edition had given Gibbings the opportunity to make minor alterations. He had agreed to a suggestion of Martin Dent's that the red on the title page should be brighter and made one or two corrections to the text but felt 'Anything further would be gilding the lily, but if you're printing a third edition before the end of the week, give me a ring!'[66] Next week was too optimistic but a third edition appeared in the following month.

Coming Down the Seine had two particular pre-occupations; an enjoyment of food and wine, and painters and painting. Gibbings had been developing a taste in wine for many years but in the company of John Hadfield and others this had matured. His travels in France had given Gibbings the perfect opportunity to visit many of the famous vineyards and wine cellars and back in England his reputation meant that he was a welcome guest at numerous wine tastings. In Paris, Robert and Patience had spent many hours visiting the Louvre and, most particularly, exhibitions of work of the Impressionists. Frustrated by the constraints of wood-engraving, Gibbings had been becoming more and more obsessed by the

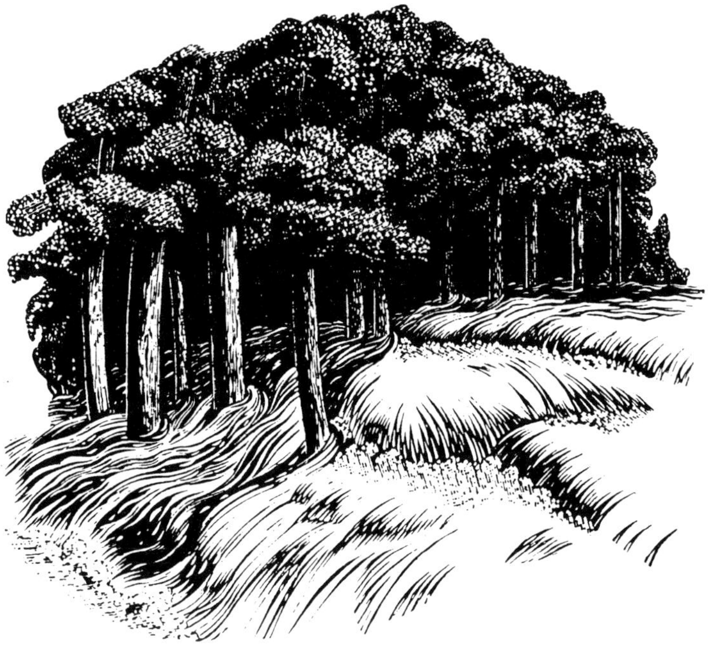

349 Flood waters on the Seine, 1953, wood-engraving, 85 x 94 mm. One of the illustrations from *Coming Down the Seine* reproduced in an article on the book by Godfrey Winn, published in *Woman's Illustrated*, July 1957.

desire to paint and even more to splash out in colour. He returns to the subject of painting and painters time and again in *Coming Down the Seine*; Poussin, Corot, Renoir, Degas, Monet and Sisley are all brought into the text and Gibbings carefully explains such theories as pointillism. He wanted the freedom to paint — to express feelings and subjects impossible with engraving:

> That lavender haze above the water was typical of many dawns; again and again the sun would rise through opalescent mists and the water wear its gossamer shroud. But the veils of morning and evening have little to offer to the wood-engraver, however generous they may be to the painter. In engraving one needs precision of form and contrasts of light and shade, for the limitations of the medium are as severe concerning variations of tone as they are austere concerning fluency of line. I incline to think that one of the earliest and most important lessons to be learnt by any art student is the recognition of those qualities most suited to his particular medium, or alternatively of the medium most suited to the qualities he wishes to express.[67]

Gibbings had tried to bring 'colour' into his black and white engravings — discussing the nature of white and black as colours, Gibbings remarked: '... as an engraver my problem was to make white paper look unlike white paper, to invest it, so to speak, with colour through the medium of black ink'.[68] During his voyage on the Seine Gibbings saw stretches of the river as Monets or Renoirs but in the city his vision had been different: '... as I made my way through the suburbs of Paris towards Montparnasse, I saw the streets only as Utrillos. How that artist loved the texture of old plaster! How those white walls of his teem with colour ...'.[69] Perhaps it was this passion for colour that persuaded him to have both the text and engravings in *Coming Down the Seine* printed in a dark green ink — in retrospect a decision that even his friend and admirer, John Hadfield, thought a mistake!

In November 1953 some reminiscences of his youth in rural Ireland were included in a review Gibbings wrote of the *Experiences* and *Further Experiences of an Irish*

R. M. by Somerville and Ross, published in the Dent journal, *Everyman*, to mark the launch of the books in the Everyman's Library series.[70] He also contributed as usual to exhibitions held by the Society of Wood Engravers at the Times Book Club in the previous month and at the Crafts Centre in Hay Hill, London, in November — both exhibitions were mentioned in an illustrated article on the Society by John Buckland-Wright, published in *The Studio*.[71]

It was a Frenchman, Pascal, who wrote, 'Rivers are roads which move, and which carry us whither we desire to go.' Gibbings adopted the phrase for the title of an article in *John O'London's Weekly* which was published in September 1953. In the article he tried to explain his love of rivers:

> I think it is the unbroken sequences of flowing water, the unchanging destinies of streams, that seem to knit a man's soul with the eternities. The rhythms of eddying pools, the rhythms of lapping wavelets, bring peace through eye and ear, emphasizing by their unceasing flow the unimportance of our passing troubles.[72]

The journey down the Seine was expected to once again provide the reflective tranquillity experienced on his other voyages but in the article he graphically described the dramatic reality:

> Forests were submerged to such a depth that the lower branches of the trees were torn from their parent stems. Tangled with their neighbours and carried with increasing momentum, they made their way across country until, halted by some remote obstacle, they formed a *barrage* that spread the cataract over a yet wider area.
>
> And there I was in a flat-bottomed boat the size of a hip-bath. The maelstrom rushed me here, swung me there; if I wasn't escaping the fate of Absalom under falling trees, I was having my flesh racked from me as I shot through the scarce open eyes of bridges. Again and again I had to wade waist deep through submerged thickets where brambles tore at my at naked limbs. Strangely enough, even in the height of the fury I couldn't but exult in the sharing of such unbridled strength and freedom.

Gibbings concluded the article: '"Time has no beginning there, no end." That is the witchery of rivers.'

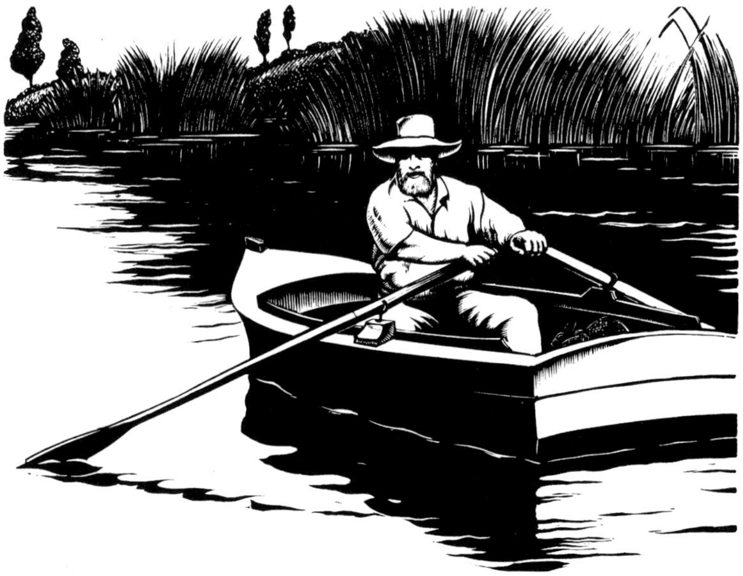

350 Gibbings enjoying a rare moment of peace on the river Seine, c. 1951, wood-engraving, 103 x 136 mm.

Chapter Twenty
The Need for Words and the Love of Paint 1953–1955

GIBBINGS NEEDED A CHANGE, he wanted to paint, and he had successfully negotiated that his next book should forgo rivers and engraving and allow him to indulge his desire to be a painter. The many months he had spent in Paris over the last few years had only fuelled that desire; he had been inspired by his visits to exhibitions of work by the Impressionists and by their use of colour, and he had mixed with the artists of the city, drawing nude models at the Académie Chaumière. He now intended to spend much of the next two years in Europe, working and living as an artist.

To this end, on 1 October 1953, he left with Douglas Eden, an Australian friend, for Paris.[1] After a week he travelled on to Venice where he was joined by Patience and together they toured the city — Gibbings drawing all the while and making colour sketches in paint. Unfortunately the weather again rather dominated their stay and Robert's health was bad. Writing to Suzanne he reported: '... I spent three weeks in Venice but between 'flu & floods didn't get as much work done as I had hoped. The weather was awful, you could have rowed a boat across the Piazza when the tides were high'.[2] Disappointed and still feeling low in health, Gibbings returned to London at the beginning of November. For the next few weeks he took things quietly, filling in with small commissions such as the redesign of the cover of the University College Calendar for his friend Denis Gwynn in Cork.[3] A more significant commission came from Charles Ede of the Folio Society, to illustrate and give editorial advice on a proposed edition of a contemporary account of the discovery of Tahiti, taken from the journal of George Robertson. Gibbings was excited by the notion; it was a subject which had personal appeal and so with clear warnings that the work would have to fit in between his travels, Gibbings signed an agreement at the end of November. He was committed to providing one block for advertising purposes by the end of May 1954, but the remainder were not needed until mid September.[4]

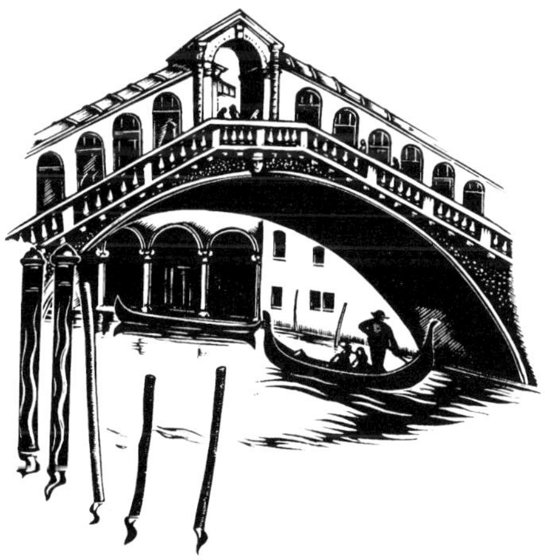

351 The Rialto bridge in Venice, 1955, wood-engraving, 82 × 84 mm. Illustration from *Trumpets from Montparnasse*.

Good news had come from Elliott Macrae, the President of Dutton; Gibbings had written to him seeking news of the *Seine*: 'I am suffering from flu, and the doctor says I need a tonic. The best one I could have would be a nice report on

'Coming Down the Seine'. I gather that it has had a splendid press in your country as over here, but I have heard nothing about how sales are going.'[5] Macrae replied that the book had had a 'fine critical reception'. To date 6,500 copies had already been sold and he expected sales to carry on over many years: 'It is pretty tough these days to get a sale of more than 7,500 copies of any book. American people do a lot of reading, but little of it is in book form.'[6]

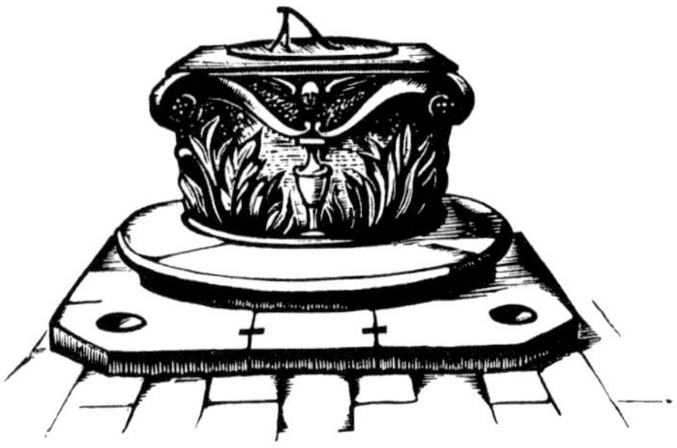

352 Well-head in Venice, 1955, wood-engraving, 40 × 65 mm. Illustration from *Trumpets from Montparnasse*.

The trip to Venice had been something of a washout but Gibbings, always adaptable and inventive in finding material, had been greatly taken by the beautifully decorated well-heads that were to be found in nearly every square, courtyard and garden in the city. Ruskin had described these marble well-heads as 'some of the most superb examples of Venetian sculpture' and Gibbings used this quotation as the opening lines of a short article for the *Saturday Book* for 1954 — it was really an introduction to a series of photographs of well-heads for which he wrote informative captions.[7] Well-heads were to feature as a section in his next book.

Earlier in 1954, two articles by Gibbings were published on the subject of Ireland and he used material and engravings from his Irish books; one was for *Everybody's* and the other for a travel journal, *Ireland of the Welcomes*.[8] Later in the year he again re-used thoughts and observations from *Coming Down the Wye* and *Sweet Thames Run Softly* in articles for the BBC's overseas journal, *London Calling*, and in the magazine *Time and Tide*.[9] Work had progressed on his new book, as yet untitled, and Gibbings had already written up his experiences in the Île de Ré and outlined his plans to Bozman at Dent:

The plot remains the same as when first discussed. Painting and the incidentals connected therewith are the main theme. But owing to the impossibility of finding a studio in Paris in 1953 the early chapters will contain rather more digressions than I visualized. You have one of them in the Ile de Ré chapter. Again and again I have thought that I had found a studio, again and again I have been disappointed. Irritating at the time, I now see that it has given me opportunities to gather a far wider range of material than I had dared hope for. Even if the early chapters are likely to be a bit Tristram Shandy-ish, it is all a good build-up for the studio which is now definite for July and August of this year. As far as I can see, there is no reason why I should not deliver on or about December 31st as agreed.[10]

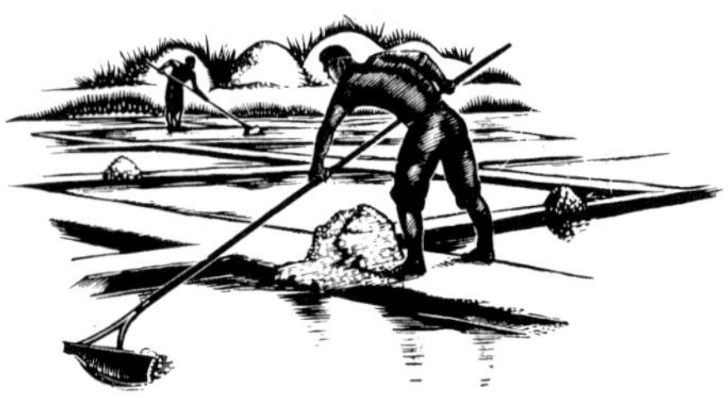

353 Salt-maker in the salt-marshes of the Île de Ré, 1955, wood-engraving, 42 × 88 mm. Illustration from *Trumpets from Montparnasse*.

Lectures and broadcasts continued to fill his diary but on 17 March 1954, St Patrick's Day, Gibbings sailed for Italy on the Orient Line ship, the *Orsova*. As in the past, the company's publicity department had been able to organise his trip and this time he was to travel in style — at short notice they had only been able to reserve him a 'stateroom'. Also on board was Sir Colin Anderson, a company director, with whom Gibbings discussed the design of the ship's menu cards. Gibbings was only too happy to promise to provide engraved illustrations for the menus in return for his passage. The publicity department had suggested life and activity on board ship as suitable subjects but Gibbings had other ideas:

... I have wondered whether a series of natural history subjects dealing with the voyage might not be appropriate. They could certainly be decorative and would lend themselves very much better to wood engravings than mere humans playing on the decks. I have

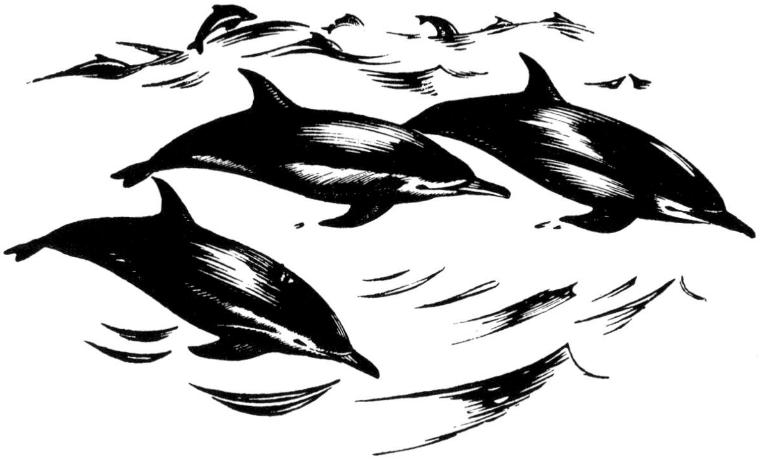

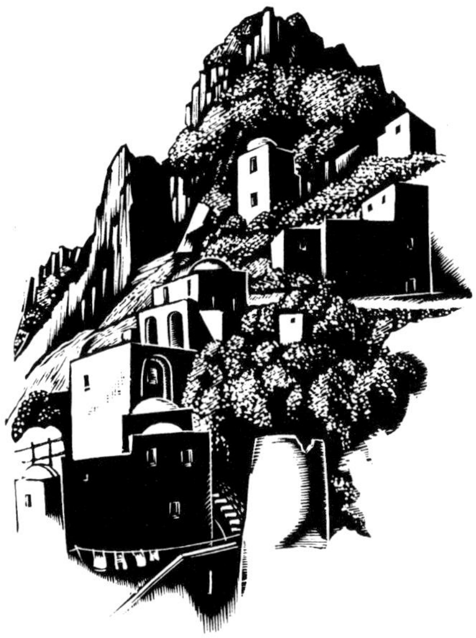

354 *left* Illustration of dolphins commissioned by the Orient Line but apparently never used, 1955, wood-engraving, 60 × 103 mm.

355 *right* View of Positano, 1955, wood-engraving, 75 × 58 mm. Illustration from *Trumpets from Montparnasse*.

thought, for instance, that albatrosses or mollyhawks might be appropriate in Australian waters, flying fish in the Indian Ocean, dolphins in the various straits where they usually appear, and for home waters some of the well-known gulls and other sea birds.[11]

Gibbings was not able to complete the commission until the August of the following year.

After a brief stop at Gibraltar, the *Orsova* 'rippled the smooth Bay of Naples' on 22 March 1954. A waiting car then drove Gibbings along the precipitous coast road to the town of Positano; its 'Plastered houses, cream coloured, white and rose, were clustered against the hillsides of a horseshoe bay, with steep flights of steps descending at every angle among them'.[12] A friend in England had recommended a hotel called the Buca di Bacco, which became his base. Artists and fishermen who congregated there proved perfect company and were a source for stories. Gibbings now had colour; the houses reminded him of nearly forty years before in Malta but instead of black and white, these plastered houses 'shone with every shade of wash. ... Doors and windows, more flamboyant, sang emerald and blue or shouted scarlet'. The view seawards also offered colour; fishing boats on the beach, 'all shades of green and white, all shades of blue and white, striped the purple sand. ... Under a boat, spread-eagled in the shade, lay a fisherman in phlox-pink shirt and turquoise trousers ...'.[13]

Enriched by mythology and history, Gibbings's senses were stimulated. After a few weeks he was offered the loan of a studio which he gratefully accepted. Situated high on the cliff, the view was magnificent — it was an 'Olympian abode'; the down side was that it was a steep descent to the beach from 'the gate of his vine-canopied terrace'.[14] Writing to John and Anna Hadfield, on 18 May, Gibbings outlined his activities:

For myself, I have learned that the world is round, I'm that giddy with trying not to slip off this ruddy hill — 500 steep steps to the beach – that I'm off to Paris next week. Immediate address unknown but from June 15th it is c/o Pierre Deval, 53 Quai Bourbon, Paris xiv, I'm told it is 'formidable'!

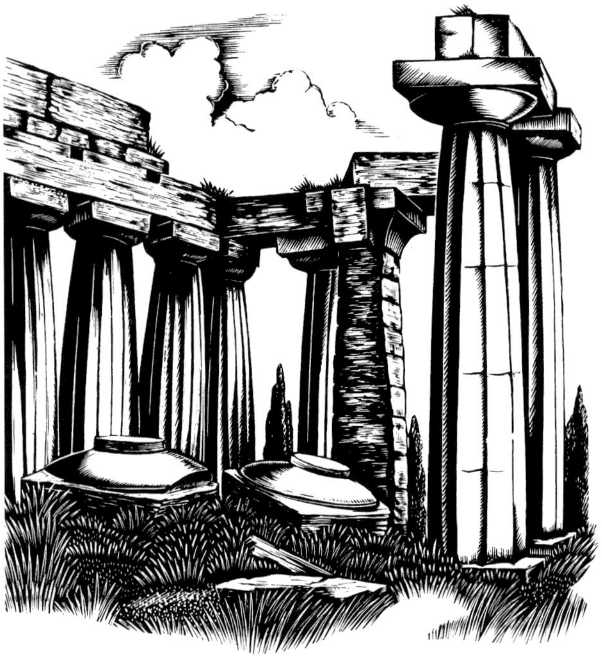

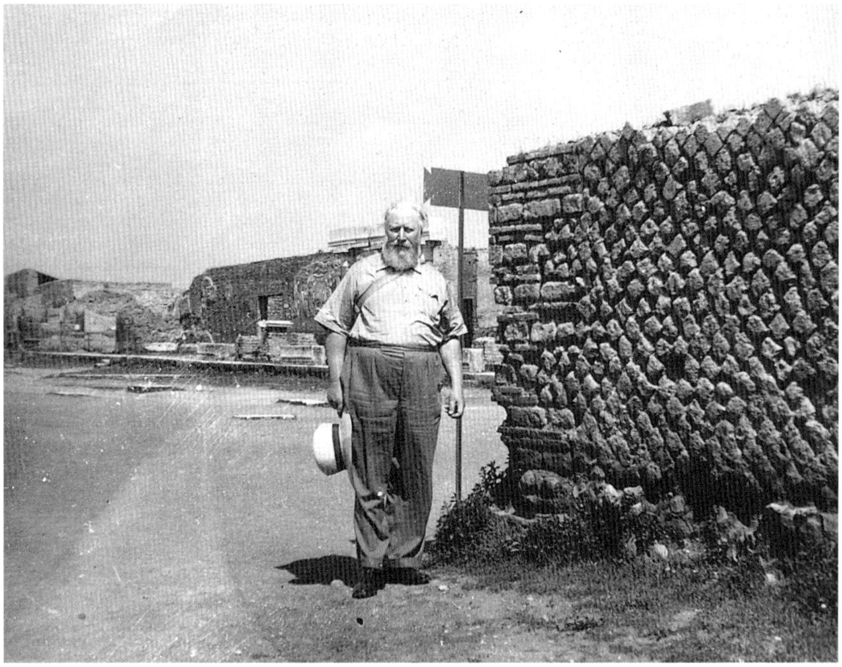

356 *left* Ancient ruins at Paestum, 1955, wood-engraving, 106 x 100 mm. Illustration from *Trumpets from Montparnasse.*

357 *right* Gibbings visiting the ruins at Pompeii in May 1954. RUL.

Work has been going well. In moments of lucidity, meaning non-giddyness [*sic*], I've visited Cuma & the Sibyll, Paestum & Pompeii & in the heat have felt contemporary with the ruins. I've done some scrumptious paintings of oranges & lemons with which I hope to enthuse you one day. ... the people of this country are very small of stature & are inclined to walk round me for a second look. The other day in the Naples museum four attendants not reaching to my shoulders surrounded me, measuring themselves against me, patting me on the chest, pinching my arms & digging me in the belly. Then they led me to a colossal statue of Hercules & pointing to it & to me said 'Simile! Simile!' I came home, a bit elated, to find my cook Nora with a plate of sardines, just purchased. Wishing to emphasize what fine fish they were she picked one up & said 'Multo grande come Papa' ('come' meaning like & Papa meaning me). From the sublime to the mac-fisheries, God forgive me, was what came into my head.[15]

These anecdotes, and many others, were elaborated on and later appeared in his book.

Patience had joined him in Positano at the end of April and soon after her arrival they went to dinner with Elliott Macrae, the head of Dutton, who was also on a trip to Italy. In addition to those sights mentioned in his letter, Robert and Patience had also toured the city of Naples, the island of Capri and the ancient city of Herculaneum. At the end of May, Patience returned to London and, as planned, Gibbings took the night train to Paris. The address he had given to the Hadfields was that of a long awaited studio which he had rented. However, Gibbings could not move in until 15 June so he booked into a small hotel in the Rue de Mazagran, not far from the ancient gates of the city, the Porte St-Denis. The weather was variable, so when it was fine Gibbings 'pottered about the streets, making odd notes in pencil or in colour';[16] when it was wet he wandered in the galleries or sketched the chorus girls at a matinée performance at the Concert Mayol — a small music hall.

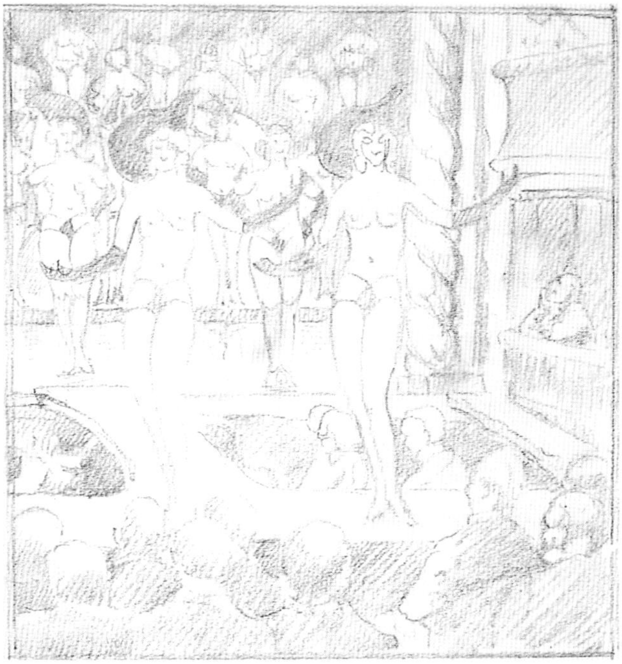

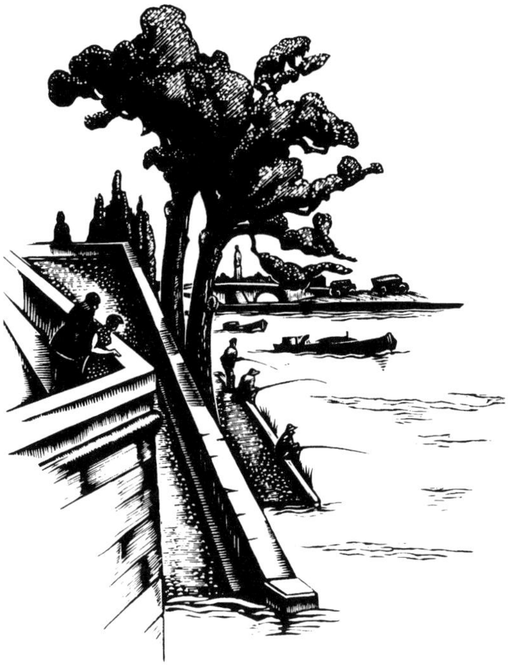

The studio was situated at the Quai de Bourbon on the Île St-Louis, a tiny island in the middle of the Seine, and one of the most prestigious and fashionable parts of the city, which had been the home of many famous artists. As soon as he moved in Gibbings felt at home and was accepted as part of the community. The position was perfect and from his fourth floor window he had views over Notre Dame and the old quarter of Paris. He could look down on to the main channel of the Seine and he was fascinated by the passing traffic of barges and their heavy cargoes; many were named after birds:

There were the *Goldfinch*, the *Curlew*, the *Green Woodpecker*, the *Oriole*, the *Wagtail*, and the *Albatross*. The piercing blasts of their hooters as they came round the point of the island were not so musical as might have been expected from such names, but they soon wove themselves into the quiet pattern of my days.[17]

Another routine that he quickly established was the hiring of life models to pose in his studio. An artist friend, known as Willy Moren in the book, introduced Gibbings to a model referred to as Nicole but really named Liliane. Soon she had a regular appointment in the afternoons to pose and Gibbings made many drawings and a painting of her. But the work of the day was organized in such a way as to allow Gibbings time to indulge in a distraction: he had noticed a pair of pigeons nesting in the poplar trees over-hanging the river close to his window. He was to spend hours observing the development of their courtship and everyday life, noting each stage of their nesting and the hatching of their eggs in his diary; it almost became an obsession — rather like following a soap opera.

On his tiny island Gibbings was enjoying solitude:

Without casting one grain of coral dust at the 'desert' islands on which I have spent idyllic days and nights, I must admit that it was this Defoe form of solitude that I found and

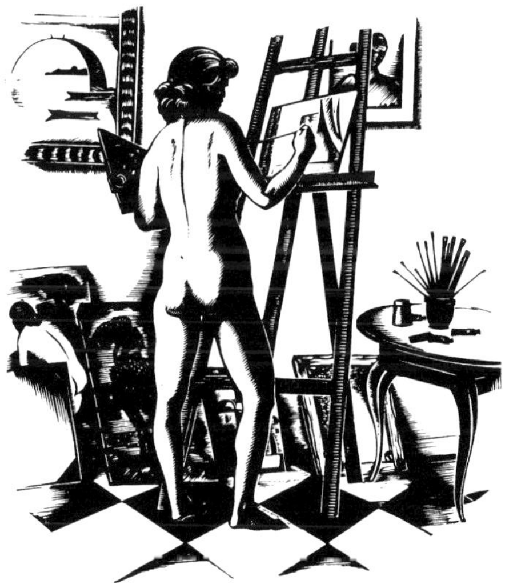

358 *left* Pencil sketch on tracing paper of dancing girls at a music hall in Paris, c. 1954, image size 197 x 190 mm. RUL.

359 *top right* The embankment in Paris, 1955, wood-engraving, 110 x 88 mm. Illustration from *Trumpets from Montparnasse*.

360 *below right* Gibbings's model, Nicole, in his studio in Paris, 1955, wood-engraving, 100 x 90 mm. Illustration from *Trumpets from Montparnasse*.

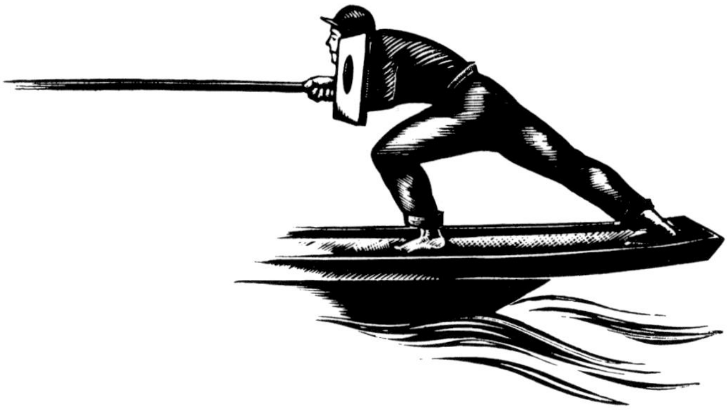

361 'Jousting' at the Grande Fête Nautique in Paris, 1955, wood-engraving, 50 x 90 mm. Illustration from *Trumpets from Montparnasse*.

enjoyed on the Île St-Louis. There in the heart of Paris, with the river flowing past on either side, I was as isolated as a lake dweller, yet within easy reach of any sophistication that might momentarily become needful to my soul.[18]

But Gibbings enjoyed company too; his daughter, Tiare, joined him for a holiday in the middle of August and a week later Patience arrived in Paris. They were in time to observe the religious Fête de St Louis and the procession of colourful banners: '... crimson, white and blue, gold-fringed, some with strange devices',[19] and the Grande Fête Nautique with its fishing competitions and 'jousting', using clashing boats rather than horses. As always, art galleries and museums, including a major exhibition of the work of Cézanne, were enjoyed.

In the middle of September, Patience returned to London and Gibbings had to vacate his beloved studio and move temporarily into the Kleinberg's flat in Montparnasse. Back in the artists' quarter, he observed his fellow painters of both sexes and all ages passing by, clutching portfolios or canvases: 'Some full of assurance though with nothing accomplished, others diffident though with much to their credit; some cynical after a few failures, others after years of disappointment convinced of ultimate success.' Gibbings was in reflective mood: 'What was it all about, I wondered, as so many others have also wondered — this urge that often is stronger than hunger? A few lines or colours in harmony can give more delight to their creator than a Lucullan feast.'[20] Despite the control and discipline demanded by his own particular medium, Gibbings was completely open in his approach to art. He was moved and influenced by art of all periods and cultures, he felt that in art there was 'no need for intellect or erudition, or even of being 'civilised'. Had not Picasso said of the cave paintings at Lascaux, 'Nothing finer has since been done'? Quoting an old sage from India, Gibbings felt that 'all art is one'.[21] His views were not those of the intellectual but they were sincere and passionate:

Of course, art has no more to do with morals than the teaching of a prelate has to do with the shape of his hat. Art is concerned only with intrinsic truth, and how and by whom the price is paid and those truths are purchased and expressed is of secondary importance. Art is the expression of the essence of reality, stripped of all accidental qualities, honest. Picasso's goat in bronze possesses every goatish quality and nothing else; that is why it is so splendid, classic in its analysis of essentials. Abstractions are made from knowledge not from ignorance.[22]

Gibbings had arranged to return to London on 20 September but was reluctant to leave the city and his 'lovely river full of stars' which had always seemed a home to him. But his stay was over; he had achieved his ambition to have time to paint; there would be time later to reflect on how successful his work had been but meantime he had 'A few small paintings and perhaps a few words.'[23]

BACK AT 91 WARWICK ROAD, Gibbings was enjoying reading a new publication that John Hadfield had recently edited. It was another in a very successful series of anthologies of writing and pictures under such themes as the *Book of Joy*. Hadfield had selected two favourite pieces from *Coming Down the Seine*. In a letter of thanks to Hadfield, Gibbings explained that 'Sitting at my unlit hearth drinking a cup of tepid tea I was warming myself with the Book of Delights.' His peace was interrupted by the postman delivering a second complimentary copy:

With your permission I will hand one of them over to PAE [Patience] who typed at least six versions of each of the R.G. rhapsodies. I think it's an awfully nice compilation John & delightfully produced. Your pairing of me with Ogden Nash was a splendid thought. Only one thing grieved me & that was that on p. vii you *apologise* for not keeping to the point. That is almost letting the side down; which reminds me, did I not tell you that a late president of the Psychological Soc. once said to me with a sigh 'there are so few points worth keeping to'.[24]

The *Book of Delights* was another 'pot pourri' of subjects and thoughts — Gibbings was in sympathy with the rich variety and wanted to champion the right to digress as he so often did in his own writing. The formula was very successful and popular although some critics saw it as a weakness. The two pieces chosen showed Gibbings's style at its best; with the economy of poetry he provides intimate description and brings the scene and mood alive for the reader. His life was often frantically busy with deadlines but Gibbings always sought moments for himself — time to reflect — it was a constant conflict of which he was aware:

There were mornings when, casting off at dawn, I drifted through long cool shadows, watching the sunlight on the trees creep down to meet the water, hearing no sound but the tremolo of the aspens, seeing no one but a chance sportsman and his dog. There were noons with cooling breezes and flocculent clouds high in the sky, and evenings when the forest rang with bird song and the river was a sheet of moving glass. There were nights when, looking skywards, the passing clouds seemed like new continents and islands marked on the inside of a mighty globe.

Hereabouts there was just enough current to keep me moving through the stretches of restful, unexciting landscape. I could relax and let fancies flitter through my brain as inconsequentially as a ladybird or a drowsy moth might rest a moment on the gunwale.

The trouble with just 'being' is that you get nothing done. The trouble with 'doing' is that it makes you unconscious of 'being'. Nothing is worth doing unless you concentrate your thoughts upon it, yet if you do that you miss the consciousness of the doing, and enjoy only the having done.[25]

The end of the year was busy. Gibbings needed to concentrate on the writing of his new book but there was the usual programme of public talks to fulfil. In October 1954 Barbara Rippon, Talks Producer for the Pacific Service of the BBC, had commissioned Gibbings to write and broadcast a series of short pieces under the title 'Letters from London', which were to be part of a programme called 'Calling the Islands' on the Overseas Service. These were to be regular contributions, going out most weeks and recorded in batches of two or three at a time. Each piece filled four to five minutes and usually consisted of reports on events which Gibbings had to attend. The subjects were diverse in the extreme and took him to places and events he would never have expected to experience. Between 12 October 1954, when his first topic was the Fête Nautique in Paris, to 18 July 1955, he recorded forty-two talks on subjects such as the Motor Show, a cattle show, Cruft's Dog Show, the Royal Horse Show, an England versus Wales football match, a wine tasting and a circus; he visited Madame Tussauds, Big Ben, the Royal Academy and London Airport and he addressed topics such as tombstones, bush doctors, criminal animals and Marco Polo as well as more reflective issues such as examples of coincidence and the seasons. Each talk was delivered with his usual light-hearted and conversational style, but, however spontaneous they seemed, the reality was that each talk involved preparation and Gibbings needed proper reward. Writing to the BBC, he put his case:

> Now I feel that we really must have a revision of the financial side. The present rate does not come near covering the time and effort involved, in particular when I have to go out specially to a lecture or a show. Yesterday I spent the morning at the Cattle Show, it took me the afternoon to prepare the script and it will break into another morning to record it. That is to say, a day and a half's work. In the case of my visit to Wembley, after failing to get into the train at Baker Street, I had to charter a taxi which cost me 22/6. I enjoy doing these broadcasts, but if I am to continue I must ask for a minimum of 10 gns. a time, with extra if I have to go far afield as for Wembley. I don't want to appear grasping but the job does cut in very seriously on my regular work which is much more remunerative.[26]

As a result of this letter Gibbings received an extra two guineas for expenses on top of his fee of six guineas for each talk!

He had frequently contributed talks to the Overseas Service over many years and valued his association with the people and the BBC itself but he was aware that his overseas audience was limited. In a letter to Suzanne he warned her of the difficulties of receiving the programmes in England: '... broadcasts I fear can only be heard on the short wave to the Pacific, at about 7am, & then they can't be heard, not in my experience anyway! There is no mention of them in the Radio T'.[27] But he had broadcast on the national networks — the Home Service and the Third Programme. He had been a guest on Women's Hour on a number of occasions and, in February 1951, Gibbings read on the programme a short folk-tale which he had collected in France and which he later included in *Coming Down the Seine*. He felt that the tale could just as easily have come from County Cork and so he 'transmogrified it into Anglo-Irish idiom and called it, "The Perfect Wife"'.[28] Gibbings's adaptation of the tale was first published in full in June 1951, in the journal *Irish Writing*, and came to the notice of Liam Miller.[29] Miller had set up his own small private press, the Dolmen Press, in Glenageary, County Dublin, and was planning a series of ballads, tales, songs and pictures under the collective title of *The Dolmen Chapbook*, to be published in parts, each in itself complete, to be followed by a bound volume. Miller admired Gibbings's work and, writing to him in November 1954, he asked if he would contribute to the project: 'Your little fable "The Perfect Wife" ... fascinates me and is the kind of thing I would like'.[30] At that time the Press was a small hand press which Miller operated in the evenings after work but he was already building a reputation in literary circles in Ireland. Gibbings readily agreed and suggested that Miller should contact Dent about the possibility of using engravings from *Sweet Cork of Thee* as he was too busy to produce anything original. *The Perfect Wife* was finally published in June 1955.[31]

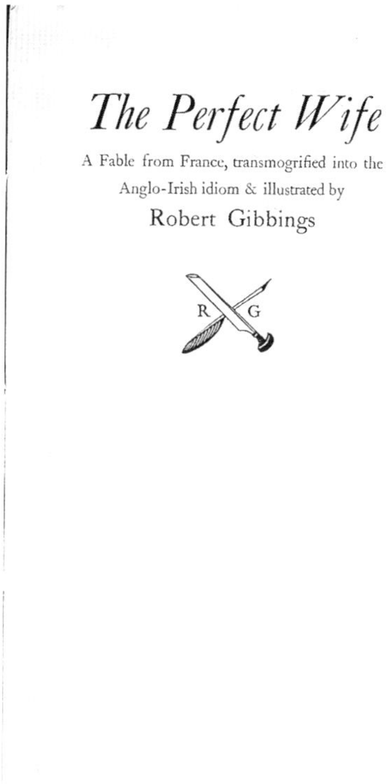

362 Cover of *The Perfect Wife*, third part of *The Dolmen Chapbook* printed by Liam Miller at the Dolmen Press in 1955. Page size 255 x 158 mm. RUL.

In the background to all his other activities, work on the engravings for Charles Ede of the Folio Society and their edition of *The Discovery of Tahiti* had progressed. As usual Gibbings had kept to the schedule, all the blocks were ready by September 1954, and the book appeared at the beginning of the new year.[32] In November 1954, Dent had published a new edition of Gibbings's little picture book, *A True Tale of Love in Tonga*.

Back in April 1954, George Macy, the director of The Limited Editions Club of New York, wrote to Robert Gibbings suggesting that he might consider illustrating another book for him. Enclosed was a list of over one hundred titles of famous books that had been circulated to members asking for their preferences for future productions — Gibbings was invited to indicate any titles that he would enjoy illustrating. The letter went astray as it was addressed to Gibbings at 'The Orchard, Waltham St Lawrence'. When Macy's letter finally reached him, four months after posting, Gibbings was living in the studio on the Quai de Bourbon in Paris. Despite the delay Gibbings received the offer with enthusiasm: 'Delighted to get your letter of April 15th *yesterday*. Where the hell has it been all this time? I would very much like to co-operate in the new venture if I am not too late in replying and if I can fit the job in between my own books.'[33]

Gibbings's passion for travel and natural history and his love of the South Seas was reflected in his selection; first choice was *The Voyages of Captain Cook* but Macy had in fact arranged for an edition of this book to be printed in Australia, illustrated by Geoffrey Ingleton and edited by Grenfell Price. By coincidence, Dr Price was also working on a definitive edition to be published by the Hakluyt Society for which Gibbings had been asked to write an essay on Cook's artists.[34]

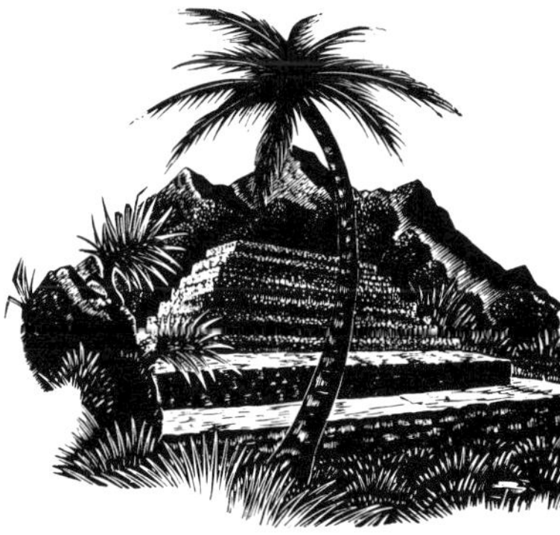

363 Tahitian altar, 1955, wood-engraving, 75 x 95 mm. Illustration from *The Discovery of Tahiti* published by The Folio Society.

Gibbings's first preference was strongly followed by Darwin's *The Voyage of the Beagle*. Gibbings had 'sailed in the same waters' as Darwin and as part of his deep interest in, and study of, marine biology he had referred to the *Beagle* 'again and again when writing and in my lectures'.[35] This was an obvious choice for Gibbings. For all his humour and spirited love of life there was also a serious and scholarly side to Gibbings's research into natural history — Macy decided that this was the book for him.

For *The Voyage of the Beagle*, Gibbings suggested that instead of just a few large engravings there should be a 'large number of little ones which can be dropped in as accents on the page to illustrate the piece of text immediately alongside. All the creatures and things of which he [Darwin] writes lend themselves admirably to small decorations and in scientific work of this kind facts are more important than fancy.'[36] Macy was in turn rather slow to respond: 'A letter which I sent you on 15 April was rewarded with a reply on 4 August; therefore, when I reply on 29 October to your letter of 4 August, I am still some weeks ahead of you', but he expressed delight that Gibbings had agreed to work on a book for The Limited Editions Club again: 'I stand ready to close with you on 'The Voyage of the Beagle'; I think you would inevitably make some excellent blocks in illustration of that book, and I would be ready to follow your lead editorially also. I have been paying the sum of six hundred pounds to artists in England for a set of illustrations for a book. I hope you will think that generous enough; if you think it too generous, I will reduce it; if you think it insufficient, I am prepared to increase it!'[37] Gibbings was delighted with the offer but could not be sure of the number of engravings that would be needed without knowing the 'format and size of the page' but was eager to reply in 'the same noble vein ... if in the end you think my acreage of boxwood is insufficient I will be prepared to increase it!' In the same letter of 2 November, he outlined his approach to the project:

> It would be great fun to edit this new edition and, if I may suggest it, it would be great fun too to design the whole thing typographically. The former would take some time and thought, but I happen to be a Fellow of the Royal Geographical Society and also of the London Zoological Society, so that I have easy access to the right material.
>
> As to typography, I don't know what the present import rules are with you, but if not too complicated I could perhaps design the book page by page in touch with the printers over here, and then get them to send you the finished unbound sheets. ... My personal feelings are that doing the whole thing would be a thoroughly enjoyable job, almost taking me back to the days of the Golden Cockerel Press.[38]

Thus with humour, warm feeling and enthusiasm the agreement was made. However, Gibbings had warned Macy that he could not start on the *Beagle* until April of the coming year by which time he hoped to have delivered everything to Dent for his own book.

At the beginning of 1955 Gibbings had sent five of his oil paintings, as illustrations for the new book, to Martin Dent who reported that he was 'enjoying the luxury of having them decorate my office'.[39] Gibbings had received a specimen page of his book showing the layout; the type had been set to a width of four inches but a slightly larger typesize than had been used in *Coming Down the Seine* was proposed. The margins were generous, giving the typography a feeling of lightness and space. Eventually the final text was to be shorter than his previous books and the page design helped to bulk up the book.

On 3 February, Patience noted in her diary that the complete manuscript of the new book had been delivered to Dent. *Coming Down the Seine* had ended with the words '... there are trumpets calling from Montparnasse', and so it had been decided to echo these words in the title of the new book — *Trumpets from Montparnasse*. The following week Bozman wrote to Gibbings giving his first reactions to the manuscript:

> I have finished my first reading of the MS and have handed it over to Martin so that he can have it prepared for the press. I have thoroughly enjoyed it, and I think that it will be

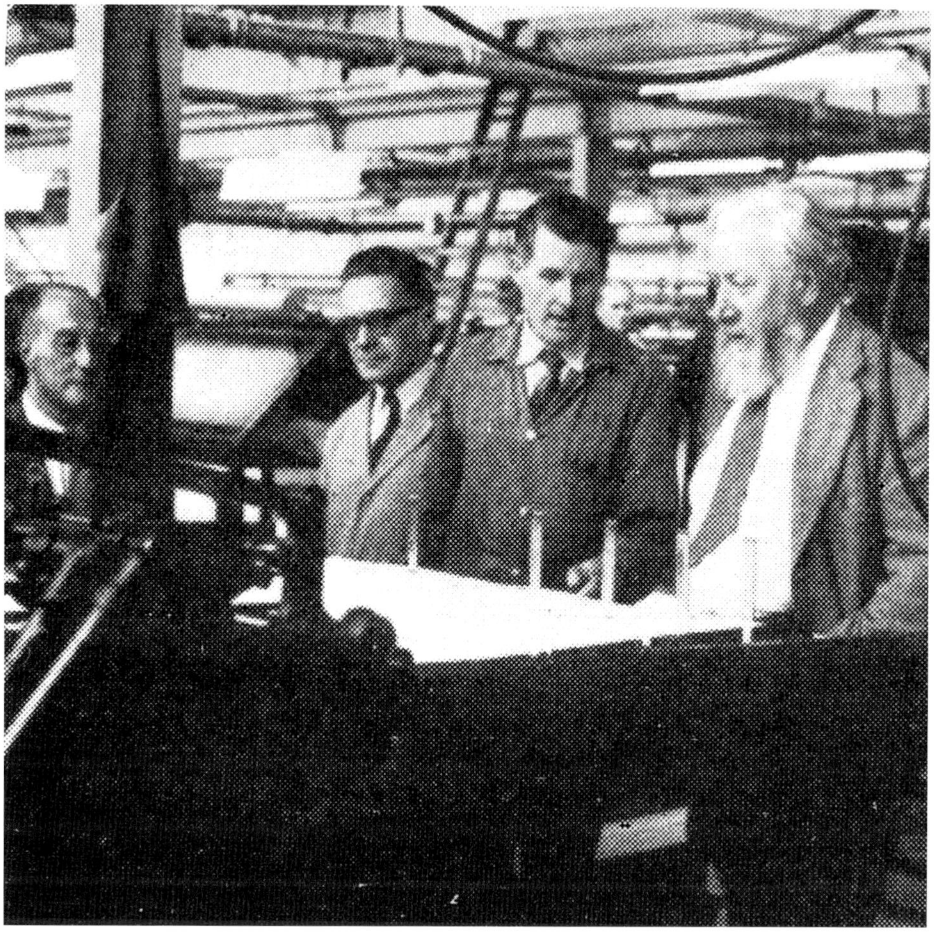

364 Gibbings in the machine room at the Aldine Press to see the printing of *Trumpets from Montparnasse* on a visit to Letchworth in September 1955. Published in *The Cog*, Dent's staff magazine, vol. 5, no. 19, December 1955.

a success. It is varied and lively and as I read on I could see how ingeniously you have brought in your reflections on painting and colour without any tedious 'aesthetic' dissertations. Your practical approach will be much more attractive to your readers than any amount of theoretical writing would be.[40]

Bozman did, however, go on to express his feeling that there was a weakness in the final chapters; he sensed that it was 'as if you were hurrying us on towards the end ...' and he also observed that certain episodes needed more integration with the main scheme of the book.

Although the main text had been submitted, Gibbings continued to add new sections:

Another 1500 to swell our pages. I have been chasing this material for more than six months and only ran it to earth last week. ... I don't anticipate any more additions of this magnitude, but I still have hopes of a few oddments which can be inserted in or before the galley proofs, according to how things go. Now that the final rush is over my brain is recovering slightly, and ideas are coming to me for a few last 'great thoughts'.[41]

In his letter he also asked for the approximate over-all dimensions of the book's dust jacket as it was proposed that he engrave a decorative design for the wrapper and he hoped to be able to re-use the woodblocks that had been used for the endpapers for *Over the Reefs*. The cost of a large woodblock at the time was such that it was much more economical to re-surface an old block after electrotype copies of the original image had been taken to print from.

Relations with Dent were generally very smooth and friendly but there was the occasional dispute. Hoppé had rightly anticipated that Gibbings might object to an advertisement for the binders Linson, which appeared in *The Bookseller* illustrated by one of his engravings.[42] The image had been 'tampered with' and a certain cartoon character, 'Bob the binder', added to the picture. Gibbings, perhaps still sensitive after the 'mattress' affair in Ireland, responded sharply and Hoppé, who had presumably given permission for the use of the image and found it rather amusing, must have been somewhat shocked at his reaction. However effective as an advertisement, Hoppé had miscalculated the strength of feeling an artist has for the integrity of his work:

> That advertisement of Linson's may be slick and clever but I think it is utterly wrong in principle and in practice. They have absolutely no right to mutilate an artist's work in that way. That was a decent engraving and their nasty little Peeping Tom has reduced it to one of utter vulgarity.[43]

This unfortunate incident, however, was immediately forgotten and relations were as good as ever. Talks and broadcasts permitting, Gibbings concentrated for the next months on completing the engravings for *Trumpets from Montparnasse*. The original intention of using pencil sketches as illustrations had been dropped and Gibbings returned to his familiar medium. Eight oil paintings were finally selected to be reproduced in full colour and fewer wood-engravings were included than in his previous books. By the end of May all the blocks had been delivered to Dent. The publication day was fixed for 20 October 1955 and at the end of September Gibbings travelled to the Dent offices to sign finished copies. The next month Dutton published the American edition, which, as with their other editions, had a different cover design, used a different typeface for the text and generally produced a less restrained feel to the book to suit the different market. Gibbings had a few qualms about the quality of the printing of his engravings for the American editions:

Cover of *Trumpets from Montparnasse* – see colour plate 8n.

Cover of the American edition of *Trumpets from Montparnasse* – see colour plate 8o.

> I gather that Dents will have sent you a set of the electros. I have not got a complete set of proofs of the blocks, but am sending you a fair collection to give an idea of the amount of colour that I like on them. Do beg of the production department to take care of the printing of the blocks: as you may remember, the printing of the early ones in the SEINE was terrible.[44]

The production manager at Dutton's accepted the criticisms and efforts were made to achieve a better result in *Trumpets from Montparnasse*. Gibbings later had to be rather humble when he sent Dutton a lengthy list of last minute corrections to the text as a result of a careful proof reading by a French acquaintance, Simone Eastman of Southampton University, who had helped Gibbings on previous occasions with his use of the French language.[45]

Generally the book had a good reception on both sides of the Atlantic – indeed, favourable reviews appeared in the Press all over the world, including India, Canada and Australia. Nearly all the critics were seduced once again by the charm of Gibbings's writing, by his optimism and his infectious love of life; others were less convinced. One critic in the *National and English Review* commented that the book revealed '... Mr. Gibbings almost as a writer in search of a subject. ... Mr. Gibbings's soufflé is feather light!'. John Gibbins in the art magazine *Apollo* was more generous:

This is one of those rare things nowadays — a wholly natural book that has no other object than to communicate pleasure, to interest and amuse, and to acknowledge its own jocund yet sensitive authority with practical sagacity and clarity of expression. Artists, when they have the gift at all, are first-rate writers, and Mr. Gibbings ranks very high.[46]

In America, one review in the *New York Times* was damning; Orville Prescott, a self-confessed fan of Gibbings's work, was less enthusiastic about this latest offering:

The sad news today is that Mr. Gibbings' new book, 'Trumpets From Montparnasse' lacks all the virtues that distinguish its charming predecessors.

These are harsh words and, as a Gibbings admirer for nearly twenty years, it pains me to record them. Nevertheless, truth must prevail. 'Trumpets From Montparnasse' is a dull, scrappy, tired collection of odds and ends entirely unworthy of the unusually handsome paper and typography in which its publishers have dressed it.[47]

One or two other critics also pointed to weaknesses and commented on the pace and patchy nature of the book. They all praised his engravings and many expressed pleasure over the richness of his paintings; but a review in the *Irish Independent* objected to the inclusion of an engraving and oil painting of a female nude. Also, it had been a risk to feature the paintings — one critic felt that they revealed Gibbings to be 'unsatisfactory as a painter'. After a run of six successful books since 1940, perhaps the formula was wearing thin, not least for Gibbings himself, who by now must have been tiring of the constant demand for new material.

Whatever the quality of the results, Gibbings had been refreshed by his painting. The opening page to *Trumpets from Montparnasse* contained a protest from Gibbings: 'I don't want to engrave. ... I've been doing that all my life. I want to paint. I want to get away from black and white and the austerities of the graver. I want the freedom and the fun of brushes and colour.' Gibbings had fulfilled his desires. He covered the surface of his canvasses with confident strokes of thick pigment, enjoying the texture and movement of oil paint; vibrant colours fill the pictures, which are post-impressionist in style. The paintings are full of energy; Gibbings was more satisfied by the *doing*, the exploring, rather than worrying whether he was producing great art. When engraving, Gibbings's portrayal of the naked human figure was often rather stiff and unconvincing, but, with the freedom of paint, his nudes became voluptuous living forms. The results of his painting were variable but his pictures are stamped with a strong, committed character, however derivative in style.

Charles Ede had taken a particular fancy to a still-life, of a large white hat filled with fruit, which was used on the dust jacket of the book. Ede offered to buy it and Gibbings was delighted but a little concerned about copyright, which might

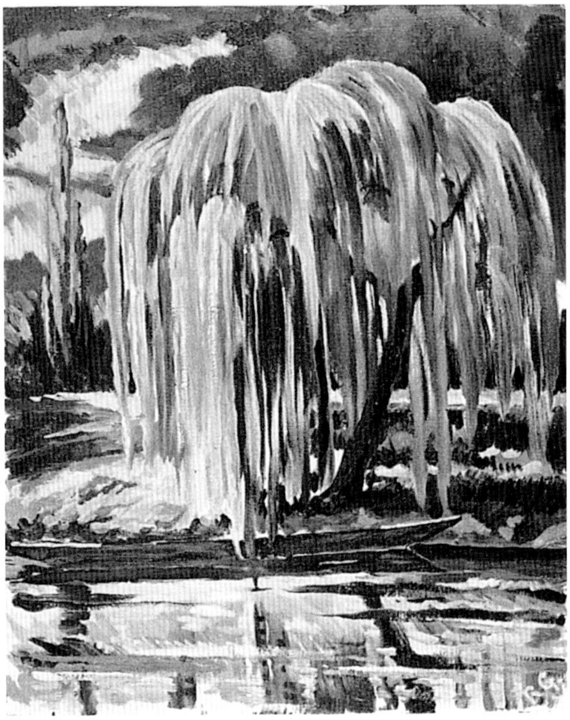

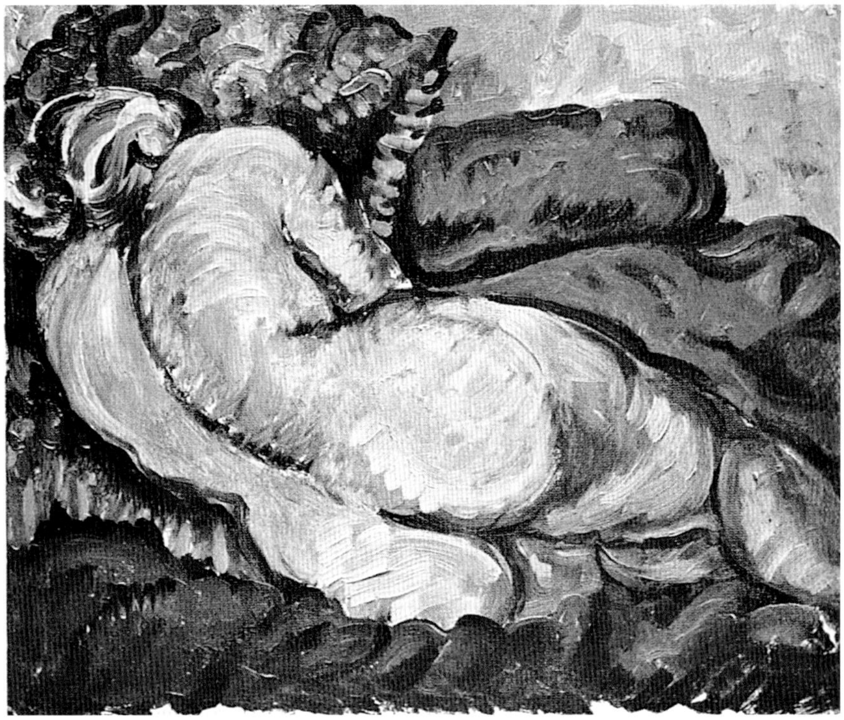

365 *left* The willow tree from the lawn at Monkey Island, 1955, oil on canvas, reproduced from a copy of *Trumpets from Montparnasse*. The original painting is in the possession of Diana Gibbings.

366 *right* Nude model, 1955, oil on canvas, reproduced from a copy of *Trumpets from Montparnasse*. The whereabouts of the original painting is unknown.

have belonged to Dent. Gibbings arranged for the picture to be collected from a display mounted by Dent at the Sunday Times Book Exhibition held at the Royal Festival Hall. This had been organised by Leon Russell and Gibbings was booked to give a lecture on his river experiences and his recent transition from black and white to colour. Ede understood the situation on reproduction rights and was just thrilled to have the picture. He assured Gibbings that it would always be available for loan to exhibitions though he stressed 'I hope not *too* often as I expect to feel very lonely without it'.[48] As a small token of his 'esteem and regard', Gibbings offered a choice of a picture of fishing boats at Positano or a still-life of 'Fruit on a chair' as a gift to his colleagues at Dent. A study of a weeping willow tree he gave to his son Patrick as it had been painted from the lawn at Monkey Island.[49]

The painting of fishing boats at Positano had for some weeks been displayed in the window of Foyle's Bookshop in London as an advertisement for the book. Christina Foyle had recently organised a small gallery in the shop and was hoping that Gibbings would hold a proper exhibition of his paintings there in the summer of 1956.[50] Although keen, Gibbings felt that he did not have enough work and suggested postponing the show until the autumn to allow him the summer to build up a better selection of work. With this in mind, in August 1955, Gibbings took a break from the noise of London and returned to the peace of the upper reaches of the Thames to spend ten days in the New Inn at Lechlade, painting and sketching by the river.

The welcome diversion as a painter was only temporary. Even while at the easel in his studio in Paris he had received the tempting offer from George Macy to illustrate *The Voyage of HMS Beagle*; 'No escape from engraving, I thought, as I sat down to accept.'[51]

Chapter Twenty-one
The Beagle: A Successful Collaboration 1954–1956

IN NOVEMBER 1954, in response to Gibbings's letter outlining his ideas for *The Voyage of HMS Beagle*, Macy wrote that 'Everything about your letter ... is a matter for rejoicing. ... I am pleased that you would like to plan the book editorially, I am pleased that you would like to plan the book typographically'. He continued:

If you want some help in the matter of setting and printing, for making sample pages and printing the book, you could turn to any of my friends who may be friends of yours: Bobby Simon of The Curwen Press, Jimmy Shand of The Shenval Press, Brooke Crutchley of Cambridge, Blair Maxwell of R & R Clark, any one of these would I think be delighted to pitch in'.[1]

In the new year, Gibbings wrote to Macy again with some questions on the format and flavour of the book:

Is it to be a semi-facsimile first edition with all the notes and addenda which are only of interest to scientists, or is it to be as readable an edition as possible, with perhaps some abridgements? It is a mighty long book, about 180,000 words. As to format, had you any preconceived idea as to size? I fancy that if only to make it readable it should not exceed Royal 8vo, and therefore would have to be in at least two volumes. If you could let me have an answer on these points it would enable me to get it all a stage further in my mind.[2]

In his letter he then approached a more 'delicate' matter; he hoped that Macy would agree to an advance on his fee: 'I'm not starving, just trying to avoid doing so in 1957.' Income from his books, although considerable, was ploughed back into his next project and also went in support of his large family. He had difficulties in 'synchronising' the financial year. Greatest expenses were incurred during his years of travel and research, during which he had a low income, and when he also incurred heavy income tax demands relating to his previous books. Macy happily agreed to an advance of two hundred pounds. As to the text, Macy felt that club members were interested in classics as literature and therefore the text should be 'readable and not pedantic', but he decided against abridgement and therefore accepted the possibility of a two volume edition. Clearly anxious to push the project along, Macy had also contacted the Cambridge University Press who had printed a number of his books:

In the matter of the format, I am now electing to put a little pressure upon you by asking the people at Cambridge to meet with you for a preliminary discussion. I am writing to John Dreyfus ... in the hope that he can by preparing specimen pages help to crystallise your ideas for the time when you get to work upon the blocks. He is a very nice young man, I am sure you will like him.[3]

At the beginning of 1955, Dreyfus was working on an edition of Thackeray's *The Newcomes*, for The Limited Editions Club, and therefore was in regular contact with Macy, who wrote to Dreyfus in January 1955: 'Because you have hinted that, once you have finished with "The Newcomes", you will be unbearably lonely, I now send this note to ask whether you would like to meet with Robert Gibbings and help him to prepare a projected edition of Charles Darwin's "The Voyage of the Beagle".'[4] Dreyfus duly contacted Gibbings and was invited to lunch at his flat in Warwick Road. Although they had not previously met, Dreyfus was obviously familiar with Gibbings's work at the Golden Cockerel Press and held him in great respect. Their first meeting went well and Gibbings reported to Macy:

... Dreyfus came along yesterday and we had a very satisfactory pow-wow about the *Beagle*. We even got as far as the design of the binding, Dreyfus being greatly taken with some Polynesian bark cloth which I showed him, and which he thought he could probably reproduce in a satisfactory way. He took it with him for experiment. He is also going to try out some sample pages. ... I liked Dreyfus very much and think he will be a pleasant collaborator.[5]

Macy was pleased to hear that Gibbings had warmed to Dreyfus and commented: 'he is not only likeable, he is an unusually fine craftsman in the world of books'. They also discussed the possibility of approaching Nora Barlow, who had already edited Darwin's diary of the voyage, to advise and perhaps write an introduction — as a grandchild of Darwin she seemed an obvious choice.

Gibbings's morale was boosted when on 11 March he received a note from Macy saying that he had decided to bring out a version of *Le Morte d'Arthur* in his cheaper, but more widely distributed, Heritage series, and consequently enclosed a banker's draft for one hundred and fifty pounds as a 'gift'. Gibbings wrote at the end of March to thank Macy for his 'noble cheque' which had reached him in time to celebrate his sixty-fifth birthday. In the same letter he reported that '... as to the minor prophet Darwin I have not been entirely idle. Apart from promises to Dreyfus to get down to the job good and proper in a few weeks' time, I have been taking certain actions about editing'.[6] Nora Barlow had been unable to help and had suggested they approach another of Darwin's descendants, Bernard Darwin, for a biographical note, but later he declined too.

In May, Gibbings found time to get away from work on *Trumpets from Montparnasse* and visited the British Museum to meet the Director of Natural History, 'Sir Gavin de Beer, F.R.S., M.A., D.Sc. (Oxon) and a lot of other things as well', to see if he would write an introduction from the 'scientific side': 'I feel that it would be a tremendous scoop if we could get him to do this job for he really is an authority and his name would look elegant on our title page.'[7] Sir Gavin later accepted the commission and his advice was sought as to which edition of Darwin's book should be used for the text. A decision was needed so that Dreyfus could go ahead with composing and preparation of sample pages. Dreyfus and Gibbings had been meeting regularly but in June their desire to keep the project moving had been unexpectedly frustrated; Gibbings moaned to Macy that 'the damn railway strike has probably kept him [Dreyfus] in Cambridge. Even letters from there are now taking four or five days'.[8] On 9 June Gibbings wrote to Dreyfus: 'I am going ahead with the first of the engravings, assuming that the measure of the page will be about 4⅞ ins.'[9] The next day Dreyfus replied, confirming the type measure and expressing the view that having a 'Knightly Fellow' to write the introduction would 'undoubtedly be sweet music to the ears of George Macy' — as indeed it was.[10]

Sir Gavin strongly advised using the second edition as he felt it embodied Darwin's ideas more accurately. Gibbings was glad of the decision for practical reasons: '... the first edition had an infinite number of notes and addenda about the place which would be a nuisance typographically'.[11] Sir Gavin's manuscript of the introduction was finished by the end of June and, to make up for the lack of a personal note from a member of the Darwin family, Gibbings suggested to Sir Gavin: 'If now you could just put in those few words about the personal side — this romantic young man setting out with a view to proving the truth of the Bible and coming back to refute it — it would be splendid.'[12] On receiving the final text Gibbings was delighted: '... how exactly it meets the case — and more so! It would make anyone want to read the book ...'.[13]

On 18 July Gibbings reported on progress to Dreyfus:

> Now as to illustrations. I have eleven designs completed of which two are half engraved. Apart from one week's work on another job, I have no other commitments until these for the *Beagle* are finished. The only delay now is on account of the holiday season, both the block-maker and my assistant [Beedham] who clears my blocks taking a fortnight off. However, I think you can count on the first half dozen blocks being with you by the 1st September and after that a steady flow until my part of the work is completed in October. With a job like this in which scientific accuracy is as necessary as decoration, it takes quite a bit of digging in the museums.[14]

The following day Gibbings wrote again:

> Further to my letter of the 18th, I have been cogitating on the difficulties of including in our new edition the wood-engravings in the 2nd Edition to which Darwin refers. Those listed below I don't feel up to re-engraving myself, and I am sure that any form of photographic reproduction would put them out of keeping with the other engravings. The best solution, therefore, seems to me to get Ralph Beedham to facsimile them for us on wood. He, as you probably know, is one of the old trade engravers and is a holy wonder at this kind of job. All that we need do is send him photos which are good enough for him to have re-photographed on to the wood. Could you get those photos done for me? In the 8th Edition, which I own, the illustrations are far too worn to work from, but in the 2nd Edition which I have on loan from the R.G.S. they are comparatively good. ... The other engravings and diagrams I can work on myself and I hope to some extent improve.[15]

Dreyfus organised the photographs and kept Macy informed of progress, passing on Gibbings's suggestion that alterations and omission of some illustrations from the original edition should be explained in the colophon. Dreyfus

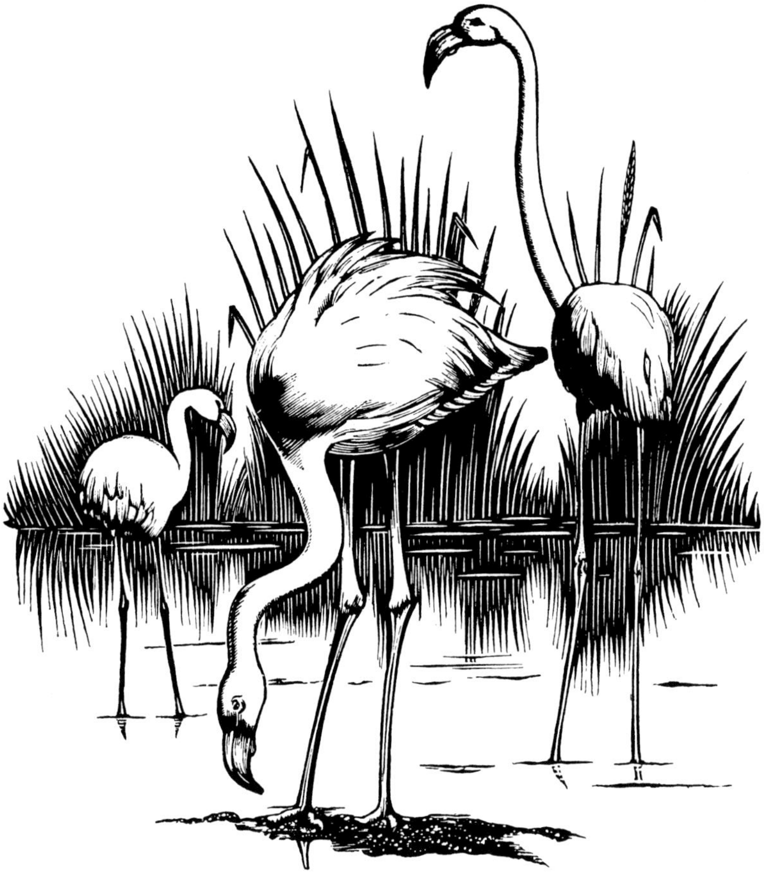

367 Flamingoes, 1956, wood-engraving, 116 x 103 mm. Illustration from *The Voyage of HMS Beagle*.

asked Gibbings for tracings of the outline of blocks already designed so that sample pages could be produced, but progress was a little delayed because Gibbings had sent the images off to be photographed onto the blocks and was awaiting their return: 'I sent them the designs a fortnight ago, and they should certainly be back in about a week. Unfortunately he [Lawrence] is devilish slow and doesn't give a damn because there is no one else who can do the job.'[16]

By 11 August Gibbings was able to send off the tracings:

Herewith proof of an unfinished block for the Puma, Chap VI, Sept. 13th., and two tracings, the Condor for Chap IX, April 27th and the Flamingoes for Chap IV, about the third page.

I suggest that the Puma might be inset in the type, with the ends of the leaves spreading on to the right-hand margin. The Condor would probably look best at the top of a page and the Flamingoes at the bottom.

Beedham, who does my clearing, is still on holiday but I hope to send you these three blocks finished and about half a dozen others by the end of the month. After that further blocks should be coming along pretty steadily: I have twenty designs now completed, including a big one of a coral reef as frontispiece.[17]

Dreyfus was on holiday in France in mid-August but Gibbings wrote to his secretary on 15 August to say that he had received the photographs needed and that they were 'splendid': 'I think now it would help still more towards accuracy if you send the negatives direct to Mr. R. J. Beedham ... as he will have to have the designs put on wood ....'[18] By the end of August Gibbings was able to report to Dreyfus:

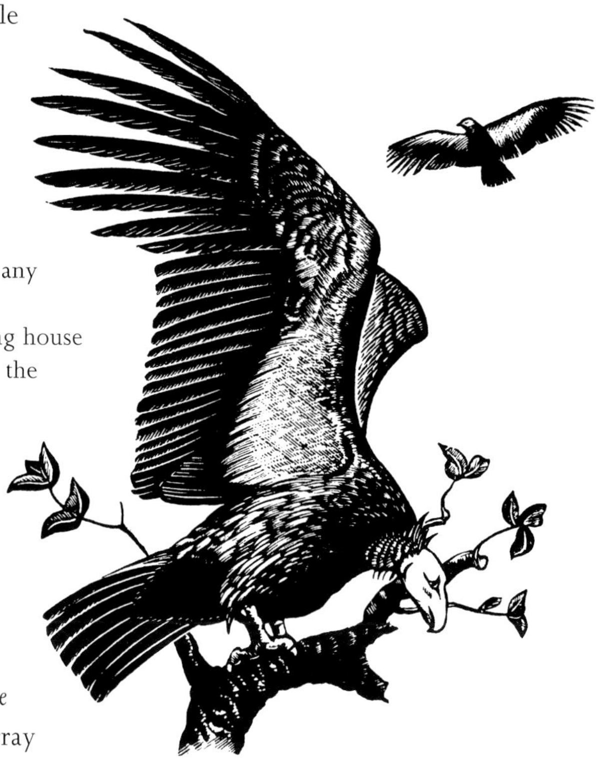

368 Condor, 1956, wood-engraving, 98 x 80 mm. Illustration from *The Voyage of HMS Beagle*.

> Herewith proofs of the first ten blocks for Macy, and under separate cover the blocks. I do hope you will think they are suitable. On each one I have written as near as possible the situation in which it should appear. I imagine that ones like the condor, the flamingoes, the scissor birds, and Moorea, will be best with the full width of the page; but the others can be inset or not as you wish. One or two of them might make appropriate tail-pieces to any particular entry.
>
> I have another ten designs on the wood, but old Beedham ... is now moving house and will be out of action for some weeks. However, I will get on with the designing so that there should not eventually be much delay.[19]

Dreyfus's reaction at seeing the engravings was very positive: 'I am bowled over by the beauty of your first engravings and I am most excited at the prospect of making this edition.'[20] Gibbings valued Dreyfus's opinion and praise; he had felt 'somewhat diffident' about the engravings and had feared that Dreyfus would be disappointed: 'Now I go ahead with renewed energy.'[21]

Dreyfus had difficulty in tracking down a second edition of the *Beagle* to work from; Gibbings had borrowed a copy, published by John Murray in 1845, from the Royal Geographical Society and felt that if they 'could both work from similar editions it would simplify references enormously' — finding the right edition to work from was eventually to be a problem. On an editorial issue, Gibbings made a 'humble suggestion' about the printing of the notes: 'They are such a damn nuisance on the page, not only spoiling its appearance but constantly distracting the reader's eye, that I wonder if we might not keep them all together at the end of each chapter or, better still, at the end of the book?'[22] Dreyfus was in full agreement.

In Cambridge Dreyfus had set up sample lines of text in three different typefaces. Eventually he decided upon Monotype 16pt Poliphilus, set solid, which he felt worked particularly well at that size and ideally matched the colour and weight of Gibbings's engravings. Gibbings queried the use of the 16pt size feeling that although it would be 'very handsome', it might be too uneconomical of space for such a long text. Dreyfus stuck to his choice and by the end of September was able to demonstrate that his judgement had been right. He sent Macy an unbound dummy of the book which extended to about 524 pages; he offered Macy the choice of having 'one handsome volume' or whether it should be divided into two.[23] Dreyfus's design, despite the large type size, worked so well and the estimated cost was so reasonable that a single volume was decided on.[24] The specimen was printed on paper which was 'identical in all respects save one to that which we would wish to use: in tone, we would prefer the paper to be a shade whiter to do fuller justice to the engravings'; the paper used was specially manufactured to Dreyfus's specifications in Scotland.[25] Dreyfus was meticulous in his care for detail, and his choice of paper, both for its printing quality and feel, was an important factor in the success of the final book.

Lawrence's dilatoriness continued to cause problems, and Gibbings was still having difficulty finding other firms that could photograph images on to the block to a sufficiently high standard and with enough speed. Dreyfus thought he might be able to help and so Gibbings sent him a sample:

> I send you herewith the proofs of the blocks which you brought along yesterday and left behind. I also send you a drawing for experiment with the wood, a clean block on which to put it, and a small block on which another design has already been photographed to show the operator the kind of surface that is the most satisfactory. This is I believe put on as a water solution because it can, with a certain amount of rubbing, be taken off with water. There is another technique, which Odhams have used occasionally on my behalf, in which the surface has to be removed with Benzol. It is a hard gritty surface and very unpleasant for cutting through, so rough that it has to be removed. This particular one that I send you can be left on even when the electro is being taken. It would be grand if someone could discover the process and do really good prints, because though this is by no means bad by present standards it is nothing like as clear as it would have been before the war.[26]

Finding a reliable source for the woodblocks themselves was also a problem. In September Dreyfus had mentioned that he had been asking around for alternative suppliers on Gibbings's behalf:

> You mentioned taking up the matter of wood with some friend of yours, and it would certainly be a good thing if there was an alternative source from the present firm of Lawrence; but to get a finish on the blocks and to get the many small pieces of wood joined up so that they don't come apart in time is a long and difficult process. Lawrence, though inclined to be cranky, is a first-rate craftsman. If, therefore, you are doing anything in this matter, please don't mention my name at all because I am already on slightly strained terms with Lawrence and if he heard that I was taking any competitive action he would certainly cut me out and I would then be stranded![27]

Macy genuinely cherished his contact with artists and could be a generous and supportive patron, but he was also a businessman and occasionally showed another side to his character. The correspondence between Macy and Gibbings was generally humorous and flattering in tone — sometimes the *bonhomie* reached an almost exaggerated level. However, at the end of September a 'small misunderstanding' took place about how many engravings had been specified for Gibbings's fee:

> When I invited you to make engravings for a book, I said that we would pay the sum of six hundred pounds for 'a set of illustrations'; I never specified the number of illustrations, it is you who have done that. Therefore, if you now choose to regard the illustrations as 'piece work', that introduces a new understanding into the deal; so, although I will undoubtedly agree with the need for each extra piece and will undoubtedly pay for each extra piece, I will curse in pure Aborigine while doing so.[28]

Gibbings had been warned of Macy's spasmodic 'cussedness' and therefore did not take offence and diplomatically pointed out that it was Macy himself who had offered an additional fee if the scale of the project increased — as it had indeed done. The matter had been proved by Patience on whom he increasingly depended as his secretary, personal assistant, sharpest critic, editor and companion. It was she who carefully filed all Gibbings's letters and could retrieve the

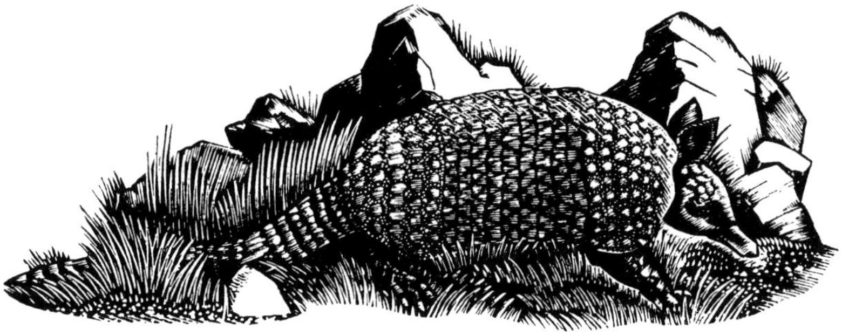

369 Armadillo, 1956, wood-engraving, 40 x 105 mm. Illustration from *The Voyage of HMS Beagle*.

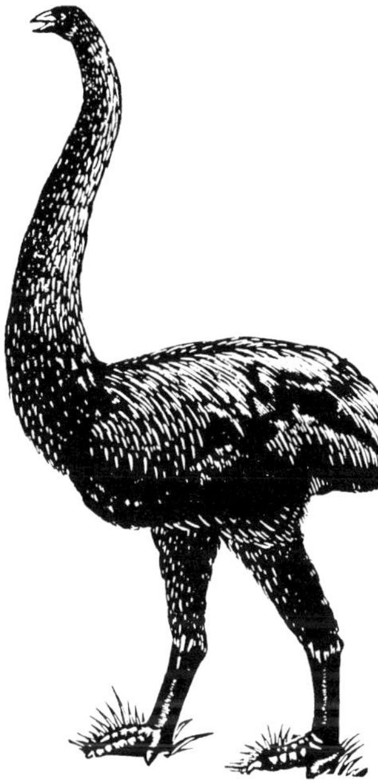

370 Moa bird, 1956, wood-engraving, 83 x 44 mm. Illustration from *The Voyage of HMS Beagle*.

appropriate evidence. Any unpleasantness was soon forgotten and Macy could only express envy over Gibbings's relationship with Patience: 'I envy you that paragon of paragons, whom I leave nameless. She is wonderfully pretty, she is wonderfully charming, she cooks wonderfully, she keeps you in order; and now, because she keeps your files of correspondence so efficiently, she is keeping *me* in order.'[29] Macy had recently met Patience when he had come to lunch with Gibbings at his flat in July 1955, during a visit to London when he stayed at the Savoy Hotel.

Patience had also been a great help in the research for the book. In the pursuit of accuracy, Gibbings referred in numerous letters to the fact that he had made frequent visits to the Natural History Museum in London to check on details. More than once, Patience was asked to do this for him and she well remembers checking the number of facets on the back of a stuffed specimen of an armadillo, or looking for images of the extinct Moa bird.

For some time Gibbings had wished to move out of London and escape to the country, and in September 1955 Patience had found a thatched, half-timbered cottage for sale in the Thameside village of Long Wittenham. Although the cottage was rather small there was a big garden with enough space to build a substantial studio. Despite the hazard of bruised heads and concussion from low beams, Gibbings fell in love with the cottage, which he described as 'about the size and shape of a thatched beehive'.[30] They moved there the following month.

Friendship, as well as a good working relationship, had developed between Gibbings and Dreyfus, who became a frequent visitor to their new home. The specimen pages of the book had reached Gibbings while he was sitting in his new garden awaiting the removal van. His only comment was 'I think they are really elegant in every way and can think of no possible improvement.'[31] At the end of November, writing to Macy, Dreyfus set out the programme of work for the book:

Sheets will be delivered by Christmas — to Gibbings in Oxfordshire. These sheets will be pasted up galleys, showing how the engravings will fall, and showing where an additional engraving would improve the make-up or adorn an inviting space.

On New Year's Day (and I mean 1 January 1956) we will start to make the book up in page form and we should complete that operation and also complete the second reading by the third week of February. Allowing for the shuttling of proofs between Cambridge, Oxfordshire and New York, we hope to finish the printing of the book by mid-April.[32]

In an attempt to solve Gibbings's continuing problems of photographing an image on to the block, Dreyfus had found a local photographer who succeeded in printing a photographic image on to the wood: 'He has found it advantageous to print down with a screen, and I would be interested to hear from you whether this is damned irritating when you come to the engraving.'[33] Gibbings had been held up by the slow service from his other suppliers and so he was pleased with the results Dreyfus had achieved:

Delighted to get that block yesterday. It seems to me a bit of alright. At first I was a little scared that the film might lift under the graver, but in fact it holds very well and so long as it can be kept as thin as it is I think it should be excellent. In a few days I will send you a new design which will be a complete try-out. If the photographer can do it in a matter of days instead of weeks, half our problems will be solved. Ten Macy designs that I sent

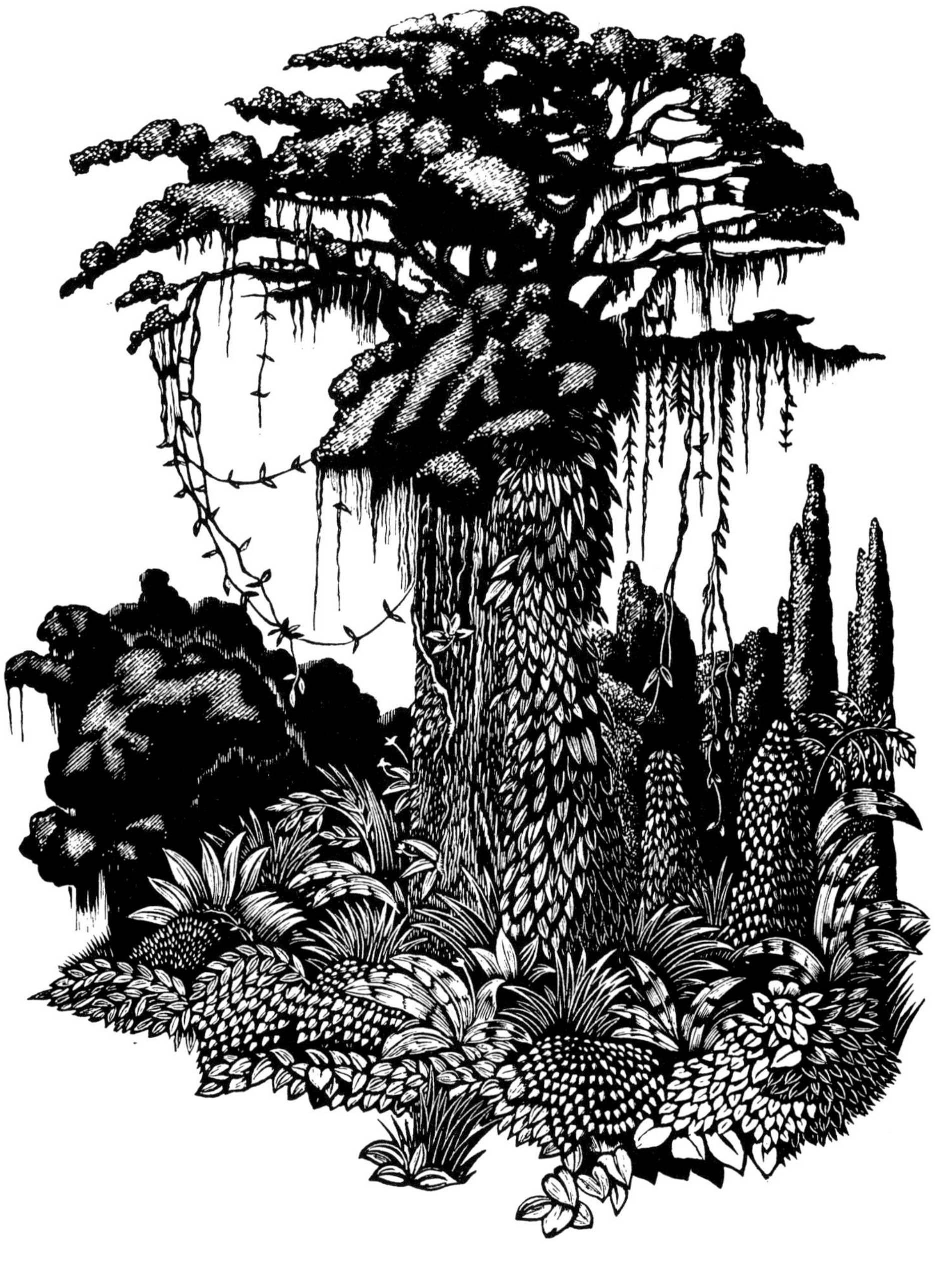

371 Brazilian forest, 1956, wood-engraving, 164 × 124 mm. Illustration from *The Voyage of HMS Beagle.*

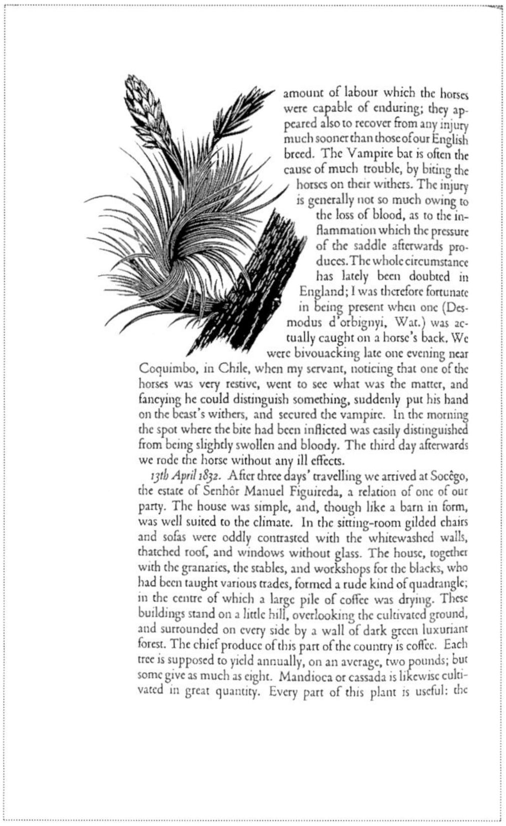

amount of labour which the horses were capable of enduring; they appeared also to recover from any injury much sooner than those of our English breed. The Vampire bat is often the cause of much trouble, by biting the horses on their withers. The injury is generally not so much owing to the loss of blood, as to the inflammation which the pressure of the saddle afterwards produces. The whole circumstance has lately been doubted in England; I was therefore fortunate in being present when one (Desmodus d'orbignyi, Wat.) was actually caught on a horse's back. We were bivouacking late one evening near Coquimbo, in Chile, when my servant, noticing that one of the horses was very restive, went to see what was the matter, and fancying he could distinguish something, suddenly put his hand on the beast's withers, and secured the vampire. In the morning the spot where the bite had been inflicted was easily distinguished from being slightly swollen and bloody. The third day afterwards we rode the horse without any ill effects.

13th April 1832. After three days' travelling we arrived at Socêgo, the estate of Senhôr Manuel Figuireda, a relation of one of our party. The house was simple, and, though like a barn in form, was well suited to the climate. In the sitting-room gilded chairs and sofas were oddly contrasted with the whitewashed walls, thatched roof, and windows without glass. The house, together with the granaries, the stables, and workshops for the blacks, who had been taught various trades, formed a rude kind of quadrangle; in the centre of which a large pile of coffee was drying. These buildings stand on a little hill, overlooking the cultivated ground, and surrounded on every side by a wall of dark green luxuriant forest. The chief produce of this part of the country is coffee. Each tree is supposed to yield annually, on an average, two pounds; but some give as much as eight. Mandioca or cassada is likewise cultivated in great quantity. Every part of this plant is useful: the

372 Page from *The Voyage of HMS Beagle* illustrated by a wood-engraving of the plant *Tillandsia Stricta*, 1956, page size 305 x 190 mm.

to Lawrence on the 13th October only came back on the wood on the 23rd November. It made me almost hopeless about getting on with the job.[34]

At the beginning of December, only three blocks remained to be engraved and Gibbings felt confident of keeping to the schedule. On 18 December he sent all but one of the proposed forty-nine blocks for Dreyfus to position in the text.

At the end of December, Dreyfus had the first thirty-two pages ready:

Herewith proposed paste-up for the first 32 pages of text. Page headings have been omitted, but they will go in, as on the specimen. But note that I would propose to drop page-head and folio from page 11, and to drop folio from page 20. This page 20 was a bit tricky; perhaps it would be better if the type bowed in slightly as shown by the wiggly lines.[35]

Both men wanted to achieve a true harmony and integration of the text and images. Page-head and folio were dropped from page 11 to allow a large illustration of a lush, Brazilian forest to spread into the space at the head of the page: a similar situation occurred on page 20, where the elegant curving fronds of the plant *Tillandsia Stricta* were allowed to spill out into the margins and, being a smaller image positioned in the top left-hand corner of the page, great care was taken to run the text around the shape of the plant. Gibbings, with only minor comments and suggestions for the distribution of images, was troubled by the beginning of the book:

As I feared, there are an awful lot of pages at the beginning without decoration, but this was practically unavoidable because for the particular subjects that I wished to illustrate I

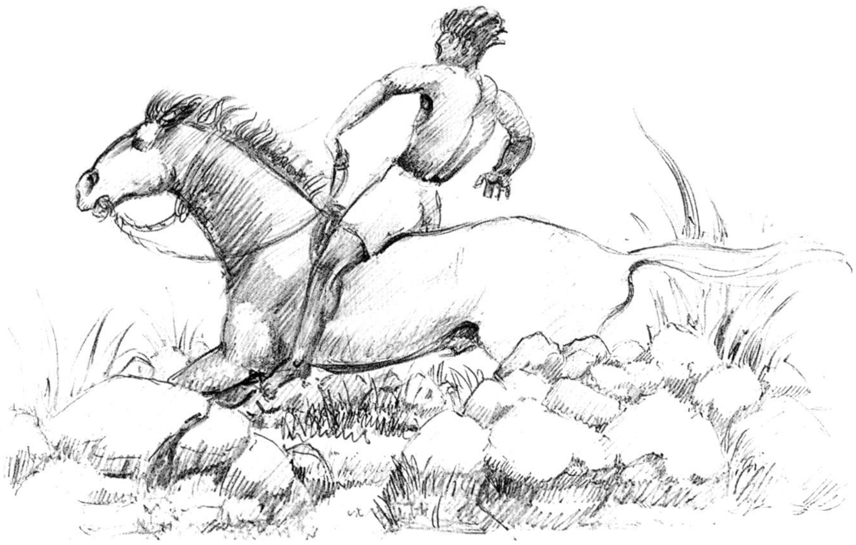

373 Drawing of bareback rider, pencil. A sketch Gibbings made on one of his trips to the Pacific islands. Clark Library.

could find no material that was fit to draw. However, I do not think it matters a bit if we can be sure of rich prelims. I therefore suggest that you shove in as many as possible of those spare oddments — the tropical fish, flower and butterfly, etc. Then the pause will be quite reasonable, all the more so as we get the sudden splodge of forest on p.11.[36]

By 30 December paste-proofs of pages up to 144 had been discussed and approved and at the end of the first week of January they had reached page 208 with only minor adjustments. Gibbings had touched up all the blocks (now a total of fifty) and had taken proofs on Japanese paper in their final state, using his table-top Albion Press. He commented to Dreyfus: 'On the machine you will probably get them still better with less of the "dirt" about the edges. I am sending Macy a duplicate set of these proofs and telling him that everything is marching at top speed.'[37]

Although Gibbings had finished the blocks for the *Beagle*, he was still experiencing difficulties with transferring the image to the block — the trial block arrived:

The block arrived by the first post this morning and I have spent a rather hectic day on it as the photographic film pulled off in great flakes, whether I wanted to cut a fine line or a broad one. ... When last I wrote, I asked you to let me know what the solvent was, but in this particular case I only had to put in the point of a penknife ... and it lifted thick as a sheet of celluloid. In many places it meant practically re-drawing and that has delayed matters a good deal. However, I hope by tomorrow evening or Saturday morning at latest to post you the finished article. Fortunately it was a simple one to do without much detail, otherwise I should have had to start all over again.[38]

Dreyfus was horrified when he heard what had happened to the photographic film and suggested another solution:

...I am sending the exhibits back to the photographer with a suitable comment. Messrs John Swain tell me that they themselves do not print down on to wood, but that they can confidently recommend Messrs Frampton & Co., of 7 Dyer's Building, London E.C.1.,

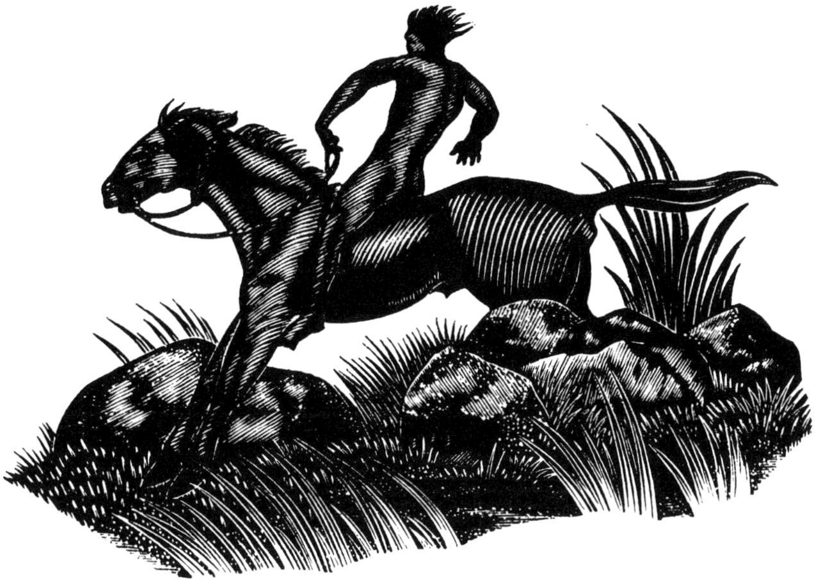

374 Bareback rider, 1956, wood-engraving, 88 × 109 mm. Illustration from *The Voyage of HMS Beagle*. John Dreyfus later recalled seeing the pencil sketch on which this engraving is based during a visit to Robert Gibbings to discuss the production of the book. Gibbings had drawn the image on one of his excursions to the Pacific islands. Gibbings had seen a man riding bareback, naked, on a horse and by chance this exactly matched the description which Darwin gives on p. 129 of the Limited Editions Club's edition: 'In the course of the day I was amused by the dexterity with which a Gaucho forced a restive horse to swim a river. He stripped off his clothes, & jumping on its back, rode into the water …. A naked man on a naked horse is a fine spectacle; I had no idea how well the two animals suited each other.' Dreyfus was particularly impressed with the way Gibbings captured the energy and movement of the scene in the resulting wood-engraving.

who do this work very well and like doing it. They are eager to do work for *you*, and would like to hear from you.[39]

Macy had been slow to respond to the proofs of the engravings and Gibbings, keen to know if he was pleased, suspected that 'the blighter' was being temperamental. However, his fears were unjustified as on 30 January he received a letter from Macy praising his work: 'These engravings are downright wonderful! Some of those which involve vegetation, making demands upon you for all kinds of textures, must rank among the very best engravings you will ever have made.'[40] Five small decorative blocks were added to enliven the prelims but Gibbings had to clear the blocks. Writing to Dreyfus on 12 February 1956, he explained:

> As Beedham has been laid up and I have had to do my own clearing, I have left the routing of several of them for your machine. You may find that the blocks of the whale, the small sea bird and the shell are rather more than type high and may need a little rubbing down on their reverse sides. You will no doubt have a gentleman with a micrometer adjustment to make any necessary alterations.[41]

It had been decided that as Macy limited the editions for the club to a relatively short run of 1500 to maintain quality and kudos, the illustrations should be printed from the original woodblocks.

Gibbings hoped that the delivery of these last blocks completed his part of the job. Dreyfus had welcomed his suggestions for layout: 'Your comments make it all the easier for me to place these delightful things',[42] yet final decisions were his. Gibbings and Dreyfus had agreed that captions to the illustrations would be disruptive to the layout of the page and that any explanation or identification of the subjects should be dealt with by a note at the beginning of the book; they also agreed that they must persuade Macy to pay for a new index to be compiled.

Gibbings was very pleased with progress; throughout February page proofs came with almost every post and he was busy answering queries from the proof readers: 'I think it's going to be an elegant book.' In his next letter he wrote: '... I think the volume is shaping well. This is the stage when it gets a bit exciting'.[43] But there were some last minute problems. Repeated textual errors led Gibbings to suspect that Cambridge had after all been working from the first edition, as there were discrepancies with his own second edition. Dreyfus soon discovered the cause – they had been using a later impression of the second edition and the compositors who had set up this later impression introduced some literal errors – a salutary warning for scholars! Dreyfus was confident that these would be corrected: 'I think that our press reader will spot them, but I have warned both the press reader and the indexer to be particularly on their guard.'[44]

By 5 March only final adjustments remained:

I think you have made a grand job of the prelims, in particular of the dedication page which is now I think one of the nicest in the book. My 'Note' also looks quite elegant.

My only suggestion is that the whale at the head of De Beer's introduction should be changed with the ship which is now over the colophon. I think the whale so close to Sir Gavin is a little inapposite, whereas the ship would be highly appropriate. The whale, too, sounding is more appropriate as a tail piece.

I think I would prefer the leaf on p.xvi inverted, but that doesn't really matter unless you agree. Otherwise I think everything is splendid and I look forward to signing 1,500 times or more![45]

The following day Gibbings received a note from Macy's office informing him that 'Mr. Macy is undergoing an enforced absence ... due to a very recent illness'. At the end of the month Gibbings received a letter signed on Macy's behalf by an assistant — the letter was full of praise and delight:

From John Dreyfus I now have, here in California where I dictate this letter for you, a complete set of the pages of 'The Voyage of the Beagle'. I think he has done wonderfully well, the book seems to my eye to be exactly right. I think he has enjoyed working with you. I think you have done wonderfully well; although I can't claim to have seen all of the thousands of engravings you have turned out in your life, I couldn't believe that at any time you could have ever turned out better engravings than these. They are downright wonderful, and anything you are being paid for them is underpayment.[46]

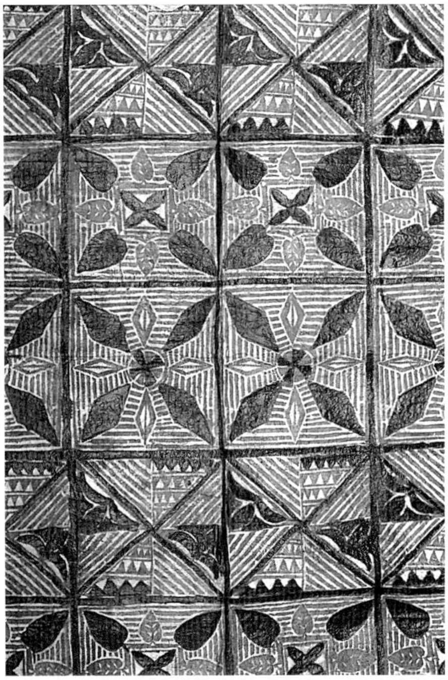

375 Piece of tapa cloth that Gibbings brought back from the islands of Polynesia. Author's collection – other examples are in the Gibbings Collection, RUL.

At the beginning of June, Gibbings wrote to Macy to report: 'I have just signed some 1550 colophon sheets of the *Beagle* and returned them to Dreyfus. If they are a sample of his final printing, the book should be "a bit of all right", impression and colour seemed to me excellent.'[47] The letter ended with a note about the binding of the book, which was to be done in New York by the Russell-Rutter Company. It was bound in a light brown sailcloth blocked in brown with a design adapted from traditional motifs taken from tapa cloth (Polynesian bark cloth). Gibbings had brought back cherished examples of the cloth from his voyages to the islands in 1946. On his very first meeting with Gibbings, two years previously, Dreyfus had been much taken by the designs and had hoped they could be used in some way for the binding.[48] The cloth was too scarce and unsuitable for bulk binding, but Gibbings suggested that Macy might wish to bind a 'few extra special copies' with an original sheet of the cloth that he had lent to Dreyfus — '... you are welcome to the piece with my blessing'.[49]

Tragically, Macy never replied to the offer, as on 12 June 1956 Gibbings received a letter informing him of his death.

Macy's widow, Helen, later wrote to Gibbings tying up contractual details but also expressing warmth and enthusiasm for the book: 'We are all eagerly awaiting the arrival of the Beagle sheets, so that we can have them bound. There is little doubt that this will be a stunning book. ... The Tapa cloth arrived a few days ago. I am touched again that you should be willing to part with it.'[50] The following year Helen Macy persuaded Gibbings to illustrate and edit another book — *Omoo* by Herman Melville. He started working on the text and drawing layouts for the title page and chapter openings but future events meant that he never completed the project.[51]

Before he fell ill, Macy had written the copy for *The Monthly Letter of The Limited Editions Club* of July 1956, which he dedicated to the launch of the book. The newsletter opened with historical background to the voyage and Darwin's career but also provided production details and warm praise of Gibbings: '... a consummate artist with a wood-block, an author of charm, and a just-short-of-professional naturalist ...'. Full credit is given to John Dreyfus, whom Macy had already said 'good words about' in previous letters, for the typographic planning and supervision of production. He ended his piece: 'The book is not one for the pocket; it is 7⅝ inches wide and one foot tall — one one-hundredth as long as the Beagle herself. You will, we trust, find it a stout and seaworthy craft.'

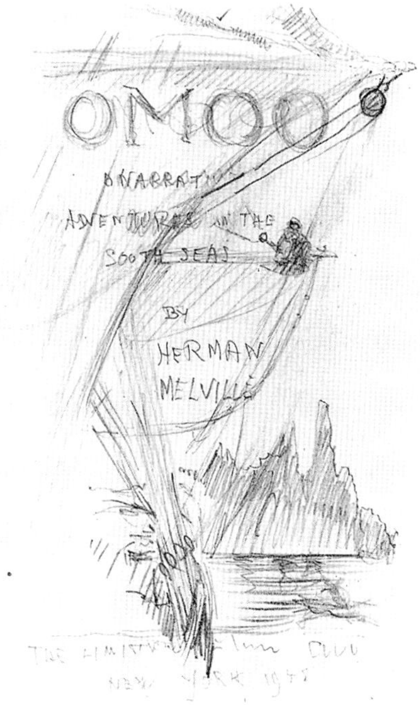

376 *above* Gibbings's sketch for the layout of the title page of Herman Melville's book *OMOO*. Clark Library.

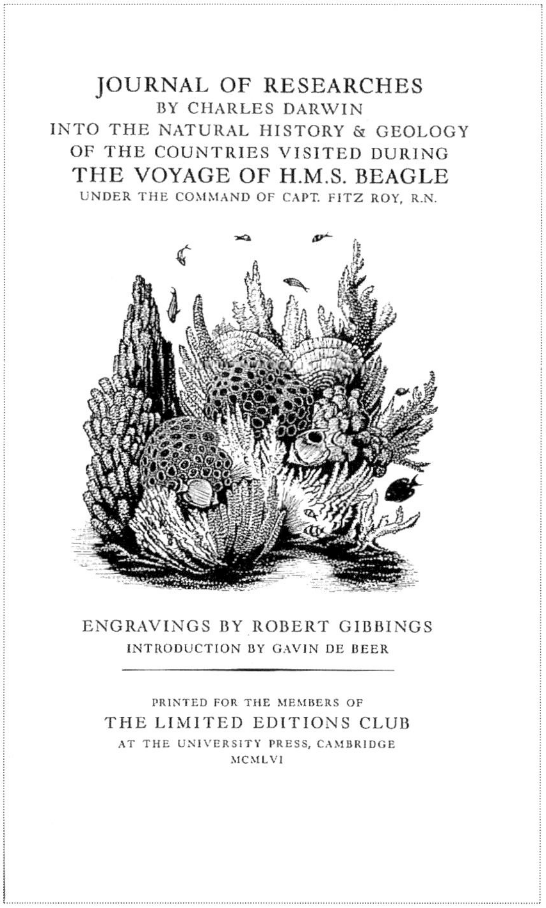

JOURNAL OF RESEARCHES
BY CHARLES DARWIN
INTO THE NATURAL HISTORY & GEOLOGY
OF THE COUNTRIES VISITED DURING
THE VOYAGE OF H.M.S. BEAGLE
UNDER THE COMMAND OF CAPT. FITZ ROY, R.N.

ENGRAVINGS BY ROBERT GIBBINGS
INTRODUCTION BY GAVIN DE BEER

PRINTED FOR THE MEMBERS OF
THE LIMITED EDITIONS CLUB
AT THE UNIVERSITY PRESS, CAMBRIDGE
MCMLVI

377 *left* Title page of *The Voyage of HMS Beagle*, 1956. The original idea of a frontispiece was eventually dropped and instead a wonderfully detailed and delicate engraving of tropical fish swimming amongst the coral was incorporated in the title page. Dreyfus designed the title page in upper case and used the typeface Goudy Modern in preference to the lighter caps of Poliphilus. Subtle changes in type size created a ripple effect which complemented the underwater illustration. The page was enriched by the use of red printing to pick out key lines in the title and a rule which 'settled' the text on the sea bed at the bottom of the page. Page size 305 x 190 mm.

THROUGHOUT 1955, Gibbings made many and varied broadcasts which included a music programme for the Overseas Service. He was asked to select three of his favourite pieces of music and talk about their particular significance in his life. Although never drawn to making music himself, Gibbings had friends in musical circles and his tastes were wide. He enjoyed popular music, from music hall songs to the singing of Danny Kaye at the Palladium. He had spent many evenings crowded around smoky fires in the pubs and cottages of Cork, taken over by the infectious rhythms of a jig played on the fiddle, enhanced by the glow from whiskey. Traditional music of all kinds appealed to him and he had been a guest at many musical festivities in the islands of Polynesia. But Gibbings also had a deep love and appreciation of classical music; works by Beethoven and Sibelius had been his choice for the programme — perhaps he recalled balmy evenings looking out on the sunset from the veranda of James Hall's native hut on the edge of the lagoon, listening to the wind-up gramophone.

In October 1955, Hoppé wrote to Gibbings announcing Dent's plans: 'We are already on to the next book of yours which we are to publish, a reprint of *John Graham, Convict*.'[52] They were anxious to take advantage of Gibbings's popularity and publish new editions of his earlier work. Following *Coconut Island* and *A True Tale of Love in Tonga*, Gibbings's agent, Pollinger, had suggested to Dent that they bring out a new edition of *The Seventh Man*. This would have meant using the original woodblocks now owned by Christopher Sandford who had taken over the rights to the book when he purchased the Golden Cockerel Press. Sandford had reacted with dismay to the proposal and in a friendly but firm letter to Gibbings stated very clearly that, in his eyes, it would be a betrayal of the customers of the Golden Cockerel Press who had bought books with the understanding that they were limited editions. Gibbings was anxious not to make this an issue: 'Don't worry one iota about *The Seventh Man*. I have been so long away from limited editions that I had forgotten, when the idea was proposed, the strictness of the old regime.'[53] In the light of Sandford's position the project was dropped.

There were no such problems with *John Graham, Convict*, which was published in September 1956. No changes were to be made to the text, but Dent had hoped that Gibbings might have kept press reviews of the original edition which could be used for publicity. True to form, Gibbings had kept nothing:

> I fear I haven't got any cuttings, though there were some damn nice ones at the time. In particular, the Times Lit. Sup. gave it a large well-placed space and amongst other things called the book 'a cameo of history' (I believe). ... I rather think the Observer also gave a good review at the time, but I can't remember. I wonder if Fabers might not have some records. ... I am sorry that I haven't got a jacket either: in fact, I haven't even got a copy of the book.[54]

Generally the re-issue was welcomed. Reviews in the press were as favourable as they had been in 1937 and the book received a surprising amount of attention.[55]

Chapter Twenty-two
Till I End My Song 1955–1958

The village of Long Wittenham and Footbridge Cottage had quickly become a real home for Gibbings — returning to the banks of the Thames, he was content. Living in London had gradually become intolerable for him; he needed peace and tranquillity and a new beginning. Patience had been instructed to look for a cottage, with a room big enough for a proper studio (a luxury he had never enjoyed in London), and a location on a river. She had stumbled upon Footbridge Cottage and, although it did not exactly fit Robert's description, she immediately felt that he would fall for its charms.

Long Wittenham is an historic village on a backwater of the river Thames, in the valley below the two tree-topped hills known locally as the Wittenham Clumps. The Clumps, with the ancient earthworks which reveal their past as hill forts, had been an inspiration for many artists, but particularly John and Paul Nash. Footbridge Cottage was situated at the end of the main street by the old village cross, with a tiny bridge over a small stream, which formed one of the boundaries to the garden, leading to the gate. Probably dating back to the fifteenth century and built as a farm labourer's cottage, the half-timbered and thatched building was charming but tiny. With only one large living room, dominated by an impressive inglenook fireplace, the cottage had two bedrooms; an extension built in the 1920s had provided a bathroom and kitchen. In most respects Gibbings, with his large frame, was out of scale with his new home, but by chance the bathroom contained an unusually large bath tub! Gibbings had in

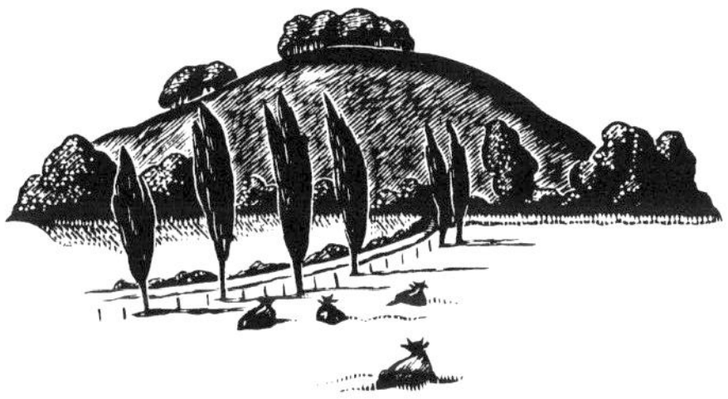

378 The Wittenham Clumps, 1957, wood-engraving, 34 x 65 mm. Illustration from *Till I End My Song*.

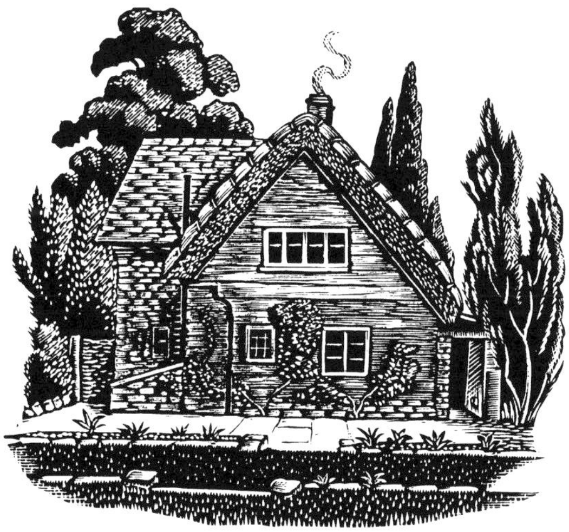

379 Footbridge Cottage, 1957, wood-engraving, 65 x 70 mm. Illustration from *Till I End My Song*. Gibbings and Patience moved here on 4 October 1955.

fact visited the village in about 1927 and knew the cottage because, by coincidence, it was the neighbour of another old house which, at one time, had been the home of A. E. Coppard: 'Little did I think then as we sun-bathed in his garden that the tumbledown bit of wattle and daub and thatch on the other side of his hedge would one day be my own snug habitat.'[1] The peaceful backwater of the Thames was only a few minutes walk across some fields, and about a mile down the road through the village was a beautiful brick bridge over the river and the picturesque village of Clifton Hampden.

Patience and Robert bought the cottage together and on 4 October 1955 they moved in. Despite the problems with the low ceilings they were very happy — a week later Gibbings reported: 'We are having a wonderful bit of fun here, except that I've got a crick in my neck from constant bending and PAE [Patience] has twice brained herself on the beams.'[2] Certain repairs to the cottage were needed straight away and Gibbings busied himself organising thatchers to put new wires on his roof and builders to modernise the tiny cabin kitchen. Patience was to split her time between Footbridge Cottage and her mother's house in Headington which the family had retained, letting out rooms to friends, after her mother's death. But at last Robert and Patience were able to enjoy creating a home together.

The cottage was small but the surrounding garden had ample space to build a studio. Since leaving the orchard at Waltham St Lawrence, Gibbings's gardening had been restricted to pot plants and access to a public garden below his flat in Warwick Road — now he luxuriated in his own private space: '... I had stood awhile in the garden. The pear-tree on my lawn was tipped with crimson, the elms beyond my boundary hedge were fringed with gold. Though it was early October a precociously minded sparrow was playing with a feather. The two tall lime-trees that overshadowed my gate seemed friendly, neighbourly, with none of the impersonal aloofness of city trees'.[3] On 28 November the builders moved in to start building a studio — this was something of a symbolic moment for Gibbings and a fulfilment of one of his dreams. A substantial but basic timber building, he designed it just as he wished, with a large skylight for the northern light. His only regret was the covering of 'living' soil, as he saw it, with concrete, but before it was 'buried' he collected masses of fossils that were turned up during the digging of the foundations. Built on the past, the studio represented a future — the promise of work to come and work full of colour. As the building progressed he '... could visualize finished canvases that were one day to hang on the cool grey walls'.[4]

In the midst of all this change, Gibbings was still hard at work on a range of projects. As well as the *Beagle*, Gibbings had completed another piece for Hadfield's *The Saturday Book* by the end of November. This time it was on one of his favourite topics — marine life. 'Thoughts on Fish', as the article was entitled, was to generate some timely cash to spend on the studio:

> Now as regards settlement, there seems no reason to drag either religion or Pollinger into it. Looking up my records I see you paid me forty Jimmies for my 'Wells'. If the same

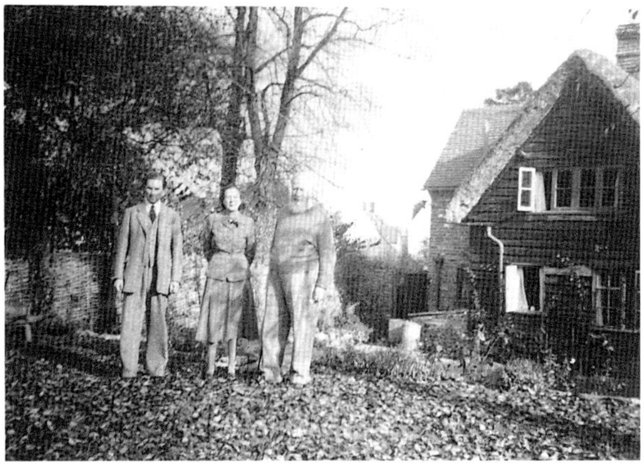

380 Gibbings with John and Anna Hadfield in the garden at Footbridge Cottage. RUL.

figure is agreeable to you it will also be to me. It would just pay for a stove and the laying on of light for my new studio. Would it not be a long and happy memory for you to think that you lit and warmed my declining years?[5]

Work on his next book had begun as soon as Gibbings moved into Footbridge Cottage. The move itself, the cottage, the building of the studio, and his new surroundings were all topics that naturally presented themselves as perfect material. The return to the Thames, the subject that was the beginning of and inspiration for his long run of successful books, seemed to bring the series to a natural end. Perhaps Gibbings instinctively felt that he had reached a conclusion and that in the future his energies should be concentrated on painting. What more appropriate title could there be for his new book than to complete Spenser's line, 'Sweet Thames run softly ...' with '... till I end my song'? It was a title that was to gain a deeper poignancy and significance.

The research for his new book frequently required visits to the library at the University of Reading, where he had a good working relationship with the Librarian — Dr Mary Kirkus. She had first met Gibbings when, as a lecturer in the Department of Fine Art, he had been a regular user of the library.[6] Robert was extremely grateful for her assistance and had given Mary copies of his books as they were published. She quickly became a friend and enthusiastic collector of his work. Even after he left the University, he regularly wrote to Mary asking for her advice and aid in finding information and locating books for him.

At the beginning of 1955, Mary wrote to Gibbings with the suggestion that she would like to compile a bibliography of his work. He was flattered and on 4 February he sent a reply:

The mere idea is a huge honour and of course if it ever got further I would help in any way I could. If it was merely the books that I have written it would be simple enough — only about a dozen in all though most of them have had many editions, if Readers Union and the various other book clubs & USA were included. If you meant to include the books by other authors that I have illustrated, the total of titles would probably be round 60. If you had thought also of engravings done for other purposes the adventure would be hell for I have never kept records and there must be dozens and dozens of which I have no memory. I am the more aware of this because Dents propose to do a 'collected works' to celebrate my 70th birthday, in 1959. ...If you did think of carrying your idea further, it would be a very nice companion to my unscholarly collection and I'm pretty sure Dents, if offered it, would jump at the publication.

But don't give it another thought unless it amuses you: if it does I'll gladly join in the laugh![7]

Gibbings was enthusiastic and wrote again a few days later to tell Mary that he was '...delighted to hear that you feel brave enough to tackle that bibliography' but concerned about the scope — he was still worried that a section devoted to 'other illustrations' would be a problem: 'I think it may be best to limit the whole thing to the *books* I have illustrated. If we get on to the cork of Eno's fruit salt, Gawd knows where we will end.'[8] Mary started to collect material and in April 1955 Bozman, on behalf of Dent, expressed delight at the prospect of publishing her book.[9] Over the next few years, Mary continued to work on the bibliography and to assist Gibbings with many enquiries about local history for *Till I End My Song*.

THE HAPPINESS AND CONTENTMENT that Gibbings felt in his new surroundings seemed to revive his spirits and bring fresh inspiration to his writing. Rather than being a tired end to the series, *Till I End My Song* had the promise of being one of the best. Bozman was delighted with the drafts of the initial chapters:

This is a promising beginning — promising particularly in that you seem to have recaptured, at once and without effort, the atmosphere of your successful river books. The peace of mind that is induced by the calm even flow of life unmistakably finds expression in the writing. ... Another *Sweet Thames*? I hope so![10]

As always the schedule was to be demanding. Bozman had been meeting with Elliott Macrae of Dutton, who felt that it was advisable to publish in the fall and was thinking of a publication date of September 1957. To achieve this, Bozman had calculated that the complete manuscript would be needed by January 1957. Dent and Dutton wanted to synchronise publication and so the schedule needed agreement before contracts were signed.[11] Gibbings replied that this was too tight and eventually it was agreed that the manuscript should be completed by January and the blocks by March, which would still allow publication in September. An important incentive, which Gibbings found hard to ignore, was offered by Macrae; Bozman reported that Macrae was 'willing to pay the entire advance due under the contract on delivery of this material, provided that you do, in fact, keep to these dates'.[12] Gibbings recognised the need for the book to be out in time to build sales for the Christmas market and to give reviewers time to read the book before being inundated by the mass of autumn publications; it was also important to have time to get the book into the overseas markets.

As the book progressed, Gibbings was able to incorporate events and happenings in his new life as they unfolded. His garden became a place of peace and reflection and also keen observation. One day, as he was sitting in his 'sunlit garden contemplating the creamy blossoms of a Mermaid rose', through the open window he drew Patience's attention to the sound of a leaf-cutting bee; an

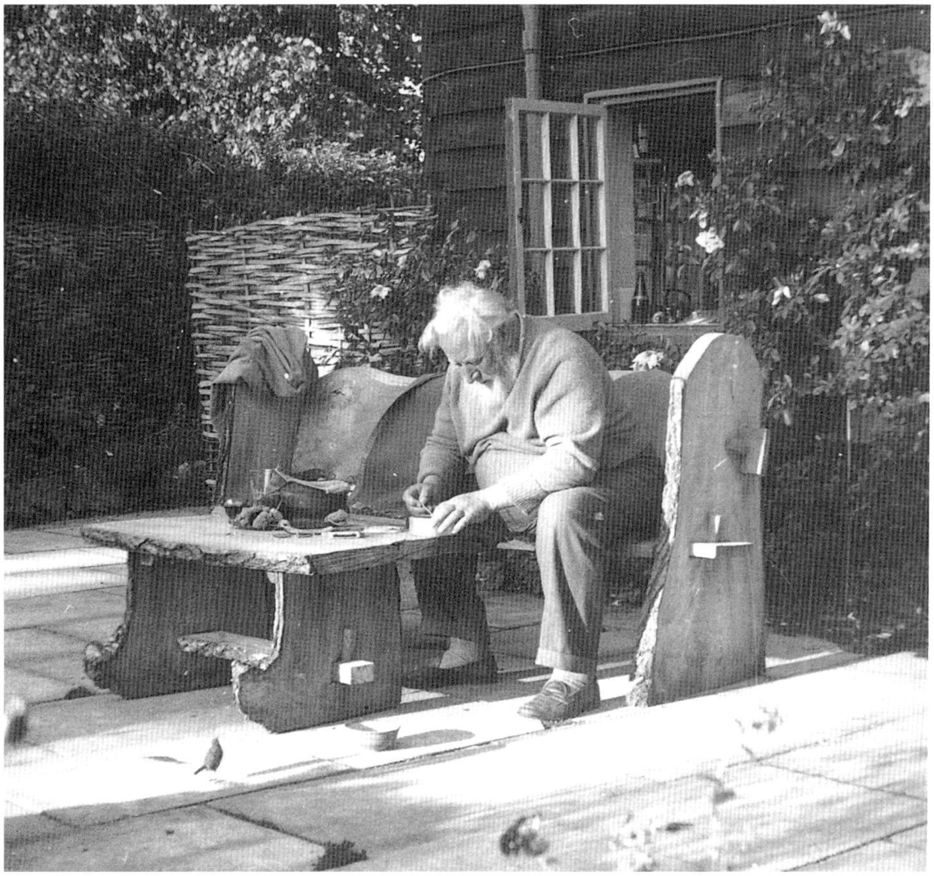

381 Gibbings sitting on the bench he made for the garden at Footbridge Cottage. RUL.

observation that he subsequently worked up for the book.[13] The only thing lacking in his garden was a comfortable seat, and to solve the problem he purchased timber from a yard in a nearby village and constructed a sturdy plank bench. This episode was also to fill a few pages of his book:

> The making of the seat was elementary. ... And then I sat back and the scent of new-sawn timber mingled with the scent of new-mown lawn. A thrush was singing from the pear-tree, two goldfinches were searching among the tulips, a sulphur yellow butterfly flittered past, and behold it was very good.[14]

In a letter to John Hadfield in September 1956, he mentioned another episode which eventually was included in his manuscript:

> ... I've fallen in love again & now have a very pretty dark haired girl come to live with me. I only met her a fortnight ago when visiting Monkey Island but I fell instantaneously for her & she made no objection at all to coming back & settling down here. Apart from the softness in her eyes & the cut of her behind I think it was the long flapping ears that got me. ... I send you a photo so that you may also love vicariously.[15]

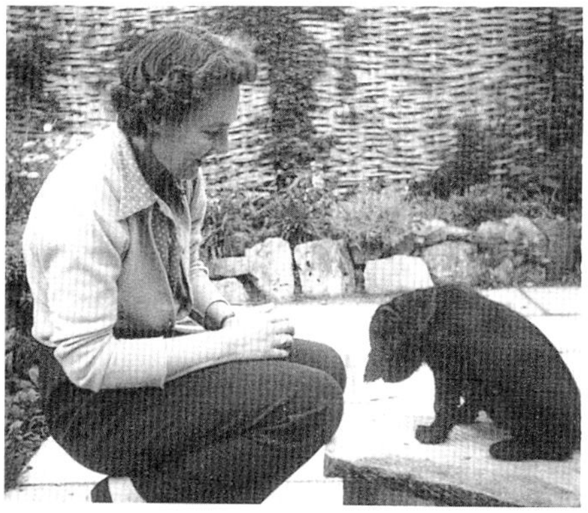

382 Patience with the spaniel pup that Robert brought home as a pet. RUL.

Gibbings had fallen for a spaniel pup whose mother belonged to Diana and Patrick; he had succumbed to her charms and had brought the tiny pup home in his pocket. Now, with a more permanent home and Patience to share the responsibilities, he had felt he could add to the family unit.

There were some interruptions to the work on *Till I End My Song*. At the end of 1956 Bozman had asked Gibbings to revise articles dealing with Polynesia for a new edition of Dent's *Everyman's Encyclopaedia*. Gibbings was hard pressed, so Patience helped with much of the research and writing and between them they completed the revisions to Bozman's satisfaction: '... there is no doubt that you have effected an immense improvement. The new articles are much more "live" than the old ones ...'.[16] Although it was Dent who had caused such distractions, they were beginning to worry that Gibbings would not be able to complete the book by the end of the year. Martin Dent wrote a long letter to Gibbings setting out again the importance and strategic significance of the publication date in terms of maximising Christmas sales — particularly for the overseas markets. Gibbings replied with a certain annoyance: 'Your Christmas card and your letter of the 18th reached me on Christmas Eve, the former giving me much pleasure, the latter not quite so much!' He pointed out that the agreement had stipulated that the manuscript should be completed by January 1957 — which he had taken to mean by the end of that month. This was still his aim, but in the circumstances he had not expected Dent to be so rigid: '... I did not expect that to be taken as a firm promise by which you could set your calendar'. Gibbings then went on to summarise the position:

When I spoke to Boz recently I told him that my total was then about 54,000 and that the main pattern of the book being complete I planned to begin forthwith on a final revise, adding wherever I could any philosophical comments that occurred to me. These and a short final summing up chapter should bring the total towards sixty thousand words. With all this he seemed to agree, emphasising that the more of the philosophy that I could put in the better. But quiet contemplative thoughts do not come overnight and cannot be forced. I cannot work harder than I have been doing. I have done seven days a week throughout the year, without a holiday, and am utterly tired. As I told Boz, I've had for months past an almost continuous pain in the end of my spine due to overstrain.

As to the illustrations, I have about thirty of the engravings well on the way, many of them wanting but a few touches to complete. I have also a painting of Lechlade bridge which I suggest as a coloured frontispiece. This I can let you have on the first opportunity of transport to town.

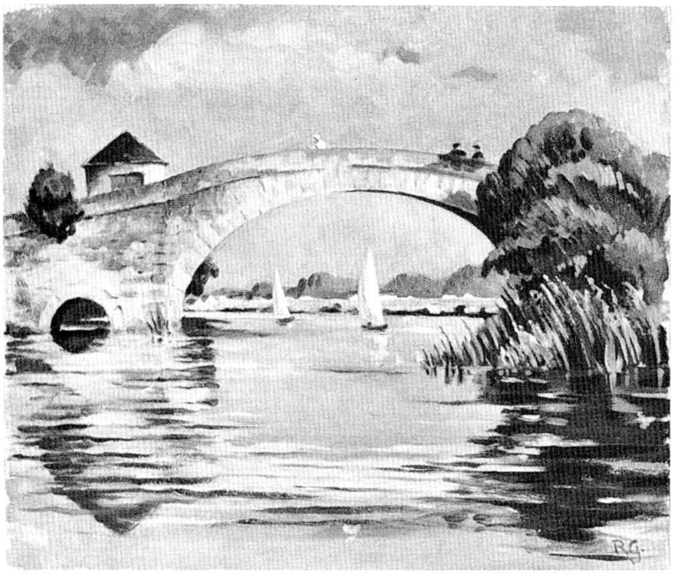

383 *Halfpenny Bridge, Lechlade*, 1956, oil painting, 382 x 458 mm., used as the frontispiece of *Till I End My Song*. In the possession of Diana Gibbings.

I suggest therefore that I do as much more as I can to the MS during the next few weeks and let you have it definitely by Jan. 31st, the same date as promised to Macrae. I will then concentrate on the blocks, most of which should be finished by the time you have the galleys ready for the paste up. As you know, the last few can only be designed when we see how the pages fall.

I do appreciate everything you say about the benefits of early publication but it is not going to help if the critics feel that the script is thin and unpolished. This is likely to be my last book of the kind and it is awfully important that it shouldn't let the others down.[17]

True to form and despite the pain from his back, Gibbings handed in the manuscript early at the beginning of January 1957. The effort had 'turned his head to jelly', but now he could concentrate on the engravings. Bozman was pleased with the manuscript: 'I have thoroughly enjoyed this. The atmosphere is clearly established from the first page and the stream flows steadily and strongly on without any falling off of interest — if anything I think that the writing gets better and better as it goes on which is as it should be.'[18]

At the beginning of March, Gibbings wrote to Hadfield that he had now completed the first batch of blocks:

... I have delivered to Martin D [Dent] a total of 27 blocks & as Renoir said in his last moments 'I think I'm improving'. I'm really quite pleased with a few of them. I think that when I get the rest of them off my chest the tension will disappear. It is most humiliating to think that one's brain is in one's bottom.[19]

Martin Dent was also full of praise when he received the blocks:

If I thought there was room for improvement I might be inclined to agree with your quotation from Renoir. These are absolutely first-class. I expect you have got most of the remaining subjects planned, but when I see, for example, that lovely one of the duck coming in to land, I begin to yearn for more action studies of birds. Whilst I don't suggest trying to overweight the book with this type of subject, I am sure they help to give it life and movement. ... you are still improving. *Sweet Thames* was a superb book but comparing many similar subjects, there is a richness and a quality in these new ones which was not always to be found in the first book. I do congratulate you ...[20]

Gibbings was producing blocks at great speed and intensity; subject matter seemed to come easily and his hand was engraving smoothly. His studio, tucked away at the end of the garden, provided a safe haven where he could disappear to work, leaving Patience to fend off inconvenient visitors. The problem with his back, which had been loosely diagnosed as lumbago, had been giving him trouble since early in the year and even the gin bottle had failed to give permanent relief. Gibbings suffered continual nagging pain which made it hard to sit for long periods — so necessary when writing and engraving.

It had been decided to reproduce the painting of the Halfpenny Bridge at Lechlade as the frontispiece, but as this was to be the only colour plate Gibbings suggested returning to the slightly smaller format used for *Coming Down the Seine*. Early in February he had snatched a few days break which he spent in a 'damn nice little pub', the May Bush in Newbridge on the Thames, sketching the view of the river from the window of his room. On his return he went to see his doctor

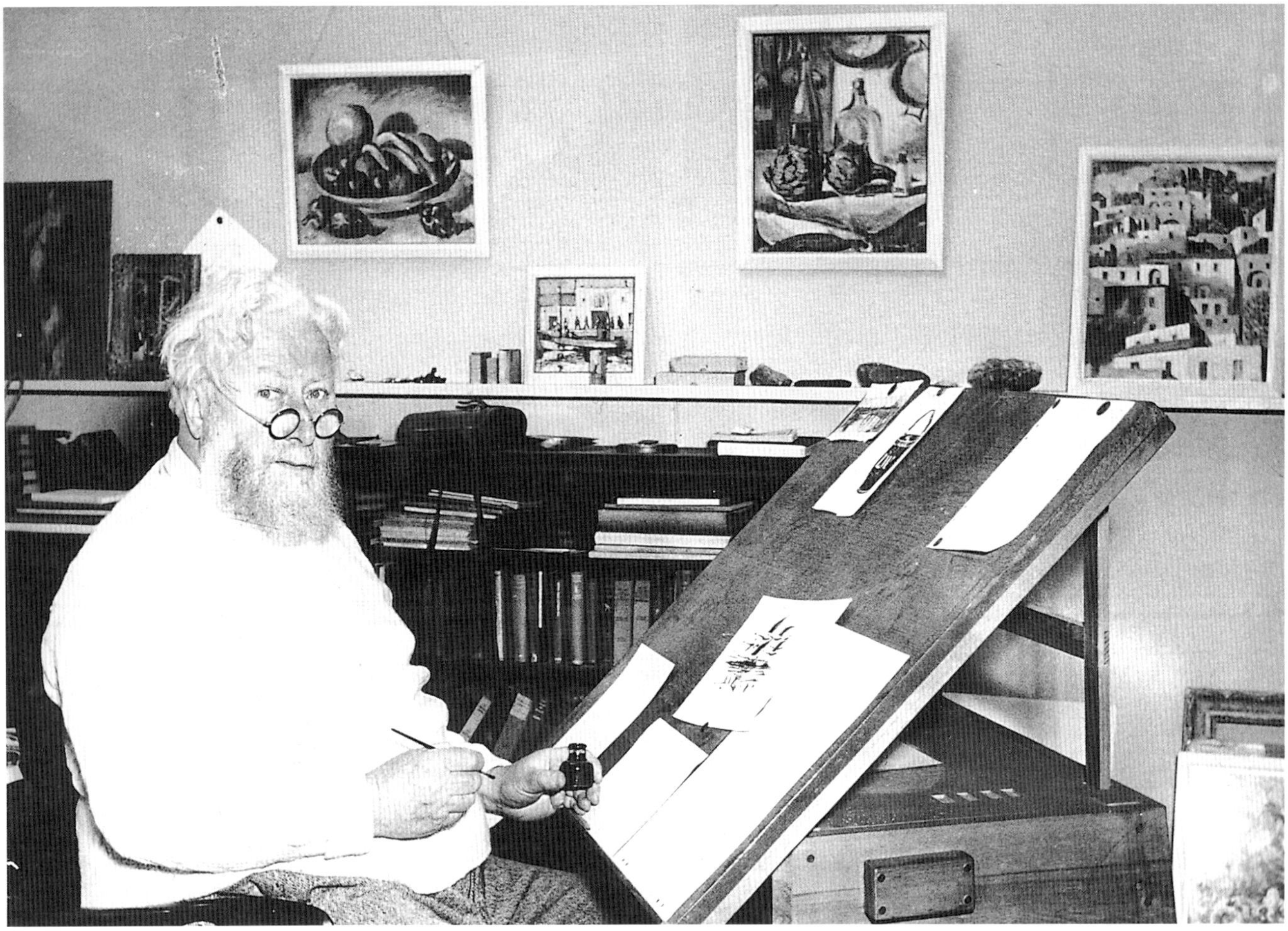

384 Gibbings working in his studio in the garden at Footbridge Cottage. RUL.

about his back and wrote to Hadfield with his news: 'First things first, beginning at the bottom I am glad to tell you that the Dr. says that my sufferings are due entirely to frustration, repression & publishers & he is going to give me some tablets that cost less than gin.' Hadfield had read Gibbings's manuscript of the book and had made some suggestions about weak sections that needed more work — Gibbings responded to his advice: 'In the few brief moments that I could spare out of doors I got some nice river stuff & indoors I got a story about a dog & a cat ... that will bring tears to every reader's eye. I have put the whole thing, 1200 words, exactly where your pencil indicated a need for home matters. I have also remembered some good associations with Coppard in this village ....'[21] Although the main text was being typeset, Gibbings was still making the odd addition where needed.

While he was in the middle of the engraving of the blocks for *Till I End My Song*, Hadfield had decided that an article on the process of wood-engraving would be splendid for the next edition of *The Saturday Book*. Gibbings had agreed and was thinking of how to create an impact with his opening paragraphs: 'I am glad to tell you that I have made a start with a story of a carpenter who once lived in this village & from there I am moving to Venezuela & South Africa.'[22] The article was eventually entitled 'Thoughts on Wood' and was beautifully illustrated by a

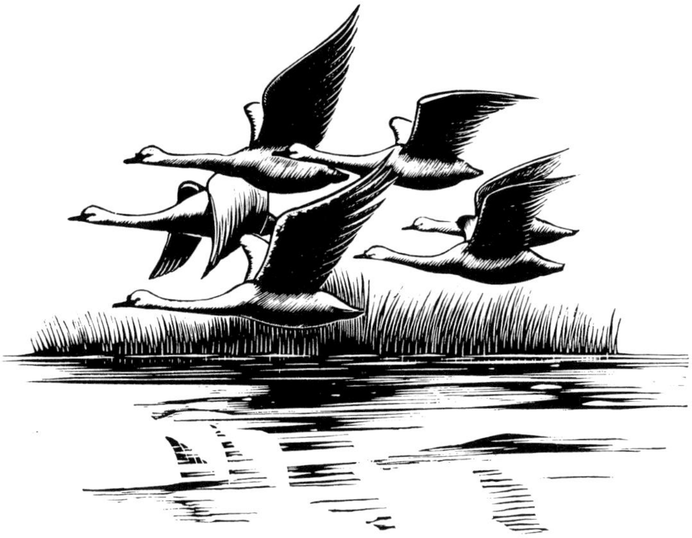

385 Swans in flight over the river Thames, 1957, wood-engraving, 70 x 93 mm. Illustration from *Till I End My Song*.

selection of engravings which showed the development of his own style of engraving. In the text, Gibbings explained the technique and described the tools and materials used and traced his career as a wood-engraver; he ended by describing his mature style and approach to the medium:

Now, with the years, I incline to austerity of outline in combination with formalized texture. I would like my engravings to partake somewhat of the quality of the low relief stone carvings from Assyria in the British Museum: Illustration and decoration combined to perfection within the limits of their medium — 'near enough' to realism as illustration, as decoration 'just right'.[23]

Although hard-pressed on his book, Gibbings had frequently received requests for other articles. In July of the previous year, the journal *Medical World* had published a humorous piece about his experiences with doctors and health entitled 'My Career in Medicine', and in March 1957, he had written another article on the 'Country of the Wye' for the BBC's journal *London Calling*, which was based on the script for one of his broadcast talks.[24]

Early in April, Gibbings was happy to report to Hadfield that he had sent the last sections of his book to Dent:

This very blessed morning I have posted to Martin the last of 50 blocks & three completely new & extra chapters ... of the text I *can* say definitely that thanks to your suggestions I have improved it by a hundred per cent.[25]

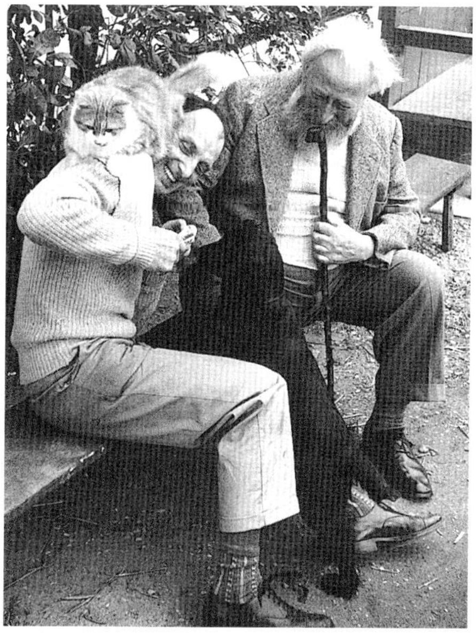

386 Gibbings and his friend Christie Seary outside The Vine in Long Wittenham. RUL.

Gibbings had been inspired in writing this new material partly as a result of a new friendship. His regular pub, the Plough, had been invaded by some newcomers to the village. For Gibbings these rather loud and domineering folk had spoilt the atmosphere and constantly pestered him for attention. As a result he had changed his drinking loyalties to a public house further down the main road of the village. Gibbings explained to Hadfield that The Vine had recently been taken over by a new publican, Christie Seary:

The new man at the 'Vine' is a holy marvel, not only for stories but for drawing out story-tellers & even in the last few weeks I have got page after page of just the bucolic, alcoholic, cynical-olic etc etc that the book needed. ... now thanks to obedience to your comments I think it *may* be the best yet. God help us. Amen.[26]

In the same letter, Gibbings had hesitantly asked his old friend if he would act as chairman at a luncheon, to be held by the National Book League, at which he was to give a talk: 'Can you bear it? again & again the same old Balls! But if we could meet between this & there we might knock up a knock-about 'script' .... Do for God's sake spit in my eye & say no if you don't feel like it.' Gibbings and Hadfield had become increasingly close as friends; they shared a sense of humour and together they could be rather schoolboyish, but Gibbings also felt he could confide in Hadfield. He felt desperate for a break and a return to Paris; he kept tempting Hadfield to join him but confessed that his 'puritan upbringing (leaving out the bank manager) tells me that I must justify my sin' — so he suggested that following 'Thoughts on Fish' and 'Thoughts on Wood' he should work on an article on his 'Thoughts on Boulevards', as his next contribution to *The Saturday Book*.[27]

Despite the doctor's diagnosis of the cause of his backpain, the pills prescribed had little beneficial effect and Gibbings had been referred to a consultant. In May 1957 he went for tests and a week of rest in a private nursing home; on his return to Footbridge Cottage he wrote to Anna Hadfield in a buoyant mood: 'Now I am back again & though still in *need* of love & sympathy am I think well on the way to resurrection. The great thing is that after x, y & z rays there is nothing wrong except "Arthritis aggravated by nervous tension."'[28] The consultant felt that he was working too hard for his age, but recommended the benefits of alcohol, to Gibbings's delight, and instructed him to drink 'as much as makes you happy, just as much as keeps you fit ...'. Gibbings had also had therapy to 'quieten the nerves', but the pain had been terrific, like 'hot blunt knives driving into my spine at one moment & into my right buttock at the next & I've lost quite a bit of weight ...'.[29]

Together with the Hadfields, Gibbings had decided on a trip to Paris in July but his condition had brought things forward; at the end of May he confided in Hadfield: 'I just can't stand any more of their gnawing into my behind & the Drs say the only way to shake 'em off is to get away for a complete change as soon as pos. So I have decided to take the wings of the morning on Monday to Paris ...'.[30] But even in Paris, Gibbings was still troubled: 'I wish I could write you a sensible constructive letter about my plans but fact is I'm fair knocked out by my back & don't know what to do. The doctors said all I needed was rest but how the hell can I rest when I can't sit stand lie walk or even think without pain.'[31]

Taking drugs more frequently did nothing to help him sleep or ease the pain and in the end Gibbings cut short his stay and returned to Footbridge Cottage. His morale had been temporarily boosted in Paris when, on more than one occasion, he had been approached for autographs by appreciative readers of *Coming Down the Seine*. At the end of July he was feeling a little better: 'I think I am at last getting the upper hand of my bum & hope soon to tread it under heel —

if you know what I mean.'[32] One piece of encouragement came from the Book Society, who were to make *Till I End My Song* a 'Recommendation' for October, the month of publication, and he had also been given a 'fillip' by Godfrey Winn's article on the *Seine*: 'He really did it awfully well & though the journal is not one to send folks rushing to the bookshops, it is, I am told, one that forms queues at the libraries.'[33]

Since January of 1956, one of Gibbings's more unusual correspondents was a nun, Sister Hildelith Cumming, of the community at Stanbrook Abbey. Sister Hildelith (soon to become Dame Hildelith Cumming) had been given the task of reviving the convent's Press. She felt that 'Quantity had taken the place of the traditional quality.'[34] She was determined to pursue quality and steer the Press away from the more obviously commercial work and to try printing 'beautiful books', taking the work of the Golden Cockerel Press as the inspiration.

Sister Hildelith had written to Gibbings asking for advice and, in particular, his opinion on the choice of a new typeface to replace their old and worn type and his view on the reproduction of coloured images. Gibbings's reply was predictable as he suggested Perpetua (the typeface used for all his Dent books); equally predictable was his support, in the form of warm encouragement. Letters were exchanged over the coming year with Gibbings advising on inks, marketing (he put them in touch with J. & E. Bumpus), and suggesting that they contact John Dreyfus as a real expert on type. Gibbings was delighted by the work of the Stanbrook Abbey Press and was generous in his praise; on the receipt of an example of their early efforts he had replied: 'I think that you have created the most perfect piece of typography that I have ever seen.'[35]

Till I End My Song WAS PUBLISHED on 3 October 1957. Gibbings dedicated the book to his old friend, Ralph Beedham, who had given him such invaluable assistance with his engraving over many years; Beedham was touched when he had seen a proof of the book: '... I am delighted with it — delighted to share (with others in previous volumes) the honour of having a page dedicated to myself'.[36]

Dutton had decided to make an offset lithographic facsimile of the Dent edition which Gibbings hoped would ensure quality. To his American publishers he was confident about the book: 'One or two people who have read the text think it is my best yet, though of that I am no judge; but I feel quite confident that the engravings are indeed the best set I have ever done.'[37] The production of *Till I End My Song* in America was delayed until November which meant that it coincided with the rush for the Christmas market. It was somewhat swamped by competition and initially sales were disappointing. In Britain sales were strong, and once again Gibbings's book received good reviews world-wide. Many reviewers expressed the hope that the title did not suggest an end to his writing and most were again won over by the charm of his book. They were only too happy to allow themselves to be carried along by his gentle cocktail of evocative description and observation, fascinating history and humorous anecdote — many

Cover of *Till I End My Song* – see colour plate 8p.

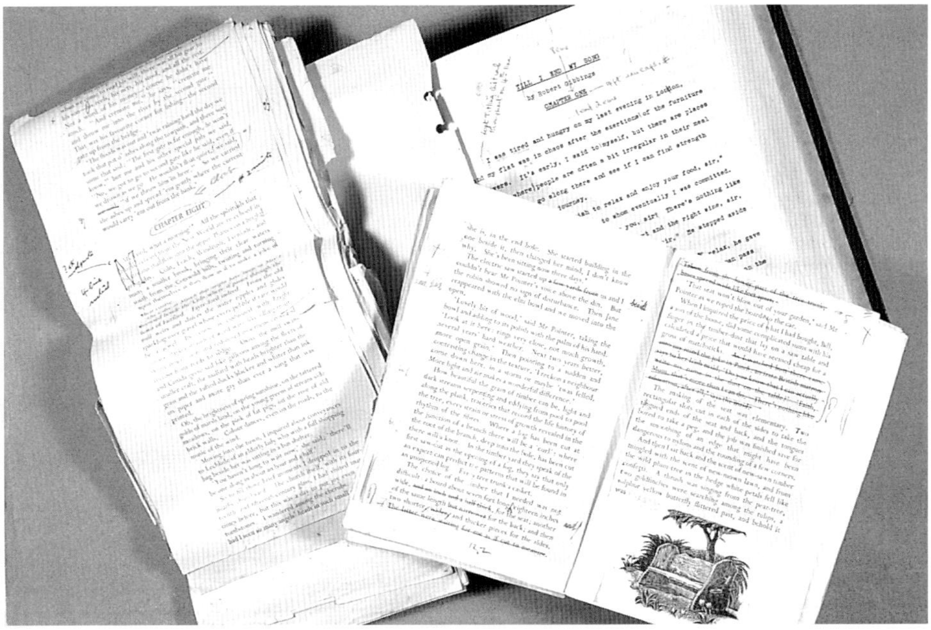

387 The typescript, galley proofs and paste-up dummy of *Till I End My Song*. RUL.

recommending the book as an obvious choice for Christmas presents. One or too critics were less easily seduced by his style. Nancy Spain, writing in the *Daily Express*, was characteristically waspish and hard hitting in her comments:

> I never thought to see the day when I would describe a book by Robert Gibbings as wishy-washy. But to tell the truth he has been Coming Down the Thames and the Lee and the Seine and the Wye and making those exquisitely meaningless wood engravings quite long enough.
>
> *Till I End My Song* is the latest of these Charm Books ... it contains many agonising remarks of the type I doubt ever truly get remarked by those country types who are supposed to remark them. ... Mind you, every now and then there is a flash of the old Gibbings charm. I delighted in the story of how Dame Nellie Melba threatened to horse-whip a critic .... And I was pleased about Mr. Gibbings's Income Tax return ... when he published a book called 'Lives of the Gallant Ladies'. ... But two moments of charm in a book of 234 pages is frankly not quite good enough.[38]

The reviewer for *The Times Literary Supplement* was less harsh but still felt that: 'His books are an excuse for the small engravings with which they are adorned', and went on to comment that Gibbings was 'shameless with his padding and his matter is thin. Yet his prose has an easy rhythm that carries the reader over the shallows, and his Irish wit is never at a loss to change the subject quickly'.[39] But these reviews were the exception. The critic in *The Times* was more appreciative of Gibbings's qualities: 'Mr. Gibbings has wit, a graceful prose, and the art of gentle surprise. As we follow him through his unhurried days we gain cumulatively a heartening sense that there is a life to be lived .... His book with its wood engravings strikes a perfect balance between verbal and pictorial expression.'[40] Gibbings had no pretensions to be an intellectual writer; his books are a sincere and genuine response to life and reflect his spirit and philosophy. He had style, sometimes rambling, sometimes sentimental, but always truthful — the descriptions of his emotional response to nature are conveyed with a sensual directness which absorbs the reader — at times with the simplicity and conciseness of poetry. His writing either appealed to the readers's taste or it did not — but Gibbings wrote as he was.

Gibbings was generally pleased with the reception of *Till I End My Song*. The pain he was suffering from his back did not intrude into the tranquillity and warmth of the book. He was content in his new home; it gave him a sense of belonging and he had found a new peace in the life he shared with Patience. But Gibbings was affected by post-publication anti-climax. Thankful to Hadfield for his compliments on the book, but always self-critical, Gibbings confessed:

> I can't tell you what balm it was to my bum & my soul — both rather closely entwined at the moment — to hear that you really think my text is not a let down. I think half my trouble has been that in 'ending my song' I had a feeling of inadequacy amounting to guilt. Everything I did I felt should have been better. As you know I love all these things of which I write & I want to make other people bloody well love them too but this time each phrase that I wrote seemed quite banal. Now your letter makes me feel that perhaps I was trying too hard — over anxious in my senility.[41]

The frequency and regularity of his trips down the road to the Vine were partly to do with the slight relief he found there but were also due to the friendship he felt towards Chris Seary, the new landlord. Gibbings was pleased to help his friend produce a publicity leaflet for the pub, the text quoting at length from *Till I End My Song* and using a selection of engravings from the book for illustration. Gibbings and Patience made many friends in the village and invitations for lunch or to dinner parties were frequent. As an easy and entertaining guest, Robert was always welcome at weekend house-parties held by their friends Pat and Chris Medley, who owned a beautiful old Manor house at the other end of the village. On one of these occasions Gerard Hoffnung was among the guests and he drew a quick cartoon of the convivial Gibbings, glass in hand. Robert genuinely loved good company but, of late, he had had to put on something of a performance. Covering up his intense pain, he would be the life and soul of the party, but

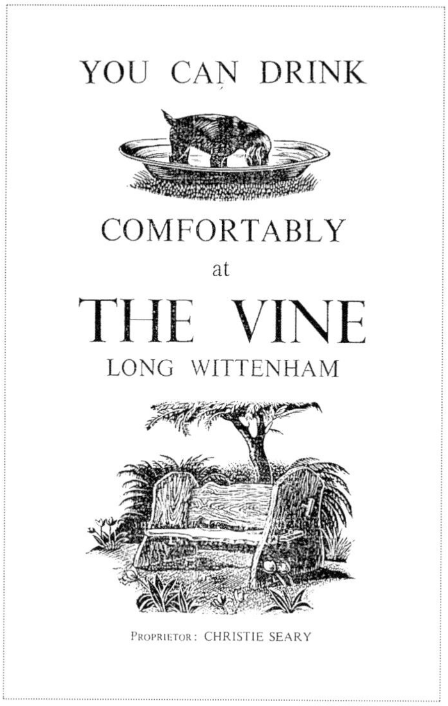

388 Cover of a publicity leaflet that Gibbings illustrated for the proprietor of The Vine. Both wood-engravings are illustrations from *Till I End My Song*; above is Gibbings's pet spaniel and below the garden bench he made. Page size 192 x 128 mm. RUL.

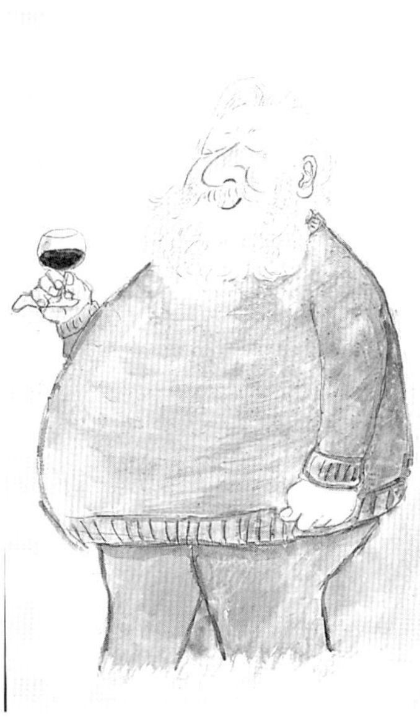

389 Cartoon of Gibbings in convivial mood by Gerard Hoffnung, c. 1956, watercolour, RUL. Gibbings is wearing a hand-knitted jumper – one of his favoured garments. He frequently wore such jumpers (usually blue) when delivering more informal public talks. Stretched over his rounded stomach, this became a world globe on which Gibbings would theatrically demonstrate his journeys around the world – much to the amusement of his audience. Reproduced by kind permission of Annetta Hoffnung.

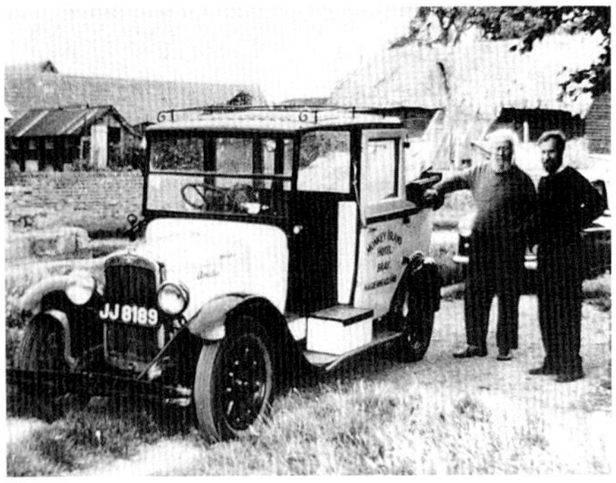

390 Gibbings and his eldest son Patrick standing outside Footbridge Cottage by the old yellow taxi, affectionately named Amelia, that was used as transport and publicity for the Monkey Island Hotel. RUL.

Patience was the sole witness to his exhaustion and suffering afterwards. She was convinced of the seriousness of his condition and she bore all the responsibility of care.

Gibbings was so anxious to please that his show of ebullient good humour was not confined to social events. Patience was frustrated by the fact that when he was visited by the doctor, he would put effort into telling stories and jokes, appearing in much better health and spirits than he really was. In such circumstances it was difficult for Patience to impart the true gravity of the situation.

Deprived of sleep and with loss of weight through a lack of appetite caused by the drugs he was taking, Gibbings felt very low. It gave him some relief to express his feelings in frequent letters to Hadfield and even now they were discussing new topics for articles — Gibbings had had an idea to focus on the subject of bird feathers. But at the beginning of November he was taken into the Churchill hospital in Oxford for further tests and investigations under anaesthetic. Once again he was reassured: '... the answer was that there is absolutely nothing wrong — to which I reply "except the pain"'.[42]

The Hadfields had invited Robert and Patience to their home for Christmas but Gibbings had other arrangements: '... this year I am breaking long custom & becoming paternal. Two large daughters are coming to sleep in the studio sawdust & between them & the dog I'll be worn out with exercise'.[43] The drugs he was taking exhausted him so much that at times he did not have the energy to get upstairs to bed and the only relief from pain came from an increasing intake of gin which, when he felt fit enough, would be provided at the bar in the Vine. On 27 December he wrote to Hadfield that he could not contribute anything to *The Saturday Book* as he was feeling 'lousy' and could no longer walk to the pub; his 'Merry Christmas' had been spent mostly in bed and Patience had started to feed him with concentrated foods. Yet Gibbings still had enough optimism to end his letter: 'I feel pretty sure that one day I'll get on top of the whole silly business.'[44] His condition had deteriorated quite suddenly, as earlier in the month he had been planning further projects with Martin Dent. For some while Dent had been negotiating with Gibbings about the possibility of publishing a large volume of his collected wood-engravings. With his latest book published, he needed a new spur: 'Now for future work, I am trying very hard to get down to business again, and one of the first items must be the Collected Works which we discussed quite a long time ago.'[45] This was to be a handsome volume and Gibbings had started on a biographical introduction and the selection of his engravings. He wanted a format which would not necessitate the reduction of some of his larger prints but he left the decision to Martin Dent: '... when you have made it could you send me some sort of a dummy, of say 300 pages, on which I can begin to build the whole story?'[46]

On 2 January Gibbings returned to the Acland Nursing Home for a barium X-ray. This time a diagnosis of bowel cancer was made and on 11 January Gibbings was taken into the Churchill Hospital in Oxford for a major operation to remove the affected parts of the colon — at that time such radical surgery was still in its early stages. Even in hospital, Gibbings was chatting to the nurses and fascinating them with his stories. One student nurse, knowing of his celebrity, rushed out to buy a copy of *Till I End My Song*, which Robert was happy to autograph. The day before Gibbings went into hospital he had received a letter from Sister Hildelith in which she had written at length of her appreciation of his help and advice but Gibbings had been unable to reply. On 26 January 1958 it was Patience who finally wrote:

I have to return to you the beautiful page from St Augustine, with the news which you may already have heard, that Robert Gibbings died on the 19th January. He had been in ill health with increasing pain for many months, but it was only a couple of weeks ago that the doctors discovered the cause. He was operated on and a growth removed, but he died four days later from heart failure.

I know he much enjoyed his correspondence with you, and seeing the lovely examples of your printing that you sent him. He had hoped one day to drive over to Stanbrook Abbey. He was a wonderful person, it is impossible to realise that he has gone.[47]

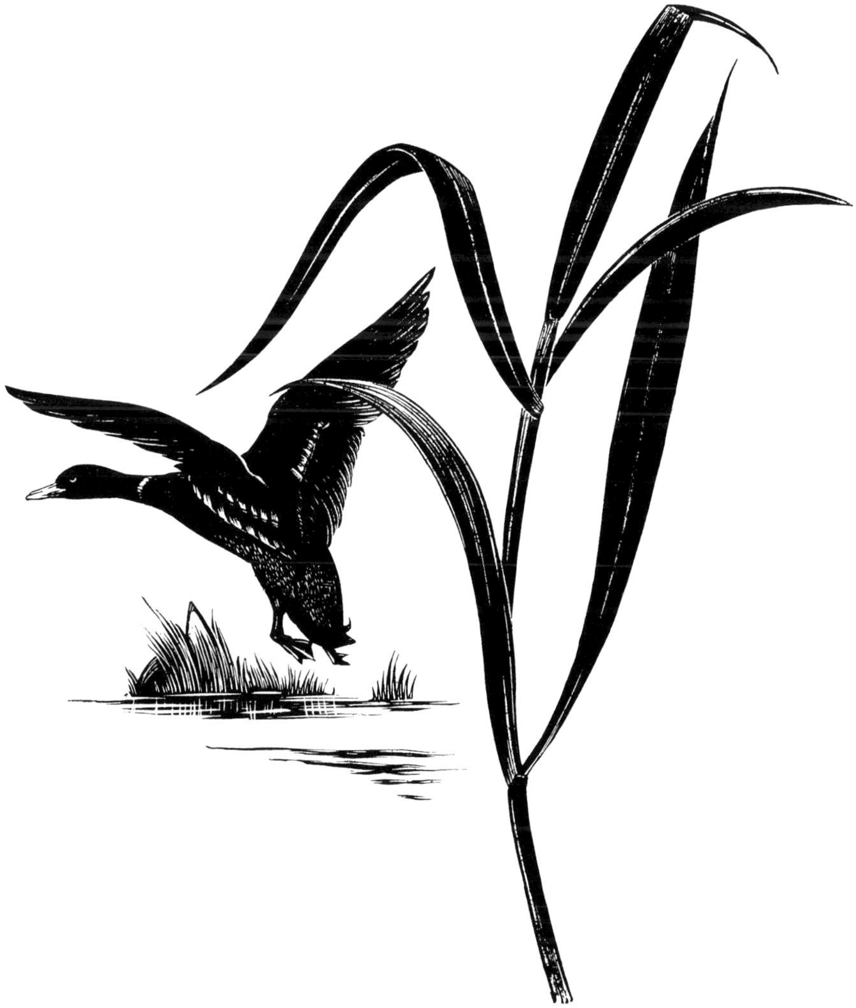

391 The engraving that followed the closing words of *Till I End My Song*: 'The dancing of a mountain stream may be as entrancing as a ballet, but the quiet of an age-old river is like the slow turning of pages in a well-loved book.' Wood-engraving, 134 x 114 mm.

Epilogue

AT ONE PARTICULAR MOMENT in his last book, Gibbings, moved by the poignancy of the single name on the War Memorial in the neighbouring village of Little Wittenham, reflects on the passing of life. Perhaps remembering his own escape from death in the trenches of Gallipoli, he muses on this lone young soldier:

> Here, on this track, he had looked his last 'on all things lovely'; the same fields ripening to harvest as I saw them, the same profusion of wild flowers starring the verges. He too would have seen the gold of yellow-hammers in the sunlight, the white rumps of wheatears as they flitted from post to post of the fence, the rainbow glints of butterflies; above them all the flocks of peewits circling high. Butterflies whose days of life are but moments in our human reckoning, lapwings whose years at best are scarce a dozen: the life span of a bird, I thought, till I too end my song.[1]

The happiness that Robert and Patience shared in their cottage in Long Wittenham had tragically only lasted for a few years and his death had been sudden and unexpected. But in that short time he had grown to love the surrounding countryside and the 'patina of age or ancestry' of the village buildings. His sense of history and continuity with the past comes out in his description of the ancient village church, built on the site of a pre-Christian burial ground, and it was here, in the graveyard of St Mary's, that he was buried on 22 January 1958. A simple gravestone marks the spot, close to a part of the boundary wall covered with honeysuckle. The stone is lettered with his name and dates, above and below his own device of an engraving tool crossed by a feather quill, beautifully carved in low relief by Michael Black, a young sculptor who was a good friend of Robert's. Obituaries appeared in newspapers and journals all over the world and the Society of Wood Engravers dedicated their twenty-ninth annual exhibition to his memory and included a special section devoted to his work.

John Hadfield had expected to publish an illustrated essay by Gibbings on 'feathers' in *The Saturday Book* for 1958. He had enjoyed the piquancy of the prospect of such a huge man 'discussing and engraving — with his characteristic finesse and lightness of touch — swansdown and wren's wings'. Hadfield still wanted Robert's name, as a regular contributor, to appear in the edition and so wrote an introduction about his friend with typical humour and affection:

> Robert's personality — his verve and volume, his stature and skill — was exceptional. But his mental and aesthetic curiosity, and his taste for the more recondite pleasures of life, were, we like to think, typically *Saturdiurnal* characteristics. He was totally uninterested in politics, careerism, commerce and keeping up with the Joneses. But he loved vintage

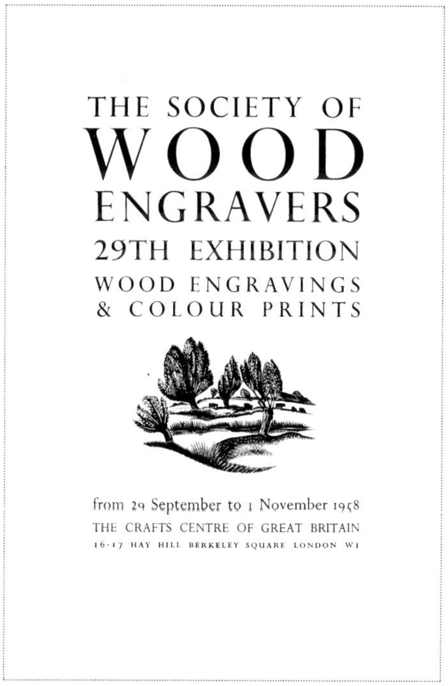

392 Cover of the catalogue for an exhibition held by the Society of Wood Engravers in 1958. As a memorial, the catalogue included an essay on Gibbings's career and a section of the exhibition was dedicated to his work. The engraving is an illustration from *Till I End My Song*. Cover size 228 x 155 mm, RUL.

traction engines and trout, microscopes, boats and birds, fossils, Sibelius, post-Impressionists and Negro dancing, rain, all things Irish, good talk and good jokes, solitude, Montparnasse and Samoa, print, paper, and pubs, flowers, claret and not wearing a tie. Although he was a most conscientious and industrious craftsman it could be said of him that all his days were Saturdays. May the Berkshire clay lie on his vast bearded frame as the swansdown from Sweet Thames that he was going to draw for us.[2]

In his will, Robert left his half-share of Footbridge Cottage to Patience and 'the thatched beehive' became her permanent home. Some of her grief at the loss of Robert was immediately channelled into a project that became a tribute to him, the book that he had left unfinished — his collected works.

It was at the beginning of 1950 that Martin Dent had first suggested to Gibbings that they would like to publish a handsome volume of his wood-engravings.[3] The idea came to him after he had seen Balston's book, *The Wood-engravings of Robert Gibbings*, which Gibbings had sent him as a Christmas greeting. Robert was very taken with the proposal and plans were laid:

> ... the idea that in a few years time we might do a properly printed book [Gibbings felt that the engravings were over-inked in the Balston book], with a rather larger selection of engravings, is a very thrilling one to me. ... It would be awfully nice to think that, round about Christmas '54, we might bring out 'The Collected Engravings of ...'.[4]

Bozman was equally enthusiastic and suggested a small edition of 1500 to be sold in this country and 500 for America. Although he was anxious that Robert should not be distracted from the book he was working on, *Trumpets from Montparnasse*, as the *Collected Works* could be done at any time, he agreed to make a dummy of the book so that Gibbings could paste in engravings of his choice and start laying out the pages. Inevitably things were delayed, but at the end of 1953 they returned to the project and it was decided that Gibbings should provide a 'running commentary' to accompany the illustrations. By November they had reached contract stage. Progress was slow, but in June 1955 Bozman wrote to say he was pleased with Gibbings's text: 'This specimen material is, *per se*, distinctly promising. It is written in your characteristic style — light, fluent, friendly, freely salted with humour and very readable.'[5] However, the project remained on hold until December 1957, when Gibbings, then very ill, was in need of a new goal. Originally the format for the book had been Crown quarto but, in order to have a page large enough to accommodate a greater number of engravings on one page, it was agreed to revise estimates to allow for Demy quarto. On 8 January 1958, only a week or so before he died, Martin Dent sent Robert two folded sections of Demy quarto for him to experiment with — Robert had already sketched out his ideas for a title page.

Robert's death only made the project seem more important, as a tribute to him, and by March 1958 Patience had agreed to take on the completion of the book and was already hard at work tracking down copies of Robert's engravings. It must have been useful therapy for her to become absorbed in the research. With her usual meticulous organization, she began the daunting task of writing hundreds of letters to museums, art galleries, friends, private collectors, book

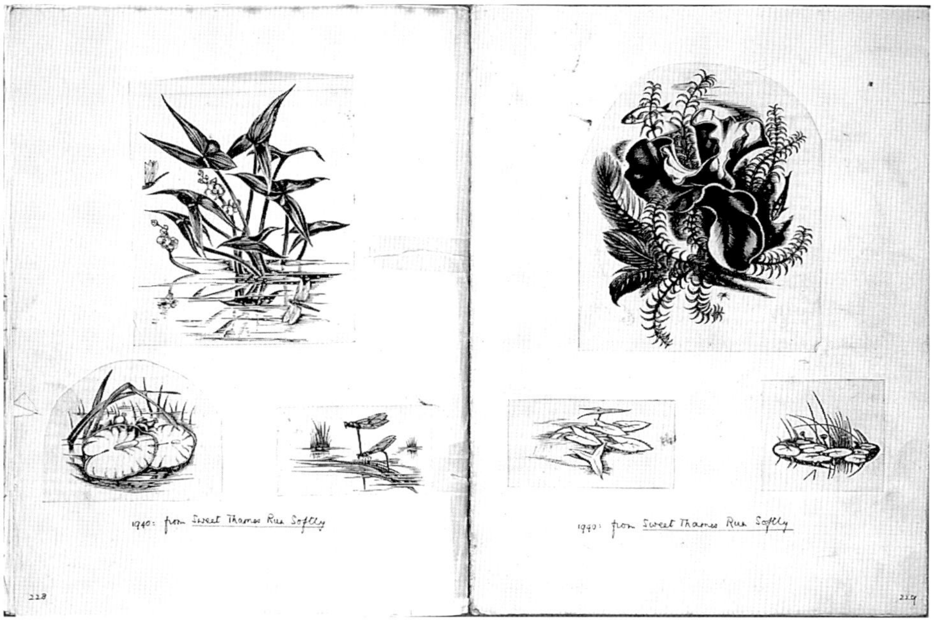

393 Double-page spread from a dummy of the *Collected Works* in which Patience Empson pasted proof pulls of the illustrations to design the layout. RUL.

dealers and libraries, gathering prints and illustrated books. Robert's early work proved to be particularly hard to find, until Patience contacted his oldest friends such as Hubert Pike and Lieutenant Colonel Robert Goodden, in Cornwall, who was able to lend, amongst other prints, a copy of *Spot*, which Robert had given him just after the First World War.

Thomas Balston had agreed to write an introduction to the *Collected Works* and Patience already had Robert's draft of his biographical notes and commentary on his work (later to be entitled 'Some Recollections'). But, sadly, these were unfinished and she agonised on how to complete his account or even if it would be appropriate for her to do so. Her confidence was boosted when Bozman wrote on 22 April to say how delighted he was with her foreword and conclusion to

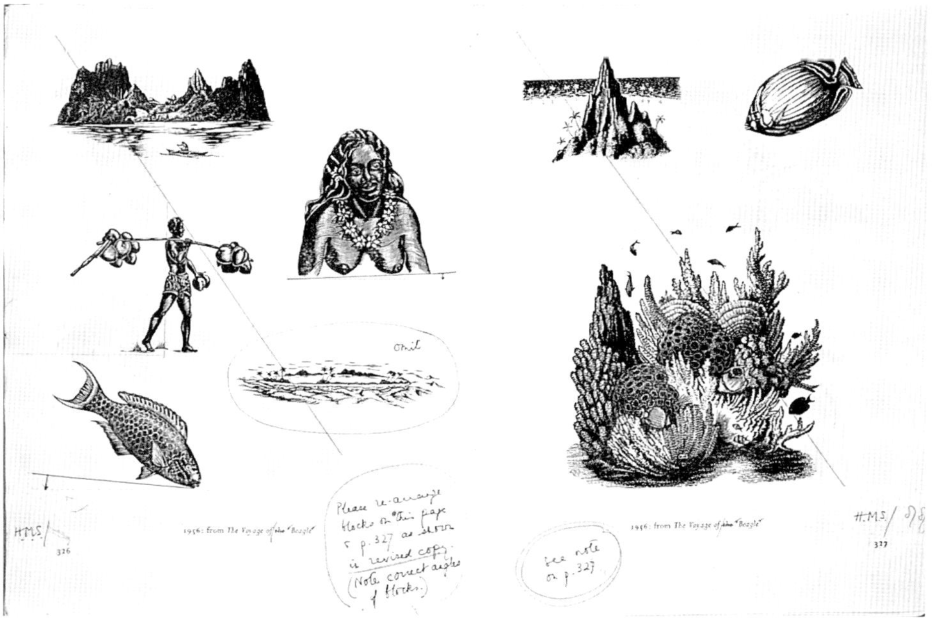

394 Proof pages of the *Collected Works* with Patience Empson's corrections and alterations. RUL.

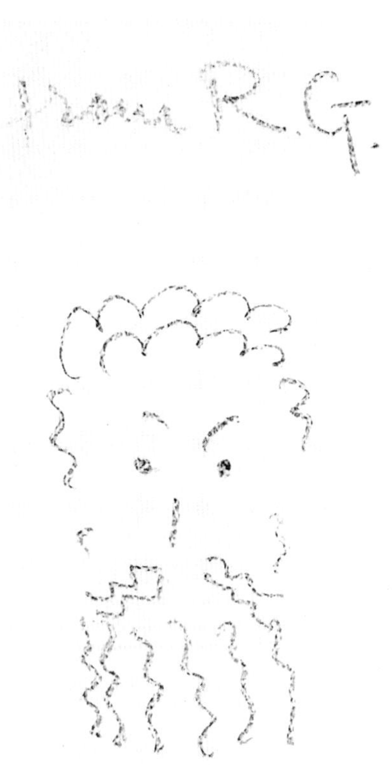

395 Cartoon self-portrait scribbled by Gibbings in pencil on the back of a library return slip and kept by Mary Kirkus after his death. Versions of this humorous image were often used by Gibbings – sometimes in place of a signature. Kirkus Collection, RUL.

Robert's recollections: 'Your draft foreword appears to me to be exactly on the right line ... Tom Balston is obviously very satisfied with your plans and progress ....'[6] Bozman had in mind that he himself would write an epilogue for the book, on the relationship between Gibbings and Dent; Balston had suggested a list of books illustrated by Robert to be included. Patience pointed out to Bozman that Dent had already commissioned a Gibbings bibliography which was being written by Dr Mary Kirkus, the Librarian at Reading University, with whom she was already collaborating and who had been of enormous help. It was therefore planned that the bibliography should form a major part of the *Collected Works*.

However, in February 1959, Mary wrote to Patience expressing concern that she had just discovered that they had both been working under a misapprehension and that Dent had reverted to the earlier plan of publishing the bibliography and *Collected Works* as two separate books. Patience tried unsuccessfully to persuade them to think again — rather thrown by the change as she had been discussing with Mary how they should acknowledge each other's contribution on the title page of her book.

For both Mary and Patience, the task of compiling information was made particularly hard by the fact that Robert had never kept proper records or even copies of his own books or prints. He had a library of reference books but otherwise he showed a cavalier attitude to his own work — often giving it away. When he became in demand as a speaker, he was obliged to scour bookshops, trying to find second-hand copies of Golden Cockerel books to take along and show as examples. It was not that he lacked pride in his work — he was just not possessive — but he was more concerned with his next project than with work from the past.

Later in 1959, a descriptive bibliographical list of sixty-seven titles was in proof form when tragically, Mary Kirkus, who had been ill for some time, suddenly died.[7] Once again, circumstances dictated that it should fall to Patience to complete the task. Mary had been an experienced and trained bibliographer, and Patience, who felt completely unqualified, was very nervous of tackling such an exacting job. She wrote to Dent at the beginning of 1960, asking if they could supply a simple manual of bibliography which she could consult. She also mentioned that John Harris, an old friend of Robert and herself, who was the Librarian of Ibadan University in Nigeria, would be visiting shortly for a week or so and had volunteered to help.

After studying Mary's proofs of the bibliography, John and Patience both came to the conclusion that some important pieces of information were missing from some of the entries and that other aspects of Gibbings's writing and engraving should be included in addition to the basic listing of illustrated books. The essential priority was a list of articles written by and about him. In the circumstances, Dent were happy to postpone publication and give Patience and Harris some time to make alterations and additions — within reason!

The *Collected Works*, now entitled *The Wood Engravings of Robert Gibbings*, was published on 5 November 1959 — in time to be included in the bibliography.

The edition was of 4,075 copies, 200 of which were issued for sale in America, with the imprint of Quadrangle Books Inc. of Chicago. On 22 March, Patience mentioned in a letter to Dent that she was pleased to see that 'it was *top* of the "Books of the week" list in the *New York Times*.'

The revisions to the bibliography became more extensive and eventually Dent agreed to a major redesign of the whole book which inevitably delayed publication. Although John Harris's expertise was of enormous help, after his return to Africa such a long-distance collaboration was bound to be difficult. However, Patience found another source of support and advice in Evan Gill, who had published his major bibliography of the work of his brother in 1953, and was working on an inventory of Eric Gill's inscriptional work. Patience had been able to provide information about the carved lintel over the door at Four Elms in Waltham.

For Robert's bibliography, in addition to Kirkus's descriptive list of books written and illustrated by Gibbings, a 'chronological check list of books, articles, and other ephemera written, illustrated, printed or published by Gibbings', and a 'chronological check list of critical and bibliographical references to Robert Gibbings', were added by Patience and John Harris. Patience had also been delighted to receive a fascinating first-hand account of printing at the Golden Cockerel Press written by Albert Cooper, the pressman. This was accompanied by a plan of the layout of the Press which she insisted on including, together with a section of illustrations showing pages from books demonstrating the integration of text and image.

The bibliography was finally published at the beginning of 1962. Evan Gill wrote to Patience in praise of the book, which he found 'neat, compact and very easy-on-the-eye .... It is sad to think that Mary Kirkus did not live to reap what she had so largely sown — I am quite certain that she would have approved whole-heartedly all that you both did to complete her work'.[8]

However taxing these projects had proved, Patience was faced with yet another challenge. The possibility of a memorial exhibition was raised in the autumn of 1958 and in February 1959 Charles Ede had written to the Victoria & Albert Museum suggesting it might be an appropriate venue. This meant more work for Patience but at least she had made useful contacts and had already tracked down important material while researching her book. In November 1959, she placed an advertisement in *The Times* asking for people with examples of Robert's work to contact her — and the response was good. When she viewed the two exhibition rooms at the V&A her heart sank — it seemed an impossibly large space to fill with such small pieces of art — however, so many items were forthcoming that in the event material was left out. A Press View was held on 28 January 1960 and the exhibition opened to the public on the following day — it closed on 28 March.[9] Reviews of the exhibition were very favourable and Patience received many letters of congratulation on its success.

Montague Weekley, an old friend, wrote an article on Gibbings and the art of wood-engraving, to publicise the Memorial Exhibition, which was published in

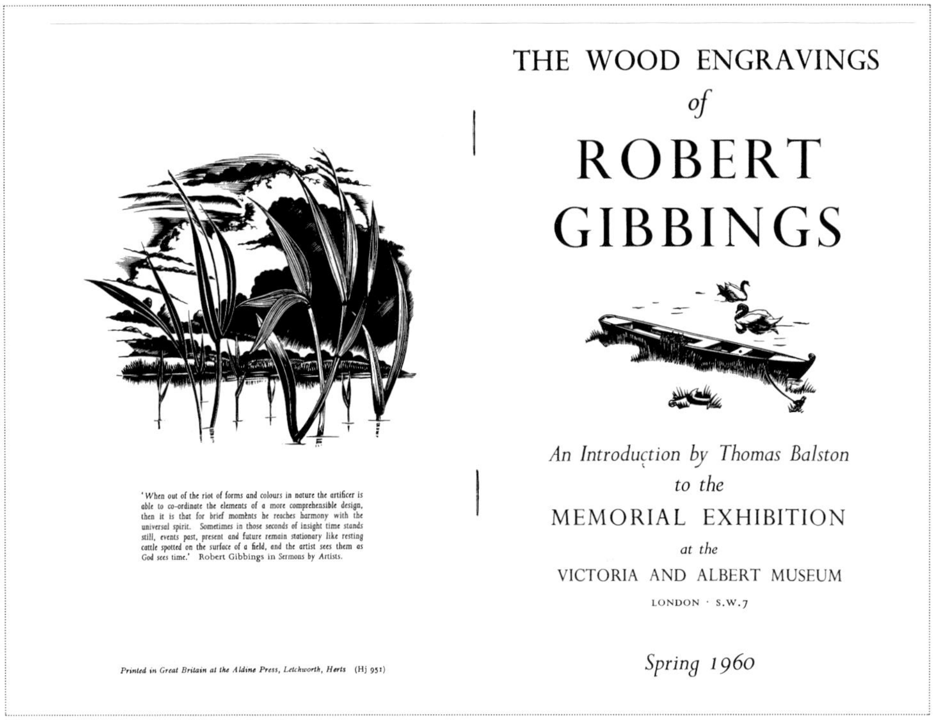

396 Cover of the booklet that was published to accompany the Memorial Exhibition held at the Victoria & Albert Museum in 1960. Under the engraving of the river Thames on the back cover is a quotation from Gibbings's essay published in *Sermons by Artists*: 'When out of the riot of forms and colours in nature the artificer is able to co-ordinate the elements of a more comprehensible design, then it is that for brief moments he reaches harmony with the universal spirit. Sometimes in those seconds of insight time stands still, events past, present and future remain stationary like resting cattle spotted on the surface of a field, and the artist sees them as God sees time'. Page size 228 x 152 mm. RUL.

The Listener. Entitled 'A Red-headed Bohemian', Weekley harked back to the 1920s when he had first met Gibbings in the artistic circles of Chelsea; impressed by his physical presence, he likened him to Augustus John: 'He and Gibbings appeared to be reincarnations of a bearded, stalwart splendour which had flourished in the preceding century's Bohemias [*sic*].'[10] John Hadfield had also proved useful in publicising the event by writing a review of Gibbings's life and work in an article which appeared in *Country Life*. He opened the article with the comment: 'The Memorial Exhibition ... is a revelation of an outsize talent, matching the outsize physique and personality of a remarkable and loveable man.'[11] That same month, Hadfield also gave a memorial lecture at the V&A, summing up Robert's career and personality:

> ... nobody who knew him — either his old friends or his chance acquaintances in pub or field or café — was ever likely to forget him as a person.
>
> In an age of Little Men, who shave their chins, wear mass-made neckties, fix their gaze on security, and seek their relaxation in the Television screen, Robert was a decidedly uncommon man ... whose philosophy of life was founded on the belief that tomorrow never comes, and who found perfect happiness in the sight of a boat or butterfly, a pebble on the path, or a group of ducks and rushes by the river's edge.
>
> Though he was, as he often said, a close-to-nature man, he was the gayest and most zestful companion any friend could have.[12]

A booklet was published to accompany the exhibition at the V&A, which contained the introductory essay Tom Balston had written for the *Collected Works*. Balston insisted on a note being attached to his essay as he wanted to explain that he had been unable, through lack of space, to say enough about the character of the man himself — to make up for this deficiency he included a quotation from the short postscript, written by Patience, to Gibbings's own 'Recollections' in the

Collected Works (*The Wood Engravings of Robert Gibbings*). It is also fitting that this biography should end with her words:

> His questing mind carried him into a diversity of worlds, and in his warm response to all whom he encountered he gave lavishly of himself — his time, his skill and his enthusiasm. His work both with the Golden Cockerel Press and the Society of Wood Engravers was of profound value to the world of book production and to his fellow artists. His handsome massive person will be remembered with gladness from Cork to the South Seas.

Notes

NOTES TO INTRODUCTION

1 Thomas Balston, *The Wood-engravings of Robert Gibbings*, London: Art and Technics, 1949. Patience Empson (ed.), *The Wood Engravings of Robert Gibbings*, introduction by Thomas Balston, London: J. M. Dent & Sons Ltd, 1959.

2 A. Mary Kirkus, Patience Empson and John Harris, *Robert Gibbings: a Bibliography*, London: J. M. Dent & Sons Ltd, 1962.

3 Simon Brett, 'Gibbings & Grey and *The Charm of Birds*', a review of a book of twenty wood-engravings printed from original blocks engraved by Gibbings, introduced and edited by Richard Landon, and published by the Friends of the Thomas Fisher Rare Book Library, Toronto, Barbarian Press, 1998. The review was published in *Parenthesis*, no. 4, April 2000, p. 47.

NOTES TO CHAPTER 1 AN IRISH CHILDHOOD 1889–1910

1 Letter from Gibbings to Nicholas Wreden, Vice-President of Dutton, Gibbings's American publisher, 6 December 1948, RUL.

2 Extract from a radio talk Gibbings gave as part of a series entitled 'I speak for myself' broadcast by the BBC on the Far Eastern Service, 23 April 1951. The script is in RUL.

3 Robert Gibbings, *Sweet Thames Run Softly*, London: J. M. Dent & Sons Ltd, 1940, pp. 202–03.

4 Robert Gibbings, *Sweet Cork of Thee*, London: J. M. Dent & Sons Ltd, 1951, pp. 43–44.

5 Robert Gibbings, *Lovely is the Lee*, London: J. M. Dent & Sons Ltd, 1945, p. 134.

6 *Sweet Cork of Thee*, p. 67.

7 Ibid.

8 Ibid. p. 72.

9 Ibid. p. 69.

10 Ibid. pp. 61–62.

11 Lennox Robinson, Tom Robinson, Nora Dorman, *Three Homes*, London: Michael Joseph Ltd, 1938, p. 70.

12 *Sweet Thames Run Softly*, p. 99.

13 Robert Gibbings, *Coming Down the Wye*, London: J. M. Dent & Sons Ltd, 1942, pp. 123–24.

14 *Sweet Cork of Thee*, p. 66.

15 Robert Gibbings, *Coming Down the Seine*, London: J. M. Dent & Sons Ltd, 1953, p. 76.

16 *Sweet Cork of Thee*, p. 197.

17 Robert Gibbings, 'Some Recollections', from *The Wood Engravings of Robert Gibbings*, ed. Patience Empson with introduction by Thomas Balston, London: J. M. Dent & Sons Ltd, 1959, p. xxxi. 'Some Recollections' are uncompleted autobiographical notes.

18 Ibid. p. xxxii.

19 *Sweet Cork of Thee*, pp. 197–98.

20 From an obituary by Stephen Farrington in *The Grammarian*, vol.1, no. 9, May 1958, p. 11.

21 *Sweet Thames Run Softly*, p. 124.

22 Ibid. p. 228.

23 Ibid. p. 51.

24 *Coming Down the Seine*, pp. 21–22. One of his pupils at the Sunday school was Patrick Hennessy who went on to be knighted as a leading industrialist and executive head of Ford. See the *Cork Examiner*, 21 March 1969.

25 Ibid. p. 14.

26 *Lovely is the Lee*, p. 134.

27 *Sweet Thames Run Softly*, p. 203.

28 *Lovely is the Lee*, p. 137.

29 Robert Gibbings, 'My Career in Medicine', *Medical World*, vol. 85, no. 1, July 1956, pp. 76 and 79–80.

30 Robert Gibbings, *Over the Reefs*, London: J. M. Dent & Sons Ltd, 1948, p. 216.

31 The buildings of the Crawford Art School now house the Crawford Art Gallery and Nelson's Place has been renamed Emmet Place.

32 Robert Gibbings, *Trumpets from Montparnasse*, London: J. M. Dent & Sons Ltd, 1955, pp. 69–70.

NOTES TO CHAPTER 2 LONDON: THE SLADE AND CSAC 1911–1913

1 George Charlton, 'The Slade School of Fine Art', *The Studio*, vol. 132, no. 643, October 1946, p. 116.

2 C. Gregory (ed.), *The Great Artists, Spencer*, part 78, vol. 4, London, 1986, p. 2490.

3 Joseph Hone, *The Life of Henry Tonks*, London: William Heinemann Ltd, 1939, p. 75.

4 John Woodson, *Mark Gertler, Biography of a Painter, 1891–1939*, London: Sidgwick & Jackson, 1972, p. 55.

5 *Coming Down the Wye*, pp. 63–64.

6 Gretchen Gerzina, *A Life of Dora Carrington*, London: John Murray, 1989, p. 20.

7 Paul Nash, *Outline, an Autobiography*, London: Faber and Faber, 1949, p. 90.

8 Ibid. p. 102.

9 Thomas Balston, *The Wood-engravings of Robert Gibbings*, London: Art and Technics Ltd, 1949, p. 14.

10 Robert Gibbings, *Till I End my Song*, London: J. M. Dent & Sons, 1957, pp. 73–75.

11 *Coming Down the Wye*, p. 63.

12 'Some Recollections', p. xxix.

13 Ibid. pp. xxix–xxxi.

14 Balston, *The Wood-engravings of Robert Gibbings*, p. 15.

15 James Hamilton, *Wood Engraving & the Woodcut in Britain c. 1890–1990*, London: Barrie & Jenkins Ltd, 1994, p. 53.

16 Rooke had joined an evening class in 1904, run by the reproductive engraver Ralph Beedham, at the Bolt Court School of Photo-engraving and Lithography. This was a technical school for process block making.

17 Joanna Selborne has pointed out that in fact Sidney Lee had introduced a class in 'Woodcuts in Colour and Wood Engraving' in 1905 but it was Rooke who eventually raised the status and recognition of the medium. See Joanna Selborne, *British Wood-engraved Book Illustration 1904–1940*, Oxford: Clarendon Press, 1998, p. 55.

18 Sylvia Backemeyer, 'The School of Book Production and its Influence', *Object Lessons*, London: Lund Humphries, 1996, p. 39.

19 'Some Recollections', pp. xxxii–xxxiii.

20 Balston made a reference to another print of this period, entitled *The Pilot Boat*. No trace of this engraving has been found but it was reputed to have hinted at the development of Gibbings's vanishing line technique. See Balston, *The Wood-engravings of Robert Gibbings*, p. 16.

21 Robert Gibbings,'Thoughts on Wood', *The Saturday Book*, no. 17, London: Hutchinson, 1957, pp. 207–13.

22 Nash, *Outline*, p. 146.

23 Ibid. p. 167.

24 Ibid. pp. 172–73.

25 Frances Spalding, *Roger Fry, Art and Life*, London: Granada Publishing, 1980, p. 154.

26 Ibid.

27 Nash, *Outline*, pp. 92–93.

28 See John Blatchly, 'The Bookplates of Robert Gibbings', *Bookplate Journal*, vol. 13, no. 2, September 1995, pp. 62–81.

29 'Some Recollections', p. xxxiii.

NOTES TO CHAPTER 3 WAR AND MARRIAGE 1914–1919

1 'Some Recollections', pp. xxxiii–xxxiv.

2 Balston, *The Wood-engravings of Robert Gibbings*, p. 16.

3 John Masefield, *Gallipoli*, London: Heinemann, 1917, p. 39.

4 'Some Recollections', p. xxxiv.

5 Letter from Gibbings to his father, 5 May 1915. Letters quoted from Gibbings to his father are from a collection of correspondence sent from the front, now in the possession of Diana Gibbings, the widow of Patrick, Robert's eldest son.

6 Letter from Gibbings to his father, 10 June 1915.

7 Letter from Gibbings to his father, 1 July 1915.

8 Ibid.

9 Records of Robert Gibbings's military service are held in the Public Records Office at Kew (WO 339/25940).

10 The photograph appeared in the *Illustrated London News*, January 15, 1916, pp. 80–81.

11 'Some Recollections', p. xxxiv.

12 Ibid. p. xxxv.

13 Ibid. p. xxxiv. Gibbings is muddled in this account of the voyage home confusing it with his earlier voyage on the *Letitia*.

14 Letter from Gibbings to his father, Bedford Hotel, 25 September 1917.

15 'Some Recollections', p. xxxiv–xxxv.

16 Ibid. p. xxxv.

17 Gibbings went before a medical board at Caxton Hall on 4 April 1918.

18 Balston, *The Wood-engravings of Robert Gibbings*, p. 17.

19 Reference from Frederick Burridge, 2 October 1918. Gibbings correspondence, Imperial War Museum, London.

20 Letter to a member of staff at the Imperial War Museum. Gibbings correspondence, Imperial War Museum, London.

21 Letter from Gibbings to the Imperial War Museum, 13 February 1920. Gibbings correspondence, Imperial War Museum, London.

22 *Daily Sketch*, 24 February 1920.

23 'Some Recollections', p. xxxv.

NOTES TO CHAPTER 4 GETTING ESTABLISHED 1920–1923

1 The bookplate appeared in *The Studio*, vol. 75, December 1918, and the anniversary address in vol. 77, September 1919.

2 The advertisement appeared in *The Studio*, vol. 77, July 1919.

3 Malcolm C. Salaman, 'The Woodcuts and Colour-prints of Captain Robert Gibbings', *The Studio*, vol. 76, February 1919, pp. 3–10.

4 Gibbings in fact made very few woodcuts in the strict definition of the term. Woodcutting involves cutting on a block made from a plank (usually of a relatively soft fruit-wood) with grain running along it, using a knife. Gibbings favoured wood-engraving, in which the block is made from a section cut across the grain of the wood (usually a hard wood — typically boxwood). Burins are used to engrave the image on the polished end-grained surface of the block. The final appearance of the print can often not show the precise technique used and confusion arises because the term woodcut is commonly used to refer to both processes. Many of Gibbings's prints, with their simple use of of black and white masses, could easily have been made as woodcuts, but he preferred the control and precision of wood-engraving.

5 Balston, *The Wood-engravings of Robert Gibbings*, p. 18.

6 The Japanese technique, printing from blocks brushed with watercolour and using pads made from the leaves of the bamboo to apply the pressure, produced delicate and expressive artisitic results where each print had an individual character and could only be reproduced commercially as half-tones. The European style, for which commercial inks could be used and the blocks printed on presses, lent itself to wider applications and opened up the potential for use as book illustration.

7 M. C. Salaman (ed.), *Modern Woodcuts and Lithographs by British and French Artists*, London: The Studio Ltd, 1919. This special number of *The Studio* included a paragraph on Gibbings's early work and four illustrations of his engravings.

8 'Some Recollections', p. xxxv. Joanna Selborne has commented that Gibbings's perception of his images 'as musical compositions echoes Kandinsky's aesthetic as translated by Wadsworth and reflects the language of Imagist poetry advocated by Ezra Pound', *British Wood-engraved Book Illustration 1904–1940*, p. 93.

9 'Some Recollections', p. xxxv.

10 Wadsworth had begun his art training in Germany, where he had been sent to study engineering draughtsmanship but found himself distracted by art classes at the Knirr Art School, where he was introduced to the German ideas on woodcutting. In 1913 he had been impressed by the Italian Futurist movement and adopted their ideas of the importance of the machine age. He met Wyndham Lewis in the same year and soon became one of the most loyal members of the Vorticist Group, contributing woodcuts to the journal *Blast* in 1914.

11 *Voices*, vol. 3, no. 1, February 1920, used a half-tone reproduction of *The Retreat from Serbia* as a frontispiece and *An Irish Question* appeared in *The Apple of Beauty and Discord*, vol. 1, 1920, p. 110.

12 Letters from Gibbings to the Dunster House Bookshop, 1919–24, are in the Clark Library.

13 The Senefelder Club was named after the inventor of lithography, Alois Senefelder.

14 Joanna Selborne,'The Society of Wood Engravers: the early years', *Craft History*, no. 1, 1988, p. 156.

15 Philip Hagreen, another engraver in the circle, looking back very late in his life, claimed, in a letter to David Knott of 19 June 1982, that it was he who made the proposal to Gibbings. A copy of the letter is in the Gibbings archive, RUL.

16 Minutes of the first meeting, 27 March 1920, The Society of Wood Engravers' archive.

17 *The Studio*, vol. 80, 1920, p. 156. Gibbings's engraving *Spot* appeared on the same page.

18 Prices were three guineas for *Melleha*, two guineas for *Clear Waters*, with small prints such as *Fowey Harbour* at one guinea — total sales for the whole exhibition amounted to £268 6s 0d, including a few sales to institutions such as the Contemporary Art Society.

19 *The Sunday Times*, November 1920.

20 *Yorkshire Post*, November 1920.

21 *Athenaeum*, November 1920.

22 'Some Recollections', p. xxxvi.

23 Ibid.

24 Ibid. Four engravings by Gibbings of London bridges were used by the St James's Advertising and Publishing Co. in a booklet entitled *Findlater's Corner* produced for Findlater, Mackie, Todd & Co., November 1921.

25 In a note on the imprint page, Gibbings advertised that most of the engravings were available in editions of twenty-five numbered and signed proofs.

26 Letter from Gibbings to the Dunster House Bookshop. The letter is dated 13 March 1922 and says that *Twelve Wood Engravings* had '... only been out about six weeks' which suggests a delay in printing as the publication date is given as 1921. Clark Library.

27 *Clear Waters* appeared in *The Studio*, vol. 81, March 1921, p. 115, and *William Walcot* in vol. 84, August 1922, p. 88.

28 Herbert Furst, 'The Modern Woodcut', *Print Collectors Quarterly*, vol. 8, no. 3, October 1921, pp. 292–96.

29 Gibbings exhibited eight engravings, most of which were editions of prints from *Twelve Wood Engravings*. Campbell Dodgson wrote another introduction for the second catalogue commenting on the rich diversity of style to be found in the work of the widening membership. Eric Gill had designed a badge for the Society depicting a box tree with the trunk pierced by an engraving tool which appeared on the cover of the catalogue. The device was also used for advertisements and a much larger version was produced for a poster printed in red, green and blue by Hilary Pepler at the St Dominic's Press in Ditchling. Philip Hagreen felt that the success of the exhibition was partly due to the poster which 'on the tube made all other posters look tawdry'. See Joanna Selborne, 'The Society of Wood Engravers: the Early Years', p. 159.

30 John Dreyfus, 'Some correspondence between Robert Gibbings and Thomas Balston', *Matrix 9*, Winter 1989, p. 38.

31 Letter from Gibbings to Balston, 21 April 1922. Clark Library.

32 Letter from Gibbings to Balston, 28 April 1922. Clark Library. Gibbings had been impressed by an article he had read in the *New York Tribune* by the American novelist, John Dos Passos, who he proposed as the author of the book.

33 See *Coming Down the Wye*, p. 1.

34 The Pilkington family had founded the famous glass manufacturing company and her father set up the successful Pilkington Tile Company. Margaret was a student at the Slade in 1913 and the next year joined Rooke's wood-engraving class at the Central School. Her father, a respected and well-known figure in Manchester, was a govenor of the Whitworth Institute. Margaret became a member of the Council of Whitworth Art Gallery in 1925 and in 1936 was to become an honorary director and take over the running of the gallery. The Whitworth became a regular venue for the Society of Wood Engravers and Margaret and Robert worked closely together on Society matters for many years.

35 Letter from Gibbings to Balston, 24 July 1922, Clark Library.

36 Letter from Gibbings to Balston, 30 December 1922, Clark Library.

37 *The Studio*, vol. 85, January 1923, p. 60.

38 John Dreyfus identified the anonymous reviewer in his article 'Some correspondence between Robert Gibbings and Thomas Balston', *Matrix 9*, Winter 1989, p. 45.

39 Letter from Gibbings to Balston, 6 March 1923, Clark Library.

40 The portfolios were covered in maroon cloth and measured 210 x 142 mm. Proofs of twelve wood-engravings used in *Erewhon*, printed by Gibbings on Japanese paper, were included in each portfolio. The edition was limited to twenty-five copies.

41 'Some Recollections', p. xxxvi.

42 Letter from Gibbings to Balston, 6 March 1923. Clark Library.

43 At a meeting on 25 February 1922, Paul Nash and Eric Daglish were accepted as full members and David Jones exhibited for the first time as a non-member at the annual exhibition. The minutes record a series of conditions and regulations passed concerning the contentious issue of the eligibility of certain categories of prints for inclusion in exhibitions: note seven stated 'No bookplates eligible for exhibition', number eight stated that 'preference will continue to be given to black & white prints'. Quotations from Society minutes that follow are all from records in the Society's archive.

44 As artists, the new wave of wood-engravers wanted to divorce themselves from the decline, as they saw it, of wood-engraved book illustration in the nineteenth-century — particularly from the work of commercial reproductive and facsimile engravers.

45 The family stayed with William and Ida Gibbings at 'Brangwyn', Libertus Road, Cheltenham.

46 'Some Recollections', p. xxxvii.

47 Ibid.

48 Ibid. pp. xxxvii–xxxviii.

NOTES TO CHAPTER 5 EARLY DAYS AT WALTHAM 1924–1925

1 Letter from Gibbings to Balston, 16 February 1924, Clark Library.

2 Ibid.

3 Letter from Gibbings to Mr Whitworth at Chatto & Windus, 29 February 1924, Chatto & Windus archive, RUL.

4 Roderick Cave has traced in detail the beginnings of the Press in his hitherto unpublished history of the Golden Cockerel Press, written in collaboration with Sarah Manson (see note 10 below). Cave graphically documents a winter of freezing cold, primitive living and cooking facilities: 'They rose shivering at five, lit the oil lamps which were their only source of light till the Winter sun came up, and boiled water for washing on a primus stove'. After tea and bread they started work on setting type with fingers numb from the cold. Also see Roderick Cave, 'Adam & Eve & Golden Cockerel', *Matrix 7*, Winter 1987, pp. 42–56.

5 A. E. Coppard, *It's Me, O Lord!*, London: Methuen & Co. Ltd, 1957, p. 236.

6 A. E. Coppard had previously trained as a book-keeper in the City but had abandoned that career in favour of becoming a professional writer. He was living in romantic poverty in a remote primitive cottage in a wood in south Oxfordshire.

7 Sue Walker and Martin Andrews, ed., 'Reminiscences of Albert Cooper, Pressman at the Golden Cockerel Press', *Matrix 9*, Winter 1989, p. 12.

8 Taylor was respected by his loyal staff, and Cooper regularly visited him in hospital, taking him fruit cake made by his wife to cheer him up. Hal never recovered and he died on 12 March 1925, leaving small legacies to his workers — Albert received fifty pounds, Taylor's overcoat and his writing desk. Cooper used the money as a deposit on a bungalow he had built in Ruscombe, a mile or so from the Press.

9 Letter from Gay Taylor to Charles T. Jacobi, 6 November 1923, Bodleian Library, University of Oxford: John Johnson, Golden Cockerel 1.

10 Roderick Cave and Sarah Manson's history of the Golden Cockerel Press, 1920–59, to be published by the British Library in 2002. Although the Gibbings family moved into the cottage in February 1924, the agreement to purchase was not signed until March and the annual rent of £40 for the house was not finalised until May. It was a very flexible arrangement, giving Gibbings the option of renting the house and the well-stocked garden on a 7, 14 or 21 year lease. This did not include all the land — about three acres of meadow land was rented on a separate short term tenancy.

11 Ibid.

12 A. C. Cooper, 'Notes on the printing methods of the Golden Cockerel Press', A. Mary Kirkus, *Robert Gibbings, a Bibliography*, London: J. M. Dent & Sons Ltd, 1962, p. 149.

13 Robert Gibbings, 'The Golden Cockerel Press', *The Colophon*, part 7, no. 6, September 1931.

14 Francis MacNamara had previously worked with Gay Taylor on the translation of *The Lives of Gallant Ladies* from the French.

15 Balston, *The Wood-engravings of Robert Gibbings*, p. 22. Thereafter, Balston commented, Gibbings generally used more harmonious papers, especially Batchelor's handmade; Van Gelder, unbleached Arnold or Kelmscott papers were also used.

16 Gibbings, 'The Golden Cockerel Press', *The Colophon*.

17 Letter from Gibbings to Balston, 6 October 1924, Clark Library.

18 Letter from Gibbings to the Dunster House Bookshop, 11 October 1924, Clark Library.

19 *Observer*, December, 1924.

20 Robert Gibbings, 'Memories of Eric Gill', *Book Collector*, vol. 2, no. 2, 1953, p. 95.

21 Letter from Eric Gill to his sister Enid Clay, 1 March 1924, Clark Library.

22 John Wilson, manager of Bumpus, was a good friend to the Press and regularly made large orders for their books. At the beginning of 1925 Gibbings was able to sell to Wilson much of the old stock which helped to pay for a new Victoria platen press. In the *Spring List* for 1925 Gibbings announced that almost all Cockerel fine editions were out of print which Cave and Manson point out helped to persuade collectors that the books were scarce and encouraged them to order new editions promptly in order to secure copies.

23 Eric Gill's diaries are in the collections of the Clark Library.

24 Fiona MacCarthy, 'Gibbings and Gill: Arcady in Berkshire', *Matrix 9*, Winter 1989, p. 27.

25 Letter from Gibbings to Colette O'Neill, 20 September 1924, Clark Library. Collette O'Neill was the stage name of an actress daughter of Lady Mabel Annesley, a recent new member of the Society of Wood Engravers, who had also learnt to engrave with Rooke at the Central School of Art and who lived quite near to Waltham. Every few lines the letter is punctuated by a wittily appropriate engraving, mostly from *Song and Poems of Henry Carey*, which are pasted onto the paper. The complete letter was reproduced in *Matrix 9*, Winter 1989, inserted between pages 36–37.

26 Robert Gibbings, 'The Golden Cockerel Press', *The Woodcut*, no. 1, 1927, p. 18.

27 Letter from Desmond Chute to Eric Gill, dated Whitsunday 1925, Clark Library.

28 Gibbings resigned from the Double Crown Club several months before the dinner at which the book received the award on 24 February 1926. He did not attend the dinner and took no part in the heated discussions over the regulation that to be eligible for a crown, the publication must be 'for ordinary sale': 'crowning' was later abandoned altogether.

29 Gibbings, *The Woodcut*, pp. 14–16.

30 Ibid., pp. 16–18.

31 *The Beacon*, vol. 1, no. 2, March 1925, p. 55.

32 *Manchester Guardian*, 23 October 1925.

33 Gibbings, *The Woodcut*, p. 18.

34 Ibid.

35 'Recollections', p. xxxviii.

36 Gibbings, *The Woodcut*, p.18

37 *Coming Down the Wye*, p. 80. Gill lived in some old monastery buildings a few miles from Llanthony Abbey.

38 Letter from Gill to Gibbings, 3 October 1925, Gleeson Library.

39 Obituary, John Murray, *Daily Telegraph*, 24 July 1993, p. 17. His son, John R. Murray, remembers his father boasting that 'he learnt the art of typography from setting type in the nude with Robert Gibbings, who evidently had a strong belief that the best results were achieved if one was unhindered by clothes'. See John G. Murray, *A Gentleman Publisher's Commonplace Book*, London: John Murray, 1996, p. 5.

NOTES TO CHAPTER 6 THE END OF THE APPRENTICESHIP 1925–1927

1 From an unpublished typescript for a lecture on the history of the Society by Margaret Pilkington, John Rylands University Library, Manchester.

2 Selborne, 'The Society of Wood Engravers: The Early Years', p. 161.

3 A wide engraving tool that has a precisely serrated cutting edge which enabled a number of fine parallel lines to be cut at the same time.

4 Selborne, 'The Society of Wood Engravers: The Early Years', p. 163.

5 Some years later, in 1931, Gibbings wrote to Pike offering to lend him money: 'There is no need to think of repayment — time enough when your [father?] leaves you something substantial & if he doesn't I'm only too glad to have made some slight difference to you seeing as how but for you we'd probably now be on the dole.' Letter from Gibbings to Pike, 23 March 1931, Clark Library.

6 The house and land had been surveyed and evaluated in December 1924 and the estimated value was £975. The Estate Agent had commented that the rent Gibbings was paying was high but the house was not for sale until after Taylor's death. In June 1926 Gibbings had to pay £1425.

7 On the legal documents she is described as Mary Holme Wiggin of '7 Lansdowne Place Cheltenham, spinster.' Documents relating to the sale and purchase of the Golden Cockerel Press are in the possession of Diana Gibbings.

8 Stanley Morison was a leading and influential typographer of his day with an international reputation. He was appointed Typographic Adviser to the Monotype Corporation in 1923.

9 Cooper obviously had a talent as an artist but had had none of the advantages of a full-time training. But even as a printing apprentice, Cooper had made time to attend evening classes in the Fine Art department at the University of Reading. Twice a week Cooper would leave work at the Press and cycle the six miles to Reading to attend classes. One of his tutors was the printmaker Professor Allen Seaby, who was a notable exponent and practitioner of the Japanese coloured woodcut and Cooper tried his hand at this technique, but it was Gibbings who encouraged him to engrave on wood. When pressed for time, Gibbings asked Cooper to clear his blocks; Gibbings engraved to the outline of his image and Cooper cut away the surrounding areas of waste that were not to print. This was a laborious process but one that demanded care and the trust of the artist.

10 Letter from Eric Gill to Desmond Chute, 5 May 1926, Gleeson Library.

11 Letter from Gill to Gibbings, 15 January 1926, Gleeson Library.

12 Gibbings, 'Memories of Eric Gill', pp. 95–96.

13 Gibbings, 'The Golden Cockerel Press', *The Colophon*, unpaginated.

14 Letter from Gill to Gibbings, 2 February 1926, Gleeson Library.

15 Letter from Gill to Desmond Chute, 5 May 1926, Gleeson Library.

16 Prospectus of forthcoming publications of the Golden Cockerel Press, 1926.

17 Letters from Mathers to the Gibbingses, RUL.

18 Gill referred to Robert's travels in a letter to Moira, 27 February 1926, Gleeson Library.

19 Entry in Gill's diary, 15 May 1926.

20 René Hague worked with Gill. Later they established the printing firm of Hague & Gill together and René married Gill's daughter, Joan.

21 In a letter to Gill, dated 28 May 1926, Gibbings asked him to design a border that could be used as a standard design on the cover of the Press's lists. Gill designed a border of leaves for the *Autumn List* but it was never used again. At the back of the publication is a list of fine editions produced by the Press since March 1923 — of twenty-six titles, nineteen are marked as out of print, indicating the success of the Press.

22 Letter from Gibbings to Gill, 25 June 1926, Gleeson Library.

23 Gibbings designed covers for: *The Danger to St Pauls*, Jonathan Cape 1925; *The Noblest Frailty*, Constable 1925; *The Crime at Vanderlynden's*, Chatto & Windus 1926, who also offered a commission to design a cover for *The Simple Guide Series* which Gibbings declined, recommending Celia Fiennes instead.

24 Eric Gill was to spend most of the winter months in Salies-de-Béarn working on engravings for *Troilus*. He rented a room above a chemist's shop as a studio.

25 This is a reference to the New London Pavilion theatre which had been famous as a music hall. Charles Cochran took it over and the Pavilion gained new fame for putting on Cochran's legendary revues. Florence Mills, a rival black singer to Josephine Baker, starred in the revue 'Blackbirds' in 1926.

26 Celia Fiennes was a pupil of Noel Rooke's and they married in 1932.

27 Letters to or from these authors are in HRHRC.

28 The correspondence with Shaw is in HRHRC.

29 Letter from Gill to Gibbings, 19 March 1927, Gleeson Library.

30 Gibbings, *Coming Down the Wye*, p. 44.

31 Note from Gibbings to Gill, 31 March 1927, Clark Library.

32 Letter from Gibbings to Balston, 17 October 1927, Clark Library.

33 Letter from Gibbings to Gill, 26 February, the year is not given but evidently 1927, Clark Library.

34 Cave and Manson, unpublished history of the Golden Cockerel Press. Lucy Cook had studied with Montessori and later worked with A. S. Neill at Summerhill, his experimental school.

35 Postcards of engravings by Mabel Annesley, Gill, David Jones, John Nash, John Farleigh, Ravilious and Gibbings himself were produced — two sets were available, post free, at a price of two shillings each.

36 Gibbings, *The Woodcut*, pp. 19–22.

37 Joanna Selborne, '*Everyman* in a Barn', *Matrix* 14, Winter 1994, pp. 235–36. From an account of the occasion recalled by Doris Pleydell-Bouverie.

38 Letter from Gibbings to Ravilious, 20 January 1927, HRHRC. A large selection of these letters covering the period 1926–1933 has been edited by Joanna Selborne and published in *Matrix 14*, Winter 1994, pp. 15–39, and *Matrix 16*, Winter 1996, pp. 67–87.

39 Letter from Gibbings to Ravilious, 25 January 1927, HRHRC.

40 Letter from Ravilious to Gibbings, 10 May 1927, HRHRC.

41 Gibbings supplied a number of American dealers but dealt principally with the Chaucer Head Bookshop in New York, Dunster House Bookshop in Cambridge, Massachusetts, and the Walden Bookshop in Chicago. Cave and Manson provide details of the distribution arrangements in their unpublished history of the Golden Cockerel Press.

42 Under Gibbings's ownership the binding of books at the Press ceased and all books were sent out to be bound.

43 Gibbings, *The Woodcut*, p. 19.

44 John Rothenstein, review of *Troilus and Criseyde* in *The Bibliophile's Almanack for 1928*, pp. 75–76.

45 Letter from Gill to R. A. Walker, 7 September 1928, Clark Library.

46 *A catalogue of an exhibition held at the Whitworth Art Gallery, Manchester, spring 1928, of engravings on wood & copper from books printed and published by the Golden Cockerel Press at Waltham Saint Lawrence Berkshire*, p. 2. The catalogue was printed at the Press. A copy is in the collections of RUL.

47 This footnote was included in the catalogue accompanying the exhibition held at the St George's Gallery from 19 October to 3 November 1927.

NOTES TO CHAPTER 7 BUILDING ON SUCCESS 1927–1928

1 Stanley Morison, *A Review of Recent Typography in England, the United States, France and Germany, 1927*, London: The Fleuron Ltd, 1927, pp. 10 and 12.

2 Gibbings had also taken on some smaller commissions including illustrations for a book entitled *The Book of the Inn*, edited by Thomas Burke and published by George H. Doran Company of New York, in 1927. Gibbings engraved a rather poor image of the George Inn, Glastonbury, which was used as the frontispiece.

3 'Some Recollections', p. xxxix.

4 By 1947 fourteen reprints accounted for 77,050 copies.

5 Letter from Ravilious to Gibbings, 20 June 1927, HRHRC. Originally Celia Fiennes was to have been the illustrator of *The Twelve Moneths* but she fell ill with meningitis and Ravilious had taken over the commission.

6 Letter from Gibbings to Ravilious, 3 August 1927, HRHRC.

7 Letter from Moira Gibbings to Ravilious, 16 May 1928, HRHRC.

8 Cave and Manson, unpublished history of the Golden Cockerel Press.

9 Letter from Gibbings to Ravilious, 27 February 1927, HRHRC.

10 *Chanticleer, a Bibliography of the Golden Cockerel Press*, London: The Golden Cockerel Press, 1936, foreword and notes by the Partners in the Press, p. 28.

11 Gibbings, *The Woodcut*, p. 19.

12 The Golden Cockerel Press had no Greek types and the daybook in the archives at Oxford University Press shows that forty pages of Greek type were set by them. In his article on the Press in *The Colophon*, 1931, Gibbings stated that 'With the exception of the Greek text in Lucian's "True History", we have never published a book which has not been completely set up and printed in our own workshops.'

13 Letter from Gibbings to Balston, undated but late 1927 or early 1928, Clark Library.

14 Letter from Gibbings to Balston, 14 December 1927, Clark Library. From this letter it seems that Gibbings was occasionally exhibiting paintings — this time at the Chenil Gallery in Chelsea.

15 *Coming Down the Wye*, p. 81.

16 Fiona MacCarthy, *Eric Gill*, London: Faber and Faber, 1989, p. 227.

17 Letter from Gibbings to Gill, undated *c.* 1928, Clark Library.

18 Penelope Hughes-Stanton, *The Wood-engravings of Blair Hughes-Stanton*, Pinner: Private Libraries Association, 1991, pp. 12–13.

19 The Gate Theatre was founded in 1925 in premises near Covent Garden but these were closed the following year and in November 1927 it re-opened as the Gate Theatre Studio, with seats for 160, in premises which had formerly been a skittle alley, and prior to that a restaurant and music hall, in Villiers Street, off the Strand.

20 Gibbings, 'Memories of Eric Gill', p. 102.

21 Letter from Gibbings to Gill, 16 January 1928, Clark Library.

22 Stanley Morison wrote to Gill admiring the sculpture he had seen at the exhibition at the Chenil Gallery and asking if his agreement with the Golden Cockerel Press would allow him to cut some initial letters for the Cambridge University Press. Letter dated 2 March 1928, Clark Library.

23 Gibbings, 'Memories of Eric Gill', p. 96.

24 Possibly a trip to Barcelona or to Venice and Florence.

25 Letter from Gill to Gibbings, 25 May 1928, Gleeson Library.

26 *Miscellaneous Poems of Jonathan Swift* was edited by Ellis Roberts who was for some time literary editor of the *New Statesman*. He was a great supporter of the Golden Cockerel Press and frequently reviewed their books.

27 Letter from Gibbings to Gill, 26 May 1928, Gleeson Library.

28 The marketing was unusual as the first edition was an autographed limited edition of only two hundred deluxe copies and included two illustrations printed direct from the woodblock that were not to be in the standard edition. The book was well printed by the Riverside Press on high quality paper, which was very sympathetic to Gibbings's engravings, and given a luxurious binding. This edition by Houghton Mifflin is not mentioned in the Kirkus bibliography.

29 An English edition of *A Mirror for Witches* was published by Heinemann in September1928.

30 'Recollections', p. xxxix.

31 Gill had suggested offering a number of copies as flat sheets or bound in paper wrappers in the French style so that owners could have the book bound to their own taste. Letter from Gill to Gibbings, 29 May 1928, Gleeson Library.

32 Letter from Gibbings to Gill, 12 June 1928, Gleeson Library.

33 Letter from Gibbings to Gill, 16 June 1928, Gleeson Library.

34 Writing to Desmond Chute, Gill explained that he was 'Frightfully busy doing engravings for Canty Tales' and went on to inform Chute that he was 'now a salaried official of the Lanston Monotype Corpn: What ho! This means advice on 'type faces'. Salary v. handsome too! & I like typography don't you know'. Letter from Gill to Chute, 10 June 1928, Gleeson Library.

35 Letter from Gibbings to Gill, 30 June 1928, Gleeson Library.

36 René Hague's involvement in the Press was short lived as he seems to have been sacked. He later married Joan Gill and with his father-in-law set up the printing firm of Hague and Gill at Pigotts.

37 *Sweet Thames Run Softly*, p. 212.

38 Even in the 'Eden' of the camp at Motzenmuhle, Gibbings retrospectively noted that he experienced some indications of the attitude towards the Jews that would emerge with full horror later. See 'Paradise Lost', *Sun Bathing Review*, vol. 8, no. 29, Spring 1940, pp. 8–9, written by Gibbings under the pseudonym 'W. St Lawrence'. Nudism was eventually banned in Nazi Germany.

39 Note in *Chanticleer* p. 32, 'An almost perfectly proportioned book, of which the Press is duly proud.'

40 Gill had designed a set of initial letters for *Lamia*, but to speed things up Ralph Beedham had been engaged to cut them.

41 *Till I End My Song*, p. 64.

42 Ibid.

43 Ibid. p. 65. The sculpture was rediscovered in 1989 by the author, abandoned in the grounds of the Hind's Head at Bray. It has since been restored and is now in the collections of The Museum of Reading.

44 Ibid.

45 Charles T. Jacobi, 'The Work of the Private Presses vii: the Golden Cockerel Press', *Penrose Annual*, vol. 30, 1928, pp. 17–18.

NOTES TO CHAPTER 8 NEW HORIZONS 1929–1931

1 'Some Recollections', pp. xxxix–xl.

2 The contract committed Gibbings to working on two books (the other to be decided) for a fee of £150 in advance and £100 on completion. Approximately twenty wood-engravings were to be provided; ten full-page and the rest to be smaller decorations. RUL.

3 *Mutiny on the Bounty* was published in 1932 and written by James Norman Hall in collaboration with Charles Nordhoff. It was the first of a trilogy which continued with *Men Against the Sea* and *Pitcairn Island* in 1934.

4 *Trumpets from Montparnasse*, p. 63.

5 'Some Recollections', p. xl.

6 Robert Gibbings, 'My Best Friend', *John O'London's Weekly*, vol. 61, January 1952, p. 90.

7 Smaller versions of this cockerel became the device generally used by the Press until 1933.

8 Letter from Moira to Gill, 21 February 1929, Clark Library.

9 Letter from Gill to Moira, 25 February 1929, Gleeson Library.

10 Letter from Moira to Gill, 28 February 1929, Gleeson Library.

11 Letter from Moira to Gill, 11 March 1929, Gleeson Library.

12 The big disadvantage of copper-engraving is that it requires a different kind of press than that used for relief printing with type and therefore it was difficult to integrate the image with the text, necessitating a second printing or, more usually, the copper-engraving appearing on a separate page. But this fact could also have its advantages. Gibbings commented: 'We are therefore able to set up the type at our own convenience & fill in delays caused by dilatory authors or artists'.

13 Gibbings, *The Colophon*, unpaginated.

14 Letter from Gibbings to Gill, 8 May 1929, Gleeson Library.

15 Letter from Gibbings to Ravilious, 2 November 1928, HRHRC.

16 Letter from Ravilious to Gibbings, 7 November 1928, HRHRC.

17 Letter from Gibbings to Ravilious, 23 November 1928, HRHRC.

18 This was partly due to a commission that Ravilious had started with Edward Bawden for a large mural for the refreshment room of Morley College in London.

19 The artist William McCance had married the wood-engraver Agnes Miller Parker in 1918. In the early twenties the couple had lived near Earl's Court — not far from the Gibbingses. They were part of a social circle that included Blair Hughes-Stanton, his wife Gertrude Hermes and the writer Naomi Mitchison. In 1930 he became controller of the Gregynog Press in Wales.

20 A method of printing coloured images based on a delicate stencil technique.

21 Robert Gibbings, 'The Art of the Book: The Golden Cockerel Press', *The Studio*, vol. 97, February 1929, pp. 98–101.

22 Gibbings, *The Woodcut*, p. 19.

23 Letter from Gill to Morison, 16 June 1928, published in Nicolas Barker, *Stanley Morison*, London: Macmillan, 1972, p. 233.

24 Ibid.

25 Gibbings had kept to the spirit of his agreement with Gill and did not object to his involvement with Monotype. His work for Monotype at this time consisted almost entirely of producing additional founts for his Gill Sans type series. Following on from Gill Sans, Morison had asked him to design a book face. For some years Gill had been working on ideas for a classical typeface which was later to be called Perpetua.

26 Also see James Mosley, 'Eric Gill and the Golden Cockerel Type', *Matrix 2*, Winter 1982, pp. 19–24.

27 Gibbings, 'Memories of Eric Gill', pp. 97–98.

28 Ravilious had designed a delightful decorative flower border to surround the title lettering by Gill on the cover of the prospectus and for the opening page he had engraved a large block of a cockerel crowing with a 'joyous expression', at Gibbings's request. The prospectus was printed on paper that carried a special watermark designed by Gill of a dove surrounded by the initials GCP, holding the P in its beak.

29 This was to have been an ambitious book, entirely illustrated by Gibbings, and designed as a uniform edition to *The Four Gospels*. The illustration on the sample page of Eve lying by the forbidden tree, shows that he intended to adopt a similar style to that which he used in *Lamia* but on a grander scale, perhaps hoping to match the achievement of Gill's work on *The Gospels*. The project was later abandoned when changes in the financial climate made such an ambitious book too risky an undertaking.

30 Letter from Gibbings to Balston, 3 June 1930, Clark Library.

31 Cave and Manson, unpublished history of the Golden Cockerel Press.

32 Maximilien Vox, 'British Wood Engraving of the Present Day', *The Studio*, vol. 99, March 1930, pp. 155–72.

33 Harold Child, 'Modern Illustrated Books: Artist and Typographer set a standard for the Connoisseur', *The Studio*, vol. 100, July 1930, pp. 33–41.

34 Malcolm Salaman, *The New Woodcut*, *The Studio*, special Spring number, 1930, p. 8.

35 Interview with Hughes-Stanton by Paul Collett, 1972, quoted in Penelope Hughes-Stanton, *The Wood-engravings of Blair Hughes-Stanton*, Pinner: Private Libraries Association, 1991, p. 15.

36 Letter from Gibbings to Ravilious, 20 October 1930, HRHRC. The letter continued: 'By the way we are holding an exhibition at Sanders in Oxford, opening next Saturday. Could you send us a few signed proofs of the Cockerel on page 1 of the Spring List … and we will exhibit 'em for sale'.

37 Letter from Gibbings to Tirzah Ravilious, 10 November 1930, HRHRC.

38 Letter from Moira Gibbings to Ravilious, 3 December 1930, HRHRC. The old wooden summerhouse that Patrick and Brigid had slept in before the extension to Four Elms had been built had been moved into the orchard and made habitable for guests.

39 Mention is made in letters of a book referred to as *Taplow* for which Tirzah had engraved a few blocks but it was never published.

40 Card in the Clark Library.

41 Churchill had published two books, both illustrated with wood-engravings by Lynton Lamb. They were limited editions printed on hand-made paper but Churchill employed printers to do the presswork for him although he involved himself in setting the type by hand.

42 Letter from John Johnson to Gibbings, 5 February 1931, the archives, Oxford University Press.

43 Letter from Moira to Chatto & Windus, 17 September 1931. Moira had previously written directly to Powys explaining that their immediate crisis in cash flow was due to the expense of work on *The Four Gospels*. A collection of correspondence between Gibbings, the Press, and Chatto & Windus is in the archives at RUL.

44 Letter from Moira to Chatto & Windus, 1 October 1931. Moira had sent a cheque for £50 which was the usual fee of approximately 10% on 475 copies but in this case they had agreed to pay 12½%.

45 Book review, *The Studio*, vol. 102, December 1931, p. 413.

46 'Some Recollections', pp. xl–xli.

47 Letter from Gibbings to Ravilious, 4 February 1931, HRHRC.

48 Letter from Gibbings to Ravilious, 11 March 1931, HRHRC.

49 Letter from Tirzah Ravilious to Gibbings, 13 March 1931, HRHRC.

50 Letter from Ravilious to Gibbings, 17 June 1931, HRHRC

51 Letter from Gibbings to Ravilious, 7 September 1931, HRHRC.

52 Ibid.

53 Letter from Gibbings to Ravilious, 11 September 1931, HRHRC.

54 Letter from Gibbings to Craig, 7 July 1931, HRHRC. A selection of the correspondence between Gibbings and Craig concerning *Preface to 'A Production'*, has been published in an article by Roderick Cave entitled 'A Cancelled Performance', *Matrix 13*, Winter 1993, pp. 80–98.

55 Letter from Gibbings to Craig, 22 September 1931, HRHRC. Robert's eldest son Patrick was suffering from 'mastoid trouble' and was waiting for an operation.

56 Letter from Gibbings to Craig, 2 December 1931, HRHRC.

57 Letter from Craig to Gibbings 26 August 1931, HRHRC.

58 'Arcady in Berkshire, South Sea Dress and Freedom in the English Countryside', *The Graphic*, 25 July 1931, p. 122.

59 Robert dug out the pool himself enlisting help from friends. The work was so exhausting that after a while Gibbings gave up and left an area in the middle of the pool as an island. The pool was circular, relatively small but deep enough to allow diving; it became the focal point for sunbathing.

60 In August 1932, Gibbings attended a naturist summer camp. Writing to Owen Rutter he reported that he had just returned from 'ten days with the Sunbathers'. Letter from Gibbings to Rutter, 17 August 1932, HRHRC.

61 Letter from Gibbings to Craig, 28 August 1931, HRHRC.

62 Unfortunately, although records of this film exist in the Pathé News archive, the film itself has been destroyed.

63 Eric Gill, *An Essay on Typography*, High Wycombe: Hague & Gill, 1931.

64 With this format the book is twice as high as it is wide and the double opening is consequently square.

65 Letter from Gill to Gibbings, 9 July 1931, Gleeson Library.

66 Letter from Gill to Desmond Chute, 15 February 1931, Gleeson Library.

NOTES TO CHAPTER 9 THE TRIUMPH BEFORE THE FALL 1931

1 John Dreyfus, *A Typographical Masterpiece*, San Francisco: The Book Club of California, 1990.

2 Gibbings, 'Memories of Eric Gill', pp. 96–97.

3 Ibid. p. 97.

4 Ibid. p. 98.

5 Ibid. pp. 98–100.

6 Ibid. p. 100.

7 Ibid. p. 98.

8 Letter from Mary Gill to Gibbings, 25 August 1931, Gleeson Library.

9 Beedham had been apprenticed to the firm of commercial engravers, Hare & Co. He had been trained as a 'facsimile' engraver and later became an instructor at the LCC School of Photo-engraving and Lithography in Bolt Court, London. As well as having immense technical skill he was also sensitive to the ideas of the

younger artists involved in the revival of wood-engraving. Amongst others he taught Joan Hassall to engrave. He had joined Gill's workshop in Ditchling in 1917 to learn about lettering and for many years was Gill's assistant, clearing his blocks and occasionally cutting floreated initials following Gill's designs. In 1921 the Ditchling Press published a little manual written by Beedham entitled *Wood Engraving* with an introduction by Gill; it was reprinted many times and an edition was published by Faber and Faber in 1946.

10 Letters quoted in Dreyfus, *A Typographical Masterpiece*, p. 44.

11 A forme is the page or pages of type assembled and secured within a chase (a metal frame) for printing at one impression.

12 On a proof of a page from *The Gospel According to Saint Mark*, Eric Gill commented about Cooper in a note pencilled in the margin: 'vid. Gibbings's original concept — and so all congratulations to the (almost) infallible Cooper!!' Quoted from entry no. 255 in *Modern Illustrated Books*, Blackwell's of Oxford Catalogue A1116, p. 31.

13 Albert Cooper recorded his reminiscences of the Press in the article 'Notes on the printing methods of the Golden Cockerel Press' published in the Kirkus bibliography and in an interview with Susan Walker and the author recorded in 1974 and published in *Matrix 9*, which have already been referred to. Ending the working day at half-past five enabled Cooper to attend evening classes at Reading University. In the arts and crafts tradition, he learnt to beat copper, design and make furniture, study letterforms, and generally dabble in the applied arts as well as attending painting and drawing classes. He had designed his own cottage, supervising the construction by a local builder, which he furnished with the products of his labours at the University. Gibbings had offered him a plot of land at Waltham, but Cooper wanted to preserve his independence and chose to live in a less isolated spot. Gibbings kept bees at Waltham and Cooper was happy to accept a hive for his garden.

14 Walker and Andrews, 'Reminiscences of Albert Cooper, Pressman at the Golden Cockerel Press', pp. 13–15.

15 Cooper, 'Notes on the Printing Methods of the Golden Cockerel Press', pp. 150–51.

16 Dreyfus, *A Typographical Masterpiece*, pp. 74–75. Harold Child was a distinguished journalist and enthusiast for fine printing. He was a founder member and a president of the Double Crown Club.

17 David Chambers, 'Sandford, Gibbings, Newbury and Rutter', *The Private Library*, vol. 8, no. 1, Spring 1985, p. 35.

18 Ibid. pp. 35–36.

NOTES TO CHAPTER 10 PEAKS AND TROUGHS 1931–1932

1 Gibbings, 'The Golden Cockerel Press', *The Colophon*, unpaginated.

2 Gertrude Hermes was also an enthusiastic sculptor and Gibbings later lent her the studio for short working holidays at Waltham with her daughters.

3 Walker and Andrews, 'Reminiscences of Albert Cooper, Pressman at the Golden Cockerel Press', p. 13.

4 Letter from Gibbings to Pilkington, 18 November 1931, RUL.

5 'Some Recollections', p. xli.

6 'Iorana' is a Tahitian word of greeting.

7 Robert Gibbings, *Iorana! a Tahitian Journal*, Boston & New York: Houghton Mifflin, 1932. The edition quoted from was published by Duckworth, London, 1932, p. 61. The book became the inspiration for a musical work by R. Nathaniel Dett (words by J. H. Quine) 1935. It was dedicated to Robert Gibbings — 'The lovely harmonies and subtle rhythms of the work evoke a tropical atmosphere which beckons the listener to dream of escape.'

8 Ibid. p. 65.

9 Ibid. pp. 65–66.

10 Ibid. p. 52.

11 Ibid. p. 74.

12 Ibid. p. 76.

13 Ibid. pp. 75–76.

14 Ibid. p. 74.

15 Robert Gibbings, *Blue Angels and Whales*, Harmondsworth: Penguin Books, 1938, p. 14.

16 Gibbings had seen a collection of Gauguin's letters in Tahiti which were the last he wrote and were claimed to have been found beside his body (see *Sweet Thames Run Softly*, pp. 101–02). An undated letter in the Clark Library from Gibbings to a Monsieur Brault shows that Gibbings was interested in buying the letters with the intention of publishing them.

17 *Iorana*, pp. 123–24.

18 *Coming Down the Wye*, p. 52. Gibbings said a friend modelled for the sculpture. He worked on it over a period of some years and later his second wife, Elisabeth, thought it was based on her as a model.

19 'Some Recollections', p. xli. Gibbings was mistaken in his account in which says he had written to the Orient Line in February.

20 Letter from Moira to John Murray, 1 February 1932, John Murray Archive.

21 Editions of the separate prints were also on sale and the Orient Line put a display of mounted prints in the window of their London office in Cockspur Street. Complimentary copies of the book were given to important clients by the managers of the Company.

22 The text of the booklet must have been based on a visit to Australia but no details of such a visit have been found. It is possible that Gibbings made such a voyage as part of one of his other expeditions. Brief references have been found to other trips but again no specific information has come to light. Gibbings makes a direct reference to a voyage to Australia with the Orient Line in *Trumpets from Montparnasse*, p. 68.

23 Gibbings began work on *Initiation* in June 1931. He wrote to Driberg on 19 June 1931, explaining that he was planning the book but had been interrupted by a horde of guests: 'Between this and Monday evening we are expecting relays of visitors amounting in all to over 50 …'. On 24 August, Gibbings explained his choice of typeface: '… Gill's Sans Serif type would be highly suitable being so to speak primitive in form …. I think it is very successful myself & will be pleasantly black to work to in the engravings' — the book was a collection of poems of the Didinga and Lango tribes translated by Driberg. Correspondence between Gibbings and Driberg concerning *Initiation* is in HRHRC.

24 Mentioned in correspondence in the Golden Cockerel Press papers, HRHRC.

25 *Sweet Thames Run Softly*, p. 72.

26 On 10 October 1932, the same month that *Consequences* was published, Gibbings wrote to Elizabeth Bowen asking if she had written anything which could be published as one of the Guinea Series. A few days later, Gibbings wrote again proposing another 'composite' book based on the deadly sins. At the beginning of November, Bowen accepted a suggestion that she be involved in a composite book, provisionally given the title *Fortunes*. In January 1933, Gibbings invited Bowen to Waltham to discuss her book in the Guinea Series and wanted to know when her manuscript would be ready. But writing on 26 January, he had to inform her that the project was off because he was selling the Press. The correspondence between Gibbings and Bowen is in HRHRC.

Gibbings had been negotiating with another of the authors contributing to *Consquences*, Séan O'Fáolain, to publish a collection of his short stories as another in the Guinea Series. However, on 24 August 1933, he had to write to O'Faoláin to explain that he was selling the Press but hoping that the new owners would carry on with the project. Unfortunately the project was dropped and O'Faoláin was disappointed. On 19 October, he wrote to Owen Rutter that he felt Gibbings had let him down '… by concealing from me the fact that this sale was contemplated'. Correspondence in HRHRC.

27 A. E. Coppard and Robert Gibbings, *Rummy, That Noble Game Expounded in Prose, Poetry, Diagram and 15 Engravings*, Waltham St Lawrence: The Golden Cockerel Press, 1932, pp. 2–3.

28 Ibid. p. 13. If Coppard was correct that the twins were three years of age, then they had gone on holiday in 1930, but if his memory was at fault, it might have been when letters from Lucy Cook show that Moira and Robert were both away in July 1929.

29 Ibid. pp. 36–37.

30 On 16 April 1932, Agnes Miller Parker wrote to Gibbings accepting the commission to illustrate *Daisy Matthews* and explaining that she had resigned from the Gregynog Press. She agreed to a fee of twenty pounds for four blocks and was excited at an opportunity to engrave an illustration of cats which was needed for one of the stories. Correspondence between Agnes Miller Parker and Gibbings concerning the production of *Daisy Matthews* is in HRHRC.

31 Ian Rogerson, *Agnes Miller Parker, Wood-engraver and Book Illustrator, 1895–1980*, Wakefield: The Fleece Press, 1990, p. 24.

32 Rupert Hart-Davis, *Hugh Walpole*, London: Hamish Hamilton, 1985, p. 60. (first published London: Macmillan & Co., 1952).

33 Letter from Gibbings to Ravilious, 11 March, 1932, HRHRC.

34 'Some Recollections', p. xli.

35 Paul Johnston (ed.), *The Book Collector's Packet*, no. 3, May 1932, p. 13.

36 Clare Leighton, *Wood-engravings and Woodcuts*, London: The Studio Ltd, 1932, p. 70.

37 Letter from Gibbings to Mary O'Sullivan, 29 July 1932, Clark Library.

38 Before Patrick was sent to St Piran's School, Robert and Moira had sent him and his sister, Brigid, to Summerhill, the boarding school run by the radical and experimental educationalist, A. S. Neill. The school had a controversial reputation as it gave pupils enormous freedom and Patrick and Brigid had spent much

of their time there climbing trees! Patrick found the old-fashioned discipline of St Piran something of a shock and was never really happy there. Later Patrick went to the naval college in Pangbourne.

39 Robert Gibbings, 'Llewelyn and Theodore', *Matrix 6*, Winter 1986, pp. 1–5. A typescript of these reminiscences written in 1953, and a letter from Llewelyn's widow Alyse, dated 19 December 1953 are in the Gibbings Collection, RUL.

40 Malcolm Elwin, *The Life of Llewelyn Powys*, London: John Lane The Bodley Head, 1946, p. 212.

41 Gibbings, 'Llewelyn and Theodore', p. 3.

NOTES TO CHAPTER 11 AN END AND A FRESH START 1933–1935

1 Letter from Gibbings to Ravilious, 31 January 1933, HRHRC.

2 Letter from Ravilious to Gibbings, 1 February 1933, HRHRC.

3 Letter from Gibbings to Ravilious, 2 February 1933, HRHRC.

4 His brother-in-law J. B. Pennefather was owner and manager of the hotel. Although Moira had left him, Gibbings still completed the order for a publicity brochure for which he used one of his own engravings and a strange image of a monkey with a book by John Farleigh. 'Jack' Pennefather had become a well-known radio announcer in South Africa after the war before returning to England.

5 Gibbings had been working on the blocks for *Lord Adrian* since October 1932. At the end of that month he wrote to Lord Dunsany apologising for a delay in sending proofs, mentioning financial and domestic difficulties. He explained that many of his American clients had gone bust or had returned large quantities of books. He also commented that his illustrations did not fit closely to the text but that 'creatures of the woods would suggest that background of nature which in the play is always present'. Correspondence between Lord Dunsany and Gibbings is in HRHRC.

6 Chambers, 'Sandford, Gibbings, Newbery and Rutter', p. 36. Much of the following account of the sale of the press is based on this article and draws upon the letters quoted.

7 Ibid.

8 Ibid.

9 Ibid. p. 37. Letter from Gibbings to Sandford, 24 May 1933.

10 Ibid. pp. 37–38. Sandford later recalled a visit to Waltham in the summer of 1933 in a review of Empson's *The Wood Engraving of Robert Gibbings* published in *John O'London* in 1959: '... I was swimming in his pool in the orchard ... he came running over the grass, golden mane and beard flowing, and dived, eighteen stone of sleek, red-gold flesh, into the deep water. The thought came to me ... was he once perhaps the benevolent river-deity of some ancient myth? But normally of course we saw him clothed — in town or country always a cosy figure in Irish tweed.

11 A few of Rutter's books were successful and one had been made into a film. A more serious aspect of his work was an interest in naval history and at one time he was President of the Writer's Circle and took part in establishing the Society of Authors.

12 Letter from Gibbings to Rutter, probably dating from November or December 1932, belonging to Joan Weatherlake, Rutter's daughter. Quoted in Cave and Manson's unpublished history of the Golden Cockerel Press.

13 Chambers, 'Sandford, Gibbings, Newbery and Rutter', p. 38.

14 Letter from Gibbings to Cooper, 5 May 1933, Cooper Collection, RUL. The 'small job for America' referred to was a book by Charles Dickens, called *Cricket on the Hearth*, which was published by the Limited Editions Club of New York in 1933. Designed by Gibbings, it was illustrated with seven watercolour plates by Hugh Thomson which Gibbings had arranged to be printed by the collotype process by John Johnson at Oxford University Press. But delay in getting a quotation from OUP meant that production was delayed. George Macy was becoming agitated and things did not improve when, on 23 June, Gibbings wrote to him in 'strictess confidence' that he was possibly getting rid of the Press and negotiating his role which was uncertain. Macy was concerned about working with the new owners; he did not want to deal with 'an unknown ... until he has proven that he is as superlative a printer as you are'. By August, Gibbings was able to send sample pages and a dummy of the book, but in September, it was Sandford who was writing to Macy to discuss the final stages of production — although Macy still hoped that Gibbings would oversee the printing. Correspondence concerning the production of *Cricket on the Hearth* is in HRHRC.

15 Letter from Gibbs to Cooper, undated, *c.* 1933, Cooper Collection, RUL.

16 Letter from Gibbings to Johnson, 31 July 1933, Bodleian Library, University of Oxford, John Johnson Collection, MS Johnson C.18 (fols 75–86).

17 Letter from Johnson to Gibbings, 28 February 1933, John Johnson Collection.

18 Letter from Gibbings to Johnson, 8 August 1933, John Johnson Collection.

19 Letter from Gibbings to Mackenzie, 5 April 1933, RUL.

20 Letter from Gibbings to Mackenzie, 10 May 1933, RUL.

21 *Sweet Thames Run Softly*, pp. 18–19.

22 Gibbings, 'A Revival in Wood Engraving', *Discovery*, vol. 14, October 1933, pp. 319–22. The article began with a useful survey of the history and the technique of wood-engraving and then documented the revival of the medium in the twentieth century. Gibbings ended by discussing his views on book illustration — the balance of wood-engraving with type and his theories on the 'unity of the page'.

23 Gibbings, 'A Garment for Sunbathing', *Sun Bathing Review*, vol. 1, no. 4, Winter 1933–34, p. 27.

24 'An Appreciation of Robert Gibbings', *Sun Bathing Review*, Spring 1958, p. 9.

25 Ibid.

26 Letter from Barford to Shaw, 25 May 1932, noted by David Knott when he saw the originals then, in the possession of J. N. Barford.

27 Fiona MacCarthy, 'Gibbings and Gill', *Matrix 9*, Winter 1989, pp. 34–35.

28 Letter from Gill to Rutter, 24 February 1934, Gleeson Library.

29 Letter from Gill to Moira, 27 December 1937, RUL.

30 Interview with Jean Harrison by the author in March 1990.

31 The print is dated 13 August 1933.

32 Gibbings became Godfather to Colonel Goodden's son, Peter.

33 *Chanticleer*, p. 40.

34 Letter from Gibbings to Walpole, undated *c.* 1934, Walpole Library, The King's School, Canterbury.

35 Rupert Hart-Davis, *Hugh Walpole*, London: Macmillan & Co. Ltd, 1952. Paperback edition London: Hamish Hamilton, 1985, p. 339.

36 It would seem that Gibbings was able to return Walpole's support as at the front of his novel *The Inquisitor*, published in 1935 and dedicated to Robert, Walpole had included a prefatory letter to 'My Dear Robert ... First I would like to acknowledge with what extreme pleasure I dedicate this book to you; modesty forbids my mentioning in public the reasons of my gratitude to you. You well know what they are.' One can only speculate on the reasons!

37 Letter from Gibbings to Rutter, 18 July 1934, HRHRC.

38 Gibbings had originally had the idea for *Sermons by Artists* in 1925. The book was to be a response to the fact that a group of clergymen (the Society of Parson Painters) held an exhibition of their pictures in Bond Street that year — Gibbings decided that artists should try their hand at writing sermons. The project was slow to develop and over the next few years many eminent artists were approached including Sir William Orpen, Jacob Epstein, C. W. R. Nevinson, Frank Dobson, A. J. Munnings, Wyndham Lewis, the cartoonist David Low, Sir William Rothenstein and Augustus John. On 28 December 1931, Henry Lamb wrote to Gibbings declining an invitation to contribute on the grounds that 'Much as I dislike Parsons my aversion from preaching is so far greater ...' — he preferred to express his feelings in his chosen medium. George Clausen felt the same and in a letter of 13 January 1932, he wrote: 'There's no reason why a parson shouldn't paint; and I think he would probably be a better parson if he did — But there is, it seems to me, every reason why a painter shouldn't preach! ... The painter has no concern of this kind; if he has anything to say it can only be through his own means of expression ...'. The project was still being worked on even while Gibbings was negotiating the sale of the Press. Eventually the new management completed the book but at least one contributor, Stanley Spencer, was rather unhappy about the change and annoyed that Gibbings had not told him about the sale of the Press and had been so secretive. Letters concerning *Sermons by Artists* are in HRHRC.

39 Sandford quoting Gibbings from *Sermons by Artists* in his article on Gibbings in *John O'Londons Weekly*, 1959.

40 A letter from Gibbings to C. B. Mortlock, dated 19 December 1932, shows how advanced plans had been. Gibbings wrote that 'We must get down to printing immediately after Christmas .... I wonder too what news you have of Munnings [the painter Alfred Munnings], it will be splendid if we could include his name in the list.' RUL.

41 Robert Gibbings, 'Exploring a Coral Reef', *Discovery*, vol.15, May 1934, p. 140.

42 'Some Recollections', p. xlii.

43 Pearn, Pollinger & Higham Ltd of Dean Street, Soho, London, were influential literary agents who represented a number of important authors including D. H. Lawrence. Later the firm moved to Maddox Street in Mayfair and later David Higham and Lawrence Pollinger formed their own companies. Pollinger remained Gibbings's agent for the rest of his life and still acts on behalf of his estate.

44 Letter from Gibbings to Johnson, 29 March 1935, Bodleian Library, University of Oxford, John Johnson Collection, MS Johnson C.18 (fols 75–86).

45 Copy of a testimonial written by Johnson concerning Gibbings, dated 8 April 1935, John Johnson Collection.

46 Letter from Gibbings to Johnson, 5 April 1935, John Johnson Collection.

47 Letter from Johnson to Gibbings, 8 September 1936, Archive of Oxford University Press.

NOTES TO CHAPTER 12 UNIVERSITY DAYS 1936–1940

1 Memorial lecture on Gibbings given by John Hadfield at the Victoria and Albert Museum in 1960.

2 Letter to the author from T. F. S. Scott, a student in the Fine Art Department at that time.

3 An interest in fine printing and the graphic and illustrative arts had been introduced at Reading by Frank Morley Fletcher, a leading exponent of Japanese wood-block printing, who was the Headmaster of the Art School 1897–1905. An Art School had been set up in Reading in the 1860s and had joined with a School of Science in the 1880s. In 1882 it had united with the Oxford University Extension Centre to form a University Extension College and by 1902 had become a full University College, covering letters (including Fine Art), Science and Agriculture.

In 1904 evening classes were set up for 'men who are engaged in the printing trade, as craftsmen, apprentices, or improvers'. The syllabuses for these classes were designed to meet the requirements of the City & Guilds of London Institute examinations and it was on this course that Albert Cooper had gained qualifications as a young apprentice. The college originally occupied buildings in Valpy Street in Reading but in 1905 moved to a purpose built campus on the London Road on land acquired through the generosity of Dr Alfred Palmer, a member of the wealthy family of biscuit manufacturers. The various departments were housed in single storey buildings of red brick bordering a central lawn and flower beds surrounding a library. The buildings were connected by covered walkways or cloisters of tiled roofs supported on timber columns — the architecture and landscaping reflecting the interest in the Arts and Crafts movement of the time. In one corner of the site airy studios and workshops were built for the School of Art. W. G. Collingwood took over from Morley Fletcher and became the first Professor of Fine Art at Reading and he supported the printing courses for the trade which continued until he retired in 1911. The Headship of the School then passed to Allen Seaby, who had been on the staff since 1889 and had been taught the art of woodcutting by Morley Fletcher. An author and artist, printmaker and illustrator, Seaby was also a keen naturalist and ornithologist and produced his best work when drawing birds and animals and making delicate prints of these subjects. Seaby did much to establish an arts and crafts tradition amongst the students and encouraged printmaking and book illustration. These enthusiasms were reflected in the choice of visitors to the School, which included Walter Crane, Joseph Pennell and W. R. Lethaby. When Anthony Betts took over the School the emphasis became focused on drawing and painting, heavily influenced by the style of the Camden Town Group and by the work of Walter Sickert, who occasionally visited Reading and received an Honorary Degree in 1938.

4 Memorandum from the Registrar, October 1934. See Michael Bott and Martin Andrews, 'Robert Gibbings and the University of Reading', *Matrix 9*, Winter 1989, pp. 63–68.

5 Ibid. p. 63.

6 'Some Recollections', p. xliii.

7 Letter from Gibbings to Johnson, 31 July 1933, Bodleian Library, University of Oxford, John Johnson Collection, MS Johnson C.18 (fols 75–86).

8 Letter from Gibbings to George Macy, 4 May 1934, HRHRC.

9 Letter from Macy to Gibbings, 24 May 1934, HRHRC.

10 Letter from Macy to Sandford, 15 January 1935, HRHRC.

11 Part of the delay was due to problems with the paper.

12 Shaun Gibbings, Robert's youngest son, has the typescript of an early version of *Coconut Island*, then called *Motu-Marama*. The contract for the book is in RUL and shows that the book was provisionally entitled *Hurroo for a Cannibal Isle* and was to be a minimum of 80,00 words in length with approx. 50 engravings; delivery was to be by 30 June 1936.

13 Robert Gibbings, *Coconut Island*, London: Faber and Faber Ltd, 1936. Revised edition published by J. M. Dent & Sons Ltd in 1949, p. 2.

14 Ibid. p. 4.

15 Ibid. p. 198.

16 Translated by Edith Vincent and published as *L'île aux cocotiers, les adventures de deux enfants dans les mers du sud*, Paris and Brussels: Editions de l'Amitié, G.-T. Rageot, part of a series of children's books called *Heures Joyeuses*.

17 Kirkus, p. 8.

18 'Robert Gibbings and the University of Reading', p. 64.

19 Ibid.

20 Ibid.

21 Background to Gibbings's classes in the Fine Art Department has been gathered from letters and interviews with students in the University at that time, notably Joan and William Wilder, T. F. S. Scott and S. Maberly Smith.

22 Each line of text was printed on a separate page in large centered type. Page size 136 x 100 mm. Donated to RUL by Margaret Randall, one of Gibbings's students who graduated in 1944 or 1945.

23 Extracts from her diary were sent to the author by Margaret Till (née Levetus).

24 Gibbings had been embarrassed at not being able to parade in academic dress with his colleagues — some students thought it was a protest by him against formality. Explaining his dilemma to friends at University College, Cork, he had jokingly suggested an honorary BA — they enthusiastically responded by putting him forward for an honorary MA. The conferring of the degree was announced in the local Cork newspapers and Robert's sister Aimée pasted an undated cutting into her scrap book in which there is mention that Gibbings had 'won distinction in the domain of Art' and that his work had been acquired by the British Museum and other public galleries at home and abroad — Harvard University had collected over twenty-four examples. The cutting also mentions that Gibbings had recently been awarded a special diploma of honour at a recent international exhibition held in Poland. Also see Gibbings's obituary published in the journal of University College Cork, *U.C.C. Record*, no. 33, Easter 1958, pp. 20–23.

25 Students who contributed illustrations for *Fatherless Oberlus* included G. Young, Margaret Webb, B. Cook, Theodore Naish, S. Green, K. Ambrose, S. Fraser and P. Andrews.

26 See Michael Bott, 'The Gibbings Collection in Reading University Library', *Matrix 9*, Winter 1989, pp. 55–59 followed by an Appendix listing books, prospectuses and ephemera printed under Gibbings in the Fine Art Department at The University of Reading, compiled by Sue Walker, pp. 59–62.

27 Four letters from William Lashly to Gibbings concerning the book, dating from October 1938 to April 1939, are in the Gibbings Collection, RUL.

28 Illustrated by S. Maberly Smith and translated by Jean Young (in collaboration with Eleanor Arkwright) of the English Department, who specialised in Anglo Saxon and was a friend of Gibbings.

29 Gibbings had met them during a visit he made to Bermuda.

30 Bott and Andrews, 'Robert Gibbings and the University of Reading', p. 64.

31 Russell Leslie, *Alpines I have Grown*, London: Lindsay Drummond, 1940, p. 7. The book was printed at the Chiswick Press and Leslie acknowledged Gibbings's support: '... I wish to record my thanks to the University of Reading, for the facilities put at my disposal while working on the book and above all to Mr. Robert Gibbings, who inspired me to undertake the task, and whose kindly guidance and invaluable criticism made the effort a pleasure.'

NOTES TO CHAPTER 13 A TIME TO WRITE 1936–1939

1 'Some Recollections', p. xlii.

2 Gibbings had written to Miss Ida Leeson, Curator of the Mitchell Library and, grateful to her for her 'unfailing generosity and help with documentary evidence', he later dedicated his book *John Graham, Convict* to her.

3 Letter from Llewelyn Powys to Gibbings, dated 1935 and sent in October or November. See Louis Wilkinson (ed), *The Letters of Llewelyn Powys*, London: John Lane, The Bodley Head, 1943, p. 202. Gibbings and Llewelyn had earlier planned to collaborate on another book to be called *The Poetry of God* which was to consist of essays on books from the Bible and the *Book of Common Prayer*. The project had been dropped when Gibbings gave up the Golden Cockerel Press but the book was to have been dedicated 'to the Glory of God and to the Memories of our two Fathers, the Rev. Canon Edward Gibbings and the Rev. Charles Francis Powys'. See Elwin, *The Life of Llewelyn Powys*, p. 212.

4 The paper specification was one issue of disagreement and Gibbings had to compromise over a Wolvercote paper from the Press's stock that was close to his preferred choice. Copies of a formal estimate sent by Johnson to Drummond on 11 August 1936 and various letters concerning the design and production of the book sent from Johnson to Gibbings are in the Archives of Oxford University Press.

5 In some critical comments on his engraving written by Gibbings for Tom Balston in 1948 (Balston was working on his book on Gibbings) he observed: 'I like the frontispiece Cormorant, and the Gannet on page 13 ... but this book makes me sick because the Publishers actually broke several of the blocks into two and printed them as separate entities. A most shocking performance on their part.' The original typescript of these comments is in the Clark Library but Dreyfus published them as an appendix to his article 'Some Correspondence between Robert Gibbings and Thomas Balston', *Matrix 9*, pp. 51–54.

6 'Some Recollections', p. xliii.

7 *Sweet Thames Run Softly*, p. 56.

8 Ian Crichton had impressed Gibbings with a sample of mud brought back from South Africa two years before — when Robert dropped the sample into distilled water he had been amazed to find a few days later that the water was 'alive' with hundreds of minute flagellates, see *Sweet Thames Run Softly*, p. 57. The Zoology department, which was in a building next to Gibbings's printing room, housed an extensive museum of biological specimens and Gibbings encouraged his students to draw items from the collection.

9 The Christmas card is amongst Allen Lane's papers in the Penguin Archive, Special Collections, Bristol University Library.

10 In a letter to the author dated 22 January 1994, Edward Young, who worked for The Bodley Head and Penguin Books, recalled meeting Gibbings and hearing his proposal — their response was enthusiastic and Young was greatly impressed by the character and stature of Gibbings. Young felt that it might well have been his own idea to start a series illustrated with wood-engravings. He knew many of the artists of the period at about that time and he lived in the same house as Gertrude Hermes.

11 Letter from Gibbings to Kenneth Hopkins, 22 May 1937, Clark Library. The young poet had visited Gibbings at Waltham earlier in the month; he later became an editor on the magazine *Everybody's* and was to commission a number of articles from Gibbings.

12 Robert Gibbings, *Blue Angels and Whales*, Harmondsworth: Penguin Books, 1938, p. 14.

13 Ibid. p. 32.

14 Ibid. p. 33.

15 Ibid. p. 36.

16 Ibid. p. 34.

17 Ibid. p. 66.

18 *Penguins Progress*, Autumn 1937, p. 1.

19 Letter from Gibbings to C. D. Wyatt, 11 October 1937, Clark Library.

20 Application letter from Gibbings to Dr S. A. Peyton, University Librarian and Secretary of the Research Board, 15 January 1938, asking for a grant, RUL.

21 Ibid.

22 Letter from Gibbings to staff at Penguin Books, 28 March 1938, Penguin Archive, Bristol University Library.

23 *Blue Angels and Whales*, p. 73.

24 Letter from Gibbings to staff at Penguin Books, 28 March 1938, Penguin Archive, Bristol University Library.

25 *Blue Angels and Whales*, p. 88.

26 *Observer*, 15 May 1938, p. 11.

27 *Blue Angels and Whales*, pp. 29–30.

28 *The Log of the 'Sea Bird'*, Reading: The School of Fine Art, 1939. Seventy-five copies were printed during the Summer term of 1939. The type was composed by S. Seward and the book was illustrated with small wood-engravings by M. E. Mills. The story had been told to Gibbings by Edwin Whitfield, one of the two young sailors who had undertaken the voyage on the *Sea Bird*, who was working at the Marine Research Station in Bermuda and was a great help and friend to him. An agreement had been signed between the two men that Whitfield should be paid a percentage of the royalties for *Blue Angels and Whales* (the story of the *Sea Bird* had formed chapter five of the book). In January 1948 Gibbings wrote to Whitfield and sent a substantial cheque as the result of the successful revised edition of *Blue Angels and Whales* published by Dent in 1946 and reprinted in 1947. Letters in RUL.

29 *Blue Angels and Whales*, p. 107.

30 *Radio Times*, vol. 51, no. 653, 3 April 1936.

31 This edition incidentally carried an advertisement for the recent publications of W. Heffer which included Doorly's *The Insect Man* which was recommended by the Junior Book Club.

32 'A Holiday under the Sea', *The Listener*, 25 May 1938, vol. 19, no. 489, p. 1114.

33 Peter Purbeck, 'Television: Matter and Manner', *The Listener*, 28 July 1938, vol. 20, no. 498, p. 207.

34 Gibbings, 'Sharks Permitting', *The Listener*, 17 November 1938, vol. 20, no. 514. pp. 1046–47.

35 Gibbings, 'Under the Coconut Palm', *The Listener*, 30 March 1939, vol. 21, no. 533, pp. 689–90.

36 See 'Penguin Illustrated Classics', *Miscellany 5*, Edinburgh: Salvia Books, 1990, published for the Penguin Collector's Society, p. 5. The whole edition is dedicated to the subject of the Illustrated Classics.

37 George Mackie, *Lynton Lamb, Illustrator*, Aldershot: Scolar Press, 1978, p. xx.

38 Letter from Gibbings to Allen Lane, 2 May 1938, Penguin Archive, Bristol University Library. In the same letter Gibbings discusses illustrations for two further books; one called *Hajji Baba* and the other an edition of the fox-hunting stories about the character Jorrocks, by R. S. Surtees, which he suggested could be illustrated by S. Maberly Smith — a 'very brilliant student' of his. Background information about the Illustrated Classics also came from an interview with Edward Young by the author, May 1994.

39 Letter from Gibbings to Lane, 8 May 1938, Penguin Archive, Bristol University Library.

40 Ibid.

41 An evening reception was organized to launch the series when guests were invited to meet the illustrators. Journalists from the *Daily Mirror*, *The Listener*, the *Manchester Evening News* and Allied Newspapers were

amongst the guests, as were many leading artists and wood-engravers. The guest list included Leon Underwood, Blair Hughes-Stanton, John Biggs, Clare Leighton, Professor Anthony Betts, Beatrice Warde, Alfred Fairbank, Gertrude Hermes, Herbert Read, Helen Binyon and Agnes Miller Parker. Penguin Archive, Bristol University Library.

42 *Penguins Progress*, May 1938, p. 4.

43 Bernard Newdigate, *The Art of the Book*, London: The Studio Ltd, Special Autumn Number 1938, pp. 56–57.

44 J. E. Morpurgo, *Allen Lane, King Penguin*, London: Hutchinson & Co. Ltd, p. 143.

45 Letter from Macy to Gibbings, 13 January 1936, HRHRC. The prestigious list of proposed illustrators included Edmund Dulac, W. A. Dwiggins, Barnett Freedman, Eric Gill, MacKnight Kauffer, Clare Leighton, Frans Masereel, Agnes Miller Parker, Arthur Rackham, Sir William Rothenstein and René Ben Sussan.

46 Letter from Gibbings to Macy, 20 January 1937, HRHRC.

47 Letter from Macy to Gibbings, 9 July 1937, HRHRC.

48 Letter from Gibbings to Macy, 15 October 1937, HRHRC.

49 Letter from Macy to Gibbings, 14 March 1938, HRHRC.

50 Letter from Gibbings to Macy, 16 April 1939, HRHRC.

51 Geoffrey Holme, *The Children's Art Book*, London: The Studio Ltd, 1938, pp. 42, 43, 50 and 92. Through his position at *The Studio*, Holme was able to select illustrations from the work of international artists, both contemporary and from the past. Holme used an ink drawing of a 'cart shed' by Gibbings and an enlarged version of an engraving of trees and farm buildings from *Where I Lived and What I Lived For*, printed in two colours; *A Street in Macedonia*, 1920, and the frog from *Count Stefan*, 1928. The choice of engravings seems very odd and does not show Gibbings's work in a favourable light — the paper and printing are poor.

52 Herbert Furst, 'Under-water Drawing', *Apollo*, vol. 29, February 1939, p. 100.

53 Tiare is the Tahitian name for a little white flower which, when tucked behind the left ear means 'I want a lover', behind the right ear means 'I've got one', *Sweet Thames Run Softly*, p. 87. Llewelyn Powys became Tiare's godfather.

54 The draft letters to Barclays Bank are in the possession of Diana Gibbings.

NOTES TO CHAPTER 14 SWEET THAMES RUN SOFTLY 1939–1941

1 Robert Gibbings, 'Rivers are Roads', *John O' London's Weekly*, vol. 62, 25 September 1953, p. 845.

2 Letter recalling his memories as a student from Professor William S. Lacy to Michael Bott, Archivist RUL, 29 January 1991, RUL.

3 *Sweet Thames Run Softly*, p. ix.

4 John Hadfield, 'A man of hills & rivers', *Picture Post*, vol. 25, no. 3, 14 October 1944, p. 19. The reference to travelling around Australia makes it very clear that Gibbings did make a lengthy trip to the country but, to date, no details of such a journey have been found except that his voyage had been with the Orient Line. See *Trumpets from Montparnasse*, p. 68.

5 Gibbings had made two earlier efforts at boat building in his youth. The first was little more than a canoe and the second (which on one occasion was stolen by salmon poachers) ended its days as the roof of a hen house near the mouth of Cork harbour. See *Lovely is the Lee*, p. 138.

6 Gibbings gave a short but detailed account of the building of his boat in one of his notebooks which is now in the collections of RUL. The account given here is based on this source and on an interview conducted by the author and Sue Walker with Norman Howard in 1975. The author and Sue Walker were both students in the Department of Typography and Graphic Communication at The University of Reading at that time and, following the tradition established by Gibbings, they wrote, handset, printed on damped hand-made paper and bound a limited edition of a short book, entitled *Robert Gibbings and the 'Willow'*, as a student project. The text was subsequently reprinted as an article in *Matrix 9*, Winter 1989, pp. 69–73.

7 *Sweet Thames Run Softly*, p. 24.

8 Ibid. p. 3.

9 Robert Gibbings, 'River Reverie', *The Listener*, vol. 22, no. 570, 14 December 1939, pp. 1168–69.

10 *Sweet Thames Run Softly*, p. 101.

11 Ibid. p. 103.

12 Ibid. p. 108.

13 A copy of the Society of Wood Engravers' newsletter, together with a draft of Gibbings's entry, written in his own hand, is part of the correspondence between Gibbings and Margaret Pilkington in the archives at The Whitworth Art Gallery, The University of Manchester.

14 Letter from Gibbings to Ralph Hartman, 3 July 1940, Clark Library.

15 Letter from Gibbings to Hartman, 21 August 1940, Clark Library.

16 Ibid.

17 Information based on interviews with Dr Ian Crichton conducted by the author in 1975 and 1991 and an article he published in the University's journal entitled 'A Wartime Log', *Reading reading*, Spring 1995, p. 13.

18 E. V. Watson, *A History of the Reading Guild of Artists*, Reading: The Reading Guild of Artists, September 1980, p. 54. Albert Cooper, the former pressman at the Golden Cockerel Press, was also a member of the Guild for many years and was a regular exhibitor.

19 *Sweet Thames Run Softly*, p. 115.

20 Ibid. pp. 130–31. Another frequent guest was C. B. Cochran. Barry Neame had invited Cochran to stay at the Hind's Head in 1940 and in his autobiography, *Cock-a-doodle-do*, published by Dent in 1941, Cochran makes a number of references to meeting Gibbings. They became friends and, in 1940, Gibbings gave Cochran a copy of *John Graham* which he inscribed, 'To C. B. Cochran from Robert Gibbings hoping we'll both escape transportation, 13-8-40'.

21 Ibid. p. 211.

22 Ibid. p. 218.

23 Hadfield, 'A man of hills & rivers', p. 20.

24 Letter from Gibbings to Hartman, 6 May 1941, Clark Library.

25 *The Times Literary Supplement*, 7 December 1940.

26 Agnes Miller Parker had met H. E. Bates through Gibbings when she illustrated his book of short stories, *The House with the Apricot & Two other Tales*, published by the Golden Cockerel Press in December 1933.

27 *The Listener*, vol. 23, no. 580, 22 February 1940.

28 Robert Gibbings, 'Peace on the River', *The Listener*, vol. 22, no. 562, 19 October 1939, pp. 768–69. The other articles were 'River Reverie'; 'River Memories', *The Listener*, vol. 23, no. 580, 22 February 1940, pp. 356–57; 'Ducks is Just Ducks', *The Listener*, vol. 23, no. 590, 2 May 1940, pp. 895–96.

29 André Maurois, *The Art of Living*, London: Hodder and Stoughton Ltd for The English Universities Press Ltd, 1940. John Waller Hills, *Summer on the Test*, London: Hodder and Stoughton, 1941. This was a new illustrated edition of a book about angling first published in 1924.

30 Robert Gibbings, 'Paradise Lost', *The Sunbathing Review*, vol. 8, no. 29, Spring 1940, pp. 8–9.

31 Robert Gibbings, 'Fleet Street to Tahiti', *Penrose Annual*, vol. 42, 1940, pp. 34–36. An earlier version of the article entitled 'Drawing Fish on the Sea Bottom' was published in *Art in New Zealand*, vol. 13, September 1940, pp. 26–29.

32 Robert Gibbings, 'English Society of Wood Engravers', *The Carnegie Magazine*, vol. 14, June 1940, pp. 85–86. In the article Gibbings outlined the revival of wood-engraving in the twentieth century and it was illustrated by a reproduction of his wood-engraving *Blue Angels and Gorgonias*.

33 Letter from Gibbings to Allen Lane, 28 February 1941, Penguin Archive, Bristol University Library.

NOTES TO CHAPTER 15 THE WYE AND THE LEE 1941–1945

1 Letter from Ian Crichton to his mother, 1 April 1941. The letter includes a detailed account of their weekend together. Copy given to the author by Dr Crichton.

2 *Coming Down the Wye*, p. 3.

3 Ibid.

4 Ibid. pp. 3–4.

5 Letter from Gibbings to John Hadfield, 9 July 1941, part of a collection of letters copied and generously given to the author by John Hadfield.

6 Letter from Gibbings to Hadfield, 11 July 1941.

7 Letter from Gibbings to Hadfield, undated but probably 14 July 1941.

8 *Coming Down the Wye*, p. 78.

9 Ibid.

10 Letter from Gibbings to Hadfield, 18 August 1941.

11 *Coming Down the Wye*, pp. 104–05.

12 Letter from Gibbings to Hadfield, 18 August 1941.

13 Letter from Gibbings to Hadfield, undated but sent from Symonds Yat in late August.

14 Letter from Gibbings to Hadfield, 8 September 1941.

15 Letter from Gibbings to Hadfield, 26 November 1941.

16 *Coming Down the Wye*, p. 140.

17 Letter from Gibbings to Hadfield, 26 November 1941.

18 Letter from Gibbings to Hadfield, 29 November 1941.

19 *Coming Down the Wye*, p. 126.

20 Ibid. pp. 122–23.

21 Ibid. pp. 124–25.

22 Letter from Gibbings to Hadfield, 8 December 1941.

23 Letter from Gibbings to Hadfield, 11 December 1941.

24 *Coming Down the Wye*, p. 140.

25 Letter from Gibbings to Moira, 30 June 1941. One of a number of letters from this period in the possession of Diana Gibbings.

26 Letter from Gibbings to Moira, 17 December 1941.

27 *Coming Down the Wye*, p. 143.

28 Ibid. p. 161.

29 Eiluned Lewis, *A Companionable Talent*, Goudhurst: The Finchcocks Press, 1996, pp. 81–82.

30 Letter from Gibbings to Mary O'Sullivan, 28 December 1942, Clark Library.

31 *Lovely is the Lee*, p. 1.

32 Ibid. p. 57.

33 Ibid. p. 86.

34 Ibid. p. 121.

35 Ibid.

36 Ibid. p. 140.

37 Ibid. p. 151.

38 Ibid. p. 157.

39 Ibid. p. 158.

40 Ibid. p. 167.

41 Ibid. p. 198.

42 Ibid. p. 199.

43 Letter from Gibbings to Eunice Frost, 18 February 1944, Penguin Archive, Bristol University Library.

44 Hadfield, 'A man of hills & rivers', p. 22.

45 Letter from Elliott B. Macrae to Gibbings, 22 August 1946, RUL. The success of this particular book could be due to the large Irish-American community keen to learn of the mother country.

NOTES TO CHAPTER 16 OVER THE REEFS 1944–1947

1 Letter from Gibbings to Cathleen Lennard Jones, 27 November 1944. A large collection of letters from Gibbings to Cathleen and George Lennard Jones between October 1944 and October 1955 was sold by Claude Cox, booksellers of Ipswich, in 1992. The author was generously given a chance to make notes from the correspondence, which is now in the collections of the National Gallery of Australia, before the sale.

2 Letter from Gibbings to Cathleen Lennard Jones, 18 March 1945.

3 A transription of the commentary was published in a postscript entitled 'Gibbings on Film' in *Matrix 15*, Winter 1995, pp. 97–98.

4 Letter from Gibbings to Cathleen Lennard Jones, undated, *c.* July or August 1945.

5 Ibid.

6 Letter from Gibbings to Cathleen Lennard Jones, 8 August 1945. It might have been Wilde's homosexuality that prompted this comment; Gibbings was strongly heterosexual but also a sensualist and free in his approach to sex, and Gill, in his diaries, implies some momentary sexual experience with Gibbings as part of one of the evenings of frolics at Waltham. See Fiona MacCarthy, *Eric Gill*, p. 191.

7 'An Irishman in cold water: Artist who draws in a diving helmet', *New Zealand Listener*, vol. 13, no. 329, 12 October 1945, pp. 6–7. Eric Ramsden, 'Robert Gibbings: Famous Illustrator-Author goes to Samoa', *Pacific Islands Monthly*, vol. 16, no. 4, 19 November 1945, p. 30.

8 Letter from Gibbings to Cathleen and George Lennard Jones, 31 October 1945. Lava lava is the Samoan version of the Tahitian pareu.

9 Ibid.

10 Letter from Gibbings to John Hadfield, 12 January 1946. Hadfield generously allowed the author to photocopy his correspondence with Gibbings.

11 The revised edition was published by Dent in February 1946. Dutton published an American edition of *Blue Angels and Whales* on the same day but sales were not expected to be high. Writing to Elliott Macrae on 27 May 1947, Gibbings specified a number of alterations to be made to the text if any further edition was to be printed. This was partly in response to a review in the *New York Herald Tribune* by Cushman Murphy, in which he slated the book. He ended his letter with the comment that he had completed two-thirds of the 'Island book' and it was promising well. He stated that he had booked a passage to England and hoped to be back in early October 1947. RUL.

12 Postcard to George Lennard Jones, 10 April 1946.

13 In fact he had heard of Shaun's birth from a 'congratulations' cable sent by one of his fans — he immediately wrote to Elisabeth but she had not replied — their relationship had become so strained that she had ceased to communicate with him or her family. Letter from Gibbings to his mother-in-law Mrs A. Empson, 30 June 1946. Private collection.

14 The boat was described as a bridal ship as it was bringing young women, many with small babies, to make a new life with New Zealand and Australian servicemen that they had recently married. Conditions on board were congested and the ship was late in docking at Wellington due to a quarantine scare; it eventually anchored on 27 May.

15 As Patience disembarked from the *Rangitata* she was greeted by a press photographer and reporter. Her celebrity took her completely by surprise but a photograph and interview about the expedition she was about to undertake with her famous brother-in-law were subsequently published in the *New Zealand Free Lance* and the *New Zealand Listener* on 14 June 1946. She was equally astonished to be treated as a distinguished visitor with an official car at her disposal — but Robert had arranged that a friend in the Department of Internal Affairs should look after her.

16 Letter from Gibbings to Hadfield, 3 September 1946.

17 Letter from Gibbings to George Lennard Jones, 10 May 1946.

18 Calling at a number of islands, to offload cargo and mail and take on bananas, Patience had her first experiences of feasts, ceremonies and dancing — they were always welcomed as honoured guests and Patience, as a young white woman, was something of a curiosity. On Nukualofa she made her first dives to observe the corals reefs and marine life.

19 Robert Gibbings, *Over the Reefs*, London: J. M. Dent & Sons Ltd, 1948, p. 82.

20 Letter from Gibbings to Cathleen Lennard Jones, 22 June 1946.

21 It was expected by the islanders that important people should be accompanied by a 'Talking Chief' or personal orator to deliver the endless speeches, on behalf of the distinguished person, that accompanied traditional kava-drinking ceremonies.

22 Letter from Gibbings to Cathleen Lennard Jones, 22 June 1946. In the event the anthropologist proved to be rather a difficult person, somewhat self-opinionated, who annoyed Robert and Patience by continually 'lecturing them', but he was very useful as an interpreter.

23 Letter from Gibbings to his mother-in-law Mrs A. Empson, 30 June 1946. Private collection.

24 Letter from Gibbings to the Lennard Joneses, 13 September 1946. Tapa cloth is made from the beaten fibres of tree bark and then decorated with strong patterns. The cloth was wrapped around the body as a simple garment. Pieces of the cloth were frequently presented as ceremonial gifts to honoured guests.

25 Many of the details of the months Robert and Patience travelled around the Polynesian Islands come from notes taken by the author of conversations with Patience Empson and notes she made at the time.

26 *Over the Reefs*, p. 189.

27 Ibid. p. 195.

28 Ibid. p. 214.

29 Ibid. p. 231–32.

NOTES TO CHAPTER 17 ... AND FAR AWAY 1947–1949

1 Robert Gibbings, *Kiwis in Captivity: as told to Robert Gibbings by F. D. Robson*, Napier: Hawkes Bay Art Gallery and Museum, 1947.

2 'Installed as a High Chief in a Samoan Island', *New Zealand Free Lance*, 7 May 1947, p. 17 and 'An Irishman sees the Islands', *New Zealand Listener*, 24 April 1947, pp. 16–17.

3 'A letter from Robert Gibbings', *The Cog*, vol. 1, no. 3, December 1947, p. 5–6.

4 With the tension over relationships with Elisabeth it was considered best for Patience to remain abroad. However, Patience had always intended to spend more time travelling on her own. She also broadcast talks on the radio in New Zealand and before setting out for South Africa she spent some time working on an

archaeological dig to unearth remains of the extinct Moa bird. She eventually wrote a colourful article about the excavations which was published in *Country Life*, 30 September 1949. While touring South Africa with her friend Rosemary Jack, Patience met up with Robert's sons, Larry and Patrick.

5 Letter from Gibbings to Charles Spencer, 21 September 1947, Clark Library.

6 Ibid.

7 Letter from Gibbings to Spencer, 15 October 1947, Clark Library.

8 Letter from Gibbings to the Lennard Joneses, 21 December 1947.

9 Letter from Gibbings to the Lennard Joneses, 22 January 1948.

10 Letter from Gibbings to the Lennard Joneses, 2 February 1948.

11 *Calling the Islands*, typescript of a broadcast for the BBC, p. 6. RUL.

12 Letter from Gibbings to George Lennard Jones, 25 February 1948.

13 Aimée Gibbings landed with the British forces at Naples and was in charge of the King George VI Club for officers in Rome during the war, where she also worked for the Y.M.C.A. She later organised a Y.M.C.A. centre outside the Schoenbrunn Palace in Vienna.

14 *Calling the Islands*, typescript of a broadcast for the BBC, pp. 1–2. RUL.

15 Letter from Gibbings to Cathleen Lennard Jones, 14 June 1948.

16 Letter from Gibbings to Cathleen Lennard Jones, 9 October 1948.

17 Letter from Gibbings to Cathleen Lennard Jones, 25 October 1948.

18 The first edition was of 17,800 copies. In 1949 Dent published an edition of 31,583 copies for the Readers Union and in 1950 an edition of 7,000 copies was published by W. & G. Foyle for members of the Travel Book Club. The book was dedicated to Gibbings's daughters Vahine and Tiare.

19 *The Cog*, vol. 2, no. 5, December 1948, p. 14. The article was reprinted from the *Citizen*, Letchworth, 29 October 1948.

20 A. R. J. Wise and R. A. Smith (ed.), *Voices on the Green*, London: Michael Joseph Ltd, 1945, pp. 62, 117 and 205.

21 Letter from Gibbings to his son, Larry Gibbings, 23 March 1948. Copy of the letter given to the author by Larry Gibbings. The letter is signed from 'Fuzz', the affectionate nickname used by the family.

22 Letters from Kay Fuller, Talks Producer at the BBC Pacific Service, to Gibbings, 5 April and 20 April 1948. RUL. The talks were scheduled to be about thirteen and a half minutes long — about 1700 words.

23 Thomas Balston, 'The River Books of Robert Gibbings', *Alphabet and Image*, no. 8, December 1948, pp. 39–49.

24 Robert Gibbings, 'Politeness to Sharks', *The Listener*, vol. 41, no. 1047, p. 260. An account, broadcast on the BBC Home Service, of shark fishing in Polynesia. On 29 March 1949, Gibbings was approached by the Talks Producer of the BBC's General Overseas Service about contributing one or two talks to a programme called 'Meet the Commonwealth'. Letter in RUL.

25 Published in an edition of 7,500 copies on 25 March 1949

26 Letter from Gibbings to Nicholas Wreden, 29 March 1949, RUL.

27 Letter from the Editor of Children's Books at Dent to Gibbings, 7 June 1949, RUL.

28 The National Book League is an independent charitable organization founded in 1925 as the National Book Council. It was renamed the National Book League in 1945.

29 *Wood-engraving in Modern English Books*, the catalogue of an exhibition arranged for the National Book League, October to November 1949. Published for the National Book League by Cambridge University Press 1949, with an introduction by Tom Balston. An article about the exhibition was written by Christopher Sandford, entitled 'The Wood-Engraved Illustration', and published in *The Studio*, vol. 139, 1950, pp. 50–55. The same year Cambridge University Press also published for the National Book League a booklet in a series of Reader's Guides entitled *Our Common Birds* by Viscount Grey of Fallodon which was illustrated with wood-engravings by Gibbings, reproduced from previous books by Fallodon, published by Constable. The overall cover design was by Joan Hassall who contributed a vignette for the title page and a tailpiece.

30 *Daily Graphic*, 20 October 1949.

31 Balston, *The Wood-engravings of Robert Gibbings*, p. 33.

32 Letter from Cyrus S. Eaton to Gibbings, 16 November 1945, RUL.

33 Letter from Gibbings to Nicholas Wreden, 6 December 1948, RUL.

NOTES TO CHAPTER 18 SWEET CORK OF THEE 1949–1951

1 The typescript of the talk, which was broadcast to New Zealand and the islands, is in the Gibbings Collection, RUL.

2 Letter from Gibbings to Wreden, 29 March 1949, RUL.

3 Kees Van Hoek was a Dutch journalist who had met Gibbings on various occasions and had written about his work. Gibbings had written to him and mentioned his caravan and probably described it as his boudoir on wheels but had not referred to the mattress.

4 Summary of Gibbings's objections as stated in the published record of the case. (See below).

5 *Summary of Evidence submitted in the case Gibbings v. O'Dea & Co. Ltd*, in the High Court, Dublin, December 1949, published by the Irish Times Ltd, p. 2. A copy of the *Summary* is in the Gibbings Collection, RUL.

6 Ibid.

7 Letter from Gibbings to the secretary of PEN, 11 December 1949, HRHRC. Gibbings had written to the association expressing interest in joining in October 1948 and was a paid-up member by the end of that year.

8 Letter from Gibbings to his son Larry, 20 December 1949. A copy of the letter was given to the author by Larry Gibbings.

9 Gibbings had written to Balston on 14 December 1949, making the same criticisms and comparing the quality of printing with that of the article in *Alphabet and Image*, which he felt had been much better. But he was generally pleased with the book: 'I think it is a pretty little child & and I am well content.' Pointing out a few misprints, he explained that the book had come out at an 'opportune' moment as the previous week had been spent in court and the publicity had been great: 'large headlines & two or three full columns a day for five days' — Gibbings expected this to create a demand for Balston's book. The previous year he had written to Balston on 21 January having read his draft manuscript; his only objection had been to the over-emphasis, as he saw it, of the 'impecunious side' of his career which he found embarrassing. Letters in the collection of Cal Hyland who gave photocopies to the author.

10 Drafts of various scripts for the programme *Private View*, along with production notes, are in the Gibbings Collection, RUL.

11 Letter from Gibbings to his son Larry Gibbings, 25 March 1950. A copy of the letter was given to the author by Larry Gibbings.

12 W. E . Williams writing a review in the *New Statesman* commented that 'Our host ... failed, however, to find many appropriate words for the occasion and therefore encouraged a similar inadequacy in the experts who presented the objects.' *New Statesman, Weekend Review*, vol. 39, no. 988, 11 February 1950. Harold Hobson wrote: '... the visit to the British Museum was enchanting. Mr. Robert Gibbings, burly, bearded, and benevolent, was a friendly and modest guide, seeming genuinely eager to look at things ... and if some of his collaborators from the Museum staff appeared to be trying to edge him off the screen this only added to the naturalness .... There was a moment of real emotion when Nelson's last letter to Lady Hamilton ... was produced. It was the best moment of the fortnight.' *The Listener*, 9 February 1950. An enthusiastic review of Gibbings's second appearance (taken from an unidentified press cutting) compared his performance with that of a rival presenter: 'Let us pay him the compliment that he out-Dimblebys Richard Dimbleby in naturalness and easy-flowing chatter.'

13 In February 1950 Gibbings had negotiated with the BBC a fee for the rights to broadcast *A True Tale of Love in Tonga* on television but it is not known whether a programme was ever made. Letters in the Gibbings Collection, RUL.

14 Herman Melville, *Typee*, London: The Folio Society, 1950. Introduction by Gibbings with pencil drawings by Jacques Bouillaire. In fact, Patience helped with much of the writing and in her own copy the title page has been amended, in Robert's hand, to read: '*Typee*, Introduction by P. A. E. assisted by Robert Gibbings in a very small way'. The original typescript and correspondence relating to the introduction to *Typee* are in the Gibbings Collection, RUL.

15 Letter from Leonard Russell to Gibbings, 16 February 1950. Russell had approached Gibbings for an article for *The Saturday Book* the previous year but Gibbings was suffering from 'flu and could not help. On this occasion Gibbings was able to reply by return of post enclosing a draft of his article. Correspondence in the Gibbings Collection, RUL. 'Autumn Night' appeared in *The Saturday Book*, no. 10, London: Hutchinson, 1950, pp. 283–88.

16 Many of the dates and details of Gibbings's activity from this period on are confirmed by entries in Patience Empson's appointment diaries which she made available to the author and which are now in the Gibbings Collection, RUL.

17 Robert Gibbings, 'Stones and Mud', *John O' London's Weekly*, vol. 59, 20 January 1950, p. 51. Also see *Sweet Cork of Thee*, p. 169.

18 The Gibbings Collection at RUL contains numerous letters to experts and authoritative bodies seeking information and confirming facts for use in his books for Dent. One example is a letter written on 3 July

1950 to the Secretary of the High Commissioner for Ireland asking for information about annual values of exports of greyhounds and cattle from Ireland; others are to the Curator at Kew Gardens, to Folk-Lore Societies both in Britain and America, national museums, ornithological and local history societies — the diversity reflecting the range of topics covered in his books.

19 *Coming Down the Seine*, pp. 126–27.

20 Gibbings's copy of the agreement is in the Gibbings Collection, RUL, along with contracts for a number of his other books.

21 Letter from Gibbings to Thomas Mason, 21 September 1950, RUL.

22 Letters covering in detail the negotiations and then the intense final design and production stages of *Sweet Cork of Thee*, and all Gibbings's subsequent books, are in the Gibbings Collection, RUL. The letters were carefully filed and stored by Patience Empson in Gibbings's studio at Footbridge Cottage, his final home in Long Wittenham, together with general correspondence dating from *c.* 1945–1958. The letters from Dent are top copies and Gibbings's typed replies are carbons and therefore unsigned. See Martin Andrews, '*Sweet Cork of Thee* and the popular books of Robert Gibbings', *Matrix 15*, Winter 1995, pp. 81–102.

23 Letter from Gibbings to Martin Dent, 11 September 1950, RUL.

24 Letter from Sandford to Gibbings, 21 November 1950, RUL.

25 Letter from Gibbings to Mary Adams at the BBC Television Service, Alexandra Palace, 3 October 1950, RUL.

26 Letter from Gibbings to James Bourlet & Sons Ltd, picture framers in London, 13 October 1950, RUL. Other letters relating to the exhibition are also in the Gibbings Collection, RUL.

27 Letter from Martin Dent to Gibbings, 14 September 1950, RUL.

28 Letter from Gibbings to E. F. Bozman, 17 October 1950, RUL.

29 Letter from Gibbings to R. J. Hall, 6 November 1950, RUL.

30 See illustrations *313*, p. 289 and *325*, p. 299, showing the Albion press. The press was purchased by RUL in February 2001.

31 Letter from Gibbings to R. J. Hall, 14 November 1950, RUL.

32 Letter from E. F. Bozman to Gibbings, 8 February 1951, RUL.

33 Letter from Gibbings to E. F. Bozman, 10 February 1951, RUL.

34 Letter from Gibbings to Martin Dent, 18 March 1951, RUL.

35 Letter from Gibbings to Martin Dent, 26 March 1951, RUL.

36 Letter from Gibbings to E. F. Bozman, 28 March 1951, RUL.

37 Letter from E. F. Bozman to Gibbings 30 March 1951, RUL.

38 In 1952 a Readers Union edition of 8,000 copies was published by Dent followed by an edition of 4,049 published by the Country Book Club.

39 Letter from Bozman to Gibbings, 21 December 1951, RUL.

40 Letter from A. J. Hoppé to Gibbings, 22 October 1951, RUL.

41 'Irish Charm', *The Times Literary Supplement*, 3 August 1951, p. 487.

42 David Marcus, A review of *Sweet Cork of Thee* in *Irish Writing*, no. 15, June 1951, pp. 25–26.

NOTES TO CHAPTER 19 COMING DOWN THE SEINE 1950–1953

1 Letter from Christopher Sandford to Gibbings, 21 November 1950, RUL.

2 Thomas Balston, *English Wood Engraving 1900–1950*, London: Art and Technics Ltd, 1951.

3 Thomas Balston, 'English Wood-Engraving, 1900–1950', *Image 5*, Autumn 1950, pp. 3–84.

4 Letter from Sandford to Gibbings, 21 November 1950, RUL.

5 Wood from the box tree is generally used to make blocks for wood-engraving but as the branches and trunk tend to be small in diameter, blocks of solid wood are also small. Large blocks are made by joining a number of blocks together using a method of tongue and grooving and glue — thus shrinking, caused by the blocks drying out, or undue pressure, can cause blocks to split along the joints. In the nineteenth century it was a common practice to bolt blocks together to make a larger surface.

6 The correspondence concerning this issue, dating from 9 February 1950 to 28 March 1951, between Gibbings and Robert Harling is in the Gibbings Collection, RUL. Also see letter from Gwen Raverat to Gibbings, 8 March 1950 or 1951 (year not given), RUL.

7 *The Times Literary Supplement*, 25 August 1950.

8 Percy Muir, *Private Presses and their Background*, London: The British Council, 1951, p. 19.

9 See letter from Eric Fullilove, Unit Manager, Crown Film Unit, to Gibbings, 26 February 1951, RUL.

10 Letter from Bozman to Gibbings, 7 November 1950, RUL.

11 Letter from Gibbings to his Aunt Suzanne, 3 April 1951. The correspondence with his aunt over a number of years is in the possession of Diana Gibbings. Gibbings was very fond of her and grateful for the financial support she gave him. Copies of the letters were given to the author.

12 Gibbings later dedicated his book to the Kleinbergs.

13 *Coming Down the Seine*, p. 3.

14 Ibid., p. 47.

15 Letter from Gibbings to the Lennard Joneses, 10 December 1951.

16 *Coming Down the Seine*, p. 57.

17 Ibid. p. 74.

18 The correspondence between Gibbings and Professor Karaghensian concerning the boat is in the Gibbings Collection, RUL.

19 Letter from Gibbings to Madame Rageot, 20 September 1951, RUL.

20 'Avec Robert Gibbings', *Terre des Jeunes*, no. 59, 1 October 1951, pp. 4–5.

21 The correspondence between Gibbings and these societies is in the Gibbings Collection, RUL.

22 Letter from Gibbings to the Secretary of The Society for Psychical Research, 24 October 1951, RUL.

23 Reply from Bernard Shaw quoted in a letter from Professor Denis Gwynn to Gibbings, 5 November (no year given but presumably 1950), RUL.

24 Letter from Gibbings to the Secretary of the Royal Society of Arts, 21 December 1952, RUL.

25 Gibbings resigned from the Royal Anthropological Institute in May 1954. See letter from the Honorary Secretary to Gibbings, 17 May 1954, RUL. According to an article published in *Arts News and Review*, 16 December 1950, he was also an Associate of the Royal Society of Painter-Etchers and a Fellow of the Royal Society of Literature.

26 Letter from Gibbings to Hoppé, 22 October 1951, RUL.

27 John Fisher, *The Midmost Waters*, London: The Naldrett Press, December 1952. Letter confirming details of commission from The Naldrett Press to Gibbings, 16 November 1951, RUL.

28 Letter from Gibbings to Bozman, 29 January, 1952, RUL.

29 Letter from Gibbings to Mr Woolley of United Rum Merchants Ltd, 29 January 1952, RUL.

30 John Harris was home on leave from his post as the Librarian of University College of Ibadan in Nigeria. In 1961 he collaborated with Patience Empson in completing the bibliography of Gibbings's work, started by Mary Kirkus.

31 Letter from Gibbings to Martin Dent, 12 February 1952, RUL.

32 Letter from Gibbings to Martin Dent, 6 April 1952, RUL.

33 Letter from Martin Dent to Gibbings, 26 November 1952, RUL.

34 Letter from Gibbings to Martin Dent, 4 December 1952, RUL.

35 Letter from Gibbings to Hopkins, 11 January 1952, RUL. The typescript for 'Drama in the Pacific' and notes about other articles are in the Gibbings Collection, RUL.

36 Robert Gibbings, 'Lost in the Loneliest Ocean', *Everybody's*, vol. 42, 6 September 1952, pp. 14 and 24, illustrated by two pencil drawings.

37 Robert Gibbings, 'Kon-Tiki Theory', *John O'London's Weekly*, vol. 61, 22 August 1952, pp. 781–82, and 'The Story behind Kon-Tiki', *The Sphere*, vol. 210, no. 2746, 27 September 1952, pp. 455–57.

38 Robert Gibbings, 'An Artist on the Seine', *The Saturday Book*, no. 12, London: Hutchinson, 1952, pp. 51–58.

39 Anna Hadfield, *A Peacock on the Lawn*, London: The Country Book Club, 1966, pp. 21–22.

40 Letter from Gibbings to Charles Ede of the Folio Society, 29 October 1952, RUL.

41 Letter from Gibbings to Erskine Childers, 26 March 1952, RUL. It was Professor Denis Gwynn who had approached Childers and suggested a stamp designed by Gibbings. See letter from Gwynn to Gibbings, 20 March (no year is given but presumably 1952), RUL.

42 The unfinished draft and typescript for the sequel to *Coconut Island* is in the Clark Library. The correspondence concerning the sequel between Dent and Gibbings is in the Gibbings Collection, RUL.

43 Letter from Hoppé to Gibbings, 23 October 1952, RUL.

44 Letter from Gibbings to Aunt Suzanne, 20 December 1952. Letters to Aunt Suzanne are in the possession of Diana Gibbings who made copies available to the author.

45 Letter from Gibbings to Christopher Bradshaw of Newman Neame Ltd, 20 March 1953, RUL.

46 Interview with John Lewis conducted by the author in November 1993.

47 Letter from Gibbings to Bradshaw, 25 March 1953, RUL.

48 Letter from Gibbings to G. Patrick Carey of Countryman Films Ltd, 8 January 1953, RUL.

49 Letter from Bozman to Gibbings, 12 February 1953, RUL.

50 Letter from Gibbings to Hoppé, 12 February 1953, RUL.

51 Letter from Gibbings to Martin Dent, 12 February 1953, RUL.

52 Letter from Gibbings to Aunt Suzanne, 21 March 1953.

53 Robert Gibbings, 'With Prince Tungi', *Overseas*, March 1953, pp. 37 and 39.

54 Letter from Prince Tungi to Gibbings, 1 January 1948, thanking Gibbings for his gift of *The Oxford Companion to Music* and describing developments on the island since Robert's visit. RUL.

55 Sir Harry Luke, *Queen Salote and Her Kingdom*, London: Putnam, 1954. Includes five engravings by Gibbings which had already been published in other books. One illustration, from *A True Tale of Love in Tonga*, is printed upside down.

56 Letter from Evan Gill to Gibbings, 25 March 1953, RUL.

57 Letter from Gibbings to Aunt Suzanne, 27 March 1953, RUL.

58 Letter from Martin Dent to Gibbings, 7 May 1953, RUL.

59 Letter from Gibbings to Cathleen Lennard Jones, August Bank Holiday 1953.

60 'Jim' Williams was the manageress at the Hind's Head and had taken over from Barry Neame. She was devoted to Robert and he dedicated *Trumpets from Montparnasse* to her.

61 John Hadfield gave the author a photocopy of the menu, signed by the guests.

62 Undated copy of the Dent reader's report, RUL.

63 Richard Church, 'One Man in a Boat', *John O'London's Weekly*, vol. 62, no. 1,522, 11 September 1953, pp. 801–02.

64 Letter from Gibbings to Richard Church, 2 September 1953, HRHRC.

65 'Godfrey Winn's Book at Bedtime: *Coming Down the Seine*', *Woman's Illustrated*, vol. 43, no. 1080, 13 July 1957, pp. 16–17.

66 Letter from Gibbings to Martin Dent, 21 September 1953, RUL.

67 *Coming Down the Seine*, p. 112.

68 Ibid. p. 72.

69 Ibid. p. 143.

70 'My View of the Irish R. M.', *Everyman*, November 1953, p. 16.

71 John Buckland-Wright, 'The Society of Wood Engravers', *The Studio*, vol. 146, 1953, pp. 134–41.

72 Robert Gibbings, 'Rivers are Roads', *John O'London's Weekly*, vol. 62, 25 September 1953, p. 845.

NOTES TO CHAPTER 20 WORDS AND PAINT 1953–1955

1 Gibbings had met Douglas Eden during his stay on the Polynesian Islands where Eden was working for the Crown Agents.

2 Letter from Gibbings to Aunt Suzanne, 27 November, 1953.

3 Letter from Gwynn to Gibbings, 27 November 1953, RUL.

4 The correspondence between Gibbings and Ede concerning this book is in the Gibbings Collection, RUL.

5 Letter from Gibbings to Macrae, 30 November 1953, RUL.

6 Letter from Macrae to Gibbings, 22 December 1953, RUL.

7 Robert Gibbings, 'The Well-heads of Venice', *The Saturday Book*, no. 12, London: Hutchinson, 1954, pp. 116–20. The photographs of well-heads were by Osvaldo Böhm.

8 Robert Gibbings, 'On Throwing Away the Cork', *Everybody's*, vol. 44, 24 April 1954, pp. 22–23 and 'A Finger of Friendship', *Ireland of the Welcomes*, May–June 1954, pp. 11–13.

9 Robert Gibbings, 'Along the Valley of the Wye', *London Calling*, no. 782, 28 October 1954, pp. 14–15 and 'Winter in Britain', *Time and Tide*, vol. 35, no. 40, 2 October 1954, pp. 1304–05.

10 Letter from Gibbings to Bozman, 1 March 1954, RUL.

11 Letter from Gibbings to the publicity department of the Orient Line, 25 February 1954, RUL.

12 Robert Gibbings, *Trumpets from Montparnasse*, London: J. M. Dent & Sons Ltd, 1955, p. 73–74.

13 Ibid. pp. 75–76.

14 Ibid. p. 81.

15 Letter from Gibbings to John and Anna Hadfield, 18 May 1954.

16 *Trumpets from Montparnasse*, p. 116.

17 Ibid. p. 140.

18 Ibid. p. 164.

19 Ibid. p. 190.

20 Ibid. p. 200.

21 Ibid.

22 Ibid. p. 71.

23 Ibid. p. 201.

24 Letter from Gibbings to Hadfield, 23 October 1954.

25 Robert Gibbings, 'A Conflict', *A Book of Delights*, London: Hulton Press, 1954, p. 74. An extract from *Coming Down the Seine*.

26 Letter from Gibbings to J. de Vries of the BBC, 8 December 1954, RUL. Many of the scripts, contracts, and the correspondence concerning Gibbings's broadcasts are in the Gibbings Collection, RUL.

27 Letter from Gibbings to Aunt Suzanne, 27 March 1953.

28 *Coming Down the Seine*, p. 128.

29 Robert Gibbings, 'The Perfect Wife', *Irish Writing*, no. 15, June 1951, pp. 25–26.

30 Letter from Liam Miller to Gibbings, 1 October 1954, RUL.

31 Robert Gibbings, *The Perfect Wife, a Fable from France, transmogrified into the Anglo-Irish idiom & illustrated by Robert Gibbings*, Glenageary, County Dublin: Dolmen Press, 1955. It was published as an eight-page booklet as the third part of *The Dolmen Chapbook*, in a limited edition of ten copies on hand-made paper and two hundred and forty ordinary copies. It was set by hand in the typeface Caslon and was illustrated by two of Gibbings's engravings.

32 Oliver Warner (ed.), *An Account of the Discovery of Tahiti, from the Journal of George Robertson, Master of H. M. S. Dolphin*, London: The Folio Society, 1955. Illustrated with eleven engravings by Gibbings.

33 Letter from Gibbings to Macy, 4 August 1954, RUL. The correspondence concerning the publication of *The Voyage of the Beagle* is in the Gibbings Collection, RUL. The letters from Macy are top copies and Gibbings's replies are carbon copies — the reverse correspondence is part of the Macy Collection in the HRHRC.

34 Gibbings had accepted the invitation in 1948 but the work had been delayed. On 2 December 1955 Gibbings wrote to the Hakluyt Society informing them that due to pressure of work he had been forced to drop the project. The correspondence between Gibbings and the Society is in the Gibbings Collection, RUL.

35 Letter from Gibbings to Macy, 4 August 1954, RUL.

36 Ibid.

37 Letter from Macy to Gibbings, 29 October 1954, RUL.

38 Letter from Gibbings to Macy, 2 November 1954, RUL.

39 Letter from Martin Dent to Gibbings, 26 January 1955, RUL.

40 Letter from Bozman to Gibbings, 9 February 1955, RUL.

41 Letter from Gibbings to Martin Dent, 7 March 1955, RUL.

42 Linson was a large commercial bindery which was frequently used by Dent.

43 Letter from Gibbings to Hoppé, 9 February 1955.

44 Letter from Gibbings to Elliott Macrae of Dutton, 22 July 1955, RUL.

45 Gibbings's knowledge of the French language was good enough for him to be understood in conversation but was weak in terms of formal grammar.

46 Review of *Trumpets from Montparnasse* by John Gibbins, *Apollo*, vol. 62, no. 369, November 1955, p. 156.

47 Review of *Trumpets from Montparnasse* by Orville Prescott in the *New York Times*, 6 December 1955.

48 Letter from Charles Ede to Gibbings, 6 October 1955, RUL.

49 Letter from Gibbings to W. G. Taylor of Dent, 2 October 1955, RUL.

50 Letter from Christina Foyle to Gibbings, 8 December 1955, RUL.

51 *Trumpets from Montparnasse*, pp. 187–88.

NOTES TO CHAPTER 21 *THE BEAGLE* 1954–1956

1 Letter from George Macy to Gibbings, 9 November 1954, RUL.

2 Letter from Gibbings to Macy, 16 January 1955 [the letter is incorrectly dated 1954], RUL.

3 Letter from Macy to Gibbings, 25 January 1955, RUL.

4 Letter from Macy to John Dreyfus, 25 January 1955, RUL.

5 Letter from Gibbings to Macy, 17 February 1955, RUL.

6 Letter from Gibbings to Macy, 21 March 1955, RUL.

7 Letter from Gibbings to Macy, 7 June 1955, RUL.

8 Ibid.

9 Letter from Gibbings to Macy, 9 June 1955, RUL.

10 Letter from Dreyfus to Gibbings, 10 June 1955, RUL.

11 Letter from Gibbings to Macy, 17 June 1955, RUL.

12 Letter from Gibbings to Sir Gavin de Beer, 30 June 1955, RUL.

13 Letter from Gibbings to Sir Gavin de Beer, 5 July 1955, RUL.

14 Letter from Gibbings to Dreyfus, 18 July 1955, RUL.

15 Letter from Gibbings to Dreyfus, 19 July 1955, RUL.

16 Letter from Gibbings to Dreyfus, 28 July 1955, RUL. The firm of T. N. Lawrence was one of the few surviving suppliers of wood-blocks, tools and materials for wood-engravers. Most of the prominent engravers of the time dealt with Mr S. T. E. Lawrence who, as well as being an authority on the medium and an excellent craftsman, also had a reputation for being rather irascible and eccentric. The firm is still going strong today although they have moved from their original premises in Bleeding Heart Yard to the Clerkenwell Road in London. See Simon Lawrence, 'My Grandfather, Stanley Thomas Lawrence', *Matrix 7*, Winter 1987, pp. 1–3.

17 Letter from Gibbings to Dreyfus, 11 August 1955, RUL.

18 Letter from Gibbings to Mrs Guilfoyle, Dreyfus's secretary, 15 August 1955, RUL.

19 Letter from Gibbings to Dreyfus, 31 August 1955, RUL.

20 Letter from Dreyfus to Gibbings, 5 September 1955, RUL.

21 Letter from Gibbings to Dreyfus, 6 September 1955, RUL.

22 Ibid.

23 Letter from Dreyfus to Macy, 30 September 1955, RUL.

24 Dreyfus was aware that the books that Gibbings had previously illustrated for Macy had all been small folio in size. Dreyfus favoured this format as he felt it would be a challenge to make the edition work as a single volume. The final page size was 12 x 7½ ins — big enough to accommodate a large text area and to allow for generous margins. In the final single volume, a frontispiece was dropped and instead a wonderfully detailed and delicate engraving of tropical fish swimming amongst the coral was incorporated in the title page. Dreyfus designed the title page in uppercase and used the typeface Goudy Modern in preference to the lighter caps of Poliphilus. Subtle changes in typesize created a ripple effect which complimented the underwater illustration and the page was enriched by the use of red printing to pick out key lines in the title and a rule which 'settled' the text on the sea bed at the bottom of the page.

25 Letter from Dreyfus to Macy 30 September 1955, RUL. The paper was manufactured by Cowan & Sons at their Valleyfield Mills at Penicuik in Midlothian, Scotland. Dreyfus reported to Gibbings on 22 February 1956 that the paper had been delivered: '... I hope you will approve of it. It has an opacity of 97 degrees, and I think the whiteness is just of the right shade.' Gibbings jokingly replied 'The sample of paper seems perfect, kindly and luminous for the blocks — who the L cares about the type?!!'

26 Letter from Gibbings to Dreyfus, 13 September 1955, RUL. The technique of photographing an image onto a woodblock had been experimented with by Henry Fox Talbot but became a common practice used by commercial engravers in the 1860s. Various formulas were used to coat the surface of the block with a light-sensitive solution — the image could then be exposed onto the block using a negative. With the decline of commercial wood-engraving at the end of the nineteenth century, companies offering this service had almost disappeared.

27 Ibid.

28 Letter from Macy to Gibbings, 27 September 1955, RUL.

29 Letter from Macy to Gibbings, 13 October 1955, RUL.

30 Robert Gibbings, *Till I End My Song*, London: J. M. Dent & Sons Ltd, 1957, p. 2.

31 Letter from Gibbings to Dreyfus, 6 October 1955, RUL.

32 Letter from Dreyfus to Macy, 28 November 1955, RUL.

33 Letter from Dreyfus to Gibbings, 28 November 1955, RUL. The use of a half tone screen presumably reproduced tones more effectively.

34 Letter from Gibbings to Dreyfus, 1 December 1955, RUL.

35 Letter from Dreyfus to Gibbings, 28 December 1955, RUL.

36 Letter from Gibbings to Dreyfus, 29 December 1955, RUL.

37 Letter from Gibbings to Dreyfus, 30 December 1955, RUL.

38 Letter from Gibbings to Dreyfus, 26 January 1956, RUL.

39 Letter from Dreyfus to Gibbings, 30 January 1956, RUL. The firm of Joseph Swain had been one of the largest and most well known commercial wood-engraving companies of the nineteenth century. The firm carried on well into the twentieth century as process engravers. Frampton & Co. was one of the only commercial wood-engraving companies to survive in business until the 1970s.

40 Letter from Macy to Gibbings, 30 January 1956, RUL.

41 Letter from Gibbings to Dreyfus, 12 February 1956, RUL.

42 Letter from Dreyfus to Gibbings, 14 February 1956, RUL.

43 Letter from Gibbings to Dreyfus, 16 February 1956, RUL.

44 Letter from Dreyfus to Gibbings, 20 February 1956, RUL.

45 Letter from Gibbings to Dreyfus, 5 March 1956, RUL.

46 Letter from Macy to Gibbings, 29 March 1956, RUL.

47 Letter from Gibbings to Macy, 4 June 1956, RUL.

48 A colleague of Dreyfus at the Cambridge University Press, John Peters, drew the decorations eventually used on the binding.

49 Letter from Gibbings to Macy, 4 June 1956, RUL.

50 Letter from Helen Macy to Gibbings, 27 July 1956, RUL.

51 The book was later published with illustrations by Reynolds Stone. An edition of *Omoo* that Gibbings had bought and begun to mark up, and his provisional sketches, were sent to Reynolds Stone after Gibbings's death in January 1958, in case they were of help to him. This material is now in the Clark Library.

52 Letter from Hoppé to Gibbings, 27 October 1955, RUL.

53 Letter from Gibbings to Sandford, 30 May 1955, RUL.

54 Letter from Gibbings to Hoppé, 30 October 1955, RUL. Gibbings was very cavalier about his books: he gave many copies away and never bothered about keeping examples of his work. His collection of Golden Cockerel Press books had been taken to South Africa by Moira and later, when he needed examples for lecturing etc., Gibbings had to buy some copies from dealers.

55 An edition of 5,200 copies was published by Dent. A further edition of 2,000 copies was printed at the Aldine Press for A. S. Barnes & Co. of New York and published in 1957.

NOTES TO CHAPTER 22 TILL I END MY SONG 1955–1958

1 Robert Gibbings, *Till I End My Song*, London: J. M. Dent & Sons Ltd. 1957, p. 13.

2 Letter from Gibbings to Charles Ede at the Folio Society, 10 October 1955, RUL.

3 *Till I End My Song*, pp. 3–4.

4 Ibid. p. 8.

5 Letter from Gibbings to Hadfield, 29 November 1955, RUL.

6 Mary Kirkus first became interested in Gibbings's engravings when her sister gave her a copy of Helen Waddell's *Beasts and Saints*, for Christmas, in 1934.

7 Letter from Gibbings to Mary Kirkus, 4 February 1955, RUL.

8 Letter from Gibbings to Mary Kirkus, 8 February 1955, RUL.

9 Dent produced a proof of the bibliography, including printed cover, which at that time was intended to be a thirty-two page paperback, measuring 223 x 144 mm. A copy of this proof is in RUL.

10 Letter from Bozman to Gibbings, 28 November 1955, RUL.

11 Letter from Bozman to Gibbings, 28 December 1955, RUL.

12 Letter from Bozman to Gibbings, 11 January 1956, RUL.

13 *Till I End My Song*, pp. 113–14.

14 Ibid. p. 123.

15 Letter from Gibbings to Hadfield, 8 September 1956.

16 Letter from Bozman to Gibbings, 4 December 1956, RUL.

17 Letter from Gibbings to Martin Dent, 27 December 1956, RUL.

18 Letter from Bozman to Gibbings, 16 January 1957, RUL.

19 Letter from Gibbings to Hadfield, 5 March 1957.

20 Letter from Martin Dent to Gibbings, 7 March 1957, RUL.

21 Letter from Gibbings to Hadfield, 12 February 1957.

22 Ibid.

23 Robert Gibbings, 'Thoughts on Wood', *The Saturday Book*, no. 17, London: Hutchinson,1957, p. 213.

24 Robert Gibbings, 'My Career in Medicine', *Medical World*, vol. 85, no. 1, July 1956, pp. 76 and 79–80. 'The Country of the Wye', *London Calling*, no. 908, 28 March 1957, pp. 14–15.

25 Letter from Gibbings to Hadfield, 2 April 1957.

26 Ibid.

27 Ibid.

28 Letter from Gibbings to Anna Hadfield, undated but presumably May 1957.

29 Letter from Gibbings to Hadfield, 8 May 1957.

30 Letter from Gibbings to Hadfield, 29 May 1957.

31 Letter from Gibbings to Hadfield, dated Wednesday 5th, presumably June.

32 Letter from Gibbings to Anna Hadfield, 20 July 1957.

33 Ibid.

34 Dame Hildelith Cumming, 'Under a Wing of the Golden Cockerel', *Matrix 2*, Winter 1982, pp. 36–49. The article includes a selection of letters from the correspondence between Dame Hildelith and Gibbings. The original letters are in the Gibbings Collection, RUL.

35 Letter from Gibbings to Dame Hildelith Cumming, 6 December 1957, *Matrix 2*, p. 44. The printing that Gibbings so admired was *Question the Beauty*, a passage from St Augustine, set in Van Krimpon's Cancelleresca Bastarda type.

36 Letter from Ralph Beedham to Gibbings, 20 August 1957, RUL. In a following letter Beedham gave Gibbings advice about another company who could photograph images onto a woodblock for engraving. The firm of S. Slinger Ltd had for some years provided this service for T. N. Lawrence and Beedham advised Gibbings to continue to send blocks to Lawrence rather than approach Slinger direct. In a letter to the author, dated 2 April 1992, the engraver Michael Renton recalled that when he worked for the firm of Slinger he had seen ink drawings by Gibbings, used for illustrations for *Till I End My Song*, being photographed onto woodblocks. Renton seemed to remember that the drawings were on tracing paper, which might suggest that they were worked up directly over sketches made on the spot, and had to be reduced to fit onto the block.

37 Letter from Gibbings to Mrs Marsh of Dutton, 29 April 1957, RUL.

38 Review of *Till I End My Song* by Nancy Spain, *Daily Express*, 4 October 1957.

39 Review of *Till I End My Song*, *The Times Literary Supplement*, 11 October 1957.

40 Review of *Till I End My Song*, *The Times*, 24 October 1957.

41 Letter from Gibbings to Hadfield, 3 October 1957.

42 Letter from Gibbings to the Hadfields, dated Sunday 10th, presumably November 1957.

43 Letter from Gibbings to Hadfield, 9 December 1957.

44 Letter from Gibbings to Hadfield, 27 December 1957.

45 Letter from Gibbings to Martin Dent, 4 December 1957, RUL.

46 Ibid.

47 Letter from Patience Empson to Dame Hildelith Cumming, 26 January 1958, *Matrix 2*, p. 46.

NOTES TO EPILOGUE

1 *Till I End My Song*, pp. 162–63.

2 John Hadfield, introduction to *The Saturday Book*, no. 18, London: Hutchinson & Co. Ltd, 1958, p. 5.

3 As early as 1934, the possibility of a volume of Gibbings's collected engravings being published by the Golden Cockerel Press had been discussed but rejected. See letter from Gibbings to Owen Rutter, 28 September 1934, HRHRC.

4 Letter from Gibbings to Martin Dent, 16 January 1950, RUL.

5 Letter from Bozman to Gibbings, 20 June 1955, RUL.

6 Letter from Bozman to Patience Empson, 22 April 1958, RUL.

7 An endowment fund which Mary Kirkus willed to the Reading University Library has often been used, most appropriately, to purchase additions to the Gibbings Collection.

8 Letter from Evan Gill to Patience Empson, 25 March 1962, RUL.

9 Following the exhibition at the V&A, some of the material was sent to the Whitworth Gallery in Manchester where it became part of another memorial exhibition which also celebrated the work of two

of Gibbings's friends and colleagues, Mabel Annesley and Gwen Raverat. Called 'Three Wood Engravers Memorial Exhibition', the exhibition was open from 20 May to 22 June 1960.

10 Montague Weekley, 'A Red-headed Bohemian', *The Listener*, vol. 62, 19 November 1959, p. 892.

11 John Hadfield, 'A Master of Wood-engraving', *Country Life*, 4 February 1960, p. 217.

12 The original typescript for Hadfield's Memorial Lecture is in the Gibbings Collection, RUL. It was published in *Matrix 1*, Winter 1981, pp. 53–59.

End Note

Gibbings's work continues to be shown in exhibitions around the world. In 1969, an exhibition of Gibbings's books and wood-engravings was held at the museum in Letchworth and in 1972, Patience Empson organized an exhibition as part of the Dorchester Abbey Festival. A major exhibition of his work was held in Reading University Library in 1975, and in 1988, the Library of the University of Ulster in Belfast mounted an exhibition of his engravings. In the centenary year of his birth, 1989, a comprehensive exhibition exploring all aspects of his life and work was held in The Museum of Reading and another, showing books, periodicals, ephemera etc. containing Gibbings's words, was mounted in the Manchester Polytechnic Library. Over the years a number of his books have been reprinted by various publishers, usually in paperback form, and his engravings have appeared as illustrations in anthologies and travel books. Eight engravings were used to illustrate an edition of *The Tailor and Ansty* by Eric Cross, which was published by Chapman & Hall Ltd in 1964 (originally published in 1942, the book gives a picture of rural Ireland told through the fireside talk of the tailor and his wife, Ansty). Engravings that had originally been intended as illustrations to Kinglake's *Eothen*, (which was to have been published by the Kynoch Press) but were used in the Kynoch Press Diary for 1941, were later used to illustrate an extract from *Eothen* published as *Engraved by Robert Gibbings: a Portrait of Lady Hester* in a limited edition by the Libanus Press in 1987.

Further Reading

WOOD-ENGRAVING, GENERAL

Balston, Thomas, *English Wood Engraving 1900–1950*, London: Art and Technics, 1951.

Brett, Simon, *The Engraver's Globe*, London: Primrose Hill Press, 2002. (Survey of contemporary engraving from around the world).

Garrett, Albert, *A History of British Wood Engraving*, London: Bloomsbury Books, 1986.

Garton, Robin, (ed.), *British Printmakers, 1855–1955*, London: Garton & Co., 1992.

Hamilton, James, *Wood Engraving & the Woodcut in Britain c. 1890–1990*, London: Barrie & Jenkins Ltd, 1994.

Selborne, Joanna, *British Wood-engraved Book Illustration 1904–1940*, Oxford: Clarendon Press, 1998.

Articles

Selborne, Joanna, 'The Wood Engraving Revival', *Object Lessons*, London: Lund Humphries and Central Saint Martin's College of Art and Design, 1996.

WOOD-ENGRAVING TECHNIQUE

Beedham, R. J., *Wood Engraving*, Ditchling: St Dominic's Press, 1921. Reprinted by Faber and Faber Ltd, 1946.

Biggs, John R., *Classic Woodcut Art and Engraving*, London: Blandford Press, 1988.

Brett, Simon, *Wood Engraving: How to do it*, London: Primrose Hill Press, 2000.

Chamberlain, Walter, *Manual of Wood Engraving*, London: Thames and Hudson Ltd, 1978.

Articles

Gibbings, Robert, 'Thoughts on Wood', *The Saturday Book*, no. 17, 1957. Reprinted in *Matrix* 9, 1989.

ROBERT GIBBINGS AND HIS CONTEMPORARIES

Balston, Thomas, *The Wood-engravings of Robert Gibbings*, London: Art and Technics, 1949.

Empson, Patience, *The Wood Engravings of Robert Gibbings*, London: J. M. Dent & Sons Ltd, 1959.

Kirkus, A. Mary, Patience Empson and John Harris, *Robert Gibbings, a bibliography*, London: J. M. Dent & Sons Ltd, 1962.

MacCarthy, Fiona, *Eric Gill*, London: Faber and Faber, 1989.

Articles

Andrews, M. J., 'Sweet Cork of Thee and the popular books of Robert Gibbings', *Matrix* 15, 1995.

—— 'The Voyage of H. M. S. Beagle', *Matrix* 19, 1999.

Balston, Thomas, 'The River Books of Robert Gibbings', *Alphabet and Image*: 8, 1948.

Bott, M. and Andrews, M. J., 'Robert Gibbings and the University of Reading', *Matrix* 9, 1989.

Dreyfus, John, (ed.), 'Some Correspondence between Robert Gibbings and Thomas Balston', *Matrix* 9, 1989.

Gibbings, Robert, 'Memories of Eric Gill', *Book Collector*, vol. 2, no. 2, 1953.

—— 'Rivers are Roads', *John O' London's Weekly*, vol. 62, September, 1953.

Hadfield, John, 'Memorial lecture to Robert Gibbings, *Matrix* 1, 1981.

MacCarthy, Fiona, 'Gibbings and Gill: Arcady in Berkshire', *Matrix* 9, 1989.

Salaman, Malcolm C., 'The Woodcuts and Colour-prints of Captain Robert Gibbings', *The Studio*, vol. 76, February 1919.

Walker, Sue and Andrews, M. J., 'Robert Gibbings and the Willow,' *Matrix* 9, 1989.

THE GOLDEN COCKEREL PRESS

Dreyfus, John, *A Typographical Masterpiece*, San Francisco: The Book Club of California, 1990.

Cave, Roderick, *The Private Press*, London: Faber and Faber Ltd, 1971, revised edition 1983.

Franklin, Colin, *The Private Presses*, London: Studio Vista, 1969, revised edition, Aldershot, 1991.

Articles

Cave , Roderick, 'The Lost Years of the Golden Cockerel Press, *Printing History*, 4, 1982.

Cooper, Albert C., 'Reminiscences of Albert Cooper, Pressman at the Golden Cockerel Press', recorded and edited by Sue Walker and Martin Andrews, *Matrix* 9, 1989.

—— 'Notes on the Printing Methods of the Golden Cockerel Press', with introduction by Patience Empson, *Matrix* 9, 1989.

Gibbings, Robert, 'The Golden Cockerel Press', *The Colophon*, part 7, no. 6, 1931.

—— 'The Golden Cockerel Press', *The Woodcut*, no. 1, 1927.

—— 'The Art of the Book: The Golden Cockerel Press', *The Studio*, vol.97, February 1929.

Mosley, James, 'Eric Gill and the Golden Cockerel Type', *Matrix* 2, 1982.

Selborne, Joanna, (ed.), 'Eric Ravilious and the Golden Cockerel Press: correspondence with Robert Gibbings, part 1: selected letters 1926–29', *Matrix* 14, 1994.

—— 'Eric and Tirzah Ravilious and the Golden Cockerel Press: correspondence with Robert and Moira Gibbings, part 2: selected letters 1929–33', *Matrix* 16, 1996.

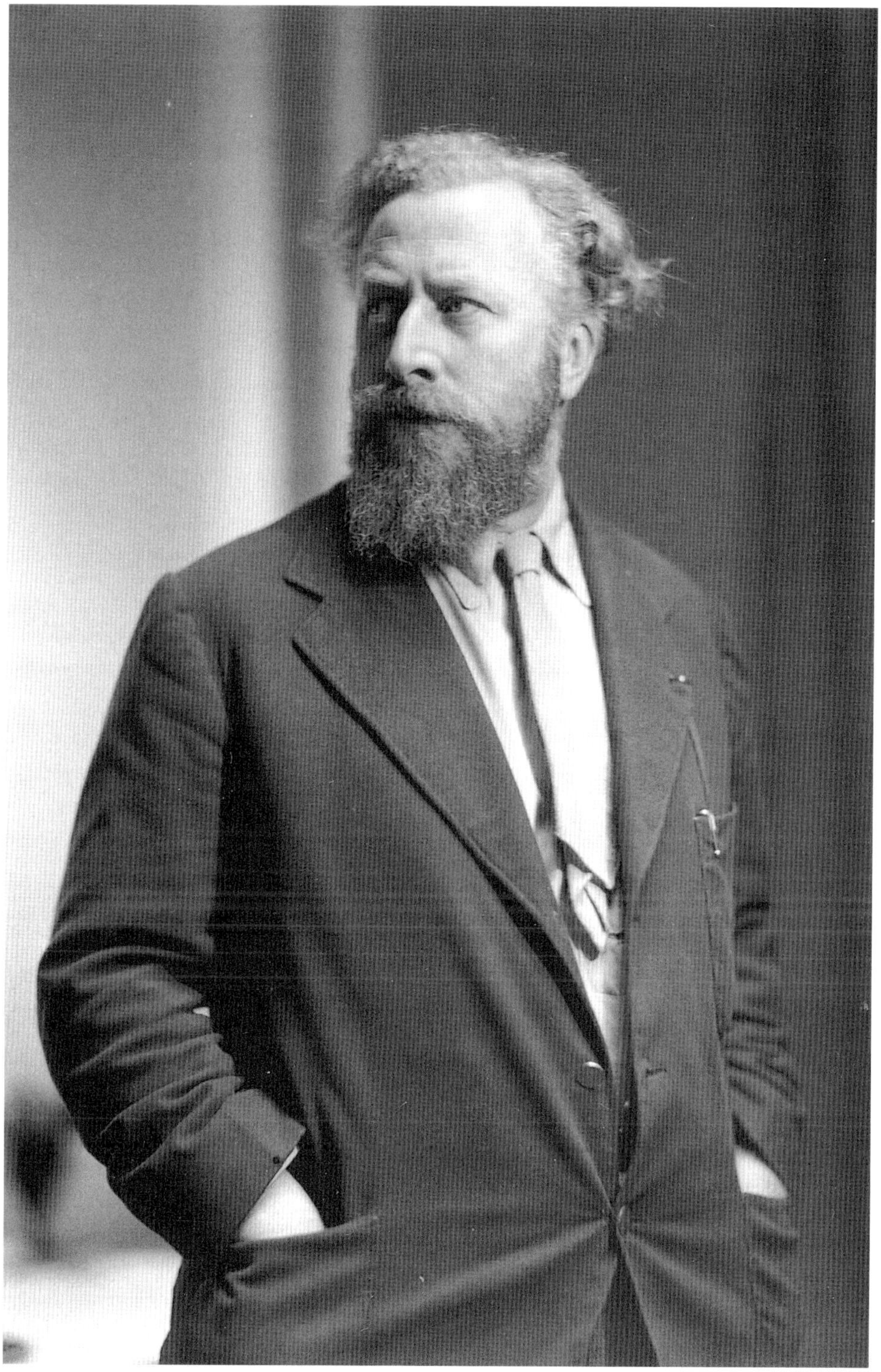

Studio portrait of Robert Gibbings by the photographer Howard Coster. Taken for publicity purposes, c. 1938. By courtesy of the National Portrait Gallery, London.

Robert Gibbings engraving a block, *c.* 1948. RUL.

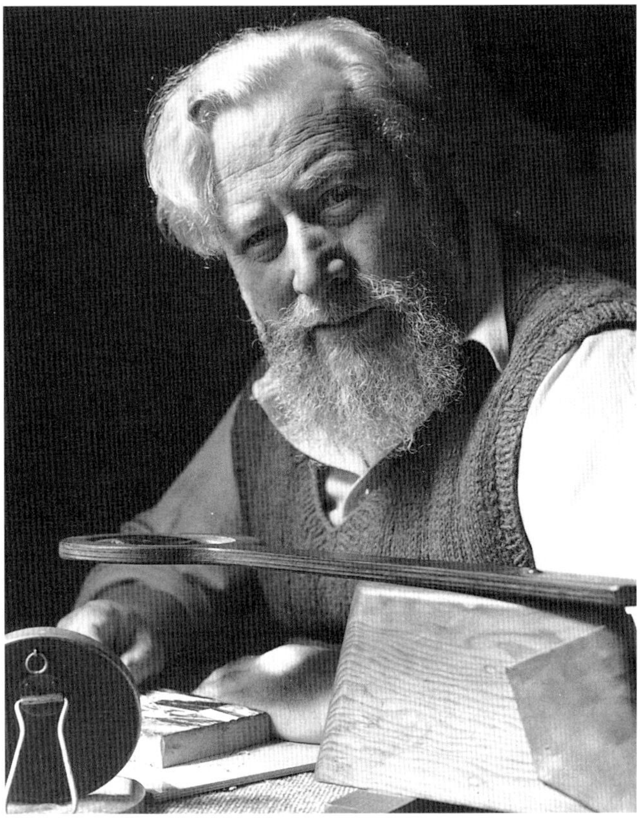

Robert Gibbings taking a proof print of one of the wood-engravings he produced to illustrate his river book *Lovely is the Lee* published in 1945. RUL.

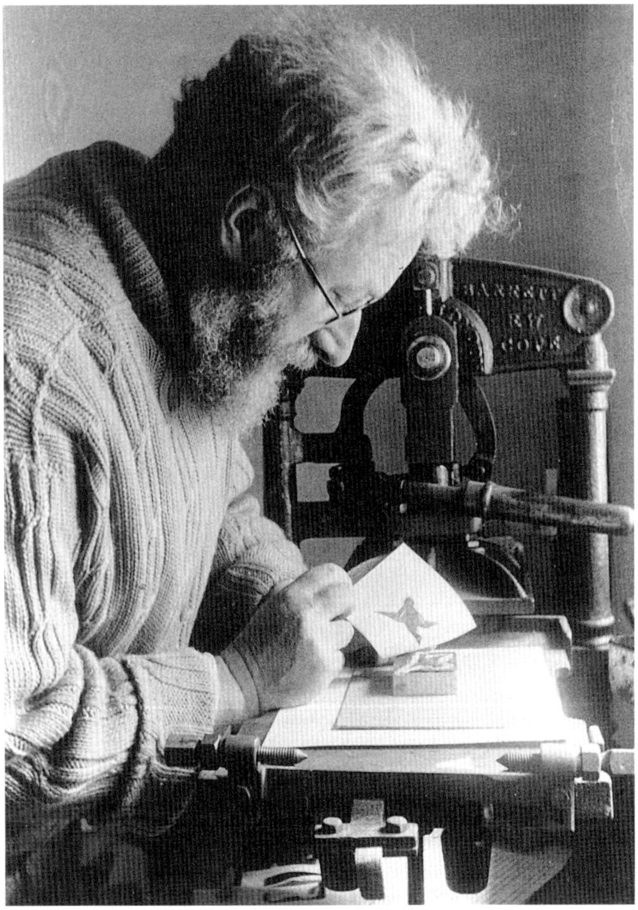

Index

KEY TO THE INDEX

Numerals in normal type refer to the page numbers of the entries. [e.g. Adams, Mary 298]

Each illustration throughout the book is numbered, and heavy, italic numerals in the index refer to the illustrations themselves, rather than to the pages on which they appear. [e.g. Aldine Press ***364***]

Numerals in heavy type, preceded by **Pl.**, refer to illustrations in the coloured plate section. [e.g. *Albert Bridge, Chelsea* 40, **Pl. 1**]

Notes to the text: If a subject in the text leads the reader to a note about the same subject, an extra index reference to the note itself is not given. In all other cases, the page number and the note in which the entry appears are shown. [eg. Ambrose, K. 397n25]

RG in an index entry refers to Robert Gibbings. [e.g. cartoon of RG 369, ***389***]

The main entry for *Gibbings, Robert* is sub-divided into entries on his *Appearance, Book Illustrations, Books, Broadcasting, Life, Travels, War Service, Work* and *Writings.*